International Management

SIXTH EDITION

International Management

Managing Across Borders and Cultures
Text and Cases

Helen Deresky

Emerita, State University of New York–Plattsburgh

PEARSON EDUCATION INTERNATIONAL

Editor-in-Chief: David Parker
Acquisitions Editor: Michael Ablassmeir
Product Development Manager: Ashley Santora
Assistant Editor, Media: Denise Vaughn
Marketing Manager: Jodi Bassett
Marketing Assistant: Ian Gold
Associate Managing Editor: Renata Butera
Project Manager, Production: Kevin H. Holm
Permissions Project Manager: Charles Morris
Senior Operations Supervisor: Arnold Vila
Senior Art Director: Jayne Conte
Cover Design: Bruce Kenselaar
Cover Illustration/Photo: Getty Images, Inc.
Director, Image Resource Center: Melinda Patelli
Manager, Rights and Permissions: Zina Arabia
Manager, Visual Research: Beth Brenzel
Manager, Cover Visual Research & Permissions: Karen Sanatar
Image Permission Coordinator: Ang'john Ferreri
Photo Researcher: Kathy Ringrose
Composition: Integra
Full-Service Project Management: BookMasters, Inc.
Printer/Binder: Courier/Kendallville, Pheonix Color Corp.
Typeface: 10/12 Times Ten Roman

Credits and acknowledgments borrowed from other sources and reproduced, with permission, in this textbook appear on appropriate page within text.

If you purchased this book within the United States or Canada you should be aware that it has been wrongfully imported without the approval of the Publisher or the Author.

Pearson Education Ltd. , London.
Pearson Education Singapore, Pte. Ltd
Pearson Education, Canada, Ltd
Pearson Education–Japan
Pearson Education Australia PTY, Limited

Pearson Education North Asia Ltd
Pearson Educación de Mexico, S.A. de C.V.
Pearson Education Malaysia, Pte. Ltd.
Pearson Education, Upper Saddle River,
  New Jersey

10 9 8 7 6 5 4 3 2 1

ISBN: 0-13-606019-6

To my husband John,
and my children, John, Mark, and Lara,
for their love and support.

Brief Contents

Contents

Preface

The sixth edition of *International Management: Managing Across Borders and Cultures* prepares students and practicing managers . . .

for careers in a dynamic global environment wherein they will be responsible for effective strategic, organizational, and interpersonal management. While managing within international and cross-cultural contexts has been the focus of this text since the first edition, the 6th edition portrays the burgeoning level, scope, and complexity of international business facing managers in the twenty-first century. This edition explores how recent developments and trends within a hypercompetitive global arena present managers with challenging situations and guides the reader as to what actions to take, and how to develop the skills necessary to design and implement global strategies, conduct effective cross-national interactions, and to manage daily operations in foreign subsidiaries. Global companies are faced with varied and dynamic environments in which they must accurately assess the political, legal, technological, competitive, and cultural factors that shape their strategies and operations. The fate of overseas operations depends greatly on the international manager's cultural skills and sensitivity, as well as the ability to carry out the company's strategy within the context of the host country's business practices.

In this 6th edition, cross-cultural management and competitive strategy are evaluated in the context of global changes—the expanding European Union (EU), the increasing trade among the Americas, and the rapidly growing economies in Asia—that require new management applications. We have added focus on how rapidly developing economies, China and India in particular, present the manager with challenging strategic decisions in an increasingly "flat world," as posited by Thomas Friedman. This edition emphasizes how the variable of culture interacts with other national and international factors to affect managerial processes and behaviors. In addition, the growing competitive influence of technology is discussed throughout the text.

This textbook is designed for undergraduate and graduate students majoring in international business or general management. Graduate students might be asked to focus more heavily on the comprehensive cases that conclude each part of the book and to complete the term project in greater detail. It is assumed, though not essential, that most students using *International Management: Managing Across Borders and Cultures*, sixth edition, will have taken a basic principles of management course. Although this text is primarily intended for business students, it is also useful for practicing managers and for students majoring in other areas, such as political science or international relations, who would benefit from a background in international management.

NEW TO THIS EDITION

- **Streamlined text** in 11 chapters, with particular focus on global strategic positioning, entry strategies and alliances, effective cross-cultural understanding and management, and developing and retaining an effective global management cadre. The sixth edition has been revised to reflect current research, current events, and global developments, and includes company examples from the popular press. In Chapter 1, for example, we introduce trends and developments facing international managers and then expand those topics in the context of the subsequent chapters. We discuss developments in globalization and also the growing nationalist backlash, the effects on global business of the rapidly growing economies of China and India and the expansion of the EU, the globalization of human capital, and the escalating effects of information technology and the global spread of e-business. We follow these trends and their effects on the role of the international manager throughout the book. For example, in Chapter 6 we have a section on Using E-Business for Global Expansion, and in Chapter 3 we examine the Internet-culture connection. In Chapter 6 we also expand our discussion of outsourcing as part of strategy and, in Chapter 7, we added a section on Implementing a Global Sourcing Strategy, later revisiting that topic in the context of HR in Chapter 9. In Chapter 2 we lead into another contemporary topic gaining increasing attention—that of CSR (corporate social resposibility)—with a new opening profile on the Enron case, new data and tables on global corruption, a new comparative section on human rights in China, and a new closing case on Nike's CSR. We have also reorganized the HR Chapters 9 and 10, adding, for example, sections on Managing Expatriates (selection, performance management, compensation), along with a new section on research on comparative IHRM in ten countries, while expanding coverage of knowledge management and virtual teams.

Other revisions to the text material include the following:

- **Comprehensive cases: Thirteen comprehensive cases are new and current;** two are favorites rolled over from the fifth edition. The selection of cases has been drawn from a broad array of geographical settings: China, Germany, India, Finland, Malaysia, France, Japan, the United States, as well as "global" cases. **The new integrative case** presents the student-manager with a variety of strategic, cultural, and political issues involved in Wal-Mart's global strategy. The cases place the student in the decision-making role of the manager regarding issues of strategy, culture, HRM, social responsibility, technology, and politics in the global arena. Examples are Google's ethical challenges in China; Coca-Cola's global CSR challenges; Nora Sakari's (Finland) joint venture negotiations in Malaysia; the global strategic challenges facing Allure Cruise Lines; the Renault (French) and Nissan (Japanese) automakers' joint venture; Starbucks' entry strategies around the world; the Infosys (India) Global Delivery Model, dealing with HRM and strategic challenges of outsourcing in the high-technology industry.

- **Chapter-Opening Profiles: We have added seven new profiles,** keeping some favorites. These give practical and current illustrations of the chapter topics, such as "India Becoming a Crucial Cog in the Machine at IBM," "Art of the Deal meets the China Syndrome," and "Adjusting Business to Saudi Arabian Culture."

- **Comparative Management in Focus sections** providing in-depth, comparative application of chapter topics in a broad range of specific countries or regions with **new or updated sections** such as "Doing Business in China—the Human Rights Challenge," "Leadership in the EU," "Joint Ventures in the Russian Federation (updated)," "Comparative IHRM Practices," and "Communicating with Arabs."

- **Management Focus Boxes: Six new focus boxes, others updated,** giving management and company examples around the world to highlight the chapter topics, such as "A Middle East Equity Giant with a Small Global Footprint," "Mittal's Marriage to Arcelor Breaks the Marwari Rules," "Procter & Gamble's Think Globally–Act Locally Structure," and "Japan's Neglected Resource—Female Workers."

- **Chapter-Ending Cases: Six *new* cases; three favorites updated.** Examples are "Under Pressure, Dubai Company Drops Port Deal," "There's Detroit and There's Trnava: the Strategic Attraction of Eastern Europe," and "Lenovo's Global Expansion."

- **Experiential Exercises** at the end of each chapter, challenging students on topics such as ethics in decision making, cross-cultural negotiations, and strategic planning.

- **Integrative Term Project** outlined at the end of the text and providing a vehicle for research and application of the course content.

- **Integrative Case: New case,** "Wal-Mart: Managing Globalization in 2007," involving students with the many challenges of operating globally—including the successes and failures.

- **Internet Study Guide** chapter quizzes are available on the text's Web site. These quizzes ask a variety of multiple choice, true/false, and essay questions that provide students with immediate feedback. Go to www.prenhall.com/deresky.

INSTRUCTOR'S RESOURCE CENTER

At **www.prenhall.com/irc,** instructors can access a variety of print, digital, and presentation resources available with this text in downloadable format. Registration is simple and gives you immediate access to new titles and new editions. As a registered faculty member, you can download resource files and receive immediate access and instructions for installing course management content on your campus server.

If you ever need assistance, our dedicated technical support team is ready to help with the media supplements that accompany this text. Visit **www.247.prenhall.com** for answers to frequently asked questions and toll-free user support phone numbers.

The following supplements are available to adopting instructors (for detailed descriptions, please visit **www.prenhall.com/irc**):

- **Instructor's Resource Center (IRC) on CD-ROM** — ISBN: 0-13-614331-8
- **Printed Instructor's Manual** — ISBN: 0-13-614328-8
- **Printed Test Item File** — ISBN: 0-13-614329-6
- **TestGen Test Generating Software** — Available at the IRC Online.
- **PowerPoint Slides** — Available at the IRC (online or on CD-ROM).
- **Custom Videos on DVD** — ISBN: 0-13-614332-6

Companion Website

This text's Companion Website at **www.prenhall.com/deresky** contains valuable resources for both students and professors, including an interactive student study guide.

SafariX eTextbooks Online

Developed for students looking to save money on required or recommended textbooks, SafariX eTextbooks Online saves students money compared to the suggested list price of the print text. Students simply select their eText by title or author and purchase immediate access to the content for the duration of the course using any major credit card. With a SafariX eText, students can search for specific keywords or page numbers, make notes online, print out reading assignments that incorporate lecture notes, and bookmark important passages for later review. For more information, or to purchase a SafariX eTextbook, visit **www.safarix.com**.

ACKNOWLEDGMENTS

The author would like to acknowledge, with thanks, the individuals who made this text possible. For the sixth edition, these people include Wanda Chaves and Steven Yacovelli, who contributed the Allure Cruise Line running case, as well as the following reviewers:

Ron Abernathy, University of North Carolina–Greensboro
Scott Boyar, University of South Alabama
Charles M. Byles, Virginia Commonwealth University
Charlie E. Mahone, Howard University
Yongsun Paik, Loyola Marymount University
Kathleen Premo, St. Bonaventure University

—Helen Deresky

CHAPTER 1

Assessing the Environment

Political, Economic, Legal, Technological

Outline

Opening Profile: India Becoming a Crucial Cog in the Machine at I.B.M.

BANGALORE, India, June 2006—The world's biggest computer services company could not have chosen a more appropriate setting to lay out its strategy for staying on top.

On the expansive grounds of the Bangalore Palace, a colonial-era mansion once inhabited by a maharajah, the chairman and chief executive of I.B.M., Samuel J. Palmisano, addressed 10,000 Indian employees. He shared the stage with A. P. J. Abdul Kalam, India's president, and Sunil Mittal, chairman of the country's largest cellular services provider, Bharti Tele-Ventures. An additional 6,500 employees looked in on the town hall-style meeting by satellite from other Indian cities.

On the same day, Mr. Palmisano and other top executives met here with investment analysts and local customers to showcase I.B.M.'s global integration capabilities in a briefing customarily held in New York. During the week, the company led the 50 analysts on a tour of its Indian operations.

IBM Human Resources Department Team having a meeting.
SOURCE: IBM India Corporate

The meetings are more than an exercise in public and investor relations. They are an acknowledgment of India's critical role in I.B.M.'s strategy, providing it with its fastest-growing market and a crucial base for delivering services to much of the world.

"A significant part of any large project that we do worldwide is today being delivered out of here," said Shanker Annaswamy, I.B.M.'s managing director for India, who presides over what is now the company's second-largest worldwide operation. In the last few years, even as the company has laid off thousands of workers in the United States and Europe, the growth in I.B.M.'s workforce in India has been remarkable. From 9,000 employees in early 2004, the number has grown to 43,000 (out of 329,000 worldwide), making I.B.M. the country's largest multinational employer.

Some of the growth has been through acquisition. In a deal valued at about $160 million in 2004, I.B.M. bought Daksh eServices of New Delhi, India's third-largest back-office outsourcing firm with 6,000 workers. Since then, that operation alone has grown to 20,000 employees.

"Now that companies such as Infosys Technologies and Cognizant have clearly demonstrated that the services marketplace is not impregnable, the new battle is for talent," said N. Lakshmi Narayanan, president and chief executive of Cognizant Technology Solutions of Teaneck, N.J. Cognizant is one of I.B.M.'s

Front of IBM corporate facility at EGL, Bangalore, India.
SOURCE: IBM India Corporate

competitors; it is incorporated in the United States but has the bulk of its 28,000 employees in India.

I.B.M. is growing not only in size by adding new hires, but also in revenue. The company's business in India grew 61 percent in the first quarter of this year, 55 percent in 2005 and 45 percent the year before.

That growth has not come just from taking advantage of the country's pool of low-cost talent. In recent months, the technology hub of Bangalore has become the center of I.B.M.'s efforts to combine high-value, cutting-edge services with its low-cost model.

For instance, the I.B.M. India Research Lab, with units in Bangalore and New Delhi and a hundred employees with Ph.D.'s, has created crucial products like a container tracking system for global shipping companies and a warranty management system for automakers in the United States. Out of the second project, I.B.M. researchers have fashioned a predictable modeling system that helps track the failure of components inside a vehicle, a potentially important tool.

In March, the company started a Global Business Solutions Center here, announcing that it would represent the "future of consulting services." I.B.M. said that it expected to invest more than $200 million a year in the new center. The company hopes to provide clients with access to the expertise of its 60,000 consultants worldwide in complex areas like supply chain management and compliance with banking rules.

But competitors are trying to gain on I.B.M. The rival consulting firm, Accenture, based in Hamilton, Bermuda, is ramping up equally rapidly in India, while another outsourcing competitor, Electronic Data Systems, based in Plano, Tex., recently made an offer for a controlling stake in Mphasis, a midsize outsourcing firm in Bangalore.

The race for India's skilled, inexpensive talent may not stop at I.B.M. "Many companies in the technology development and support niche covet and value these workers highly," said Kevin M. Moss, a New York-based special counsel in Kramer Levin Naftalis & Frankel's outsourcing and technology transactions group.

On the pricing front, rivals like Tata Consultancy Services of Mumbai and Infosys Technologies of Bangalore have pioneered and perfected the low-cost model. Infosys Technologies, with 52,700 employees, has $2.15 billion in annual revenues, a figure that is growing 30 percent annually.

But the depth, breadth and geographic spread of I.B.M.'s global operations—which generated $91 billion in sales last year, $47 billion from services—keep it ahead of its competitors for now. For example, I.B.M. manages a system it developed for a large American oil company, which it would not identify, that keeps track of consumption and oversees financial and administrative processes as well as the technical help desk, data network and servers. I.B.M. is also researching tools to track company assets and reduce costs.

"All this is done for one customer seamlessly from three of our centers in Bangalore, Chicago and outside of London," said Amitabh Ray, director of global delivery, I.B.M. Global Services. "These kinds of capabilities and global scale are unmatched."

But smaller rivals are playing catch-up here, too, by talking to customers about their needs and then developing custom-built software. Infosys Technologies, for instance, has a consulting unit with headquarters in Fremont, Calif., near Silicon Valley, where it now has 200 consultants, and an additional 1,800 consultants in India.

Meanwhile, Mr. Annaswamy, I.B.M.'s chief executive in India, acknowledged that growth was difficult because thousands of recruits had to be quickly integrated into the company. Salaries are rising, and employee costs are also moving up, he said.

Even so, the Indian operation is becoming more and more strategic for the company. "Both in terms of size and scale, India has become the focal point," Mr. Ray, of I.B.M. Global Services, said.

Managers in the twenty-first century are being challenged to operate in an increasingly complex, interdependent, and dynamic global environment. Those involved in global business have to adjust their strategies and management styles to those regions of the world in which they want to operate, whether directly or through some form of alliance. Typical challenges that managers must face involve politics, culture, global competition, terrorism, and technology. In addition, the opportunities and risks of the global marketplace increasingly bring with them the societal obligations of operating in a global community. An example is the dilemma faced by Western drug manufacturers of how to fulfill their responsibilities to stockholders, acquire capital for research, and protect their patents while also being good global citizens by responding to the cry for free or low-cost drugs for AIDS in poor countries. Managers in those companies are struggling to find ways to balance their social responsibilities, their images, and their competitive strategies.

To compete aggressively, firms must make considerable investments overseas—not only capital investment but also investment in well-trained managers with the skills essential to working effectively in a multicultural environment. In any foreign environment, managers need to handle a set of dynamic and fast-changing variables, including the all-pervasive variable of culture that affects every facet of daily management. Added to that "behavioral software" are the challenges of the burgeoning use of technological software and the borderless Internet, which are rapidly changing the dynamics of competition and operations.

Global management, then, is the process of developing strategies, designing and operating systems, and working with people around the world to ensure sustained competitive advantage. Those management functions are shaped by the prevailing conditions and ongoing developments in the world, as outlined in the following sections.

THE GLOBAL BUSINESS ENVIRONMENT

Following is a summary of some of the global situations and trends that managers need to monitor and incorporate in their strategic and operational planning.

Globalism

"The World Is Flat"

THOMAS FRIEDMAN[1]

Business competitiveness has now evolved to a level of sophistication that many term **globalism** (though more commonly called globalization)—global competition characterized by networks of international linkages that bind countries, institutions, and people in an interdependent global economy. The invisible hand of global competition is being propelled by the phenomenon of an increasingly borderless world, by technological advancements, and by the rise of developing economies such as China and India—a process that Thomas Friedman refers to as "leveling the playing field" among countries—or the "flattening of the world."[2]

One person described globalization in the context of the situation surrounding the death of Princess Diana of England:

> *Princess Diana was an English princess*
> *With an Egyptian boyfriend*
> *Who crashed in a French tunnel,*
> *Driving a German car*
> *With a Dutch engine,*
> *Driven by a Belgian who was drunk*
> *On Scottish whisky,*
> *Followed closely by Italian Paparazzi,*
> *On Japanese motorcycles.*
> *She was treated by an American doctor,*
> *Using Brazilian medicines.*
> *This description is sent to you by an American Indian,*
> *Using Bill Gates's technology,*

And you are probably reading this on your computer,
That uses Taiwanese chips,
and a Korean monitor,
assembled by Bangladeshi workers
in a Singapore plant,
transported by Indian lorry-drivers,
unloaded by Sicilian longshoremen,
and trucked to you by Mexican immigrants.[3]

Globalization has led to the narrowing of differences in regional output growth rates as economic activity increased, driven largely by increases led by China, India, and Russia (China's growth, 10.7 percent in 2006, continues its escalation into 2007).[4] It is clear that world trade is phenomenal and growing and, importantly, is increasingly including the developing nations. However, there are important aspects of globalism other than economic factors, though these aspects are intertwined. Exhibit 1-1 shows the top 20 countries as measured by four comprehensive factors—trade, travel, technology, and links to the rest of the world; the details for those categories are given below the chart. As you can see, although the United States leads the world in technology, it falls behind a number of countries on the other three factors.

EXHIBIT 1-1   Measuring Globalilzation

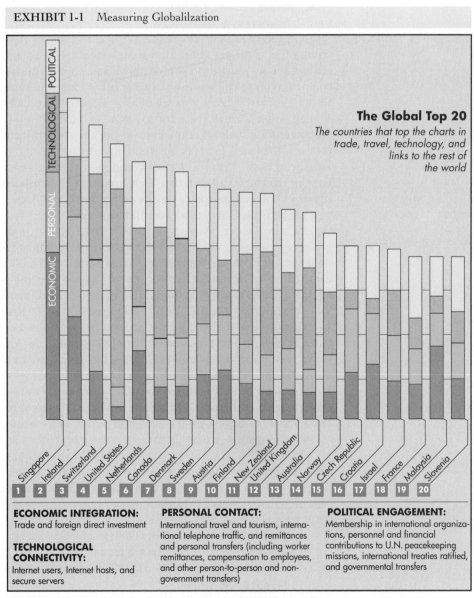

The Global Top 20
The countries that top the charts in trade, travel, technology, and links to the rest of the world

ECONOMIC INTEGRATION:
Trade and foreign direct investment

TECHNOLOGICAL CONNECTIVITY:
Internet users, Internet hosts, and secure servers

PERSONAL CONTACT:
International travel and tourism, international telephone traffic, and remittances and personal transfers (including worker remittances, compensation to employees, and other person-to-person and non-government transfers)

POLITICAL ENGAGEMENT:
Membership in international organizations, personnel and financial contributions to U.N. peacekeeping missions, international treaties ratified, and governmental transfers

As we consider the many facets of globalism and how they intertwine, we observe how economic power and shifting opinions and ideals about politics and religion, for example, result in an increasing backlash against globalism and a rekindling of nationalism. Globalism has been propelled by capitalism and open markets, most notably by Western companies. Now

> *. . . economic power is shifting fast to the emerging nations of the south. China and India are replacing the U.S. as the engines of world economic growth.*
>
> FINANCIAL TIMES,
> *March 3, 2006*[5]

The rising nationalist tendencies are evident as emerging and developing nations—wielding their economic power in attempted takeovers and inroads around the world—encounter protectionism. There is hostility to takeovers such as the Indian company Mittal Steel's bid for Europe's largest steel company, Arcelor. At times Europe seems to be closing its borders; and even the United States reacted to an attempted takeover of the British P&O by Dubai Ports World early in 2006, as detailed in the chapter-ending case. For example, as the demand on energy resources burgeons with heightened industrial activity in China, we see increased protectionism of those resources around the world as Russia, Venezuela, and Bolivia privatized their energy resources in 2005.

In returning to our discussion at the corporate level, we can see that almost all firms around the world are affected to some extent by globalism. Firms from any country now compete with your firm both at home and abroad, and your domestic competitors are competing on price by outsourcing or offshoring resources and services anywhere in the world. Often it is difficult to tell which competing products of services are of domestic or foreign origin. While Ford, for example, is pushing it's Mustang with the slogan "buy American," only about 65 percent of the car content comes from the United States or Canada—the rest is purchased abroad. In contrast, Japan's Toyota Sienna model is far more American, with 90 percent local components being assembled in Indiana.[6] This didn't happen overnight. Toyota has been investing in North America for 20 years in plants, suppliers, and dealerships, as well as design, testing, and research centers. Their patience has paid off, with the Camry model continuing its popularity, and with the company closing in on the declining General Motors on its own turf. Clearly, competition is borderless, with most global companies producing and selling more of their global brands and services abroad than domestically. Avon, for example, estimates it employs 5 million sales representatives globally, and believes a large share of future revenues will come from China, where it hired an additional 399,000 sales representatives in 2006.[7] Nestlé has 50 percent of its sales outside of its home market, Coca-Cola has 80 percent, and Procter & Gamble has 65 percent. Investment by global companies around the world means that this aspect of globalism benefits developing economies—through the transfer of financial, technological, and managerial resources, as well as through the development of local allies that later become self-sufficient and have other operations. Global companies are becoming less tied to specific locations, and their operations and allies are spread around the world as they source and coordinate resources and activities in the most suitable areas, and as technology facilitates faster and more flexible interactions and greater efficiencies.

It is essential, therefore, for managers to go beyond operating only in their domestic market. If they do not, they will be even further behind the majority of managers who have already recognized that they must have a global vision for their firms, beginning with preparing themselves with the skills and tools of managing in a global environment. Companies that desire to remain globally competitive and to expand their operations to other countries will have to develop a cadre of top management with experience operating abroad and an understanding of what it takes to do business in other countries and to work with people of other cultures.

Small companies are also affected by, and in turn affect, globalism. They play a vital role in contributing to their national economies—through employment, new job creation, development of new products and services, and international operations, typically exporting. The vast majority (about 98 percent) of businesses in developed economies are small and medium-sized enterprises (SMEs), which are typically referred to as those companies having fewer than 500 employees. Small businesses are rapidly discovering foreign markets. Although many small businesses are affected by globalism only to the extent that they face competing products from abroad, an increasing number of entrepreneurs are being approached by potential offshore customers, thanks to the burgeoning number of trade shows, federal and state export initiatives, and the growing use of Web sites, with the ease of making contact and placing orders online.[8] In fact, there has never been a better time for SMEs to go global; the Internet is as valid a tool for small companies to find customers and suppliers around the world as it is for large companies. By using the Internet, email, and web-conferencing, small companies can inexpensively contact customers and set up their global businesses. One example of a very small global business (two people) is that of Gayle Warwick, based in London, as described in the accompanying Management Focus.

Management Focus

Small Company, Global Approach

Gayle Warwick Fine Linen is a multinational player. Its high-end, handmade bed and table linens are woven in Europe, embroidered in Vietnam, and sold in Britain and the United States. Sales are soaring, and its full-time staff recently doubled—to two: Gayle Warwick and the assistant she hired in March.

Just because you are a U.S. citizen does not mean your business has to be based in the United States. Ms. Warwick discovered that with barriers to trade and investment falling everywhere, she was free to roam the world to make the contacts she needed to put her business together, then to return to her home base in London to run the show. At first, Ms. Warwick, who is fifty, operated from an office and a dining-room-turned-showroom in her London home in the Pimlico district. Then in September, the upscale British retailer Thomas Goode did away with its linen department in the Mayfair district and turned the space over to her company.

The catalyst was a social encounter in the early 1990s with the Vietnamese wife of one of her husband's business colleagues, a woman who showed her a hand-embroidered tablecloth from her native country and invited Ms. Warwick to visit her in Vietnam. The two women made the trip in 1995, had samples made, and ordered other linens, which they shipped home and sold at charity Christmas fairs.

It was a start—but just a start. "I thought there might be something in this, but I wasn't sure what," Ms. Warwick said. "There was no connect-the-dots from my past to that moment and idea."

When the Vietnamese woman moved away the next year, Ms. Warwick decided to go to Vietnam on her own to explore the possibility of setting up a linen business. That trip convinced her that she needed to do more research. With the help of $16,000 in savings, she spent the next three years traveling to Italy, Ireland, and Switzerland to talk with linen and organic-cotton spinners, weavers, and

Gayle Warwick's company, which is based in London, has its handmade bed and table linens woven in Europe, embroidered in Vietnam, and sold in Britain and the United States.
SOURCE: Courtesy of Jonathan Player.

finishers; to France and Germany to attend textile trade fairs; and to Vietnam to find embroiderers. "You have to be really tenacious," she said of her learning experience.

Her increasing expertise and the contacts she made paid off. For example, executives of a French quality-control company in Ho Chi Minh City, once known as Saigon, put her in touch with exporters in Hanoi, who in turn helped her find skilled craftspeople in northern Vietnamese villages to work on her designs. She hired a French freight forwarder, SDV International Logistics, to handle her far-flung business by shipping unfinished and finished fabrics within Europe and to Vietnam, then delivering the embroidered linens to London and the United States. Although they do not do so for Ms. Warwick, freight forwarders can also manage payments, a potential godsend for small exporters dealing with partners scattered around the globe.

Regional Trading Blocs

> *The dominance of the United States is already over. What is emerging is a world economy of blocs represented by the North American Free Trade Agreement (NAFTA), the EU, and the Association of Southeast Asian Nations (ASEAN). There's no one center in this world economy.*
>
> (the late) PETER DRUCKER[9]

Much of today's world trade takes place within three regional free-trade blocs (Western Europe, Asia, and the Americas) grouped around the three dominant currencies (the euro, the yen, and the dollar). These trade blocs are continually expanding their borders to include neighboring countries, either directly or with separate agreements.

The European Union

The European Union (EU) now comprises a 27-nation unified market of over 400 million people. The map in Exhibit 1-2 shows the 25 as of December 2006; Bulgaria and Romania joined in January of 2007.

This "borderless" market now includes ten Central and Eastern Europe (CEE) countries—the Czech Republic, Estonia, Hungary, Latvia, Lithuania, Poland, the Slovak Republic, and Slovenia—as well as Malta and Cyprus. They joined the EU in May 2004, having met the EU accession requirements, including privatizing state-run businesses, improving the infrastructure, and revamping their finance and banking systems.[10] Bulgaria and Romania joined in January 2007; Turkey is an official candidate but unlikely to meet the requirements before 2015.

With the euro now a legally tradable currency, Europe's business environment is being transformed. The vast majority of legislative measures have been adopted to create an internal market with free movement of goods and people among the EU countries. The elimination of internal tariffs and customs, as well as financial and commercial barriers, has not eliminated national pride. Although most people in Europe are thought of simply as Europeans, they still think of themselves first as British, French, Danish, Italian, etc., and are wary of giving too much power to centralized institutions or of giving up their national

EXHIBIT 1-2 EU Member States, 2007 Admissions, and Candidate Countries

SOURCE: http://en.wikipedia.org

culture. The continuing enlargement of the EU to include many less prosperous countries has also promoted divisions among the "older" members.[11]

Global managers face two major tasks. One is strategic (dealt with more fully in Chapter 6): How firms outside of Europe can deal with the implications of the EU and of what some have called a "Fortress Europe"—that is, a market giving preference to insiders. The other task is cultural: How to deal effectively with multiple sets of national cultures, traditions, and customs within Europe, such as differing attitudes about how much time should be spent on work versus leisure activities.

Asia

> *The next phase of globalization will most likely have an Asian face. Americans and Europeans will not find it comfortable . . .*

> U.S. National Intelligence Council, quoted in Financial Times,
> *March 3, 2006*[12]

Japan and the Four Tigers—Singapore, Hong Kong, Taiwan, and South Korea, each of which has abundant natural resources and labor—have provided most of the capital and expertise for Asia's developing countries. Indeed, Japan is the world's second largest economy, and China is its biggest trading partner. Now the focus is on China's role in driving closer integration in the region through its rapidly growing exports. Japan continues to negotiate trade agreements with its neighbors; China is negotiating with the entire thirteen-member ASEAN, while ASEAN is negotiating for earlier development of its own free trade area, Asean Free Trade Area (AFTA).[13]

> *The Chinese market offers big opportunities for foreign investment, but you must learn to tolerate ambiguity and find a godfather to look after your political connections.*

> Financial Times[14]

China has enjoyed recent success as an export powerhouse, a status built on its strengths of low costs and a constant flow of capital. Having achieved its quest to join the World Trade Organization (WTO) in 2002, its gross domestic product (GDP) growth rate (10.7 percent in 2006) has been the fastest growth rate in the world for several consecutive years. Its vast population of low-wage workers and massive consumer market potential has attracted offshoring of manufacturing from companies around the world. In fact there are 49,000 U.S. companies alone operating in China.[15] It is estimated that China has over 160 cities with populations of over 1 million:

> *One town manufactures most of the eyeglass frames in the world, while the town next door produces most of the portable cigarette lighters in the world, and the next one is doing most of the computer screens for Dell, and another is specializing in mobile phones.*

> Thomas Friedman, 2005[16]

While considerable differences are found among the country's regions, making for quite varied markets, it is clear that China is slowly opening its doors. China seems to be stuck halfway between a command economy and a market economy, with capital allocation still largely state-controlled.[17] Central, regional, and local political influences create unpredictability for businesses, as do the arbitrary legal systems, suspect data, and underdeveloped infrastructure. In addition to foreign investment, China continues to enjoy significant inflows of money from the ethnic Chinese outside of China, often called the "Bamboo Network" or the "Overseas Chinese" network (further discussed in Chapter 8).

While China is known as the world's factory (Wal-Mart is China's eighth biggest trading partner), **India** is becoming known as the world's services supplier. India is the world's leader for outsourced back-office services, and increasingly for high-tech services. India is the fastest-growing free market democracy, with an estimated growth of 8.1 percent through March 2006.[18] Yet its biggest hindrance to growth, in particular for the manufacturing sector, remains its poor infrastructure. The Comparative Management in Focus section, later in this chapter, as well as the chapter opening profile, highlights the growth and changes in India's economy.

In **South Asia** an agreement was signed to form the South Asia Association of Regional Cooperation (SAARC), a free trade pact among seven South Asian nations: Bangladesh, Bhutan, India, the Maldives, Nepal, Pakistan, and Sri Lanka, effective January 1, 2006. The agreement will lower tariffs to 25 percent within three to five years and eliminate them within seven years. The member nations comprise 1.5 billion people, with an estimated one-third of them living in poverty. Trade in South Asia is estimated at $14 billion, though the majority of that trade will be between India and Pakistan, the two largest countries in the region.[19] Officials in those countries hope to follow the success of the other Asian regional bloc, the ASEAN.

The Americas

The goal of the NAFTA between the United States, Canada, and Mexico was to bring faster growth, more jobs, better working conditions, and a cleaner environment for all as a result of increased exports and trade. This trading bloc—"one America"—has 421 million consumers. Now, many years since the 1993 agreement, the debate continues about the extent to which those goals have been accomplished. That perspective varies, of course, among the three NAFTA countries and also varies according to how it has affected individual business firms and employees in various parts of those countries.

However, some changes for Mexico in those years are not debatable, whether or not they all are attributable to the NAFTA. Mexican trade policy is among the most open in the world, and Mexico has become an important exporting and importing power. Trade with the United States and Canada has tripled since NAFTA was ratified in 1994. In recent years almost 85 percent of Mexico's exports have gone to the United States, making the Mexican economic cycles very dependent on the American economic behavior. Mexico, however, has signed 12 trade agreements with 43 nations, putting 90 percent of its trade under free trade regulations; the latest agreement was made with Japan in 2005.[20]

The trade agreements have resulted in an increase in GDP from $403 billion in 1993 to $717 billion in 2005, with exports of $213.4 billion. Mexico's 3 percent GDP growth in 2005 also included an increase in remittances by migrants—those contributions made by Mexicans living abroad both legally and illegally, mostly in the United States, to their families at home in Mexico; they comprised $18 billion in 2005, up from $2.4 billion in 1994.[21] One has to wonder this then: If more jobs are available in Mexico and if people are being paid fairly, why are so many crossing the border to find jobs? Certainly, recent competition from China for offshored jobs from foreign firms has put downward pressure on opportunities for Mexico, as manufacturing facilities and some service facilities migrate from Mexico to China in a race for the lowest cost operations.[22]

Modeled after the NAFTA agreement, the goal of the U.S.-Central America Free Trade Agreement (CAFTA) was to promote trade liberalization between the United States and five Central American countries: Costa Rica, El Salvador, Guatemala, Honduras, and Nicaragua. In 2004, the Dominican Republic joined the negotiations, and the agreement was renamed DR-CAFTA. The treaty must be approved by the U.S. Congress and by National Assemblies in the Central American countries before it becomes law. CAFTA is considered to be a stepping-stone to the larger Free Trade Area of the Americas (FTAA) that would encompass 34 economies, but which has met with considerable resistance.[23]

Other Regions in the World

Sweeping political, economic, and social changes around the world present new challenges to global managers. The worldwide move away from communism, together with the trend toward privatization, has had an enormous influence on the world economy. Economic freedom is a critical factor in the relative wealth of nations.

One of the most striking changes today is that almost all nations have suddenly begun to develop decentralized, free market systems in order to manage a global economy of intense competition, the complexity of high-tech industrialization, and an awakening hunger for freedom.

The Russian Federation

Foreign investment in Russia, as well as its consumers' climbing confidence and affluence, bode well for the economy. However corruption and government interference persist . . .

The investment climate is clouded by the increasing willingness . . . of the Russian government to intervene in the economy.

THE FINANCIAL TIMES,
May 16, 2006[24]

Until recently, Russia has been regarded as more politically stable. New land, legal and labor codes, as well as the now-convertible ruble have encouraged foreign firms to take advantage of opportunities in that immense area, in particular the vast natural resources and the well-educated population of 145 million. Moscow, in particular, is teeming with new construction sites, high-end cars, and new restaurants. Growth has been steady, and in 2006 alone there was about $17 billion in foreign direct investment. The real GDP growth for Russia is considered to be controlled by the so-called business "oligarchs"—a small group of businesspeople with political influence who capitalized on the privatization of Russia's economy and who limit competitive opportunities for small businesses. However, foreign investors became very wary after the break up of the Yukos oil group, including jailing its head Mikhail Khodorkovsky with an eight-year sentence; this made foreign investors reluctant to propose new deals that would require political approval. The forced government auction, resulting in bankruptcy, was viewed as President Putin's way to quell the political ambitions of Khodorkovsky. About two dozen Russian companies have come under the control of the Kremlin in the last few years, including newspapers and banks.[25]

Less … change that has come about more slow … NP) and low per capita income, as well … s and high international debt. Their econo … vernment intervention discourage the f … al and South America, the Middle East … ent to stimulate economic growth. Afric … f the world's investors, although it recei … rica, which has the region's biggest econo … ey have a competitive edge on the Afric … parts of the world.[26] Vodacom of Sout … Kindu, Congo.

… l risks, LDCs offer considerable pote … rn trade-offs and keeping up with polit … e two of the many demands on

An ad on a shop in Kindu, Congo, promotes cell phone service from Vodacom of South Africa
SOURCE: Copyright Adam Roberts, Reprinted by permission.

international managers. India is one country whose economy is booming as a result of opening up to global business and providing highly skilled and educated workers to foreign companies. (For further discussion of the effects of globalization on India's landscape and culture see the Comparative Management in Focus: Opening Economy Revitalizes India.)

Comparative Management in Focus

Opening Economy Revitalizes India

Map 1-1 India

Gurgaon, India—Tarun Narula, a 25-year-old computer instructor, celebrated Mohandas K. Gandhi's birthday on Oct. 2 by going to the Metropolitan Mall. So did so many thousands of others that the parking lot was full, as were those of the other two malls across and down the street. Indian-made sport utility vehicles, cars, and motorcycles fought for space, choking the roads of this satellite city south of Delhi.

Inside the malls, young people sipped coffee at Barista Coffee, the Starbucks of India. They wandered through Indian department stores, Marks and Spencer, Lacoste, and Reebok. Families took children to McDonald's or the Subway sandwich shop. Moviegoers chose between "Boom," a Bollywood film with a decidedly Western touch of vulgarity, and "2 Fast 2 Furious."

This is no longer the India of Gandhi, among history's most famous ascetics.

The change in values, habits and options in India—not just from his day, but from a mere decade ago—is undeniable, and so is the sense of optimism about India's economic prospects.

He's everywhere. McDonalds is in Gurgaon, India—indicative of the global economy.
SOURCE: Amy Waldman, NYTimes

Much of India is still mired in poverty, but just over a decade after the Indian economy began shaking off its statist shackles and opening to the outside world, it is booming. The surge is based on strong industry and agriculture, rising Indian and foreign investment and American-style consumer spending by a growing middle class, including the people under age 25 who now make up half the country's population. India's economy is the second fastest growing in the world, after China.

The growth of the past decade has put more money in the pockets of an expanding middle class, 250 million to 300 million strong, and more choices in front of them. Their appetites are helping to fuel demand-led growth for the first time in decades.

India is now the world's fastest growing telecom market, with more than one million new mobile phone subscriptions sold each month. Indians are buying about 10,000 motorcycles a day. Banks are now making $15 billion a year in home loans, with the lowest interest rates in decades helping to spur the spending, building and borrowing. Credit and debit cards are slowly gaining. The potential for even more market growth is enormous, a fact recognized by multinationals and Indian companies alike. After huffing and puffing in place for eight or nine years, "the train has left the station," C. K. Prahalad, a professor at the University of Michigan Business School, said of the Indian economy.

More than a decade after India began opening its economy by reducing protectionism and red tape, slowly lifting restrictions on foreign investment and reforming its financial sector, the changes are starting to show substantial results.

Companies that stumbled in the face of recession and new competitive pressures in the 1990s have increased productivity and are showing record profits. India is slowly making a name not just for software exports and service outsourcing, but also as an exporter of autos, auto parts, and motorcycles.

Nature has played a part as well. The seasonal monsoon that ended recently was the best this agriculture-dependent economy has seen in at least five years, with normal or excess rainfall in 33 of 36 of the country's sub-regions. That, in turn, is putting income and credit in rural pockets, spurring a run on consumer goods that will only strengthen when the harvest comes in later this year.

In some places, the economic transformation is startling. Look at islands of prosperity like Gurgaon, or Bangalore, and you see an India that many Americans—not to speak of Indians—would not recognize.

It is a place where a young fashion designer like Swati Bhargava, 27, who works for a company that exports clothes to American and French chains, can buy stylish Indian clothes, eat at Pizza Hut, drink at Barista, and contemplate the country mutating around her.

SOURCE: Amy Waldman, "Sizzling Economy Revitalizes India," *New York Times*, October 20, 2003. Copyright © 2003 by The New York Times Co. Reprinted with permission.

Information Technology

Of all the developments propelling global business today, the one that is transforming the international manager's agenda more than any is the rapid advance in information technology (IT). The speed and accuracy of information transmission are changing the nature of the global manager's job by making geographic barriers less relevant. Indeed, the necessity of being able to access IT is being recognized by managers and families around the world, who are giving priority to being "plugged in" over other lifestyle accoutrements.

Information can no longer be totally controlled by governments; political, economic, market, and competitive information is available almost instantaneously to anyone around the world, permitting informed and accurate decision making. Even cultural barriers are being lowered gradually by the role of information in educating societies about one another. Indeed, as consumers around the world become more aware, through various media, of how people in other countries live, their tastes and preferences begin to converge.

The explosive growth of information technology is both a cause and an effect of globalism. The information revolution is boosting productivity around the world. In addition, use of the Internet is propelling electronic commerce around the world (as discussed later in this chapter). Companies around the world are linked electronically to their employees, customers, distributors, suppliers, and alliance partners in many countries. Technology, in all its forms, gets dispersed around the world by **multinational corporations (MNCs)** and their alliance partners in many countries. However, some of the information intended for electronic transmission is currently subject to export controls by an EU directive intended to protect private information about its citizens. So, perhaps IT is not yet "borderless" but rather is subject to the same norms, preferences, and regulations as "human" cross-border interactions.

The Globalization of Human Capital

Firms around the world have been offshoring manufacturing jobs to low-cost countries for decades—that is, they close down all or part of a factory, say, in Detroit and open it back up in China or Mexico. An increasing number of firms are producing or assembling parts of their products in many countries and then integrating them into their global supply chains. More recently many are now also outsourcing white-collar jobs to India, China, Mexico, and the Phillippines: customer support, medical analysis, technical work, computer programming, form filling and claims processing—all these jobs can now move around the globe in the same way that farming and factory jobs could a century ago.[27] We have all experienced talking to someone in India when we call the airlines or a technology support service; now increasingly sophisticated jobs are being outsourced, leaving many people in developed economies to worry about job retention. IBM's India staff, for example, jumped from 9,000 to 43,000 from 2004 through mid-2006, making it's staff the second largest behind the United States.[28]

Forrester Research predicted that 3.3 million (U.S.) jobs would be lost in service-sector outsourcing by 2015, and added that "the information technology industry will lead the initial overseas exodus."[29] A programmer in India, for example—well educated, skilled, and English-speaking—earns about $20,000 a year, compared to $80,000 in the United States. In Bangalore, India, MNCs such as Intel, Dell, IBM, Yahoo!, and AOL employ workers in chip design, software, call centers, and tax processing.[30] In March 2006, Dell, the world's largest maker of personal computers, announced plans to double the size of its workforce in India, to 20,000, and is looking for a site for its manufacturing unit in the country. Dell has four call centers in India, where the bulk of its 10,000 employees work, as well as software development and product testing centers. Referring to the country's highly educated and English-speaking workers in technological fields, Michael Dell addressed a news conference during his visit to Bangalore, India's outsourcing capital, saying:

> *There is a fantastic opportunity to attract talent. We will ensure a major recruitment push in engineering talents. The company plans to double its hardware engineering staff to 600 in a year.*
>
> MICHAEL DELL,
> *March 21, 2006*[31]

In China—long the world's low-cost manufacturing hub—jobs are on the upswing for back-office support for financial services and for telecom and retail companies in Asia. Such employees communicate to people in Hong Kong and Taiwan in local languages.[32] While backlash from some firms' clients has resulted in them repatriating high-end jobs, white-collar job migration is still on the rise for firms around the world, bringing with it a new phase in economic globalization and competition.

The Global Manager's Role

Whatever your level of involvement, it is important to understand the global business environment and its influence on the manager's role. This complex role demands a contingency approach to dynamic environments, each of which has its own unique requirements. Within the larger context of global trends and competition, the rules of the game for the global manager are set by each country (see Exhibit 1-3): its political and economic agenda, its technological status and level of development, its regulatory environment, its comparative and competitive advantages, and its cultural norms. The astute manager will analyze the new environment, anticipate how it may affect the future of the home company, and then develop appropriate strategies and operating styles.

THE POLITICAL AND ECONOMIC ENVIRONMENT

Proactive globally-oriented firms maintain an up-to-date profile of the political and economic environment of the countries in which they maintain operations (or have plans for future investment).

An important aspect of the political environment is the phenomenon of ethnicity—a driving force behind political instability around the world. In fact, many uprisings and conflicts that are thought to be political in nature are actually expressions of differences among ethnic groupings. Often, religious disputes lie at the heart of those differences. Uprisings based on religion operate either in conjunction with ethnic differences (as probably was the case in the former Yugoslavia) or as separate from them (as in Northern Ireland). Many terrorist activities are also based on religious differences, as in the Middle

EXHIBIT 1-3   An Open System Model

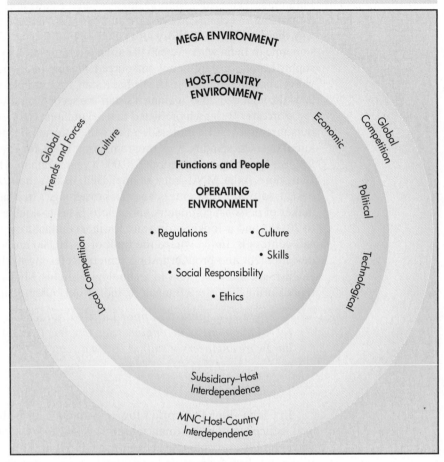

East. Managers must understand the ethnic and religious composition of the host country in order to anticipate problems of general instability, as well as those of an operational nature, such as effects on the workforce, on production and access to raw materials, and on the market. For example, consider the following:

> *In Pakistan one must understand the differences between Punjabi and Sindi. In Malaysia it is essential to recognize the special economic relationship between Chinese and Malay. In the Philippines it is important to understand the significant and lead financial role played by the Filipino-Chinese.*[33]

Political Risk

> *In a dramatic sign of how high energy prices have sparked a resurgence of nationalism from Caracas to Moscow, Bolivia nationalized its natural-gas industry, ordering foreign companies to give up control of fields and accept much tougher operating terms within six months or leave the country.*
>
> WALL STREET JOURNAL,
> *May 2, 2006*[34]

Bolivian President Evo Morales' move to nationalize the national gas industry followed that in Venezuela, where Mr. Chavez, in a move against Big Oil, forced major oil companies to accept a minority stake in fields that they had owned, also giving more money for higher taxes and royalties.[35]

The managers of a global firm need to investigate the political risks to which they expose their company in certain countries—and the implications of those risks for the economic success of the firm. **Political risks** are any governmental action or politically motivated event that could adversely affect the long-run profitability or value of a firm. The Middle East, as we have seen, has traditionally been an unstable area where political risk heavily influences business decisions.

In unstable areas, multinational corporations weigh the risks of nationalization or expropriation, as in Bolivia and Venezuela in the examples previously cited. **Nationalization** refers to the forced sale of an MNC's assets to local buyers, with some compensation to the firm, perhaps leaving a minority ownership with the MNC. **Expropriation**, very rare in the last decade, occurs when a local government seizes and provides inadequate compensation for the foreign-owned assets of an MNC; when no compensation is provided, it is confiscation. In countries that have a proven history of stability and consistency, the political risk to a multinational corporation is relatively low. The risk of expropriation is highest in countries that experience continuous political upheaval, violence, and change. An event that affects all foreign firms doing business in a country or region is called a **macropolitical risk event**. In the Middle East, Iraq's invasion of Kuwait in 1990 abruptly halted all international business with and within both of those countries and caught businesses wholly unprepared.

In many regions, **terrorism** poses a severe and random political risk to company personnel and assets and can, obviously, interrupt the conduct of business. According to Micklous, terrorism is "the use, or threat of use, of anxiety-inducing . . . violence for ideological or political purposes."[36] The increasing incidence of terrorism around the world concerns MNCs. In particular, the kidnapping of business executives has become quite common. An event that affects one industry or company or only a few companies is called a **micropolitical risk event**.[37] Such events have become more common than macropolitical risk events. Such micro action is often called "creeping expropriation," indicating a government's gradual and subtle action against foreign firms.[38] This is when a "death from 1,000 cuts" comes in—"when you haven't been expropriated, but it takes ten times longer to do anything."[39] Typically, such continuing problems with an investment present more difficulty for foreign firms than do major events that are insurable by political-risk insurers. The following list describes seven typical political risk events common today (and possible in the future):

1. Expropriation of corporate assets without prompt and adequate compensation
2. Forced sale of equity to host-country nationals, usually at or below depreciated book value
3. Discriminatory treatment against foreign firms in the application of regulations or laws
4. Barriers to **repatriation** of funds (profits or equity)
5. Loss of technology or other intellectual property (such as patents, trademarks, or trade names)
6. Interference in managerial decision making
7. Dishonesty by government officials, including canceling or altering contractual agreements, extortion demands, and so forth[40]

Political Risk Assessment

International companies must conduct some form of political risk assessment to manage their exposure to risk and to minimize financial losses. Typically, local managers in each country assess potentially destabilizing issues and evaluate their future impact on their company, making suggestions for dealing with possible problems. Corporate advisers then establish guidelines for each local manager to follow in handling these problems. Dow Chemical has a program in which it uses line managers trained in political and economic analysis, as well as executives in foreign subsidiaries, to provide risk analyses of each country.[41]

Risk assessment by multinational corporations usually takes two forms. One uses experts or consultants familiar with the country or region under consideration. Such consultants, advisers, and committees usually monitor important trends that may portend political change, such as the development of opposition or destabilizing political parties. They then assess the likelihood of political change and develop several plausible scenarios to describe possible future political conditions.

A second and increasingly common means of political risk assessment used by MNCs is the development of internal staff and in-house capabilities. This type of assessment may be accomplished by having staff assigned to foreign subsidiaries, by having affiliates monitor local political activities, or by hiring people with expertise in the political and economic conditions in regions critical to the firm's operations. Frequently, all means are used. The focus must be on monitoring political issues before they become headlines; the ability to minimize the negative effects on the firm—or to be the first to take advantage of opportunities—is greatly reduced once a major media source, such as CNN, has put out the news.

No matter how sophisticated the methods of political risk assessment become, nothing can replace timely information from people on the front line. In other words, sophisticated techniques and consultations are useful as an addition to, but not as a substitute for, the line managers in foreign subsidiaries, many of whom are host-country nationals. These managers represent the most important resource for current information on the political environment, and how it might affect their firm, because they are uniquely situated at the meeting point of the firm and the host country. Prudent MNCs, however, weigh the subjectivity of these managers' assessments and also realize that similar events will have different effects from one country to another.

An additional technique, the assessment of political risk through the use of computer modeling, is now becoming fairly common. One firm, American Can, uses a program called PRISM (Primary Risk Investment Screening Matrix), which digests information from overseas managers and consultants on 200 variables and reduces them to an index of economic desirability and an index of political and economic stability. Those countries with the most favorable PRISM indices are then considered by American Can for investment.[42] Such a program, of course, is only as good as its input data—which is often of doubtful quality because of inadequate information systems in many countries and because the information is processed subjectively.

To analyze their data regarding potential risks, some companies attempt to quantify variables into a ranking system for countries. They use their staff or outside consultants to allocate a minimum and a maximum score for criteria they deem important to them on (1) the political and economic environment, (2) domestic economic conditions, and (3) external economic relations. The sum of the individual scores for each variable represents a total risk evaluation range for each country.[43] One drawback of these quantitative systems is that they rely on information based primarily on past events. They are therefore limited in their ability to predict political events in a volatile environment.

Still another method, more rapidly responsive to and predictive of political changes, is the early-warning system. This system uses lead indicators to predict possible political dangers, such as signs of violence or riots, developing pressure on the MNC to hire more local workers, or pending import–export restrictions.[44] The early-warning analysis is typically separated into macrorisk and microrisk elements.

In addition to assessing the political risk facing a firm, alert managers also examine the specific types of impact that such risks may have on the company. For an autonomous international subsidiary, most of the impact from political risks (nationalization, terrorism) will be at the level of the ownership and control of the firm because its acquisition by the host country would provide the state with a fully operational business.[45] For global firms, the primary risks are likely to be from restrictions (on imports, exports, currency, and so forth), with the impact at the level of the firm's transfers (or exchanges) of money, products, or component parts.[46]

Managing Political Risk

After assessing the potential political risk of investing or maintaining current operations in a country, managers face perplexing decisions on how to manage that risk. On one level, they can decide to suspend their firm's dealings with a certain country at a given point—either by the avoidance of investment or by the withdrawal of current investment (by selling or abandoning plants and assets). On another level, if they decide that the risk is relatively low in a particular country or that a high-risk environment is worth the potential returns, they may choose to start (or maintain) operations there and to accommodate that risk through adaptation to the political regulatory environment. That adaptation can take many forms, each designed to respond to the concerns of a particular local area. Some means of adaptation suggested by Taoka and Beeman are as follows:

1. Equity sharing includes the initiation of joint ventures with nationals (individuals or those in firms, labor unions, or government) to reduce political risks.

2. Participative management requires that the firm actively involve nationals, including those in labor organizations or government, in the management of the subsidiary.

3. Localization of the operation includes the modification of the subsidiary's name, management style, and so forth, to suit local tastes. Localization seeks to transform the subsidiary from a foreign firm to a national firm.

4. Development assistance includes the firm's active involvement in infrastructure development (foreign-exchange generation, local sourcing of materials or parts, management training, technology transfer, securing external debt, and so forth).[47]

In addition to avoidance and adaptation, two other means of risk reduction available to managers are dependency and hedging. Some means that managers might use to maintain *dependency*—keeping the subsidiary and the host nation dependent on the parent corporation—are as follows:

1. Input control means that the firm maintains control over key inputs, such as raw materials, components, technology, and know-how.

2. Market control requires that the firm keep control of the means of distribution (for instance, by only manufacturing components for the parent firm or legally blocking sales outside the host country).

3. Position control involves keeping certain key subsidiary management positions in the hands of expatriate or home-office managers.

4. Staged contribution strategies mean that the firm plans to increase, in each successive year, the subsidiary's contributions to the host nation (in the form of tax revenues, jobs, infrastructure development, hard-currency generation, and so forth). For this strategy to be most effective, the firm must inform the host nation of these projected contributions as an incentive.[48]

Finally, even if the company cannot diminish or change political risks, it can minimize the losses associated with these events by hedging. Some means of **hedging** are as follows:

1. Political risk insurance is offered by most industrialized countries. In the United States, the Overseas Private Investment Corporation (OPIC) provides coverage for new investments in projects in friendly, less developed countries. Insurance minimizes losses arising from specific risks—such as the inability to repatriate profits, expropriation, nationalization, or confiscation—and from damage as a result of war, terrorism, and so forth.[49] The Foreign Credit Insurance Association (FCIA) also covers political risks caused by war, revolution, currency inconvertibility, and the cancellation of import or export licenses. However, political risk insurance covers only the loss of a firm's assets, not the loss of revenue resulting from expropriation.[50]

2. Local debt financing (money borrowed in the host country), where available, helps a firm hedge against being forced out of operation without adequate compensation. In such instances, the firm withholds debt repayment in lieu of sufficient compensation for its business losses.

Multinational corporations also manage political risk through their global strategic choices. Many large companies diversify their operations both by investing in many countries and by operating through joint ventures with a local firm or government or through local licensees. By involving local people, companies, and agencies, firms minimize the risk of negative outcomes due to political events. (See Chapters 6 and 7 for further discussion of these and other global strategies.)

Managing Terrorism Risk

No longer is the risk of terrorism for global businesses focused only on certain areas such as South America or the Middle East. That risk now has to be considered in countries such as the United States, which had previously been regarded as safe. Eighty countries lost citizens in the World Trade Center attack on September 11, 2001. Many companies from Asia and Europe had office branches in the towers of the World Trade Center; most of those offices, along with the employees from those countries, were destroyed in the attack. Thousands of lives and billions of dollars were lost, not only by those immediately affected by the attack but also by countless small and large businesses impacted by the ripple effect; global airlines and financial markets were devastated.

As incidents of terrorism accelerate around the world, many companies are increasingly aware of the need to manage the risk of terrorism. In high-risk countries, both IBM and Exxon try to develop a benevolent image through charitable contributions to the local community. They also try to maintain low profiles and minimize publicity in the host countries by using, for example, discreet corporate signs at company sites.[51]

Some companies have put together teams to monitor the patterns of terrorism around the world. Kidnappings are common in Latin America (as a means of raising money for political activities). Abductions in Colombia hit a record 3,029 in 2000.[52] In the Middle East, airplane hijackings, kidnapping of foreigners, and blackmail (for the release of political prisoners) are common. In Western Europe, terrorists typically aim bombs at U.S.-owned banks and computer companies. Almost all MNCs have stepped up their security measures abroad, hiring consultants in counterterrorism (to train employees to cope with the threat of terrorism) and advising their employees to avoid U.S. airlines when flying overseas. For many firms, however, the opportunities outweigh the threats, even in high-risk areas.

Economic Risk

Closely connected to a country's political stability is its economic environment—and the relative risk that it may pose to foreign companies. A country's level of economic development generally determines its economic stability and, therefore, its relative risk to a foreign firm. Most industrialized nations pose little risk of economic instability; less developed nations pose more risk. This risk was illustrated when Argentina's economic woes, estimated to result in the country's economy shrinking up to 15 percent in 2002, negatively affected foreign firms doing business there.

A country's ability or intention to meet its financial obligations determines its economic risk. The economic risk incurred by a foreign corporation usually falls into one of two main categories. Its subsidiary (or other investment) in a specific country may become unprofitable if (1) the government abruptly changes its domestic monetary or fiscal policies or (2) the government decides to modify its foreign-investment policies. The latter situation would threaten the company's ability to repatriate its earnings and would create a financial or interest-rate risk. Furthermore, the risk of exchange-rate volatility results in currency translation exposure to the firm when the balance sheet of the entire corporation is consolidated, and may cause a negative cash flow from the foreign subsidiary. Currency translation exposure occurs when the value of one country's currency changes relative to that of another. For a U.S. company operating in Mexico, the peso devaluation in the late 1990s meant that the company's assets in that country were worth less when translated into dollars on the financial statements, but the firm's liabilities in Mexico were also less. When exchange-rate changes are radical, repercussions are felt around the world. For example, when the Russian ruble was devalued in 1998, it was unfortunate for the Russian people because their money bought much less and for Russian firms because they did not have enough buying power to purchase products from overseas, which meant that the sales of foreign companies declined. On the other hand, foreign companies suddenly had more purchasing power in Russia to outsource raw materials, labor, and so on.

Because every MNC operating overseas exposes itself to some level of economic risk, often affecting its everyday operational profitability, managers constantly reassess the level of risk their companies may face in any specific country or region of the world. Four methods of analyzing economic risk, or a country's creditworthiness, are recommended by John Mathis, a professor of international economics who has also served as senior financial policy analyst for the World Bank. These methods are (1) the quantitative approach, (2) the qualitative approach, (3) a combination of both of these approaches, and (4) the checklist approach.

The *quantitative approach*, says Mathis, "attempts to measure statistically a country's ability to honor its debt obligation."[53] This measure is arrived at by assigning different weights to economic variables in order to produce a composite index used to monitor the country's creditworthiness over time and to make comparisons with other countries. A drawback of this approach is that it does not take into account different stages of development among the countries it compares.

The **qualitative approach** evaluates a country's economic risk by assessing the competence of its leaders and analyzing the types of policies they are likely to implement. This approach entails a subjective assessment by the researcher in the process of interviewing those leaders and projecting the future direction of the economy.

The **checklist approach** relies on a few easily measurable and timely criteria believed to reflect or indicate changes in the creditworthiness of the country. Researchers develop various vulnerability indicators that categorize countries in terms of their ability to withstand economic volatility. Most corporations recognize that neither this, nor any single approach, can provide a comprehensive economic risk profile of a country. Therefore, they try to use a combination of approaches.

THE LEGAL ENVIRONMENT

The prudent global manager consults with legal services, both locally and at headquarters, to comply with host-country regulations and to maintain cooperative long-term relationships in the local area. If the manager waits until a problem arises, little legal recourse may be available outside of local interpretation and enforcement. Indeed, this has been the experience of many foreign managers in China, where financial and legal systems remain rudimentary in spite of attempts to show the world a capitalist face. Managers there often simply ignore their debts to foreign companies as they did under the old socialist system. The lesson to many foreign companies in China is that they are losing millions because Beijing often does not stand behind the commitments of its state-owned enterprises. David Ji, a Chinese-American electronics entrepreneur, experienced this painful lesson:

> *A year after the Chinese police apprehended him in his hotel room during a business trip, Mr. Ji remains in China as a pawn—his colleagues say a hostage— in a commercial dispute that pits Changhong, China's largest television manufacturer, against Apex Digital, Mr. Ji's electronics trading company based in Los Angeles.*

> THE NEW YORK TIMES,
> *November 1, 2005*[54]

Changhong claimed that Apex owed it $470 million, but Mr. Ji claimed the amount is less than $150 million. Mr. Ji, after two months in custody, had no recourse under China's judicial system, which fiercely protects its powerful companies like Changhong. There is heavy pressure from foreign companies for Beijing to embrace global legal norms with the same determination that it has pursued foreign trade.[55]

Although no guarantee is possible, the risk of massive losses may be minimized, among other ways, by making sure you get approval from related government offices (national, provincial, and local), seeing that you are not going to run amok of long-term government goals, and getting loan guarantees from the headquarters of one of Beijing's main banks. Some of the contributing factors in cases like Mr. Ji's are often the personal connections—guanxi—involved and the fact that some courts offer their services to the business community for profit. In addition, many judges get their jobs through nepotism rather than by virtue of a law degree.[56]

Although the regulatory environment for international managers consists of the many local laws and the court systems in those countries in which they operate, certain other legal issues are covered by international law, which governs relationships between sovereign countries, the basic units in the world political system. One such agreement, which regulates international business by spelling out the rights and obligations of the seller and the buyer, is the United Nations Convention on Contracts for the International Sale of Goods (CISG). This applies to contracts for the sale of goods between countries that have adopted the convention.

Generally speaking, the manager of the foreign subsidiary or foreign operating division will comply with the host country's legal system. Such systems, derived from common law, civil law, or Muslim law, are a reflection of the country's culture, religion, and traditions. Under **common law**, used in the United States and 26 other countries of English origin or influence, past court decisions act as precedents to the interpretation of the law and to common custom. **Civil law** is based on a comprehensive set of laws organized into a code. Interpretation of these laws is based on reference to codes and statutes. About 70 countries, predominantly in Europe (e.g., France and Germany), are ruled by civil law, as is Japan. In Islamic countries, such as Saudi Arabia, the dominant legal system is **Islamic law**; based on religious beliefs, it dominates all aspects of life. Islamic law is followed in approximately 27 countries and combines, in varying degrees, civil, common, and indigenous law.

Contract Law

A **contract** is an agreement by the parties concerned to establish a set of rules to govern a business transaction. Contract law plays a major role in international business transactions because of the complexities arising from the differences in the legal systems of participating countries and because the host government in many developing and communist countries is often a third party in the contract. Both common law and civil law countries enforce contracts, although their means of resolving disputes differ. Under civil law, it is assumed that a contract reflects promises that will be enforced without specifying the details in the contract; under common law, the details of promises must be written into the contract to be enforced. Astute international managers recognize that they will have to draft contracts in legal contexts different from their own, and they prepare themselves accordingly by consulting with experts in international law before going overseas. In some countries "The risk is, you could have a contract torn up or changed. We're just going to have to adjust to that in the West," says Robert Broadfoot, who heads the Political & Economic Risk Consultancy in Hong Kong. He says that Western companies think they can avoid political risk by spelling out every detail in a contract, but "in Asia, there is no shortcut for managing the relationship."[57] In other words, the contract is in the relationship, not on the paper, and the way to ensure the reliability of the agreement is to nurture the relationship.

Even a deal that has been implemented for some time may start to get watered down at a time when you cannot do anything about it. A Japanese-led consortium experienced this problem after it built an expressway in Bangkok. The Thai government later lowered the toll that it had agreed could be charged for use of the road. This is a subtle form of expropriation, since a company cannot simply pack up a road and leave.[58] Neglect regarding contract law may leave a firm burdened with an agent who does not perform the expected functions, or a firm may be faced with laws that prevent management from laying off employees (often the case in Belgium, the Netherlands, Germany, Sweden, and elsewhere).

Other Regulatory Issues

Differences in laws and regulations from country to country are numerous and complex. These and other issues in the regulatory environment that concern multinational firms are briefly discussed here.

Countries often impose protectionist policies, such as tariffs, quotas, and other trade restrictions, to give preference to their own products and industries. The Japanese have come under much criticism for protectionism, which they use to limit imports of foreign goods while they continue exporting consumer goods (e.g., cars and electronics) on a large scale. The U.S. auto industry continues to ask the U.S. government for protection from Japanese car imports. Calls to "Buy American," however, are thwarted by the difficulty of identifying cars that are truly U.S.-made; the intricate web of car-manufacturing alliances between Japanese and American companies often makes it difficult to distinguish the maker.

A country's tax system influences the attractiveness of investing in that country and affects the relative level of profitability for an MNC. Foreign tax credits, holidays, exemptions, depreciation allowances, and taxation of corporate profits are additional considerations the foreign investor must examine before acting. Many countries have signed tax treaties (or conventions) that define such terms as "income," "source," and "residency" and spell out what constitutes taxable activities.

The level of government involvement in the economic and regulatory environment varies a great deal among countries and has a varying impact on management practices. In Canada, the government has a significant involvement in the economy. It has a powerful role in many industries, including transportation, petrochemicals, fishing, steel, textiles, and building materials—forming partly owned or wholly owned enterprises. Wholly owned businesses are called Crown Corporations (Petro Canada, Ontario Hydro Corporation, Marystown Shipyard, Saskatchewan Telephones, and so forth), many of which are as large as major private companies. The government's role in the Canadian economy, then, is one of both control and competition.[59] Government policies, subsidies, and regulations directly affect the manager's planning process, as do other major factors in the Canadian legal environment, such as the high proportion of unionized workers (30 percent). In Quebec, the law requiring official bilingualism imposes considerable operating constraints and expenses. For a foreign subsidiary, this regulation forces managers to speak both French and English and to incur the costs of language training for employees, translators, the administration of bilingual paperwork, and so on.[60]

THE TECHNOLOGICAL ENVIRONMENT

The effects of technology around the world are pervasive—both in business and in private lives. In many parts of the world, whole generations of technological development are being skipped over. For example, many people will go straight to a digital phone without ever having had their houses wired under the analog system. Even in a remote village such as Bario, Malaysia—still lacking many traditional roads—an information highway is underway.[61] Advances in information technology are bringing about increased productivity—for employees, for companies, and for countries.[62] As noted by Thomas Friedman, technology, as well as other factors that are opening up borders—"the opening of the Berlin Wall, Netscape, work flow, outsourcing, offshoring, open-sourcing, insourcing, supply-chaining, in-forming"—have converged to create a more level playing field. The result of this convergence was

> *The creation of a global, Web-enabled playing field that allows for multiple forms of collaboration—the sharing of knowledge and work—in real time, without regard to geography, distance, or, in the near future, even language.*
>
> THOMAS FRIEDMAN,
> *The World Is Flat, 2005*[63]

Now that we are in a global information society, it is clear that corporations must incorporate into their strategic planning and their everyday operations the accelerating macro-environmental phenomenon of technoglobalism—in which the rapid developments in information and communication technologies (ICTs) are propelling globalization and vice versa.[64] Investment-led globalization is leading to global production networks, which results in global diffusion of technology to link parts of the value-added chain in different countries. That chain may comprise parts of the same firm, or it may comprise suppliers and customers, or technology-partnering alliances among two or more firms. Either way, technological developments are facilitating, indeed necessitating, the network firm structure that allows flexibility and rapid response to local needs. Clearly, the effects of technology on global trade and business transactions cannot be ignored; in addition, the Internet is propelling electronic commerce around the world. The ease of use and pervasiveness of the Internet raise difficult questions about ownership of intellectual property, consumer protection, residence location, taxation, and other issues.

New technology specific to a firm's products represents a key competitive advantage to firms and challenges international businesses to manage the transfer and diffusion of proprietary technology, with its attendant risks. Whether it is a product, a process, or a management technology, an MNC's major concern is the **appropriability of technology**—that is, the ability of the innovating firm to profit from its own technology by protecting it from competitors.

An MNC can enjoy many technological benefits from its global operations. Advances resulting from cooperative research and development (R&D) can be transferred among affiliates around the world, and specialized management knowledge can be integrated and shared. However, the risks of technology transfer and pirating are considerable and costly. Although firms face few restrictions on the creation and dissemination of technology in developed countries, less developed countries often impose restrictions on licensing agreements, royalties, and so forth, as well as on patent protection.

In Germany, for example, royalties on patents are limited to 10 percent of sales, but the patent and trademark durations are 20 years and 10 years, respectively, with 45 percent being the highest tax bracket allowed on royalties. Less developed countries tend to be comparatively more restrictive on the patent and trademark durations and on the range of unpatentable items. Egypt has no limits on royalties but will only patent production processes, and then only for 15 years.

In most countries, governments use their laws to some extent to control the flow of technology. These controls may be in place for reasons of national security. Other countries, LDCs in particular, use their investment laws to acquire needed technology (usually labor-intensive technology to create jobs), increase exports, use local technology, and train local people.

The most common methods of protecting proprietary technology are the use of patents, trademarks, trade names, copyrights, and trade secrets. Various international conventions afford some protection in participating countries; more than 80 countries adhere to the International Convention for the Protection of Industrial Property, often referred to as the Paris Union, for the protection of patents. However, restrictions and differences in the rules in some countries not signatory to the Paris Union, as well as industrial espionage, pose continuing problems for firms trying to protect their technology.

One risk to a firm's intellectual property is the inappropriate use of the technology by joint-venture partners, franchisees, licensees, and employees (especially those who move to other companies). Some countries rigorously enforce employee secrecy agreements.

Another major consideration for global managers is the need to evaluate the appropriateness of technology for the local environment—especially in less developed countries. Studying the possible cultural consequences of the transfer of technology, managers must assess whether the local people are ready and willing to change their values, expectations, and behaviors on the job to use new technological methods, whether applied to production, research, marketing, finance, or some other aspect of business. Often, a decision regarding the level of technology transfer is dominated by the host government's regulations or requirements. In some instances, the host country may require that foreign investors import only their most modern machinery and methods so that the local area may benefit from new technology. In other cases, the host country may insist that foreign companies use only labor-intensive processes, which can help to reduce high unemployment in an area. When the choice is left to international managers, experts in economic development recommend that managers make informed choices about appropriate technology. The choice of technology may be capital intensive, labor intensive, or intermediate, but the key is that it should suit the level of development in the area and the needs and expectations of the people who will use it.[65]

Global e-Business

In spite of global trade's slower-than-expected pace of advancement over the Internet, without doubt the Internet has had a considerable impact on how companies buy and sell goods around the world—mostly raw materials and services going to manufacturers. Internet-based electronic trading and data exchange are changing the way companies do business, while breaking down global barriers of time, space, logistics, and culture. However, the Internet is not totally open; governments still make sure that their laws are obeyed in cyberspace. This was evidenced when France forced Yahoo! to stop displaying Nazi trinkets for sale where French people could view them.[66] The reality is that

Different nations, and different peoples, may want a different kind of Internet – one whose language, content and norms conform more closely to their own.

FINANCIAL TIMES,
May 17, 2006[67]

There is no doubt, however, that the Internet has introduced a new level of global competition by providing efficiencies through reducing numbers of suppliers and slashing administration costs throughout the value chain. **E-business** is "the integration of systems, processes, organizations, value chains, and entire markets using Internet-based and related technologies and concepts."[68] **E-commerce** refers directly to the marketing and sales process via the Internet. Firms use e-business to help build new relationships between businesses and customers.[69] The Internet and e-business provide a number of uses and advantages in global business, including the following:

1. Convenience in conducting business worldwide; facilitating communication across borders contributes to the shift toward globalization and a global market.
2. An electronic meeting and trading place, which adds efficiency in conducting business sales.
3. A corporate Intranet service, merging internal and external information for enterprises worldwide.
4. Power to consumers as they gain access to limitless options and price differentials.
5. A link and efficiency in distribution.[70]

Although most early attention was on e-commerce, experts now believe the real opportunities are in business-to-business (**B2B**) transactions. In addition, while the scope, complexity, and sheer speed of the B2B phenomenon, including e-marketplaces, have global executives scrambling to assess the impact and their own competitive roles, estimates for growth in the e-business marketplace may have been overzealous because of the global economic slowdown and its resultant dampening of corporate IT spending. While we hear mostly about large companies embracing B2B, it is noteworthy that a large proportion of current and projected B2B use is by small and medium-sized firms, for three common purposes: supply chain, procurement, and distribution channel.

A successful Internet strategy—especially on a global scale—is, of course, not easy to create. Potential problems abound, as experienced by the European and U.S. companies surveyed by Forrester Research. Such problems include internal obstacles and politics, difficulties in regional coordination and in balancing global versus local e-commerce, and cultural differences. Such a large-scale change in organizing business clearly calls for absolute commitment from the top, empowered employees with a willingness to experiment, and good internal communications.[71] Barriers to the adoption and progression of e-business around the world include lack of readiness of partners in the value chain, such as suppliers. If companies want to have an effective marketplace, they usually must invest in increasing their trading partners' readiness and their customers' capabilities. Other barriers are cultural. In Europe, for example, "Europe's e-commerce excursion has been hindered by a laundry list of cultural and regulatory obstacles, like widely varying tax systems, language hurdles, and currency issues."[72]

In other areas of the world, barriers to creating global e-businesses include differences in physical, information, and payment infrastructure systems. In such countries, innovation is required to use local systems for implementing a Web strategy. In Japan, for example, very few transactions are conducted using credit cards. Typically, bank transfers and COD are used to pay for purchases. Also, many Japanese use convenience stores, such as 7-Eleven Japan, to pay for their online purchases by choosing that option online.[73]

For these reasons, B2B e-business is likely to expand globally faster than **B2C** (business-to-consumer) transactions. In addition, consumer e-commerce depends on each country's level of access to computers and the Internet, as well as the relative efficiency of home delivery. Clearly, companies who want to go global through e-commerce must localize to globalize, which means much more than just presenting online content in local languages.

Localizing . . . also means recognizing and conforming to the nuances, subtleties and tastes of multiple local cultures, as well as supporting transactions based on each country's currency, local connection speeds, payment preferences, laws, taxes and tariffs.[74]

In spite of various problems, use of the Internet to facilitate and improve global competitiveness continues to be explored and discovered. In the public sector in Europe, for example, the European Commission advertises tender invitations online in order to transform the way public sector contracts are awarded, using the Internet to build a truly single market.

It is clear that e-business is not only a new Web site on the Internet but also a source of significant strategic advantage. Hoping to capture this strategic advantage, the European Airbus venture—a public and private sector combination—has joined a global aerospace B2B exchange for aircraft parts. The exchange illustrates two major trends in global competition: (1) those of cooperative global alliances, even among competitors, to achieve synergies and (2) the use of technology to enable those connections and synergies.

CONCLUSION

A skillful global manager cannot develop a suitable strategic plan or consider an investment abroad without first assessing the environment—political, economic, legal, and technological—in which the company will operate. This assessment should result not so much in a comparison of countries as in a comparison of (1) the relative risk and (2) the projected return on investments among these countries. Similarly, for ongoing operations, both the subsidiary manager and headquarters management must continually monitor the environment for potentially unsettling events or undesirable changes that may require the redirection of certain subsidiaries or the entire company. Some of the critical factors affecting the global manager's environment (and therefore requiring monitoring) are listed in Exhibit 1-4.

EXHIBIT 1-4   The Environment of the Global Manager

Political Environment	**Economic Environment**
■ Form of government	■ Economic system
■ Political stability	■ State of development
■ Foreign policy	■ Economic stability
■ State companies	■ GNP
■ Role of military	■ International financial standing
■ Level of terrorism	■ Monetary/fiscal policies
■ Restrictions on imports/exports	■ Foreign investment
Regulatory Environment	**Technological Environment**
■ Legal system	■ Level of technology
■ Prevailing international laws	■ Availability of local technical skills
■ Protectionist laws	■ Technical requirements of country
■ Tax laws	■ Appropriability
■ Role of contracts	■ Transfer of technology
■ Protection for proprietary property	■ Infrastructure
■ Environmental protection	
Cultural Environment (see Part II)	

Environmental risk has become the new frontier in global business. The skills of companies and the measures taken to manage their exposure to environmental risk on a world scale will soon largely replace their ability to develop, produce, and market global brands as the key element in global competitive advantage.

The pervasive role of culture in international management will be discussed fully in Part II, with a focus on how the managerial functions and the daily operations of a firm are also affected by a subtle, but powerful, environmental factor in the host country—that of culture.

Chapter 2 presents some more subtle, but critical, factors in the global environment—those of social responsibility and ethical behavior. We will consider a variety of questions: What is the role of the firm in the future of other societies and their people? What stakeholders must managers consider in their strategic and operational decisions in other countries? How do the expectations of firm behavior vary around the world, and should those expectations influence the international manager's decisions? What role does long-term global economic interdependence play in the firm's actions in other countries?

Summary of Key Points

1. Competing in the twenty-first century requires firms to invest in the increasingly refined managerial skills needed to perform effectively in a multicultural environment. Managers need a global orientation to meet the challenges of world markets and rapid, fundamental changes in a world of increasing economic interdependence.
2. Global management is the process of developing strategies, designing and operating systems, and working with people around the world to ensure sustained competitive advantage.
3. One major direction in world trade is the rise of newly developing economies, such as China and India.
4. Drastic worldwide changes present dynamic challenges to global managers, including the political and economic trend toward the privatization of businesses, rapid advances in information technology, and the management of offshore human capital.
5. Global managers must be aware of political risks around the world. Political risks are any governmental actions or politically motivated events that adversely affect the long-run profitability or value of a firm.
6. The risk of terrorist activity represents an increasing risk around the world. Managers have to decide how to incorporate that risk factor in their strategic and operational plans.
7. Political risk assessment by MNCs usually takes two forms: consultation with experts familiar with the area and the development of internal staff capabilities. Political risk can be managed through (1) avoiding or withdrawing investment, (2) adapting to the political regulatory environment, (3) maintaining the host country's dependency on the parent corporation, and (4) hedging potential losses through political risk insurance and local debt financing.
8. Economic risk refers to a country's ability to meet its financial obligations. The risk is that the government may change its economic policies, thereby making a foreign company unprofitable or unable to repatriate its foreign earnings.
9. The regulatory environment comprises the many different laws and courts of those nations in which a company operates. Most legal systems derive from the common law, civil law, or Islamic law.
10. Use of the Internet in e-commerce—in particular, in business-to-business (B2B) transactions—and for intracompany efficiencies is rapidly becoming an important factor in global competitiveness.
11. The appropriability of technology is the ability of the innovating firm to protect its technology from competitors and to obtain economic benefits from that technology. Risks to the appropriability of technology include technology transfer and pirating and legal restrictions on the protection of proprietary technology. Intellectual property can be protected through patents, trademarks, trade names, copyrights, and trade secrets.

Discussion Questions

1. Poll your classmates about their attitudes towards "globalization." What are the trends and opinions around the world that underlie those attitudes?
2. Discuss examples of recent macropolitical risk events and the effect they have or might have on a foreign subsidiary. What are micropolitical risk events? Give some examples and explain how they affect international business.
3. What means can managers use to assess political risk? What do you think is the relative effectiveness of these different methods? At the time you are reading this, what countries or areas do you feel have political risk sufficient to discourage you from doing business there?
4. Can political risk be "managed"? If so, what methods can be used to manage such risk, and how effective are they? Discuss the lengths to which you would go to manage political risk relative to the kinds of returns you would expect to gain.

5. Explain what is meant by the economic risk of a nation. Use a specific country as an example. Can economic risk in this country be anticipated? How?

6. Discuss the importance of contracts in international management. What steps must a manager take to ensure a valid and enforceable contract?

7. Discuss the effects of various forms of technology on international business. What role does the Internet play? Where is all this leading? Explain the meaning of the "appropriability of technology." What role does this play in international competitiveness? How can managers protect the proprietary technology of their firms?

8. Discuss the risk of terrorism. What means can managers use to reduce the risk or the effects of terrorism? Where in the world, and from what likely sources, would you anticipate terrorism?

Application Exercises

1. Do some further research on the technological environment. What are the recent developments affecting businesses and propelling globalization? What problems have arisen regarding use of the Internet for global business transactions, and how are they being resolved?

2. Consider recent events and the prevailing political and economic conditions in the Russian Federation. As a manager who has been considering investment there, how do you assess the political and economic risks at this time? What should be your company's response to this environment?

Experiential Exercise

In groups of three, represent a consulting firm. You have been hired by a diversified multinational corporation to advise on the political and economic environment in different countries. The company wants to open one or two manufacturing facilities in Asia. Choose a specific type of company and two specific countries in Asia and present them to the class, including the types of risks that would be involved and what steps the firm could take to manage those risks.

Internet Resources

Visit the Deresky Companion Website at www.prenhall.com/deresky for this chapter's Internet resources.

Under Pressure, Dubai Company Drops Port Deal

The state-owned Dubai company seeking to manage some terminal operations at six American ports dropped out of the deal on March 9, 2006, bowing to an unrelenting bipartisan attack in the U.S. Congress that swept aside President Bush's efforts.

The company, DP World, said that at the direction of Dubai's ruler it would "transfer" to a still-unnamed American company the leases to manage some of the busiest terminals in the United States, including some in New York, Newark, Baltimore and Miami.

Under questioning, the company declined to say whether it planned to sell the American operations or had some other transaction in mind.

The action averted a showdown with Congress that Mr. Bush was all but certain to lose, as signaled on March 8 by a 62-to-2 vote of the House Appropriations Committee to reject the transfer, because it allowed the sale of some terminal operations to an Arab state company.

Senator John W. Warner, Republican of Virginia, announced the change on the Senate floor two hours before the Senate had been scheduled to vote on a motion that could have paved the way for a Democratic proposal to scuttle the deal.

Mr. Warner made his announcement amid indications that the White House was looking for a way out of the confrontation. A delegation of Republican Congressional leaders told Mr. Bush on Thursday morning that his threat to veto Congressional action against transferring control of the terminals would not stop Congress from blocking the deal.

The outcome did nothing to solve the underlying issue exposed by an uproar that has consumed the capital for weeks. A vast majority of containers that flow daily into the United States remain uninspected and vulnerable to security gaps at many points.

Some experts suggested that DP World's quick surrender might take pressure off the administration, Congress and nations around the world to solve that problem.

DP World announced its decision after the White House appeared to signal that Mr. Bush wanted a face-saving way out of the shift by declining to repeat his veto threat.

The company said the decision had been made by the prime minister of the United Arab Emirates, who is also the ruler of Dubai, Sheikh Mohammed bin Rashid al Maktoum.

"This was clearly not a business decision made by DP World," a senior administration official said. "It was a strategic decision made by the U.A.E. to avoid further damage."

In Dubai, a senior political official with intimate knowledge of the deliberations, said: "A political decision was taken to ask DP World to try and defuse the situation. We have to help our friends."

The official sought anonymity because he was not authorized to speak for the record. He was referring to Mr. Bush, who backed the initial deal, and several Republican senators who did as well.

The company's decision drew sighs of relief from officials in New York and other cities where the imminent transfer had stirred cries of alarm. But the announcement left those officials wondering which American companies might want to buy the American terminal operations. The company that DP World outbid to buy the current operator, Peninsular & Oriental Steam Navigation, a British company, for $6.8 billion, is Singaporean.

"If it's a U.S. company, it should alleviate some of the concerns about security which have been talked about over the last few weeks," Charles A. Gargano, vice chairman of the Port Authority of New York and New Jersey, said. "I don't know how successful they'll be."

The Port Authority owns terminals in the New York metropolitan region.

Foreign companies have long dominated the business of loading and unloading cargo ships, and few American operators remain. "This is a case where we were arguing about the wrong part of the problem," said Stephen Flynn, a former Coast Guard officer and port security expert who has argued that the nationality of the port operations manager has little to do with the gaping holes in security. "Americans were shocked to learn that the vast majority of port operations in this country are handled by foreign firms. But transportation is a global network, and we're not going to own all of it."

Private equity firms, including the Blackstone Group in New York and KKR, have been named as potential buyers of the American terminal operations, which are a small and not particularly lucrative slice of the $6.85 billion Dubaian purchase.

The collapse of the deal is the second time in less than a year in which a foreign acquisition raised protests about the economic security of the United States. Cnooc, a Chinese government-owned oil company, dropped a bid to buy Unocal in July, after it was clear that opposition would run high. Chevron took over the company instead, for $18 billion.

What appeared to set off Democrats and Republicans this time, against the backdrop of concern about possible terrorist attacks, was that the buyer was a state-owned Arab company. Mr. Bush and his aides issued a strong defense, suggesting that racial bias lay at the core of the objections and warning that an undercurrent of isolationism would ultimately harm American efforts to enlist other nations in antiterrorism campaigns.

Those objections were washed away in a tidal wave of opposition in which Republicans and Democrats competed to position themselves as greater protectors of American security.

Democrats like Senator Charles E. Schumer of New York warned that the port operations could be "infiltrated" by terrorists exploiting the ownership in Dubai, an emirate known for its open trade. Dubai had been the transfer point starting in the late 1990s for nuclear components shipped by the largest illicit nuclear technology network in the world.

The chairman of the House Armed Services Committee, Representative Duncan Hunter, Republican of California, introduced a bill that would require American ports and other strategic assets to be returned to American hands.

"Our longer-term goal is to identify long-range foreign investment in our critical infrastructure, reform the process for approving foreign investment in the United States and ensure 100 percent cargo inspection," Mr. Hunter said on Thursday.

From the start of the controversy, the White House appeared to have been caught flat-footed. Mr. Bush and his top advisers said they learned about the transfer late last month, one month after the Committee on Foreign Investments in the United States, an interagency committee that passes judgment on foreign acquisitions, approved the shift, after resolving minimal objections raised by the Coast Guard, part of the Homeland Security Department. The uproar over the deal, fanned in part by talk radio, led the White House and DP World into concessions. Ten days ago, DP World agreed to a more thorough investigation by the interagency group and said it would hold the American operations separate from the rest of the company until the review was completed.

By Thursday morning, Mr. Bush's press secretary, Scott McClellan, appeared to signal that the White House was backing away from its position, by refusing to repeat the veto threat.

At the time, Mr. Bush was meeting with the Senate majority leader, Bill Frist, and Speaker J. Dennis Hastert, both of whom had vocally split with Mr. Bush on the deal.

"It was a tactical discussion by that point," a participant said. "Look, the president didn't fall off a turnip truck. He understood the political reality."

Another participant, the House majority leader, Representative John A. Boehner, Republican of Ohio, was unapologetic about the uprising.

"House Republicans," Mr. Boehner said, "were obligated to take action to respond to the concerns Americans have expressed about the proposed deal."

It was unclear who a buyer might be for the assets now on the block. Experts said ports businesses threw off a predictable amount of cash, a quality often attractive to private equity buyers.

Because DP World is desperate to sell, some experts said, the terminal leases could be dumped at a bargain price.

"There are a lot of private equity firms that focus on logistics businesses, and operating a port might be a logical extension of that," said Andrew Sommer, a partner with Debevoise & Plimpton in New York who often works with private equity firms.

Three private equity firms named as potential suitors, Blackstone, KKR and the Texas Pacific Group, had no comment.

DP World issued its decision hours after its side won a round in a legal dispute with the Port Authority. The authority had asked a New Jersey state court in Newark to allow it to break quickly its 30-year lease on the Port Newark Container Terminal, half operated by P&O Ports North America.

Judge Patricia K. Costello of Superior Court in Essex County ruled that she did not know enough about the transaction to make an immediate decision about whether the transfer was a transaction that required the consent of the Port Authority. Judge Costello ordered an expedited review of the complaint because of the "high level of public interest" in the "security and workings of the port."

SOURCE: D. Sanger, "Under Pressure, Dubai Company Drops Port Deal," www.nytimes.com, March 10, 2006. Copyright © 2006 by The New York Times Co. Reprinted with permission.

Update: LONDON, Dec. 11: Under political pressure, DP World sold its United States holdings to the American International Group. The DP World sale is the final chapter in a politically charged deal that many financial advisers say helped drive Middle East petrodollars away from the United States and into developing market areas like Asia instead. (www.nytimes.com, December 11, 2006.)

CASE QUESTIONS

1. Discuss the role that political factors—both in the United States and in Dubai—played in the reversal of the ports deal.
2. How did the concerns of the U.S. public result in a business decision by a Dubai company?
3. Do you agree with the decision, accepting that transportation takes place through a global network of companies?
4. What are the implications of DP World's withdrawal for global business and investment?

CHAPTER 2

Managing Interdependence

Social Responsibility and Ethics

Outline

Opening Profile: In Enron Case, a Verdict on an Era

Guilty of crimes—and a whole lot more.

Regardless of whether the jury verdict against Kenneth L. Lay and Jeffrey K. Skilling is upheld, testimony from 56 days of trial has sealed what is sure to be history's judgment—one that is unlikely to be vulnerable to appeal. (Note: Subsequent to this report, Ken Lay died of heart failure before imprisonment.)

The Enron case will forever stand as the ultimate reflection of an era of near madness in finance, a time in the late 1990s when self-certitude and spin became a substitute for financial analysis and coherent business models. Controls broke down and management deteriorated as arrogance overrode careful judgment, allowing senior executives to blithely push aside their critics.

Indeed, it could be argued that the most significant lesson from the trial had nothing to do with whether the defendants, both former Enron chief executives, committed the crimes charged in their indictments. Instead, the testimony and the documents admitted during the case painted a broad and disturbing portrait of a corporate culture poisoned by hubris, leading ultimately to a recklessness that placed the business's survival at risk.

"Enron is one of the great frauds in American business history," said James Post, a professor of management at Boston University. "But it is also a symbol of a particular era of management practice. The excesses of Enron point pretty clearly to what was going on in mainstream companies across the business landscape in the 1990s."

That may go a long way toward explaining how corporate America became infused in the late 1990s by what appeared to be a near endless amount of greed and criminality, leading to scandal at an array of corporate giants, from Enron to WorldCom, and from Adelphia to HealthSouth.

It was not simply that the ethics of the corporate world changed overnight; the ever-rising bubble of market prices created a sense of invincibility among corporate executives, who read market delusions as proof of their own genius. Arrogance gave way to recklessness, which in turn opened the door to criminality.

That message was repeated throughout the trial of Mr. Skilling and Mr. Lay. Paula Rieker, an executive with the company's investor relations group, testified to her fear of correcting Mr. Skilling when he made what she considered to be false statements to investors. Vince Kaminski, a top risk analyst, spoke of how Mr. Skilling became increasingly difficult to contradict as Enron won plaudits from the marketplace. And Ben F. Glisan Jr., the treasurer, portrayed an "Emperor's New Clothes" culture, where no one was willing to challenge the rule-bending and recklessness as the company's executives charged into one ill-considered business line after another.

"I would think that most observers of this trial would be shocked and surprised that Enron was such a poorly run company for so long," said Stephen Meagher, a former federal prosecutor who now represents corporate whistle-blowers. "But as long as the checks kept coming in and the stock price kept going up, it was easy to look the other way and ignore the obvious clues that there were deep problems there."

Attention to the mundane details of business—debt maturity schedules, available cash, company-wide risk—appeared to be almost second thoughts among the senior ranks of the company, if thought about at all. Instead, the focus was centered on marketing the image, not only of the company, but also of its senior executives. It was an approach that met widespread success and was emulated throughout corporate America.

"This was the era of the story, the shtick, the celebrity," said Mr. Post of Boston University. "Lay and Skilling delighted in that, they loved becoming business and civic celebrities. They created the model for that kind of superexecutive C.E.O. in the 1990s. Meanwhile, they left all the details to people who were being driven by a troubled culture."

In the end, although many in the public seem to believe this was a case about the collapse of Enron, that had little to do with the criminal charges. In the closing arguments, the government made sure to separate allegations of criminality from responsibility for Enron's collapse.

The testimony suggested that the bankruptcy was much more about a company gone out of control, with executives pushing to the financial edge on deals that received little attention and supervision once the transactions closed. But as that recklessness rotted the company from the inside, the jury found, Mr. Skilling and Mr. Lay falsely portrayed a corporate ship where everything remained steady.

The testimony and evidence suggested that Enron executives could not even agree on what the company's business was. There was no doubt that Enron made the bulk of its profits from trading natural gas contracts. But trading companies rarely win stratospheric stock prices; the risks and requirements for credit in such businesses temper potential market enthusiasm. So some executives argued that Enron was not a trading company, but a logistics business—one involved in every step of the production and delivery of commodities—and therefore deserved its once-lofty stock price.

Putting new labels on the old wine didn't change the financial underpinnings of the business. Most trading companies, because of the knowledge that a sudden market bump can cause available cash to disappear, maintain credit ratings of A and above to protect them in the downdrafts. Enron chose instead to maintain a credit rating just notches above junk, apparently in the belief that a bad day would never arrive.

That freed capital and allowed for borrowings that otherwise would not have been available, driving Enron's supposed "growth" strategy into new business lines, which almost all proved to be debacles. Throughout the trial, there was repeated testimony about Enron's disastrous forays into international power plants and water operations, which led to the company's acquiring billions of dollars in assets that lost huge value, becoming a financial albatross.

A result, when Enron finally faced a crisis, was that it was financially unable to weather the storm. Credit lines were largely tapped out, few assets had the equity necessary for additional borrowings and the liquidity needed for the trading business rapidly dried up. Those factors combined to push Enron toward collapse.

The trial underscores that neither defendant fully accepted what happened at the company. Mr. Lay testified that the collapse was largely caused by short sellers, critical articles in the *Wall Street Journal*, and a resulting panic in the marketplace.

But short selling, negative press and market concerns are issues that scores of companies deal with every year, without collapsing. Indeed, to some degree, Mr. Lay's argument was a bit like blaming a match for igniting a basement filled with gasoline. In this case, the accelerant was the poor condition of Enron's financial structure.

Those lessons about the importance of quality management and strong finances in avoiding scandal, experts said, have not been lost on the audiences that perhaps matter most: the managers of corporate America and the government regulators who keep an eye on them.

"Some people say this is the end of an era, but I don't think it is," said George A. Stamboulidis, a partner with Baker & Hostetler who was appointed a monitor at Merrill Lynch as part of that firm's settlement of an Enron-related case. "This fuels the government and boards and investors to continue to push for more accountability, more transparency and better management."

Those continued efforts, coupled with the changes of the past, should mean that the kind of troubles that emerged at Enron are less likely to appear on the corporate landscape.

"Hopefully," Mr. Stamboulidis said, "the ways businesses are run in 2006 are very different from the ways the businesses were run in the 1990s."

But others expressed fear that as long as huge sums of money can be earned by executives for cutting corners and being dishonest, collapses and scandals like Enron will continue to be part of corporate America.

"One of the things we know from social psychology is that incentives and greed really blind corporate executives," said Arthur P. Brief, a professor at the A. B. Freeman School of Business at Tulane University. "And those incentives are still with us."

Global interdependence is a compelling factor in the global business environment, creating demands on international managers to take a positive stance on issues of social responsibility and ethical behavior, economic development in host countries, and ecological protection around the world.

Managers today are usually quite sensitive to issues of social responsibility and ethical behavior because of pressures from the public, from interest groups, from legal and governmental concerns, and from media coverage. In August 2003, for example, the

United Nations published draft guidelines for the responsibilities of transnational corporations and called for companies to be subject to monitoring, verification, and censure. Though many companies agree with the guidelines, they resist the notion that corporate responsibility should be regulated and question where to draw the line between socially responsible behavior and the concerns of the corporation's other stakeholders.[1] In the domestic arena, managers are faced with numerous ethical complexities. In the international arena, such concerns are compounded by the larger numbers of stakeholders involved, including customers, communities, allies, and owners in various countries.

This chapter's discussion focuses separately on issues of social responsibility and ethical behavior, though considerable overlap can be observed. The difference between the two is a matter of scope and degree. Whereas ethics deals with decisions and interactions on an individual level, decisions about social responsibility are broader in scope, tend to be made at a higher level, affect more people, and reflect a general stance taken by a company or a number of decision makers.

THE SOCIAL RESPONSIBILITY OF MNCs

Multinational corporations (MNCs) have been and—to a lesser extent—continue to be at the center of debate regarding **corporate social responsibility (CSR)**, particularly the benefits versus harm wrought by their operations around the world, especially in less developed countries. The criticisms of MNCs have been lessened in recent years by the decreasing economic differences among countries, by the emergence of less developed countries' (LDCs) multinationals, and by the greater emphasis on social responsibility by MNCs.

Issues of social responsibility continue to center on the poverty and lack of equal opportunity around the world, the environment, consumer concerns, and employee safety and welfare. Many argue that, since MNCs operate in a global context, they should use their capital, skills, and power to play proactive roles in handling worldwide social and economic problems and that, at the least, they should be concerned with host-country welfare. Others argue that MNCs already have a positive impact on LDCs by providing managerial training, investment capital, and new technology, as well as by creating jobs and improving infrastructure. Certainly, multinational corporations constitute a powerful presence in the world economy and often have a greater capacity than local governments to induce change. The sales, debts, and resources of the largest multinationals exceed the gross national product, the public and private debt, and the resources, respectively, of some nations.

The concept of **international social responsibility** includes the expectation that MNCs concern themselves with the social and economic effects of their decisions. The issue is how far that concern should go and what level of planning and control that concern should take. Such dilemmas are common for MNC managers. Del Monte managers, for example, realize that growing pineapples in the rich coastal lands of Kenya brings mixed results there. Although badly needed foreign-exchange earnings are generated for Kenya, poor Kenyans living in the region experience adverse effects because less land is available for subsistence agriculture to support them.[2]

Opinions on the level of social responsibility that a domestic firm should demonstrate range from one extreme—the only responsibility of a business is to make a profit, within the confines of the law, in order to produce goods and services and serve its shareholders' interests[3]—to another extreme—companies should anticipate and try to solve problems in society. Between these extremes are varying positions described as socially reactive, in which companies respond, to some degree of currently prevailing social expectations, to the environmental and social costs of their actions.

The stance toward social responsibility that a firm should take in its international operations, however, is much more complex—ranging perhaps from assuming some responsibility for economic development in a subsidiary's host country to taking an active role in identifying and solving world problems. The increased complexity regarding the social responsibility and ethical behavior of firms across borders is brought about by the additional stakeholders in the firm's activities through operating overseas. As illustrated in Exhibit 2-1, managers are faced with not only considering stakeholders in the host country but also with weighing their rights against the rights of their domestic stakeholders. Most

EXHIBIT 2-1   MNC Stakeholders

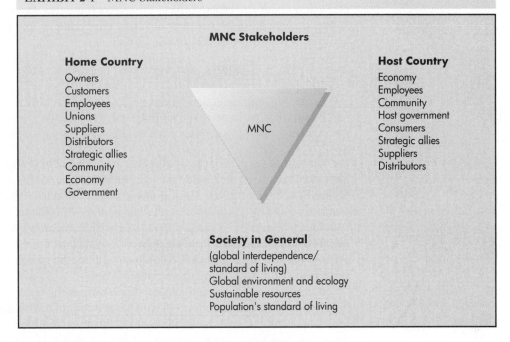

managerial decisions will have a trade-off of the rights of these stakeholders—at least in the short term. For example, a decision to discontinue using children in Pakistan to sew soccer balls means the company will pay more for adult employees and will, therefore, reduce the profitability to its owners. That same decision—while taking a stand for human rights according to the social and ethical expectations in the home country and bowing to consumers' demands—may mean that those children and their families go hungry or are forced into worse working situations. Another decision to keep jobs at home to satisfy local employees and unions will mean higher prices for consumers and less profit for stakeholders. In addition, if competitors take their jobs to cheaper overseas factories, a company may go out of business, which will mean no jobs at all for the domestic employees and a loss for the owners. In spite of conflicting agendas, there is some consensus about what **CSR** means at a basic level—that "corporate activity should be motivated in part by a concern for the welfare of some non-owners, and by an underlying commitment to basic principles such as integrity, fairness and respect for persons."[4]

CSR: Global Consensus or Regional Variation?

With the growing awareness of the world's socioeconomic interdependence, global organizations are beginning to recognize the need to reach a consensus on what should constitute moral and ethical behavior. Some think that such a consensus is emerging because of the development of a **global corporate culture**—an integration of the business environments in which firms currently operate.[5] This integration results from the gradual dissolution of traditional boundaries and from the many intricate interconnections among MNCs, internationally linked securities markets, and communication networks. Nevertheless, there are commonly acknowledged regional variations in how companies respond to corporate social responsibility (CSR):

> *The U.S. and Europe adopt strikingly different positions that can be traced largely to history and culture. In the U.S., CSR is weighted more towards "doing business right" by following basic business obligations; . . . in Europe, CSR is weighted more towards serving—or at least not conflicting with—broader social aims, such as environmental sustainability.*

THE FINANCIAL TIMES,
June 3, 2005[6]

While making good faith efforts to implement CSR, companies operating abroad face confusion about the cross-cultural dilemmas it creates, especially how to behave in host countries, which have their own differing expectations and agendas. Recommendations about how to deal with such dilemmas include:

- Engaging stakeholders (and sometimes nongovernmental organizations, or NGOs) in a dialogue.
- Establishing principles and procedures for addressing difficult issues such as labor standards for suppliers, environmental reporting, and human rights.
- Adjusting reward systems to reflect the company's commitment to CSR.[7]

Although it is very difficult to implement a generalized code of morality and ethics in individual countries, such guidelines do provide a basis of judgment regarding specific situations. Bowie uses the term **moral universalism** to address the need for a moral standard that is accepted by all cultures.[8] Although, in practice, it seems unlikely that a universal code of ethics will ever be a reality, Bowie says that this approach to doing business across cultures is far preferable to other approaches, such as ethnocentrism or ethical relativism. With an **ethnocentric approach**, a company applies the morality used in its home country—regardless of the host country's system of ethics.

A company subscribing to **ethical relativism**, on the other hand, simply adopts the local moral code of whatever country in which it is operating. With this approach, companies run into value conflicts, such as continuing to do business in China despite home-country objections to China's continued violation of human rights. In addition, public pressure in the home country often forces the MNC to act in accordance with ethnocentric value systems anyway. In one instance, public outcry in the United States and most of the world resulted in major companies (IBM, General Motors, Coca-Cola, and Eastman Kodak) either selling or discontinuing their operations in South Africa during the 1980s to protest that country's apartheid policies. More recently, the Food and Drug Administration (FDA) has been pressuring U.S. manufacturers of silicone-filled breast implants (prohibited in the United States for cosmetic surgery because of health hazards) to adopt a voluntary moratorium on exports. While Dow Corning has ceased its foreign sales—citing its responsibility to apply the same standards internationally as it does domestically—other major manufacturers continue to export the implants, often from their factories in other countries.

The difficulty, even in adopting a stance of moral universalism, is in deciding where to draw the line: Which kinds of conflicts of values, asks Wicks, are "conversation stoppers" or "cooperation enders"?[9] Individual managers must at some point decide, based on their own morality, when they feel a situation is simply not right and to withdraw their involvement.

There are practical limitations on our ability to act in the modern world, but a systematic infringement of basic personal rights is generally grounds for ending cooperation. Less blatant violations, or practices that are not abhorrent to our basic values, are treated as items that are negotiable.[10] One fact is inescapable, however, and that is that, in a globalized market economy, CSR is part of modern business.

MNC Responsibility Toward Human Rights

> With almost all tech products now made by contract manufacturers in low-wage nations where sweatshops are common, . . . Hewlett Packard, Dell, IBM, Intel, and twelve other tech companies decided to unite to create the Electronic Industry Code of Conduct (EICC)

> BUSINESS WEEK,
> June 19, 2006[11]

Whereas many situations regarding the morality of the MNC's presence or activities in a country are quite clear, other situations are not, especially when dealing with human rights. The role of MNCs in pulling out of South Africa in the 1980s as part of the movement against apartheid has now played out, and many are cautiously returning to the now multiracial democracy. In many other areas of the world, the question of what role MNCs should play regarding human rights is at the forefront. So loud has been the cry about products coming from so-called sweatshops around the world that (former) President Clinton established an Anti-Sweatshop Code of Conduct, which includes a ban on forced labor, abuse, and discrimination, and it requires companies to provide a healthy and safe work environment and to pay at least the prevailing local minimum wage, among other requirements. A group has been named to monitor compliance; enforcement is difficult, of course, but publicity helps. The Department of Labor publishes the names of companies that comply with the code, including Nike, Reebok, Liz Claiborne, Wal-Mart, and Phillips-Van Heusen.[12] Nike's efforts to address its problems include publishing its entire list of contract manufacturers on the Internet in order to gain transparency. The company admits that it is difficult to keep track of what goes on at its 800 plus contracted factories around the world.[13] (See the case at the end of this chapter for a review of Nike's approach to human rights in its factories.)

What constitutes "human rights" is clouded by the perceptions and priorities of people in different countries. While the United States often takes the lead in the charge against what it considers human rights violations around the world, other countries point to the homelessness and high crime statistics in the United States. Often the discussion of human rights centers around Asia because many of the products in the West are imported from Asia by Western companies using manufacturing facilities located there. It is commonly held in the West that the best chance to gain some ground on human rights issues is for large MNCs and governments around the world to take a unified stance; many global players now question the morality of trading for goods that have been produced by forced labor or child labor. Although laws in the United States ban prison imports, shady deals between the manufacturers and companies acting as intermediaries make it difficult to determine the origin of many products—and make it easy for companies wanting access to cheap products or materials to ignore the law. However, under pressure from their labor unions (and perhaps their consciences), a number of large image-conscious companies, such as Reebok and Levi Strauss, have established corporate codes of conduct for their buyers, suppliers, and contractors and have instituted strict procedures for auditing their imports.[14] In addition, some companies are uniting with others in their industry to form their own code for responsible action. One of these is the Electronic Industry Code of Conduct (EICC), which comprises Hewlett-Packard, Dell, IBM, Intel, and 12 other tech companies who have agreed on the following policies:

- The EICC bans forced and child labor and excessive overtime.
- The EICC requires contract manufacturers to follow some basic environmental requirements.
- The EICC requires each company to audit its overseas suppliers to ensure compliance, following a common factory inspection system for all members.[15]

Codes of Conduct

A considerable number of organizations have developed their own codes of conduct; some have gone further to group together with others around the world to establish standards to improve the quality of life for workers around the world. Companies such as Avon, Sainsbury Plc., Toys "R" Us, and Otto Versand have joined with the Council on Economic Priorities (CEP) to establish SA8000 (Social Accountability 8000, on the lines of the manufacturing quality standard ISO9000). Their proposed global labor standards would be monitored by outside organizations to certify whether plants are meeting those standards, among which are the following:

- Do not use child or forced labor.
- Provide a safe working environment.
- Respect workers' rights to unionize.
- Do not regularly require more than 48-hour work weeks.
- Pay wages sufficient to meet workers' basic needs.[27]

In addition, four **international codes of conduct** provide some consistent guidelines for multinational enterprises (MNEs). These codes were developed by the International Chamber of Commerce, the Organization for Economic Cooperation and Development, the International Labor Organization, and the United Nations

Comparative Management in Focus

Doing Business in China—The Human Rights Challenge

Map 2-1 China

> *It's easy to be mesmerized by China: the double-digit growth, the ambitious space program, the shining new cities along its teeming shore, the prospect of selling to the largest and one day perhaps the richest market on earth.*
>
> THE ECONOMIST,
> *April 22, 2006*[16]

It seems that China's high-speed economic train has left the station, but left many of its people and their basic rights largely behind. As discussed in Chapter 1, China retains a strong appeal, in particular for manufacturers, with its cheap labor rates and an expanding market of over one billion people. It is now the world's third biggest manufacturer after the United States and Japan, with that part of its economy having quadrupled in size since 1990—a rate ten times faster than for the whole of global industry.[17] Growth in higher skilled jobs and in services is now well under way. However, there is a swelling tide among MNCs about the pitfalls of operating in China—among them the uncertain legal climate; the difficulty of protecting intellectual property there; the repression of free speech; and the difficulty of monitoring, let alone correcting, human rights violations in factories. As discussed in detail in the Nike case at the end of this chapter, the company found rampant violations of workers' rights in many of its factories throughout Asia, including making workers work 60 hours a week, forcing overtime, and ignoring laws on minimum wages and child labor.[18] MNCs like Nike face considerable pressure in their home markets to address human rights in China and elsewhere.

Consumers boycott their products, and trade unions in the United States, for example, complain that repression of workers' rights has enabled Chinese companies to push down labor costs, causing considerable loss of manufacturing jobs at home.[19]

In 2006, the crackdown over what President Hu Jintao's government calls "propaganda" escalated with reporters being jailed, editorial staffs fired, and publications closed.[20] The PRC Communist Party "exerts near complete control over China's 358 television stations and 2,119 newspapers, according to the nonprofit group Freedom House."[21] In 2005, China ranked 159th out of 167 countries in a survey of press freedom, according to Reporters Without Borders, the Paris-based international rights group.[22]

> *. . . a vast security network and compliant multinationals keep the mainland's Net under Beijing's thumb.*
>
> BUSINESS WEEK,
> *January 23, 2006*[23]

Freedom of information took a particularly hard hit with the news that Google had agreed to China's demands to apply censors' blacklists to its search engine there. In spite of Google's founding principle "Don't be evil," their business interests apparently clashed with their principles, leading many to conclude that Google is putting it's own freedoms at risk in China; however, that is also occurring with Microsoft and Yahoo! in China.[24] (The Google case is discussed in detail in the Part I ending cases.)

While Internet and technology executives were called to Capitol Hill in February 2006 to defend their companies' practices in China, it was clear that the future of American corporations and foreign policy interests would prevail.[25] Rather, the debate continues over how Internet companies can engage more effectively with Beijing on human rights issues. But, in a blow to the industry, in July 2006, Amnesty International accused Yahoo! Microsoft, and Google of overlooking their human rights obligations in order to tap into China's dynamic online market, stating that "all three companies have in different ways facilitated or participated in the practice of government censorship in China."[26]

Commission on Transnational Corporations. Getz has integrated these four codes and organized their common underlying principles, thereby establishing MNE behavior toward governments, publics, and people, as shown in Exhibit 2-2 (the originating

---

EXHIBIT 2-2   International Codes of Conduct for MNEs

MNE and Host Governments

Economic and developmental policies

- MNEs should consult with governmental authorities and national employers' and workers' organizations to ensure that their investments conform to the economic and social development policies of the host country. (ICC; OECD; ILO; UN/CTC)
- MNEs should not adversely disturb the balance-of-payments or currency exchange rates of the countries in which they operate. They should try, in consultation with the government, to resolve balance-of-payments and exchange rate difficulties when possible. (ICC; OECD; UN/CTC)
- MNEs should cooperate with governmental policies regarding local equity participation. (ICC; UN/CTC)
- MNEs should not dominate the capital markets of the countries in which they operate. (ICC; UN/CTC)
- MNEs should provide the information necessary for correctly assessing taxes to be paid to host government authorities. (ICC; OECD)

- MNEs should not engage in transfer pricing policies that modify the tax base on which their entities are assessed. (OECD; UN/CTC)
- MNEs should give preference to local sources for components and raw materials if prices and quality are competitive. (ICC; ILO)
- MNEs should reinvest some profits in the countries in which they operate. (ICC)

Laws and regulations

- MNEs are subject to the laws, regulations, and jurisdiction of the countries in which they operate. (ICC; OECD; UN/CTC)
- MNEs should respect the right of every country to exercise control over its natural resources, and to regulate the activities of entities operating within its territory. (ICC; OECD; UN/CTC)
- MNEs should use appropriate international dispute settlement mechanisms, including arbitration, to resolve conflicts with the governments of the countries in which they operate. (ICC; OECD)

(continued)

EXHIBIT 2-2 (cont.)

- MNEs should not request the intervention of their home governments in disputes with host governments. (UN/CTC)
- MNEs should resolve disputes arising from expropriation by host governments under the domestic law of the host country. (UN/CTC)

Political involvement

- MNEs should refrain from improper or illegal involvement in local political activities. (OECD; UN/CTC)
- MNEs should not pay bribes or render improper benefits to any public servant. (OECD; UN/CTC)
- MNEs should not interfere in intergovernmental relations. (UN/CTC)

MNEs and the Public

Technology transfer

- MNEs should cooperate with governmental authorities in assessing the impact of transfers of technology to developing countries and should enhance the technological capacities of developing countries. (OECD; UN/CTC)
- MNEs should develop and adapt technologies to the needs and characteristics of the countries in which they operate. (ICC; OECD; ILO)
- MNEs should conduct research and development activities in developing countries, using local resources and personnel to the greatest extent possible. (ICC; UN/CTC)
- When granting licenses for the use of industrial property rights, MNEs should do so on reasonable terms and conditions. (ICC; OECD)
- MNEs should not require payment for the use of technologies of no real value to the enterprise. (ICC)

Environmental protection

- MNEs should respect the laws and regulations concerning environmental protection of the countries in which they operate. (OECD; UN/CTC)
- MNEs should cooperate with host governments and with international organizations in the development of national and international environmental protection standards. (ICC; UN/CTC)
- MNEs should supply to appropriate host governmental authorities information concerning the environmental impact of the products and processes of their entities. (ICC; UN/CTC)

MNEs and Persons

Consumer protection

- MNEs should respect the laws and regulations of the countries in which they operate with regard to consumer protection. (OECD; UN/CTC)
- MNEs should preserve the safety and health of consumers by disclosure of appropriate information, proper labeling, and accurate advertising. (UN/CTC)

Employment practices

- MNEs should cooperate with host governments' efforts to create employment opportunities in particular localities. (ICC)
- MNEs should support representative employers' organizations. (ICC; ILO)
- MNEs should try to increase employment opportunities and standards in the countries in which they operate. (ILO)
- MNEs should provide stable employment for their employees. (ILO)
- MNEs should establish nondiscriminatory employment policies and promote equal employment opportunities. (OECD; ILO)
- MNEs should give priority to the employment and promotion of nationals of the countries in which they operate. (ILO)
- MNEs should ensure that adequate training is provided to all employees. (ILO)
- MNEs should contribute to the managerial and technical training of nationals of the countries in which they operate, and should employ qualified nationals in managerial and professional capacities. (ICC; OECD; UN/CTC)
- MNEs should respect the right of employees to organize for the purpose of collective bargaining. (OECD; ILO)
- MNEs should provide workers' representatives with information necessary to assist in the development of collective agreements. (OECD; ILO)
- MNEs should consult with workers' representatives in all matters directly affecting the interests of labor. (ICC)
- MNEs, in the context of negotiations with workers' representatives, should not threaten to transfer the operating unit to another country. (OECD; ILO)
- MNEs should give advance notice of plant closures and mitigate the resultant adverse effects. (ICC; OECD; ILO)
- MNEs should cooperate with governments in providing income protection for workers whose employment has been terminated. (ILO)
- MNEs should provide standards of employment equal to or better than those of comparable employers in the countries in which they operate. (ICC; OECD; ILO)
- MNEs should pay, at minimum, basic living wages. (ILO)
- MNEs should maintain the highest standards of safety and health, and should provide adequate information about work-related health hazards. (ILO)

Human rights

- MNEs should respect human rights and fundamental freedoms in the countries in which they operate. (UN/CTC)
- MNEs should not discriminate on the basis of race, color, sex, religion, language, social, national and ethnic origin, or political or other opinion. (UN/CTC)
- MNEs should respect the social and cultural objectives, values, and traditions of the countries in which they operate. (UN/CTC)

International agency sources:

OECD: The Organization for Economic Cooperation and Development Guidelines for Multinational Enterprises

ILO: The International Labor Office Tripartite Declarations of Principles Concerning Multinational Enterprises and Social Policy

ICC: The International Chamber of Commerce Guidelines for International Investment

UN/CTC: The United Nations Universal Declaration of Human Rights

The UN Code of Conduct on Transnational Corps.

institutions are in parentheses). Getz concludes, "As international organizations and institutions (including MNEs themselves) continue to refine the codes, the underlying moral issues will be better identified, and appropriate MNE behavior will be more readily apparent."[28]

ETHICS IN GLOBAL MANAGEMENT

National, as well as corporate, cultures need to be taken into account if multinationals are to enforce their codes across different regions.

FINANCIAL TIMES,
March 7, 2005[29]

Globalization has multiplied the ethical problems facing organizations. However, business ethics have not yet been globalized. Attitudes toward ethics are rooted in culture and business practices. Swee Hoon Ang found, for example, that while East Asians tended to be less ethical than their expatriate counterparts from the United States and Britain, it was because they considered deception as amoral and acceptable if it has a positive effect on larger issues such as the company, the extended family, or the state.[30] For an MNC, it is difficult to reconcile consistent and acceptable behavior around the world with home-country standards. One question, in fact, is whether it should be reconciled. It seems that, while the United States has been the driving force to legislate moral business conduct overseas, perhaps more scrutiny should have been applied to those global MNCs headquartered in the United States, such as Enron and WorldCom, that so greatly defrauded their investors, employees, and all who had business with them.

The term **international business ethics** refers to the business conduct or morals of MNCs in their relationships with individuals and entities. Such behavior is based largely on the cultural value system and the generally accepted ways of doing business in each country or society, as we have discussed throughout this book. Those norms, in turn, are based on broadly accepted guidelines from religion, philosophy, professional organizations, and the legal system. The complexity of the combination of various national and cultural factors in a particular host environment that combine to determine ethical or unethical societal norms is illustrated in Exhibit 2-3. The authors, Robertson and Crittenden, note,

Varying legal and cultural constraints across borders have made integrating an ethical component into international strategic decisions quite challenging.[31]

Should managers of MNC subsidiaries, then, base their ethical standards on those of the host country or those of the home country—or can the two be reconciled? What is the moral responsibility of expatriates regarding ethical behavior, and how do these issues affect business objectives? How do expatriates simultaneously balance their responsibility to various stakeholders—to owners, creditors, consumers, employees, suppliers, governments, and societies? The often conflicting objectives of host and home governments and societies also must be balanced.

The approach to these dilemmas varies among MNCs from different countries. While the American approach is to treat everyone the same by making moral judgments based on general rules, managers in Japan and Europe tend to make such decisions based on shared values, social ties, and their perceptions of their obligations. According to many U.S. executives, there is little difference in ethical practices among the United States, Canada, and Northern Europe. According to Bruce Smart, former U.S. Undersecretary of Commerce for International Trade, the highest ethical standards seem to be practiced by the Canadians, British, Australians, and Germans. As he says, "a kind of noblesse oblige still exists among the business classes in those countries"—compared with the prevailing attitude among many U.S. managers that

EXHIBIT 2-3   A Moral Philosophy of Cross-cultural Societal Ethics

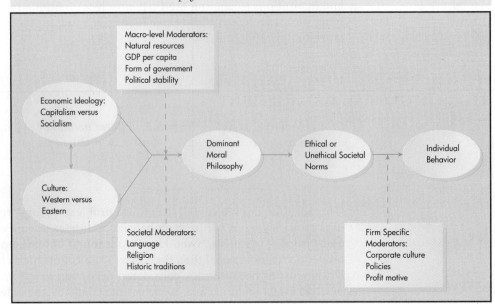

SOURCE: C. J. Robertson and W. F. Crittenden, "Mapping Moral Philisophies: Strategic Implications for Multinational Firms," *Strategic Management Journal*, 24: 385–392 (2003) © John Wiley & Sons, Inc. Reproduced with permission.

condones "making it" whatever way one can.[32] Another who experienced few problems with ethical practices in Europe is Donald Petersen, former CEO of Ford Motor Company. However, he warns us about underdeveloped countries, in particular those under a dictatorship where bribery is a generally accepted practice.[33] Petersen's experience has been borne out by research, which draws on 14 surveys from seven independent institutions, by Transparency International, a German nongovernmental organization (NGO) that fights corruption. The organization's year 2005 Global Corruption Barometer (selections are shown in Exhibit 2-4) shows results of research into the extent that business and other sectors of their society are affected by corruption, as perceived by businesspeople, academics, and risk analysts in 69 countries. The survey was conducted for Transparency International (TI) by Gallup International, with 54,260 respondents. As part of their conclusions, TI states that:

> *In terms of the impact of corruption on different spheres of life, respondents clearly stated that the political spheres in their countries are affected by corruption. However, a high percentage of people also thought that the business sector was similarly affected. This was particularly the case for citizens in Africa and Western Europe. Conversely, fewer people in Latin America had this opinion.*

> TRANSPARENCY INTERNATIONAL,
> *December 9, 2005*[34]

By following the column marked "Business/private sector," we can see some average scores for different regions—the "worst" being Central and Eastern Europe, with 3.7 out of 4, and the lowest being Africa, with 3.1. We can also look at individual countries—for example, Canada has a score of 3.0, and Turkey has the highest (worst) score of 4.0.[35]

The biggest single problem for MNCs in their attempt to define a corporate-wide ethical posture is the great variation of ethical standards around the world. Many practices that are considered unethical or even illegal in some countries are accepted ways of doing

EXHIBIT 2-4   Global Corruption Barometer 2005 Full Country Tables

National institutions and sectors, corrupt or clean?								
To what extent do you perceive the following sectors in this country/territory to be affected by corruption? (1: not at all corrupt, . . . 5: extremely corrupt)	Political parties	Parliament/ legislature	Police	Legal system judiciary	Tax revenues	Business/private sector	Customs	Medical services
Cambodia	2.9	2.4	3.2	3.9	3.1	2.6	3.8	2.8
Hong Kong	3.1	2.5	2.9	2.4	2.1	3.2	2.6	2.2
India	4.7	4.4	4.7	4.3	3.8	3.4	4.1	3.8
Indonesia	4.2	4.0	4.0	3.8	3.8	3.5	4.0	2.7
Japan	4.2	3.7	3.8	3.0	3.5	3.3	2.9	3.6
Malaysia	3.7	3.1	4.0	2.9	2.8	3.1	3.4	2.3
Pakistan	3.9	3.7	4.3	4.0	3.9	3.4	4.0	3.7
Philippines	4.2	4.2	4.0	3.4	3.7	3.2	3.7	2.9
Singapore	2.2	1.8	2.0	2.1	1.8	2.7	2.0	1.7
South Korea	4.4	4.4	3.7	3.7	3.5	3.5	3.6	3.3
Taiwan	4.1	4.3	3.4	3.4	3.1	3.2	3.6	3.1
Thailand	3.9	2.8	3.8	2.8	2.8	2.9	3.2	2.4
ASIA—average	4.2	3.9	3.9	3.4	3.5	3.3	3.4	3.3
Cameroon	3.9	3.3	4.7	4.3	4.0	3.7	4.4	3.7
Ethiopia	3.6	3.2	3.7	3.7	3.8	3.8	3.6	3.4
Ghana	4.1	3.1	4.7	3.8	3.7	3.2	4.2	2.9
Kenya	3.7	3.8	4.1	3.6	3.4	2.9	3.7	3.2
Nigeria	4.5	4.1	4.7	3.8	3.6	3.2	4.2	3.0
Senegal	3.6	3.1	3.7	3.2	2.8	2.8	3.6	2.7
South Africa	4.0	3.7	4.0	3.3	2.7	3.0	2.9	3.0
Togo	3.6	3.5	3.9	3.9	3.4	3.3	4.2	3.0
AFRICA—average	4.2	3.8	4.4	3.7	3.5	3.1	4.0	3.0
Austria	3.6	3.1	2.8	2.8	2.8	3.0	2.7	2.5
Denmark	2.7	2.5	2.0	2.0	1.8	2.8	1.8	2.1
Finland	3.1	2.7	1.7	2.0	1.9	2.8	1.8	2.0
France	4.1	3.4	3.1	3.1	2.5	3.5	2.7	2.3
Germany	3.7	3.2	2.4	2.7	2.9	3.2	2.6	2.8
Greece	4.1	3.5	3.3	3.7	3.8	3.4	3.5	3.6
Iceland	3.3	2.6	2.0	2.3	1.8	3.1	2.0	1.9
Ireland	3.7	3.1	2.7	3.2	2.8	3.1	2.2	2.4
Italy	4.2	3.6	2.5	3.2	3.5	3.5	2.9	3.5
Luxembourg	3.4	2.8	2.7	2.6	2.4	3.3	2.3	2.1
Netherlands	3.0	2.8	2.9	2.7	2.4	3.1	2.7	2.3
Norway	3.2	2.7	2.4	2.2	2.0	3.5	2.2	2.6
Portugal	3.9	3.3	3.0	3.3	3.7	3.4	3.3	2.9
Spain	3.4	3.2	3.1	3.2	3.3	3.3	2.8	2.9
Switzerland	3.2	2.7	2.2	2.3	2.5	2.9	2.1	2.3
United Kingdom	3.5	3.2	2.8	2.9	2.5	3.0	2.4	2.2
W. EUROPE—average	3.7	3.3	2.7	2.9	2.9	3.3	2.7	2.7

EXHIBIT 2-4   (cont.)

To what extent do you perceive the following sectors in this country/territory to be affected by corruption? (1: not at all corrupt, . . . 5: extremely corrupt)	Political parties	Parliament/legislature	Police	Legal system judiciary	Tax revenues	Business/private sector	Customs	Medical services
Bosnia and Herzegovina	4.5	4.2	4.0	4.1	3.5	3.8	3.9	3.9
Bulgaria	4.3	4.2	3.8	4.3	3.4	3.8	4.5	4.1
Croatia	4.0	3.8	3.3	3.9	3.3	3.6	3.3	3.5
Czech Republic	3.7	3.3	3.7	3.4	2.7	3.1	3.4	2.9
Georgia	3.6	3.6	2.9	3.9	3.5	3.4	3.6	3.1
Kosovo	3.1	2.5	1.9	3.0	2.7	3.0	3.4	3.4
Lithuania	4.3	4.1	4.1	4.2	3.3	3.6	4.2	3.9
Macedonia	4.1	4.0	3.5	4.3	3.4	3.5	4.2	3.9
Moldova	3.8	3.6	4.2	3.8	2.9	3.5	4.2	4.0
Poland	4.2	4.1	3.9	4.0	3.1	3.8	2.7	4.1
Romania	3.8	3.6	3.6	3.7	2.4	3.4	3.8	3.6
Russia	4.0	3.9	4.2	3.9	3.8	3.8	3.7	3.5
Serbia	4.2	3.6	4.0	4.1	3.2	3.8	4.2	4.0
Ukraine	3.9	3.8	4.1	4.1	3.6	3.8	4.1	4.0
CE EUROPE—average	4.0	3.9	4.0	3.9	3.5	3.7	3.7	3.7
Argentina	4.6	4.5	4.3	4.3	3.4	3.6	4.2	3.0
Bolivia	4.8	4.6	4.7	4.3	3.5	3.4	4.4	3.2
Chile	4.2	3.8	3.5	4.1	3.2	3.5	3.3	2.5
Colombia	4.4	4.2	3.8	3.8	3.6	3.1	3.6	3.2
Costa Rica	4.6	4.2	3.8	3.6	4.1	3.5	4.0	3.5
Dominican Republic	4.3	3.7	4.3	3.8	3.8	3.3	3.7	3.4
Ecuador	4.9	4.9	4.3	4.6	3.7	3.4	4.5	3.5
Guatemala	4.2	4.0	4.2	3.9	4.0	3.7	3.8	3.6
Mexico	4.7	4.4	4.7	4.5	3.9	3.5	4.2	3.2
Nicaragua	4.6	4.4	4.3	4.4	4.4	3.9	4.1	4.0
Panama	4.7	4.7	4.4	4.5	3.9	3.5	4.0	3.2
Paraguay	4.8	4.7	4.7	4.6	4.1	3.5	4.6	3.9
Peru	4.5	4.5	4.4	4.5	3.9	3.4	3.4	3.6
Uruguay	4.0	3.4	3.9	3.5	3.0	3.2	4.0	3.2
Venezuela	3.7	3.7	3.7	3.4	3.2	3.3	3.4	3.3
LAC—average	4.5	4.4	4.3	4.3	3.7	3.5	4	3.2
Israel	4.5	4.2	3.3	2.9	3.2	3.2	3.0	3.0
Turkey	4.1	3.9	4.0	4.0	4.2	4.0	4.1	4.1
Canada	3.9	3.6	2.7	3.2	2.9	3.0	2.5	2.5
USA	3.9	3.5	3.1	3.5	3.4	3.2	3.0	3.1
Total	4.0	3.7	3.6	3.5	3.4	3.4	3.3	3.2

SOURCE: www.Transparency.org, August 6, 2006.

Note: The results presented here rely on data from the TI Corruption perceptions Index, 2005, provided by Transparency International—the global coalition against corruption. Used with permission.

business in others. More recently, this dilemma has taken on new forms because of the varied understandings of the ethical use of technology around the world, as illustrated by the electronic data privacy laws in Europe. The EU Directive on Data Protection guarantees European citizens absolute control over data concerning them. A U.S. company wanting personal information must get permission from that person and explain what the information will be used for; the company must also guarantee that the information won't be used for anything else without the person's consent.

Bribery

There are few other areas where a single employee can, with one instance of misjudgment, create huge embarrassment [for the company].

FINANCIAL TIMES,
February 2, 2006[36]

The computer is on the dock, it's raining, and you have to pay $100 [bribe] to get it picked up.

WILLIAM C. NORRIS,
Control Data Corporation

MNCs are often caught between being placed at a disadvantage by refusing to go along with a country's accepted practices, such as bribery, or being subject to criticism at home for using "unethical" tactics to get the job done. Large companies that have refused to participate have led the way in taking a moral stand because of their visibility, their potential impact on the local economy, and, after all, their ability to afford such a stance. Whereas the upper limits of ethical standards for international activities are set by the individual standards of certain leading companies—or, more realistically, by the moral values of their top managers—it is more difficult to set the lower limits of those standards; that limit gets set by whether the laws are actually enforced in that location.

The bribery of officials is prohibited by law in all countries, but it still goes on as an accepted practice; often, it is the only way to get anything done. In such cases, the MNC managers have to decide which standard of behavior they will follow. What about the $100 bribe to get the computer off the rainy dock? William Norris says he told his managers to pay the $100 because to refuse would be taking things too far. Generally, Control Data did not yield to such pressure, though it said sales were lost as a result.[37]

A specific ethical issue for managers in the international arena is that of **questionable payments**. These are business payments that raise significant questions of appropriate moral behavior either in the host nation or in other nations. Such questions arise out of differences in laws, customs, and ethics in various countries, whether the payments in question are political payments, extortion, bribes, sales commissions, or "grease money"—payments to expedite routine transactions. Other common types of payments are made to speed the clearance of goods at ports of entry and to obtain required certifications. They are called different names in different countries: tokens of appreciation, *la mordida* (the bite, in Mexico), *bastarella* ("little envelope" in Italy), *pot-de-vin* (jug of wine in France). For the sake of simplicity, all these different types of questionable payments are categorized in this text as some form of bribery. In Mexico, for example, companies make monthly payments to the mail carriers or their mail gets "lost."

Most managers perceive bribery as "endemic in business and government in parts of Africa and south and east Asia. Corruption and bribery are considered to be part of the culture and environment of certain markets, and will not simply go away."[38] In some parts of Latin America, for example, customs officers are paid poorly and so are encouraged to take bribes to supplement their incomes. However, developed countries are not immune to bribery—as demonstrated in 2002 when several members of the International Olympic

Committee were expelled for accepting bribes during Salt Lake City's campaign to host the 2002 Winter Olympics.

The dilemma for Americans operating abroad is how much to adhere to their own ethical standards in the face of foreign customs or how much to follow local ways to be competitive. Certainly, in some societies, gift giving is common to bind social and familial ties, and such gifts incur obligation. Nevertheless, a bribe is different from a gift or other reciprocation, and those involved know that by whether it has a covert nature. According to Noonan:

> *Bribery is universally shameful. Not a country in the world that does not treat bribery as criminal on its books. . . . In no country do bribetakers speak publicly of their bribes, nor do bribegivers announce the bribes they pay. No newspaper lists them. No one advertises that he can arrange a bribe. No one is honored precisely because he is a big briber or bribee. No one writes an autobiography in which he recalls the bribes he has taken or paid. . . . Not merely the criminal law—for the transaction could have happened long ago and prosecution be barred by time—but an innate fear of being considered disgusting restrains briber and bribee from parading their exchange. Significantly, it is often the Westerner with ethnocentric prejudice who supposes that a modern Asian or African society does not regard the act of bribery as shameful in the way Westerners regard it.*[39]

However, Americans must be able to distinguish between harmless practices and actual bribery, between genuine relationships and those used as a cover-up. To help them distinguish, the **Foreign Corrupt Practices Act** (FCPA) of 1977 was established, which prohibits U.S. companies from making illegal payments, other gifts, or political contributions to foreign government officials for the purposes of influencing them in business transactions. The goal was to stop MNCs from contributing to corruption in foreign government and to upgrade the image of the United States and its companies operating overseas. The penalties include severe fines and sometimes imprisonment. Many managers feel the law has given them a more even playing field, and so they have been more willing to do business in certain countries where it seemed impossible to do business without bribery and kickbacks.

Since then, in 1997 the Organisation for Economic Co-operation and Development Convention on Bribery was signed by 36 countries in an attempt to combat corruption.[40] However, evidential problems continue to hinder prosecution. Unless there is a complaint or whistle-blowing, there are few avenues for regulators to ferret out incidents in bribery in corporations. Unfortunately, bribery continues, mostly on a small scale, where it often goes undetected. In any event, it is prudent (and hopefully honorable) for companies to set in place processes to minimize the risk of prosecution, including:

- Having a global compliance system which shows that employees have understood, and signed off on, the legal obligations regarding bribery and corruption in the countries where they do business.
- Making employees aware of the penalties and ramifications for lone actions, such as criminal sanctions.
- Having a system in place to investigate any foreign agents and overseas partners who will be negotiating contracts.
- Keeping an effective whistle-blowing system in place.[41]

As far as the actions that individual managers take when doing business overseas, if we agree with Carson that "accepting a bribe involves the violation of an implicit or explicit promise or understanding associated with one's office or role, and that, therefore, accepting (or giving) a bribe is always prima facie wrong,"[42] then our decisions as managers, salespersons, and so on are always clear, no matter where we are.

If, however, we acknowledge that in some cases—in "morally corrupt contexts," as Philips calls them—" there may be no prima facie duty to adhere to the agreements implicit in one's role or position," then the issue becomes situational and a matter of judgment, with few consistent guidelines. If our perspective, continues Philips, is that "the action purchased from the relevant official does not count as a violation of his [or her] duty," then the U.S. managers or other foreign managers involved are actually victims of extortion rather than guilty of bribery.[43] That is the position taken by Gene Laczniak of Marquette Company, who says that it is just part of the cost of doing business in many countries to pay small bribes to get people simply to do their jobs. However, he is against paying bribes to persuade people to make decisions that they otherwise would not have made.[44]

Whatever their professed beliefs, many businesspeople are willing to engage in bribery as an everyday part of meeting their business objectives. Many corporate officials, in fact, avoid any moral issue by simply "turning a blind eye" to what goes on in subsidiaries. Some companies avoid these issues by hiring a local agent who takes care of the paperwork and pays all the so-called fees in return for a salary or consultant's fee.[45] However, while the FCPA does allow "grease" payments to facilitate business in a foreign country, if those payments are lawful there, other payments prohibited by the FCPA remain subject to prosecution even if the company says it did not know that its agents or subsidiaries were making such payments—the so-called "reason to know" provision.[46]

Critics of the FCPA contend that the law represents an ethnocentric attempt to impose U.S. standards on the rest of the world and puts U.S. firms at a competitive disadvantage. In any event, many feel that business activities that cannot stand scrutiny are clearly unethical, corrupt, and, in the long run, corrupting. Bribery fails three important tests of ethical corporate actions: (1) Is it legal? (2) Does it work (in the long run)? (3) Can it be talked about?[47]

Many MNCs have decided to confront concerns about ethical behavior and social responsibility by developing worldwide practices that represent the company's posture. Among those policies are the following:

- Develop worldwide codes of ethics.
- Consider ethical issues in strategy development.
- Develop periodic "ethical impact" statements.
- Given major, unsolvable, ethical problems, consider withdrawal from the problem market.[48]

Making the Right Decision

How is a manager operating abroad to know what is the "right" decision when faced with questionable or unfamiliar circumstances of doing business? The first line of defense is to consult the laws of both the home and the host countries—such as the FCPA. If any of those laws would be violated, then you, the manager, must look to some other way to complete the business transaction, or withdraw altogether.

Second, you could consult the International Codes of Conduct for MNEs (see Exhibit 2-2). These are broad and cover various areas of social responsibility and ethical behavior; even so, many issues are subject to interpretation.

If legal consultation does not provide you with a clear answer about what to do, you should consult the company's code of ethics (if there is one). You, as the manager, should realize that you are not alone in making these kinds of decisions. It is also the responsibility of the company to provide guidelines for the actions and decisions made by its employees. In addition, you are not the first, and certainly not the last, to be faced with this kind of situation—which also sets up a collective experience in the company about what kinds of decisions your colleagues typically make in various circumstances. Those norms or expectations (assuming they are honorable) can supplement the code of ethics or substitute for the lack of a formal code. If your intended action runs contrary to the norms or the formal code, discontinue that plan.

If you are still unsure of what to do, you have the right and the obligation to consult your superiors. Unfortunately, often the situation is not that clear-cut, or your boss will tell you to "use your own judgment." Sometimes your superiors in the home office just want you to complete the transaction to the benefit of the company and don't want to be involved in what you have to do to consummate the deal.

If your dilemma continues, you must fall back upon your own moral code of ethics. One way to consider the dilemma is to ask yourself what the rights of the various stakeholders involved are (see Exhibit 2-1), and how you should weigh those rights. First, does the proposed action (rigged contract bid, bribe, etc.) harm anyone? What are the likely consequences of your decision in both the short run and long run? Who would benefit from your contemplated action? What are the benefits to some versus potential harm to others? In the case of a rigged contract bid through bribery, for example, people are put at a disadvantage, especially over the long term, with a pattern of this behavior. This is because, if competition is unfair, not only are your competitors harmed by losing the bid, but also the consumers of the products or services are harmed because they will pay more to attain them than they would under an efficient market system.

In the end, you have to follow your own conscience and decide where to draw the line in the sand in order to operate with integrity—otherwise the line moves further and further away with each transgression. In addition, what can start with a small bribe or cover-up here—a matter of personal ethics—can, over time, and in the aggregate of many people covering up, result in a situation of a truly negligent, and perhaps criminal, stance toward social responsibility to society, like that revealed by investigations of the tobacco industry in the United States. Indeed, executives are increasingly being held personally and criminally accountable for their decisions; this is true even for people operating on the board of directors of a company. Criminal charges were brought against 15 executives of WorldCom in 2003, for example, and the noose was thrown around the world after the Enron convictions in 2006 (see this chapter's opening case profile), as international banks such as Citigroup and JP Morgan Chase were charged with taking part in sham deals to disguise Enron's financial problems.

Richard Rhodes, CEO of Rhodes Architectural Stone, Inc., is one executive who has drawn a line in the sand for himself and his company, and who holds himself and his employees accountable to a high moral standard when it comes to issues of bribery and human rights. He explains how they deal with difficult situations abroad in the accompanying Management Focus, "CEO Speaks Out: Ethics Abroad—Business Fundamentals, Value Judgments."

Management Focus

CEO Speaks Out: Ethics Abroad—Business Fundamentals, Value Judgments

You've just finished negotiating the deal, and it's time for a celebration, drinks and dinner all around, and you go to bed only to wake up the next morning to learn that the other side wants to start all over again.

Or, you try to buy something—say a collection of antique vessels for resale for decorative uses—and you're told that the artifacts are yours but only for a price. You wonder, should I agree to pay a bribe just this once?

So it goes sometimes when it comes to the business of doing business abroad, which has been the case for my company, Rhodes Architectural Stone, Inc., ever since its launch (under another name) in 1998. Ours is the business of buying artifacts slated for demolition in areas of the world, such as Africa, China, India, and Indonesia, and, in turn, selling to discriminating clients in the United States.

If there is one thing we've learned, it is that the ethical landscape is different in the third world. In the United States—notwithstanding the recent spate of corporate scandals that have set a woefully new low for ethical business behavior—the fact remains that standards do exist against which improprieties can be measured.

Not so in some other countries. The tenets that underlie our U.S. business language—that your word is your bond, that transparency is expected in joint ventures and contractual engagements, that each party walks away from the table getting as well as giving something—are not always understood in all parts of the world.

This inherent conflict between first- and third-world business standards has meant that our journey as a design-driven firm has been at times extremely difficult. A core value of the company, which we call "value in the round," meaning that value must be created for all parties in the deal, has involved familiarizing ourselves with an alien environment in order to establish business fundamentals. Needing to respect cultural differences must be carefully investigated and evaluated while all the time taking care not to cross the line to engage in practices we abhor.

BUSINESS BLACK AND WHITE

In short, in the world of grays that characterizes business dealings in countries in which ethics are at best rudimentary by U.S. standards, and at worst nonexistent, we've taken the position that we must establish a black and white.

Let me explain. Take the word "transparency," for example, which in the United States involves a baseline understanding of capitalism, allowing that each party is able to get something in a negotiation without necessarily having cheated another. With that common understanding, negotiators don't need to resort to taking money out of the game—bribing, to be precise—because all of the money is in the game.

Nor is there a need to have to renegotiate a deal that has already been agreed upon because of a belief that the deal that was struck couldn't be good—or why would the parties have agreed to it?

In countries whose business laws are nascent, if they exist at all, and whose thinking has been shaped by philosophies vastly different from our own, our first challenge is to take what I call the "entry-level" business players, who disproportionately populate the developing countries in which we do business, and bring them up to speed in the business fundamentals of the U.S.

In the all-too-common instance of being asked that a deal be renegotiated, we see it as our duty to teach the fundamentals that underlie the business practices of the West, such as your word is your bond, and that, while it's all right to take as much time as you need to negotiate a deal, once you've agreed, you stand by it.

In the wake of a request to go back to the table after the celebratory dinner, for example, I begin by outlining what it's going to take for them to do business with us. We put it down in writing, even though I've learned that such documents are unenforceable. And, if they ask again to renegotiate, we walk.

In short, in a world in which business fundamentals are shades of gray, we've determined a black-and-white process that is our blueprint for doing business.

MORAL BLACK AND WHITE

Back to the bribes: Simply put, we don't do them. In the case of our wanting to buy the collection of antique vessels, for example, we walked when told we would have to make such a payment. The good news in that case was that we were actually invited back a year later to make the purchase on our terms.

The matter of bribes, however, is more than just shall we or shall we not. It goes to the heart of the other issue underlying doing business in the third world, and that is the need for a way to respect cultural differences without crossing the line to engage in practices that are inappropriate or immoral by Western standards.

Looked at this way, Rhodes Architectural Stone not only draws the line at paying bribes, but also at child labor and the mistreatment of women. The matter of child labor will serve to illustrate the dilemma. Imagine an American entrepreneur, traveling in the bitter cold in the remote countryside dressed in a Gore-Tex® parka, Thinsulate socks, and the most comfortable and technologically advanced clothing money can buy. We arrive and state that we will not buy anything fabricated or procured with child labor. Now contrast that with the local reality of the labor of the entire family required to put bread on the table and a roof over one's head.

If my children were starving, I suppose I would do the same. In fact, our own forbearers in the United States did employ children in factories well into the twentieth century, and because of that, we don't have to do it any more.

Into this moral gray area, we've established another black and white: namely, that we cannot and will not do business with entities that engage in the practice of child labor, but we will not go the next step and preach. In other words, we will not tell them they are wrong.

Surely, we bring a powerful lever when it comes to backing up this moral stance. Unlike foreign companies that go into native countries to sell products to people who can't afford to buy them, we are there to buy what they have to sell. We bring the twin carrots of hard currency and jobs.

That advantage notwithstanding, the decision to establish a moral black and white wasn't easy. It's one thing to come to that imperative in the matter of formulating business standards where none exist, for that involves the neutral task of teaching. It's quite another to tread into territory in which the actions are criminal or immoral by Western standards and, yet, understandable within the context of the foreign culture.

The decision to do so, therefore, is actually a process, one of thought and reflection and, in the final analysis, leadership.

PUTTING IT ALL TOGETHER

In coming to the imperatives that Rhodes Architectural Stone has determined for its business dealings overseas, I was fortunate to have the counsel of a member of our board, a former Whirlpool executive, who had extensive business experience throughout the world.

This individual taught me that when dealing with the grays that characterize the business landscape in the third world, it is necessary to establish a black and white, both for the way you will conduct business and account for your moral imperatives. And, if the reality differs considerably when you are actually at the table, it is necessary to be strong enough to walk away.

In sum, you must ask yourself questions such as: Who am I? How do I feel about this or that action? Can I sleep at night if I so engage in this or that behavior?

In the milieu of grays that characterizes the world beyond our oceans, be strong enough to formulate your black and whites, which, in turn, will become your guiding principles.

SOURCE: Ewing Marion Kauffman Foundation, www.entreworld.org, copyright © 2003 Richard Rhodes. Used with permission. All rights reserved.

This article is the opinion of the author, and does not necessarily represent the opinion of EntreWorld or the Ewing Marion Kauffman Foundation.

MANAGING INTERDEPENDENCE

Because multinational firms (or other organizations, such as the Red Cross) represent global interdependency, their managers at all levels must recognize that what they do, in the aggregate, has long-term implications for the socioeconomic interdependence of nations. Simply to describe ethical issues as part of the general environment does not address the fact that managers must control their activities at all levels—from simple, daily business transactions involving local workers, intermediaries, or consumers to global concerns of ecological responsibility—for the future benefit of all concerned. Whatever the situation, the powerful long-term effects of MNC and MNE action (or inaction) should be planned for and controlled—not haphazardly considered part of the side effects of business. The profitability of individual companies depends on a cooperative and constructive attitude toward global interdependence.

Foreign Subsidiaries in the United States

Much of the preceding discussion has related to U.S. subsidiaries around the world. However, to globally highlight the growing interdependence and changing balance of business power, foreign subsidiaries in the United States should also be considered. Since much criticism about a lack of responsibility has been directed toward MNCs with headquarters in the United States, we must think of these criticisms from an outsider's perspective. The number of foreign subsidiaries in the United States has grown and continues to grow dramatically; **foreign direct investment (FDI)** in the United States by other countries is, in many cases, far more than U.S. investment outward. Americans are thus becoming more sensitive to what they perceive as a lack of control over their own country's business.

Things look very different from the perspective of Americans employed at a subsidiary of an overseas MNC. Interdependence takes on a new meaning when people "over there" are calling the shots regarding strategy, expectations, products, and personnel. Often, Americans' resentment about different ways of doing business by "foreign" companies in the United States inhibits cooperation, which gave rise to the companies' presence in the first place.

Today, managers from all countries must learn new ways, and most MNCs are trying to adapt. Sadahei Kusumoto, president and CEO of Minolta Corporation, says that Japanese managers in the United States must recognize that they are "not in Honshu [Japan's largest island] anymore" and that one very different aspect of management in the United States is the idea of corporate social responsibility.[49]

In Japan, corporate social responsibility has traditionally meant that companies take care of their employees, whereas in the United States the public and private sectors are expected to share the responsibility for the community. Part of the explanation for this difference is that U.S. corporations get tax deductions for corporate philanthropy, whereas Japanese firms do not; nor are Japanese managers familiar with community needs. For these and other reasons, Japanese subsidiaries in the United States have not been active in U.S. philanthropy. However, Kusumoto pinpoints why they should become more involved in the future:

> *In the long run, failure to play an active role in the community will brand these companies as irresponsible outsiders and dim their prospects for the future.*[50]

Whether Kusomoto's motives for change are humanitarian or just good business sense does not really matter. The point is that he recognizes interdependence in globalization and acts accordingly.

Managing Subsidiary–Host-Country Interdependence

When **managing interdependence**, international managers must go beyond general issues of social responsibility and deal with the specific concerns of the MNC subsidiary–host-country relationship. Outdated MNC attitudes that focus only on profitability and autonomy are shortsighted and usually result in only short-term realization of those goals. MNCs must learn to accommodate the needs of other organizations and countries:

> *Interdependence rather than independence, and cooperation rather than confrontation are at the heart of that accommodation . . . the journey from independence to interdependence managed badly leads to dependence, and that is an unacceptable destination.*[51]

Most of the past criticism levied at MNCs has focused on their activities in LDCs. Their real or perceived lack of responsibility centers on the transfer in of inappropriate technology, causing unemployment, and the transfer out of scarce financial and other resources, reducing the capital available for internal development. In their defense, MNCs help LDCs by contributing new technology and managerial skills, improving the infrastructure, creating jobs, and bringing in investment capital from other countries by exporting products. The infusion of outside capital provides foreign-exchange earnings that can be used for further development. The host government's attitude is often referred to as a love–hate relationship: It wants the economic growth that MNCs can provide, but it does not want the incursions on national sovereignty or the technological dependence that may result. Most criticisms of MNC subsidiary activities, whether in less developed or more developed countries, are along the following lines:

1. MNCs locally raise their needed capital, contributing to a rise in interest rates in host countries.
2. The majority (sometimes even 100 percent) of the stock of most subsidiaries is owned by the parent company. Consequently, host-country people do not have much control over the operations of corporations within their borders.
3. MNCs usually reserve the key managerial and technical positions for expatriates. As a result, they do not contribute to the development of host-country personnel.
4. MNCs do not adapt their technology to the conditions that exist in host countries.
5. MNCs concentrate their research and development activities at home, restricting the transfer of modern technology and know-how to host countries.
6. MNCs give rise to the demand for luxury goods in host countries at the expense of essential consumer goods.
7. MNCs start their foreign operations by purchasing existing firms rather than by developing new productive facilities in host countries.
8. MNCs dominate major industrial sectors, thus contributing to inflation, by stimulating demand for scarce resources and earning excessively high profits and fees.
9. MNCs are not accountable to their host nations but only respond to home-country governments; they are not concerned with host-country plans for development.[52]

Specific MNCs have been charged with tax evasion, union busting, and interference in host-country politics. Of course, MNCs have both positive and negative effects on different economies. For every complaint about MNC activities (whether about capital

EXHIBIT 2-5 Potential Benefits and Costs to Host Countries of MNC Operations There

Benefits	Costs
Capital Market Effects	
■ Broader access to outside capital	■ Increased competition for local scarce capital
■ Economic growth	■ Increased interest rates as supply of local capital decreases
■ Foreign-exchange earnings	■ Capital service effects of balance of payments
■ Import substitution effects allow governments to save foreign exchange for priority projects	
■ Risk sharing	
Technology and Production Effects	
■ Access to new technology and R&D developments	■ Technology is not always appropriate
■ Employee training in new technology	■ Plants are often for assembly only and can be dismantled
■ Infrastructure development and support	■ Government infrastructure investment is higher than expected benefits
■ Export diversification	■ Increased pollution
■ Introduction of new management techniques	
Employment Effects	
■ Direct creation of new jobs	■ Limited skill development and creation
■ Introduction of more humane employment standards	■ Competition for scarce skills
■ Opportunities for indigenous management development	■ Low percentage of managerial jobs for local people
■ Income multiplier effects on local community business	■ Employment instability because of ability to move production operations freely to other countries

SOURCE: Adapted from R. H. Mason and R. S. Spich, *Management: An International Perspective,* (202) (Homewood, IL: Irwin, 1987).

markets, technology transfer, or employment practices), we can identify potential benefits (see Exhibit 2-5).

Numerous conflicts arise between MNC companies or subsidiaries and host countries, including conflicting goals (both economic and noneconomic) and conflicting concerns, such as the security of proprietary technology, patents, or information. Overall, the resulting trade-offs create an interdependent relationship between the subsidiary and the host government, based on relative bargaining power. The power of MNCs is based on their large-scale, worldwide economies, their strategic flexibility, and their control over technology and production location. The bargaining chips of the host governments include their control of raw materials and market access and their ability to set the rules regarding the role of private enterprise, the operation of state-owned firms, and the specific regulations regarding taxes, permissions, and so forth.

MNCs run the risk of their assets becoming hostage to host control, which may take the form of nationalism, protectionism, or governmentalism. Under **nationalism**, for example, public opinion is rallied in favor of national goals and against foreign influences. Under **protectionism**, the host institutes a partial or complete closing of borders to withstand competitive foreign products, using tariff and nontariff barriers, such as those used by Japan. Under **governmentalism**, the government uses its policy-setting role to favor national interests, rather than relying on market forces. An example is Britain's decision to privatize its telephone system.[53]

The intricacies of the relationship and the relative power of an MNC subsidiary and a host-country government are situation specific. Clearly, such a relationship should be managed for mutual benefit; a long-term, constructive relationship based on the MNC's socially responsive stance should result in progressive strategic success for the MNC and economic progress for the host country. The effective management of subsidiary–host-country interdependence must have a long-term perspective. Although temporary strategies to reduce interdependence via controls on the transnational flows by firms (for example, transfer-pricing tactics) or by governments (such as new residency requirements for skilled workers) are often successful in the short run, they result in inefficiencies that must be absorbed by one or both parties, with negative long-term results.[54] In setting up and maintaining subsidiaries, managers are wise to consider the long-term trade-offs between strategic plans and operational management. By finding out for themselves the pressing local concerns and understanding the sources of past conflicts, they can learn from mistakes and recognize the consequences of the failure to manage problems. Furthermore, managers should implement policies that reflect corporate social responsibility regarding local economic issues, employee welfare, or natural resources.[55] At the least, the failure to effectively manage interdependence results in constraints on strategy. In the worst case, it results in disastrous consequences for the local area, for the subsidiary, and for the global reputation of the company.

The interdependent nature of developing economies and the MNCs operating there is of particular concern when discussing social responsibility because of the tentative and fragile nature of the economic progression in those countries. MNCs must set a high moral standard and lay the groundwork for future economic development. At the minimum, they should ensure that their actions will do no harm. Some recommendations by De George for MNCs operating in and doing business with developing countries are as follows:

1. Do no intentional harm. This includes respect for the integrity of the ecosystem and consumer safety.
2. Produce more good than harm for the host country.
3. Contribute by their activity to the host country's development.
4. Respect the human rights of their employees.
5. To the extent that local culture does not violate ethical norms, respect the local culture and work with and not against it.
6. Pay their fair share of taxes.
7. Cooperate with the local government in developing and enforcing just background (infrastructure) institutions (i.e., laws, governmental regulations, unions, and consumer groups, which serve as a means of social control).[56]

Managing Environmental Interdependence

International managers—and all people for that matter—can no longer afford to ignore the impact of their activities on the environment. As Ward and Dubois put it:

> *Now that mankind is in the process of completing the colonization of the planet, learning to manage it intelligently is an urgent imperative. [People] must accept responsibility for the stewardship of the earth. The word stewardship implies, of course, management for the sake of someone else. . . . As we enter the global phase of human evolution, it becomes obvious that each [person] has two countries, his [or her] own and the planet earth.*[57]

Effectively **managing environmental interdependence** includes considering ecological interdependence as well as the economic and social implications of MNC activities. There is an ever-increasing awareness of, and a mounting concern worldwide about, the effects of global industrialization on the natural environment. Government regulations and powerful interest groups are demanding ecological responsibility regarding the use of scarce natural resources and production processes that threaten permanent damage to the planet. MNCs have to deal with each country's different policies and techniques for environmental and health protection. Such variations in approach reflect different levels of industrialization, living standards, government–business relations, philosophies of collective intervention, patterns of industrial competition, and degrees of sophistication in public policy.[58]

In recent years, the export of hazardous wastes from developed countries to less developed ones has increased considerably. One instance was the dumping of over 8,000 drums of waste, including drums filled with polychlorinated biphenyl (PCB), a highly toxic compound, in Koko, Nigeria.[59] While not all dumping is illegal, the large international trade in hazardous wastes (as a result of the increasing barriers to domestic disposal) raises disturbing questions regarding social responsibility. Although the importer of waste must take some blame, it is the exporter who shoulders the ultimate responsibility for both generation and disposal. Often, companies choose to dispose of hazardous waste in less developed countries to take advantage of weaker regulations and lower costs. Until we have strict international regulation of trade in hazardous wastes, companies should take it upon themselves to monitor their activities, as Singh and Lakhan demand:

> To export these wastes to countries which do not benefit from waste-generating industrial processes or whose citizens do not have lifestyles that generate such wastes is unethical. It is especially unjust to send hazardous wastes to lesser-developed countries which lack the technology to minimize the deleterious effects of these substances.[60]

The exporting of pesticides poses a similar problem, with the United States and Germany being the main culprits. The United States exports about 200 million pounds of pesticides each year that are prohibited, restricted, or not registered for use in the United States.[61] One MNC, Monsanto Chemical Corporation, for example, sells DDT to many foreign importers, even though its use in the United States has been essentially banned. Apart from the lack of social responsibility toward the people and the environment in the countries that import DDT, this action is also irresponsible to U.S. citizens because many of their fruits and meat products are imported from those countries.[62]

These are only two of the environmental problems facing countries and large corporations today. According to Graedel and Allenby, the path to truly sustainable development is for corporations to broaden their concept of industrial ecology:

> The concept [of industrial ecology] requires that an industrial system be viewed not in isolation from its surrounding systems, but in concert with them. It is a systems view in which one seeks to optimize the total materials cycle from virgin material, to finished material, to component, to product, to obsolete product, and to ultimate disposal.[63]

Essentially, this perspective supports the idea that environmental citizenship is necessary for a firm's survival as well as responsible social performance.[64]

It is clear, then, that MNCs must take the lead in dealing with ecological interdependence by integrating environmental factors into strategic planning. Along with an investment appraisal, a project feasibility study, and operational plans, such planning should include an environmental impact assessment.[65] At the least, MNC managers must deal with the increasing scarcity of natural resources in the next few decades by (1) looking for alternative raw materials, (2) developing new methods of recycling or disposing of used materials, and (3) expanding the use of by-products.[66]

Multinational corporations already have had a tremendous impact on foreign countries, and this impact will continue to grow and bring about long-lasting changes. Even now, U.S. MNCs alone account for about 10 percent of the world's gross national product (GNP). Because of interdependence at both the local and global level, it is not only moral but also in the best interest of MNCs to establish a single clear posture toward social and ethical responsibilities worldwide and to ensure that it is implemented. In a real sense, foreign firms enter as guests in host countries and must respect the local laws, policies, traditions, and culture as well as those countries' economic and developmental needs.

CONCLUSION

When research findings and anecdotal evidence indicate differential attitudes toward ethical behavior and social responsibility across cultures, MNCs must take certain steps. For example, they must be careful when placing a foreign manager in a country whose values are incongruent with his or her own because this could lead to conflicts with local managers, governmental bodies, customers, and suppliers. As discussed earlier, expatriates should be oriented to the legal and ethical ramifications of questionable foreign payments, the differences in environmental regulations, and the local expectations of personal integrity. They should also be supported as they attempt to integrate host-country behaviors with the expectations of the company's headquarters.

Social responsibility, ethical behavior, and interdependence are important concerns to be built into management control—not as afterthoughts but as part of the ongoing process of planning and controlling international operations for the long-term benefit of all.

Part II focuses on the pervasive and powerful influence of culture in the host-country environment in which the international manager operates. Chapter 3 examines the nature of culture—what are its various dimensions and roots? How does culture affect the behavior and expectations of employees, and what are the implications for how managers operating in other countries should behave?

Summary of Key Points

1. The concept of international social responsibility (known in business circles as CSR—corporate social responsibility) includes the expectation that MNCs should be concerned about the social and economic effects of their decisions on activities in other countries, and should build appropriate provisions into their strategic plans to deal with those potential effects.

2. Moral universalism refers to the need for a moral standard that is accepted around the world; however, varying cultural attitudes and business practices make this goal unattainable at this time. A number of groups of corporations within industries have collaborated on sets of policies for CSR both for their companies and those in their supply chains. Such collaborations help to raise the standard in host countries and to level the playing field for managers within those industries.

3. Concerns about MNC social responsibility revolve around issues of human rights in other countries, such as South Africa and China. Many organizations develop codes of conduct that specifically deal with human rights in their operations around the world.

4. International business ethics refers to the conduct of MNCs in their relationships to all individuals and entities with whom they come into contact. Ethical behavior is judged and based largely on the cultural value system and the generally accepted ways of doing business in each country or society. MNC managers must decide whether to base their ethical standards on those of the host country or those of the home country and whether these different standards can be reconciled.

5. MNCs must balance their responsibility to various stakeholders, such as owners, creditors, consumers, employees, suppliers, governments, and societies. Firms with a long-term perspective recognize the need to consider all of their stakeholders in their business plans.

6. Managers operating abroad are often faced with differing attitudes towards bribery or other payments that raise significant questions about appropriate moral behavior in either the host nation or other nations, and yet frequently are demanded to conduct business. The Foreign Corrupt Practices Act prohibits most questionable payments by U.S. companies doing business in other countries.

7. Managers must control their activities relative to interdependent relationships at all levels—from simple, daily business transactions involving local workers, intermediaries, or consumers to global concerns of ecological responsibility.

8. The failure to effectively manage interdependence will result in constraints on strategy, in the least, or in disastrous consequences for the local area, the subsidiary, and the global reputation of the company.

9. Managing environmental interdependence includes the need to consider ecological interdependence as well as the economic and social implications of MNC activities.

10. The MNC–host-country relationship is generally a love–hate relationship from the host country's viewpoint in that it wants the economic growth that the MNC can provide but does not want the dependency and other problems that result.

Discussion Questions

1. Discuss the concept of international social responsibility. What role does it play in the relationship between a company and its host country?
2. Discuss the criticisms that have been leveled against MNCs in the past regarding their activities in less developed countries. What counterarguments are there to those criticisms?
3. What does moral universalism mean? Discuss your perspective on this concept. Do you think the goal of moral universalism is possible? Is it advisable?
4. What do you think should be the role of MNCs toward human rights issues in other countries—for example, China or South Africa? What are the major human rights concerns at this time? What ideas do you have for dealing with these problems? What is the role of corporate codes of conduct in dealing with these concerns?
5. What is meant by international business ethics? How does the local culture affect ethical practices? What are the implications of such local norms for ethical decisions by MNC managers?
6. As a manager in a foreign subsidiary, how can you reconcile local expectations of questionable payments with the Foreign Corrupt Practices Act? What is your stance on the problem of "payoffs?" How does the degree of law enforcement in a particular country affect ethical behavior in business?
7. Explain what is meant by managing interdependence in the global business arena. Discuss the love–hate relationship between MNCs and host countries.
8. What do you think are the responsibilities of MNCs toward the global environment? Give some examples of MNC activities that run counter to the concepts of ecological interdependence and environmental responsibility.
9. Discuss the ethical issues that have developed regarding the use of IT in cross-border transactions. What new conflicts have developed since the printing of this book? What solutions can you suggest?

Application Exercise

Do some research to determine the codes of conduct of two MNCs. Compare the issues that they cover and share your findings with the class. After several students have presented their findings, prepare a chart showing the commonalities and differences of content in the codes presented. How do you account for the differences?

Experiential Exercise

Consider the ethical dilemmas in the following situation and decide what you would do. Then meet in small groups of students and come to a group consensus. Discuss your decisions with the class.

I am CEO of an international trading company in Turkey. One state-owned manufacturing company (Company A) in one of the Middle East countries opened a tender for 15,000 tons PVC granule K value 70. Company A makes all its purchases through tenders. For seven years in that market, my company has never been able to do any business with Company A (though we have sold many bulk materials to other state-owned companies in that market). One of our new managers had a connection with the purchasing manager of Company A, who promised to supply us with all of our competitors' bids if we pay him a 2 percent commission on all of our sales to his company. Our area manager accepted this arrangement. He got the competing bids, made our offer, and we got the tender. I learned of this situation when reviewing our income and expenses chart, which showed the 2 percent commission.

What shall I do, given the following: (1) If I refuse to accept the business without any legitimate reasons (presently there are none) my company will be blacklisted in that country—where we get about 20 percent of our gross yearly profit. (2) If I accept the business and do not pay the 2 percent commission, the purchasing manager will make much trouble for us when he receives our shipment. I am sure that he will not release our 5 percent bank guarantee letter about the quality and quantity of the material. (3) If I accept the business and pay the 2 percent commission, it will go against everything I have achieved in the 30 years of my career.

You have three ethical problems here: First, your company has won a rigged bid. Second, you must pay the person who rigged it or he will make life miserable for you. Third, you have to decide what to do with the area manager who accepted this arrangement.

SOURCE: J. Delaney and D. Sockell, "Ethics in the Trenches," *Across the Board* (October 1990): 17.

Internet Resources

Visit the Deresky Companion Website at www.prenhall.com/deresky for this chapter's Internet resources.

Nike's CSR Challenge

IN 2005 NIKE returned to reporting on its social and environmental practices after a couple of years of silence due to legal concerns. The sports and clothing company is very important to countries such as Vietnam, where it is the largest private-sector employer with more than 50,000 workers producing shoes through subcontractors. (1) Nike's new report makes sobering reading, as it describes widespread problems in Asian factories. The company said it audited hundreds of factories in 2003 and 2004 and found cases of abusive treatment in more than a quarter of its South Asian plants. For example, between 25% and 50% of the factories in the region restrict access to toilets and drinking water during the workday. The same percentage of factories deny workers at least one day off in seven. In more than half of Nike's factories employees work more than 60 hours per week. In up to 25%, workers refusing overtime were punished. Wages were below the legal minimum at up to 25% of factories. (2)

For the first time in a major corporate report the details of all the factories were published. The report was significant for this transparency and being so candid about the problems that workers for Nike still face, and therefore the challenges that remain for the management. The NGOs working on these issues know that Nike is not alone in facing such problems. Indeed, they realise that the company has invested more in improving conditions than many of its competitors. Studies of voluntary corporate attempts at improving labor standards in global supply chains have suggested that they are delivering widespread improvements, and instead new approaches are needed that engage governments, NGOs, and local businesses. (3)

This realization has led to a new strategy from Nike. In May Nike's Vice President of Corporate Responsibility, Hannah Jones, told delegates at the Ethical Trading Initiative (ETI) conference that, whereas the company had previously been looking into how to solve problems for themselves, now they are exploring how to create systemic change in the industry. She explained that "premium brands are in a lonely leadership position" because "consumers are not rewarding us" for investments in improved social performance in supply chains. Like other companies, they have realized that the responsibility of one is to work towards the accountability of all. Consequently, one of Nike's new corporate citizenship goals is "to effect positive, systemic change in working conditions within the footwear, apparel and equipment industries." This involves the company engaging labor ministries, civil society and competitors around the world to try to raise the bar so that all companies have to attain better standards of social and environmental performance. One example is its involvement in the Multi-Fibre Agreement (MFA) Forum to help countries, unions and others plan for the consequences of the end of the MFA.

This new strategy is beyond what many consultants, media commentators and academics currently understand. By claiming to be an advance in thinking, an article in *The Economist* in May, by the worldwide managing director of McKinsey & Company, illustrated the limits of current consulting advice. It suggested that seeking good societal relations should be seen as both good for society and good for profitability. "Profits should not be seen as an end in themselves," suggested Ian Davis, "but rather as a signal from society that their company is succeeding in its mission of providing something people want." (4) However, those who have experience working in this field for some years, including Nike realise that, however we may wish to talk about the compatibility of profits with people and planet, the current societal frameworks for business are not making this a reality. The implication is that we have to make this so by changing those frameworks.

The key strategic shift for Nike's management is that they no longer regard the company as a closed system. Instead, they understand its future depends on the way customers, suppliers, investors, regulators and others relate to it. Their challenge is to reshape the signals being given out by those groups to itself and its competitors, so that the company can operate in a sustainable and just way, which is also financially viable.

Nike's experience is pertinent to other companies, whose voluntary efforts are failing to address the root causes of the problems associated with their industry. Unilever, for example, was criticised by ActionAid for profiting from worsening conditions for workers on plantations. (5) Falling prices have led to plantations laying off workers and wages going unpaid—a trend that has seen a consequent increase in attacks against owners and managers. Applying a systems view to the situation would suggest that Unilever reconsider how it influences the global political economy that is driving down prices for tea.

The challenge is not only one of strategy but also leadership. Traditionally, analysts and educators on corporate leadership have assumed that it involves leading people towards the goal of their employer, the company. In May an article on leadership in Conference Board Canada's *Organizational Performance Review* quoted the thoughts of leaders from World War II and the Korean War. (6) This reflects what Mark Gerzon describes as a focus on "leadership within borders", when what the world needs is "leaders beyond borders". (7) This means people who can see across borders created by others, such as the borders of their job, and reach across such borders to engage others in dialogue and action to address systemic problems. We could call this "transcending leadership", which was alluded to by James McGregor Burns, in his path-breaking book *Leadership*. (8) It is a form of leadership that transcends the boundaries of one's professional role and the limits of one's own situation to engage people on collective goals. It is a form of leadership that transcends a limited conception of self, as the individual leader identifies with ever-greater wholes. It is a form of leadership that transcends the need for a single leader, by helping people to transcend their limited states of consciousness and concern and inspire them to lead.

Perhaps the best modern example of transcending leadership is Gandhi, who aroused and elevated the hopes and demands of millions of Indians and whose life and personality were enhanced in the process. It is an irony of our times that this anti-imperialist who chose to spin his own cloth could be an inspiration for the future direction of executives in large companies sourcing clothes from factories across Asia. Gandhi called on us to understand our connectedness to "all that lives", and identify with ever-greater wholes. There is a lesson here for Nike and others. The apparel sector is an open system, and so wider issues of trade flows, governance, media, financial markets and politics impact on the potential of the sector, and thus Nike, to become sustainable and just. Without changes to the financial markets, Nike may find its efforts are in vain.

REFERENCES

1. www.csr-asia.com/index.php?p=1925
2. www.csr-asia.com/index.php?p=1855
3. BSR and PWC, "Public Sector Support for the Implementation of Corporate Social Responsibility (CSR) in Global Supply Chains: Conclusions From Practical Experience" (2004); bsr.org/Meta/BSR_worldbankscm.pdf.
4. Ian Davis, "The Biggest Contract," *The Economist*, 26 May 2005.
5. www.mallenbaker.net/csr/nl/82.html
6. Jeffrey Gandz, "Leadership Character and Competencies," Organizational Performance Review, Spring/ Summer 2005 (Conference Board Canada).
7. M. Gerzon, Leaders beyond Borders (2004); www.mediatorsfoundation.org.
8. J. M. Burns, *Leadership* (New York: Harper & Row, 1978).

SOURCE: "Nike Says Time to Team Up," *The Journal of Corporate Citizenship*, Autumn 2005, i19 p. 10(3). By *Jem Bendell*. Auckland University of Technology, Director, Lifeworth. COPYRIGHT 2005 Greenleaf Publishing, reprinted with permission.

CASE QUESTIONS

1. What are the challenges regarding corporate social responsibility that companies in the apparel industry face in its supply chains around the world?
2. Discuss the meaning and implications of the statement by a Nike representative that "consumers are not rewarding us for investments in improved social performance in supply chains."
3. What does it mean to have an industry open-systems approach to social responsibility? What parties are involved? Who are the stakeholders?
4. What is meant by "leadership beyond borders"?
5. Is it possible to have "a compatibility of profits with people and planet"? Whose responsibility is it to achieve that state?

SOURCE: Helen Deresky

Case 1   Coca-Cola's Business Practices: Facing the Heat in a Few Countries

The University of Michigan has said it is committed to working only with companies that have ethical and responsible practices, yet the Coca-Cola Company is in obvious violation of these standards. Coca-Cola needs to be accountable for their actions, and until they are, we demand that they are taken off our campus. We refuse to support businesses that are unable to promote basic human rights amongst their employees and the public.[1]

KRISTIN PURDY,
The Coke Coalition, University of Michigan, in 2005

Coca-Cola is a frequent violator of union rights and that's why several universities in the United States have decided to protest their conduct.[2]

FABIO ARIAS,
Vice President, CUT Trade Union Confederation, Colombia, in 2006

It is very unfortunate. The actual volume in terms of sales is small but it is the larger issue of our reputation. These allegations are false but we do share the concerns with issues.[3]

KARI BJORHUS,
Spokeswoman for the Coca-Cola Company, in 2006

INTRODUCTION

From January 1, 2006, the University of Michigan in the United States put on hold the sale of the products of The Coca-Cola Company (Coca-Cola) in all its campuses, thus becoming the tenth U.S. university to do so. The ban was the outcome of a relentless campaign by student activists and trade union groups, who accused Coca-Cola of violent labor practices in Colombia and of creating environmental problems in India.

To order copies, call 0091-40-2343-0462/63 or write to ICFAI Center for Management Research, Plot #49, Nagarjuna Hills, Hyderabad 500 082, India or email icmr@icfai.org. Web site: www.icmrindia.org.

This case was written by Soorya Tejomoortula under the direction of Rajiv Fernando, ICFAI Center for Management Research (ICMR). It is intended to be used as a basis for class discussion rather than to illustrate either effective or ineffective handling of a management situation. It was compiled from published sources.

[1]"Students campaign to ban Coca-Cola products on campuses," www.indiaresource.org, April 19, 2005.
[2]"Colombian workers support U.S. universities' ban on Coca-Cola," www.timesleader.com, January 02, 2006.
[3]"Univ in US to toss Coca-Cola," www.financialexpress.com, January 02, 2006.

University of Michigan issued the orders for the ban based on the recommendation of its University Dispute Board. This was following the inability of Coca-Cola to meet the deadline of December 31, 2005, that required agreeing on a protocol on the findings of the commission formed by a set of universities in the United States. The commission had offered to investigate the company's labor practices and that of its bottlers in Colombia. Coca-Cola did not want the findings of the commission to have any legal consequences but the attorneys in an earlier lawsuit against Coca-Cola and its bottlers in Colombia insisted that the findings should be legally admissible in court of law in the US.

Other prominent U.S. universities that had banned Coca-Cola on similar grounds were the New York University, the largest private university in the United States; Rutgers University in New Jersey; and the Santa Clara University in California. The University of Michigan and The New York University were Coca-Cola's largest campus markets in the United States. Coca-Cola's annual contracts with the University of Michigan, which had over 50,000 students, were worth around US$1.4 million in sales in 2005.

The campaign by student activists and trade union groups to ban Coca-Cola had been going on for several years in different countries. Coca-Cola was accused, along with its bottling partners, of hiring paramilitary death squads in Colombia to kidnap, intimidate, or kill its union leaders and other workers at its bottling plants. Since

1989, approximately eight union leaders of Coca-Cola's plants in Colombia had been murdered and many others abducted and tortured.

In India, Coca-Cola had to face opposition from the local people around its factory in Plachimada, Kerala,[4] who charged that the company was responsible for the draining of the underground water table. In 2003, a BBC[5] report revealed that Coca-Cola was distributing improperly treated sludge containing toxic carcinogens and heavy metals, such as cadmium and lead, as fertilizer to farmers in the region. Coca-Cola shut down this plant in March 2004 owing to mounting pressure. The company then decided to shift its operations to a nearby industrial zone, the Kanjikode Industrial Area.

There were also protests at Coca-Cola's Mehdiganj plant in North India over similar issues. In addition to these accusations, in 2003 the Center for Science and Environment (CSE)[6] made public the findings of its study wherein it reported that the products of both Coca-Cola and PepsiCo Inc. (Pepsi) that were sold in India contained a cocktail of harmful pesticide residues.

In an official statement, Coca-Cola denied that it had used death squads in Colombia. The company said that two judicial investigations in the country had not found any evidence in support of such allegations. Coca-Cola also claimed that there was no evidence linking it or its bottlers with the groundwater problems at its factory locations in India. Responding to the allegation that its products contained pesticide residues, it said that the products that it sold in India were perfectly safe and were in accordance with global quality standards.

Over the years, Coca-Cola, one of the largest non-alcoholic beverage companies and the world's most widely recognized brand, had been facing a string of problems that could seriously damage its brand image. The company had also faced allegations related to anti-competitive business practices in Mexico and had to pay heavy fines and penalties.

BACKGROUND NOTE

The Coca-Cola drink, popularly referred to as "Coke," is a kind of cola, a sweet carbonated[7] drink containing caramel[8] and other flavoring agents. It was invented by Dr. John Smith Pemberton (Pemberton) on May 8, 1886, at Atlanta, Georgia. The beverage was named Coca-Cola because at that time it contained extracts of coca leaves and kola nuts.[9] Frank M. Robinson (Robinson), Pemberton's bookkeeper and partner who came up with the name for the drink, suggested that it be spelled Coca-Cola rather than Coca-Kola because he thought the two Cs would look better while advertising. Robinson designed the now world famous Coca-Cola trademark as well.

Pemberton later sold the business to a group of businessmen, one of whom was Griggs Candler (Candler). By 1888, several forms of Coca-Cola were in the market competing against each other. Candler acquired these businesses from the other businessmen and established The Coca-Cola Company in 1892. He aggressively marketed the product through advertising, distribution of coupons and souvenirs, and promoted the brand name Coca-Cola. Sales grew rapidly. and by 1895 the product was being sold across the United States.

In the initial years, Coca-Cola was sold through soda fountains[10] wherein the Coca-Cola syrup, carbon dioxide, and water were mixed and given to customers. In 1894, a fountain seller named Joseph A. Biedenharn introduced the concept of selling the prepared drink in bottles. He thus became the first bottler for Coca-Cola. In 1899, large-scale bottling of Coca-Cola began when Benjamin Thomas and Joseph Whitehead won a contract from Candler to sell Coca-Cola throughout America in bottles. They started subcontracting the task of bottling and distribution, which led to easy availability and rapid growth of sales. The Coca-Cola bottling system grew to become one of the largest, widest production and distributions networks in the world.

However, the rapid increase of Coca-Cola's popularity led to many counterfeits flooding the market, and Coca-Cola had to spend huge sums of money on educating its customers on how to recognize the genuine product. The company realized that it needed a uniquely designed bottle that the customer would instantly recognize. In 1916, the hobble-skirt design bottle was designed by Root Glass Company, Indiana,[11] and was approved by the bottlers (Refer to Exhibit I for a photograph of the hobble-skirt design bottle). The design of the bottle was so distinctive that it would be instantly recognizable as a Coca-Cola bottle by the customer even it was felt in the dark or if the bottle was broken. The design of the Coca-Cola bottle became as famous as the Coca-Cola trademark.

In 1919, a group of investors headed by Ernest Woodruff and W. C. Bradley purchased Coca-Cola for US$25 million. In 1923, Robert Winship Woodruff (Woodruff), son of Ernest Woodruff, was elected company

---

[4]Kerala is a state in the southern part of India.
[5]The British Broadcasting Corporation (BBC) is a publicly funded radio and television broadcasting corporation of the United Kingdom. (Source: http://en.wikipedia.org/wiki/BBC)
[6]Center for Science and Environment (CSE) is an independent, non-governmental organization that aims to increase public awareness on science, technology, environment, and development. CSE was established in 1980 and is based in New Delhi.
[7]Carbonation, which involves dissolving carbon dioxide, is used in aqueous solutions like soft drinks to make them effervescent.
[8]Caramel is a food that has a brown color and a sweet toasted flavor. Caramel can be made from sugar by heating it slowly to around 170°C.

[9]The kola nut has a bitter flavor and high caffeine content, and is primarily obtained from some West African or Indonesian trees.
[10]Historically, soda fountains referred to soda shops and the part of a drugstore (pharmacy) where sodas, ice cream, sundaes, hot beverages, iced beverages, baked goods, and light meals were prepared and served. Now the term refers to the carbonated drink dispensers found in fast-food restaurants and convenience stores in the United States and Canada.
[11]Indiana is a U.S. state with Indianapolis as the capital.

EXHIBIT I   Hobble-Skirt Design Bottle

SOURCE: http://www.brandine.com/images

EXHIBIT II   Bell Shaped Fountain Glass

SOURCE: http://wingers.info/menu/Coke

president. He was widely credited with making Coca-Cola one of the world's most recognized brands and a multinational company with huge revenues and profits. Woodruff believed in product quality and started a "Quality Drink" campaign using a staff of highly trained service people. The main focus of the campaign was to encourage and assist fountain outlets in aggressively selling and correctly serving Coca-Cola. To make the campaign more successful, a distinctive bell-shaped fountain glass was introduced along the lines of the popular Coca-Cola bottle. This design also became very famous (Refer to Exhibit II for a photograph of the bell shaped fountain glass). In 1933, Coca-Cola introduced automatic fountain dispensers that automatically prepared the finished drink.

Woodruff also initiated steps to increase sale of Coca-Cola in bottles. With the assistance of the bottlers, he established quality standards for every phase of bottling. Advertising and marketing support was also increased and by the end of 1928, Coca-Cola's bottle sales exceeded fountain sales for the first time. Innovative merchandising concepts were introduced for bottles. Six-bottle cardboard cartons were introduced to make it easier for the consumer to take Coca-Cola home. A metal, open-top cooler was introduced to serve ice-chilled Coca-Cola at retail outlets. The coolers were later modified and became self-operated automatic coin control machines. They were installed at factories, offices, railway stations, and other institutions.

Under Woodruff's leadership, Coca-Cola took several initiatives to expand rapidly into international markets. Earlier, Coca-Cola's international operations had not been properly organized. In 1926, Woodruff established the Foreign Department to organize the international operations; this later became a subsidiary known as The

Coca-Cola Export Corporation. Coca-Cola sponsored the Amsterdam Olympic Games in 1928 to promote its product in other countries. From then on, it regularly sponsored the Olympic Games.

During the World War II, there was difficulty in shipping the Coca-Cola syrup to Germany. This led to the birth of the brand Fanta in Germany, which was manufactured locally. Coca-Cola also positioned itself as an American drink when it supplied Coca-Cola for a nominal price of five cents to American soldiers during the war and later identified with the American way of life. World War II also provided an ideal platform for Coca-Cola to expand to other countries by setting up bottling plants to serve the American soldiers stationed there. After the war, these plants were used to establish its operations in those countries.

The period 1940 to 1970 was one of rapid international growth, and Coca-Cola became a symbol of friendliness and refreshment across the world. In 1955, Coca-Cola became the first company to introduce the sale of the soft drinks in metal tins, a concept originally developed for the American soldiers. In 1960, Coca-Cola acquired the Minute Maid Corporation to add fruit juices to its product portfolio. In 1977, PET (Polyethylene Terephthalate)[12] bottles were introduced. During this time, the company also introduced various brands like Sprite and TAB, which went on to become bestselling soft drink brands.

In 1980, Roberto Goizueta[13] became the Chairman and CEO of Coca-Cola. Business analysts described him as

---

[12]PET (Polyethylene terephthalate) is a thermoplastic resin of the polyester family that is used to make beverage, food, and other liquid containers; synthetic fibers; as well as for some other thermoforming applications.
[13]Roberto C. Goizueta, a Cuban immigrant, had worked up the ranks at Coca-Cola and was its Chairman and CEO from 1980 to 1997. Under his leadership, Coca-Cola's stock value increased by more than 7,200 percent.

a man with a global vision and credited him with taking steps that made Coca-Cola popular across the world. In 1985, Coca-Cola changed its old formula to make its product taste sweeter and to compete more effectively with Pepsi. This new formula was launched with a lot of publicity and was marketed as the "New Coca-Cola." However, the new product was a commercial failure and was described as one of the biggest marketing blunders ever. Customers were vociferous in their demand for the original taste and demonstrations were held against the company. Coca-Cola reintroduced the original taste as "Coca-Cola Classic." In 1982, "Diet Coke" was introduced as a low-calorie soft drink for health-conscious customers.

In 1986, Coca-Cola merged the company-owned distribution network with two large ownership groups that were for sale—the John T. Lupton franchises and BCI Holding Corporation's bottling holdings—to form an independent entity, Coca-Cola Enterprises Inc. (CCE). CCE, which mainly operated in America and Europe, distributed two billion physical cases of products, representing 21 percent of Coca-Cola's volume worldwide, in 2004. The total revenues of CCE for the same year were US$18 billion.

In 2005, Coca-Cola had operations in over 200 countries selling more than 400 brands in categories like packaged drinking water, coffees, juices, sports drinks, and teas, apart from its main soft drink products. The company owned four of the top five soft drink brands in the world, Coca-Cola, Diet Coke, Fanta, and Sprite. It also had other popular brands like Barq's, Fruitopia, Minute Maid, POWERade, and Dasani water.

Coca-Cola had became one of the biggest beverage companies in the world by 2005, selling around 1.3 billion beverage servings per day. The main reasons for Coca-Cola's enormous success were its advertising campaigns (refer to Exhibit III for a list of popular advertising slogans of Coca-Cola) and its massive production and distribution operations spread across the world (Refer to Exhibit IV for brief financial information).

COCA-COLA'S BUSINESS PRACTICES

Coca-Cola had always believed that it conducted its business with responsibility and ethics. The company's business practices were aimed at creating value at the marketplace, providing excellent working conditions, protecting the environment, and strengthening the communities in the places of operation. Commitment to quality and a code of business conduct were evolved to ensure good business practices.

According to Coca-Cola, its commitment to quality was reflected in every facet of its business. These included commitment to product quality, quality in business processes, and in its relationships with suppliers and retailers. The quality system was reviewed constantly so that the performance bar for these standards was always kept high. The quality guidelines were communicated to all business units and their implementation reviewed. The company introduced the Coca-Cola Quality System (TCCQS) to achieve these quality objectives (Refer to Exhibit V for details on TCCQS).

Coca-Cola prepared a code of business conduct for all its employees that incorporated the company's core values such as honesty, integrity, diversity, quality, respect, responsibility, and accountability. The code of

EXHIBIT III Popular Advertising Slogans of Coca-Cola

Year	Slogan
1886	Drink Coca-Cola
1929	Pause that Refreshes
1936	It's the Refreshing Thing to Do
1942	It's the Real Thing
1944	Global High Sign
1950s	Sign of Good Taste
1950s	Be Really Refreshed
1950s	Go Better Refreshed
1963	Things Go Better with Coke
1969	It's the Real Thing (revived from 1942)
1971	I'd Like to Buy the World a Coke
1979	Have a Coke and a Smile
1985	We've Got a Taste for You (New Coke)
1985	America's Real Choice (Coca-Cola Classic)
1993	Always Coca-Cola
1999	Enjoy Coca-Cola
2001	Life Tastes Good
2005	Make It Real

Note: The list is not exhaustive.
Compiled from various sources.

EXHIBIT IV Comparison of Key Financials for the Years 2003, 2004, and 2005 (In US$ million)

Year	December 31, 2005	December 31, 2004	December 31, 2003
Total Revenues	23,104	21,962	21,044
Gross Profit	14,909	14,324	13,282
Operating Profit	6,085	5,698	5,221
Net Profit	4,972	4,847	4,347

Compiled from various resources.

EXHIBIT V   The Coca-Cola Quality System (TCCQS)

The Coca-Cola Quality System (TCCQS) was developed by a global team of professionals and approved by the senior management of top franchise bottling partners. The quality system reflected the integrated approach to managing quality, the environment, and health and safety. The system formed the guiding principles encompassing all the business processes and activities, helped the management in decision making, and drove the company toward continuous improvement and quality.

Based on the quality system, four guideline books were published in the key areas of quality, environment safety, and suppliers. They were *Quality Management System Standard, Environmental Management System Standard, Safety Management System Standard, and Supplier Expectations.* TCCQS was found to be on a par with ISO in quality standards (ISO 9001: 2000), environmental standards (ISO 14001:1996), and occupational health and safety standards (OHSAS 18001:1999).

The quality system was constantly revised to meet the latest and most stringent food and safety regulations including the Global Food Safety Initiative[14] (GFSI) Guidance Document. Coca-Cola believed in the promise of refreshing and benefiting the customers and strove to keep up this promise through the Quality System.

SOURCE: Adapted from www2.coca-cola.com.

business conduct was uniform for all the company's operations across the world and it clearly defined policies and procedures to help employees handle various contingencies. Coca-Cola believed that the company's most valuable asset was its trademark brand and that the

EXHIBIT VI   Coca-Cola's Code of Business Conduct

Coca-Cola considered its employees to be the representatives of the company and expected them to act with honesty and integrity in all the matters pertaining to the company. The code of conduct covered various aspects such as:

- Employee responsibilities
- Conflicts of interest
- Financial records
- Use of company assets
- Working with customers and suppliers
- Working with governments
- Protecting information
- Administration of code

Employees were encouraged to ask for guidance when in doubt on issues relating to the code of business conduct, ethics, and compliance matters and to report possible violations. The company created an exclusive Internet Web site, www.KOethics.com, and had an international toll-free telephone number for guidance and reporting of such issues. The company arranged for translators for employees who could not speak English over the provided telephone line. The employees also had the choice of remaining anonymous and were required to cooperate with any investigations of code of business conduct.

Managers had the primary responsibility to maintain the code of conduct in the company. Managers had to understand the code of conduct and report suspected violations. If any employee violated the code of conduct with the knowledge of the manager, then both would be held equally responsible for the offence.

SOURCE: Adapted from www2.coca-cola.com.

[14]In April 2000, a group of international retailer CEOs identified the need to enhance food safety, ensure consumer protection, and strengthen consumer confidence, to set requirements for food safety schemes and to improve cost efficiency throughout the food supply chain. Following their lead, the Global Food Safety Initiative (GFSI) was launched in May 2000.

value of this brand had been built over a century by the commitment and integrity of its employees (Refer to Exhibit VI for Coca-Cola's code of business conduct).

Coca-Cola also laid out extensive policies and procedures with respect to labor relations. The company's policy was to comply with all applicable labor and employment laws of the countries in which it operated. In its labor policies, the company said that it respected the workplace human rights of its employees in accordance with international labor standards. The company was also committed to its employees' right to form unions and their right to join the union or not. The company said that it ensured these rights were exercised without fear of retaliation, repression, or any other form of discrimination from the management.

Coca-Cola also believed that any disputes relating to labor relations were best solved in the place of origin. Through experience, it had learnt that labor relations were matters that were best handled at the place of origin because the best capability and knowledge to manage such issues existed at that level. However, any local issues having broader implications (both nationally and internationally), would be reviewed at the higher management levels depending on the merit of the case.

However, while Coca-Cola held that it was completely committed to ethical practices, there were several moderate to severe allegations made against it regarding trade practices and labor relations over the years. The allegations about Coca-Cola's business practices ranged from monopolistic and anti-competitive trade practices, discriminatory employment practices, depletion of groundwater tables, and environmental pollution. In 2005, the campaign against Coca-Cola's business practices became intensified with more student activists, labor unions, and environmental organizations actively supporting a campaign to ban Coca-Cola's products at various colleges, schools, and organizations in Europe and North America.

LABOR PRACTICES IN COLOMBIA

Colombia is widely considered as one of the most dangerous countries in the world for trade union activists and union leaders. The country was in the midst of a four-decade-old civil war involving leftist guerrillas,[15] right-wing paramilitary groups,[16] and government forces. The civil war claimed approximately three thousand lives a year, including those of many trade union leaders and workers. It was reported that in 2000, three out of every five trade unionists killed in the world were from Colombia.

In 2001, SINALTRAINAL,[17] a Colombian labor union, charged that Coca-Cola and its bottlers Panamerican Beverages (Panamaco), Bebidas y Alimentos De Uraba, and Coca-Cola Femsa were linked to the violence against its union members in Colombia. Around eight union leaders of Coca-Cola's plants in Colombia had been murdered since 1989, and many others had been abducted and tortured. Coca-Cola was accused of hiring paramilitary death squads to kidnap, torture, or kill union leaders and intimidate worker union activists at its bottling plants.

Of the total of eight murders, four occurred at the bottling plant Bebidas y Alimentos De Uraba in Carepa City between 1995 and 1996. Of these four, the most widely publicized was the killing of Isidro Segundo Gil (Isidro), a member of the union executive board, on December 5, 1996, at the entrance of the plant. It was alleged that after killing Isidro, paramilitary squads kidnapped another union leader from his home and torched the union offices.

It was further alleged that the following day the paramilitary squads returned to the plant and made the workers sign a statement on Coca-Cola letterhead that they were resigning from their membership of the union. The workers were given a deadline and threatened with dire consequences if they refused to sign. The union members alleged that since they had no choice, most of them resigned on the spot. It was further said that some members quit their jobs and fled to other cities fearing for their lives. Another allegation was that the then president of the union had been summoned by the plant manager and, in the presence of paramilitary men, asked to leave the city along with other union leaders.

SINALTRAINAL charged that apart from these eight killings, 48 members had been forced into hiding and 65 members had received death threats. In 1995, five union members working in a Coca-Cola plant at the city of Bucaramanga were jailed for six months on charges of terrorism. They were accused of planting an explosive device in the factory. However, these charges could not be proved and were later dropped for lack of evidence. The trade union also alleged that the bottlers were systematically targeting permanent workers so that they could be replaced by contract workers, who would do more work for lower wages.

In January 2004, a New York City Fact-Finding Delegation[18] went to Colombia to verify these allegations. The delegation concluded that Coca-Cola's involvement in the violation of human rights and labor rights could not be excluded. The report estimated that there had been 179 major human rights violations of Coca-Cola's workers including the murders. Union members and their family members had been kidnapped and tortured; workers had been fired for attending union meetings; many had been asked to denounce their legal rights.

According to the report, the violence and intimidation had occurred with the knowledge or under the directions of the company's managers at the bottling plants. The paramilitary groups had had free access to the plants and had cordial relations with the plant managers. The report said that Coca-Cola's Colombian managers had admitted that they had never investigated the relationship between the plant managers of their local bottlers and paramilitary groups in spite of so many complaints and allegations. The report concluded that this lack of action on Coca-Cola's part clearly showed the company's utter disregard for human rights and the well-being of its labor personnel in Colombia.

TRADE PRACTICES IN MEXICO

Mexico was an important market for Coca-Cola as the country was second, after the United States, in terms of per capita consumption of soft drinks in the world. The Mexican market for soft drinks was estimated at US$6.6 billion for the year 2004. Over the years, some of the highest profit margins for Coca-Cola in its overseas operations came from Mexico. Coca-Cola was the number one seller of soft drinks in Mexico, with a 70 percent market share. Coca-Cola's largest bottler in Mexico was Coca-Cola Femsa (CCF), in which Coca-Cola had a 40 percent stake. Its stock was listed on the New York Stock Exchange.

The chief competitor for Coca-Cola in Mexico was Pepsi. However, Coca-Cola also faced stiff competition from Big Cola, a beverage manufactured by the Ajegroup.[19] Big Cola was priced very low when compared to the price of Coca-Cola. This low-pricing strategy made a big impact on the Mexican soft drink market because half the population was poor and had low purchasing power. By 2004, it was estimated that Big Cola had cornered around 5 percent of the market and was growing rapidly. To counter Big Cola's rising popularity,

---

[15]Leftist guerrillas were armed groups with socialistic ideologies waging a war against the Colombian government.

[16]Right-wing paramilitary groups were armed groups supporting capitalistic ideologies opposing leftist guerrillas.

[17]Sindicato Nacional de Trabajadores de Industrias Alimenticias (SINALTRAINAL) is the National Food Workers' Union, which represents Coca-Cola employees in Columbia.

[18]In January 2004, New York City Council Member Hiram Monserrate and a delegation of union workers as well as student and community activists traveled to Colombia to investigate allegations against Coca-Cola.

[19]Ajegroup, a privately held company based in Peru, is involved in the beverage business.

Coca-Cola resorted to lowering its prices, which led to a fall in its profit margins.

It was alleged that CCF resorted to monopolistic and anti-competitive trade practices to deal with the threat of Big Cola. Small retail operators were warned to stock and sell only Coca-Cola's products. Failure to do so would result in supplies being stopped. These retailers would also stand to lose freebies like refrigerators and other gifts that they otherwise received. Operators who did not heed these warnings were lured to exchange their Big Cola stock for Coca-Cola. CCF was accused of insulting Big Cola and its customers, most of whom belonged to the poorer sections, with advertisements like, "You are not ugly, you have personality, drink Coca-Cola."[20] CCF was also accused of bribing local government officials with gifts to get permissions for setting up bottling plants.

On July 4, 2005, the Federal Competition Commission (FCC)[21] in Mexico charged Coca-Cola and its bottlers for violation of anti-monopoly laws and indulging in anti-competitive business practices. Fines of US$15 million and US$53 million were imposed in two separate cases, which amounted to one of the largest fines ever imposed in Mexico. The US$15 million fine was imposed in response to a complaint by a small retail operator, Raquel Chavez (Raquel), when Coca-Cola refused to sell her its products because she was selling Big Cola's products. FCC investigated her complaint and found evidence in similar incidents, some of which were documented by Big Cola, which supported the lawsuit against Coca-Cola in the later stages. Raquel's victory was hailed as the victory of David over Goliath.

ENVIRONMENT & PRODUCT ISSUES IN INDIA

In India, Coca-Cola was accused of draining the underground water table, of releasing improperly treated industrial effluents, and of selling products containing pesticide residues above standard limits. The focal point of the environmental accusations in India was the Coca-Cola plant located in Kerala. Coca-Cola, through its subsidiary in India, The Hindustan Coca-Cola Beverages Pvt. Ltd., had established a bottling plant at the Plachimada locality in the Palakkad district in Kerala. The unit was established in 1998–1999 in a 40-acre plot that had previously been used for irrigation of rice paddy and other food crops.

The factory site was located in the proximity of a main irrigation canal that drew water from a nearby barrage and reservoir. It was alleged that Coca-Cola had dug more than 65 bore-wells in the plot to extract the groundwater for production and operations. The daily production was estimated at 85 truckloads of beverages wherein each load contained 550–600 cases and each case contained 24 bottles, each of 300 ml volume. It was estimated that every day, 15 million liters of ground water were extracted free of cost and used for production and bottle washing.[22]

Many local residents in the villages surrounding the factory site alleged that over the years they had been faced with depleted underground water levels, leading to water scarcity. In addition, the bottle-washing operation involved the use of chemicals and generation of effluents. These effluents were allegedly released without adequate treatment, leading to the contamination of groundwater. As a result, it was reported that the groundwater turned turbid or milky on boiling and was unfit for consumption. Another by-product of bottle washing was a foul-smelling dry sediment sludge waste. It was said that the waste was initially sold to unsuspecting farmers as a fertilizer. When there were no takers, Coca-Cola allegedly offered it free of charge.

In 2003, BBC Radio 4's Face the Facts program revealed that a separate study conducted by it has shown that the sludge contained high levels of carcinogenic heavy metals like cadmium and lead. It was alleged that when the farmers came to know that it was toxic and raised protests, the waste was dumped on the wayside and on the lands at night. In the same year, the Center for Science and Environment (CSE) published a report which revealed that 12 soft drink brands sold by Coca-Cola and Pepsi in India had pesticide levels far higher (almost 36 times more) than what was permitted by the European Economic Commission (EEC).[23]

Some of the main pesticides found were Lindane,[24] DDT,[25] Malathion,[26] and Chlorpyriphos.[27] It was believed that the use of groundwater which had high pesticide residues and which had not been properly treated by the companies was the main reason for such high pesticide levels. These residues could cause cancer, damage to the nervous and reproductive systems, birth defects, and severe disruption of the immune system in the long run. The same study concluded that no such residues were found in the

---

[20]"Coca-Cola in Chiapas labour rights," www.ciepac.org/bulletins, January 13, 2005.

[21]The Federal Competition Commission (FCC), created in 1993, is an agency in the Ministry of Economy with technical and operational autonomy that is responsible for the implementation of the Federal Economic Competition Law in Mexico.

[22]"Struggle against Coca-Cola in Kerala," www.zmag.org, September 10, 2002.

[23]The European Economic Commission is a branch of the governing body of the European Union (EU) possessing executive and some legislative powers. It is located in Brussels, Belgium.

[24]Lindane is an insecticide, which has been banned in 52 countries across the world as it is believed to cause cancer.

[25]DDT (Dichloro-Diphenyl-Trichloroethane) was the first modern pesticide and is the most well known. It is also believed to cause cancer.

[26]Malathion is an insecticide with relatively low human toxicity. However, malathion breaks down, especially in indoor environments, into malaoxon, which is 60 times more toxic than malathion.

[27]Chlorpyriphos is a toxic insecticide that is widely used in pest control.

EXHIBIT VII Other Allegations Against Coca-Cola

In 1998, Coca-Cola was accused of discriminating against its African-American employees in pay and promotions and a class action race discrimination lawsuit was filed against it by its African-American employees. In 2000, after an 18-month-long litigation, Coca-Cola was ordered by the court to settle the lawsuit for US$192.5 million. Of the total amount, US$36 million was allocated to monitoring the company's employment practices and stopping discrimination. Of the remaining amount, US$113 million would be paid as cash payment and US$43.5 million would be adjusted in salaries. Also, Coca-Cola had to agree to form an outside task force that would ensure that the company maintained fair practices in pay, promotions, and performance evaluation.

In 2002, there were fresh allegations that the company's African-American employees continued to remain underrepresented in top management of the company. They were also paid less and dismissed more often than white employees. In its operations in African countries, Coca-Cola was accused of having only white employees at the managerial levels while Africans were employed at lower levels as factory workers and in distribution operations. White employees were predominantly granted medical coverage for HIV/AIDS, while the local workers were ignored. Coca-Cola workers in the Cincinnati plant in the United States also accused the company of creating a hostile, intimidating, offensive, and abusive workplace environment, and they filed a lawsuit against the company.

In June 1999, Coca-Cola products were banned for a brief period in Belgium after about 100 students in Belgium fell ill after drinking its products. The illness was attributed to the use of "wrong" carbon dioxide gas in the products manufactured in a plant at Antwerp, Belgium. The ban was lifted after Coca-Cola withdrew all its products from Belgium, Luxembourg, The Netherlands, and other countries where the products manufactured in Belgium were being sold. During the same period, in France, the sale of canned Coca-Cola drinks was suspended briefly following fears that they had been contaminated with a fungicide used to treat a small number of transportation pallets.

In June 2005, an investigation authorized by the European Union found that Coca-Cola had entered into deals with shops and bars to exclusively stock Coca-Cola products, and it concluded that these agreements were anti-competitive in nature. Coca-Cola in Europe had to agree to end the deals. In 1998, Pepsi made a similar complaint in the United States that Coca-Cola was illegally entering into agreements under which only Coca-Cola brands would be sold at the fountain sales in restaurants and other businesses. However the complaint was dismissed.

Matthew Whitley (Whitley), a former employee of Coca-Cola, filed lawsuits against Coca-Cola for improper dismissal from the service. He claimed that he had been dismissed after he had brought to the notice of Coca-Cola's top management certain improper accounting practices. During the course of the lawsuit, it was revealed that Tom Moore (Moore), a former head of Coca-Cola's Burger King[31] account, had been aware of a fraudulent test used by one of his direct subordinates, John Fisher, to boost sales of Frozen Coke at Burger King's outlets. Coca-Cola later apologized to Burger King and Moore was forced to resign. Among the other allegations in the lawsuit was one which said that Coca-Cola had conspired with its suppliers and artificially boosted sales. Whitley demanded US$44 million to drop the lawsuits against the company. Finally, Coca-Cola settled these lawsuits by agreeing to pay US$540,000 to Whitley.

SOURCE: Compiled from various sources.

same brands that were sold in the United States. (Refer to Exhibit VII for other allegations against Coca-Cola.)

BOYCOTT OF COCA-COLA PRODUCTS

In July 2001, SINALTRAINAL, with the help of United Steelworkers of America (USWA)[28] and the International Labor Rights Fund (ILRF),[29] filed a lawsuit against Coca-Cola and its Colombian bottlers at a court in Miami, Florida, under the Alien Tort Claims Act (ATCA)[30] of the American Judicial System. It accused them of being responsible for a campaign of murder and intimidation against its unionized workers and charged that it was using right-wing paramilitary groups for the purpose. The U.S. judge dismissed these charges against Coca-Cola in Colombia but approved the charges against the local bottlers in Colombia.

This prompted SINALTRAINAL to issue an international appeal for the boycott of Coca-Cola's products until it got justice in Colombia. On July 22, 2003, a boycott campaign was started by major trade unions in Colombia and it was supported by the World Social Forum,[32] student activists, and other various social activist organizations around the world. The call for the boycott attracted instant attention from student groups, trade unions, and other organizations all over the world.

In October 2003, in response to the boycott, the student union of the University of Dublin, the largest university in Ireland, decided to ban Coca-Cola's products from outlets that were controlled by it. An attempt by Coca-Cola to reverse the ban failed and the boycott spread to other colleges like Trinity College and the National College of Art and Design. The Union of Students in Ireland, which represented 250,000 students,

---

[28]The United Steelworkers of America (USWA), established in May 22, 1942, has over 1.2 million active and retired workers as members. The union is headquartered at Pittsburgh, Pennsylvania.

[29]The International Labor Rights Fund (ILRF), established in 1986, is an advocacy organization dedicated to achieving just and humane treatment for workers worldwide.

[30]The Alien Tort Claims Act (ATCA) of 1789 grants jurisdiction to U.S. Federal Courts over "any civil action by an alien for a tort (breach of civil contract) only, committed in violation of the law of nations or a treaty of the United States."

[31]The Burger King Corporation, a large international chain of fast-food restaurants, predominantly sells hamburgers, French fries, and soft drinks.

[32]World Social Forum is an annual meeting against globalization. It is a platform for information exchange on anti-globalization movements and campaigns around the world.

passed a resolution to support the ban on Coca-Cola. After this, the Teachers' Union of Ireland, the Irish National Teachers Organization, and a number of other trade unions and political organizations supported the boycott of Coca-Cola.

The call for the boycott of Coca-Cola's products also had a significant impact in England. In 2004, UNISON,[33] the largest trade union in the United Kingdom, passed a resolution during its National Delegate Conference to support the boycott. In March 2005, ECOSY,[34] an organization for young European socialists and a member of the federation of youth wings of all mainstream socialist and social democratic parties in the European Union, voted to support the boycott following a motion tabled by the Irish Labor Youth delegation. In addition, a number of other trade unions and organizations joined the Coca-Cola boycott campaign. (Refer to Exhibit VIII for a list of organizations that boycotted Coca-Cola.)

England also witnessed an active student campaign to boycott Coca-Cola. The National Union of Students, which represented 750 unions, passed a resolution to verify the allegations against Coca-Cola in Colombia and India. The National Union of Students held a 25 percent stake in the procurement agency that had contracts with Coca-Cola; therefore the decision was significant in monetary terms for the company. If these allegations were proved to be true, then Coca-Cola

could be possibly banned from almost every college and university in England.

In May 2005, following agitations from student unions and other organizations, 12 universities in America, including large universities such as the University of Michigan, New York State University, Rutgers University, and Santa Carla University, formed a Commission and discussed the issue with Coca-Cola. The Commission offered to investigate the allegations against Coca-Cola in Colombia. However, Coca-Cola and the Commission failed to reach an agreement on whether the Commission's findings would be admissible in the earlier lawsuit against Coca-Cola in Florida. While Coca-Cola did not want the findings to be admissible, the plaintiffs of the lawsuit insisted that they should be admissible.

Coca-Cola spokeswoman Kari Bjorhus said, "Although we have reached an impasse on the Commission's assessment protocol, we are exploring other ways that we might be able to conduct an additional credible, objective, and impartial independent, third-party assessment in Colombia without incurring legal risks."[35] The negotiations between the universities' Commission and Coca-Cola reached a deadlock and hence Coca-Cola's products were banned from those universities in America.

The boycott of Coca-Cola also had an impact in Canada. In October 2005, the students union of McMaster University voted to reject a renewal of the US$6 million a year exclusive deal the university had with Coca-Cola. Coca-Cola sent senior executives for negotiations with the student union but they failed in the effort. Similarly, students at the University of British Colombia, University of Guelph, and Ryerson University started their campaign against Coca-Cola and were considering a boycott.

Coca-Cola tried to contain the campaign by saying that it could lead to a loss of local jobs due to lack of demand. Kerry Kerr, public relations coordinator for Coca-Cola, said, "We're always concerned that these allegations could continue to spread. One of the main concerns, especially for our bottlers in areas like Canada, is that these boycotts are actually affecting workers in the local area."[36]

The City Council of Turin, Italy, took a controversial decision when it approved a boycott of Coca-Cola products. The city of Turin hosted the February 2006 Winter Olympic games. The decision created a controversy because Coca-Cola had donated US$10 million to the Torino (Turin) Olympic Committee and was the sponsor of these Games. In another setback to Coca-Cola, the organizers of the Live

EXHIBIT VIII   List of Organizations that Boycotted Coca-Cola

Name of the Organization	Membership
UNISON (United Kingdom)	1.3 million
Service Employees International Union (SEIU)	1.7 million
Communications Workers of America (CWA)	0.7 million
American Postal Workers Union (APWU)	0.27 million
Labor Council for Latin American Advancement (LCLAA)	1.7 million
American Federation of Teachers (AFT)	1.3 million
International Longshore and Warehouse Union	0.06 million
Northern Ireland Public Services Association	Not Available

Note: The list is not exhaustive.
SOURCE: Adapted from www.educationnews.org/for-christmas.htm.

---

[33]UNISON is the largest trade union in the United Kingdom, with over 1.3 million members. It was formed in 1993 by the merger of three previous public sector trade unions—the National and Local Government Officers Association (NALGO), the National Union of Public Employees (NUPE), and the Confederation of Health Service Employees (COHSE).
[34]ECOSY or Young European Socialists is an association of socialist and social democratic youth organizations in the European Union. It is the youth arm of the Party of European Socialists (PES) and is a member of the International Union of Socialist Youth (IUSY) based in Brussels, Belgium.

---

[35]"University of Michigan gives Coca-Cola the boot," www.billingsgazette.com, December 31, 2005.
[36]Colin Perkel, "Coca Cola hits back as boycott over alleged human-rights abuses gathers steam," www.cbc.ca, December 27, 2005.

EXHIBIT IX Interbrand Top Ten Brand Rankings from 2001 to 2005

Brand Name	2005	2004	2003	2002	2001
Coca-Cola	1	1	1	1	1
Microsoft	2	2	2	2	2
IBM	3	3	3	3	3
GE	4	4	4	4	4
Intel	5	5	5	5	6
Nokia	6	8	6	6	5
Disney	7	6	7	7	7
McDonald's	8	7	8	8	9
Toyota	9	9	11	12	14
Marlboro	10	10	9	9	11

SOURCE: bwnt.businessweek.com/brand/2005

8 concerts[37] pulled out of negotiations with the company over sponsorship deals because of public opposition. Coca-Cola was also banned from the Make Poverty History March[38] held at Edinburgh, Scotland, on July 2, 2005, attended by approximately 300,000 people.

The impact of these bans and boycotts on Coca-Cola in terms of sales and profits was very little when compared to its overall business revenues and profits. However the impact was far greater in terms of the company's brand image and public relations. Coca-Cola was one of the most widely recognized brands in the world and had been consistently ranked by Interbrand[39] as the number one brand in the world from 2001 to 2005. (Refer to Exhibit IX for the Interbrand top ten brand rankings from 2001 to 2005.)

COCA-COLA'S RESPONSE

Coca-Cola opened an exclusive Web site, www.cokefacts. org, to address these allegations, especially those related to Colombia and India. In an official statement featured on the Web site, Coca-Cola claimed that the allegations against the business practices in Colombia were false. Two different judicial enquiries in Colombia, one by a

Colombian court and the other by the Colombia Attorney General, had found no evidence against Coca-Cola or its bottlers linking them to the murders of the union members. Coca-Cola also quoted a judgment in the lawsuit in Miami, Florida,[40] wherein the judge had dismissed the charges against Coca-Cola, Columbia. A workplace assessment conducted in Colombia by Cal Safety Compliance Corporation,[41] a respected, independent third-party assessor, too had found no instances of anti-union violence or intimidation at the bottling plants.

Coca-Cola and its bottlers conducted an internal investigation and said that they found no evidence regarding the allegations. The company claimed that on the contrary, the bottlers enjoyed normal relations with 12 separate unions in Colombia and had collective bargaining agreements in place with all the unions that covered wages, benefits, and working conditions. The local bottlers were working along with local unions and the Colombian government for the workers' safety and uplift. They provided transportation to and from work to any worker who felt unsafe. The bottlers were providing loans for secure housing of the workers and increasing the security of union offices. Employees were also given paid cellular phones for emergency use and were protected from shift and job changes with legal aid.

The Colombian Vice President, Francisco Santos, who was in charge of improving the government's human rights record, including investigating cases of violence against trade union activists, said, "This (SINALTRAINAL vs. Coca-Cola) is not a labor union fight, it's a political fight. You can't justify the death of a union leader. (But) they took a myth and built a campaign out of it. They found a model that works, and they've been very successful at (promoting) it. They've been able to build this (martyrdom) image."[42] He declared that the government was committed to investigating and stopping the killings of the labor union leaders. "We know there are problems, we're trying to solve them. It's not as easy to get away with killing a labor leader as it was five years ago. But we're (still) not satisfied at all with the results."[43]

Coca-Cola also rejected the allegations made against it of monopolistic business practices and anti-competitive trade practices in Mexico. The company said that it would appeal to a higher authority against the fines imposed by the FCC. Company spokesman Charlie Sutlive said, "As we stated before, we respect the decisions. However, we have used the appeal processes open to us to present arguments that our business practices

---

[37]Live 8 was a series of concerts that took place in July 2005 in the G8 nations and South Africa. They were timed to precede the G8 Conference and Summit that was held in Perthshire, Scotland, from July 6–8, 2005. The objective of these concerts was to pressure world leaders to write off the debt of the world's poorest nations, increase and improve aid, and negotiate for fairer trade rules in the interest of poorer countries.

[38]Make Poverty History March was a program organized by The Make Poverty History campaign. The campaign is a British and Irish coalition of charities, religious groups, trade unions, campaigning groups, and celebrities committed to increasing awareness and pressuring governments into taking action to alleviate poverty.

[39]Interbrand is a company dedicated to identifying, building, and expressing the right idea for a brand. The company was established in 1974 at London and is now headquartered in New York.

[40]Florida is a state in the Southeastern region of the United States.

[41]Cal Safety Compliance Corporation (CSCC), based in Los Angeles, is a global provider of socially responsible supply chain consulting services, which include monitoring, training and education, program development and management, and research capabilities. The company has operations in 110 countries.

[42]Geri Smith, "Inside Coca-Cola's labor struggles," www.businessweek.com, January 23, 2006.

[43]Geri Smith, "Inside Coca-Cola's labor struggles," www.businessweek.com, January 23, 2006.

comply with Mexican competition laws, and to demonstrate that our commercial practices are fair."[44]

In another official statement, Coca-Cola rebutted the charges against its bottling plant at Plachimada, Kerala. The company said the plant was not responsible for the depletion of the underground water table. The company quoted a study conducted in October 2002 by Dr. R.N. Athvale, emeritus scientist at the National Geophysical Research Institute (NGRI),[45] which concluded that there was no field evidence of overexploitation of the groundwater reserves in the area surrounding the plant. The report added that any underground depletion could not be attributed to the water extraction in the plant area.

Coca-Cola also quoted another report prepared by the Palakkad District Environmental Protection Council and Guidance Society in June 2002. The report had concluded that the factory did not cause any environmental damage at any level. A report prepared by the Kerala State Groundwater Department too had rejected these allegations and attributed the depletion to a decrease in rainfall over the years. Coca-Cola claimed that the plant had established an advanced system for rain water harvesting to replenish the under groundwater table at the plant.

The company also rejected the allegation that its factory had released untreated industrial effluents. Coca-Cola stated that the technology used for wastewater treatment at the plant was among the most advanced in the world, equivalent to the technology used at its bottling plants in America and Europe. Moreover, the procedures for treatment and discharge of effluents complied with the standards and norms set by the Kerala State Pollution Control Board (KSPCB).

In response to the allegations that it supplied toxic sludge to farmers as fertilizer, Coca-Cola said that the dry sediment slurry waste or sludge, a by-product of its operations, was not harmful. The sludge was made up of organic and inorganic material that would not contaminate the land. The sludge was used around the world, including by Coca-Cola, as a soil enhancer. The generation of sludge in all the company's plants was monitored for composition and was disposed of properly. Further, the KSPCB had concluded in a detailed study that the concentration of cadmium and other heavy metals in the sludge were below prescribed limits and therefore could not be considered hazardous.

Coca-Cola also rejected the charge that its products in India contained high levels of pesticides and insecticides. The company said that testing for pesticides in finished soft drinks was a complex process and often produced unreliable and unrepeatable results. The accurate way of carrying out the test was to test each of the separate ingredients for its soft drinks before they were combined to make a finished soft drink. Coca-Cola routinely tested its ingredients in this way to ensure that the final soft drink product remained safe.

Furthermore, the company quoted a study conducted by the Department of Family and Child Welfare, Central Government of India, after the allegations were made in August 2003, which found that the products sold by the company were perfectly safe. Coca-Cola said that it was a responsible corporate citizen in India and mentioned that it had won many awards with regard to environment management and community development in India. (Refer to Exhibit X for awards won by Coca-Cola in India.)

EXHIBIT X   Awards Won by Coca-Cola in India

Category	Award
Community Development	Coca-Cola received the Bhagidari Award from Chief Minister of Delhi Sheila Dikshit for the company's efforts and contributions toward community development programs.
Environment	The World Environment Foundation (WEF) awarded the prestigious Golden Peacock Environment Management Award 2005 (GPEMA) to the bottling plant at Kaladera, near Jaipur, India, in recognition of its world-class environment practices.
	Coca-Cola's Dasna[46] plant in India received the Golden Peacock Environment Management Award 2004.
	Coca-Cola received a water conservation and pollution control award from the Andhra Pradesh Government on World Environment Day in June 2003.
	The Golden Peacock Award was given by the World Environment Foundation for effective environmental management at the plant at Ameenpur Village, near Hyderabad, India.
Health	Coca-Cola was recognized by the Rajiv Gandhi Foundation (RGF)[47] for participation in a motorized tri-wheeler scheme for the disabled.

Note: The list is not exhaustive.
SOURCE: Adapted from www.cokefacts.org.

[44]"Mexican woman battles Coke, wins," www.english.aljazeera.net, November 15, 2005.
[45]NGRI, based in Hyderabad, India, is an institute dedicated to basic and applied research in the field of geophysics, groundwater exploration, environmental information, etc.

[46]Dasna is a city in the state of Uttar Pradesh in North India.
[47]The Rajiv Gandhi Foundation (RGF), established in 1991, aims to work and act as a catalyst in promoting effective, practical, and sustainable programs in areas of national development in India.

Atul Singh, Coca-Cola India President and CEO, felt that the environmental and pesticide allegations against the company in India were still being debated because of Coca-Cola India's failure to communicate with its consumers, nongovernment organizations (NGOs), and even its own local employees. He said, "It's (communication failure) not just with consumers and NGOs on the pesticide controversy; even staffers were not getting the message."[48]

QUESTIONS FOR DISCUSSION

1. Discuss the nature of the allegations that led to the boycott of Coca-Cola's products by many U.S. universities.
2. Was the boycott by student activists and trade unions against Coca-Cola justified? Will it have a significant impact on the company in the long run? What should Coca-Cola do to protect its brand image in light of these allegations?
3. Discuss the company's stance towards CSR (corporate social responsibility) around the world. Who are Coca-Cola's many stakeholders, and what is the company's relative responsibility to each of them?
4. Discuss the company's reputation (justified or not) in light of the concept of "managing interdependence around the world." What does it take to be a "good citizen" in host countries? How well has Coca-Cola fared in this regard? What does the company need to do now?

ADDITIONAL READINGS AND REFERENCES

"World: Europe Belgium considers lifting Coke ban," http://news.bbc.co.uk, January 16, 1999.

"Coca-Cola to pay out $192.5 million to employees," www.wndu.com, November 16, 2000.

"Struggle against Coca-Cola in Kerala," www.zmag.org, September 10, 2002.

"Toxic pesticides found in Indian soft drinks," www.ens-newswire.com, August 05, 2003.

"Pepsi, Coke contain pesticides: CSE," http://in.rediff. com, August 05, 2003.

"Coke, Pepsi India fight pesticide residue claims in court," www.ens-newswire.com, August 08, 2003.

John F. Borowski, "For Christmas, will Coca-Cola stop acting like Big Tobacco?" www.educationnews.org, December 22, 2004.

"Coca-Cola in Chiapas labour rights," www.ciepac.org, January 13, 2005.

"Students campaign to ban Coca-Cola products on campuses," www.indiaresource.org, April 19, 2005.

"US: Coke to examine overseas labor practices," www.corpwatch.org, June 20, 2005.

"Did Coca-Cola torture and kill workers in Latin America?" www.straightdope.com, November 04, 2005.

"Mexican woman battles Coke, wins," english.aljazeera. net, November 15, 2005.

Chad Terhune, "Isdell could lose Coke's cola crown," www.laborrights.org/, December 7, 2005.

Thomas Gary, "Coke ban heats up across country," www.nyunews.com, December 08, 2005.

Colin Perkel, "Coca Cola hits back as boycott over alleged human-rights abuses gathers steam," www.cbc.ca, December 27, 2005.

Marla Dickerson, "Upstart firm in Peru taking fizz out of cola giants Coke, Pepsi face unlikely challenger," www.sfgate.com, December 30, 2005.

"University of Michigan gives Coca-Cola the boot," www. billingsgazette.com, December 31, 2005.

"School bans Coca-Cola," www.chicagotribune.com, December 31, 2005.

Gaurav, "Coca-Cola banned from University of Michigan," http://gbytes.gsood.com, December 31, 2005.

"US varsity suspends Coke sale," http://inhome.rediff.com, December 31, 2005.

"Colleges boycott Coke over labor concerns," www.taipeitimes. com, January 01, 2006.

"Univ in US to toss Coca-Cola," www.financialexpress.com, January 02, 2006.

"Colombian workers support U.S. universities' ban on Coca-Cola," www.timesleader.com, January 02, 2006.

"Coke should make U-M pay for cola ban," www.detnews.com, January 11, 2006.

Geri Smith, "Inside Coca-Cola's labor struggles," www.businessweek.com, January 23, 2006.

Elizabeth Woyke, "How NYU chose Colombia over Coke," www.businessweek.com, January 23, 2006.

"'Killer Coke' or innocent abroad? Controversy over anti-union violence in Colombia has colleges banning Coca-Cola," www.businessweek.com, January 23, 2006.

"We just failed to communicate—Interview with Atul Singh," *Business Standard,* February 7, 2006.

"Questions and Answers re: Coca-Cola," www.umich.edu, April 11, 2006.

Benjamin L. Weintraub, "University of Michigan retracts Coke ban," www.thecrimson.com, April 12, 2006.

Parama Majumder, "Michigan University revokes ban on Coke," www.merinews.com, April 18, 2006.

---

[48]Interview with Atul Singh, "We just failed to communicate," *Business Standard*, February 7, 2006.

"Another "Classic Coke" move to deny and delay account- ability for Human Rights violations in Colombia," www.laborrights.org, May 2006.

www.brandine.com/images/

http://bwnt.businessweek.com/brand/2005/

www2.coca-cola.com/heritage/chronicle_birth_refreshing_ idea.html

www2.coca-cola.com/ourcompany/pdf/business_conduct_ guidelines.pdf

www2.coca-cola.com/ourcompany/commitment_ quality.html

www2.coca-cola.com/presscenter/viewpointsmichigan_ bor.html

www.cokefacts.org/citizenship/cit_aw_recognition.shtml

www.cokefacts.org/index.shtml

www.educationnews.org/for-christmas.htm

http://en.wikipedia.org/wiki/Coca-Cola_slogans

http://finance.yahoo.com/q/bc?s=KO

http://finance.yahoo.com/q/is?s=KO&annual

www.killercoke.org/report.htm

Case 2   Google in China: The Big Disconnect

For many young people in China, Kai-Fu Lee is a celebrity. Not quite on the level of a movie star like Edison Chen or the singers in the boy band F4, but for a 44-year-old com- puter scientist who invariably appears in a somber dark suit, he can really draw a crowd. When Lee, the new head of operations for Google in China, gave a lecture at one Chinese university about how young Chinese should com- pete with the rest of the world, scalpers sold tickets for $60 apiece. At another, an audience of 8,000 showed up; students sprawled out on the ground, fixed on every word.

It is not hard to see why Lee has become a cult figure for China's high-tech youth. He grew up in Taiwan, went to Columbia and Carnegie-Mellon and is fluent in both English and Mandarin. Before joining Google last year, he worked for Apple in California and then for Microsoft in China; he set up Microsoft Research Asia, the company's research-and-development lab in Beijing. In person, Lee exudes the cheery optimism of a life coach; last year, he pub- lished "Be Your Personal Best," a fast-selling self-help book that urged Chinese students to adopt the risk-taking spirit of American capitalism. When he started the Microsoft lab seven years ago, he hired dozens of China's top graduates; he will now be doing the same thing for Google. "The stu- dents of China are remarkable," he told me when I met him in Beijing in February. "There is a huge desire to learn."

Lee can sound almost evangelical when he talks about the liberating power of technology. The Internet, he says, will level the playing field for China's enormous rural underclass; once the country's small villages are connected, he says, students thousands of miles from Shanghai or Beijing will be able to access online course materials from M.I.T. or Harvard and fully educate themselves. Lee has been with Google since only last summer, but he wears the company's earnest, utopian ethos on his sleeve: when he was hired away from Microsoft, he published a gushingly emotional open letter on his personal Web site, praising

Google's mission to bring information to the masses. He concluded with an exuberant equation that translates as "youth + freedom + equality + bottom-up innovation + user focus + don't be evil = The Miracle of Google."

When I visited with Lee, that miracle was being con- ducted out of a collection of bland offices in downtown Beijing that looked as if they had been hastily rented and occupied. The small rooms were full of eager young Chinese men in hip sweatshirts clustered around enor- mous flat-panel monitors, debugging code for new Google projects. "The ideals that we uphold here are really just so important and noble," Lee told me. "How to build stuff that users like, and figure out how to make money later. And 'Don't Do Evil'"—he was referring to Google's bold motto, "Don't Be Evil"—"all of those things. I think I've always been an idealist in my heart."

Yet Google's conduct in China has in recent months seemed considerably less than idealistic. In January, a few months after Lee opened the Beijing office, the company announced it would be introducing a new version of its search engine for the Chinese market. To obey China's censorship laws, Google's representatives explained, the company had agreed to purge its search results of any Web sites disapproved of by the Chinese government, including Web sites promoting Falun Gong, a government-banned spiritual movement; sites promoting free speech in China; or any mention of the 1989 Tiananmen Square massacre. If you search for "Tibet" or "Falun Gong" most anywhere in the world on google.com, you'll find thousands of blog entries, news items and chat rooms on Chinese repression. Do the same search inside China on google.cn, and most, if not all, of these links will be gone. Google will have erased them completely.

Google's decision did not go over well in the United States. In February, company executives were called into Congressional hearings and compared to Nazi collabora- tors. The company's stock fell, and protesters waved plac- ards outside the company's headquarters in Mountain View, Calif. Google wasn't the only American high-tech company to run aground in China in recent months, nor

SOURCE: Clive Thompson, "Google in China: the Big Disconnect," www.nytimes.com, April 23, 2006. Copyright @ 2006 The New York Times Company, used with permission.

was it the worst offender. But Google's executives were supposed to be cut from a different cloth. When the company went public two years ago, its telegenic young founders, Sergey Brin and Larry Page, wrote in the company's official filing for the Securities and Exchange Commission that Google is "a company that is trustworthy and interested in the public good." How could Google square that with making nice with a repressive Chinese regime and the Communist Party behind it?

It was difficult for me to know exactly how Lee felt about the company's arrangement with China's authoritarian leadership. As a condition of our meeting, Google had demanded that I not raise the issue of government relations; only the executives in Google's California head office were allowed to discuss those matters. But as Lee and I talked about how the Internet was transforming China, he offered one opinion that seemed telling: the Chinese students he meets and employs, Lee said, do not hunger for democracy. "People are actually quite free to talk about the subject," he added, meaning democracy and human rights in China. "I don't think they care that much. I think people would say: 'Hey, U.S. democracy, that's a good form of government. Chinese government, good and stable, that's a good form of government. Whatever, as long as I get to go to my favorite Web site, see my friends, live happily.'" Certainly, he said, the idea of personal expression, of speaking out publicly, had become vastly more popular among young Chinese as the Internet had grown and as blogging and online chat had become widespread. "But I don't think of this as a political statement at all," Lee said. "I think it's more people finding that they can express themselves and be heard, and they love to keep doing that."

It sounded to me like company spin—a curiously deflated notion of free speech. But spend some time among China's nascent class of Internet users, as I have these past months, and you begin to hear such talk somewhat differently. Youth + freedom + equality + don't be evil is an equation with few constants and many possible solutions. What is freedom, just now, to the Chinese? Are there gradations of censorship, better and worse ways to limit information? In America, that seems like an intolerable question—the end of the conversation. But in China, as Google has discovered, it is just the beginning.

CULTURAL DIFFERENCES

Google was not, in fact, a pioneer in China. Yahoo was the first major American Internet company to enter the market, introducing a Chinese-language version of its site and opening up an office in Beijing in 1999. Yahoo executives quickly learned how difficult China was to penetrate—and how baffling the country's cultural barriers can be for Americans. Chinese businesspeople, for example, rarely rely on e-mail, because they find the idea of leaving messages to be socially awkward. They prefer live exchanges, which means they gravitate to mobile phones and short

text messages instead. (They avoid voicemail for the same reason; during the weeks I traveled in China, whenever I called a Chinese executive whose phone was turned off, I would get a recording saying that the person was simply "unavailable," and the phone would not accept messages.) The most popular feature of the Internet for Chinese users—much more so than in the United States—is the online discussion board, where long, rollicking arguments and flame wars spill on for thousands of comments. Baidu, a Chinese search engine that was introduced in 2001 as an early competitor to Yahoo, capitalized on the national fervor for chat and invented a tool that allows people to create instant discussion groups based on popular search queries. When users now search on baidu.com for the name of the Chinese N.B.A. star Yao Ming, for example, they are shown not only links to news reports on his games; they are also able to join a chat room with thousands of others and argue about him. Baidu's chat rooms receive as many as five million posts a day.

As Yahoo found, these cultural nuances made the sites run by American companies feel simply foreign to Chinese users—and drove them instead to local portals designed by Chinese entrepreneurs. These sites, including Sina.com and Sohu.com, had less useful search engines, but they were full of links to chat rooms and government-approved Chinese-language news sites. Nationalist feelings might have played a role, too, in the success Chinese-run sites enjoyed at Yahoo's expense. "There's now a very strong sense of pride in supporting the local guy," I was told by Andrew Lih, a Chinese-American professor of media studies at the University of Hong Kong.

Yahoo also was slow to tap into another powerful force in Chinese life: rampant piracy. In most parts of the West, after the Napster wars, movie and music piracy is increasingly understood as an illicit activity; it thrives, certainly, but there is now a stigma against taking too much intellectual content without paying for it. (Hence the success of iTunes.) In China, downloading illegal copies of music, movies and software is as normal and accepted as checking the weather online. Baidu's executives discovered early on that many young users were using the Internet to hunt for pirated MP3's, so the company developed an easy-to-use interface specifically for this purpose. When I sat in an Internet cafe in Beijing one afternoon, a teenager with mutton-chop sideburns a few chairs over from me sipped a Coke and watched a samurai movie he'd downloaded free, while his friends used Baidu to find and pull down pirated tracks from the 50 Cent album "Get Rich or Die Tryin'." Almost one-fifth of Baidu's traffic comes from searching for unlicensed MP3's that would be illegal in the United States. Robin Li, Baidu's 37-year-old founder and C.E.O., is unrepentant. "Right now I think that the record companies may not be happy about the service we are offering," he told me recently, "but I think digital music as a trend is unstoppable."

At first, Google took a different approach to the Chinese market than Yahoo did. In early 2000, Google's engineers quietly set about creating a version of their search engine that could understand character-based Asian languages like Chinese, Japanese and Korean. By the end of the year, they had put up a clunky but service-able Chinese-language version of Google's home page. If you were in China and surfed over to google.com in 2001, Google's servers would automatically detect that you were inside the country and send you to the Chinese-language search interface, much in the same way google.com serves up a French-language interface to users in France.

While Baidu appealed to young MP3 hunters, Google became popular with a different set: white-collar urban professionals in the major Chinese cities, aspirational types who follow Western styles and sprinkle English words into conversation, a class that prides itself on being cosmopoli-tan rather than nationalistic. By pulling in that audience, Google by the end of 2002 achieved a level of success that had eluded Yahoo: it amassed an estimated 25 percent of all search traffic in China—and it did so working entirely from California, far outside the Chinese government's sphere of influence.

THE GREAT FIREWALL

Then on Sept. 3, 2002, Google vanished. Chinese work-ers arrived at their desks to find that Google's site was down, with just an error page in its place. The Chinese government had begun blocking it. China has two main methods for censoring the Web. For companies inside its borders, the government uses a broad array of penalties and threats to keep content clean. For Web sites that originate anywhere else in the world, the government has another impressively effective mechanism of con-trol: what techies call the Great Firewall of China.

When you use the Internet, it often feels placeless and virtual, but it's not. It runs on real wires that cut through real geographical boundaries. There are three main fiber-optic pipelines in China, giant underground cables that provide Internet access for the public and connect China to the rest of the Internet outside its borders. The Chinese government requires the private-sector companies that run these fiber-optic networks to specially configure "router" switches at the edge of the network, where sig-nals cross into foreign countries. These routers—some of which are made by Cisco Systems, an American firm—serve as China's new censors.

If you log onto a computer in downtown Beijing and try to access a Web site hosted on a server in Chicago, your Internet browser sends out a request for that specific Web page. The request travels over one of the Chinese pipelines until it hits the routers at the border, where it is then examined. If the request is for a site that is on the government's blacklist—and there are lots of them—it won't get through. If the site isn't blocked wholesale, the routers then examine the words in the requested page's Internet address for blacklisted terms. If the address con-tains a word like "falun" or even a coded term like

"198964" (which Chinese dissidents use to signify June 4, 1989, the date of the Tiananmen Square massacre), the router will block the signal. Back in the Internet cafe, your browser will display an error message. The filters can be surprisingly sophisticated, allowing certain pages from a site to slip through while blocking others. While I sat at one Internet cafe in Beijing, the government's filters allowed me to surf the entertainment and sports pages of the BBC but not its news section.

Google posed a unique problem for the censors: Because the company had no office at the time inside the country, the Chinese government had no legal authority over it—no ability to demand that Google voluntarily withhold its search results from Chinese users. And the firewall only half-worked in Google's case: it could block sites that Google pointed to, but in some cases it would let slip through a list of search results that included banned sites. So if you were in Shanghai and you searched for "human rights in China" on google.com, you would get a list of search results that included Human Rights in China (hrichina.org), a New York-based organization whose Web site is banned by the Chinese government. But if you tried to follow the link to hrichina.org, you would get nothing but an error message; the firewall would block the page. You could see that the banned sites existed, in other words, but you couldn't reach them. Government officials didn't like this situation—Chinese citizens were receiving constant reminders that their leaders felt threat-ened by certain subjects—but Google was popular enough that they were reluctant to block it entirely.

In 2002, though, something changed, and the Chinese government decided to shut down all access to Google. Why? Theories abound. Sergey Brin, the co-founder of Google, whose responsibilities include government relations, told me that he suspects the block might have been at the instigation of a competitor—one of its Chinese rivals. Brin is too diplomatic to accuse anyone by name, but various American Internet execu-tives told me they believe that Baidu has at times bene-fited from covert government intervention. A young Chinese-American entrepreneur in Beijing told me that she had heard that the instigator of the Google block-ade was Baidu, which in 2002 had less than 3 percent of the search market compared with Google's 24 percent. "Basically, some Baidu people sat down and did hundreds of searches for banned materials on Google," she said. (Like many Internet businesspeople I spoke with in China, she asked to remain anonymous, fearing retribution from the authorities.) "Then they took all the results, printed them up and went to the government and said, 'Look at all this bad stuff you can find on Google!' That's why the government took Google offline." Baidu strongly denies the charge, and when I spoke to Guo Liang, a professor at the Chinese Academy of Social Sciences in Beijing, he dismissed the idea and argued that Baidu is simply a stronger com-petitor than Google, with a better grasp of Chinese desires. Still, many Beijing high-tech insiders told me that it is common for domestic Internet firms to complain to the government about the illicit content of competitors, in the hope that their rivals will suffer the consequences. In China, the censorship regime is not only a political tool; it is also a competitive one—a cudgel that private firms use to beat one another with.

SELF-DISCIPLINE AWARDS

When I visited a dingy Internet cafe one November evening in Beijing, its 120 or so cubicles were crammed with teenagers. (Because computers and home Internet connections are so expensive, many of China's mostly young Internet users go online in these cafes, which charge mere pennies per hour and provide fast broadband—and cold soft drinks.) Everyone in the cafe looked to be settled in for a long evening of lightweight entertainment: young girls in pink and yellow Hello Kitty sweaters juggled multiple chat sessions, while upstairs a gang of young Chinese soldiers in olive-drab coats laughed as they crossed swords in the medieval fantasy game World of Warcraft. On one wall, next to a faded kung-fu movie poster, was a yellow sign that said, in Chinese characters, "Do not go to pornographic or illegal Web sites." The warning seemed almost beside the point; nobody here looked even remotely likely to be hunting for banned Tiananmen Square retrospectives. I asked the cafe manager, a man with huge aviator glasses and graying hair, how often his clients try to view illegal content. Not often, he said with a chuckle, and when they do, it's usually pornography. He said he figured it was the government's job to keep banned materials inaccessible. "If it's not supposed to be seen," he said, "it's not supposed to be seen."

One mistake Westerners frequently make about China is to assume that the government is furtive about its censorship. On the contrary, the party is quite matter of fact about it—proud, even. One American businessman who would speak only anonymously told me the story of attending an award ceremony last year held by the Internet Society of China for Internet firms, including the major Internet service providers. "I'm sitting there in the audience for this thing," he recounted, "and they say, 'And now it's time to award our annual Self-Discipline Awards!' And they gave 10 companies an award. They gave them a plaque. They shook hands. The minister was there; he took his picture with each guy. It was basically like Excellence in Self-Censorship—and everybody in the audience is, like, clapping." Internet censorship in China, this businessman explained, is presented as a benevolent police function. In January, the Shenzhen Public Security Bureau created two cuddly little anime-style cartoon "Internet Police" mascots named "Jingjing" and "Chacha"; each cybercop has a blog and a chat window where Chinese citizens can talk to them. As a Shenzhen official candidly told The Beijing Youth Daily, "The main function of Jingjing and Chacha is to intimidate." The article went on to explain that the characters are there "to publicly remind all Netizens to be conscious of safe and healthy use of the Internet, self-regulate their online behavior and maintain harmonious Internet order together."

Intimidation and "self-regulation" are, in fact, critical to how the party communicates its censorship rules to private-sector Internet companies. To be permitted to offer Internet services, a private company must sign a license agreeing not to circulate content on certain subjects, including material that "damages the honor or interests of the state" or "disturbs the public order or destroys public stability" or even "infringes upon national customs and habits." One prohibition specifically targets "evil cults or superstition," a clear reference to Falun Gong. But the language is, for the most part, intentionally vague. It leaves wide discretion for any minor official in China's dozens of regulatory agencies to demand that something he finds offensive be taken offline.

Government officials from the State Council Information Office convene weekly meetings with executives from the largest Internet service companies—particularly major portals that run news stories and host blogs and discussion boards—to discuss what new topics are likely to emerge that week that the party would prefer be censored. "It's known informally as the 'wind-blowing meeting'—in other words, which way is the wind blowing," the American businessman told me. The government officials provide warnings for the days ahead, he explained. "They say: 'There's this party conference going on this week. There are some foreign dignitaries here on this trip.'"

American Internet firms typically arrive in China expecting the government to hand them an official blacklist of sites and words they must censor. They quickly discover that no master list exists. Instead, the government simply insists the firms interpret the vague regulations themselves. The companies must do a sort of political mind reading and intuit in advance what the government won't like. Last year, a list circulated online purporting to be a blacklist of words the government gives to Chinese blogging firms, including "democracy" and "human rights." In reality, the list had been cobbled together by a young executive at a Chinese blog company. Every time he received a request to take down a posting, he noted which phrase the government had objected to, and after a while he developed his own list simply to help his company avoid future hassles.

The penalty for noncompliance with censorship regulations can be serious. An American public-relations consultant who recently worked for a major domestic Chinese portal recalled an afternoon when Chinese police officers burst into the company's offices, dragged the C.E.O. into a conference room and berated him for failing to block illicit content. "He was pale with fear afterward," she said. "You have to understand, these people are terrified, just terrified. They're seriously worried about slipping up and going to jail. They think about it every day they go into the office."

As a result, Internet executives in China most likely censor far more material than they need to. The Chinese system relies on a classic psychological truth: self-censorship is always far more comprehensive than formal censorship. By having each private company assume responsibility for its corner of the Internet, the government effectively outsources the otherwise unmanageable task of monitoring the billions of e-mail messages, news stories and chat postings that circulate every day in China. The government's preferred method seems to be to leave the companies guessing, then to call up occasionally with angry demands that a Web page be taken down in 24 hours. "It's the panopticon," says James Mulvenon, a China specialist who is the head of a Washington policy group called the Center for Intelligence Research and Analysis. "There's a randomness to their enforcement, and that creates a sense that they're looking at everything."

The government's filtering, while comprehensive, is not total. One day a banned site might temporarily be visible, if the routers are overloaded—or if the government suddenly decides to tolerate it. The next day the site might disappear again. Generally, everyday Internet users react with caution. They rarely push the government's limits. There are lines that cannot be crossed, and without actually talking about it much, everyone who lives and breathes Chinese culture understands more or less where those lines are. This is precisely what makes the environment so bewildering to American Internet companies. What's allowed? What's not allowed?

In contrast to the confusion most Americans experience, Chinese businessmen would often just laugh when I asked whether the government's censorship regime was hard to navigate. "I'll tell you this, it's not more hard than dealing with Sarbanes and Oxley," said Xin Ye, a founding executive of Sohu.com, one of China's biggest Yahoo-like portals. (He was referring to the American law that requires publicly held companies to report in depth on their finances.) Another evening I had drinks in a Shanghai jazz bar with Charles Chao, the president of Sina, the country's biggest news site. When I asked him how often he needs to remove postings from the discussion boards on Sina.com, he said, "It's not often." I asked if that meant once a week, once a month or less often; he demurred. "I don't think I can talk about it," he said. Yet he seemed less annoyed than amused by my line of questioning. "I don't want to call it censorship," he said. "It's like in every country: they have a bias. There are taboos you can't talk about in the U.S., and everyone knows it."

Jack Ma put it more bluntly: "We don't want to annoy the government." Ma is the hyperkinetic C.E.O. of Alibaba, a Chinese e-commerce firm. I met him in November in the lobby of the China World Hotel in Beijing, just after Ma's company had closed one of the biggest deals in Chinese Internet history. Yahoo, whose share of the Chinese search-engine market had fallen (according to one academic survey) to just 2.3 percent, had paid $1 billion to buy 40 percent of Alibaba and had given Ma complete control over all of Yahoo's services in China, hoping he could do a better job with it. From his seat on a plush sofa, Ma explained Alibaba's position on online speech. "Anything that is illegal in China—it's not going to be on our search engine. Something that is really no good, like Falun Gong?" He shook his head in disgust. "No! We are a business! Shareholders want to make money. Shareholders want us to make the customer happy. Meanwhile, we do not have any responsibilities saying we should do this or that political thing. Forget about it!"

A BIT OF A REVOLUTION

Last fall, at a Starbucks in Beijing, I met with China's most famous political blogger. Zhao Jing, a dapper, handsome 31-year-old in a gray sweater, seemed positively exuberant as he explained how radically China had changed since the Web arrived in the late 1990's. Before, he said, the party controlled every single piece of media, but then Chinese began logging onto discussion boards and setting up blogs, and it was as if a bell jar had lifted. Even if you were still too cautious to talk about politics, the mere idea that you could publicly state your opinion about anything—the weather, the local sports scene—felt like a bit of a revolution.

Zhao (who now works in the Beijing bureau of The New York Times) pushed the limits further than most. After college, he took a job as a hotel receptionist in a small city. He figured that if he was lucky, he might one day own his own business. When he went online in 1998, though, he realized that what he really wanted to do was to speak out on political questions. He began writing essays and posting them on discussion boards. Soon after he started his online writing, a newspaper editor offered him a job as a reporter.

"This is what the Internet does," Zhao said, flashing a smile. "One week after I went on the Internet, I had a reputation all over the province. I never thought I could be a writer. But I realized the problem wasn't me—it was my small town." Zhao lost his reporting job in March 2003 after his paper published an essay by a retired official advocating political reform; the government retaliated by shutting the paper down. Still eager to write, in December 2004 Zhao started his blog, hosted on a blogging service with servers in the U.K. His witty pro-free-speech essays, written under the name Michael Anti, were soon drawing thousands of readers a day. Last August, the government used the Great Firewall to block his site so that no one in China could read it; defiant, he switched over to Microsoft's blogging tool, called MSN Spaces. The government was almost certainly still monitoring his work, but remarkably, he continued writing. Zhao knew he was safe, he told me, because he knew where to draw the line.

"If you talk every day online and criticize the government, they don't care," he said. "Because it's just talk. But if you organize—even if it's just three or four people—that's what they crack down on. It's not speech; it's organizing. People say I'm brave, but I'm not." The Internet brought Zhao a certain amount of political influence, yet he seemed less excited about the way his blog might transform the government and more excited about the way it had transformed his sense of himself. Several young Chinese told me the same thing. If the Internet is bringing a revolution to China, it is experienced mostly as one of self-actualization: empowerment in a thousand tiny, everyday ways.

One afternoon I visited with Jiang Jingyi, a 29-year-old Chinese woman who makes her living selling clothes on eBay. When she opened the door to her apartment in a trendy area of Shanghai, I felt as if I'd accidentally stumbled into a chic SoHo boutique. Three long racks full of puffy winter jackets and sweaters dominated the center of the living room, and neat rows of designer running shoes and boots ringed the walls. As she served me tea in a bedroom with four computers stacked on a desk, Jiang told me, through an interpreter, that she used to work as a full-time graphic designer. But she was a shopaholic, she said, and one day decided to take some of the cheap clothes she'd found at a local factory and put them up for auction online. They sold quickly, and she made a 30 percent profit. Over the next three months, she sold more and more clothes, until one day she realized that her eBay profits were outstripping her weekly paycheck. She quit her job and began auctioning full time, and now her monthly sales are in excess of 100,000 yuan, or about $12,000.

"My parents can't understand it," she said with a giggle, as she clicked at the computer to show me one of her latest auctions, a winter jacket selling for 300 yuan. (Her description of the jacket translated as "Very trendy! You will look cool!") At the moment, Jiang sells mostly to Chinese in other major cities, since China's rudimentary banking system and the lack of a reliable credit-card network mean there is no easy way to receive payments from outside the country. But when Paypal—eBay's online payment system—finally links the global market with the Chinese market, she says she will become a small international business, marketing cut-rate clothes directly to hipsters in London or Los Angeles.

COMPROMISES AND DISCLAIMERS

Google never did figure out exactly why it was knocked offline in 2002 by the Chinese government. The blocking ended abruptly after two weeks, as mysteriously as it had begun. But even after being unblocked, Google still had troubles. The Great Firewall tends to slow down all traffic coming into the country from the world outside. About 15 percent of the time, Google was simply unavailable in China because of data jams. The firewall also began punishing curious minds: whenever someone inside China searched for a banned term, the firewall would often retaliate by sending back a command that tricked the user's computer into believing Google itself had gone dead. For several minutes, the user would be unable to load Google's search page—a digital slap on the wrist, as it were. For Google, these delays and shutdowns were a real problem, because search engines like to boast about delivering results in milliseconds. Baidu, Google's chief Chinese-language rival, had no such problem, because its servers were located on Chinese soil and thus inside the Great Firewall. Worse, Chinese universities had virtually no access to foreign Web sites, which meant that impressionable college students—in other countries, Google's most ardent fans—were flocking instead to Baidu.

Brin and other Google executives realized that the firewall allowed them only two choices, neither of which they relished. If Google remained aloof and continued to run its Chinese site from foreign soil, it would face slowdowns from the firewall and the threat of more arbitrary blockades—and eventually, the loss of market share to Baidu and other Chinese search engines. If it opened up a Chinese office and moved its servers onto Chinese territory, it would no longer have to fight to get past the firewall, and its service would speed up. But then Google would be subject to China's self-censorship laws.

What eventually drove Google into China was a carrot and a stick. Baidu was the stick: by 2005, it had thoroughly whomped its competition, amassing nearly half of the Chinese search market, while Google's market share remained stuck at 27 percent. The carrot was Google's halcyon concept of itself, the belief that merely by improving access to information in an authoritarian country, it would be doing good. Certainly, the company's officials figured, it could do better than the local Chinese firms, which acquiesce to the censorship regime with a shrug. Sure, Google would have to censor the most politically sensitive Web sites—religious groups, democracy groups, memorials of the Tiananmen Square massacre—along with pornography. But that was only a tiny percentage of what Chinese users search for on Google. Google could still improve Chinese citizens' ability to learn about AIDS, environmental problems, avian flu, world markets. Revenue, Brin told me, wasn't a big part of the equation. He said he thought it would be years before Google would make much if any profit in China. In fact, he argued, going into China "wasn't as much a business decision as a decision about getting people information. And we decided in the end that we should make this compromise."

He and his executives began discussing exactly which compromises they could tolerate. They decided that—unlike Yahoo and Microsoft—they would not offer e-mail or blogging services inside China, since that could put them in a position of being forced to censor blog postings or hand over dissidents' personal information to the secret police. They also decided they would not take down the existing, unfiltered Chinese-language version of the google.com engine. In essence, they would offer two search engines in Chinese. Chinese surfers could still access the old google.com; it would produce uncensored search results, though controversial links would still lead to dead ends, and the site would be slowed down and occasionally blocked entirely by the firewall. The new option would be google.cn, where the results would be censored by Google—but would arrive quickly, reliably and unhindered by the firewall.

Brin and his team decided that if they were going to be forced to censor the results for a search for "Tiananmen Square," then they would put a disclaimer at the top of the search results on google.cn explaining that information had been removed in accordance with Chinese law. When Chinese users search for forbidden terms, Brin said, "they can notice what's missing, or at least notice the local control." It is precisely the solution you'd expect from a computer scientist: the absence of information is a type of information. (Google displays similar disclaimers in France and Germany, where they strip out links to pro-Nazi Web sites.)

Brin's team had one more challenge to confront: how to determine which sites to block? The Chinese government wouldn't give them a list. So Google's engineers hit on a high-tech solution. They set up a computer inside China and programmed it to try to access Web sites outside the country, one after another. If a site was blocked by the firewall, it meant the government regarded it as illicit—so it became part of Google's blacklist.

The Google executives signed their license to become a Chinese Internet service in December 2005. They never formally sat down with government officials and received permission to put the disclaimer on censored search results. They simply decided to do it—and waited to see how the government would react.

THE CHINA STORM

Google.cn formally opened on Jan. 27, 2006, and human-rights activists immediately logged onto the new engine to see how it worked. The censorship was indeed comprehensive: the first page of results for "Falun Gong," they discovered, consisted solely of anti-Falun Gong sites. Google's image-searching engine—which hunts for pictures—produced equally skewed results. A query for "Tiananmen Square" omitted many iconic photos of the protest and the crackdown. Instead, it produced tourism pictures of the square lighted up at night and happy Chinese couples posing before it.

Google's timing could not have been worse. Google.cn was introduced into a political environment that was rapidly souring for American high-tech firms in China. Last September, Reporters Without Borders revealed that in 2004, Yahoo handed over an e-mail user's personal information to the Chinese government. The user, a business journalist named Shi Tao, had used his Chinese Yahoo account to leak details of a government document on press restrictions to a pro-democracy Web site run by Chinese exiles in New York. The government sentenced him to 10 years in prison. Then in December, Microsoft obeyed a government request to delete the writings of Zhao Jing—the free-speech blogger I'd met with in the fall. What was most remarkable about this was that Microsoft's blogging service has no servers located in China; the company effectively allowed China's censors to reach across the ocean and erase data stored on American territory.

Against this backdrop, the Google executives probably expected to appear comparatively responsible and ethical. But instead, as the China storm swirled around Silicon Valley in February, Google bore the brunt of it. At the Congressional hearings where the three companies testified—along with Cisco, makers of hardware used in the Great Firewall—legislators assailed all the firms, but ripped into Google with particular fire. They asked how a company with the slogan "Don't Be Evil" could conspire with China's censors. "That makes you a functionary of the Chinese government," said Jim Leach, an Iowa Republican. "So if this Congress wanted to learn how to censor, we'd go to you."

ZHAO JING'S RANKINGS

In February, I met with Zhao Jing again, two months after his pro-democracy blog was erased by Microsoft. We ordered drinks at a faux-Irish pub in downtown Beijing. Zhao was still as energetic as ever, though he also seemed a bit rueful over his exuberant comments in our last conversation. "I'm more cynical now," he said. His blog had been killed because of a single post. In December, a Chinese newspaper editor was fired, and Zhao called for a boycott of the paper. That apparently crossed the line. It was more than just talk; Zhao had now called for a political action. The government contacted Microsoft to demand the blog be shuttered, and the company complied—earning it a chorus of outrage from free-speech advocates in the United States, who accused Microsoft of having acted without even receiving a formal legal request from the Chinese government.

Microsoft seemed chastened by the public uproar; at the Congressional hearings, the company's director of government relations expressed regret. To try to save face, Microsoft executives pointed out that they had saved a copy of the deleted blog postings and sent them to Zhao. What they did not mention, Zhao told me, is that they refused to e-mail Zhao the postings; they offered merely to burn them onto a CD and mail them to any address in the United States Zhao requested. Microsoft appeared to be so afraid of the Chinese government, Zhao noted with a bitter laugh, that the company would not even send the banned material into China by mail. (Microsoft declined to comment for this article.)

I expected Zhao to be much angrier with the American Internet companies than he was. He was surprisingly philosophical. He ranked the companies in order of ethics, ticking them off with his fingers. Google, he said, was at the top of the pile. It was genuinely improving the quality of Chinese information and trying to do its best within a bad system. Microsoft came next; Zhao was obviously unhappy with its decision, but he said that it had produced such an easy-to-use blogging tool that, on balance, Microsoft was helping Chinese people to speak publicly. Yahoo came last, and Zhao had nothing but venom for the company.

"Google has struck a compromise," he said, and compromises are sometimes necessary. Yahoo's behavior, he added, put it in a different category: "Yahoo is a sellout. Chinese people hate Yahoo." The difference, Zhao said, was that Yahoo had put individual dissidents in serious danger and done so apparently without thinking much about the human damage. (Yahoo did not respond to requests for comment.) Google, by contrast, had avoided introducing any service that could get someone jailed. It was censoring information, but Zhao considered that a sin of omission, rather than of commission.

THE DISTORTED UNIVERSE

Zhao's moral calculus was striking, not least because it is so foreign to American ways of thinking. For most Americans, or certainly for most of those who think and write about China, there are no half-measures in democracy or free speech. A country either fully embraces these principles, or it disappears down the slippery slope of totalitarianism. But China's bloggers and Internet users have already lived at the bottom of the slippery slope. From their perspective, the Internet—as filtered as it is—has already changed Chinese society profoundly. For the younger generation, especially, it has turned public speech into a daily act. This, ultimately, is the perspective that Google has adopted, too. And it raises an interesting question: Can an imperfect Internet help change a society for the better?

One Internet executive I spoke to summed up the conundrum of China's Internet as the "distorted universe" problem. What happens to people's worldviews when they do a Google search for Falun Gong and almost exclusively find sites opposed to it, as would happen today on google.cn? Perhaps they would trust Google's authority and assume there is nothing to be found. This is the fear of Christopher Smith, the Republican representative who convened the recent Congressional hearings. "When Google sends you to a

Chinese propaganda source on a sensitive subject, it's got the imprimatur of Google," he told me recently. "And that influences the next generation—they think, Maybe we can live with this dictatorship. Without your Lech Walesas, you never get democracy." For Smith, Google's logic is the logic of appeasement. Like the companies that sought to "engage" with apartheid South Africa, Google's executives are too dedicated to profits ever to push for serious political change. (Earlier this month, Google's C.E.O., Eric Schmidt, visited Kai-Fu Lee in Beijing and told journalists that it would be "arrogant" of Google to try to change China's censorship laws.)

But perhaps the distorted universe is less of a problem in China, because—as many Chinese citizens told me—the Chinese people long ago learned to read past the distortions of Communist propaganda and media control. Guo Liang, the professor at the Chinese social sciences academy, told me about one revealing encounter. "These guys at Harvard did a study of the Chinese Internet," Guo said. "I talked to them and asked, 'What were your results?' They said, 'We think the Chinese government tries to control the Internet.' I just laughed. I said, 'We know that!'" Google's filtering of its results was not controversial for Guo because it was nothing new.

Andrew Lih, the Chinese-American professor at the University of Hong Kong, said that many in China take a long-term perspective. "Chinese people have a 5,000-year view of history," he said. "You ban a Web site, and they're like: 'Oh, give it time. It'll come back.'" Or consider the position of a group of Chinese Internet geeks trying to get access to Wikipedia, the massive free online encyclopedia where anyone can write an entry. Currently, all of wikipedia.com is blocked; the group is trying to convince Wikipedia's overseers to agree to the creation of a sanitized Chinese version with the potentially illegal entries removed. They argue that this would leave 99.9 percent of Wikipedia intact, and if that material were freely available in China, they say, it would be a great boon for China, particularly for underfinanced and isolated schools. (So far, Wikipedia has said it will not allow the creation of a censored version of the encyclopedia.)

Given how flexible computer code is, there are plenty of ways to distort the universe—to make its omissions more or less visible. At one point while developing google.cn, Google considered blocking all sites that refer to controversial topics. A search for Falun Gong in China would produce no sites in favor of it, but no sites opposing it either. What sort of effect would that have had? Remember too that when Google introduced its censored google.cn engine, it also left its original google.com Chinese-language engine online. Which means that any Chinese citizen can sit in a Net cafe, plug "Tiananmen Square" into each version of the search engine and then compare the different results—a trick that makes the blacklist somewhat visible. Critics have suggested that Google should go even further and actually publish its blacklist online in the United States, making its act of censorship entirely transparent.

THE SUPER GIRL THEORY

When I spoke to Kai-Fu Lee in Google's Beijing offices, there were moments that to me felt jarring. One minute he sounded like a freedom-loving Googler, arguing that the Internet inherently empowers its users. But the next minute he sounded more like Jack Ma of Alibaba—insisting that the Chinese have no interest in rocking the boat. It is a circular logic I encountered again and again while talking to China's Internet executives: we don't feel bad about filtering political results because our users aren't looking for that stuff anyway.

They may be right about their users' behavior. But you could just as easily argue that their users are incurious because they're cowed. Who would openly search for illegal content in a public Internet cafe—or even at home, since the government requires that every person with personal Internet access register his name and phone number with the government for tracking purposes? It is also possible that the government's crackdown on the Internet could become more intense if the country's huge population of poor farmers begins agitating online. The government is reasonably tolerant of well-educated professionals online. But the farmers, upset about corrupt local officials, are serious activists, and they pose a real threat to Beijing; they staged 70,000 demonstrations in 2004, many of which the government violently suppressed.

In the eyes of critics, Google is lying to itself about the desires of Chinese Internet users and collaborating with the Communist Party merely to secure a profitable market. To take Lee at his word is to take a leap of faith: that the Internet, simply through its own inherent properties, will slowly chip away at the government's ability to control speech, seeding a cultural change that strongly favors democracy. In this view, there will be no "great man" revolution in China, no Lech Walesa rallying his oppressed countrymen. Instead, the freedom fighters will be a half-billion mostly apolitical young Chinese, blogging and chatting about their dates, their favorite bands, video games—an entire generation that is growing up with public speech as a regular habit.

At one point in our conversation, Lee talked about the "Super Girl" competition televised in China last year, the country's analogue to "American Idol." Much like the American version of the show, it featured young women belting out covers of mainstream Western pop songs amid a blizzard of corporate branding. (The full title of the show was "Mongolian Cow Sour Yogurt Super Girl Contest," in honor of its sponsor.) In each round, viewers could vote for their favorite competitor via text message from their mobile phones. As the season ran its course, it began to resemble a presidential election campaign, with delirious fans setting up Web sites urging voters to pick their favorite singer. In the final episode, eight million young Chinese used their mobile phones to vote; the winner was Li Yuchun, a 21-year-old who dressed like a schoolgirl and sang "Zombie," by the Irish band the Cranberries.

"If you think about a practice for democracy, this is it," Lee said. "People voted for Super Girls. They loved it—they went out and campaigned." It may not be a revolution, in other words, but it might be a start.

QUESTIONS FOR DISCUSSION

1. This interview illustrates the complex environment faced by companies who want to operate in other countries—political, technological, cultural, and ethical. Discuss in detail the specific environmental differences and difficulties that Google is facing in China.
2. What is the "Great Firewall" of China? Explain the role of the "firewall" in convincing Google to begin operating from within China instead of from foreign soil.
3. Discuss the different methods by which the Chinese government obtains censorship of Internet sites. What compromises did Google's executives make about how to operate in China? What services does the company offer and what have they decided not to offer in China? How did they decide which services to eliminate? What did Google learn from Yahoo's experience?
4. Who are the stakeholders in this case? Discuss the concerns and rights of each set of stakeholders.

   How should Google prioritize the relative obligation that the company has towards those stakeholders?
5. What role and responsibility does a technology company such as Google have towards society in general? Should the home company culture, ethics, and politics impact how the company operates in China? To what extent do you agree with those critics about how Google is going along with China's censorship of the company's sites?
6. To what extent does a company like Google promote cultural convergence around the world? Is this a good thing or not?
7. On balance, do you agree or disagree with Google's operating model in China? Can an imperfect Internet help change a society for the better? Whose role or responsibility is that? What, if anything, would you do differently?

Case 3 Allure Cruise Line*—Challenges of Strategic Growth and Organizational Effectiveness: Part 1

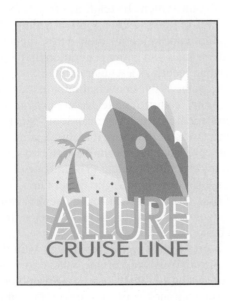

LEARNING OBJECTIVES AND OVERALL CASE STUDY GOAL

The Student's Role

You are the Organizational Development consulting team that has been hired by the senior leadership team of Allure Cruise Line to help them facilitate the expansion of their business and to address other issues the organization is currently facing.

Learning Objectives

Upon completion of this Case Study, you will be able to:

- Give examples of the variables organizations engaged internationally that have diverse workforces need to consider in order to ensure their success and effectiveness, within the context of three key strategies: *Business, Organizational,* and *People Strategies.*
- Explain and apply the international strategy development and implementation process and the factors that organizations must take into account and evaluate when

considering international expansion of their business and be able to apply these to a real life case study *(Business Strategy).*

- Describe how organizations need to consider their structure, organizational culture, and their processes to compete internationally *(Organizational Strategy).*
- Articulate how organizations can and need to set up and address their human resources management functions when working internationally and when sending employees abroad *(People Strategy).*
- Give examples of the current challenges with the people issues facing human resource managers and organizational leaders of Allure Cruise Line.
- Develop and present a plan to address the identified people challenges in a timely and business-focused manner.
- Articulate how the situation affecting Allure is similar to or different than other corporate environments.

THE BUSINESS—ALLURE CRUISE LINE

Overview

Allure Cruise Line is a small North American cruise line. It currently has three ships in its fleet and is in the process of planning to add new ships and itineraries in the upcoming several years. Allure Cruise Line has been in existence since 1993, and during this time, has grown to develop a reputation for providing one of the highest quality cruise experiences available. Figure 1 notes the overall Vision and Mission of Allure Cruise Line.

Allure Cruise Line's three ships have a passenger capacity of 2,500. Currently, the ships sail out of Fort

*Note: The data used to develop this case study was garnered through the managers of an existing cruise line. The name of the cruise line, as well as the individuals in the case study, and some data have been changed to protect the confidentiality of the cruise line; specific data changes can be found in Section 4 of this study.

SOURCE: Wanda V. Chaves, PhD., University of Tampa, and Steven R. Yacovelli, Ed.D., TopDog Learning Center.

FIGURE 1 Allure's Vision and Mission Statements

OUR VISION

Our vision is to continuously provide unforgettable experiences for our passengers and be the customer service leader in the cruise industry.

OUR MISSION

Our mission is to deliver unique vacation experiences characterized by exceptional guest service and a wide array of itineraries that cater to a variety of different lifestyles.

Lauderdale, Florida, and have several itineraries within the Caribbean from which passengers can choose, including destinations such as San Juan, Puerto Rico; St. Thomas, U.S.V.I.; Nassau, Bahamas; St. Croix, U.S.V.I.; and others. Their corporate offices are in Miami, Florida, and their operating offices are in Fort Lauderdale. The cruise line is flagged in Liberia.

Workforce

Each ship has a crew of 1,000 of which 190 are officers on board. The crew represents 40 different countries and nationalities. The captain and his executive leadership team are all from Greece. Typically, crew members sign contracts for six to ten months. Their contracts are renewed, after a four-week to two-month break, based on the company's wish to rehire them as well as the immigration and visa regulations of their country. Officers sign contracts for up to three to six months and typically renew their contracts after taking a two-month break. Due to the fact that the staffing on the ship is handled through short-term contracts, the makeup of the crew is in a state of constant change.

Ship's Organizational Structure

The organization within the ships is structured hierarchically. The captain is the senior ranking officer on board. His senior leadership team includes three executive officers: the staff captain, the hotel director, and the chief engineer.

The staff captain, who is second in command on board, is in charge of the bridge team, navigation team, deck department, safety, and sanitation. The staff captain also oversees the managing of the crew, including all of the morale and discipline issues with the crew.

The hotel director oversees all of the areas within the ship pertaining to the purser or guest services, including the rooms, restaurants, casinos, and entertainment onboard.

The chief engineer is in charge of all the operations pertaining to the ship's infrastructure, including the engine room, mechanical maintenance, shipboard computers, plumbing, and electrical.

Reporting to the executive officers on the ship are several other layers of officers (titled "officers" and "petty officers") who are directly in charge of the crew members. The organization is non-unionized. Figure 2 depicts this relationship and areas of responsibility.

Organizational Culture Onboard

As with other cruise lines, the culture on board the ships is very complex. It is characterized by three co-existing different cultures:

(1) *Safety and Readiness*
Influenced primarily by the cultures of the marine and military, the culture on the ships, as previously stated, is a hierarchical one in which crew members are expected

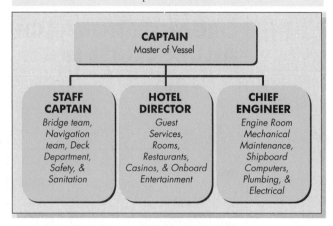

FIGURE 2   Allure's Shipboard Executive Committee

to follow orders, primarily to maintain the safety of the guests on the ships.

(2) *Service*
The primary focus on board is to provide the highest level of guest service available. The crew is trained and instructed on how to ensure that the guests' needs and expectations are exceeded during their trip.

(3) *Management*
The culture of the senior leadership team, and the country from which the team members originate, has a great influence on the way in which the ship and its crew are managed.

As on all cruise ships, in addition to the dynamics of the presence of these three coexisting organizational norms, the complexity of life onboard is magnified due to the close quarters within which the crew live and work. For example, a crew member who works in the dining room may share a cabin with three other dining room servers. If personal conflicts arise in the shared cabin, this can greatly impact the working relationship among the crew members.

These potential conflicts are not limited to roommate situations either. Crew members socialize and fraternize together, and they dine together regardless of their rank (either in an Officer's Mess or a Crew Member's Mess area). The space in which the crew can spend time during non-working hours is extremely limited. There are usually only one or two social areas for crew to enjoy onboard since the majority of the space onboard is typically reserved for the passenger entertainment and revenue-generating areas. At Allure, however, because the ships are slightly older, space is even more limited than on newer designed ships.

In addition, other factors influencing the culture on board, which cannot be underestimated, include the exceptional diversity of cultural backgrounds among the crew members as well as the constant rotations and changes in the makeup of the crew.

Allure Cruise Line's Company Structure

The Executive Leadership Team of the Allure Cruise Line company is comprised of seven senior executives

FIGURE 3 Allure's Organizational Structure

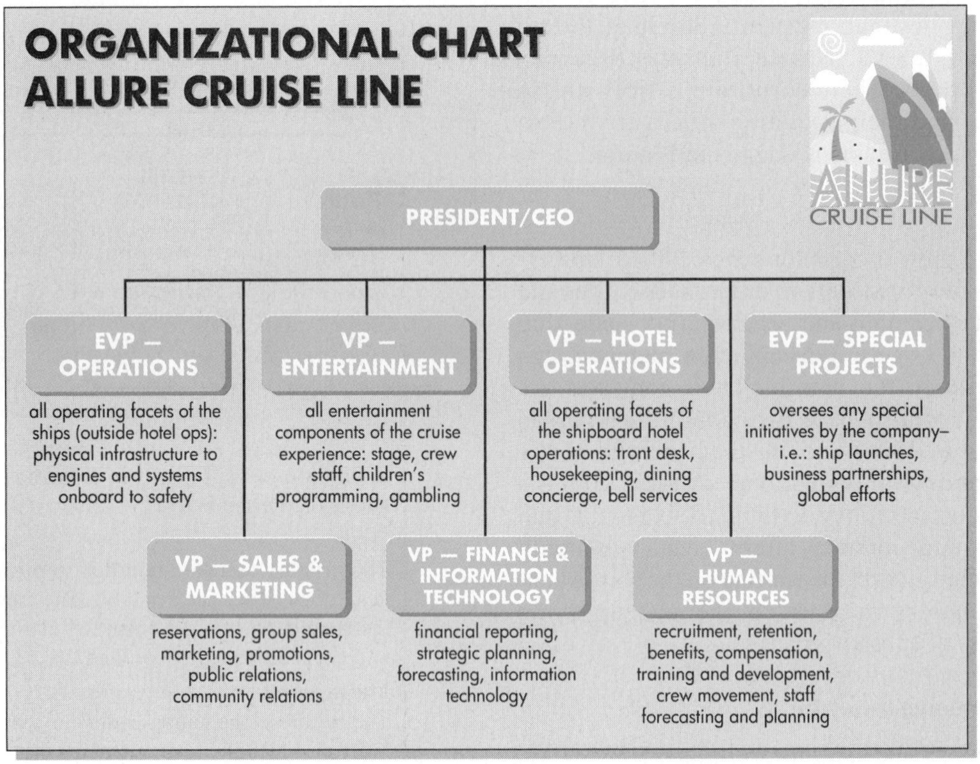

ORGANIZATIONAL CHART
ALLURE CRUISE LINE

who work at Allure's corporate offices in Miami and report to the president/CEO of the organization.

The executive vice president of operations is responsible for all of the operations on the ships with the exception of the hotel operations. He oversees the physical infrastructure, engines, operating systems, as well as the safety operations onboard.

The vice president of hotel operations is in charge of all of the hotel operations onboard including the front desk, housekeeping, dining, concierge, and bell services.

The vice president of entertainment manages all of the entertainment components of the cruise experience including the stage, crew staff, children's programming, and gambling in the casinos onboard.

The executive vice president of special projects oversees any special initiatives including new ship launches, business partnerships, and any global efforts that are pursued by the organization.

The vice president of sales and marketing is in charge of group sales, marketing, promotions, public relations, and community relations.

The vice president of finance and information technology is in charge of Allure's financial reporting, strategic planning, forecasting, and information technology.

The vice president of human resources oversees all of the HR functions for the ships, including recruitment and retention, compensation and benefits, training and development, career movement, and staff forecasting and planning.

Figure 3 depicts the reporting structure of the Allure Cruise Line organization.

Corporate Goals

The organization is planning the expansion of its business to the Mediterranean. It would like to add two new ships to its fleet within the next five years. Also, the organization is currently experiencing some morale issues among its crew and some cross-cultural challenges on board the three existing ships. These issues are beginning to have an impact on the service that is being provided to the passengers.

The leadership team is concerned and has hired your team to help them address these issues as well as to help them with the strategic planning and implementation process for their expansion.

INTERVIEW WITH ALLURE CRUISE LINE EXECUTIVE

Interviews were conducted with several members of Allure's senior leadership team to obtain more information regarding the cruise industry and Allure's current challenges.

Following you will find the dialogues from the interview with Rebecca Brandon, Vice President of Operations, who works as part of Allure's offshore team. She provided a historical perspective of the cruise industry and Allure Cruise Lines:

> *"At the start of the cruise industry, there was a divided market: for the rich and poor (if you've seen 'Titanic' you know about the term* steerage*). It was a very class-based means of travel and vacationing. Today, however, the distinctions are blurred, but they still exist based on the service and packages provided to customers.*

> *"Today everyone is a VIP, but distinctions come in the packages they receive. At the end of the 1980s and beginning of the 1990s, the cruise industry took off, and there were many different cruise lines available to passengers.*

> *"As for the history of Allure, we ordered its first ship in 1990, which took two and a half years to build. That ship, the 'Allure Regent,' set sail in 1993, and our fleet has expanded to three ships in operation today. Since the launching of the 'Regent,' Allure has really become quite a wealthy company, and we are privately funded (as opposed to being publicly traded).*

> *"Since the launching of the 'Regent,' our customer base has developed to about 60 percent repeat customers and 40 percent new customers. We have a very loyal, strong customer base with a higher level of disposable income (in the older cruiser market), and we want to continue to focus on them. About 60 percent of our customers are U.S. customers. Interestingly, 80 percent of the people in the U.S. have never been on a cruise. So there is a lot of opportunity to expand our reach and target these potential customers.*

> *"The main reason we retain this returning business is through our competitive advantage: We strive to provide the highest level of service provided to our passengers. Therefore, we really need to hire high-quality people who are very service oriented; it is Allure's service and name that distinguish it in the market. In addition, we try to change itineraries often—in summer and winter. Since our passengers are mostly returning folks, they tend to wait for a change to travel. We provide the service they expect with new and exciting itineraries, and they keep coming back to sail with us.*

> *"The support for sustaining this has many variables, one of which is around our technological infrastructure (our VP of HR can address the 'people' side of the operation better than I). In today's market, passengers want technology onboard (e.g., high-speed Internet in their cabins). Now since our ships are already over ten years old, we have had to retrofit the ships to increase the technology on board, but we are still not where we need to be. One of our challenges is we are losing in the market due to our being behind on technology. We need to find a way to keep up.*

> *"More technically speaking, the engines on cruise vessels today have different propulsion systems that are much more efficient and cost effective than when the 'Regent' was designed. Those ships, like ours, that still have fuel-burning systems are not set up to be the most competitive and run as cost-effectively as newer designs. New ships today also have high-end designs: large atriums, malls, large open spaces. Our ships are more comfortable, but maybe not as 'fancy.'*

> *"For the rest of the operation, we have some other logistical issues that may be preventing us from being the most efficient. For example, in our dining options for passengers: Many of the more modern ships have what is called 'freestyle dining' (e.g., have 11 restaurants onboard, and passengers can choose any of them in which to dine versus the more restrictive assignment to a specific dining time and restaurant each evening). Allure is not able to provide this option to our passengers because we simply do not have the space. In order to have freestyle dining onboard, we would need to increase the number of crew members working in the restaurants, and we do not have any extra living space to accommodate the necessary increase in crew. One of the challenges we need your help in addressing is how do we determine how we can improve our dining experience with our existing labor.*

> *"Another operational issue is the entertainment we provide passengers. Whereas in the past casinos were the main entertainment onboard, this is no longer the case. Passengers want fireworks, high-tech Broadway-style theatrical productions, etc. However, we are limited again in what we can provide in terms of these high-tech experiences. Our casinos still bring in the most revenue; therefore, we have no plans of taking them off our ships.*

> *"In conjunction with these operational issues are the world events and their impact on the travel industry overall. Due to recent events, such as the September 11th attacks in the United States and the crisis in the Middle East, more cruise lines are leaving from closer destinations because many passengers prefer to drive to reach the ports of departure. Also, security measures onboard have significantly increased (i.e., metal detectors, baggage screening, increased scrutiny of documentation—birthdays, Social Security Number, names, family groups, etc.). The crew has had to be trained on these new security measures that Allure is now taking. Allure is not the cheapest package on the market. Since people are finding themselves with less disposable income,*

our loyal customers are traveling less frequently. However, Allure is still doing well financially.

"But at Allure, we do not want to rest on our current good fortune. We want to continue to develop new itineraries and expand our business. We have surveyed our loyal customers, and there is a strong interest on their part to see us add some European itineraries. Therefore, we want to move to the Mediterranean. We are closely watching the financial markets. If we decide to build new ships, it will have a big impact on their price. Not only do price fluctuations affect the building of the ships, but they also impact anything else that will be onboard (e.g., carpeting, furniture, art). We would like to focus on our 60 percent repeat customers.

"With the new expansion of our company and when we add the two new ships, there may be increased challenges for the three current, older ships. First, we know that we could potentially cause the cannibalization of our own customer base with customers wanting to sail only on our new ships. In addition, our crew members will more than likely want to work on the new ships, which could impact our overall service and their morale.

"Several questions arise from this decision to expand our fleet. We need to determine where the new ships would sail. Would we send them to the Mediterranean or send the older ships there? How will we market these new ships and set ourselves up to compete in that market? We could potentially put the new ships on our current frequent routes and the older ships on the new itineraries (this would keep the mileage down on the new ships and help control depreciation of assets). Do we tailor different ships (the newer and the older) and cruise experiences to different customers? Will we establish a separate division, a new cruise line, or expand the current organization? We want to be careful not to dilute our product nor change what has worked in the past; we need to maintain our guest service standards high. We do not want to play with it at all.

"From you, our O.D. Consulting team, we could use your expertise to help develop this expansion strategy."

ASSIGNMENT

Dynamics of the Cruise Industry

The cruise industry is the epitome of an international operation and business: (1) Ships travel to and from ports of calls around the world, (2) the crew members working onboard come from a wide variety of countries, and (3) they serve customers from all over the globe. This presents many opportunities but also complex challenges for the cruise business.

Your assignment for this part of the case study is to spend some time studying the cruise industry. In order to effectively help Allure with its expansion and current challenges, you need to be knowledgeable about the history, dynamics, major players, and challenges of the cruise line industry.

As a team, you are to conduct research regarding the cruise industry and business. You are to educate yourself about the following questions/issues:

- ✓ Who are the "major players" in the North American cruise industry?
- ✓ What are the business statistics about these "players"? Asset size? Fleet size? Passenger volume? Crew to passenger ratios? Where are they located? Organizational structure?
- ✓ What are the route structures? Where do they sail to?
- ✓ Where are these major players flagged? Where are their corporate offices? Where are their operating offices?
- ✓ What are the plans for expansion for the major players?
- ✓ What factors distinguish the major players from one another?
- ✓ What is the shipboard organizational structure? What types of positions are on these cruise lines?
- ✓ What is the historical perspective of the cruise industry? Who were the first lines? What were they like? Is there any correlation with the cruise industry and other organizations?
- ✓ What are the major "laws" that the cruise industries need to abide by? Are there any laws specific to operating in North America/the United States?
- ✓ What is the state of the cruise industry? Is it growing or shrinking? How does the world economy and political climate affect the cruise industry? How does this affect fleet deployment and route selection/ports of call?

The following is a list of recommended websites and books, current as of this writing:

WEBSITES

www.imo.org/Conventions/contents.asp?doc_id=651&topic_id=257
www.cruising.org/
www.cruisejobline.com/
www.shipyards.com/

www.hal-pc.org/~nugent/company.html
www.cybercruises.com/orderbook.htm
www.shipsandcruises.com/
www.cruiseindustrynews.com/
www.courts.state.ny.us/tandv/cruiserights.html

BOOKS

Cartwright, R. & Baird, C. (1999). *Development and Growth of the Cruise Industry.* Butterworth-Heinemann.

Cudahy, B. (2001). *The Cruise Ship Phenomenon in North America.* Cornell Maritime Press.

Dickinson, B., & Vladimir, A. (1996). *Selling the Sea: An Inside Look at the Cruise Industry.* Wiley Publishers.

Israel, G. (1999). *Dictionary of the Cruise Industry: Terms Used in Cruise Industry Management, Operations,* *Law, Finance, Management, Ship Design & Construction.* Seatrade Cruise Academy.

Klein, R. (2002). *Cruise Ship Blues: A Guide to the Underside of the Cruise Ship Industry.* Consortium.

Mancini, M. (2003). *Cruising: A Guide to the Cruise Line Industry.* Delmar Publishers.

Ward, D. (2004). *Berlitz Ocean Cruising & Cruise Ships 2004 (Berlitz Complete Guide to Cruising and Cruise Ships).* Berlitz Guides.

CHAPTER

3

Understanding the Role of Culture

Outline

Opening Profile: Adjusting Business to Saudi Arabian Culture

For most outsiders, Saudi Arabia is a land of contrasts and paradoxes. (Map 3-1 shows its location.) It has supermodern cities, but its strict Islamic religious convictions and ancient social customs, on which its laws and customs depend, often clash with modern economic and technical realities. Saudi Arabians sometimes employ latitude in legal formation and enforcement to ease these clashes and sometimes accommodate different behaviors from foreigners. Nevertheless, many foreigners misunderstand Saudi laws and customs or find them contrary to their own value systems. Foreign companies have had mixed success in Saudi Arabia, due in large part to how well they understood and adapted imaginatively to Saudi customs.

Companies from countries with strict separation between state and religion or where few people actively engage in religion find Saudi Arabia's pervasiveness of religion daunting. Religious decrees have sometimes made companies rescind activities. For example, an importer halted sales of the children's game Pokémon because the game might encourage the un-Islamic practice of gambling, and a franchisor was forced to remove the face under the crown in Starbucks' logo because Saudi authorities felt the public display of a woman's face was religiously immoral. However, most companies know the requirements in advance. For instance, Coty Beauty omits models' faces on point-of-purchase displays that it depicts in other countries. Companies know that they must remove the heads and hands from mannequins and must not display them scantily clad. Companies, such as McDonald's, dim their lights, close their doors, and stop attending to customers

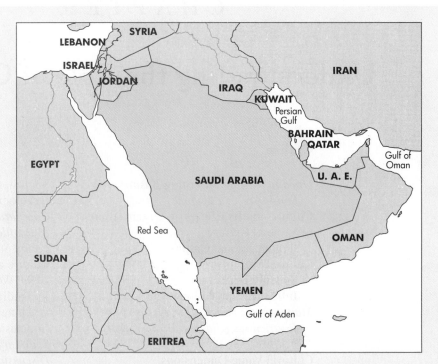

Map 3-1   Saudi Arabia comprises most of the Arabian peninsula. All of the countries bordering Saudi Arabia are Arab countries (meaning that the first language is Arabic), and all are predominately Islamic.

during the five times per day that men are called to pray. Companies also adjust voluntarily to gain the good will of customers—for example, by converting revenue-generating space to prayer areas. (Saudi Arabian Airlines does this in the rear of its planes, and the U.K.'s Harvey Nichols does this in its department store.) During the holy period of Ramadan, people are less active during the day because they fast, so many stores shift some operating hours to the evenings when people prefer to shop.

In 2000, Saudi Arabia ratified an international agreement designed to eliminate the discrimination of women; however, its prescribed behaviors for women appear paradoxical to outsiders. On the one hand, women now outnumber men in Saudi Arabian universities and own about 20 percent of all Saudi businesses. (There are separate male and female universities, and female-owned businesses can sell only to women.) Women also comprise a large portion of Saudi teachers and doctors. On the other hand, women account for only about 7 percent of the workforce. They cannot have private law or architectural firms, nor can they be engineers. They are not permitted to drive, because this may lead to evil behavior. They must wear abayas (robes) and cover their hair completely when in public. They cannot work alongside men except in the medical profession, and they cannot sell directly to male customers. If they are employed where men work, they must have separate work entrances and be separated from males by partitions. They must be accompanied by an adult male relative when dealing with male clerks.

The female prescriptions have implications for business operations. For example, the Saudi American Bank established branches for and staffed only by women. Pizza Hut installed two dining rooms—one for single men and one for families. (Women do not eat there without their families.) Both Harvey Nichols and Saks Fifth Avenue have created women-only floors in their department stores. On lower levels, there is mixed shopping, all male salespeople (even for products like cosmetics and bras), and no changing rooms or places to try cosmetics. On upper floors, women can check their *abayas* and shop in jeans, spandex, or whatever. The stores have also created drivers' lounges for their chauffeurs.

A downside is that male store managers can visit upper floors only when the stores are closed, which limits their observations of situations that might improve service and performance. Similarly, market research companies cannot rely on discussions with family-focused groups to determine marketing needs. Because men do much more of the household purchasing, companies target them more in their marketing than in other countries.

Why do high-end department stores and famous designers operate in Saudi Arabia where women cover themselves in *abayas* and men typically wear *thobes* (long robes)? Simply, the many very rich people in Saudi Arabia are said to keep Paris couture alive. Even though Saudi Arabia prohibits fashion magazines and movies, this clientele knows what is in fashion. (The government also prohibits satellite dishes, but some estimates say that two-thirds of Saudi homes have them.) Women buy items from designers' collections, which they wear abroad or in Saudi Arabia only in front of their husbands and other women. Underneath their *abayas*, they often wear very expensive jewelry, makeup, and clothing. Wealthy men also want the latest high-end fashions when traveling abroad.

Another paradox is that about 60 percent of the Saudi private workforce is foreign, even though the unemployment rate is about 30 percent. Changing economic conditions are at least partially responsible for this situation. In the early 1980s, Saudi oil revenues caused per capita income to jump to about $28,000, but this plummeted below $7,000 by the early 2000s. When incomes were high, Saudis brought in foreigners to do most of the work. At the same time, the government liberally supported university training, including study abroad. Saudis developed a mentality of expecting foreigners to do all the work, or at least some of the work, for them. The New Zealand head of National Biscuits & Confectionery said that Saudis now want only to be supervisors and complain if they have to work at the same level as people from Nepal, Bangladesh, and India. Although the government has taken steps to replace foreign workers with Saudis, prevailing work attitudes impede this transition. For example, the acceptance by a Saudi of a bellboy job at the Hyatt Regency hotel in Jidda was so unusual that Saudi newspapers put his picture on their front pages.

Saudi Arabian legal sanctions seem harsh to many outsiders. Religious patrols may hit women if they show any hair in public. The government carries out beheadings and hand-severances in public and expects passers-by to observe the punishments, some of which are for crimes that would not be offenses in other countries. For example, the government publicly beheaded three men in early 2002 for being homosexuals. However, there are inconsistencies. For example, religious patrols are more relaxed about women's dress codes in some Red Sea resorts, and they are more lenient toward the visiting female executives of MNEs than toward Saudi women. Whereas they don't allow Saudi women to be flight attendants on Saudi Arabian Airlines because they would have to work alongside men, they permit women from other Arab countries to do so. Further, in foreign investment compounds where almost everyone is a foreigner, these religious patrols make exceptions to most of the strict religious prescriptions.

Interesting situations concern the charging of interest and the purchase of accident insurance, both of which are disallowed under strict Islamic interpretations of the Koran. In the case of interest, the Saudi government gives interest-free loans for mortgages. This worked well when Saudi Arabia was awash with oil money, but borrowers must now wait about 10 years for a loan. In the case of accident insurance (by strict Islamic doctrine, there are no accidents, only preordained acts of God), the government eliminated prohibitions because businesses needed the insurance.

Personal interactions between cultures are tricky, and those between Saudis and non-Saudis are no exception. For example, Parris-Rogers International (PRI), a British publishing house, sent two salesmen to Saudi Arabia and paid them on a commission basis. They expected that by moving aggressively, the two men could make the same number of calls as they could in the United Kingdom. They were used to working eight-hour days, to having the undivided attention of potential clients, and to restricting conversation to the business transaction. To them, time was money. However, they found that appointments seldom began at the scheduled time and most often took place at cafés where the Saudis would engage in what the salesmen considered idle chitchat. Whether in a café or in the office, drinking coffee or tea and talking to acquaintances seemed to take precedence over business matters. The salesmen began showing so much irritation at "irrelevant" conversations, delays, and interruptions from friends that they caused irrevocable damage to the company's objectives. The Saudi counterparts considered them rude and impatient.

Whereas businesspersons from many countries invite counterparts to social gatherings at their homes to honor them and use personal relationships to cement business arrangements, Saudis view the home as private and even consider questions about their families as rude and an invasion of privacy. In contrast, Saudi businessmen seldom regard business discussions as private; they thus welcome friends to sit in. The opposite is true in many countries.

In spite of contrasts and paradoxes, foreign companies find ways to be highly successful in Saudi Arabia. In some cases, legal barriers to some products, such as to alcoholic beverages and pork products, have created boons for other products, such as soft drinks and turkey ham. In addition, some companies have developed specific practices in response to Saudi conditions and have later benefited from them in their home countries. For example, companies, such as Fuji and Kodak, created technology for while-you-wait photo development for Saudi Arabia because customers wanted to retrieve photos without anyone else seeing them. They transferred this technology to the United States several years later.

SOURCE: John D. Daniels, Lee H. Radebaugh, and Daniel P. Sullivan, *International Business: Environments and Operations*, 10th ed. © 2004. Reprinted by permission of Pearson Education, Inc., Upper Saddle River, NJ.

This chapter's opening profile describes how an understanding of the local culture and business environment can give managers an advantage in competitive industries. Foreign companies—no matter how big—can ignore those aspects to their peril. Such differences in culture and the way of life in other countries necessitate that managers develop international expertise to manage on a contingency basis according to the host-country environment. Powerful, interdependent factors in that environment—political, economic, legal, technological, and cultural—influence management strategy, functions, and processes.

A critical skill for managing people and processes in other countries is **cultural savvy**—that is, a working knowledge of the cultural variables affecting management decisions. Managers have often seriously underestimated the significance of cultural factors. According to numerous accounts, many blunders made in international operations can be attributed to a lack of cultural sensitivity.[1] Examples abound. Scott Russell, senior vice president for human resources at Cendant Mobility in Danbury, Connecticut, recounts the following:

> *An American company in Japan charged its Japanese HR manager with reducing the workforce. The Japanese manager studied the issue but couldn't find a solution within cultural Japanese parameters; so when he came back to the Americans, he reduced the workforce by resigning—which was not what they wanted.[2]*

Cultural sensitivity, or **cultural empathy**, is an awareness and an honest caring about another individual's culture. Such sensitivity requires the ability to understand the perspective of those living in other (and very different) societies and the willingness to put oneself in another's shoes.

International managers can benefit greatly from understanding the nature, dimensions, and variables of a specific culture and how these affect work and organizational processes. This cultural awareness enables them to develop appropriate policies and determine how to plan, organize, lead, and control in a specific international setting. Such a process of adaptation to the environment is necessary to successfully implement strategy. It also leads to effective interaction in a workforce of increasing cultural diversity, in both the United States and other countries.

Company reports and management studies make it clear that a lack of cultural sensitivity costs businesses money and opportunities. One study of U.S. multinational corporations found that poor intercultural communication skills still constitute a major management problem. Managers' knowledge of other cultures lags far behind their understanding of other organizational processes.[3] In a synthesis of the research on cross-cultural training, Black and Mendenhall found that up to 40 percent of expatriate managers leave their assignments early because of poor performance or poor adjustment to the local environment. About half of those who remain are considered only marginally effective. Furthermore, they found that cross-cultural differences are the cause of failed negotiations and interactions, resulting in losses to U.S. firms of over $2 billion a year for failed expatriate assignments alone.[4]

Other evidence indicates, however, that cross-cultural training is effective in developing skills and enhancing adjustment and performance. In spite of such evidence, U.S. firms do little to take advantage of such important research and to incorporate it into their ongoing training programs, whose purpose is ostensibly to prepare managers before sending them overseas. Too often, the importance of such training in developing cultural sensitivity is realized much too late, as seen in the following account of the unhappy marriage between America's AT&T and Italy's Olivetti, the office-equipment maker:

> One top AT&T executive believes that most of the problems in the venture stemmed from cultural differences. "I don't think we or Olivetti spent enough time understanding behavior patterns," says Robert Kayner, AT&T group executive. "We knew the culture was different, but we never really penetrated. We would get angry, and they would get upset." Mr. Kayner says AT&T's attempts to fix the problems, such as delays in deliveries, were transmitted in curt memos that offended Olivetti officials. "They would get an attitude, 'Who are you to tell us what to do,'" he says. Or, the Olivetti side would explain its own problems, and AT&T managers would simply respond, "Don't tell me about your problems. Solve them." AT&T executives are the first to admit, now, that one of the greatest challenges of putting a venture together is that partners frequently see the world in very different—and potentially divisive—ways.[5]

This chapter provides a conceptual framework with which companies and managers can assess relevant cultural variables and develop cultural profiles of various countries. This framework is then used to consider the probable effects of cultural differences on an organization and their implications for management. To do this, the powerful environmental factor of cultural context is examined. The nature of culture and its variables and dimensions are first explored, and then specific differences in cultural values and their implications for the on-the-job behavior of individuals and groups are considered. Cultural variables, in general, are discussed in this chapter. The impact of culture on specific management functions and processes is discussed in later chapters as appropriate.

CULTURE AND ITS EFFECTS ON ORGANIZATIONS

Societal Culture

As generally understood, the **culture** of a society comprises the shared values, understandings, assumptions, and goals that are learned from earlier generations, imposed by present members of a society, and passed on to succeeding generations. This shared outlook results, in large part, in common attitudes, codes of conduct, and expectations that subconsciously guide and control certain norms of behavior.[6] One is born into, not with, a given culture, and gradually internalizes its subtle effects through the socialization process. Culture results in a basis for living grounded in shared communication, standards, codes of conduct, and expectations.[7] Over time, cultures evolve as societies adapt to transitions in their external and internal environments and relationships. A manager assigned to a foreign subsidiary, for example, must expect to find large and small differences in the behavior of individuals and groups within that organization. As depicted in Exhibit 3-1, these differences result from the societal, or sociocultural, variables of the culture, such as religion and language, in addition to prevailing national variables, such as economic, legal, and political factors. National and sociocultural variables, thus, provide the context for the development and perpetuation of cultural variables. These cultural variables, in turn, determine basic attitudes toward work, time, materialism, individualism, and change. Such attitudes affect an individual's motivation and expectations regarding work and group relations, and they ultimately affect the outcomes that can be expected from that individual.

Organizational Culture

Compared to societal culture, which is often widely held within a region or nation, **organizational culture** varies a great deal from one organization, company, institution, or group to another. Organizational culture represents those expectations, norms, and goals held in common by members of that group. For a business example, consider the oft-quoted comparison between IBM—considered traditionally to be very formal, hierarchical, and rules-bound, and with its employees usually in suits—and Apple Computer, whose organizational culture is very organic, or "loose" and informal, with its employees typically wearing casual clothes and interacting informally.

A policy change made by KLM Royal Dutch Airlines, with which the organizational culture responded to national cultural values and accepted practices, illustrated the way these sets of variables can interact, and how societal culture can influence organizational culture. The culture of social responsiveness in the Netherlands was incorporated into business policy when the airline revised its travel-benefits policy for families of employees. For some time, many KLM stewards had protested the rule that

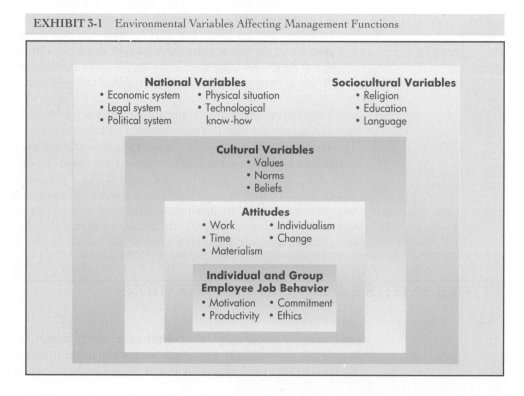

EXHIBIT 3-1 Environmental Variables Affecting Management Functions

National Variables
- Economic system
- Legal system
- Political system
- Physical situation
- Technological know-how

Sociocultural Variables
- Religion
- Education
- Language

Cultural Variables
- Values
- Norms
- Beliefs

Attitudes
- Work
- Time
- Materialism
- Individualism
- Change

Individual and Group Employee Job Behavior
- Motivation
- Productivity
- Commitment
- Ethics

only immediate family members were eligible for low fares on KLM flights. They found it discriminatory that even just-married heterosexual spouses received the benefit, whereas long-term homosexual partners were not eligible. Upon reconsideration, KLM responded that any couple who formally registered as living together, which is a normal legal practice in the Netherlands, would be eligible for the low fares. However, a year had to elapse between partners before a new partner could be registered. By changing its policy, KLM put the emphasis on committed relationships rather than on marital status or sexual preference.[8]

McDonald's provides another example, with its 58 restaurants in Russia. The company's experience with setting up businesses there since the first restaurant opened in Moscow demonstrates the combined effects of national and cultural variables on work. In Russia, local employees require lengthy training to serve up "Bolshoi Maks" in the "McDonald's way." Unfortunately, Russians are still, for the most part, not familiar with working under the capitalist system; they have been victims of the inertia brought about by the old system of central planning for so long that productivity remains low. As a result, most Russians have few goods to buy, and the new free-market prices are so high that there is little motivation for them to work for rubles that won't buy anything.[9]

Which organizational processes—technical and otherwise—are most affected by cultural differences, and how, is the subject of ongoing cross-cultural management research and debate.[10] Some argue that the effects of culture are more evident at the individual level of personal behavior than at the organizational level, as a result of convergence.[11] **Convergence** describes the phenomenon of the shifting of individual management styles to become more similar to one another. The convergence argument is based on the belief that the demands of industrialization, worldwide coordination, and competition tend to factor out differences in organizational-level processes, such as choice of technology and structure. In a 2000 study of Japanese and Korean firms, Lee, Roehl, and Choe found that globalization and firm size were sources of convergence of management styles.[12] These factors are discussed in more detail later in this chapter.

The effects of culture on specific management functions are particularly noticeable when we attempt to impose our own values and systems on another society. Exhibit 3-2 gives some examples of the values typical of U.S. culture, compares some common perspectives held by people in other countries, and shows which management functions might be affected, clearly implying the need for the differential management of organizational processes. For example, American managers plan activities, schedule them, and judge their timely completion based on the belief that people influence and control the future, rather than assuming that events will occur only at the will of Allah, as managers in an Islamic nation might believe.

Many people in the world understand and relate to others only in terms of their own culture. This unconscious reference point of one's own cultural values is called a **self-reference criterion**.[13] The result of such an attitude is illustrated in the following story:

> *Once upon a time there was a great flood, and involved in this flood were two creatures, a monkey and a fish. The monkey, being agile and experienced, was lucky enough to scramble up a tree and escape the raging waters. As he looked down from his safe perch, he saw the poor fish struggling against the swift current. With the very best of intentions, he reached down and lifted the fish from the water. The result was inevitable.*[14]

The monkey assumed that its frame of reference applied to the fish and acted accordingly. Thus, international managers from all countries must understand and adjust to unfamiliar social and commercial practices—especially the practices of that mysterious and unique nation, the United States. Japanese workers at a U.S. manufacturing plant learned to put courtesy aside and interrupt conversations with Americans when there were problems. Europeans, however, are often confused by Americans' apparent informality, which then backfires when the Europeans do not get work done as the Americans expect.[15]

EXHIBIT 3-2   U.S. Values and Possible Alternatives

Aspects of U.S. Culture*	Alternative Aspect	Examples of Management Function Affected
The individual can influence the future (where there is a will there is a way).	Life follows a preordained course, and human action is determined by the will of God.	Planning and scheduling
The individual can change and improve the environment.	People are intended to adjust to the physical environment rather than to alter it.	Organizational environment, morale, and productivity
An individual should be realistic in his or her aspirations.	Ideals are to be pursued regardless of what is "reasonable."	Goal setting and career development
We must work hard to accomplish our objectives (Puritan ethic).	Hard work is not the only prerequisite for success; wisdom, luck, and time are also required.	Motivation and reward system
Commitments should be honored (people will do what they say they will do).	A commitment may be superseded by a conflicting request, or an agreement may only signify intention and have little or no relationship to the capacity for performance.	Negotiating and bargaining
One should effectively use one's time (time is money that can be saved or wasted).	Schedules are important, but only in relation to other priorities.	Long- and short-range planning
A primary obligation of an employee is to the organization.	The individual employee has a primary obligation to his or her family and friends.	Loyalty, commitment, and motivation
The employer or employee can terminate the relationship.	Employment is for a lifetime.	Motivation and commitment to the company
The best-qualified people should be given the positions available.	Family, friendship, and other considerations should determine employment practices.	Employment, promotions, recruiting selection, and reward

*Aspect here refers to a belief, value, attitude, or assumption that is a part of a culture in that it is shared by a large number of people in that culture.
SOURCE: Excerpted from *Managing Cultural Differences* by Philip R. Harris and Robert T. Moran, 5th ed. Copyright © 2000 by Gulf Publishing Company, Houston, TX. Used with permission. All rights reserved.

As a first step toward cultural sensitivity, international managers should understand their own cultures. This awareness helps to guard against adopting either a parochial or an ethnocentric attitude. **Parochialism** occurs, for example, when a Frenchman expects those from or in another country to automatically fall into patterns of behavior common in France. **Ethnocentrism** describes the attitude of those who operate from the assumption that their ways of doing things are best—no matter where or under what conditions they are applied. Companies both large and small have demonstrated this lack of cultural sensitivity in countless subtle (and not so subtle) ways, with varying disastrous effects.

Procter & Gamble (P&G) was one such company. In an early Japanese television commercial for Camay soap, a Japanese woman is bathing when her husband walks into the bathroom. She starts telling him about her new beauty soap. Her husband, stroking her shoulder, hints that he has more on his mind than suds. The commercial, which had been popular in Europe, was a disaster in Japan. For the man to intrude on his wife "was considered bad manners," says Edwin L. Artzt, P&G's vice chairman and international chief. "And the Japanese didn't think it was very funny." P&G has learned from its mistakes and now generates about half of its revenue from foreign sales.[16]

After studying his or her own culture, the manager's next step toward establishing effective cross-cultural relations is to develop cultural sensitivity. Managers not only must be aware of cultural variables and their effects on behavior in the workplace, but also must appreciate cultural diversity and understand how to build constructive working relationships anywhere in the world. The following sections explore cultural variables and dimensions. Later chapters suggest specific ways in which managers can address these variables and dimensions to help build constructive relationships.

CULTURAL VARIABLES

Given the great variety of cultures and subcultures around the world, how can a student of cross-cultural management, or a manager wishing to be culturally savvy, develop an understanding of the specific nature of a certain people? With such an understanding, how can a manager anticipate the probable effects of an unfamiliar culture within an organizational setting and thereby manage human resources productively and control outcomes?

One approach is to develop a cultural profile for each country or region with which the company does or is considering doing business. Developing a cultural profile requires some familiarity with the cultural variables universal to most cultures. From these universal variables, managers can identify the specific differences found in each country or people—and hence anticipate their implications for the workplace.

Managers should never assume that they can successfully transplant American, or Japanese, or any other country's styles, practices, expectations, and processes. Instead, they should practice a basic tenet of good management—contingency management. Contingency management requires managers to adapt to the local environment and people and to manage accordingly. That adaptation can be complex because the manager may confront differences not only in culture, but also in business practices.

Subcultures

Managers should recognize, of course, that generalizations in cultural profiles will produce only an approximation, or stereotype, of national character. Many countries comprise diverse subcultures whose constituents conform only in varying degrees to the national character. In Canada, distinct subcultures include anglophones and francophones (English-speaking and French-speaking people) and indigenous Canadians. The United States, too, has varying subcultures. Americans abroad are almost always dealt with in the context of the stereotypical American, but at home Americans recognize differences among themselves due to ethnic, geographic, or other subcultural backgrounds. Americans should apply the same insight toward people in other countries and be extremely careful not to overgeneralize or oversimplify. For example, although Americans tend to think of Chinese as homogeneous in their culture, considerable differences among Chinese people occur owing to regional diversity—including distinct ethnic groups with their own local customs and a multitude of dialects. A study by Ralston, Yu Kai-Ceng, Xun Wang, Terpstra, and He Wei, concluded that, although adherence to traditional Confucian values was common to all regions, regions differed considerably on variables such as individualism and openness to change (with Guangzhou and Shanghai ranking the highest on those dimensions, followed by Beijing and Dalian and then Chengdu and Lanzhou).[17] This implies that Chinese in Guangzhou and Shanghai may be somewhat more "westernized" and more open to doing business with westerners.

Above all, good managers treat people as individuals, and they consciously avoid any form of **stereotyping**. However, a cultural profile is a good starting point to help managers develop some tentative expectations—some cultural context—as a backdrop to managing in a specific international setting. It is useful, then, to look at what cultural variables have been studied and what implications can be drawn from the results.

Influences on National Culture

Before we can understand the culture of a society, we need to recognize that there are subsystems in a society which are a function of where people live; these subsystems influence, and are influenced by, people's cultural values and dimensions and so affect their behaviors, both on and off the job. Harris and Moran identified eight categories that form the subsystems in any society.[18] This systems approach to understanding cultural and national variables—and their effects on work behavior—is consistent with the model shown in Exhibit 3-1 that shows those categories as a broad set of influences on societal culture. The following sections describe these eight categories and explain their implications for workplace behavior.

Kinship   A kinship system is the system adopted by a given society to guide family relationships. Whereas in the United States this system consists primarily of the nuclear family (which is increasingly represented by single-parent families), in many other parts of the world the kinship system consists of an extended family with many members, spanning several generations. This extended, closely knit family, typical in many Eastern nations, may influence corporate activities in cases where family loyalty is given primary consideration—such as when contracts are awarded or when employees are hired (and a family member is always selected over a more suitable candidate from outside the family). In these family-oriented societies, such practices are pervasive and are taken for granted. Foreign managers often find themselves locked out of important decisions when dealing with family businesses. If, however, they take the time to learn the local cultural expectations regarding families, they will notice predictable patterns of behavior and be better prepared to deal with them. Such traditional practices are exemplified in the experience of an Asian MBA, educated in the United States, when he presented a more up-to-date business plan to his uncle, the managing director of a medium-sized firm in India:

> *The family astrologer attended the meeting and vetoed the plan. Later, the nephew persisted and asked the astrologer to reconsider the plan. The astrologer recommended various ceremonies after which the astral signs would probably bend toward the plan.*[19]

Education   The formal or informal education of workers in a foreign firm, received from whatever source, greatly affects the expectations placed on those workers in the workplace. It also influences managers' choices about recruitment and staffing practices, training programs, and leadership styles. Training and development programs, for example, need to be consistent with the general level of educational preparation in that country.

Economy   Whatever the economic system, the means of production and distribution in a society (and the resulting effects on individuals and groups) has a powerful influence on such organizational processes as sourcing, distribution, incentives, and repatriation of capital. At this time of radically changing political systems, it appears that the drastic differences between capitalist and socialist systems will have less effect on multinational corporations (MNCs) than in the past.

Politics   The system of government in a society, whether democratic, communist, or dictatorial, imposes varying constraints on an organization and its freedom to do business. The influence of such political actions on culture is illustrated in the accompanying Management Focus: China Issues New Restrictions Aimed at Protecting Its Culture. It is the manager's job to understand the political system and how it affects organizational processes to negotiate positions within that system and to manage effectively the mutual concerns of the host country and guest company. This kind of compromise was made by Google and other companies in 2006 when they had to bow to China's state control of Web sites in order to do business there.

Religion   The spiritual beliefs of a society are often so powerful that they transcend other cultural aspects. Religion commonly underlies both moral and economic norms. In the United States, the effects of religion in the workplace are limited (other than a generalized belief in hard work, which stems from the Protestant work ethic), whereas in other countries religious beliefs and practices often influence everyday business transactions and on-the-job behaviors. For example, in India, McDonald's does not serve

---

Management Focus

China Issues New Restrictions Aimed at Protecting Its Culture

New regulations proposed by the Chinese government would keep additional foreign satellite broadcasters from entering the market and would strengthen restrictions on foreign television programs, books, newspapers and theater performances, all in an effort to tighten control over the country's culture.

The regulations were announced by China's Propaganda Department, the Ministry of Culture and four other regulators, and were published on Wednesday, August 4, 2005.

They spell out what parts of China's government are responsible for overseeing what parts of the media and entertainment industry, and they promise to make it more difficult for foreign companies to bring in books, the Internet and video games, and performing acts at a time when many multinationals are turning to China for growth.

"Import of cultural products contrary to regulations will be punished according to the circumstances, and in serious cases the import license will be revoked," the rules state. "In the near future there will be no more approvals for setting up cultural import agencies."

"We must strengthen censorship of and volume controls on imported television dramas, cartoons and television programs," the regulations say.

Co-productions between Chinese and foreign film and television makers will face stricter censorship, and foreign publications will be able to be sold only through government-controlled agencies, with strict punishment of unregulated sales. A preface says the rules are intended to help China's "opening up" to the outside world. But analysts and broadcasters said they were part of an effort to clamp down on foreign influence on culture.

David Wolf, a specialist in Beijing on China's media for Burson-Marsteller, the public relations company, said the rules "add greater clarity and specificity to rules we already know but weren't as clear."

In early July 2005, China issued a ban on Chinese broadcasters and foreign investors jointly operating television channels, and earlier that year the government froze Chinese-foreign co-production of TV programs.

SOURCE: C. Buckley, "China Issues New Restrictions Aimed at Protecting Its Culture," www.nytimes.com, August 3, 2005, p. C4. Copyright © The New York Times Co., reprinted with permission.

---

beef or pork out of respect for Hindu and Muslim customers. Also, in a long-standing tradition based on the Qur'an and the sayings of Muhammad, Arabs consult with senior members of the ruling families or the community regarding business decisions. Hindus, Buddhists, and some Muslims believe in the concept of destiny, or fate. In Islamic countries, the idea of *insha Allah,* that is, "God willing," prevails. In some Western countries, religious organizations, such as the Roman Catholic Church, play a major cultural role through moral and political influence.

One of the ways that the Islamic faith affects the operations of international firms involves the charging of interest:

> *The kingdom of Saudi Arabia observes Sharia, which is Islamic law based on both the Qur'an and the Hadith—the traditions of the Prophet Muhammad. Under these codes, interest is banned, and both the giver and the taker of interest are equally damned. This means that the modern Western banking system is technically illegal. A debate has begun on the interpretation of the concept of interest. The kingdom's religious scholars, the ulema, view all interest, or rib'a, as banned. Some have challenged that interpretation as too restrictive, however, and have called for a more liberal interpretation. Their view is that Muhammad referred only to excessive interest when he condemned usury. Should something come of this debate, it would help establish a legal framework for dealing with Saudi Arabia's banking problems, such as steep drops in profits, and end the legal limbo of Western-style banking in the kingdom.[20]*

Associations   Many and various types of associations arise out of the formal and informal groups that make up a society. Whether these associations are based on religious, social, professional, or trade affiliations, managers should be familiar with them and the role they may play in business interactions.

Health   The system of health care in a country affects employee productivity, expectations, and attitudes toward physical fitness and its role in the workplace. These expectations will influence managerial decisions regarding health care benefits, insurance, physical facilities, sick days, and so forth.

Recreation   Closely associated with other cultural factors, recreation includes the way in which people use their leisure time, as well as their attitudes toward leisure and their choice of with whom to socialize. Workers' attitudes toward recreation can affect their work behavior and their perception of the role of work in their lives.

CULTURAL VALUE DIMENSIONS

Cultural variables result from unique sets of shared values among different groups of people. Most of the variations between cultures stem from underlying value systems, which cause people to behave differently under similar circumstances. **Values** are a society's ideas about what is good or bad, right or wrong—such as the widespread belief that stealing is immoral and unfair. Values determine how individuals will probably respond in any given circumstance. As a powerful component of a society's culture, values are communicated through the eight subsystems just described and are passed from generation to generation. Interaction and pressure among these subsystems (or more recently from foreign cultures) may provide the impetus for slow change. The dissolution of the Soviet Union and the formation of the Commonwealth of Independent States is an example of extreme political change resulting from internal economic pressures and external encouragement to change.

Project GLOBE Cultural Dimensions

Recent research results on cultural dimensions have been made available by the GLOBE (Global Leadership and Organizational Behavior Effectiveness) Project team. The team comprises 170 researchers who have collected data over seven years on cultural values and practices and leadership attributes from 18,000 managers in 62 countries. Those managers were from a wide variety of industries and sizes of organizations from every corner of the globe. The team identified nine cultural dimensions that distinguish one society from another and have important managerial implications: assertiveness, future orientation, performance orientation, humane orientation, gender differentiation, uncertainty avoidance, power distance, institutional collectivism versus individualism, and in-group collectivism. Only the first four are discussed here; this avoids confusion for readers since the other five dimensions are similar to those researched by Hofstede, which are presented in the next section. (Other research results from the GLOBE Project are presented in subsequent chapters where applicable, such as in the Leadership section in Chapter 11.) The descriptions are as follows and selected results are shown in Exhibit 3-3.[21]

Assertiveness   This dimension refers to how much people in a society are expected to be tough, confrontational, and competitive versus modest and tender. Austria and Germany, for example, are highly assertive societies that value competition and have a "can-do" attitude. This compares with Sweden and Japan, less assertive societies, which tend to prefer warm and cooperative relations and harmony. The GLOBE team concluded that those countries have sympathy for the weak and emphasize loyalty and solidarity.

Future Orientation   This dimension refers to the level of importance a society attaches to future-oriented behaviors such as planning and investing in the future. Switzerland and Singapore, high on this dimension, are inclined to save for the future and have a longer time horizon for decisions. This perspective compares with societies such as Russia and Argentina, which tend to plan more in the shorter term and place more emphasis on instant gratification.

EXHIBIT 3-3   Selected Cultural Dimensions Rankings from the GLOBE Research Project

Country Rankings on Assertiveness

Least Assertive Countries in GLOBE		Medium Assertive Countries in GLOBE		Most Assertive Countries in GLOBE	
Sweden	3.38	Egypt	3.91	Spain	4.42
New Zealand	3.42	Ireland	3.92	United States	4.55
Switzerland	3.47	Philippines	4.01	Greece	4.58
Japan	3.59	Ecuador	4.09	Austria	4.62
Kuwait	3.63	France	4.13	Germany (Former East)	4.73

Country Rankings on Performance Orientation

Least Performance-Oriented Countries in GLOBE		Medium Performance-Oriented Countries in GLOBE		Most Performance-Oriented Countries in GLOBE	
Russia	2.88	Sweden	3.72	United States	4.49
Argentina	3.08	Israel	3.85	Taiwan	4.56
Greece	3.20	Spain	4.01	New Zealand	4.72
Venezuela	3.32	England	4.08	Hong Kong	4.80
Italy	3.58	Japan	4.22	Singapore	4.90

Country Rankings on Future Orientation

Least Future-Oriented Countries in GLOBE		Medium Future-Oriented Countries in GLOBE		Most Future-Oriented Countries in GLOBE	
Russia	2.88	Slovenia	3.59	Denmark	4.44
Argentina	3.08	Egypt	3.86	Canada (English-speaking)	4.44
Poland	3.11	Ireland	3.98	Netherlands	4.61
Italy	3.25	Australia	4.09	Switzerland	4.73
Kuwait	3.26	India	4.10	Singapore	5.07

Country Rankings on Humane Orientation

Least Humane-Oriented Countries in GLOBE		Medium Humane-Oriented Countries in GLOBE		Most Humane-Oriented Countries in GLOBE	
Germany (Former West)	3.18	Hong Kong	3.90	Indonesia	4.69
Spain	3.32	Sweden	4.10	Egypt	4.73
France	3.40	Taiwan	4.11	Malaysia	4.87
Singapore	3.49	United States	4.17	Ireland	4.96
Brazil	3.66	New Zealand	4.32	Philippines	5.12

SOURCE: Adapted from Mansour Javidan and Robert J. House, "Cultural Acumen for the Global Manager: Lessons from Project GLOBE," *Organizational Dynamics* (Spring 2001): 289–305, with permission from Elsevier.

Performance Orientation   This dimension measures the importance of performance improvement and excellence in society and refers to whether or not people are encouraged to strive for continued improvement. Singapore, Hong Kong, and the United States score high on this dimension; typically, this means that people tend to take initiative and have a sense of urgency and the confidence to get things done. Countries like Russia and Italy have low scores on this dimension; they hold other priorities ahead of performance, such as tradition, loyalty, family, and background, and they associate competition with defeat.

Humane Orientation   This dimension measures the extent to which a society encourages and rewards people for being fair, altruistic, generous, caring, and kind. Highest on this dimension are the Philippines, Ireland, Malaysia, and Egypt, indicating a focus on sympathy and support for the weak. In those societies paternalism and patronage are important, and people are usually friendly and tolerant and value harmony. This compares with Spain, France, and the former West Germany, which scored low on this dimension; people in these countries give more importance to power and material possessions, as well as self-enhancement.

Clearly, research results such as these are helpful to managers seeking to be successful in cross-cultural interactions. Anticipating cultural similarities and differences allows managers to develop the behaviors and skills necessary to act and decide in a manner appropriate to the local societal norms and expectations.

Cultural Clusters

Gupta et al (2002), from the GLOBE research team, also analyzed their data on the nine cultural dimensions to determine where similarities cluster geographically. Their results support the existence of ten cultural clusters: South Asia, Anglo, Arab, Germanic Europe, Latin Europe, Eastern Europe, Confucian Asia, Latin America, Sub-Sahara Africa, and Nordic Europe. They point out the usefulness to managers of these clusters:

> *Multinational corporations may find it less risky and more profitable to expand into more similar cultures rather than those which are drastically different.*[22]

These clusters are shown in Exhibit 3-4. To compare two of their cluster findings, for example, Gupta et al (2002) describe the Germanic cluster as masculine, assertive, individualistic, and result-oriented. This compares with the Latin American cluster, which they characterize as practicing high power distance, low performance orientation, uncertainty avoidance, and collective:

> *Latin American societies tend to enact life as it comes, taking its unpredictability as a fact of life, and not overly worrying about results.*[23]

Hofstede's Value Dimensions

Earlier research resulted in a pathbreaking framework for understanding how basic values underlie organizational behavior; this framework was developed by Hofstede, based on his research on over 116,000 people in 50 countries. He proposed four value dimensions: power distance, uncertainty avoidance, individualism, and masculinity.[24] We should be cautious when interpreting these results, however, because his research findings are based on a sample drawn from one multinational firm, IBM, and because he does not account for within-country differences in multicultural countries. Although we introduce these value dimensions here to aid in the understanding of different cultures, their relevance and application to management functions will be discussed in later chapters.

The first of these value dimensions, **power distance**, is the level of acceptance by a society of the unequal distribution of power in institutions. In the workplace, inequalities in power are normal, as evidenced in hierarchical boss–subordinate relationships. However, the extent to which subordinates accept unequal power is societally determined. In countries in which people display high power distance (such as Malaysia, the Philippines, and Mexico), employees acknowledge the boss's authority simply by respecting that individual's formal position in the hierarchy, and they seldom

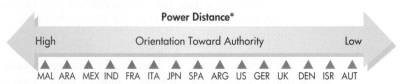

Power Distance*

High ← Orientation Toward Authority → Low

MAL ARA MEX IND FRA ITA JPN SPA ARG US GER UK DEN ISR AUT

*Not to scale—indicates relative magnitude.
Note: ARA = Arab Countries
      AUT = Austria

SOURCE: Based on G. Hofstede, "National Cultures in Four Dimensions,"
International Studies of Management and Organization, (Spring–Summer 1983).

EXHIBIT 3-4 Geographic Culture Clusters

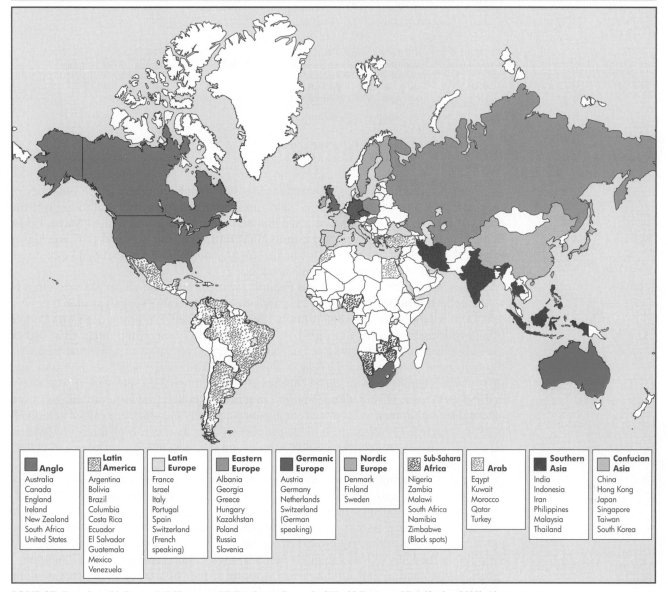

Anglo	**Latin America**	**Latin Europe**	**Eastern Europe**	**Germanic Europe**	**Nordic Europe**	**Sub-Sahara Africa**	**Arab**	**Southern Asia**	**Confucian Asia**
Australia	Argentina	France	Albania	Austria	Denmark	Nigeria	Eqypt	India	China
Canada	Bolivia	Israel	Georgia	Germany	Finland	Zambia	Kuwait	Indonesia	Hong Kong
England	Brazil	Italy	Greece	Netherlands	Sweden	Malawi	Morocco	Iran	Japan
Ireland	Columbia	Portugal	Hungary	Switzerland		South Africa	Qatar	Philippines	Singapore
New Zealand	Costa Rica	Spain	Kazakhstan	(German		Namibia	Turkey	Malaysia	Taiwan
South Africa	Ecuador	Switzerland	Poland	speaking)		Zimbabwe		Thailand	South Korea
United States	El Salvador	(French	Russia			(Black spots)			
	Guatemala	speaking)	Slovenia						
	Mexico								
	Venezuela								

SOURCE: Data from V. Gupta, P. J. Hanes, and P. Dorfman, *Journal of World Business,* 37, 1 (Spring 2002): 13.

bypass the chain of command. This respectful response results, predictably, in a centralized structure and autocratic leadership. In countries where people display low power distance (such as Austria, Denmark, and Israel), superiors and subordinates are apt to regard one another as equal in power, resulting in more harmony and cooperation. Clearly, an autocratic management style is not likely to be well received in low power distance countries.

The second value dimension, **uncertainty avoidance**, refers to the extent to which people in a society feel threatened by ambiguous situations. Countries with a high level of uncertainty avoidance (such as Japan, Portugal, and Greece) tend to have strict laws and procedures to which their people adhere closely, and a strong sense of nationalism prevails. In a business context, this value results in formal rules and procedures designed to provide more security and greater career stability. Managers have a propensity for low-risk decisions, employees exhibit little aggressiveness, and lifetime employment is common. In countries with lower levels of uncertainty avoidance (such as Denmark, Great Britain, and, to a lesser extent, the United States), nationalism is less pronounced, and protests and other such activities are tolerated. As a consequence, company activities are less structured and less formal, some managers take more risks, and high job mobility is common.

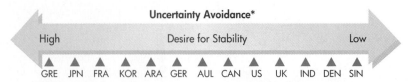

*Not to scale—indicates relative magnitude.
Note: AUL = Australia
SOURCE: Based on G. Hofstede, 1983.

The third of Hofstede's value dimensions, **individualism**, refers to the tendency of people to look after themselves and their immediate families only and to neglect the needs of society. In countries that prize individualism (such as the United States, Great Britain, and Australia) democracy, individual initiative, and achievement are highly valued; the relationship of the individual to organizations is one of independence on an emotional level, if not on an economic level.

In countries such as Pakistan and Panama, where low individualism prevails—that is, where **collectivism** predominates—one finds tight social frameworks, emotional dependence on belonging to "the organization," and a strong belief in group decisions. People from a collectivist country, like Japan, believe in the will of the group rather than that of the individual, and their pervasive collectivism exerts control over individual members through social pressure and the fear of humiliation. The society valorizes harmony and saving face, whereas individualistic cultures generally emphasize self-respect, autonomy, and independence. Hiring and promotion practices in collectivist societies are based on paternalism rather than achievement or personal capabilities, which are valued in individualistic societies. Other management practices (such as the use of quality circles in Japanese factories) reflect the emphasis on group decision-making processes in collectivist societies.

Hofstede's findings indicate that most countries scoring high on individualism have both a higher gross national product and a freer political system than those countries scoring low on individualism—that is, there is a strong relationship among individualism, wealth, and a political system with balanced power. Other studies have found that the output of individuals working in a group setting differs between individualistic and collectivist societies. In the United States, a highly individualistic culture, social loafing is common—that is, people tend to perform less when working as part of a group than when working alone.[25] In a comparative study of the United States and the People's Republic of China (a highly collectivist society), Earley found that the Chinese did not exhibit as much social loafing as the Americans.[26] This result can be attributed to Chinese cultural values, which subordinate personal interests to the greater goal of helping the group succeed.

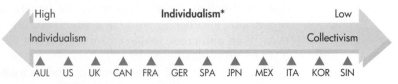

*Not to scale—indicates relative magnitude.
SOURCE: Based on G. Hofstede, 1983.

The fourth value dimension, **masculinity**, refers to the degree of traditionally "masculine" values—assertiveness, materialism, and a lack of concern for others—that prevail in a society. In comparison, femininity emphasizes "feminine" values—a concern for others, for relationships, and for the quality of life. In highly masculine societies (Japan and Austria, for example), women are generally expected to stay home and raise a family. In organizations, one finds considerable job stress, and organizational interests generally encroach on employees' private lives. In countries with low masculinity (such as Switzerland and New Zealand), one finds less conflict and job stress, more women in high-level jobs, and a reduced need for assertiveness. The United States lies somewhat in the middle, according to Hofstede's research. American women typically are encouraged to work, and families often are able to get some support for child care (through day-care centers and maternity leaves).

High					Masculinity*					Low
Assertive/Materialistic										Relational
JPN	MEX	GER	UK	US	ARA	FRA	KOR	POR	CHC	DEN	SWE

*Not to scale—indicates relative magnitude.

SOURCE: Based on G. Hofstede, 1983.

The four cultural value dimensions proposed by Hofstede do not operate in isolation; rather, they are interdependent and interactive—and thus complex—in their effects on work attitudes and behaviors. For example, in a 2000 study of small to medium-sized firms in Australia, Finland, Greece, Indonesia, Mexico, Norway, and Sweden, based on Hofstede's dimensions, Steensma, Marino, and Weaver found that "entrepreneurs from societies that are masculine and individualistic have a lower appreciation for cooperative strategies as compared to entrepreneurs from societies that are feminine and collectivist. Masculine cultures view cooperation in general as a sign of weakness and individualistic societies place a high value on independence and control."[27] In addition, they found that high levels of uncertainty avoidance prompted more cooperation, such as developing alliances to share risk.

Long-term/Short-term Orientation   Later research in 23 countries, using a survey developed by Bond and colleagues called the Chinese Value Survey, led Hofstede to develop a fifth dimension called the Confucian work dynamism, which he labeled a long-term/short-term dimension. He defined long-term orientation as "the extent to which a culture programs its members to accept delayed gratification of their material, social, and emotional needs."[28] In other words, managers in most Asian countries are more future-oriented and so stride towards long-term goals; they value investment in the future and are prepared to sacrifice short-term profits. Those countries such as Great Britain, Canada, and the United States place a higher value on short-term results and profitability, and evaluate their employees accordingly.

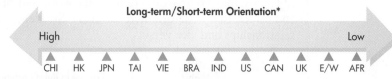

		Long-term/Short-term Orientation*								
High										Low
CHI	HK	JPN	TAI	VIE	BRA	IND	US	CAN	UK	E/W	AFR

*Not to scale—indicates relative magnitude.

SOURCE: Based on G. Hofstede, 2001.

Trompenaars's Value Dimensions

Fons Trompenaars also researched value dimensions; his work was spread over a ten-year period, with 15,000 managers from 28 countries representing 47 national cultures. Some of those dimensions, such as individualism, people's attitude towards time, and relative inner- versus outer-directedness, are similar to those discussed elsewhere in this chapter and others, and so are not presented here; other selected findings from Trompenaars's research that affect daily business activities are explained next, along with the placement of some of the countries along those dimensions, in approximate relative order.[29] If we view the placement of these countries along a range from personal to societal, based on each dimension, some interesting patterns emerge.[30] One can see that the same countries tend to be at similar positions on all dimensions, with the exception of the emotional orientation.

Looking at Trompenaars's dimension of **universalism versus particularism**, we find that the universalistic approach applies rules and systems objectively, without consideration for individual circumstances, whereas the particularistic approach—more common in Asia and in Spain, for example—puts the first obligation on relationships and is more subjective. Trompenaars found, for example, that people in particularistic societies are more likely to pass on insider information to a friend than those in universalistic societies.

High	Obligation*	Low
Universalistic		Particularistic

US   GER SWE UK ITA   FRA   JPN SPA CHI

*Not to scale—indicates relative magnitude.
SOURCE: Data based on F. Trompenaars, 1993.

In the **neutral versus affective** dimension, the focus is on the emotional orientation of relationships. The Italians, Mexicans, and Chinese, for example, would openly express emotions even in a business situation, whereas the British and Japanese would consider such displays unprofessional; they, in turn would be regarded as "hard to 'read'."

High	Emotional Orientation in Relationships*	Low
Neutral		Affective

JPN   UK GER SWE   UK   FRA SPA ITA   CHI

*Not to scale—indicates relative magnitude.
SOURCE: Data based on F. Trompenaars, 1993.

As far as involvement in relationships goes, people tend to be either **specific or diffuse** (or somewhere along that dimension). Managers in specific-oriented cultures—the United States, United Kingdom, France—separate work and personal issues and relationships; they compartmentalize their work and private lives, and they are more open and direct. In diffuse-oriented cultures—Sweden, China—work spills over into personal relationships and vice versa.

High	Privacy in Relationships*	Low
Specific		Diffuse

UK US FRA   GER   ITA JPN SWE   SPA CHI

*Not to scale—indicates relative magnitude.
SOURCE: Data based on F. Trompenaars, 1993.

In the **achievement versus ascription** dimension, the question that arises is "What is the source of power and status in society?" In an achievement society, the source of status and influence is based on individual achievement—how well one performs the job and what level of education and experience one has to offer. Therefore, women, minorities, and young people usually have equal opportunity to attain position based on their achievements. In an ascription-oriented society, people ascribe status on the basis of class, age, gender, and so on; one is more likely to be born into a position of influence. Hiring in Indonesia, for example, is more likely to be based on who you are than is the case in Germany or Australia.

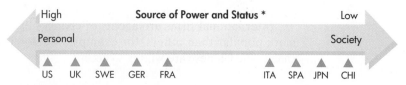

*Not to scale—indicates relative magnitude.
SOURCE: Data based on F. Trompenaars, 1993.

It is clear, then, that a lot of what goes on at work can be explained by differences in people's innate value systems, as described by Hofstede, Trompenaars, and the GLOBE researchers. Awareness of such differences and how they influence work behavior can be very useful to you as a future international manager.

Critical Operational Value Differences

After studying various research results about cultural variables, it helps to identify some specific culturally based variables that cause frequent problems for Americans in international management. Important variables are those involving conflicting orientations toward time, change, material factors, and individualism. We try to understand these operational value differences because they strongly influence a person's attitudes and probable response to work situations.

Time   Americans often experience much conflict and frustration because of differences in the concept of time around the world—that is, differences in temporal values. To Americans, time is a valuable and limited resource; it is to be saved, scheduled, and spent with precision, lest we waste it. The clock is always running—time is money. Therefore, deadlines and schedules have to be met. When others are not on time for meetings, Americans may feel insulted; when meetings digress from their purpose, Americans tend to become impatient. Similar attitudes toward time are found in Western Europe and elsewhere.

In many parts of the world, however, people view time from different and longer perspectives, often based on religious beliefs (such as reincarnation, in which time does not end at death), on a belief in destiny, or on pervasive social attitudes. In Latin America, for example, a common attitude toward time is *mañana,* a word that literally means "tomorrow." A Latin American person using this word, however, usually means an indefinite time in the near future. Similarly, the word *bukra* in Arabic can mean "tomorrow" or "some time in the future." While Americans usually regard a deadline as a firm commitment, Arabs often regard a deadline imposed on them as an insult. They feel that important things take a long time and therefore cannot be rushed. To ask an Arab to rush something, then, is to imply that you have not given him an important task or that he would not treat that task with respect. International managers have to be careful not to offend people—or lose contracts or employee cooperation—because they misunderstand the local language of time.

Change   Based largely on long-standing religious beliefs, values regarding the acceptance of change and the pace of change can vary immensely among cultures. Western people generally believe that an individual can exert some control over the future and can manipulate events, particularly in a business context—that is, individuals feel they have some internal control. In many non-Western societies, however, control is considered external; people generally believe in destiny, or the will of their God, and therefore adopt a passive attitude or even feel hostility toward those introducing the "evil" of change. In societies that place great importance on tradition (such as China), one small area of change may threaten an entire way of life. Webber describes just how difficult it is for an Asian male, concerned about tradition, to change his work habits:

> *To the Chinese, the introduction of power machinery meant that he had to throw over not only habits of work but a whole ideology; it implied dissatisfaction with the ways of his father's way of life in all its aspects. If the old loom must be discarded, then 100 other things must be discarded with it, for there are somehow no adequate substitutes.*[31]

International firms are agents of change throughout the world. Some changes are more popular than others; for example, McDonald's hamburgers are apparently one change the Chinese are willing to accept.

The New Idea
SOURCE: Courtesy McDonald's Corporation.

Material Factors   In large part, Americans consume resources at a far greater rate than most of the rest of the world. Their attitude toward nature—that it is there to be used for their benefit—differs from the attitudes of Indians and Koreans, for example, whose worship of nature is part of their religious beliefs. Whereas Americans often value physical goods and status symbols, many non-Westerners find these things unimportant; they value the aesthetic and the spiritual realm. Such differences in attitude have implications for management functions, such as motivation and reward systems, because the proverbial carrot must be appropriate to the employee's value system.

Individualism   In general, Americans tend to work and conduct their private lives independently, valuing individual achievement, accomplishments, promotions, and wealth above any group goals. In many other countries, individualism is not valued (as discussed previously in the context of Hofstede's work). In China, for example, much more of a "we" consciousness prevails, and the group is the basic building block of social life and

EXHIBIT 3-5   Fundamental Differences Between Japanese and Mexican Culture that Affect Business Organizations

Dimension	Japanese Culture	Mexican Culture
Hierarchical nature	Rigid in rank and most communication; blurred in authority and responsibility	Rigid in all aspects
Individualism vs. collectivism	Highly collective culture; loyalty to work group dominates; group harmony very important	Collective relative to family group; don't transfer loyalty to work group; individualistic outside family
Attitudes toward work	Work is sacred duty; acquiring skills, working hard, thriftiness, patience, and perseverance are virtues	Work is means to support self and family; leisure more important than work
Time orientation	Balanced perspective; future oriented; monochronic in dealings with outside world	Present oriented; time is imprecise; time commitments become desirable objectives
Approach to problem solving	Holistic, reliance on intuition, pragmatic, consensus important	Reliance on intuition and emotion, individual approach
Fatalism	Fatalism leads to preparation	Fatalism makes planning, disciplined routine unnatural
View of human nature	Intrinsically good	Mixture of good and evil

SOURCE: J. J. Lawrence and Ryh-song Yeh, "The Influence of Mexican Culture on the Use of Japanese Manufacturing Techniques in Mexico," *Management International Review* 34, no. 1 (1994): 49–66.

work. For the Chinese, conformity and cooperation take precedence over individual achievement, and the emphasis is on the strength of the family or community—the predominant attitude being, "We all rise or fall together."

International managers often face conflicts in the workplace as a result of differences in these four basic values of time, change, materialism, and individualism. If these operational value differences and their likely consequences are anticipated, managers can adjust expectations, communications, work organization, schedules, incentive systems, and so forth to provide for more constructive outcomes for the company and its employees. Some of these operational differences are shown in Exhibit 3-5, using Japan and Mexico as examples. Note in particular the factors of time, individualism change (fatalism), and materialism (attitudes toward work) expressed in the exhibit.

THE INTERNET AND CULTURE

Koreans are an impatient people, and we like technology. So everyone wants the fastest Internet connection.

HWANG KYU-JUNE[32]

We would be remiss if we did not acknowledge the contemporary phenomenon of the increasingly pervasive use of the Internet in society, for it seems to be encroaching on many of the social variables discussed earlier—in particular associations, education, and the economy. In South Korea, for example, where information technology makes up about 30 percent of the gross domestic product (GDP), there is an obsession for anything digital. Over 70 percent of homes are connected to a high-speed Internet service. That compares with 50 percent in Canada—the next highest user—and 23 percent in the United States.[33] This phenomenon seems to be changing the lives of many Koreans. Teenagers, used to hanging out at the mall, now do so at the country's 20,000 personal computer (PC) parlors to watch movies, check email, and surf the Net for as little as US$1. Korean housewives are on a waiting list for ADSL lines when the $35 billion high-speed government telecommunications project is completed. By then 95 percent of Korean households will have Internet access.[34]

At the same time that the Internet is affecting culture, culture is also affecting how the Internet is used. One of the pervasive ways that culture is determining how the Internet may be used in various countries is through the local attitude to **information privacy**—the right to control information about oneself—as observed in the following quote:

You Americans just don't seem to care about privacy, do you?

SWEDISH EXECUTIVE[35]

While Americans collect data about consumers' backgrounds and what they buy, often trading that information with other internal or external contacts, the Swedes, for example, are astounded that this is done, especially without governmental oversight.[36] The Swedes are required to register all databases of personal information with the Data Inspection Board (DIB), their federal regulatory agency for privacy, and to get permission from that board before that data can be used. Indeed, the Swedish system is typical of most countries in Europe in their societal approaches to privacy.[37] One example of a blocked data transfer occurred when Sweden would not allow U.S. airlines to transmit passenger information, such as wheelchair need and meal preferences, to the United States.[38]

Generally in Europe, each person must be informed, and given the chance to object, if the information about that person is going to be used for direct marketing purposes or released to another party. That data cannot be used for secondary purposes if the consumer objects.

> *In Italy, data cannot be sent outside—even to other EU countries—without the explicit consent of the data subject.*
> *In Spain, all direct mail has to include the name and address of the data owner so that the data subject is able to exercise his rights of access, correction, and removal.*[39]

The manner in which Europe views information privacy has its roots in culture and history, leading to a different value set regarding privacy. The preservation of privacy is considered a human right, perhaps partially as a result of an internalized fear about how personal records were used in war times in Europe. In addition, research by Smith on the relationship between level of concern about privacy and Hofstede's cultural dimensions revealed that high levels of uncertainty avoidance were associated with the European approach to privacy, whereas higher levels of individualism, masculinity, and power distance were associated with the U.S. approach.[40]

It seems, then, that societal culture and the resultant effects on business models can render the assumptions about the "global" nature of information technology incorrect. U.S. businesspeople, brought up on a strong diet of the market economy, need to realize that they will often need to "localize" their use of IT to different value sets about its use. This advice applies in particular to the many e-commerce companies doing business overseas. With 75 percent of the world's Internet market living outside the United States, multinational e-businesses are learning the hard way that their Web sites must reflect local markets, customs, languages, and currencies to be successful in foreign markets. Different legal systems, financial structures, tastes, and experiences necessitate attention to every detail to achieve global appeal. In other words, e-businesses must localize to globalize, which means much more than translating online content to local languages. Lycos Europe, for example, based its privacy policies upon German law since it is the most stringent.

One problem area often beyond the control of e-business is the costs of connecting to the Internet for people in other countries. In Asia, for example, such costs are considerably higher than in the United States. Other practical problems in Asia, as well as in Germany, the Netherlands, and Sweden, include the method of payment, which in most of these places still involves cash or letters of credit and written receipts. Dell tackled this problem by offering debit payments from consumers' checking accounts. Some companies have learned the hard way that they need to do their homework before launching sites aimed at overseas consumers. Dell, for example, committed a faux pas when it launched an e-commerce site in Japan with black borders on the site; black is considered negative in the Japanese culture, so many consumers took one look and didn't want anything else to do with it. Dell executives learned that the complexity of language translation into Japanese was only one area in which they needed to localize.

DEVELOPING CULTURAL PROFILES

Managers can gather considerable information on cultural variables from current research, personal observation, and discussions with people. From these sources, managers can develop cultural profiles of various countries—composite pictures of working environments, people's attitudes, and norms of behavior. As we have previously discussed, these profiles are often highly generalized; many subcultures, of course, may exist within a country. However, managers can use these profiles to anticipate drastic differences in the level of motivation, communication, ethics, loyalty, and individual and group productivity that may be encountered in a given country. More such homework may have helped Wal-Mart's expansion efforts into Germany and South Korea, from which it withdrew in 2006. Wal-Mart's executives simply did not do enough research about the culture and shopping habits of people there; for example:

> *In Germany, Wal-Mart stopped requiring sales clerks to smile at customers—a practice that some male shoppers interpreted as flirting—and scrapped the morning Wal-Mart chant by staff members. "People found these things strange; Germans just don't behave that way," said Hans-Martin Poschmann, the secretary of the Verdi union, which represents 5,000 Wal-Mart employees here.*
>
> NEW YORK TIMES,
> *July 31, 2006*[41]

It is relatively simple for Americans to pull together a descriptive profile of U.S. culture, even though regional and individual differences exist, because Americans know themselves and because researchers have thoroughly studied U.S. culture. The results of one such study by Harris and Moran are shown in Exhibit 3-6, which provides a basis of comparison with other cultures and, thus, suggests the likely differences in workplace behaviors.

It is not so easy, however, to pull together descriptive cultural profiles of peoples in other countries unless one has lived there and been intricately involved with those people. Still, managers can make a start by using what comparative research and literature are available.

EXHIBIT 3-6   Americans at a Glance

1. *Goal and achievement oriented*—Americans think they can accomplish just about anything, given enough time, money, and technology.
2. *Highly organized and institutionally minded*—Americans prefer a society that is institutionally strong, secure, and tidy or well kept.
3. *Freedom-loving and self-reliant*—Americans fought a revolution and subsequent wars to preserve their concept of democracy, so they resent too much control or interference, especially by government or external forces. They believe in an ideal that all persons are created equal; though they sometimes fail to fully live that ideal, they strive through law to promote equal opportunity and to confront their own racism or prejudice.
   They also idealize the self-made person who rises form poverty and adversity, and think they can influence and create their own futures. Control of one's destiny is popularly expressed as "doing your own thing." Americans think, for the most part, that with determination and initiative, one can achieve whatever one sets out to do and thus, fulfill one's individual human potential.
4. *Work oriented and efficient*—Americans possess a strong work ethic, though they are learning in the present generation to constructively enjoy leisure time. They are conscious of time and efficient in doing things. They tinker with gadgets and technological systems, always searching for easier, better, more efficient ways to accomplish tasks.
5. *Friendly and informal*—Americans reject the traditional privileges of royalty and class but defer to those with affluence and power. Although informal in greeting and dress, they are a noncontact culture (e.g., usually avoid embracing in public) and maintain a certain physical/psychological distance with others (e.g., about 2 feet).
6. *Competitive and aggressive*—Americans in play or business generally are so oriented because of their drives to achieve and succeed. This is partially traced to their heritage of having to overcome a wilderness and hostile elements in their environment.
7. *Values in transition*—Traditional American values of family loyalty, respect and care of the aged, marriage and the nuclear family, patriotism, material acquisition, forthrightness, and the like are undergoing profound reevaluation as people search for new meanings.
8. *Generosity*—Although Americans seemingly emphasize material values, they are a sharing people, as has been demonstrated in the Marshall Plan, foreign aid programs, refugee assistance, and their willingness at home and abroad to espouse a good cause and to help neighbors in need. They tend to be altruistic and some would say naive as a people.

SOURCE: From *Managing Cultural Differences* by Philip R. Harris and Robert T. Moran, 5th ed. Copyright © 2000 by Gulf Publishing Company, Houston, TX. Used with permission. All rights reserved.

The following Comparative Management in Focus provides brief, generalized country profiles based on a synthesis of research, primarily from Hofstede[42] and England,[43] as well as numerous other sources.[44] These profiles illustrate how to synthesize information and gain a sense of the character of a society—from which implications may be drawn about how to manage more effectively in that society. More extensive implications and applications related to managerial functions are drawn in later chapters.

Recent evidence points to some convergence with Western business culture resulting from Japan's economic contraction and subsequent bankruptcies. Focus on the group, lifetime employment, and a pension has given way to a more competitive business environment with job security no longer guaranteed and an emphasis on performance-based pay. This has led Japan's "salarymen" to recognize the need for personal responsibility on the job and in their lives. Although only a few years ago emphasis was on the group, Japan's long economic slump seems to have caused some cultural restructuring of the individual. Corporate Japan is changing from a culture of consensus and groupthink to one touting the need for an "era of personal responsibility" as a solution to revitalize its competitive position in the global marketplace.[45]

To tell you the truth, it's hard to think for yourself, says Mr. Kuzuoka . . . [but, if you don't] . . . in this age of cutthroat competition, you'll just end up drowning.[46]

Comparative Management in Focus

Profiles in Culture—Japan, Germany, and South Korea

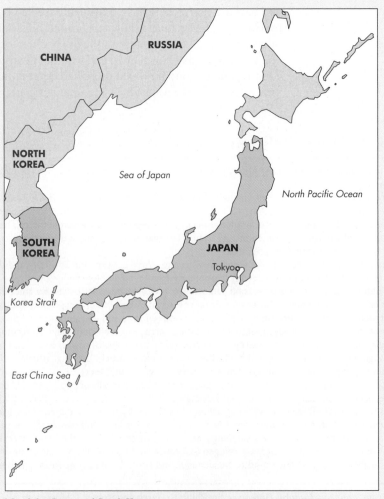

Map 3-2   Japan and South Korea

JAPAN

The traditional Japanese business characteristics of politeness and defer-ence have left companies without the thrusting culture needed to succeed internationally.

FINANCIAL TIMES,
October 10, 2005[47]

With intense global competition many Japanese companies are recognizing the need for more assertiveness and clarity in their business culture in order to expand abroad. As a result, many Japanese employees are recognizing the need to manage their own careers as companies move away from lifetime employment to be more competitive. Only a handful of large businesses, such as Toyota, Komatsu, and Canon, have managed to become indisputable global leaders by maintaining relationships and a foundation for their operations around the world.[48] For the majority of Japanese, the underlying cultural values still predominate—for now anyway.

Much of Japanese culture—and the basis of working relationships—can be explained by the principle of *wa*, "peace and harmony." This principle, embedded in the value the Japanese attribute to *amae* ("indulgent love"), probably origi-nated in the Shinto religion, which focuses on spiritual and physical harmony. *Amae* results in *shinyo,* which refers to the mutual confidence, faith, and honor necessary for successful business relationships. Japan ranks high on pragmatism, masculinity, and uncertainty avoidance, and fairly high on power distance. At the same time, much importance is attached to loyalty, empathy, and the guidance of subordinates. The result is a mix of authoritarianism and humanism in the work-place, similar to a family system. These cultural roots are evident in a homoge-neous managerial value system, with strong middle management, strong working relationships, strong seniority systems that stress rank, and an emphasis on look-ing after employees. The principle of *wa* carries forth into the work group—the building block of Japanese business. The Japanese strongly identify and thus seek to cooperate with their work groups. The emphasis is on participative manage-ment, consensus problem solving, and decision making with a patient, long-term perspective. Open expression and conflict are discouraged, and it is of paramount importance to avoid the shame of not fulfilling one's duty. These elements of work culture result in a devotion to work, collective responsibility, and a high degree of employee productivity.

If we extend this cultural profile to its implications for specific behaviors in the workplace, we can draw a comparison with common American behaviors. Most of those behaviors seem to be opposite to those of their counterparts; it is no wonder that many misunderstandings and conflicts in the workplace arise between Americans and Japanese (see Exhibit 3-7). For example, a majority of the attitudes and behaviors of many Japanese stems from a high level of collectivism, compared with a high level of individualism common to Americans. This contrast is highlighted in the center of Exhibit 3-7—"Maintain the group"—compared with "Protect the individual." In addition, the strict social order of the Japanese permeates the work-place in adherence to organizational hierarchy and seniority and in loyalty to the firm. This contrasts markedly with the typical American responses to organizational relationships and duties based on equality. In addition, the often blunt, outspoken American businessperson offends the indirectness and sensitivity of the Japanese for whom the virtue of patience is paramount, causing the silence and avoidance that so frustrates Americans. As a result, Japanese businesspeople tend to think of American organizations as having no spiritual quality and little employee loyalty, and of Americans as assertive, frank, and egotistic. Their American counterparts, in turn, respond with the impression that Japanese businesspeople have little experi-ence and are secretive, arrogant, and cautious.[49]

EXHIBIT 3-7 The American–Japanese Cultural Divide

Japanese	American
Man within nature	Man controlling nature
Caution	Risk-taking
Incremental improvement	Bold initiative
Deliberation	Spontaneity
Adherence to form	Improvisation
Silence	Outspokenness
Memorization	Critical thinking
Emotional sensitivity	Logical reasoning
Indirectness	Clarity and frankness
Assuaging	Confronting
Avoiding	Threatening
Consensus building	Decisiveness
Conformity	Individuality
Group convention	Personal principle
Trusted relationships	Legal safeguards
Collective strength	Individual independence
Maintain the group	Protect the individual
Modest resignation	Righteous indignation
Saving face	Being heard
Oppressive unanimity	Chaotic anarchy
Humble cooperation	Proving oneself
Rewarding seniority	Rewarding performance
Loyalty	Track record
Generalists	Specialists
Obligations	Opportunities
Untiring effort	Fair effort
Shame	Guilt
Dependency	Autonomy
Dutiful relationships	Level playing field
Industrial groups	Industrial competition
Strict ranking	Ambiguous/informal ranking
Racial differentiation	Racial equality
Gender differentiation	Gender equality

(Left categories: Patience, Harmony, Hierarchy. Right categories: Action, Freedom, Equality.)

SOURCE: R. G. Linowes, "The Japanese Manager's Traumatic Entry into the United States: Understanding the American–Japanese Cultural Divide," *The Academy of Management Executive,* VII, no. 4 (November 1993): 24.

GERMANY

The reunited Germany is somewhat culturally diverse inasmuch as the country borders several nations. Generally, Germans rank quite high on Hofstede's dimension of individualism, although their behaviors seem less individualistic than those of Americans. They score fairly high on uncertainty avoidance and masculinity and have a relatively small need for power distance. These cultural norms show up in the Germans' preference for being around familiar people and situations; they are also reflected in their propensity to do a detailed evaluation of business deals before committing themselves.

Christianity underlies much of German culture—more than 96 percent of Germans are Catholics or Protestants. This may be why Germans tend to like rule and order in their lives, and why there is a clear public expectation of acceptable and the unacceptable ways to act. Public signs everywhere in Germany dictate what is allowed or *verboten* (forbidden). Germans are very strict with their use of time, whether for business or pleasure, frowning on inefficiency or on tardiness. In business, Germans tend to be assertive, but they downplay aggression. Decisions are not as centralized as one would expect, with hierarchical processes often giving way to consensus decision making. However, strict departmentalization is present in organizations, with centralized and final authority at the departmental manager level. Hall and Hall describe the German preference for closed doors and private space as evidence of the affinity for compartmentalization in organizations and in their own lives. They also prefer more physical space around them in conversation than do most other Europeans, and they seek privacy so as not to be overheard. German law prohibits loud noises in public areas on weekend afternoons. Germans are conservative, valuing privacy, politeness, and formality; they usually use last names and titles for all except those close to them.

In negotiations, Germans want detailed information before and during discussions, which can become lengthy. They give factors such as voice and speech control much weight. However, since Germany is a low-context society, communication is explicit, and Americans find negotiations easy to understand.[50]

SOUTH KOREA

Koreans rank high on collectivism and pragmatism, fairly low on masculinity, moderate on power distance, and quite high on uncertainty avoidance. Although greatly influenced by U.S. culture, Koreans are still very much bound to the traditional Confucian teachings of spiritualism and collectivism. Korea and its people have undergone great changes, but the respect for family, authority, formality, class, and rank remain strong. Koreans are demonstrative, friendly, quite aggressive and hard-working, and very hospitable. For the most part, they do not subscribe to participative management. Family and personal relationships are important, and connections are vital for business introductions and transactions. Business is based on honor and trust; most contracts are oral. Although achievement and competence are important to Koreans, the priority of guarding both parties' social and professional reputations is a driving force in relationships. Thus, praise predominates, and honest criticism is rare.

Further insight into the differences between U.S. and Korean culture can be derived from the following excerpted letter from Professor Jin K. Kim in Plattsburgh, New York, to his high school friend, MK, in South Korea, who just returned from a visit to the United States. MK, whom Dr. Kim had not seen for 20 years, planned to emigrate to the United States, and Dr. Kim wanted to help ward off his friend's culture shock by telling him about U.S. culture from a Korean perspective.

Dear MK,

I sincerely hope the last leg of your trip home from the five-week fact-finding visit to the United States was pleasant and informative. Although I may not have expressed my sense of exhilaration about your visit through the meager lodging accommodations and "barbaric" foods we provided, it was sheer joy to spend four weeks with you and Kyung-Ok. (Please refrain from hitting the ceiling. My use of your charming wife's name, rather than the usual Korean expression "your wife" or "your house person," is not an indication of my amorous intentions toward her as any red-blooded Korean man would suspect. Since you are planning to immigrate to this country soon, I thought you might as well begin to get used to the idea of your wife exerting her individuality. Better yet, I thought you should be warned that the moment the plane touches U.S. soil, you will lose your status as the center of your familial universe.) At any rate, please be assured that during your stay here my heart was filled with memories of our three years together in high school when we were young in Pusan.

During your visit, you called me, on several occasions, an American. What prompted you to invoke such a reference is beyond my comprehension. Was it my rusty Korean expressions? Was it my calculating mind? Was it my pitifully subservient (at least when viewed through your cultural lens) role that I was playing in my family life? Or, was it my familiarity with some facets of the cultural landscape? This may sound bewildering to you, but it is absolutely true that through all the years I have lived in this country, I never truly felt like an American. Sure, on the surface, our family followed closely many ritualistic routines of the American culture: shopping malls, dining out, PTA, Little League, picnics, camping trips, credit card shopping sprees, hot dogs, and so on. But mentally I remained stubbornly in the periphery. Naturally, then, my subjective cultural attitudes stayed staunchly Korean. Never did the inner layers of my Korean psyche yield to the invading American cultural vagaries, I thought. So, when you labeled me an American for the first time, I felt a twinge of guilt.

Several years ago, an old Korean friend of mine, who settled in the United States about the same time I did, paid a visit to Korea for the first time in some fifteen years. When he went to see his best high school friend, who was now married and had two sons, his friend's wife made a bed for him and her husband in the master bedroom, declaring that she would spend the night with the children. It was not necessarily the sexual connotation of the episode that made my friend blush; he was greatly embarrassed by the circumstance in which he imposed himself to the extent that the couple's privacy had to be violated. For his high school friend and his wife, it was clearly their age-old friendship to which the couple's privacy had to yield. MK, you might empathize rather easily with this Korean couple's state of mind, but it would be a gross mistake even to imagine there may be occasions in your adopted culture when a gesture of friendship breaks the barrier of privacy. Zealously guarding their privacy above all, Americans are marvelously adept at drawing the line where friendship—that elusive "we" feeling—stops and privacy begins. . . .

Indeed, one of the hardest tasks you will face as an "alien" is how to find that delicate balance between your individuality (for example, privacy) and your collective identity (for example, friendship or membership in social groups).

Privacy is not the only issue that stems from this individuality–collectivity continuum. Honesty in interpersonal relationships is another point that may keep you puzzled. Americans are almost brutally honest and frank about issues that belong to public domains; they are not afraid of discussing an embarrassing topic in most graphic details as long as the topic is a matter of public concern. Equally frank and honest gestures are adopted when they discuss their own personal lives once the presumed benefits from such gestures are determined to outweigh the risks involved. Accordingly, it is not uncommon to encounter friends who volunteer personally embarrassing and even shameful information lest you find it out from other sources. Are Americans equally straightforward and forthcoming in laying out heartfelt personal criticisms directed at their friends? Not likely. Their otherwise acute sense of honesty becomes significantly muted when they face the unpleasant task of being negative toward their personal friends. The fear of an emotion-draining confrontation and the virtue of being polite force them to put on a facade or mask.

The perfectly accepted social behavior of telling "white lies" is a good example. The social and personal virtues of accepting such lies are grounded in the belief that the potential damage that can be inflicted by directly telling a friend the hurtful truth far outweighs the potential benefit that the friend could gain from it. Instead of telling a hurtful truth directly, Americans use various indirect communication channels to which their friend is likely to be tuned. In other words, they publicize the information in the form of gossip or behind-the-back recriminations until it is transformed into a sort of collective criticism against the target individual. Thus objectified and collectivized, the "truth" ultimately reaches the target individual with a minimal cost of social discomfort on the part of the teller. There is nothing vile or insidious about this communication tactic, since it is deeply rooted in the concern for sustaining social pleasantry for both parties.

This innocuous practice, however, is bound to be perceived as an act of outrageous dishonesty by a person deeply immersed in the Korean culture. In the Korean cultural context, a trusted personal relationship precludes such publicizing prior to direct, "honest" criticism to the individual concerned, no matter what the cost in social and personal unpleasantry. Indeed, as you are well aware, MK, such direct reproach and even recrimination in Korea is in most cases appreciated as a sign of one's utmost love and concern for the target individual. Stressful and emotionally draining as it is, such a frank expression of criticism is done out of "we" feeling. Straight-talking friends did not want me to repeat undesirable acts in front of others, as it would either damage "our reputation" or go against the common interest of "our collective identity." In Korea, the focus is on the self-discipline that forms a basis for the integrity of "our group." In America, on the other hand, the focus is on the feelings of two individuals. From the potential teller's viewpoint, the primary concern is how to maintain social politeness, whereas from the target person's viewpoint, the primary concern is how to maintain self-esteem. Indeed, these two diametrically opposed frames of reference—self-discipline and self-esteem—make one culture collective and the other individualistic.

It is rather amazing that for all the mistakes I must have made in the past twenty years, only one non-Korean American friend gave me such an "honest" criticism. In a sense, this concern for interpersonal politeness conceals disapproval of my undesirable behavior for a time and ultimately delays the adjustment or realignment of my behavior, since it is likely to take quite a while for the collective judgment to reach me through the "publicized" channels of communication. So many Korean immigrants express their indignation about their U.S. colleagues who smile at them but who criticize them behind their backs. If you ever become a victim of such a perception, MK, please take heart that you are not the only one who feels that pain.

MK, the last facet of the individualism–collectivism continuum likely to cause a great amount of cognitive dissonance in the process of your assimilation to American life is the extent to which you have to assert your individuality to other people. You probably have no difficulty remembering our high school principal, K. W. Park, for whom we had a respect–contempt complex. He used to lecture, almost daily at morning assemblies, on the virtue of being modest. As he preached it, it was a form of the Confucian virtue of self-denial. Our existence or presence among other people, he told us, should not be overly felt through communicated messages (regardless of whether they are done with a tongue or pen). . . . One's existence, we were told, should be noticed by others in the form of our acts and conduct. One is obligated to provide opportunities for others to experience one's existence through what he or she does. Self-initiated effort for public recognition or self-aggrandizement was the most shameful conduct for a person of virtue.

This idea is interesting and noble as a philosophical posture, but when it is practiced in America, it will not get you anywhere in most circumstances. The lack of self-assertion is translated directly into timidity and lack of self-confidence. This is a culture where you must exert your individuality to the extent that it would make our high school principal turn in his grave out of shame and disgust. Blame the size of the territory or the population of this country. You may even blame the fast-paced cadence of life or the social mobility that moves people around at a dizzying speed. Whatever the specific reason might be, Americans are not waiting to experience you or your behaviors as they exist. They want a "documented" version of you that is eloquently summarized, decorated, and certified. What they are looking for is not your raw, unprocessed being with rich texture; rather, it is a slickly processed self, neatly packaged, and, most important, conveniently delivered to them. Self-advertising is encouraged almost to the point of pretentiousness. Years ago in Syracuse, I had an occasion to introduce a visiting Korean monk–scholar to a gathering of people who wanted to hear something about Oriental philosophies. After taking an elegantly practiced bow to the crowd, this humble monk declared, "My name is. . . . Please teach me, as I do not know anything." It took quite a bit of probing and questioning for us to extract something to chew on from that monk with the mysterious smile. Contrast this with an American colleague of mine applying for a promotion several years ago, who literally hauled in two cabinets full of documented evidence of his scholarly achievements.

The curious journey toward the American end of the individualism–collectivism continuum will be inevitable, I assure you. The real question is whether it will be in your generation, your children's, or their children's. Whenever it happens, it will be a bittersweet revenge for me, since only then will you realize how it feels to be called an American by your best high school chum.

SOURCE: Excerpted from a letter by Dr. Jin K. Kim, State University of New York—Plattsburgh. Copyright © 2001 by Dr. Jin K. Kim. Used with permission of Dr. Kim.

CULTURE AND MANAGEMENT STYLES AROUND THE WORLD

As an international manager, once you have researched the culture of a country in which you may be going to work or with which to do business, and after you have developed a cultural profile, it is useful then to apply that information to develop an understanding of the expected management styles and ways of doing business that predominate in that region, or with that type of business setting. Two examples follow: Saudi Arabia and Chinese Small Family Businesses.

Saudi Arabia

Understanding how business is conducted in the modern Middle East requires an understanding of the Arab culture, since the Arab peoples are the majority there and most of them are Muslim. As discussed in the opening profile, the Arab culture is intertwined with the pervasive influence of Islam. Even though not all Middle Easterners are Arab, Arab culture and management style predominate in the Arabian Gulf region. Shared culture, religion, and language underlie behavioral similarities throughout the Arab world. Islam "permeates Saudi life—Allah is always present, controls everything, and is frequently referred to in conversation."[51] Employees may spend more than two hours a day in prayer as part of the life pattern that intertwines work with religion, politics, and social life.

Arab history and culture are based on tribalism, with its norms of reciprocity of favors, support, obligation, and identity passed on to the family unit, which is the primary structural model. Family life is based on closer personal ties than in the West. Arabs value personal relationships, honor, and saving face for all concerned; these values take precedence over the work at hand or verbal accuracy. "Outsiders" must realize that establishing a trusting relationship and respect for Arab social norms has to precede any attempts at business discussions. Honor, pride, and dignity are at the core of "shame" societies, such as the Arabs. As such, shame and honor provide the basis for social control and motivation. Circumstances dictate what is right or wrong and what is acceptable behavior.[52]

Arabs avoid open admission of error at all costs because weakness (*muruwwa*) is a failure to be manly. It is sometimes difficult for westerners to get at the truth because of the Arab need to avoid showing weakness; instead, Arabs present a desired or idealized situation. Shame is also brought on someone who declines to fulfill a request or a favor; therefore, a business arrangement is left open if something has yet to be completed.

The communication style of Middle Eastern societies is high context (that is, implicit and indirect), and their use of time is polychronic: Many activities can be taking place at the same time, with constant interruptions commonplace. The imposition of deadlines is considered rude, and business schedules take a backseat to the perspective that

EXHIBIT 3-8   Behavior that Will Likely Cause Offense in Saudi Arabia

- Bringing up business subjects until you get to know your host, or you will be considered rude.
- Commenting on a man's wife or female children over 12 years of age.
- Raising colloquial questions that may be common in your country but possibly misunderstood in Saudi Arabia as an invasion of privacy.
- Using disparaging or swear words and off-color or obscene attempts at humor.
- Engaging in conversations about religion, politics, or Israel.
- Bringing gifts of alcohol or using alcohol, which is prohibited in Saudi Arabia.
- Requesting favors from those in authority or esteem, for it is considered impolite for Arabs to say no.
- Shaking hands too firmly or pumping—gentle or limp handshakes are preferred.
- Pointing your finger at someone or showing the soles of your feet when seated.

SOURCE: P. R. Harris and R. T. Moran, *Managing Cultural Differences*, 5th ed. (Houston: Gulf Publishing, 2000).

events will occur "sometime" when Allah wills *(bukra insha Allah)*. Arabs give primary importance to hospitality; they are cordial to business associates and lavish in their entertainment, constantly offering strong black coffee (which you should not refuse) and banquets before considering business transactions. Westerners must realize the importance of personal contacts and networking, socializing and building close relationships and trust, practicing patience regarding schedules, and doing business in person. Exhibit 3-8 gives some selected actions and nonverbal behaviors that may offend Arabs. The relationship between cultural values and norms in Saudi Arabia and managerial behaviors is illustrated in Exhibit 3-9.

Chinese Small Family Businesses

The predominance of small businesses in China and the region highlights the need for managers from around the world to gain an understanding of how such businesses operate. Many small businesses—most of which are family or extended-family businesses—become part of the value chain (suppliers, buyers, retailers, etc.) within industries in which "foreign" firms may compete.

Some specifics of Chinese management style and practices in particular are presented here as they apply to small businesses. (Further discussion of the Chinese culture continues in Chapter 5 in the context of negotiation.) It is important to note that no matter the size of a company, but especially in small businesses, it is the all-pervasive presence and use of *guanxi* that provides the little red engine of business transactions in China. *Guanxi* means "connections"—the network of relationships the Chinese cultivate through friendship and affection; it entails the exchange of favors and gifts to provide an obligation to reciprocate favors. Those who share a *guanxi* network share an unwritten code.[53] The philosophy and structure of Chinese businesses comprise paternalism, mutual obligation, responsibility, hierarchy, familialism, personalism, and connections.[54] Autocratic leadership is the norm, with the owner using his or her power—but with a caring about other people that may predominate over efficiency.[55]

According to Lee, the major differences between Chinese management styles and those of their Western counterparts are human-centeredness, family-centeredness, centralization of power, and small size.[56] Their human-centered management style puts people ahead of a business relationship and focuses on friendship, loyalty, and trustworthiness.[57] The family is extremely important in Chinese culture, and any small business tends to be run like a family.

The centralized power structure in Chinese organizations, unlike those in the West, splits into two distinct levels: At the top are the boss and a few family members, and at the bottom are the employees, with no ranking among the workers.[58]

As Chinese firms in many modern regions in the Pacific Rim seek to modernize and compete locally and globally, a tug of war has begun between the old and the new: the

EXHIBIT 3-9   The Relationship Between Culture and Managerial Behaviors in Saudi Arabia

Cultural Values	Managerial Behaviors
Tribal and family loyalty	Work group loyalty
	Paternal sociability
	Stable employment and a sense of belonging
	A pleasant workplace
	Careful selection of employees
	Nepotism
Arabic language	Business as an intellectual activity
	Access to employees and peers
	Management by walking around
	Conversation as recreation
Close and warm friendships	A person rather than task and money orientation
	Theory Y management
	Avoidance of judgment
Islam	Sensitivity to Islamic virtues
	Observance of the Qur'an and Sharia
	Work as personal or spiritual growth
	Consultative management
	A full and fair hearing
	Adherence to norms
Honor and shame	Clear guidelines and conflict avoidance
	Positive reinforcement
	Training and defined job duties
	Private correction of mistakes
	Avoidance of competition
An idealized self	Centralized decision making
	Assumption of responsibility appropriate to position
	Empathy and respect for the self-image of others
Polychronic use of time	Right- and left-brain facility
	A bias for action
	Patience and flexibility
Independence	Sensitivity to control
	Interest in the individual
Male domination	Separation of sexes
	Open work life; closed family life

SOURCE: R. R. Harris and R. T. Moran, *Managing Cultural Differences* 4th ed. (Houston: Gulf Publishing, 1996).

traditional Chinese management practices and the increasingly "imported" Western management styles. As discussed by Lee, this struggle is encapsulated in the different management perspectives of the old and young generations. A two-generational study of Chinese managers by Ralston et al. also found generational shifts in work values in China. They concluded that the new generation manager is more individualistic, more independent, and takes more risks in the pursuit of profits. However, they also found the new generation holding on to their Confucian values, concluding that the new generation may be viewed as "crossverging their Eastern and Western influences, while on the road of modernization."[59]

CONCLUSION

This chapter has explored various cultural values and how managers can understand them with the help of cultural profiles. The following chapters focus on application of this cultural knowledge to management in an international environment (or, alternatively in a domestic multicultural environment)—especially as relevant to cross-cultural communication (Chapter 4), negotiation and decision making (Chapter 5), and motivating and leading (Chapter 11). Culture and communication are essentially synonymous; what happens when people from different cultures communicate, and how can international managers understand the underlying process and adapt their styles and expectations accordingly? For the answers, read the next chapter.

Summary of Key Points

1. The culture of a society comprises the shared values, understandings, assumptions, and goals that are passed down through generations and imposed by members of the society. These unique sets of cultural and national differences strongly influence the attitudes and expectations and therefore the on-the-job behavior of individuals and groups.
2. Managers must develop cultural sensitivity to anticipate and accommodate behavioral differences in various societies. As part of that sensitivity, they must avoid parochialism—an attitude that assumes one's own management techniques are best in any situation or location and that other people should follow one's patterns of behavior.
3. Harris and Moran take a systems approach to understanding cultural and national variables and their effects on work behavior. They identify eight subsystems of variables: kinship, education, economy, politics, religion, associations, health, and recreation.
4. From his research in 50 countries, Hofstede proposes four underlying value dimensions that help to identify and describe the cultural profile of a country and affect organizational processes: power distance, uncertainty avoidance, individualism, and masculinity.
5. Through his research, Fons Trompenaars confirmed some similar dimensions, and found other unique dimensions: obligation, emotional orientation, privacy, and source of power and status.
6. The GLOBE project team of 170 researchers in 62 countries concluded the presence of a number of other dimensions, and ranked countries on those dimensions, including assertiveness, performance orientation, future orientation, and humane orientation. Gupta et al. from that team found geographical clusters on nine of the GLOBE project cultural dimensions.
7. On-the-job conflicts in international management frequently arise out of conflicting values and orientations regarding time, change, material factors, and individualism.
8. Managers can use research results and personal observations to develop a character sketch, or cultural profile, of a country. This profile can help managers anticipate how to motivate people and coordinate work processes in a particular international context.

Discussion Questions

1. What is meant by the culture of a society, and why is it important that international managers understand it? Do you notice cultural differences among your classmates? How do those differences affect the class environment? Your group projects?
2. Describe the four dimensions of culture proposed by Hofstede. What are the managerial implications of these dimensions? Compare the findings with those of Trompenaars and the GLOBE project team.
3. Discuss the types of operational conflicts that could occur in an international context because of different attitudes toward time, change, material factors, and individualism. Give examples relative to specific countries.
4. Give some examples of countries in which the family and its extensions play an important role in the workplace. How are managerial functions affected, and what can a manager do about this influence?
5. Discuss collectivism as it applies to the Japanese workplace. What managerial functions does it affect?
6. Discuss the role of Islam in cross-cultural relations and business operations.

Application Exercises

1. Develop a cultural profile for one of the countries in the following list. Form small groups of students and compare your findings in class with those of another group preparing a profile for another country. Be sure to compare specific findings regarding religion, kinship, recreation, and other subsystems. What are the prevailing attitudes toward time, change, material factors, and individualism?

   Any African country
   People's Republic of China
   Saudi Arabia
   Mexico
   France
   India

2. In small groups of students, research Hofstede's findings regarding the four dimensions of power distance, uncertainty avoidance, masculinity, and individualism for one of the following countries in comparison to the United States. (Your instructor can assign the countries to avoid duplication.) Present your findings to the class. Assume you are a U.S. manager of a subsidiary in the foreign country and explain how differences on these dimensions are likely to affect your management tasks. What suggestions do you have for dealing with these differences in the workplace?

Brazil
Italy
People's Republic of China
Russia

Experiential Exercises

1. A large Baltimore manufacturer of cabinet hardware had been working for months to locate a suitable distributor for its products in Europe. Finally invited to present a demonstration to a reputable distributing company in Frankfurt, it sent one of its most promising young executives, Fred Wagner, to make the presentation. Fred not only spoke fluent German but also felt a special interest in this assignment because his paternal grandparents had immigrated to the United States from the Frankfurt area during the 1920s. When Fred arrived at the conference room where he would be making his presentation, he shook hands firmly, greeted everyone with a friendly *guten tag,* and even remembered to bow the head slightly as is the German custom. Fred, an effective speaker and past president of the Baltimore Toastmasters Club, prefaced his presentation with a few humorous anecdotes to set a relaxed and receptive atmosphere. However, he felt that his presentation was not well received by the company executives. In fact, his instincts were correct, for the German company chose not to distribute Fred's hardware products.
   What went wrong?

2. Bill Nugent, an international real estate developer from Dallas, had made a 2:30 P.M. appointment with Mr. Abdullah, a high-ranking government official in Riyadh, Saudi Arabia. From the beginning things did not go well for Bill. First, he was kept waiting until nearly 3:45 P.M. before he was ushered into Mr. Abdullah's office. When he finally did get in, several other men were also in the room. Even though Bill felt that he wanted to get down to business with Mr. Abdullah, he was reluctant to get too specific because he considered much of what they needed to discuss sensitive and private. To add to Bill's sense of frustration, Mr. Abdullah seemed more interested in engaging in meaningless small talk than in dealing with the substantive issues concerning their business.
   How might you help Bill deal with his frustration?

3. Tom Forrest, an up-and-coming executive for a U.S. electronics company, was sent to Japan to work out the details of a joint venture with a Japanese electronics firm. During the first several weeks, Tom felt that the negotiations were proceeding better than he had expected. He found that he had very cordial working relationships with the team of Japanese executives, and in fact, they had agreed on the major policies and strategies governing the new joint venture. During the third week of negotiations, Tom was present at a meeting held to review their progress. The meeting was chaired by the president of the Japanese firm, Mr. Hayakawa, a man in his mid-forties, who had recently taken over the presidency from his 82-year-old grandfather. The new president, who had been involved in most of the negotiations during the preceding weeks, seemed to Tom to be one of the strongest advocates of the plan that had been developed to date. Hayakawa's grandfather, the recently retired president, also was present at the meeting. After the plans had been discussed in some detail, the octogenarian past president proceeded to give a long soliloquy about how some of the features of this plan violated the traditional practices on which the company had been founded. Much to Tom's amazement, Mr. Hayakawa did nothing to explain or defend the policies and strategies that they had taken weeks to develop. Feeling extremely frustrated, Tom then gave a fairly strong argued defense of the plan. To Tom's further amazement, no one else in the meeting spoke up in defense of the plan. The tension in the air was quite heavy, and the meeting adjourned shortly thereafter. Within days the Japanese firm completely terminated the negotiations on the joint venture.
   How could you help Tom better understand this bewildering situation?

SOURCE: Gary P. Ferraro, *The Cultural Dimensions of International Business,* 2nd ed. (Upper Saddle River, NJ: Prentice Hall, 1994).

Internet Resources

Visit the Deresky Companion Website at www.prenhall.com/deresky for this chapter's Internet resources.

Moto: Coming to America from Japan

Moto arrived in Chicago in the middle of winter, unprepared for the raw wind that swept off the lake. The first day he bought a new coat and fur-lined boots. He was cheered by a helpful salesgirl who smiled as she packed his lined raincoat into a box. Americans were nice, Moto decided. He was not worried about his assignment in America. The land had been purchased, and Moto's responsibility was to hire a contracting company and check on the pricing details. The job seemed straightforward.

Moto's firm, KKD, an auto parts supplier, had spent a year and a half researching U.S. building contractors. Allmack had the best record in terms of timely delivery and liaisons with good architects and the best suppliers of raw materials. That night Moto called Mr. Crowell of Allmack, who confirmed the appointment for the next morning. His tone was amiable.

Moto arrived at the Allmack office at nine sharp. He had brought a set of *kokeshi* dolls for Crowell. The dolls, which his wife had spent a good part of a day picking out, were made from a special maple in the mountains near his family home in Niigata. He would explain that to Crowell later, when they knew each other. Crowell also came from a hilly, snowy place, which was called Vermont.

When the secretary ushered him in, Crowell stood immediately and rounded the desk with an outstretched hand. Squeezing Moto's hand, he roared, "How are you? Long trip from Tokyo. Please sit down, please."

Moto smiled. He reached in his jacket for his card. By the time he presented it, Crowell was back on the other side of the desk. "My card," Moto said seriously.

"Yes, yes," Crowell answered. He put Moto's card in his pocket without a glance.

Moto stared at the floor. This couldn't be happening, he thought. Everything was on that card: KKD, Moto, Michio, Project Director. KKD meant University of Tokyo and years of hard work to earn a high recommendation from Dr. Iwasa's laboratory. Crowell had simply put it away.

"Here." Crowell handed Moto his card.

"Oh, John Crowell, Allmack, President," Moto read aloud, slowly trying to recover his equilibrium. "Allmack is famous in Japan."

"You know me," Crowell replied and grinned. "All those faxes. Pleased to meet you, Moto. I have a good feeling about this deal."

Moto smiled and laid Crowell's card on the table in front of him.

"KKD is pleased to do business with Allmack," Moto spoke slowly. He was proud of his English. Not only had he been a top English student in high school and university, but he had also studied English in a *juku* (an after-school class) for five years. As soon as he received this assignment, he took an intensive six-week course taught by Ms. Black, an American, who also instructed him in U.S. history and customs.

Crowell looked impatient. Moto tried to think of Ms. Black's etiquette lessons as he continued talking about KKD and Allmack's history. "We are the best in the business," Crowell interrupted. "Ask anyone. We build the biggest and best shopping malls in the country."

Moto hesitated. He knew Allmack's record—that's why he was in the room. Surely Crowell knew that. The box of *kokeshi* dolls pressed against his knees. Maybe he should give the gift now. No, he thought, Crowell was still talking about Allmack's achievements. Now Crowell had switched to his own achievements. Moto felt desperate.

"You'll have to come to my house," Crowell continued. "I live in a fantastic house. I had an architect from California build it. He builds for all the stars, and for me." Crowell chuckled. "Built it for my wife. She's the best wife, the very best. I call her my little sweetheart. Gave the wife the house on her birthday. Took her right up to the front door and carried her inside."

Moto shifted his weight. Perhaps if he were quiet, Crowell would change the subject. Then they could pretend the conversation never happened. "Moto-san, what's your first name? Here, we like to be on a first-name basis."

"Michio," Moto whispered.

"Michio-san, you won't get a better price than from me. You can go down the block to Zimmer or Casey, but you got the best deal right here."

"I brought you a present," Moto said, handing him the box of *kokeshi* dolls.

"Thanks," Crowell answered. He looked genuinely pleased as he tore open the paper. Moto looked away while Crowell picked up a *kokeshi* doll in each hand. "They look like Russian dolls. Hey, thanks a lot, my daughter will love them."

Moto pretended that he hadn't heard. I'll help by ignoring him, Moto thought, deeply embarrassed.

Crowell pushed the *kokeshi* dolls aside and pressed a buzzer. "Send George in," he said.

The door opened and a tall, heavyset man with a dark crew cut stepped inside the room.

"George Kubushevsky, this is Moto-san, Michio. . . ."

"How do you do?" Kubushevsky's handshake was firm.

Moto took out his card.

"Thanks," Kubushevsky said. "Never carry those." He laughed and hooked his thumbs in his belt buckle. Moto nodded. He was curious. Kubushevsky must be a Jewish name—or was it Polish, or maybe even German? In Japan he'd read books about all three groups. He looked at Kubushevsky's bone structure. It was impossible to tell. He was too fat.

"George, make sure you show Michio everything. We want him to see all the suppliers, meet the right people, you understand?"

"Sure." George grinned and left the room.

Moto turned to Crowell. "Is he a real American?" Moto asked.

"A real American? What's that?"

Moto flushed. "Is he first generation?" Moto finished lamely. He remembered reading that Jews, Lebanese, and Armenians were often first generation.

"How do I know? He's just Kubushevsky."

During the next few weeks Moto saw a great deal of Kubushevsky. Each morning he was picked up at nine and taken to a round of suppliers. Kubushevsky gave him a rundown on each supplier before they met. He was amiable and polite, but never really intimate. Moto's response was also to be polite. Once he suggested that they go drinking after work, but Kubushevsky flatly refused, saying that he had to work early the next morning. Moto sighed, remembering briefly his favorite bar and his favorite hostess in Tokyo. Yuko-san must be nearly fifty now, he thought affectionately. She could make him laugh. He wished he were barhopping with his colleagues from his *ringi* group at KKD. Moto regretted that he had not brought more *kokeshi* dolls, since Kubushevsky had not seemed delighted with the present of the KKD pen.

One morning they were driving to a cement outlet.

"George."

"Yes, Michio-san."

Moto paused. He still found it difficult to call Kubushevsky by his first name. "Do you think I could have some papers?"

"What kind of papers?" Kubushevsky's voice was friendly. Unlike Crowell, he kept an even tone. Moto liked that.

"I need papers on the past sales of these people."

"We're the best."

"I need records for the past five years on the cement place we are going to visit."

"I told you, Michio-san, I'm taking you to the best! What do you want?"

"I need some records."

"Trust me, I know what I'm doing."

Moto was silent. He didn't know what to say. What did trust have to do with anything? His *ringi* group in Tokyo needed documentation so they could discuss the issues and be involved in the decisions. If the decision to go with one supplier or the other was correct, that should be reflected in the figures.

"Just look at what's going on now," George said. "Charts for the last five years, that's history."

Moto remained silent. George pressed his foot to the gas. The car passed one truck, and then another. Moto looked nervously at the climbing speedometer. Suddenly Kubushevsky whistled and released his foot. "Alright, Michio-san, I'll get you the damned figures."

"Thanks," Moto said softly.

"After we see the cement people, let's go for a drink."

Moto looked uneasily at the soft red lightbulb that lit the bar. He sipped his beer and ate a few peanuts. Kubushevsky was staring at a tall blonde at the other end of the bar. She seemed to notice him also. Her fingers moved across the rim of the glass.

"George," Moto said gently. "Where are you from, George?"

"Here and there," Kubushevsky said idly, still eyeing the blonde.

Moto laughed. "Here and there."

Kubushevsky nodded. "Here and there," he repeated.

"You Americans," Moto said. "You must have a home."

"No home, Michio-san."

The blonde slid her drink down the bar and slipped into the next seat. Kubushevsky turned more toward her.

Moto felt desperate. Last week Crowell had also acted rudely. When Imai, KKD's vice president, was visiting from Japan, Crowell had dropped them both off at a golf course. What was the point?

He drained his beer. Immediately the familiar warmth of the alcohol made him buoyant. "George," he said intimately. "You need a wife. You need a wife like Crowell has."

Kubushevsky turned slowly on his seat. He stared hard at Moto. "You need a muzzle," he said quietly.

"You need a wife," Moto repeated. He had Kubushevsky's full attention now. He poured Kubushevsky another beer. "Drink," he commanded.

Kubushevsky drank. In fact they both drank. Then suddenly Kubushevsky's voice changed. He put his arm around Moto and purred in his ear. "Let me tell you a secret, Moto-san. Crowell's wife is a dog. Crowell is a dog. I'm going to leave Allmack, just as soon as possible. Want to join me, Michio-san?"

Moto's insides froze. Leave Crowell. What was Kubushevsky talking about? He was just getting to know him. They were a team. All those hours in the car together, all those hours staring at cornfields and concrete. What was Kubushevsky talking about? Did Crowell know? What was Kubushevsky insinuating about joining him? "You're drunk, George."

"I know."

"You're very drunk."

"I know."

Moto smiled. The blonde got restless and left the bar. Kubushevsky didn't seem to notice. For the rest of the night he talked about his first wife and his two children, whom he barely saw. He spoke of his job at Allmack and his hopes for a better job in California. They sat at a low table. Moto spoke of his children and distant wife. It felt good to talk, almost as good as having Yuko next to him.

As they left the bar, Kubushevsky leaned heavily on him. They peed against a stone wall before getting in the car. All the way home Kubushevsky sang a song about a folk here named Davy Crockett, who "killed himself a bear when he was only three." Moto sang a song from Niigata about the beauty of the snow on the rooftops in winter. Kubushevsky hummed along.

They worked as a team for the next four months. Kubushevsky provided whatever detailed documentation Moto asked for. They went drinking a lot. Sometimes they both felt a little sad, sometimes happy, but Moto mostly felt entirely comfortable. Kubushevsky introduced him to Porter, a large, good-natured man in the steel business who liked to hunt and cook gourmet food, to Andrews, a tiny man who danced the polka as if it were a waltz and to many others.

Just before the closing, Kubushevsky took him to a bar and told him of a job offer in California. He had tears in his eyes and hugged Moto good-bye. Moto had long since accepted the fact that Kubushevsky would leave.

Two weeks later Moto looked around the conference room at Allmack. Ishii, KKD's president, and Imai had flown in from Tokyo for the signing of the contract for the shopping mall, the culmination of three years of research and months of negotiation. John Crowell stood by his lawyer, Sue Smith. Sue had been on her feet for five hours. Mike Apple, Moto's lawyer, slammed his fist on the table and pointed at the item in question. The lawyers argued a timing detail that Moto was sure had been worked out weeks before. Moto glanced nervously at Ishii and Imai. Ishii's eyes were closed. Imai stared at the table.

Moto shifted uneasily in his seat. Sue was smarter than Mike, he thought. Perhaps a female lawyer wouldn't have been so terrible. While it was not unusual to see females in professional positions in Japan, this was America. Tokyo might have understood. After all, this was America, he repeated to himself. Internationalization required some adjustment. A year ago he would have had total loss of face if confronted with this prolonged, argumentative closing. Today he did not care. He could not explain to Tokyo all he'd learned in that time, all the friends he'd made. When he tried to communicate about business in America, the home office sent him terse notes by fax.

Now the lawyers stood back. President Ishii opened his eyes. Crowell handed a pen to Ishii. They signed the document together. The lawyers smiled. Sue Smith looked satisfied. She should be pleased, Moto thought. Her extensive preparation for the case made him realize again that the Japanese stereotype of the "lazy" American was false. Sue's knowledge of the case was perfect in all details. I'll have to use her next time, Moto thought. She's the smart one. Yes, he thought, his friend Kubushevsky had taught him many things. Suddenly he felt Kubushevsky's large presence. Moto lowered his head in gratitude.

CASE QUESTIONS

1. What was Moto's purpose and agenda for the first meeting with Crowell? How does he try to implement his agenda?

2. What communication problems were there between Moto and Crowell?

3. What was the significance of the dolls? What went wrong?

4. Why did Crowell's remarks about Allmack threaten a loss of face from Moto's perspective?

5. How did Moto feel about Kubushevsky's behavior early on? How did their relationship change?

SOURCE: Patricia Cercik, *On Track with the Japanese, 1992* (New York: Kodansha International, 114 Fifth Ave., NY, NY, 10011) (OR Kudanske America).

CHAPTER

Communicating Across Cultures

4

Outline

Opening Profile: On Keeping Your Foot Safely Out of Your Mouth

Joe Romano found out on a business trip to Taiwan how close a one-syllable slip of the tongue can come to torpedoing a deal.

Mr. Romano, a partner of High Ground, an emerging technology-marketing company in Boston, has been traveling to Asia for ten years and speaks fluent Mandarin and Taiwanese. Or so he thought, until he nearly blew an important deal when he met the chief executive of a major Taiwanese manufacturer.

"You're supposed to say 'Au-ban,' which means basically, 'Hello, No. 1 Boss,'" Mr. Romano explained. "But being nervous, I slipped and said 'Lau-ban ya,' which means, 'Hello, wife of the boss.'"

"So I basically called him a woman in front of twenty senior Taiwanese executives, who all laughed," he said. "He looked at me like he was going to kill me because in Asia, guys are hung up on being seen as very manly. I had to keep asking them to forgive 'the stupid American' before the C.E.O. would accept my apologies."

This is why translators are worth the investment for delicate business negotiations overseas, suggests Heike Estey, who leads cultural-sensitivity training as director of sales for Express Visa Service in Washington.

Even in the same language, communication miscues can occur. Lee Bowden, the managing director of the Sagamore, was staying at a 350-room resort on Lake George in Bolton Landing, New York, where he overheard a British guest ask the desk clerk for "a rubber." While the clerk hemmed and hawed, Mr. Bowden, having worked in Britain, knew that the guest was requesting an eraser, not a condom. The confusion was quickly erased, and the requested device was delivered to the guest.

Stephen Schechter, professor of political science at the Sage Colleges in Troy, New York, and co-director of Civitas, an international civic education group, recalls a bilingual blooper so stark that it could have caused a permanent rift. At the end of a visit to Syracuse in the early 1990's, Yakov Sokolov, a Russian partner in the organization, raised a glass to his local hosts. "My dear friends, thank you so much for your hostility," he said, flubbing the word "hospitality."

"It could have been a terrible diplomatic error," Dr. Schechter said, "but thanks to good humor it has become a thing of beauty, a metaphor for our ability to overcome cultural misunderstandings."

It is not just spoken language that can create havoc for those trying to make their way in an unfamiliar culture. Body language can also send out the wrong signals.

Neil Alumkal, an associate vice president of 5W Public Relations, a Manhattan firm, recounted the time he and some associates were in Bangkok taking a motorcycle taxi known as a *tuk tuk* to the Royal Dragon, a restaurant so large that waiters use roller skates to move around. Giving directions, they tried to demonstrate which establishment they meant by raising their feet toward the non-English-speaking driver and pointing to them, as though they were wearing skates.

He immediately pulled over in a rage and ordered them out of his vehicle. Unbeknownst to them, showing the soles of your feet to someone is a serious insult in Thailand and most other Asian countries as well as in much of the Middle East.

Even ingrained mannerisms that no one would pay attention to at home can make an unfavorable impression abroad. For Stacie Krajchir, who has worked on TV commercial shoots around the world and is a co-author of *The Itty Bitty Guide to Business Travel*, it was the posture she took when she was engaged in conversations that got her in hot water.

"I have a habit of putting my hands on my hips when I talk," said Ms. Krajchir, who lives in Venice Beach, California. "But in Bali, it was politely but pointedly noted that when you stand that way it's seen as a sign of rudeness or defiance."

She committed an even worse blunder in Thailand. While working on a commercial with children, she affectionately patted one of them on the head. Alas, in that country, she said, the gesture was seen as "a grave offense because the head is considered sacred." Once again, the cultural gaffe was brought to her attention, and she apologized.

The question of physical contact is one of the great imponderables of international travel. The rules on whom to touch, where, when, why, for how long, and with what degree of enthusiasm vary starkly from country to country.

"With touching, it's very complicated because it's so deeply embedded not just as a cultural thing but as an emotional thing," said Sheida Hodge, the worldwide managing director of the cross-cultural division of Berlitz International in Princeton, New Jersey. "Generally, American culture is not a touching culture, so when we are abroad we just have to watch closely and try to adapt."

For example, in France, a relationship-oriented culture, good friends greet members of the opposite sex with a peck on each cheek. To the French, a handshake is much more than a simple ritual for saying hello or goodbye but rather a means of making a personal connection, Ms. Hodge said. The Japanese bow to one another at varying angles, depending on their relative social standing, she said, but "because they are familiar with American habits, a handshake is O.K." Latin Americans like to throw their arms around colleagues' backs or grab them by the arm to show their friendliness, physical acts that can startle or discomfit Yankee visitors.

In general, she said, people in southern Europe and the Middle East are much more physical than Americans, though in most Muslim countries, social touching never takes place between the sexes.

With so many cultural land mines out there, is there any hope for the untutored American business traveler? Ms. Hodge, who is the author of *Global Smarts: The Art of Communicating and Deal Making Anywhere in the World* has a reassuring answer. "None of these faux pas are deal breakers," she said. "People think, 'Oh, I crossed my legs. There goes the contract.' It's not true."

Ms. Estey suggested that "it behooves anyone doing business in a country that is foreign to them to do some cultural homework." One source she recommended is a Web site called CultureGrams.com, a primer on the customs and geography of 180 countries ($199 a year for up to five users).

When Americans do make the effort to learn their international colleagues' communication styles, it can pay off. Donald C. Dowling, Jr.—a senior counsel at Proskauer Rose, a Manhattan law firm—speaks fluent Spanish, but he admits his French "is awful." So it was all the more surprising when the head of the Paris office, where he was doing a stint, toasted him at a Christmas party, throwing his arm around Mr. Dowling and announcing, "I love this guy because he speaks French."

"It took me a minute to figure out he wasn't making fun of me," Mr. Dowling said. "I think he just appreciated that I tried, unlike one American stationed in that office for two years, who managed to pick up a total of three words."

SOURCE: Perry Garfinkel, "On Keeping Your Foot Safely Out of Your Mouth," www.nytimes.com, July 13, 2004. Reprinted by permission of The New York Times Co.

Cultural communications are deeper and more complex than spoken or written messages. The essence of effective cross-cultural communication has more to do with releasing the right responses than with sending the "right" messages.

HALL AND HALL[1]

Multi-local online strategy . . . is about meeting global business objectives by tuning in to the cultural dynamics of their local markets.

"THINK GLOBALLY, INTERACT LOCALLY,"
New Media Age[2]

As the opening profile suggests, communication is a critical factor in the cross-cultural management issues discussed in this book, particularly those of an interpersonal nature, involving motivation, leadership, group interactions, and negotiation. Culture is conveyed and perpetuated through communication in one form or another. Culture and communication are so intricately intertwined that they are, essentially, synonymous.[3] By understanding this relationship, managers can move toward constructive intercultural management.

Communication, whether in the form of writing, talking, listening, or via the Internet, is an inherent part of a manager's role and takes up the majority of a manager's time on the job. Studies by Mintzberg demonstrate the importance of oral communication; he found that most managers spend between 50 and 90 percent of their time talking to people.[4] The ability of a manager to effectively communicate across cultural boundaries will largely determine the success of international business transactions or the output of a culturally diverse workforce. It is useful, then, to break down the elements involved in the communication process, both to understand the cross-cultural issues at stake and to maximize the process.

THE COMMUNICATION PROCESS

The term **communication** describes the process of sharing meaning by transmitting messages through media such as words, behavior, or material artifacts. Managers communicate to coordinate activities, to disseminate information, to motivate people, and to negotiate future plans. It is of vital importance, then, for a receiver to interpret the meaning of a particular communication in the way the sender intended. Unfortunately, the communication process (see Exhibit 4-1) involves stages during which meaning can be distorted. Anything that serves to undermine the communication of the intended meaning is typically referred to as **noise**.

The primary cause of noise stems from the fact that the sender and the receiver each exist in a unique, private world thought of as her or his life space. The context of that private world, largely based on culture, experience, relations, values, and so forth, determines the interpretation of meaning in communication. People filter, or selectively understand, messages consistent with their own expectations and perceptions of reality and their values and norms of behavior. The more dissimilar the cultures of those involved, the more the likelihood of misinterpretation. In this way, as Samovar, Porter, and Jain state, cultural factors pervade the communication process:

> *Culture not only dictates who talks with whom, about what, and how the communication proceeds, it also helps to determine how people encode messages, the meanings they have for messages, and the conditions and circumstances under which various messages may or may not be sent, noticed, or interpreted. In fact, our entire repertory of communicative behaviors is dependent largely on the culture in which we have been raised. Culture, consequently, is the foundation of communication. And, when cultures vary, communication practices also vary.*[5]

Communication, therefore, is a complex process of linking up or sharing the perceptual fields of sender and receiver; the perceptive sender builds a bridge to the life space of the receiver.[6] After the receiver interprets the message and draws a conclusion about what the sender meant, he or she will, in most cases, encode and send back a response, making communication a circular process.

The communication process is rapidly changing, however, as a result of technological developments, therefore propelling global business forward at a phenomenal growth rate. These changes are discussed later in this chapter.

EXHIBIT 4-1   The Communication Process

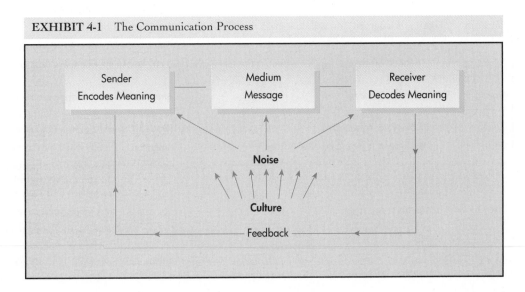

Cultural Noise in the Communication Process

In Japanese there are several words for "I" and several words for "you" but their use depends on the relationship between the speaker and the other person. In short, there is no "I" by itself; the "I" depends on the relationship.

H. C. TRIANDIS,
The Blackwell Handbook of Cross-cultural Management[7]

Because the focus in this text is on effective cross-cultural communication, it is important to understand what cultural variables cause noise in the communication process. This knowledge of **cultural noise**—the cultural variables that undermine the communications of intended meaning—will enable us to take steps to minimize that noise and so to improve communication.

When a member of one culture sends a message to a member of another culture, **intercultural communication** takes place. The message contains the meaning intended by the encoder. When it reaches the receiver, however, it undergoes a transformation in which the influence of the decoder's culture becomes part of the meaning.[8] Exhibit 4-2 provides an example of intercultural communication in which the meaning got all mixed up. Note how the attribution of behavior differs for each participant. **Attribution** is the process in which people look for an explanation of another person's behavior. When they realize that they do not understand another, they tend, say Hall and Hall, to blame their confusion on the other's "stupidity, deceit, or craziness."[9]

In the situation depicted in Exhibit 4-2, the Greek employee becomes frustrated and resigns after experiencing communication problems with his American boss. How could

EXHIBIT 4-2   Cultural Noise in International Communication

Behavior		Attribution	
American:	"How long will it take you to finish this report?"	American:	I asked him to participate.
		Greek:	His behavior makes no sense. He is the boss. Why doesn't he tell me?
Greek:	"I don't know. How long should it take?"	American:	He refuses to take responsibility.
		Greek:	I asked him for an order.
American:	"You are in the best position to analyze time requirements."	American:	I press him to take responsibility for his actions.
		Greek:	What nonsense: I'd better give him an answer.
Greek:	"10 days."	American:	He lacks the ability to estimate time; this time estimate is totally inadequate.
American:	"Take 15. Is it agreed? You will do it in 15 days?"	American:	I offer a contract.
		Greek:	These are my orders: 15 days.
In fact, the report needed 30 days of regular work. So the Greek worked day and night, but at the end of the 15th day, he still needed to do one more day's work.			
American:	"Where is the report?"	American:	I am making sure he fulfills his contract.
		Greek:	He is asking for the report.
		(Both attribute that it is not ready.)	
Greek:	"It will be ready tomorrow."		
American:	"But we agreed it would be ready today."	American:	I must teach him to fulfill a contract.
		Greek:	The stupid, incompetent boss! Not only did he give me the wrong orders, but he doesn't even appreciate that I did a 30-day job in 16 days.
The Greek hands in his resignation.		The American is surprised.	
		Greek:	I can't work for such a man.

SOURCE: Adapted from H. C. Triandis, *Interpersonal Behavior* (Monterey, California Brooks/Cole, 1997), 248; reported in Simcha Ronen, *Comparative and Multinational Management* (New York: John Wiley and Sons, 1986), 101–102.

this outcome have been avoided? We do not have much information about the people or the context of the situation, but we can look at some of the variables that might have been involved and use them as a basis for analysis.

THE CULTURE–COMMUNICATION LINK

The following sections examine underlying elements of culture that affect communication. The degree to which one is able to effectively communicate largely depends on how similar the other person's cultural expectations are to our own. However, cultural gaps can be overcome by prior learning and understanding of those variables and how to adjust to them.

Trust in Communication

The key ingredient in a successful alliance is trust.

JAMES R. HOUGHTON,
Former Chairman, Corning, Inc.[10]

Effective communication, and therefore collaboration in alliances across national boundaries, depends on the informal understandings among the parties that are based on the trust that has developed between them. However, the meaning of trust and how it is developed and communicated vary across societies. In China and Japan, for example, business transactions are based on networks of long-standing relationships based on trust rather than on the formal contracts and arm's-length relationships typical of the United States. When there is trust between parties, implicit understanding arises within communications. This understanding has numerous benefits in business, including encouraging communicators to overlook cultural differences and minimize problems. It allows communicators to adjust to unforeseen circumstances with less conflict than would be the case with formal contracts, and it facilitates open communication in exchanging ideas and information.[11] From his research on trust in global collaboration, John Child suggests the following guidelines for cultivating trust:

- Create a clear and calculated basis for mutual benefit. There must be realistic commitments and good intentions to honor them.
- Improve predictability: Strive to resolve conflicts and keep communication open.
- Develop mutual bonding through regular socializing and friendly contact.[12]

What can managers anticipate with regard to the level of trust in communications with people in other countries? If trust is based on how trustworthy we consider a person to be, then it must vary according to that society's expectations about whether that culture supports the norms and values that predispose people to behave credibly and benevolently. Are there differences across societies in those expectations of trust? Research by the World Values Study Group of 90,000 people in 45 societies provides some insight on cultural values regarding predisposition to trust. When we examine the percentage of respondents in each society who responded that "most people can be trusted," we can see that the Nordic countries and China had the highest predisposition to trust, followed by Canada, the United States, and Britain, while Brazil, Turkey, Romania, Slovenia, and Latvia had the lowest level of trust in people.[13]

The GLOBE Project

Results from the GLOBE research on culture, discussed in Chapter 3, provide some insight into culturally appropriate communication styles and expectations for the manager to use abroad. GLOBE researchers Javidan and House make the following observations:[14] For people in societies that ranked high on performance orientation—for example, the United States—presenting objective information in a direct and explicit way is an important and expected manner of communication; this compares with people in Russia or Greece—which ranked low on performance orientation—for whom hard facts and figures are not readily available or taken seriously. In those cases, a more indirect approach is preferred. People from countries ranking low on assertiveness, such as Sweden, also recoil from explicitness; their preference is for much two-way discourse and friendly relationships.

People ranking high on the "humane" dimension, such as those from Ireland and the Philippines, make avoiding conflict a priority and tend to communicate with the goal of being supportive of people rather than of achieving objective end results. This compares to people from France and Spain whose agenda is achievement of goals.

The foregoing provides examples of how to draw implications for appropriate communication styles from the research findings on cultural differences across societies. Astute global managers have learned that culture and communication are inextricably linked and that they should prepare themselves accordingly. Most will also suggest that you carefully watch and listen to how your hosts are communicating and to follow their lead.

Cultural Variables in the Communication Process

On a different level, it is also useful to be aware of cultural variables that can affect the communication process by influencing a person's perceptions; some of these variables have been identified by Samovar and Porter and discussed by Harris and Moran, and others.[15] These variables are as follows: attitudes, social organization, thought patterns, roles, language (spoken or written), nonverbal communication (including kinesic behavior, proxemics, paralanguage, and object language), and time. Although these variables are discussed separately in this text, their effects are interdependent and inseparable—or, as Hecht, Andersen, and Ribeau put it, "Encoders and decoders process nonverbal cues as a conceptual, multichanneled gestalt."[16]

Attitudes   We all know that our attitudes underlie the way we behave and communicate and the way we interpret messages from others. Ethnocentric attitudes are a particular source of noise in cross-cultural communication. In the incident described in Exhibit 4-2, both the American and the Greek are clearly attempting to interpret and convey meaning based on their own experiences of that kind of transaction. The American is probably guilty of stereotyping the Greek employee by quickly jumping to the conclusion that he is unwilling to take responsibility for the task and the scheduling.

This problem, **stereotyping**, occurs when a person assumes that every member of a society or subculture has the same characteristics or traits. Stereotyping is a common cause of misunderstanding in intercultural communication. It is an arbitrary, lazy, and often destructive way to find out about people. Astute managers are aware of the dangers of cultural stereotyping and deal with each person as an individual with whom they may form a unique relationship.

Social Organization   Our perceptions can be influenced by differences in values, approach, or priorities relative to the kind of social organizations to which we belong. These organizations may be based on one's nation, tribe, or religious sect, or they may consist of the members of a certain profession. Examples of such organizations include the Academy of Management or the United Auto Workers (UAW).[17]

Thought Patterns   The logical progression of reasoning varies widely around the world and greatly affects the communication process. Managers cannot assume that others use the same reasoning processes, as illustrated by the experience of a Canadian expatriate in Thailand:

> *While in Thailand a Canadian expatriate's car was hit by a Thai motorist who had crossed over the double line while passing another vehicle. After failing to establish that the fault lay with the Thai driver, the Canadian flagged down a police-man. After several minutes of seemingly futile discussion, the Canadian pointed out the double line in the middle of the road and asked the policeman directly, "What do these lines signify?" The policeman replied, "They indicate the center of the*

road and are there so I can establish just how far the accident is from that point."
The Canadian was silent. It had never occurred to him that the double line might
not mean "no passing allowed."[18]

In the Exhibit 4-2 scenario, perhaps the American did not realize that the Greek employee had a different rationale for his time estimate for the job. Because the Greek was not used to having to estimate schedules, he just took a guess, which he felt he had been forced to do.

Roles   Societies differ considerably in their perceptions of a manager's role. Much of the difference is attributable to their perceptions of who should make the decisions and who has responsibility for what. In the Exhibit 4-2 example, the American assumes that his role as manager is to delegate responsibility, to foster autonomy, and to practice participative management. He prescribes the role of the employee without any consideration of whether the employee will understand that role. The Greek's frame of reference leads him to think that the manager is the boss and should give the order about when to have the job completed. He interprets the American's behavior as breaking that frame of reference, and therefore he feels that the boss is "stupid and incompetent" for giving him the wrong order and for not recognizing and appreciating his accomplishment. The manager should have considered what behaviors Greek workers would expect of him and then either should have played that role or discussed the situation carefully, in a training mode.

Language   Spoken or written language, of course, is a frequent cause of miscommunication, stemming from a person's inability to speak the local language, a poor or too-literal translation, a speaker's failure to explain idioms, or a person missing the meaning conveyed through body language or certain symbols. Even among countries that share the same language, problems can arise from the subtleties and nuances inherent in the use of the language, as noted by George Bernard Shaw: "Britain and America are two nations separated by a common language." This problem can exist even within the same country among subcultures or subgroups.[19]

Many international executives tell stories about lost business deals or lost sales because of communication blunders:

> *When Pepsi Cola's slogan "Come Alive with Pepsi" was introduced in*
> *Germany, the company learned that the literal German translation of "come alive"*
> *is "come out of the grave."*
> *   A U.S. airline found a lack of demand for its "rendezvous lounges" on its*
> *Boeing 747s. They later learned that "rendezvous" in Portuguese refers to a room*
> *that is rented for prostitution.*[20]

More than just conveying objective information, language also conveys cultural and social understandings from one generation to the next.[21] Examples of how language reflects what is important in a society include the 6,000 different Arabic words used to describe camels and their parts and the 50 or more classifications of snow used by the Inuit, the Eskimo people of Canada.

Inasmuch as language conveys culture, technology, and priorities, it also serves to separate and perpetuate subcultures. In India, 14 official and many unofficial languages are used, and over 800 languages are spoken on the African continent.

Because of increasing workforce diversity around the world, the international business manager will have to deal with a medley of languages. For example, assembly-line workers at the Ford plant in Cologne, Germany, speak Turkish and Spanish as well as German. In Malaysia, Indonesia, and Thailand, many of the buyers and traders are Chinese. Not all Arabs speak Arabic; in Tunisia and Lebanon, for example, French is the language of commerce.[22]

International managers need either a good command of the local language or competent interpreters. The task of accurate translation to bridge cultural gaps is fraught with difficulties, as Schermerhorn discovered in his study of 153 Hong Kong Chinese bilinguals. He found a considerable difference in interpretation and response according to whether the medium used was Chinese or English, even after many experts were involved in the translation process.[23]

Even the direct translation of specific words does not guarantee the congruence of their meaning, as with the word "yes" used by Asians, which usually means only that they have heard you, and, often, that they are too polite to disagree. The Chinese, for example, through years of political control, have built into their communication culture a cautionary stance to avoid persecution by professing agreement with whatever opinion was held by the person questioning them.[24]

Politeness and a desire to say only what the listener wants to hear create noise in the communication process in much of the world. Often, even a clear translation does not help a person to understand what is meant because the encoding process has obscured the true message. With the poetic Arab language—replete with exaggeration, elaboration, and repetition—meaning is attributed more to how something is said rather than what is said.

For the American supervisor and Greek employee cited in Exhibit 4-2, it is highly likely that the American could have picked up some cues from the employee's body language, which probably implied problems with the interpretation of meaning. How might body language have created noise in this case?

Nonverbal Communication Behavior that communicates without words (although it often is accompanied by words) is called **nonverbal communication**. People will usually believe what they see over what they hear—hence the expression, "A picture is worth a thousand words." Studies show that these subtle messages account for between 65 and 93 percent of interpreted communication.[25] Even minor variations in body language, speech rhythms, and punctuality, for example, often cause mistrust and misperception of the situation among cross-national parties.[26] The media for such nonverbal communication can be categorized into four types: (1) kinesic behavior, (2) proxemics, (3) paralanguage, and (4) object language.

The term **kinesic behavior** refers to communication through body movements—posture, gestures, facial expressions, and eye contact. Although such actions may be universal, often their meaning is not. Because kinesic systems of meaning are culturally specific and learned, they cannot be generalized across cultures. Most people in the West would not correctly interpret many Chinese facial expressions; sticking out the tongue expresses surprise, a widening of the eyes shows anger, and scratching the ears and cheeks indicates happiness.[27] Research has shown for some time, however, that most people worldwide can recognize displays of the basic emotions of anger, disgust, fear, happiness, sadness, surprise, and contempt.[28]

Many businesspeople and visitors react negatively to what they feel are inappropriate facial expressions, without understanding the cultural meaning behind them. In his studies of cross-cultural negotiations, Graham observed that the Japanese feel uncomfortable when faced with the Americans' eye-to-eye posture. They are taught since childhood to bow their heads out of humility, whereas the automatic response of Americans is "look at me when I'm talking to you!"[29]

Subtle differences in eye behavior (called *oculesics*) can throw off a communication badly if they are not understood. Eye behavior includes differences not only in eye contact but also in the use of eyes to convey other messages, whether or not that involves mutual gaze. Edward T. Hall, author of the classic *The Silent Language*, explains the differences in eye contact between the British and the Americans. During speech, Americans will look straight at you, but the British keep your attention by looking away. The British will look at you when they have finished speaking, which signals that it is your turn to talk. The implicit rationale for this is that you can't interrupt people when they are not looking at you.[30]

It is helpful for U.S. managers to be aware of the many cultural expectations regarding posture and how they may be interpreted. In Europe or Asia, a relaxed posture in business meetings may be taken as bad manners or the result of poor upbringing. In

Korea you are expected to sit upright, with feet squarely on the floor, and to speak slowly, showing a blending of body and spirit.

Managers can also familiarize themselves with the many different interpretations of hand and finger signals around the world, some of which may represent obscene gestures. Of course, we cannot expect to change all of our ingrained, natural kinesic behavior, but we can be aware of what it means to others. We also can learn to understand the kinesic behavior of others and the role it plays in their society, as well as how it can affect business transactions. Misunderstanding the meanings of body movements—or an ethnocentric attitude toward the "proper" behavior—can have negative repercussions, as illustrated in the opening profile of this chapter.

Proxemics deals with the influence of proximity and space on communication—both personal space and office space or layout. Americans expect office layout to provide private space for each person, and usually a larger and more private space as one goes up the hierarchy. In much of Asia, the custom is open office space, with people at all levels working and talking in close proximity to one another. Space communicates power in both Germany and the United States, evidenced by the desire for a corner office or one on the top floor. The importance of French officials, however, is made clear by a position in the middle of subordinates, communicating that they have a central position in an information network, where they can stay informed and in control.[31]

Do you ever feel vaguely uncomfortable and start moving backward slowly when someone is speaking to you? This is because that person is invading your "bubble"—your personal space. Personal space is culturally patterned, and foreign spatial cues are a common source of misinterpretation. When someone seems aloof or pushy, it often means that she or he is operating under subtly different spatial rules.

Hall and Hall suggest that cultural differences affect the programming of the senses and that space, perceived by all the senses, is regarded as a form of territory to be protected.[32] South Americans, Southern and Eastern Europeans, Indonesians, and Arabs are **high-contact cultures**, preferring to stand close, touch a great deal, and experience a "close" sensory involvement. On the other hand, North Americans, Asians, and Northern Europeans are **low-contact cultures** and prefer much less sensory involvement, standing farther apart and touching far less. They have a "distant" style of body language.[33]

Interestingly, high-contact cultures are mostly located in warmer climates, and low-contact cultures in cooler climates. Americans are relatively nontouching, automatically standing at a distance so that an outstretched arm will touch the other person's ear.[34] Standing any closer than that is regarded as invading intimate space. However, Americans and Canadians certainly expect a warm handshake and maybe a pat on the back from closer friends, though not the very warm double handshake of the Spaniards (clasping the forearm with the left hand). The Japanese, considerably less **haptic (touching)**, do not shake hands; an initial greeting between a Japanese and a Spanish businessperson would be uncomfortable for both parties if they were untrained in cultural haptics.

When considering high- and low-contact cultures, we can trace a correlation between Hofstede's cultural variables of individualism and collectivism and the types of kinesic and proxemic behaviors people display. Generally, people from individualistic cultures are more remote and distant, whereas those from collectivist cultures are interdependent: They tend to work, play, live, and sleep in close proximity.[35]

The term **paralanguage** refers to how something is said rather than the content—the rate of speech, the tone and inflection of voice, other noises, laughing, or yawning. The culturally aware manager learns how to interpret subtle differences in paralanguage, including silence. Silence is a powerful communicator. It may be a way of saying no, of being offended, or of waiting for more information to make a decision. There is considerable variation in the use of silence in meetings. While Americans get uncomfortable after 10 or 15 seconds of silence, Chinese prefer to think the situation over for 30 seconds before speaking. The typical scenario between Americans and Chinese, then, is that the American gets impatient, says something to break the silence, and offends the Chinese by interrupting his or her chain of thought and comfort level with the subject.[36] Graham, a researcher on international negotiations, taped a bargaining session held at Toyota's U.S. headquarters in California. The U.S. executive had made a proposal to open a new production facility in Brazil and was waiting for a response from the three Japanese executives, who sat with lowered eyes and hands folded on the table. After about 30 seconds—an eternity to Americans, accustomed to a conversational response time of a few tenths of a second— the American blurted out that they were getting nowhere—and the meeting ended in a stalemate. More sensitivity to cultural differences in communication might have led him to wait longer or perhaps to prompt some further response through another polite question.[37]

The term **object language**, or **material culture**, refers to how we communicate through material artifacts, whether architecture, office design and furniture, clothing, cars, or cosmetics. Material culture communicates what people hold as important. In Mexico, a visiting international executive or salesperson is advised to take time out, before negotiating business, to show appreciation for the surrounding architecture, which is prized by Mexicans.

Time   Another variable that communicates culture is the way people regard and use time (see also Chapter 3). To Brazilians, relative punctuality communicates the level of importance of those involved. To Middle Easterners, time is something controlled by the will of Allah.

To initiate effective cross-cultural business interactions, managers should know the difference between *monochronic time systems* and *polychronic time systems* and how they affect communications. Hall and Hall explain that in **monochronic cultures** (Switzerland, Germany, and the United States), time is experienced in a linear way, with a past, a present, and a future, and time is treated as something to be spent, saved, made up, or wasted. Classified and compartmentalized, time serves to order life. This attitude is a learned part of Western culture, probably starting with the Industrial Revolution. Monochronic people, found in individualistic cultures, generally concentrate on one thing at a time, adhere to time commitments, and are accustomed to short-term relationships.

In contrast, **polychronic cultures** tolerate many things occurring simultaneously and emphasize involvement with people. Two Latin friends, for example, will put an important conversation ahead of being on time for a business meeting, thus communicating the priority of relationships over material systems. Polychronic people—Latin Americans, Arabs, and those from other collectivist cultures—may focus on several things at once, be highly distractible, and change plans often.[38]

The relationship between time and space also affects communication. Polychronic people, for example, are likely to hold open meetings, moving around and conducting transactions with one party and then another, rather than compartmentalizing meeting topics, as do monochronic people.

The nuances and distinctions regarding cultural differences in nonverbal communication are endless. The various forms are listed in Exhibit 4-3; wise intercultural managers will take careful account of the role that such differences might play.

EXHIBIT 4-3   Forms of Nonverbal Communication

- Facial expressions
- Body posture
- Gestures with hands, arms, head, etc.
- Interpersonal distance (proxemics)
- Touching, body contact
- Eye contact
- Clothing, cosmetics, hairstyles, jewelry
- Paralanguage (voice pitch and inflections, rate of speech, and silence)
- Color symbolism
- Attitude toward time and the use of time in business and social interactions
- Food symbolism and social use of meals

What aspects of nonverbal communication might have created noise in the interactions between the American supervisor and the Greek employee in Exhibit 4-2? Undoubtedly, some cues could have been picked up in the kinesics behavior of each person. It was the responsibility of the manager, in particular, to notice any indications from the Greek that could have prompted him to change his communication pattern or assumptions. Face-to-face communication permits the sender of the message to get immediate feedback, verbal and nonverbal, and thus to have some idea as to how that message is being received and whether additional information is needed. What aspects of the Greek employee's kinesic behavior or paralanguage might have been evident to a more culturally sensitive manager? Did both parties' sense of time affect the communication process?

Context

East Asians live in relatively complex social networks with prescribed role relations; attention to context is, therefore, important for their effective functioning. In contrast, westerners live in less constraining social worlds that stress independence and allow them to pay less attention to context.

RICHARD E. NISBETT,
September 2005[39]

A major differentiating factor that is a primary cause of noise in the communication process is that of context—which actually incorporates many of the variables discussed earlier. The **context** in which the communication takes place affects the meaning and interpretation of the interaction. Cultures are known to be high- or low-context cultures, with a relative range in between.[40] In **high-context cultures** (Asia, the Middle East, Africa, and the Mediterranean), feelings and thoughts are not explicitly expressed; instead, one has to read between the lines and interpret meaning from one's general understanding. Two such high-context cultures are those of South Korea and Arab cultures. In such cultures, key information is embedded in the context rather than made explicit. People make assumptions about what the message means through their knowledge of the person or the surroundings. In these cultures, most communication takes place within a context of extensive information networks resulting from close personal relationships. See the following Management Focus for further explanation of the Asian communication style.

In **low-context cultures** (Germany, Switzerland, Scandinavia, and North America), where personal and business relationships are more compartmentalized, communication media have to be more explicit. Feelings and thoughts are expressed in words, and information is more readily available. Westerners focus more on the individual, and therefore tend to view events as the result of specific agents, while easterners view events in a broader and longer-term context.[41]

In cross-cultural communication between high- and low-context people, a lack of understanding may preclude reaching a solution, and conflict may arise. Germans, for example, will expect considerable detailed information before making a business decision, whereas Arabs will base their decisions more on knowledge of the people involved—the information is present, but it is implicit.

People in high-context cultures expect others to understand unarticulated moods, subtle gestures, and environmental clues that people from low-context cultures simply do not process. Misinterpretation and misunderstanding often result.[42] People from high-context cultures perceive those from low-context cultures as too talkative, too obvious, and redundant. Those from low-context cultures perceive high-context people as nondisclosing, sneaky, and mysterious. Research indicates, for example, that Americans find talkative people more attractive, whereas Koreans, high-context people, perceive less verbal people as more attractive. Finding the right balance between low- and high-context communication can be tricky, as Hall and Hall point out: "Too much

Management Focus

Oriental Poker Face: Eastern Deception or Western Inscrutability?

Among many English expressions that are likely to offend those of us whose ancestry may be traced to the Far East, two stand out quite menacingly for me: "Oriental poker face" and "idiotic Asian smile." The former refers to the supposedly inscrutable nature of a facial expression that apparently reflects no particular state of mind, while the latter pokes fun at a face fixed with a perpetually friendly smile. Westerners' perplexity, when faced with either, arises from the impression that these two diametrically opposed masquerading strategies prevent them from extracting useful information—at least the type of information that at least they could process with a reasonable measure of confidence—about the feelings of the person before them. An Asian face that projects no signs of emotion, then, seems to most Westerners nothing but a facade. It does not matter whether that face wears an unsightly scowl or a shining ray; a facial expression they cannot interpret poses a genuine threat.

Compassionate and sympathetic to their perplexity as I may be, I am also insulted by the Western insensitivity to the significant roles that subtle signs play in Asian cultures. Every culture has its unique modus operandi for communication. Western culture, for example, apparently emphasizes the importance of direct communication. Not only are the communicators taught to look directly at each other when they convey a message, but they also are encouraged to come right to the point of the message. Making bold statements or asking frank questions in a less than diplomatic manner (i.e., "That was really a very stupid thing to do!" or "Are you interested in me?") is rarely construed as rude or indiscreet. Even embarrassingly blunt questions such as "Senator Hart, have you ever had sexual intercourse with anyone other than your wife?" are tolerated most of the time. Asians, on the other hand, find this direct communicative communication style quite unnerving. In many social interactions, they avoid direct eye contact. They "see" each other without necessarily looking directly at each other, and they gather information about inner states of mind without asking even the most discreet or understated questions. Many times they talk

around the main topic, and, yet, they succeed remarkably well in understanding one another's position. (At least they believe they have developed a reasonably clear understanding.)

To a great extent, Asian communication is listening-centered; the ability to listen (and a special talent for detecting various communicative cues) is treated as equally important as, if not more important than, the ability to speak. This contrasts clearly with the American style of communication that puts the utmost emphasis on verbal expression; the speaker carries most of the burden for ensuring that everyone understands his or her message. An Asian listener, however, is prone to blame himself or herself for failing to reach a comprehensive understanding from the few words and gestures performed by the speaker. With this heavier burden placed on the listener, an Asian speaker does not feel obliged to send clearly discernible message cues (at least not nearly so much as he or she is obliged to do in American cultural contexts). Not obligated to express themselves without interruption, Asians use silence as a tool in communication. Silence, by most Western conventions, represents discontinuity of communication and creates a feeling of discomfort and anxiety. In the Orient, however, silence is not only comfortably tolerated but is considered a desirable form of expression. Far from being a sign of displeasure or animosity, it serves as an integral part of the communication process, used for reflecting on messages previously exchanged and for carefully crafting thoughts before uttering them.

It is not outlandish at all, then, for Asians to view Americans as unnecessarily talkative and lacking in the ability to listen. For the Asian, it is the American who projects a mask of confidence by being overly expressive both verbally and nonverbally. Since the American style of communication places less emphasis on the act of listening than on speaking, Asians suspect that their American counterparts fail to pick up subtle and astute communicative signs in conversation. To one with a cultural outlook untrained in reading those signs, an inscrutable face represents no more than a menacing or amusing mask.

SOURCE: Dr. Jin Kim, State University of New York–Plattsburgh. Copyright © 1995 by Dr. Jin Kim. Used with permission of Dr. Kim.

information leads people to feel they are being talked down to; too little information can mystify them or make them feel left out."[43] Exhibit 4-4 shows the relative level of context in various countries.

The importance of understanding the role of context and nonverbal language to avoid misinterpretation is illustrated in the Comparative Management in Focus: Communicating with Arabs.

EXHIBIT 4-4   Cultural Context and Its Effects on Communication

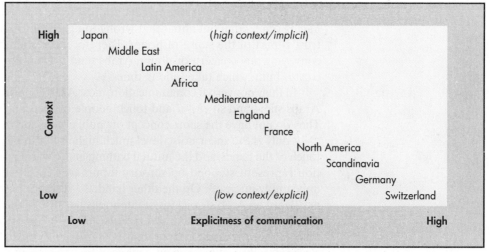

SOURCE: Based on information drawn from Edward T. Hall and M. R. Hall, *Understanding Cultural Differences* (Yarmouth, ME: Intercultural Press, 1990); and Martin Rosch, "Communications: Focal Point of Culture," *Management International Review* 27, no. 4 (1987): 60.

Comparative Management in Focus

Communicating with Arabs

In the Middle East, the meaning of a communication is implicit and interwoven, and consequently much harder for Americans, accustomed to explicit and specific meanings, to understand.

Arabs are warm, emotional, and quick to explode: "Sounding off" is regarded as a safety valve.[44] In fact, the Arabic language aptly communicates the Arabic culture, one of emotional extremes. The language contains the means for overexpression, many adjectives, words that allow for exaggeration, and metaphors to emphasize a position. What is said is often not as important as how it is said.[45] Eloquence and flowery speech are admired for their own sake, regardless of the content. Loud speech is used for dramatic effect.

At the core of Middle Eastern culture are friendship, honor, religion, and traditional hospitality. Family, friends, and connections are very important on all levels in the Middle East and will take precedence over business transactions. Arabs do business with people, not companies, and they make commitments to people, not contracts. A phone call to the right person can help to get around seemingly insurmountable obstacles. An Arab expects loyalty from friends, and it is understood that giving and receiving favors is an inherent part of the relationship; no one says no to a request for a favor. A lack of follow-through is assumed to be beyond the friend's control.[46]

Because hospitality is a way of life and highly symbolic, a visitor must be careful not to reject it by declining refreshment or rushing into business discussions. Part of that hospitality is the elaborate system of greetings and the long period of getting acquainted, perhaps taking up the entire first meeting. While the handshake may seem limp, the rest of the greeting is not. Kissing on the cheeks is common among men, as is hand-holding between male friends. However, any public display of intimacy between men and women is strictly forbidden by the Arab social code.

Women play little or no role in business or entertainment; the Middle East is a male-dominated society, and it is impolite to inquire about women. Other nonverbal taboos include showing the soles of one's feet and using the left (unclean) hand to eat or pass something. In discussions, slouching in a seat or leaning against a wall communicates a lack of respect.

The Arab society also values honor. Harris and Moran explain: "Honor, social prestige, and a secure place in society are brought about when conformity is achieved. When one fails to conform, this is considered to be damning and leads to a degree of shame."[47] Shame results not just from doing something wrong but from having others find out about that wrongdoing. Establishing a climate of honesty and trust is part of the sense of honor. Therefore, considerable tact is needed to avoid conveying any concern or doubt. Arabs tend to be quite introverted until a mutual trust is built, which takes a long time.[48]

In their nonverbal communication, most Arab countries are high-contact cultures. Arabs stand and sit closer and touch people of the same sex more than Westerners. They do not have the same concept of "public" and "private" space, or as Hall puts it, "Not only is the sheer noise level much higher, but the piercing look of the eyes, the touch of the hands, and the mutual bathing in the warm moist breath during conversation represent stepped-up sensory inputs to a level which many Europeans find unbearably intense.[49] On the other hand, the distance preferred by North Americans may leave an Arab suspicious of intentions because of the lack of olfactory contact.[50]

The Muslim expression *Bukra insha Allah*—"Tomorrow if Allah wills"—explains much about the Arab culture and its approach to business transactions. A cultural clash typically occurs when an American tries to give an Arab a deadline. "I am going to Damascus tomorrow morning and will have to have my car tonight," is a sure way to get the mechanic to stop work," explains Hall, "because to give another person a deadline in this part of the world is to be rude, pushy, and demanding."[51] In such instances, the attitude toward time communicates as loudly as words.

In verbal interactions, managers must be aware of different patterns of Arab thought and communication. Compared to the direct, linear fashion of American communication, Arabs tend to meander: They start with social talk, discuss business for a while, loop round to social and general issues, then back to business, and so on.[52] American impatience and insistence on sticking to the subject will "cut off their loops," triggering confusion and dysfunction.

Exhibit 4-5 illustrates some of the sources of noise that are likely to interfere in the communication process between Americans and Arabs.

EXHIBIT 4-5   Miscommunication Between Americans and Arabs Caused by Cross-cultural Noise

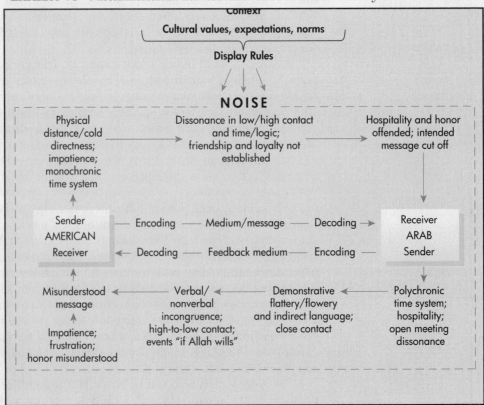

For people doing business in the Middle East, the following are some useful guidelines for effective communication:

- Be patient. Recognize the Arab attitude toward time and hospitality—take time to develop friendship and trust, for these are prerequisites for any social or business transactions.

- Recognize that people and relationships matter more to Arabs than the job, company, or contract—conduct business personally, not by correspondence or telephone.

- Avoid expressing doubts or criticism when others are present—recognize the importance of honor and dignity to Arabs.

- Adapt to the norms of body language, flowery speech, and circuitous verbal patterns in the Middle East, and don't be impatient to "get to the point."

- Expect many interruptions in meetings, delays in schedules, and changes in plans.[53]

Communication Channels

In addition to the variables related to the sender and receiver of a message, the variables linked to the channel itself and the context of the message must be taken into consideration. These variables include fast or slow messages and information flows, as well as different types of media.

Information Systems   Communication in organizations varies according to where and how it originates, the channels, and the speed at which it flows, whether it is formal or informal, and so forth. The type of organizational structure, the staffing policies, and the leadership style will affect the nature of an organization's information system.

As an international manager, it is useful to know where and how information originates and the speed at which it flows, both internally and externally. In centralized organizational structures, as in South America, most information originates from top managers. Workers take less responsibility to keep managers informed than in a typical company in the United States, where delegation results in information flowing from the staff to the managers. In a decision-making system where many people are involved, such as the **ringi system** of consensus decision making in Japan, the expatriate needs to understand that there is a systematic pattern for information flow.[54]

Context also affects information flow. In high-context cultures (such as in the Middle East), information spreads rapidly and freely because of the constant close contact and the implicit ties among people and organizations. Information flow is often informal. In low-context cultures (such as Germany or the United States), information is controlled and focused, and thus it does not flow so freely.[55] Compartmentalized roles and office layouts stifle information channels; information sources tend to be more formal.

It is crucial for an expatriate manager to find out how to tap into a firm's informal sources of information. In Japan, employees usually have a drink together on the way home from work, and this becomes an essential source of information. However, such communication networks are based on long-term relationships in Japan (and in other high-context cultures). The same information may not be readily available to "outsiders." A considerable barrier in Japan separates strangers from familiar friends, a situation that discourages communication.

Americans are more open and talk freely about almost anything, whereas Japanese will disclose little about their inner thoughts or private issues. Americans are willing to have a wide "public self," disclosing their inner reactions verbally and physically. In contrast, the Japanese prefer to keep their responses largely to their "private self." The Japanese expose only a small portion of their thoughts; they reduce, according to Barnlund, "the unpredictability and emotional intensity of personal encounters."[56] Cultural clashes between the public and private selves in intercultural communication between Americans and Japanese result when each party forces its cultural norms of communication on the other. In the American style, the American's cultural norms of explicit communication impose on the Japanese by invading the person's private self. The

Japanese style of implicit communication causes a negative reaction from the American because of what is perceived as too much formality and ambiguity, which wastes time.[57]

Cultural variables in information systems and context underlie the many differences in communication style between Japanese and Americans. Exhibit 4-6 shows some specific differences. The Japanese *ningensei* ("human beingness") style of communication

EXHIBIT 4-6   Difference Between Japanese and American Communication Styles

Japanese *Ningensei* Style of Communication	U.S. Adversarial Style of Communication
1. Indirect verbal and nonverbal communication	1. More direct verbal and nonverbal communication
2. Relationship communication	2. More task communication
3. Discourages confrontational strategies	3. Confrontational strategies more acceptable
4. Strategically ambiguous communication	4. Prefers more to-the-point communication
5. Delayed feedback	5. More immediate feedback
6. Patient, longer-term negotiators	6. Shorter-term negotiators
7. Uses fewer words	7. Favors verbosity
8. Distrustful of skillful verbal communicators	8. Exalts verbal eloquence
9. Group orientation	9. More individualistic orientation
10. Cautious, tentative	10. More assertive, self-assured
11. Complementary communicators	11. More publicly critical communication
12. Softer, heartlike logic	12. Harder, analytic logic preferred
13. Sympathetic, empathetic, complex use of pathos	13. Favors logos, reason
14. Expresses and decodes complex relational strategies and nuances	14. Expresses and decodes complex logos, cognitive nuances
15. Avoids decision making in public	15. Frequent decision making in public
16. Makes decisions in private venues, away from public eye	16. Frequent decision in public at negotiating tables
17. Decisions via *ringi* and *nemawashi* (complete consensus process)	17. Decisions by majority rule and public compromise is more commonplace
18. Uses go-betweens for decision making	18. More extensive use of direct person-to-person, player-to-player interaction for decisions
19. Understatement and hesitation in verbal and nonverbal communication	19. May publicly speak in superlatives, exaggerations, nonverbal projection
20. Uses qualifiers, tentativeness, humility as communicator	20. Favors fewer qualifiers, more ego-centered
21. Receiver/listening-centered	21. More speaker- and message-centered
22. Inferred meanings, looks beyond words to nuances, nonverbal communication	22. More face-value meaning, more denotative
23. Shy, reserved communicators	23. More publicly self-assertive
24. Distaste for purely business transactions	24. Prefers to "get down to business" or "nitty gritty"
25. Mixes business and social communication	25. Tends to keep business negotiating more separated from social communication
26. Utilizes *matomari* or "hints" for achieving group adjustment and saving face in negotiating	26. More directly verbalizes management's preference at negotiating tables
27. Practices *haragei* or "belly logic" and communication	27. Practices more linear, discursive, analytical logic; greater reverence for cognitive than for affective

SOURCE: Reprinted from A. Goldman, "The Centrality of 'Ningensei' to Japanese Negotiating and Interpersonal Relationships: Implications for U.S.-Japanese Communication," *International Journal of Intercultural Relations* 18, no. 1 (Winter 1994), with permission from Elsevier.

refers to the preference for humanity, reciprocity, a receiver orientation, and an underlying distrust of words and analytic logic.[58] The Japanese believe that true intentions are not readily revealed in words or contracts but are, in fact, masked by them. In contrast to the typical American's verbal agility and explicitness, Japanese behaviors and communications are directed to defend and give face for everyone concerned; to do so, they avoid public disagreements at all costs. In cross-cultural negotiations, this last point is essential.

The speed with which we try to use information systems is another key variable that needs attention to avoid misinterpretation and conflict. Americans expect to give and receive information very quickly and clearly, moving through details and stages in a linear fashion to the conclusion. They usually use various media for fast messages—letters or emails giving all the facts and plans up front, faxes, and familiar relationships. In contrast, the French use the slower message channels of deep relationships, culture, and sometimes mediators to exchange information. A French written communication will be tentative, with subsequent letters slowly building up to a new proposal. The French preference for written communication, even for informal interactions, echoes the formality of their relationships—and results in a slowing down of message transmission that often seems unnecessary to Americans. Jean-Louis Reynal, a plant manager at Citröen, explains that "it wouldn't be too much of an exaggeration to say that, until they are written, until they are entrusted to the blackboard, the notepad, or the flip chart, ideas have no reality for the French manager. You could even say that writing is an indispensable aid to 'being' for us."[59]

In short, it behooves Americans to realize that, because most of the world exchanges information through slower message media, it is wise to schedule more time for transactions, develop patience, and learn to get at needed information in more subtle ways—after building rapport and taking time to observe the local system for exchanging information.

We have seen that cross-cultural misinterpretation can result from noise in the actual transmission of the message—the choice or speed of media. Interpreting the meaning of a message can thus be as much a function of the transmission channel (or medium) as it is of examining the message itself.

INFORMATION TECHNOLOGY: GOING GLOBAL AND ACTING LOCAL

> *All information is local; IT systems can connect every corner of the globe, but IT managers are learning they have to pay attention to regional differences.*
>
> COMPUTERWORLD[60]

> *Deploying B2B e-commerce technology [globally] . . . becomes exponentially more difficult because systems must address concerns not germane to domestic networks, such as language translation, currency conversion and even cultural differences.*
>
> INTERNETWEEK[61]

Using the Internet as a global medium for communication has enabled companies of all sizes to quickly develop a presence in many markets around the world—and, in fact, has enabled them to "go global." However, their global reach cannot alone translate into global business. Those companies are learning that they have to adapt their e-commerce and their enterprise resource planning (ERP) applications to regional idiosyncrasies beyond translation or content management issues; even asking for a name or an email address can incur resistance in many countries where people do not like to give out personal information.[62] While communication over the Internet is clearly not as personal as face-to-face cross-cultural communication, those transactions must still be regionalized and personalized to adjust to differences in language, culture, local laws, and business models, as well as differences in the level of development in the local telecommunications infrastructure. Yet, if the Internet is a global medium for communication, why do so many U.S. companies treat the Web as a U.S.-centric phenomenon? Giving preference to some geographic regions, languages, and cultures is "a short-sighted business decision that will result in diminished brand equity, market share, profits and global leadership."[63] With an annual predicted growth rate of 70 percent in non–English-language sites and usage, this soon puts English-language sites in the minority.[64]

It seems essential, then, that a global online strategy must also be multilocal. The impersonal nature of the Web must somehow be adapted to local cultures to establish relationships and create customer loyalty. Effective technological communication requires even more cultural sensitivity than face-to-face communication because of the inability to assess reactions and get feedback, or even to retain contact in many cases. It is still people, after all, who respond to and interact with other people through the medium of the Internet, and those people interpret and respond according to their own languages and cultures, as well as their local business practices and expectations. In Europe, for example, significant differences in business cultures and e-business technology have slowed e-business progress there. However, some companies are making progress in pan-European integration services, such as *leEurope*, which aims to cross language, currency, and cultural barriers. Specifically, *leEurope* is building a set of services "to help companies tie their back-end e-business systems together across European boundaries through a series of mergers involving regional e-business integrators in more than a dozen countries."[65]

MANAGING CROSS-CULTURAL COMMUNICATION

Steps toward effective intercultural communication include the development of cultural sensitivity, careful encoding, selective transmission, careful decoding, and appropriate follow-up actions.

Developing Cultural Sensitivity

When acting as a sender, a manager must make it a point to know the receiver and to encode the message in a form that will most likely be understood as intended. On the manager's part, this requires an awareness of his or her own cultural baggage and how it affects the communication process. In other words, what kinds of behaviors does the message imply, and how will they be perceived by the receiver? The way to anticipate the most likely meaning that the receiver will attach to the message is to internalize honest cultural empathy with that person. What is the cultural background—the societal, economic, and organizational context—in which this communication is taking place? What are this person's expectations regarding the situation, what are the two parties' relative positions, and what might develop from this communication? What kinds of transactions and behaviors is this person used to? Cultural sensitivity (discussed in Chapter 3) is really just a matter of understanding the other person, the context, and how the person will respond to the context. Americans, unfortunately, have a rather negative reputation overseas of not being culturally sensitive. One not-for-profit group, called Business for Diplomatic Action, has the following advice for Americans when doing business abroad, in its attempts to counteract the stereotypical American traits such as boastfulness, loudness, and speed:

- **Read a map:** Familiarize yourself with the local geography to avoid making insulting mistakes.
- **Dress up:** In some countries, casual dress is a sign of disrespect
- **Talk small:** Talking about wealth, power, or status—corporate or personal—can create resentment.
- **No slang:** Even casual profanity is unacceptable
- **Slow down:** Americans talk fast, eat fast, move fast, live fast. Many cultures do not.
- **Listen as much as you talk:** Ask people you're visiting about themselves and their way of life.
- **Speak lower and slower:** A loud voice is often perceived as bragging.
- **Religious restraint:** In many countries, religion is not a subject for public discussion.
- **Political restraint:** Steer clear of this subject. If someone is attacking U.S. politicians or policies, agree to disagree.[66]

Careful Encoding

In translating his or her intended meaning into symbols for cross-cultural communication, the sender must use words, pictures, or gestures that are appropriate to the receiver's frame of reference. Of course, language training is invaluable, but senders should also avoid idioms and regional sayings (such as "Go fly a kite" or "Foot the bill") in a translation, or even in English when speaking to a non-American who knows little English.

Literal translation, then, is a limited answer to language differences. Even for people in English-speaking countries, words may have different meanings.[67] Ways to avoid problems are to speak slowly and clearly, avoid long sentences and colloquial expressions, and explain things in several different ways and through several media, if possible.[68] However, even though English is in common use around the world for business transactions, the manager's efforts to speak the local language will greatly improve the climate. Sometimes people from other cultures resent the assumption by English-speaking executives that everyone else will speak English.

Language translation is only part of the encoding process; the message also is expressed in nonverbal language. In the encoding process, the sender must ensure congruence between the nonverbal and the verbal message. In encoding a message, therefore, it is useful to be as objective as possible and not to rely on personal interpretations. To further clarify their messages, managers can hand out written summaries of verbal presentations and use visual aids, such as graphs or pictures. A good general guide is to move slowly, wait, and take cues from the receivers.

Selective Transmission

The type of medium chosen for the message depends on the nature of the message, its level of importance, the context and expectations of the receiver, the timing involved, and the need for personal interaction, among other factors. Typical media include email, letters or memos, reports, meetings, telephone calls, teleconferences, videoconferences, or face-to-face conversations. The secret is to find out how communication is transmitted in the local organization—how much is downward versus upward or vertical versus horizontal, how the grapevine works, and so on. In addition, the cultural variables discussed earlier need to be considered: whether the receiver is from a high- or low-context culture, whether he or she is used to explicit or implicit communication, and what speed and routing of messages will be most effective.

For the most part, it is best to use face-to-face interaction for relationship building or for other important transactions, particularly in intercultural communications, because of the lack of familiarity between parties. Personal interactions give the manager the opportunity to get immediate verbal and visual feedback and to make rapid adjustments in the communication process.

International dealings are often long-distance, of course, limiting the opportunity for face-to-face communication. However, personal rapport can be established or enhanced through telephone calls or videoconferencing and through trusted contacts. Modern electronic media can be used to break down communication barriers by reducing waiting periods for information, clarifying issues, and allowing instant consultation. Global telecommunications and computer networks are changing the face of cross-cultural communication through the faster dissemination of information within the receiving organization. Ford of Europe uses videoconferencing for engineers in Britain and Germany to consult about quality problems. Through the video monitors, they examine one another's engineering diagrams and usually find a solution that gets the factory moving again in a short time.[69]

Careful Decoding of Feedback

Timely and effective feedback channels can also be set up to assess a firm's general communication about the progression of its business and its general management principles. The best means for getting accurate feedback is through face-to-face interaction because this allows the manager to hear, see, and immediately sense how a message is being interpreted.

When visual feedback on important issues is not possible or appropriate, it is a good idea to use several means of attaining feedback, in particular, employing third parties.

Decoding is the process of translating the received symbols into the interpreted message. The main causes of incongruence are (1) the receiver misinterprets the message, (2) the receiver encodes his or her return message incorrectly, or (3) the sender misinterprets the feedback. Two-way communication is thus essential for important issues so that successive efforts can be made until an understanding has been achieved. Asking other colleagues to help interpret what is going on is often a good way to break a cycle of miscommunication.

Perhaps the most important means for avoiding miscommunication is to practice careful decoding by improving one's listening and observation skills. A good listener practices projective listening, or empathetic listening—listening without interruption or evaluation to the full message of the speaker, attempting to recognize the feelings behind the words and nonverbal cues, and understanding the speaker's perspective.

At the multinational corporation (MNC) level, avenues of communication and feedback among parent companies and subsidiaries can be kept open through telephone calls, regular meetings and visits, reports, and plans—all of which facilitate cooperation, performance control, and the smooth running of the company. Communication among far-flung operations can be best managed by setting up feedback systems and liaison people. The headquarters people should maintain considerable flexibility in cooperating with local managers and allowing them to deal with the local context as they see fit.

Follow-up Actions

Managers communicate through both action and inaction. Therefore, to keep open the lines of communication, feedback, and trust, managers must follow through with action on what has been discussed and then agreed upon—typically a contract, which is probably the most important formal business communication. Unfortunately, the issue of contract follow-through is a particularly sensitive one across cultures because of the different interpretations regarding what constitutes a contract (perhaps a handshake, perhaps a full legal document) and what actions should result. Trust, future communications, and future business are based on such interpretations, and it is up to managers to understand them and to follow through on them.

The management of cross-cultural communication depends largely on a manager's personal abilities and behavior. Those behaviors that researchers indicate to be most important to intercultural communication effectiveness (ICE) are listed here, as reviewed by Ruben:

1. Respect (conveyed through eye contact, body posture, voice tone, and pitch)
2. Interaction posture (the ability to respond to others in a descriptive, nonevaluative, and nonjudgmental way)
3. Orientation to knowledge (recognizing that one's knowledge, perception, and beliefs are valid only for oneself and not for everyone else)
4. Empathy
5. Interaction management
6. Tolerance for ambiguity
7. Other-oriented role behavior (one's capacity to be flexible and to adopt different roles for the sake of greater group cohesion and group communication)[70]

Whether at home or abroad, certain personal capabilities facilitate effective intercultural communication; these abilities can help the expatriate to adapt to the host country and enable productive working relations to develop in the long term. Researchers have established a relationship between personality traits and behaviors and the ability to adapt to the host-country's cultural environment.[71] What is seldom pointed out, however, is that communication is the mediating factor between those behaviors and the relative level of adaptation the expatriate achieves. The communication process facilitates cross-cultural adaptation through this process, expatriates learn the dominant communication patterns of the host society. Therefore, we can link those personality factors shown by research to ease adaptation with those necessary for effective intercultural communication.

Kim has consolidated the research findings of these characteristics into two categories: (1) **openness**—traits such as open-mindedness, tolerance for ambiguity, and extrovertedness; and (2) **resilience**—traits such as having an internal locus of control, persistence, a tolerance of ambiguity, and resourcefulness.[72] These personality factors, along with the expatriate's cultural and racial identity and the level of preparedness for change, comprise that person's potential for adaptation. The level of preparedness can be improved by the manager before his or her assignment by gathering information about the host country's verbal and nonverbal communication patterns and norms of behavior. Kim explains that the major variables that affect the level of communication competence achieved between the host and the expatriate are the adaptive predisposition of the expatriate and the conditions of receptivity and conformity to pressure in the host environment. These factors affect the process of personal and social communication, and, ultimately, the adaptation outcome. Explains Kim, "Three aspects of strangers' adaptive change—increased functional fitness, psychological health, and intercultural identity—have been identified as direct consequences of prolonged communication-adaptation experiences in the host society."[73] Chapter 10 explores areas where the firm has responsibility to improve the employee/managerial ability to adapt.

In identifying personal and behavioral specifics that facilitate ICE, however, we cannot lose sight of the whole picture. We must remember the basic principle of contingency management, which is that managers operate in a system of many interacting variables in a dynamic context. Studies show that situational factors—such as the physical environment, time constraints, degree of structure, feelings of boredom or overwork, and anonymity—are strong influences on intercultural communication competence.[74]

It is this interdependence of many variables that makes it difficult for intercultural researchers to isolate and identify factors for success. Although managers try to understand and control up front as many factors as possible that will lead to management effectiveness, often they only find out what works from the results of their decisions.

CONCLUSION

Effective intercultural communication is a vital skill for international managers and domestic managers of multicultural workforces. Because miscommunication is much more likely to occur among people from different countries or racial backgrounds than among those from similar backgrounds, it is important to be alert to how culture is reflected in communication—in particular through the development of cultural sensitivity and an awareness of potential sources of cultural noise in the communication process. A successful international manager is thus attuned to these variables and is flexible enough to adjust his or her communication style to best address the intended receivers—that is, to do it "their way."

Cultural variables and the manner in which culture is communicated underlie the processes of negotiation and decision making. How do people around the world negotiate: What are their expectations and their approach to negotiations? What is the importance of understanding negotiation and decision-making processes in other countries? Chapter 5 addresses these questions and makes suggestions for the international manager to handle these important tasks.

Summary of Key Points

1. Communication is an inherent part of a manager's role, taking up the majority of the manager's time on the job. Effective intercultural communication largely determines the success of international transactions or the output of a culturally diverse workforce.
2. Culture is the foundation of communication, and communication transmits culture. Cultural variables that can affect the communication process by influencing a person's perceptions include attitudes, social organizations, thought patterns, roles, language, nonverbal language, and time.
3. Language conveys cultural understandings and social norms from one generation to the next. Body language, or nonverbal communication, is behavior that communicates without words. It accounts for 65 to 93 percent of interpreted communication.

4. Types of nonverbal communication around the world are kinesic behavior, proxemics, paralanguage, and object language.
5. Effective cross-cultural communication must take account of whether the receiver is from a country with a monochronic or a polychronic time system.
6. Variables related to channels of communication include high- and low-context cultures, fast or slow messages and information flows, and various types of media.
7. In high-context cultures, feelings and messages are implicit and must be accessed through an understanding of the person and the system. In low-context cultures, feelings and thoughts are expressed, and information is more readily available.
8. The effective management of intercultural communication necessitates the development of cultural sensitivity, careful encoding, selective transmission, careful decoding, and follow-up actions.
9. Certain personal abilities and behaviors facilitate adaptation to the host country through skilled intercultural communication.
10. Communication via the Internet must still be localized to adjust to differences in language, culture, local laws, and business models.

Discussion Questions

1. How does culture affect the process of attribution in communication?
2. What is stereotyping? Give some examples. How might people stereotype you? How does a sociotype differ from a stereotype?
3. What is the relationship between language and culture? How is it that people from different countries who speak the same language may still miscommunicate?
4. Give some examples of cultural differences in the interpretation of body language. What is the role of such nonverbal communication in business relationships?
5. Explain the differences between monochronic and polychronic time systems. Use some examples to illustrate their differences and the role of time in intercultural communication.
6. Explain the differences between high- and low-context cultures, giving some examples. What are the differential effects on the communication process?
7. Discuss the role of information systems in a company, how and why they vary from country to country, and the effects of these variations.

Application Exercises

1. Form groups in your class—multicultural groups, if possible. Have each person make notes about his or her perceptions of (1) Mexican-Americans, (2) Native Americans, (3) African-Americans, and (4) Americans of European descent. Discuss your notes and draw conclusions about common stereotypes. Discuss any differences and why stereotyping occurs.
2. Invite some foreign students to your class. Ask them to bring photographs, slides, and so forth of people and events in their native countries. Have them explain the meanings of various nonverbal cues, such as gestures, dress, voice inflections, architecture, and events. Discuss with them any differences between their explanations and the attributions you assigned to those cues.
3. Interview a faculty member or a businessperson who has worked abroad. Ask him or her to identify factors that facilitated or inhibited adaptation to the host environment. Ask whether more preparation could have eased the transition and what, if anything, that person would do differently before another trip.

Experiential Exercise: Script for Juan Perillo and Jean Moore

Scene I: February 15, San Juan, Puerto Rico

JUAN: Welcome back to Puerto Rico, Jean. It is good to have you here in San Juan again. I hope that your trip from Dayton was a smooth one.

JEAN: Thank you, Juan. It's nice to be back here where the sun shines. Fred sends his regards and also asked me to tell you how important it is that we work out a firm production schedule for the next three months. But first, how is your family? All doing well, I hope.

JUAN: My wife is doing very well, but my daughter, Marianna, broke her arm and has to have surgery to repair the bone. We are very worried about that because the surgeon says she may have to have several operations. It is very difficult to think about my poor little daughter in the operating room. She was out playing with some other children when it happened. You know how roughly children sometimes play with each other. It's really amazing that they don't have more injuries. Why, just last week, my son . . .

JEAN: Of course I'm very sorry to hear about little Marianna, but I'm sure everything will go well with the surgery. Now, shall we start work on the production schedule?

JUAN: Oh, yes, of course, we must get started on the production schedule.

JEAN: Fred and I thought that June 1 would be a good cutoff date for the first phase of the schedule. And we also thought that 100 A-type computers would be a reasonable goal for that phase. We know that you have some new assemblers whom you are training, and that you've had some problems getting parts from your suppliers in the past few months. But we're sure you have all those problems worked out by now and that you are back to full production capability. So, what do you think? Is 100 A-type computers produced by June 1 a reasonable goal for your people?

JUAN: (Hesitates a few seconds before replying) You want us to produce 100 of the newly designed A-type computers by June 1? Will we also be producing our usual number of Z-type computers, too?

JEAN: Oh, yes. Your regular production schedule would remain the same as it's always been. The only difference is that you would be producing the new A-type computers, too. I mean, after all, you have a lot of new employees, and you have all the new manufacturing and assembling equipment that we have in Dayton. So, you're as ready to make the new product as we are.

JUAN: Yes, that's true. We have the new equipment, and we've just hired a lot of new assemblers who will be working on the A-type computer. I guess there's no reason we can't meet the production schedule you and Fred have come up with.

JEAN: Great, great. I'll tell Fred you agree with our decision and will meet the goal of 100 A-type computers by June 1. He'll be delighted to know that you can deliver what he was hoping for. And, of course, Juan, that means that you'll be doing just as well as the Dayton plant.

Scene II: May 1, San Juan, Puerto Rico

JEAN: Hello, Juan. How are things here in Puerto Rico? I'm glad to have the chance to come back and see how things are going.

JUAN: Welcome, Jean. It's good to have you here. How is your family?

JEAN: Oh, they're fine, just fine. You know, Juan, Fred is really excited about that big order we just got from the Defense Department for 50 A-type computers. They want them by June 10, so we will ship them directly to Washington from San Juan as the computers come off your assembly line. Looks like it's a good thing we set your production goal at 100 A-type computers by June 1, isn't it?

JUAN: Um, yes, that was certainly a good idea.

JEAN: So, tell me, have you had any problems with the new model? How are your new assemblers working out? Do you have any suggestions for changes in the manufacturing specs? How is the new quality control program working with this model? We're always looking for ways to improve, you know, and we appreciate any ideas you can give us.

JUAN: Well, Jean, there is one thing . . .

JEAN: Yes? What is that?

JUAN: Well, Jean, we have had a few problems with the new assemblers. Three of them have had serious illnesses in their families and have had to take off several days at a time to nurse a sick child or elderly parent. And another one was involved in a car accident and was in the hospital for several days. And you remember my daughter's surgery? Well, her arm didn't mend properly, and we had to take her to Houston for additional consultations and therapy. But, of course, you and Fred knew about that.

JEAN: Yes, we were aware that you had had some personnel problems and that you and your wife had had to go to Houston with Marianna. But what does that have to do with the 50 A-type computers for the Defense Department?

JUAN: Well, Jean, because of all these problems, we have had a few delays in the production schedule. Nothing serious, but we are a little bit behind our schedule.

JEAN: How far behind is "a little bit"? What are you trying to tell me, Juan? Will you have 50 more A-type computers by June 1 to ship to Washington to fill the Defense Department order?

JUAN: Well, I certainly hope we will have that number ready to ship. You know how difficult it can be to predict a precise number for manufacturing, Jean. You probably have many of these same problems in the Dayton plant, don't you?

SOURCE: L. Catlin and T. White, *International Business: Cultural Sourcebook and Case Studies* (Cincinnati, Ohio: South-Western, 1994), used with permission.

Exercise Questions

1. What went wrong for Jean in Puerto Rico? Could this have been avoided? What should she have done differently?
2. Replay the role of Jean and Juan during their conversation, establishing a more constructive communication and management style than Jean did previously.

Internet Resources

Visit the Deresky Companion Website at www.prenhall.com/deresky for this chapter's Internet resources.

Elizabeth Visits GPC's French Subsidiary

Elizabeth Moreno is looking out the window from her business-class seat somewhere over the Indian Ocean on Thai Air en route to Paris's Orly International Airport from the Philippines, where she has just spent a week of meetings and problem solving in a pharmaceutical subsidiary of the Global Pharmaceutical Company (GPC).

GPC has the lion's share of the worldwide market in ethical pharmaceutical products. Ethical drugs are those that can be purchased only through a physician's prescription. In the United States, GPC has research and manufacturing sites in New York, New Jersey, Pennsylvania, and Michigan. The company also has subsidiaries in Canada, Puerto Rico, Australia, the Philippines, Brazil, England, and France. GPC has its administrative headquarters in Pennsylvania.

Because of the geographically dispersed locations of its subsidiaries, GPC's top scientists and key managers log thousands of jet miles a year visiting various offices and plants. Its top specialists and executives regularly engage in multisite real-time video and telephone conferences, and they also use electronic mail, faxes, modems, and traditional mail to keep in touch with key personnel.

Despite these technological advances, face-to-face meetings and on-site consultations are used widely. In the case of the French subsidiary, nothing can take the place of face-to-face consultations. The French manager is suspicious of figures in the balance sheet, of the telephone, of his subordinates, of what he reads in the newspaper, and of what Americans tell him in confidence. In contrast, the American trusts all these (Hill 1994, 60). This is the reason GPC regularly sends its scientists and executives to France.

Elizabeth Moreno is one of the key specialists within GPC. Her expertise in chemical processing is widely known not only within her company but also in the pharmaceutical industry worldwide. She has been working at GPC for more than twelve years since finishing her advanced degree in chemistry from a university in the Midwest. While working for GPC, she has been given more and more responsibilities leading to her current position as vice president of chemical development and processing.

From a hectic visit in the Philippines, her next assignment is to visit the French subsidiary plant for one week to study a problem with shelf-life testing of one of its newest anti-allergy capsules. It seems that the product's active ingredient is degrading sooner than the expiration date. During her stay, she will conduct training for chemists in state-of-the-art techniques for testing and for training local managers in product statistical quality control. These techniques are now currently used in other GPC locations.

To prepare for her foreign assignments, Elizabeth attended a standard three-hour course given by her company's human resource management department on dealing with cross-cultural issues. Moreover, she recalls reading from a book on French management about the impersonal nature of French business relations. This was so much in contrast with what she just has experienced during her visit to the Philippine subsidiary. The French tend to regard authority as residing in the role and not in the person. It is by the power of the position that a French manager gets things done (Hill 1994, 58). With this knowledge, she knows that her expertise and her position as vice president will see her through the technical aspects of the meetings that are lined up for the few days she will be in Paris.

French managers view their work as an intellectual challenge that requires application of individual brainpower. What matters to them is the opportunity to show one's ability to grasp complex issues, analyze problems, manipulate ideas, and evaluate solutions (Hill 1994, 214).

There are a few challenges for Elizabeth on this assignment. She is not fluent in French. Her only exposure to France and the language was a two-week vacation with her husband in Paris a couple of years ago. However, in her highly technical field, the universal language is English. Thus, she believes she will not have much difficulty communicating with the French management to get her assignment successfully completed.

Americans place high value on training and education. In the United States, the field of management has principles that are generally applicable and can be taught and learned. In contrast, the French place more emphasis on the person who can adapt to any situation by virtue of his intellectual quality (Hill 1994, 63). Expertise and intellectual ability are inherent in the individual and cannot be acquired simply through training or education.

It appears that Elizabeth will be encountering very different ways of doing business in France. While she thought about the challenges ahead, her plane landed at Orly International Airport. She whisked through customs and immigration without any delays. No limousine was waiting for her curbside at the arrival. Instead she took the train to downtown Paris and checked into an apartment hotel that was reserved for her in advance of her arrival.

After a week in Paris, she is expected back in her home office to prepare reports to GPC management about her foreign assignments.

CASE QUESTIONS

1. What can Elizabeth Moreno do to establish a position of power in front of French managers to help her accomplish her assignment in five days? Explain.
2. What should Elizabeth know about high-context versus low-context cultures in Europe? Explain.
3. What should Elizabeth include in her report, and what should be the manner in which it is communicated, so that future executives and scientists avoid communications pitfalls? Explain.
4. How can technical language differ from everyday language in corporate communications? Explain.

Case Bibliography

Richard Hill, *Euro-Managers and Martians: The Business Cultures of Europe's Trading Nations* (Brussels: Europulications, Division of Europublic, SA/NV, 1994).

SOURCE: This case was prepared by Edwin J. Portugal, MBA, Ph.D., who teaches multinational management at State University of New York–Potsdam. It is intended to be used as a basis for discussion on the complexity of multicultural management and not to illustrate effective versus ineffective management styles. Copyright © 2004 by Edwin J. Portugal.

CHAPTER 5

Cross-cultural Negotiation and Decision Making

Outline

Opening Profile: Art of the Deal Meets the China Syndrome

The party invitations were sent, the bags were packed and the executives of Millicom International Cellular were ready to leave for Beijing to celebrate the sale of their company to China Mobile Communications.

But shortly before Millicom executives could leave for Luxembourg Airport, China was on the line and the $5.3 billion deal was off.

That was the conclusion in July, 2006, after months of negotiations between the Chinese company, hungry for acquisitions in emerging market industries, and Millicom, a mobile phone company with nine million subscribers in developing countries.

Why the Chinese got cold feet is open for debate, but financial advisers on both sides, who spent months shuttling Chinese executives to Millicom offices stretching from Chad to El Salvador, were shocked.

Millicom issued a statement that day, July 3, saying it had terminated "all discussions concerning a potential sale." Its stock promptly fell 25 percent.

The demise of the closely watched deal, which would have been the largest overseas transaction for a Chinese government-owned company, is exposing a chasm between deal-making styles in China and those in Europe and the United States.

China Mobile's last-minute exit is viewed in its homeland as smart corporate strategy. Many analysts and deal makers say China Mobile narrowly avoided overpaying for a disparate group of assets that would have been tough to manage.

In European and American deal-making circles, though, the way the exit was handled prompted gnashing of teeth at investment banks and boardrooms. Had China Mobile warned Millicom earlier, it might have avoided upsetting the stock market, deal-makers said, and permitted the telecom company to come up with a face-saving new bidder. Some financial advisers warn that Chinese companies could find their buying prospects drying up as a result.

"For a lot of prospective targets, they have lost credibility," said a European banker who spoke on the condition of anonymity because he did not want to alienate any prospective Chinese clients.

The debate exposes an uncomfortable truth for deal-makers salivating over the promise of Chinese expansion: corporate China's outward growth may be pegged to a strategy of mergers and acquisitions, particularly of brand-name Western companies, but executing those deals will not be easy.

Wall Street's biggest investment banks have paid multimillion-dollar salaries to hire Chinese bankers with top connections in recent years. While deal volume and equity offerings within the country have been brisk, big deals outside China have been scarce, particularly outside of the energy sector.

Acquisitions by Chinese companies (not including those in Hong Kong) outside the country fell in 2005 to $4.9 billion, from $7.2 billion a year earlier, according to Thomson Financial. Countries a fraction of China's size were well ahead of that pace. Companies based in Belgium, for example, bought $8.65 billion worth of companies outside the country in 2005.

Some high-profile deals have been struck recently, but they have been modest compared to the booming cross-border merger scene in the rest of the world. Lenovo bought I.B.M.'s personal computer unit for $1.75 billion, and Nanjing Automobile bought the MG Rover Group for a price estimated at less than $100 million, both in 2005. The oil company Cnooc reached an agreement to buy Unocal for $18.5 billion, also in 2005, but was forced to drop the bid after American politicians objected.

Chinese companies are on track for record overseas deal-making this year, with more than $9.8 billion in purchases completed already. But some bankers warn against expecting a flood of big-name overseas acquisitions and say that the Millicom-China Mobile outcome might be the norm rather than the exception.

Liang Meng, co-head of China investment banking at J. P. Morgan, expects just a few major deals out of China each year. The reason, he said, is largely that Chinese managers tend to proceed more slowly than their counterparts in the West.

"They are more cautious, either because they have not done much of it or because they are entering into totally new markets or totally new environments," Mr. Meng said.

These executives have usually been in their job for 20 or 30 years, much of that time solely in China.

"They have usually moved up because they are right most of the time or all of the time," Mr. Meng said, and they want to be absolutely certain a deal is the right move.

It should not be a surprise that overseas merger volume has been subdued, some analysts said.

"We are talking about a culture of doing business that has been learned over many centuries," said Jay Berry, a professor of business studies in China at Jilin University-Lambton College and a former consultant at McKinsey & Company.

Chinese companies are "absolutely" slower to make deals than their foreign counterparts, Mr. Berry said. "They are much absorbed by internal problems, tied to the wrong products, fragmented, unprofitable, uncompetitive, highly political and drowning in debt," he said.

The negotiations between China Mobile and Millicom were complicated and often frustrating for the European advisers and executives. They said that their Chinese counterparts were difficult to pin down for meetings and that establishing a schedule to get the deal done was virtually impossible.

"If they agreed to a date, they seemed to see that as a concession," one adviser said.

Veteran China deal makers found the Europeans' discomfort amusing and said they had encountered a common negotiating tactic.

"When Kissinger and Nixon went to China, they didn't know when they were going to meet Mao," said Jack Huang, head of the Greater China practice at the law firm Jones Day. "That game has been played by the Chinese over and over."

Still, Mr. Huang cautioned against saying Chinese executives would not be able to close deals overseas.

"The Chinese know very well if you want to do deals on the international arena, you have to move expeditiously," he said. "This is not a situation where the bureaucrats don't know the realities outside of China."

Nonetheless, Chinese companies may be operating at a disadvantage to their multinational competitors on the deal front. Multinational companies outside China generally have a special team that deals with mergers and acquisitions, notes Oded Shenkar, author of "The Chinese Century" and a professor of management at Ohio State University.

"They have experience and routines as to how you look at a deal, and they'd abort it fairly early on" if it was not going to work, he said.

"The Chinese do not have that yet," Mr. Shenkar said.

That will change as their experience in the energy business spreads to other industries, said Angus Barker, head of mergers and acquisitions for Asia at UBS. UBS was an adviser to Andes Petroleum, a group of Chinese oil companies, when it acquired $1.42 billion worth of oil fields in Ecuador in 2005.

Judging from the energy transactions, Mr. Barker said, Chinese companies have "shown they can mix it with all comers from around the world in auctions and win."

SOURCE: H. Timmons and D. Greenlees, "The Art of the Deal Meets the China Syndrome," *New York Times*, July 7, 2006, C.6, copyright © The New York Times Co., reprinted with permission.

Global managers negotiate with parties in other countries to make specific plans for strategies (exporting, joint ventures, acquisitions, and so forth) and for continuing operations. While the complexities of cross-cultural negotiations among firms around the world present challenge enough, managers may also be faced with negotiating with government-owned companies. Such a situation is illustrated in the opening profile about the difficulties experienced by Millicom International Cellular in negotiating and trying to secure a deal with Chinese Mobile Telecommunications.

The high-level political negotiations between the United States and China to gain the return of the U.S. military crew from the plane that was forced to land there after flying into Chinese airspace in April 2001 is another example of complex situations fraught with both political agenda and cultural nuances, such as the need for the Chinese to "save face" by demanding an apology.[1]

Managers must prepare for strategic negotiations. Next the operational details must be negotiated—the staffing of key positions, the sourcing of raw materials or component parts, and the repatriating of profits, to name a few. As globalism burgeons, the ability to conduct successful cross-cultural negotiations cannot be overemphasized. Failure to negotiate productively will result in lost potential alliances and lost business at worst, and confusion and delays at best.

During the process of negotiation—whether before, during, or after negotiating sessions—all kinds of decisions are made, both explicitly and implicitly. A consideration of cross-cultural negotiations must therefore include the various decision-making processes that occur around the world. Negotiations cannot be conducted without decisions being made.

This chapter examines the processes of negotiation and decision making as they apply to international and domestic cross-cultural contexts. The objective is a better understanding of successful management.

NEGOTIATION

Implementing strategy depends on management's ability to negotiate productively—a skill widely considered one of the most important in international business. In the global arena, cultural differences produce great difficulties in the negotiation process. Ignorance of native bargaining rituals, more than any other single factor, accounts for unimpressive sales efforts.[2] Important differences in the negotiation process from country to country include (1) the amount and type of preparation for a negotiation, (2) the relative emphasis on tasks versus interpersonal relationships, (3) the reliance on general principles rather than specific issues, and (4) the number of people present and the extent of their influence.[3] In every instance, managers must familiarize themselves with the cultural background and underlying motivations of the negotiators—and the tactics and procedures they use—to control the process, make progress, and therefore maximize company goals.

The term **negotiation** describes the process of discussion by which two or more parties aim to reach a mutually acceptable agreement. For long-term positive relations, the goal should be to set up a win–win situation—that is, to bring about a settlement beneficial to all parties concerned. This process, difficult enough when it takes place among people of similar backgrounds, is even more complex in international negotiations because of differences in cultural values, lifestyles, expectations, verbal and nonverbal language, approaches to formal procedures, and problem-solving techniques. The complexity is heightened when negotiating across borders because of the greater number of stakeholders involved. These stakeholders are illustrated in Exhibit 5-1. In preparing for negotiations, it is critical to avoid projective cognitive similarity—that is, the assumption that others perceive, judge, think, and reason in the same way when, in fact, they do not because of differential cultural and practical influences. Instead, astute negotiators empathetically enter into the private world or cultural space of their counterparts, while willingly sharing their own view of the situation.[4]

EXHIBIT 5-1   Stakeholders in Cross-cultural Negotiations

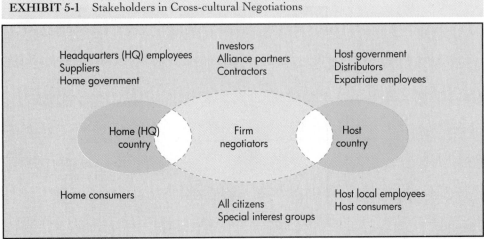

THE NEGOTIATION PROCESS

The negotiation process comprises five stages, the ordering of which may vary according to the cultural norms; for most people, relationship building is part of a continuous process in any event: (1) preparation, (2) relationship building, (3) the exchange of task-related information, (4) persuasion, and (5) concessions and agreement.[5] Of course, in reality these are seldom distinct stages but rather tend to overlap; negotiators may also temporarily revert to an earlier stage. With that in mind, it is useful to break down the negotiation process into stages to discuss the issues relevant to each stage and what international managers might expect, so that they might more successfully manage this process. These stages are shown in Exhibit 5-2 and discussed in the following sections.

Stage One: Preparation

The importance of careful preparation for cross-cultural negotiations cannot be overstated. To the extent that time permits, a distinct advantage can be gained if negotiators familiarize themselves with the entire context and background of their counterparts (no matter where the meetings will take place) in addition to the specific subjects to be negotiated. Because most negotiation problems are caused by differences in culture, language, and environment, hours or days of tactical preparation for negotiation can be wasted if these factors are not carefully considered.[6]

To understand cultural differences in negotiating styles, managers first must understand their own styles and then determine how they differ from the norm in other countries. They can do this by comparing profiles of those perceived to be successful negotiators in different countries. Such profiles reflect the value system, attitudes, and expected behaviors inherent in a given society. Other sections of this chapter describe and compare negotiating styles around the world.

Variables in the Negotiating Process

Adept negotiators conduct research to develop a profile of their counterparts so that they know, in most situations, what to expect, how to prepare, and how to react. Exhibit 5-3 shows 12 variables to consider when preparing to negotiate. These variables can, to a great degree, help managers understand the deep-rooted cultural and national motivations and traditional processes underlying negotiations with people from other countries.

After developing thoughtful profiles of the other party or parties, managers can plan for the actual negotiation meetings. Prior to the meetings, they should find out as much as

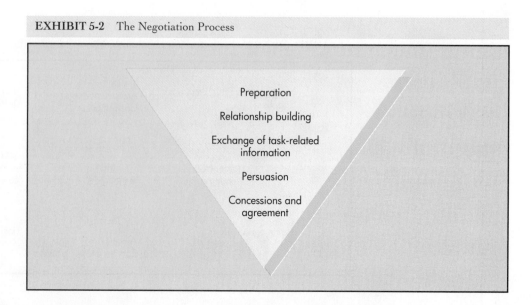

EXHIBIT 5-2   The Negotiation Process

Preparation

Relationship building

Exchange of task-related information

Persuasion

Concessions and agreement

EXHIBIT 5-3 Variables in the Negotiation Process

1. *Basic conception of negotiation process:* Is it a competitive process or a problem-solving approach?
2. *Negotiator selection criteria:* Is selection based on experience, status, expertise, personal attributes, or some other characteristic?
3. *Significance of type of issues:* Is it specific, such as price, or is the focus on relationships or the format of talks?
4. *Concern with protocol:* What is the importance of procedures, social behaviors, and so forth in the negotiation process?
5. *Complexity of communicative context:* What degree of reliance is placed on nonverbal cues to interpret information?
6. *Nature of persuasive arguments:* How do the parties attempt to influence each other? Do they rely on rational arguments, on accepted tradition, or on emotion?
7. *Role of individuals' aspirations:* Are motivations based on individual, company, or community goals?
8. *Bases of trust:* Is trust based on past experience, intuition, or rules?
9. *Risk-taking propensity:* How much do the parties try to avoid uncertainty in trading information or making a contract?
10. *Value of time:* What is each party's attitude toward time? How fast should negotiations proceed, and what degree of flexibility is there?
11. *Decision-making system:* How does each team reach decisions—by individual determination, by majority opinion, or by group consensus?
12. *Form of satisfactory agreement:* Is agreement based on trust (perhaps just a handshake), the credibility of the parties, commitment, or a legally binding contract?

SOURCE: Adapted from S. E. Weiss and W. Stripp, *Negotiation with Foreign Business Persons: An Introduction for Americans with Propositions on Six Cultures* (New York University Faculty of Business Administration, February 1985).

possible about (1) the kinds of demands that might be made, (2) the composition of the "opposing" team, and (3) the relative authority that the members possess. After this, the managers can gear their negotiation strategy specifically to the other side's firm, allocate roles to different team members, decide on concessions, and prepare an alternative action plan in case a negotiated solution cannot be found.[7]

In some situations, however, the entire negotiation process is something people have to learn from scratch. After the splintering of the Soviet Union into 15 independent republics, managers from the Newmont Mining Corporation of Denver, wishing to form a joint venture to refine gold deposits in Uzbekistan, found themselves at a standstill. Officials in Uzbekistan had never negotiated a business contract and had no one to tell them how to proceed.[8]

Following the preparation and planning stage, which is usually done at the home office, the core of the actual negotiation takes place on-site in the foreign location (or at the manager's home office if the other team has decided to travel there). In some cases, a compromise on the location for negotiations can signal a cooperative strategy, which Weiss calls "Improvise an Approach: Effect Symphony"—a strategy available to negotiators familiar with each other's culture and willing to put negotiation on an equal footing. Weiss gives the following example of this negotiation strategy:

> *For their negotiations over construction of the tunnel under the English Channel, British and French representatives agreed to partition talks and alternate the site between Paris and London. At each site, the negotiators were to use established, local ways, including the language . . . thus punctuating approaches by time and space.*[9]

In this way, each side was put into the context and the script of the other culture about half the time.

The next stage of negotiation—often given short shrift by Westerners—is that of relationship building. In most parts of the world, this stage usually has already taken place or is concurrent with other preparations.

Stage Two: Relationship Building

Relationship building is the process of getting to know one's contacts in a host country and building mutual trust before embarking on business discussions and transactions. This process is regarded with much more significance in most parts of the world than it is in the United States. U.S. negotiators are, generally speaking, objective about the specific matter at hand and usually want to waste no time in getting down to business and making progress. This approach, well understood in the United States, can be disastrous if the foreign negotiators want to take enough time to build trust and respect as a basis for negotiating contracts. In such cases, American efficiency interferes with the patient development of a mutually trusting relationship—the very cornerstone of an Asian business agreement.[10]

In many countries, such as Mexico and China, personal commitments to individuals, rather than the legal system, form the basis for the enforcement of contracts. Effective negotiators allow plenty of time in their schedules for such relationship building with bargaining partners. This process usually takes the form of social events, tours, and ceremonies, along with much **nontask sounding** (nemawashi)—general, polite conversation and informal communication before meetings—while all parties get to know one another. In such cultures, one patiently waits for the other party to start actual business negotiations, aware that relationship building is, in fact, the first phase of negotiations.[11] It is usually recommended that managers new to such scenarios use an intermediary— someone who already has the trust and respect of the foreign managers and who therefore acts as a "relationship bridge." Middle Easterners, in particular, prefer to negotiate through a trusted intermediary, and for them as well, initial meetings are only for the purpose of getting acquainted. Arabs do business with the person, not the company, and therefore mutual trust must be established.

In their bestseller on negotiation, *Getting to Yes,* Fisher and Ury point out the dangers of not preparing well for negotiations:

> *In Persian, the word "compromise" does not have the English meaning of a midway solution which both sides can accept, but only the negative meaning of surrendering one's principles. Also, "mediator" means "meddler," someone who is barging in uninvited. In 1980, United Nations Secretary-General Kurt Waldheim flew to Iran to deal with the hostage situation. National Iranian radio and television broadcast in Persian a comment he was to have made upon his arrival in Tehran: "I have come as a mediator to work out a compromise." Less than an hour later, his car was being stoned by angry Iranians.[12]*

As a bridge to the more formal stages of negotiations, such relationship building is followed by posturing—that is, general discussion that sets the tone for the meetings. This phase should result in a spirit of cooperation. To help ensure this result, negotiators must use words like "respect" and "mutual benefit" rather than language that would suggest arrogance, superiority, or urgency.

Stage Three: Exchanging Task-Related Information

In the next stage—exchanging task-related information—each side typically makes a presentation and states its position; a question-and-answer session usually ensues, and alternatives are discussed. From an American perspective, this represents a straightforward, objective, efficient, and understandable stage. However, Copeland and Griggs point out that negotiators from other countries continue to take a more indirect approach at this stage. Mexican negotiators are usually suspicious and indirect, presenting little substantive material and more lengthy, evasive conversation. French negotiators enjoy debate and conflict and will often interrupt presentations to argue about an issue even if it has little relevance to the topic being presented. The Chinese also ask many questions of their counterparts, and delve specifically and repeatedly into the details at hand; conversely, Chinese presentations contain only vague and ambiguous material. For instance, after about 20 Boeing officials spent six weeks presenting masses of literature and technical demonstrations to the Chinese, the Chinese said, "Thank you for your introduction."[13]

The Russians also enter negotiations well prepared and well versed in the specific details of the matter being presented. To answer their (or any other side's) questions, it is generally a good idea to bring along someone with expertise to answer any grueling technical inquiries. Russians also put a lot of emphasis on protocol and expect to deal only with top executives.

Adler suggests that negotiators should focus not only on presenting their situation and needs but also on showing an understanding of their opponents' viewpoint. Focusing on the entire situation confronting each party encourages the negotiators to assess a wider range of alternatives for resolution, rather than limiting themselves to their preconceived, static positions. She suggests that to be most effective, negotiators should prepare for meetings by practicing role reversal.[14]

Stage Four: Persuasion

In the next phase of negotiations—persuasion—the hard bargaining starts. Typically, both parties try to persuade the other to accept more of their position and to give up some of their own. Often, some persuasion has already taken place beforehand in social settings and through mutual contacts. In the Far East, details are likely to be worked out ahead of time through the backdoor approach *(houmani)*. For the most part, however, the majority of the persuasion takes place over one or more negotiating sessions. International managers usually find that this process of bargaining and making concessions is fraught with difficulties because of the different uses and interpretations of verbal and nonverbal behaviors. Although variations in such behaviors influence every stage of the negotiation process, they can play a particularly powerful role in persuasion, especially if they are not anticipated.

Studies of negotiating behavior have revealed the use of certain tactics, which skilled negotiators recognize and use. A study by John Graham comparing the use of various tactics (promises, threats, and so forth) among Japanese, Americans, and Brazilians indicates that the Japanese and Americans tend to be more alike in the use of these behaviors, whereas the Japanese and Brazilians are less alike. For example, Brazilians use fewer promises and commitments than the Japanese or Americans (only half as many), but they use commands far more often. The Japanese and Americans use threats twice as often as Brazilians, and they use commands only about half as often as Brazilians. Brazilians and the Japanese seldom behave similarly.[15]

Other, less savory tactics are sometimes used in international negotiations. Often called "dirty tricks," these tactics, according to Fisher and Ury, include efforts to mislead "opponents" deliberately.[16] Some negotiators may give wrong or distorted factual information or use the excuse of ambiguous authority—giving conflicting impressions about who in their party has the power to make a commitment. In the midst of hard bargaining, the prudent international manager will follow up on possibly misleading information before taking action based on trust.

Other rough tactics are designed to put opposing negotiators in a stressful situation physically or psychologically so that their giving in is more likely. These include uncomfortable room temperatures, too-bright lighting, rudeness, interruptions, and other irritations. Specific bargaining pressures include extreme or escalating demands, threats to stop negotiating, calculated delays, and a take-it-or-leave-it attitude. In a survey of 18 U.S.–Korean joint ventures, for example, U.S. executives reported that the behavior of the Koreans during the course of negotiations was often "abusive," resulting in "shouting matches, desk pounding, and chest beating."[17]

International negotiators must keep in mind, however, that what might seem like dirty tricks to Americans is simply the way other cultures conduct negotiations. In some South American countries, for example, it is common to start negotiations with misleading or false information.

The most subtle behaviors in the negotiation process, and often the most difficult to deal with, are usually the nonverbal messages—the use of voice intonation, facial and body expressions, eye contact, dress, and the timing of the discussions. Nonverbal behaviors are ingrained aspects of culture used by people in their daily lives; they are not specifically changed for the purposes of negotiation. In his comparative study of the nonverbal negotiating behaviors of Japanese, Americans, and Brazilians, Graham assessed the relative frequency of the use of silent periods, conversational overlaps, facial gazing (staring at people's faces), and touching. He found that Brazilians interrupted conversation about twice as often as the Japanese and Americans, and used much more touching and facial gazing. Needless to say, they scored low on silent periods. The Japanese tended to use more silent periods and interruptions than Americans but less facial gazing. The Japanese and Americans evidenced no touching whatsoever, other than handshaking, during a 30-minute period.[18]

Although persuasion has been discussed as if it were always a distinct stage, it is really the primary purpose underlying all stages of the negotiation process. In particular, persuasion is an integral part of the process of making concessions and arriving at an agreement.

Stage Five: Concessions and Agreement

In the last stage of negotiation—concessions and agreement—tactics vary greatly across cultures. Well-prepared negotiators are aware of various concession strategies and have decided ahead of time what their own concession strategy will be. Familiar with the typical initial positions that various parties are likely to take, they know that Russians and Chinese generally open their bargaining with extreme positions, asking for more than they hope to gain, whereas Swedes usually start with what they are prepared to accept.

Research in the United States indicates that better end results are attained by starting with extreme positions. With this approach, the process of reaching an agreement involves careful timing of the disclosure information and of concessions. Most people who have studied negotiations believe that negotiators should disclose only the information that is necessary at a given point and that they should try to obtain information piece by piece to gradually get the whole picture without giving away their goals or concession strategy. These guidelines will not always work in intercultural negotiations because the American process of addressing issues one at a time, in a linear fashion, is not common in other countries or cultures. Negotiators in the Far East, for example, approach issues in a holistic manner, deciding on the whole deal at the end, rather than making incremental concessions.

Again, at the final stage of agreement and contract, cultural values determine how these agreements will be honored. Whereas Americans take contracts very seriously, Russians often renege on their contracts. The Japanese, on the other hand, consider a formal contract to be somewhat of an insult and a waste of time and money in legal costs, since they prefer to operate on the basis of understanding and social trust.[19]

UNDERSTANDING NEGOTIATION STYLES

Global managers can benefit from studying differences in negotiating behaviors (and the underlying reasons for them), which can help them recognize what is happening in the negotiating process. Exhibit 5-4 shows some examples of differences among North American, Japanese, and Latin American styles. Brazilians, for example, generally have a spontaneous, passionate, and dynamic style. They are very talkative and particularly use the word "no" extensively—more than 40 times per half hour compared with 4.7 times for Americans, and only 1.9 times for the Japanese. They also differ markedly from Americans and the Japanese by their use of extensive physical contact.[20]

The Japanese are typically skillful negotiators. They have spent a great deal more time and effort studying U.S. culture and business practices than Americans have spent studying Japanese practices. A typical example of this contrast was apparent when Charlene Barshefsky—a tough American international lawyer who had never visited

EXHIBIT 5-4   Comparison of Negotiation Styles—Japanese, North American, and Latin American

Japanese	North American	Latin American
Emotional sensitivity highly valued	Emotional sensitivity not highly valued	Emotional sensitivity valued
Hiding of emotions	Dealing straightforwardly or impersonally	Emotionally passionate
Subtle power plays; conciliation	Litigation not so much as conciliation	Great power plays; use of weakness
Loyalty to employer; employer takes care of employees	Lack of commitment to employer; breaking of ties by either if necessary	Loyalty to employer (who is often family)
Face-saving crucial; decisions often on basis of saving someone from embarrassment	Decisions made on a cost-benefit basis; face-saving does not always matter	Face-saving crucial in decision making to preserve honor, dignity
Decision makers openly influenced by special interests	Decision makers influenced by special interests but often not considered ethical	Execution of special interests of decision expected, condoned
Not argumentative; quiet when right	Argumentative when right or wrong, but impersonal	Argumentative when right or wrong; passionate
What is down in writing must be accurate, valid	Great importance given to documentation as evidential proof	Impatient with documentation as obstacle to understanding general principles
Step-by-step approach to decision making	Methodically organized decision making	Impulsive, spontaneous decision making
Good of group is the ultimate aim	Profit motive or good of individual is the ultimate aim	What is good for group is good for the individual
Cultivate a good emotional social setting for decision making; get to know decision makers	Decision making impersonal; avoid involvements, conflict of interest	Personalism necessary for good decision making

SOURCE: From Pierre Casse, *Training for the Multicultural Manager: A Practical and Cross-cultural Approach to the Management of People* (Washington, D.C.: Society for Intercultural Education, Training, and Research, 1982).

Japan before—was sent there as a trade negotiator and had little knowledge of its counterparts. But Mr. Okamatsu, like most Japanese negotiators, was very familiar with America. He had lived with his family in New York for three years and had spent many years handling bilateral trade disputes between the two countries. The different styles of the two negotiators were apparent in the negotiations. Ms. Barshefsky wanted specific import goals. Mr. Okamatsu wanted to talk more about the causes of trade problems rather than set specific targets, which he called the "cooperative approach." Ms. Barshefsky snapped that the approach was nonsense and "would analyze the past to death, with no link to future change."[21]

Such differences in philosophy and style between the two countries reflect ten years of anger and feelings of betrayal in trade negotiations. John Graham, a California professor who has studied international negotiating styles, says that the differences between U.S. and Japanese styles are well illustrated by their respective proverbs: The American believes that "The squeaking wheel gets the grease," and the Japanese say that "The pheasant would not be shot but for its cry."[22] The Japanese are calm, quiet, patient negotiators; they are accustomed to long, detailed negotiating sessions. Whereas Americans often plunge straight to the matter at hand, the Japanese instead prefer to develop long-term, personal relationships. The Japanese want to get to know those on the other side and will spend some time in nontask sounding.

In negotiations, the Japanese culture of politeness and hiding of emotions can be disconcerting to Americans when they are unable to make straightforward eye contact or when the Japanese maintain smiling faces in serious situations. It is important that Americans understand what is polite and what is offensive to the Japanese—and vice versa. Americans must avoid anything that resembles boasting because the Japanese value humility, and physical contact or touching of any sort must be avoided.[23] Consistent with the culture-based value of maintaining harmony, the Japanese are likely to be evasive or even leave the room rather than give a direct negative answer.[24] Fundamental to Japanese culture is a concern for the welfare of the group; anything that affects one member or part of society affects the others. Thus, the Japanese view decisions carefully in light of long-term consequences; they use objective, analytic thought patterns; and they take time for reflection.[25]

Further insight into negotiating styles around the world can be gained by comparing the North American, Arab, and Russian styles. Basic cultural values often shed light on the way information is presented, whether and how concessions will be made, and the general nature and duration of the relationship.

For North Americans, negotiations are businesslike; their factual appeals are based on what they believe is objective information, presented with the assumption that it is understood by the other side on a logical basis. Arabs use affective appeals based on emotions and subjective feelings. Russians employ axiomatic appeals—that is, their appeals are based on the ideals generally accepted in their society. The Russians are tough negotiators; they stall for time until they unnerve Western negotiators by continuously delaying and haggling. Much of this approach is based on the Russians' different attitude toward time. Because Russians traditionally do not subscribe to the Western belief that "time is money," they are more patient, more determined, and more dogged negotiators. They try to keep smiles and other expressions of emotion to a minimum to present a calm exterior.[26]

In contrast to the Russians, Arabs are more interested in long-term relationships and are, therefore, more likely to make concessions. Compared with Westerners, Arabs have a casual approach to deadlines, and frequently the negotiators lack the authority to finalize a deal.[27]

Successful Negotiators Around the World

Following are selected profiles of what it takes to be a successful negotiator, as perceived by people in their home countries. These are profiles of American, Indian, Arab, Swedish, and Italian negotiators, according to Pierre Casse, and give some insight into what to expect from different negotiators and what they expect from others.[28]

American Negotiators

According to Casse, a successful American negotiator acts as follows:

1. Knows when to compromise
2. Takes a firm stand at the beginning of the negotiation
3. Refuses to make concessions beforehand
4. Keeps his or her cards close to his or her chest
5. Accepts compromises only when the negotiation is deadlocked
6. Sets up the general principles and delegates the detail work to associates
7. Keeps a maximum of options open before negotiation
8. Operates in good faith
9. Respects the "opponents"
10. States his or her position as clearly as possible
11. Knows when he or she wishes a negotiation to move on
12. Is fully briefed about the negotiated issues
13. Has a good sense of timing and is consistent
14. Makes the other party reveal his or her position while keeping his or her own position hidden as long as possible
15. Lets the other negotiator come forward first and looks for the best deal

Indian Negotiators

Indians, says Casse, often follow Gandhi's approach to negotiation, which Gandhi called *satyagraha,* "firmness in a good cause." This approach combines strength with the love of truth. The successful Indian negotiator thus acts as follows:

1. Looks for and says the truth
2. Is not afraid of speaking up and has no fears
3. Exercises self-control ("The weapons of the *satyagraha* are within him.")
4. Seeks solutions that will please all the parties involved ("*Satyagraha* aims to exalt both sides.")
5. Respects the other party ("The opponent must be weaned from error by patience and sympathy. Weaned, not crushed; converted, not annihilated.")
6. Neither uses violence nor insults
7. Is ready to change his or her mind and differ with himself or herself at the risk of being seen as inconsistent and unpredictable
8. Puts things into perspective and switches easily from the small picture to the big one
9. Is humble and trusts the opponent
10. Is able to withdraw, use silence, and learn from within
11. Relies on himself or herself, his or her own resources and strengths
12. Appeals to the other party's spiritual identity ("To communicate, the West moves or talks. The East sits, contemplates, suffers.")
13. Is tenacious, patient, and persistent
14. Learns from the opponent and avoids the use of secrets
15. Goes beyond logical reasoning and trusts his or her instinct as well as faith

Arab Negotiators

Many Arab negotiators, following Islamic tradition, use mediators to settle disputes. A successful Arab mediator acts in the following way:

1. Protects all the parties' honor, self-respect, and dignity
2. Avoids direct confrontations between opponents
3. Is respected and trusted by all
4. Does not put the parties involved in a situation where they have to show weakness or admit defeat
5. Has the necessary prestige to be listened to
6. Is creative enough to come up with honorable solutions for all parties
7. Is impartial and can understand the positions of the various parties without leaning toward one or the other
8. Is able to resist any kind of pressure that the opponents could try to exercise on him
9. Uses references to people who are highly respected by the opponents to persuade them to change their minds on some issues ("Do it for the sake of your father.")
10. Can keep secrets and in so doing gains the confidence of the negotiating parties
11. Controls his temper and emotions (or loses it when and where necessary)
12. Can use conferences as mediating devices
13. Knows that the opponents will have problems in carrying out the decisions made during the negotiation
14. Is able to cope with the Arab disregard for time
15. Understands the impact of Islam on the opponents who believe that they possess the truth, follow the Right Path, and are going to "win" because their cause is just

Swedish Negotiators

Swedish negotiators, according to Casse, are:

1. Very quiet and thoughtful
2. Punctual (concerned with time)
3. Extremely polite
4. Straightforward (they get straight down to business)

5. Eager to be productive and efficient
6. Heavy going
7. Down to earth and overcautious
8. Rather flexible
9. Able to and quite good at holding emotions and feelings
10. Slow at reacting to new (unexpected) proposals
11. Informal and familiar
12. Conceited
13. Perfectionist
14. Afraid of confrontations
15. Very private

Italian Negotiators

Italians, says Casse, value a negotiator who acts as follows:

1. Has a sense of drama (acting is a main part of the culture)
2. Does not hide his or her emotions (which are partly sincere and partly feigned)
3. Reads facial expressions and gestures very well
4. Has a feeling for history
5. Does not trust anybody
6. Is concerned about the *bella figura*—the "good impression"—he or she can create among those who watch his or her behavior
7. Believes in the individual's initiatives, not so much in teamwork
8. Is good at being obliging and simpatico at all times
9. Is always on the *qui vive*—the "lookout"
10. Never embraces definite opinions
11. Is able to come up with new ways to immobilize and eventually destroy his or her opponents
12. Handles confrontations of power with subtlety and tact
13. Has a flair for intrigue
14. Knows how to use flattery
15. Can involve other negotiators in complex combinations

Comparing Profiles

Comparing such profiles is useful. Indian negotiators, for example, are humble, patient, respectful of the other parties, and very willing to compromise, compared with Americans, who are firmer about taking stands. An important difference between Arab negotiators and those from most other countries is that the negotiators are mediators, not the parties themselves; hence, direct confrontation is made impossible. Successful Swedish negotiators are conservative and careful, dealing with factual and detailed information. This profile contrasts with Italian negotiators, who are expressive and exuberant but less straightforward than their Swedish counterparts.

The accompanying Management Focus highlights Arif Masood Naqvi, a successful negotiator and decision maker doing business in the Arab world with a clear focus on expanding his firm Abraaj Capital in the Middle East and Southeast Asia.

MANAGING NEGOTIATION

Skillful global managers must assess many factors when managing negotiations. They must understand the position of the other parties in regard to their goals—whether national or corporate—and whether these goals are represented by principles or specific details. They should have the ability to recognize the relative importance

Management Focus

A Middle East Equity Giant with a Small Global Footprint

Arif Masood Naqvi, the chief executive of the private equity firm Abraaj Capital, has an ambitious goal that may sound familiar to New York bankers.

He wants to create a one-stop financial services shop, serving up everything that companies and investors need, from lending to investment banking to brokerage.

But unlike, say, Citigroup, this bank will focus on serving the Middle East and Southeast Asia.

Right now, "there isn't such an institution in the Arab world," Mr. Naqvi said during a recent interview in London. Creating one is the only way to fend off the big Wall Street and London banks that are rapidly expanding in the region, he said.

He has already taken the first steps: In September, 2006, Abraaj bought 25 percent of EFG-Hermes Holding, a securities broker, investment bank and asset manager, with a market value of $2.5 billion and offices in Egypt and Dubai.

Abraaj intends to increase that stake, and eventually get management control, Mr. Naqvi said. The plan has the backing of EFG-Hermes's management.

Banks like Goldman Sachs and Citigroup are rapidly picking up licenses to do business in Dubai's growing financial center and are applying for permission in other countries in the Middle East as well, so Abraaj has to expand, Mr. Naqvi said.

"The only way we can compete is to add scale and mass," he said.

The Middle East is awash with opportunities for deal makers and investors. Not only is the region generating billions in petrodollars, but industries and infrastructure are rapidly privatizing. Mr. Naqvi estimates that some $300 billion to $400 billion in assets in the region, from

roads to banks to oil pipelines, will be turned over to private hands in coming years. "We're seeing a lot of investment come into our part of the world," he said.

The Middle Eastern banking market, meanwhile, is fragmented, made up of government-backed banks and family-controlled lenders, and smaller institutions like Abraaj. Global banks like HSBC, Deutsche Bank and Citigroup are pushing for a bigger share of the market.

Analysts and economists say there is good reason to be bullish on the region. "We're not expecting economies there to suffer," said Philip Smith, an analyst with Fitch Ratings. "There is a lot of expansion and a lot of investment, and on that basis, there is significant potential" for a regional bank.

Capital flows in the region are already quite high, said Simon Williams, an HSBC economist based in Dubai, but they are going to grow in size and scope.

Private capital has a huge role to play in the region, particularly in project financing, Mr. Williams said. "Given the scale of the projects, the strength of the region's creditworthiness and long-term access to low-cost funds, I would expect that to continue," he added.

Abraaj has a long list of Middle Eastern investors, including Sheik Abdulrahman al-Turki of Saudi Arabia, who is also chairman of Abraaj; Sheik Nawaf Nasser bin Khalid al-Thani of Qatar; and Al Jaber Group of the United Arab Emirates.

Mr. Naqvi, who founded Abraaj in 2002, has spent most of his career investing in the Middle East, North Africa and South Asia. After stints at Arthur Anderson in London and the Olayan Group, a Saudi investment and manufacturing conglomerate, he founded the investment firm Cupola Group in 1994.

The group has $400 million in assets under management and focuses on consumer brands in Pakistan, where Mr. Naqvi was born. It has invested in 35 KFC fast-food franchises there, as well as cafes and restaurants.

Abraaj's managers include former employees from Lehman Brothers, Deutsche Bank and Goldman Sachs.

What may curtail Mr. Naqvi's ambitious plans is competition, which is increasing by the day. EFG-Hermes ranked 20th in mergers and acquisitions in the region in 2005, but is not in the top 20 this year. Citigroup has dominated deals in the Middle East since 2004.

The big banks have strong balance sheets and the global reach to sell products like debt and equity for companies that are going private. But their contacts can be weak on the ground, and their ability to expand is limited: most countries in the Middle East limit foreign ownership of financial institutions.

Mr. Naqvi said his focus on the region would give him an edge. "We don't have ambitions to go global," he said. "We're obsessive about driving value in the region." Competition is coming on the private equity front as well. Western private equity shops have recently started to do more than just raise money in the Middle East, they are looking to invest there as well. The Carlyle Group is raising a $1 billion fund for Middle East investments, for example.

Not surprisingly, Mr. Naqvi thinks they are beatable.

Their "timing is all wrong," Mr. Naqvi said. A fund like Carlyle may be a giant in the rest of the world, but they're the "smaller guys on the block," in the Middle East, he said. "We have 110 investment professionals," Mr. Naqvi said. "What are they going to do, put four people on the ground?"

attached to completing the task versus developing interpersonal relationships. Managers also must know the composition of the teams involved, the power allotted to the members, and the extent of the teams' preparation. In addition, they must grasp the significance of personal trust in the relationship. As stated earlier, the culture of the parties involved affects their negotiating styles and behavior and thus the overall process of negotiation. However, whatever the culture, research by Tse, Francis, and Walls has found person-related conflicts to "invite negative, more relation-oriented (versus information-oriented) responses," leading them to conclude that "The software of negotiation—that is, the nature and the appearance of the relationship between the people pursuing common goals—needs to be carefully addressed in the negotiation process.[29]

This is particularly true when representatives of individual-focused cultures (such as the Americans) and group-focused cultures (such as the Chinese) are on opposite sides of the table. Many of these culture-based differences in negotiations came to light in Husted's recent study on Mexican negotiators' perceptions of the reasons for the failure of their negotiations with U.S. teams. (The summary findings are shown in Exhibit 5-5.) However, Husted believes that "many of the perceived differences relate to the typical differences found between high-context and low-context cultures."[30] In other words, the Mexican managers' interpretations were affected by their high-context culture, with the characteristics of an indirect approach, patience in discussing ideas, and maintenance of dignity. Instead, the low-context Americans conveyed an impatient, cold, blunt communicative style. To maintain the outward dignity of their Mexican counterparts, Americans must approach negotiations with Mexicans with patience and tolerance and refrain from attacking ideas because these attacks may be taken personally.

The relationships among the factors of cross-cultural negotiation discussed in this chapter are illustrated in Exhibit 5-6.

The successful management of intercultural negotiations requires that a manager go beyond a generalized understanding of the issues and variables involved. She or he must

EXHIBIT 5-5 Bargaining with the Gringos: Mexican Managers' Perceptions of Causes of Failure of Negotiations with Americans

	Very Important (%)	Important (%)	Moderately Important (%)	Total (%)
Problems with U.S. team				
Lack of authority of U.S. team to make decisions	37.0	20.0	15.0	72.0
U.S. team's failure to resolve doubts of Mexican team	34.0	26.0	14.0	74.0
U.S. team's lack of sincerity	41.0	20.0	9.0	70.0
Eigenvalue: 2.9009/Percent of var.: 26.4/Cum. var.: 26.4				
Negotiation process				
Differences in negotiation styles	26.5	28.4	22.5	77.4
U.S. team quoting unreasonable prices	52.5	17.8	8.9	79.2
Mexican lack of knowledge of delivery systems	42.0	19.0	11.0	72.0
Mexican lack of preparation	40.6	21.8	9.9	72.3
Eigenvalue: 2.3577/Percent of var.: 21.4/Cum. var.: 47.8				
Cultural barriers				
Differences in business practices	24.5	29.4	22.5	76.4
Communication barriers	37.3	17.6	12.7	67.6
Eigenvalue: 1.7976/Percent of var.: 16.3/Cum. var.: 64.1				
Language problems	41.2	21.6	5.9	68.7
Eigenvalue: 1.0763/Percent of var.: 9.8/Cum. var.: 73.9				
Price constraints				
Mexican team's inability to lower the price	32.0	22.0	18.0	72.0
Eigenvalue: 1.0433/Percent of var.: 9.5/Cum. var.: 83.4				

SOURCE: Bryan W. Husted, "Bargaining with the Gringos: An Exploratory Study of Negotiations between Mexican and U.S. Firms," *International Executive* 36(5) (September–October 1994): 625–644.

EXHIBIT 5-6 Cross-cultural Negotiation Variables

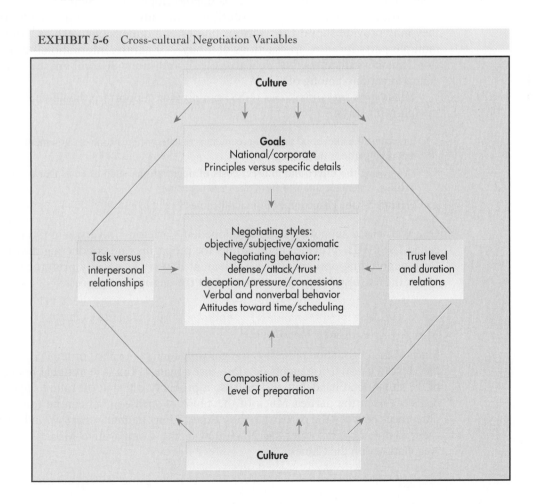

(1) gain specific knowledge of the parties in the upcoming meeting, (2) prepare accordingly to adjust to and control the situation, and (3) be innovative.[31]

Research has shown that a problem-solving approach is essential to successful cross-cultural negotiations, whether abroad or in the home office, although the approach works differently in various countries.[32] This problem-solving approach requires that a negotiator treat everyone with respect, avoid making anyone feel uncomfortable, and not criticize or blame the other parties in a personal way that may make someone feel shame—that is, lose face.

Research by the Huthwaite Research Group reveals how successful negotiators, compared to average negotiators, manage the planning process and their face-to-face behavior. The group found that during the planning process, successful negotiators consider a wider range of options and pay greater attention to areas of common ground. Skillful negotiators also tend to make twice as many comments regarding long-term issues and are more likely to set upper and lower limits regarding specific points. In their face-to-face behavior, skillful negotiators make fewer irritating comments—such as "We're making you a generous offer," make counterproposals less frequently, and use fewer reasons to back up arguments. In addition, skilled negotiators practice active listening—asking questions, clarifying their understanding of the issues, and summarizing the issues.[33] The accompanying Comparative Management in Focus section illustrates the challenges faced when negotiating with the Chinese.

Using the Web to Support Negotiations

Modern technology can provide support for the negotiating process, though it can't take the place of the essential face-to-face ingredient in many instances. A growing component for electronic commerce is the development of applications to support the negotiation of contracts and resolution of disputes. As Web applications develop, they may provide support for various phases and dimensions, such as "Multiple issue, multiple party business transactions of a buy–sell nature; international dispute resolution (business disputes, political disputes); and internal company negotiations and communications, among others.[34]

Negotiation support systems (NSS) can provide support for the negotiation process in the following ways:

- Increasing the likelihood that an agreement is reached when a zone of agreement exists (solutions that both parties would accept)
- Decreasing the direct and indirect costs of negotiations, such as costs caused by time delays (strikes, violence), and attorneys' fees, among others
- Maximizing the chances for optimal outcomes[35]

One Web-based support system, developed at Carleton University in Ottawa, Canada—called INSPIRE—provides applications for preparing and conducting negotiations and for renegotiating options after a settlement. Users can specify preferences and assess offers; the site also has graphical displays of the negotiation process.[36]

Managing Conflict Resolution

Much of the negotiation process is fraught with conflict—explicit or implicit—and such conflict can often lead to a standoff, or a lose–lose situation. This is regrettable, not only because of the situation at hand, but also because it probably will shut off future opportunities for deals between the parties. Much of the cause of such conflict can be found in cultural differences between the parties—in their expectations, in their behaviors, and particularly in their communication styles—as illustrated in the Comparative Management in Focus, Negotiating with the Chinese.

Comparative Management in Focus

Negotiating with the Chinese

The Chinese think in terms of process that has no culmination. Americans think in terms of concrete solutions to specific problems . . . The Chinese approach is impersonal, patient and aloof . . . To Americans, Chinese leaders seem polite but aloof and condescending. To the Chinese, Americans appear erratic and somewhat frivolous.

HENRY KISSINGER,
Newsweek, May, 2001[37]

The Chinese way of making decisions begins with socialization and initiation of personal guanxi rather than business discussion. The focus is not market research, statistical analysis, facts, PowerPoint presentations, or to-the-point business discussion. My focus must be on fostering guanxi.

SUNNY ZHOU,
General Manager of Kunming Lida Wood and Bamboo Products[38]

When Westerners initiate business negotiations with representatives from the People's Republic of China, cultural barriers confront both sides. As noted in this chapter's

Map 5-1:   China

opening profile, "the demise of the deal [between Millicom International Celluar and Chinese Mobile Communications in July 2006] is exposing a chasm between deal-making styles in China and those in Europe and the United States."[39]

The negotiation process used by the Chinese—although there are variations among the Cantonese, Shanghainese, and northern Chinese—is mystifying to Westerners. For instance, the Chinese put much greater emphasis than Americans on respect and friendship, on saving face, and on group goals. Long-term goals are more important to the Chinese than the specific current objectives typical of Western negotiators. Even though market forces are starting to have more influence in China, political and economic agendas are still expected to be considered in negotiations. Research by Xinping Shi of 198 managers in Beijing, 185 in Shanghai, and 189 in Guangzhou shows that prevailing economic conditions, political pervasiveness, and "constituent shadow" (the influence that constituents, such as political and state agencies, have on the negotiating parties in China) are key practical factors that, added to cultural factors, make up the context affecting Chinese negotiations. These antecedent factors, when filtered through the specific negotiator's profile, result in various behaviors, processes, and outcomes from those negotiations. Moreover, little difference in those factors was found among the different regions in China. Exhibit 5-7 shows these environmental factors and the relationships among the factors involved in Western–Chinese business negotiation.

Businesspeople report two major areas of conflict in negotiating with the Chinese: (1) The amount of detail the Chinese want about product characteristics, and (2) their apparent insincerity about reaching an agreement. In addition, Chinese negotiators frequently have little authority, frustrating Americans who do have the authority and are ready to conclude a deal.[40] This situation arises because Chinese companies report to the government trade corporations, which are involved in the negotiations and often have a representative on the team. The goals of Chinese negotiators remain primarily within the framework of state planning and political ideals. Although China is tending to become more profit-oriented, most deals are still negotiated within the confines of the state budget allocation for that project rather than on the basis of a project's profitability or value. It is crucial, then, to find out which officials—national, provincial, local—have the power to make, and keep, a deal. According to James Broering of Arthur Andersen, who does much business in China, "companies have negotiated with government people for months, only to discover that they were dealing with the wrong people."[41]

Research shows that for the Chinese, the negotiation process is greatly affected by three cultural norms: their ingrained politeness and emotional restraint, their emphasis on social obligations, and their belief in the interconnection of work, family, and friendship. Because of the Chinese preference for emotional restraint and saving face, aggressive or emotional attempts at persuasion in negotiation are likely to fail. Instead, the Chinese tendency to avoid open conflict will more likely result in negative strategies such as discontinuing or withdrawing from negotiation.[42] The concept of

EXHIBIT 5-7 Influences on Western–Chinese Business Negotiations

SOURCE: Xinping Shi, "Antecedent Factors of International Business Negotiations in the China Context," *Management International Review*, no. 2 (April 2001): 182.

face is at the heart of this kind of response—it is essential for foreigners to recognize the role that face behavior plays in negotiations. There are two components of face—*lien* and *mien-tzu*. *Lien* refers to a person's moral character; it is the most important thing defining that person, and without it one cannot function in society. It can only be earned by fulfilling obligations to others. *Mien-tzu* refers to one's reputation or prestige, earned through accomplishments or through bureaucratic or political power.[43] Giving others one's time, gifts, or praise enhances one's own face. In negotiations, it is vital that you do not make it obvious that you have "won" because that means that the other party has "lost" and will lose face. One must, therefore, make token concessions and other attempts to show that respect must be demonstrated, and modesty and control must be maintained; otherwise anyone who feels he or she has "lost face" will not want to deal with you again. The Chinese will later ignore any dealings or incidents that caused them to lose face, maintaining the expected polite behavior out of social consciousness and concern for others. When encountering an embarrassing situation, they will typically smile or laugh in an attempt to save face, responses that are confusing to Western negotiators.[44]

Research by Kam-hon Lee et al. in 2006 explored sources of tension felt by Chinese and Americans during negotiations. For the Americans, sources of tension and lack of trust were attributed to what they referred to as Chinese misrepresentations, and to the Chinese not following what the Americans considered normative negotiation procedures. Generally, the Americans felt that the Chinese team was not being truthful with them and were not giving straight answers. From the perspective of the Chinese, tension on the part of the Americans damaged the interpersonal relationships between the parties, which are so important to the Chinese; this resulted in the Chinese not trusting the Americans and having negative expectations about the Americans' cooperativeness in the future. Further, Lee et al. found that intransigence was the most frequent cause of tension in both the Chinese and the American parties.[45]

The emphasis on social obligations underlies the strong orientation of the Chinese toward collective goals. Therefore, appeals to individual members of the Chinese negotiating team, rather than appeals to benefit the group as a whole, will probably backfire. The Confucian emphasis on the kinship system and the hierarchy of work, family, and friends explains the Chinese preference for doing business with familiar, trusted people and trusted companies. "Foreign" negotiators, then, should focus on establishing long-term, trusting relationships, even at the expense of some immediate returns.

Deeply ingrained in the Chinese culture is the importance of harmony for the smooth functioning of society. Harmony is based primarily on personal relationships, trust, and ritual. After the Chinese establish a cordial relationship with foreign negotiators, they use this relationship as a basis for the give-and-take of business discussions. This implicit cultural norm is commonly known as *guanxi*, which refers to the intricate, pervasive network of personal relations that every Chinese carefully cultivates. It is the primary means of getting ahead, in the absence of a proper commercial legal system.[46] In other words, *guanxi* establishes obligations to exchange favors in future business activities.[47] Even within the Chinese bureaucracy, *guanxi* prevails over legal interpretations. Although networking is important anywhere to do business, the difference in China is that "*guanxi* networks are not just commercial, but also social, involving the exchange both of favor and affection."[48] Firms that have special *guanxi* connections and give preferential treatment to one another are known as members of a *guanxihu* network.[49] Sunny Zhou, general manager of Kumming Lida Wood and Bamboo Products, states that when he shops for lumber, "The lumber price varies drastically, depending on whether one has strong *guanxi* with the local administrators."[50]

Western managers should thus anticipate extended preliminary visiting (relationship building), in which the Chinese expect to learn more about them and their trustworthiness. The Chinese also use this opportunity to convey their deeply held principles. They attach considerable importance to mutual benefit.[51] The Chinese expect Western firms to sacrifice corporate goals and above-average profits to Chinese national goals and principles, such as meaningful friendship, Chinese national development, and the growth and enhancement of the Chinese people. Misunderstandings occur when Americans show polite acceptance of these general principles without understanding their significance—because they do not have any obvious relationship to American corporate goals, such as profit. Nor do such principles seem relevant to practical decisions on plant locations, employee practices, or sourcing.[52]

Americans often experience two negotiation stages with the Chinese: the technical and the commercial. During the long technical stage, the Chinese want to hammer out every detail of the proposed product specifications and technology. If there are two teams of negotiators, it may be several days before the commercial team is actually called in to deal with aspects of production, marketing, pricing, and so forth. However, the commercial team should sit in on the first stage to become familiar with the Chinese negotiating style.[53] The Chinese negotiating team is usually about twice as large as the Western team; about a third of the time is spent discussing technical specifications, and another third on price negotiations, with the rest devoted to general negotiations and posturing.[54]

The Chinese are among the toughest negotiators in the world. American managers must anticipate various tactics, such as their delaying techniques and their avoidance of direct, specific answers: Both ploys are used to exploit the known impatience of Americans. The Chinese frequently try to put pressure on Americans by "shaming" them, thereby implying that the Americans are trying to renege on the friendship—the basis of the implicit contract. Whereas Westerners come to negotiations with specific and segmented goals and find it easy to compromise, the Chinese are reluctant to negotiate details. They find it difficult to compromise and trade because they have entered negotiations with a broader vision of achieving development goals for China, and they are offended when Westerners don't internalize those goals.[55] Under these circumstances, the Chinese will adopt a rigid posture, and no agreement or contract is final until the negotiated activities have actually been completed.

Patience, respect, and experience are necessary prerequisites for anyone negotiating in China. For the best outcomes, older, more experienced people are more acceptable to the Chinese in cross-cultural negotiations. The Chinese want to deal with the top executive of an American company, under the assumption that the highest officer has attained that position by establishing close personal relationships and trust with colleagues and others outside the organization. Western delegation practices are unfamiliar to them, and they are reluctant to come to an agreement without the presence of the Chinese foreign negotiator.[56] From the Western perspective, confusing jurisdictions of government ministries hamper decisions in negotiations.[57] Americans tend to send specific technical personnel with experience in the task at hand; therefore, they have to take care in selecting the most suitable negotiators. In addition, visiting negotiating teams should realize that the Chinese are probably negotiating with other foreign teams, often at the same time, and will use that setup to play one company's offer against the others. On an interpersonal level, Western negotiators must also realize that, while a handshake is polite, physical contact is not acceptable in Chinese social behavior, nor are personal discussion topics such as one's family. However, it is customary to give and take small gifts as tokens of friendship. Pye offers the following additional tips to foreigners conducting business with the Chinese:[58]

- Practice patience
- Accept prolonged periods of stalemate
- Refrain from exaggerated expectations and discount Chinese rhetoric about future prospects
- Expect the Chinese to try to manipulate by shaming
- Resist the temptation to believe that difficulties may have been caused by one's own mistakes
- Try to understand Chinese cultural traits, but realize that a foreigner cannot practice them better than the Chinese

As discussed in Chapter 4, much of the difference in communication styles is attributable to whether you belong to a high-context or low-context culture (or somewhere in between, as shown in Exhibit 4-4). In low-context cultures such as that in the United States, conflict is handled directly and explicitly. It is also regarded as separate from the person negotiating— that is, the negotiators draw a distinction between the people involved and the information or opinions they represent. They also tend to negotiate on the basis of factual information and logical analysis. That approach to conflict is called **instrumental-oriented conflict**.[59] In high-context cultures, such as in the Middle East, the approach to conflict is called **expressive-oriented conflict**—that is, the situation is handled indirectly and implicitly, without clear delineation of the situation by the person handling it. Such negotiators do not want to get in a confrontational situation because it is regarded as insulting and would cause a loss of "face," so they tend to use evasion and avoidance if they cannot reach agreement through emotional appeals. Their avoidance and inaction conflict with the expectations of the low-context negotiators who are looking to move ahead with the business at hand and arrive at a solution.

The differences between high- and low-context cultures that often lead to conflict situations are summarized in Exhibit 5-8. Most of these variables were discussed previously in this chapter or in Chapter 4. They overlap because the subjects, culture, and communication are inseparable and because negotiation differences and conflict situations arise from variables in culture and communication.

The point here is, how can a manager from France, Japan, or Brazil, for example, manage conflict situations? The solution, as discussed previously, lies mainly in one's ability to know and understand the people and the situation to be faced. Managers must be prepared by developing an understanding of the cultural contexts in which they will be operating. What are the expectations of the persons with whom they will be negotiating? What kinds of communication styles and negotiating tactics should they expect, and how will they differ from their own? It is important to bear in mind one's own expectations and negotiating style, as well as to be aware of the other parties' expectations. Managers ought to consider in advance what it will take to arrive at a win–win solution. Often it helps to use the services of a host-country adviser or mediator, who may be able to help with early diffusion of a conflict situation.

EXHIBIT 5-8   Sources of Conflict Between Low-Context and High-Context Cultures

Key Questions	Low-Context Conflict	High-Context Conflict
Why	Analytic, linear logic; instrumental oriented; dichotomy between conflict and conflict parties	Synthetic, spiral logic; expressive oriented; integration of conflict and conflict parties
When	Individualistic oriented; low collective normative expectations; violations of individual expectations create conflict potentials	Group oriented; high collective normative expectations; violations of collective expectations create conflict potentials
What	Revealment; direct, confrontational attitude; action and solution oriented	Concealment; indirect nonconfrontational attitude; "face" and relationship oriented
How	Explicit communication codes; line-logic style: rational-factual rhetoric; open, direct strategies	Implicit communication codes; point-logic style: intuitive-effective rhetoric; ambiguous, indirect strategies

SOURCE: W. Gudykunst, L. Stewart, and S. Ting-Toomey, *Communication, Culture, and Organizational Processes*. Copyright © 1985 by Sage Publications, Inc. Reprinted by permission of Sage Publications, Inc.

DECISION MAKING

Negotiation actually represents the outcome of a series of small and large decisions. The decisions include those made by each party before actual negotiations start—for example, in determining the position of the company and what fallback proposals it may suggest or accept. The decisions also include incremental decisions, made during the negotiation process, on how to react and proceed, when to concede, and on what to agree or disagree. Negotiation can thus be seen as a series of explicit and implicit decisions, and the subjects of negotiation and decision making become interdependent.

For instance, sometimes just the way a decision is made during the negotiation process can have a profound influence on the outcome, as this example shows:

> *In his first loan negotiation, a banker new to Japan met with seven top Japanese bankers who were seeking a substantial amount of money. After hearing their presentation, the American agreed on the spot. The seven Japanese then conferred among themselves and told the American they would get back to him in a couple of days regarding whether they would accept his offer or not. The American banker learned a lesson he never forgot.*[60]

The Japanese bankers expected the American to negotiate, to take time to think it over, and to consult with colleagues before giving the final decision. His immediate decision made them suspicious, so they decided to reconsider the deal.

There is no doubt that the speed and manner of decision making affect the negotiation process. In addition, how well negotiated agreements are implemented is affected by the speed and manner of decision making. In that regard, it is clear that the effective use of technology is playing an important role, especially when dealing with complex cross-border agreements in which the hundreds of decision makers involved are separated by time and space.

The role of decision making in management, however, goes far beyond the finite occasions of negotiations. It is part of the manager's daily routine—from operational-level, programmed decisions requiring minimal time and effort to those nonprogrammed decisions of far broader scope and importance, such as the decision to enter into a joint venture in a foreign country.

The Influence of Culture on Decision Making

It is crucial for international managers to understand the influence of culture on decision-making styles and processes. Culture affects decision making both through the broader context of the nation's institutional culture, which produces collective patterns of decision making, and through culturally based value systems that affect each individual decision maker's perception or interpretation of a situation.[61]

The extent to which decision making is influenced by culture varies among countries. For example, Hitt, Tyler, and Park have found a "more culturally homogenizing influence on the Korean executives' cognitive models" than on those of U.S. executives, whose individualistic tendencies lead to different decision patterns.[62] The ways that culture influences an executive's decisions can be studied by looking at the variables involved in each stage of the rational decision-making process. These stages are (1) defining the problem, (2) gathering and analyzing relevant data, (3) considering alternative solutions, (4) deciding on the best solution, and (5) implementing the decision.

One of the major cultural variables affecting decision making is whether a people tend to assume an objective approach or a subjective approach. Whereas the Western approach is based on rationality (managers interpret a situation and consider alternative solutions based on objective information), this approach is not common throughout the world. Latin Americans, among others, are more subjective, basing decisions on emotions.

Another cultural variable that greatly influences the decision-making process is the risk tolerance of those making the decision. Research shows that people from Belgium, Germany, and Austria have a considerably lower tolerance for risk than people from Japan or the Netherlands—whereas American managers have the highest tolerance for risk.[63]

Another important variable in the decision-making process is the manager's perception of the locus of control over outcomes—whether that locus is internal or external. Some managers feel they can plan on certain outcomes because they are in control of events that will direct the future in the desired way. In contrast, other managers believe that such decisions are of no value because they have little control over the future—which lies in the hands of outside forces, such as fate, God, or nature. American managers believe strongly in self-determination and perceive problem situations as something they can control and should change. However, managers in many other countries, Indonesia and Malaysia among them, are resigned to problem situations and do not feel that they can change them. Obviously, these different value systems will result in a great difference in the stages of consideration of alternative actions and choice of a solution, often because certain situations may or may not be viewed as problems in the first place.

Another variable that affects the consideration of alternative solutions is how managers feel about staying with familiar solutions or trying new ones. Many managers, particularly those in Europe, value decisions based on past experiences and tend to emphasize quality. Americans, on the other hand, are more future oriented and look toward new ideas to get them there.

Approaches to Decision Making

In addition to affecting different stages of the decision-making process, value systems influence the overall approach of decision makers from various cultures. The relative level of utilitarianism versus moral idealism in any society affects its overall approach to problems. Generally speaking, utilitarianism strongly guides behavior in the Western world. Research has shown that Canadian executives are more influenced by a short-term, cost–benefit approach to decision making than their Hong Kong counterparts. Canadian managers are considerably more utilitarian than leaders from the People's Republic of China, who approach problems from a standpoint of moral idealism; they consider the problems, alternatives, and solutions from a long-term, societal perspective rather than an individual perspective.[64]

Another important variable in companies' overall approach to decision making is that of autocratic versus participative leadership. In other words, who has the authority to make what kinds of decisions? A society's orientation—whether it is individualistic or collectivist (see Chapter 3)—influences the level at which decisions are made. In many countries with hierarchical cultures—Germany, Turkey, and India, among others—authorization for action has to be passed upward through echelons of management before final decisions can be made. Most employees in these countries simply expect the autocrat—the boss—to do most of the decision making and will not be comfortable otherwise. Even in China, which is a highly collectivist society, employees expect autocratic leadership because their value system presupposes the superior to be automatically the most wise. In comparison, decision-making authority in Sweden is very decentralized. Americans talk a lot about the advisability of such participative leadership, but in practice they are probably near the middle between autocratic and participative management styles.

Arab managers have long traditions of consultative decision making, supported by the Qur'an and the sayings of Muhammad. However, such consultation occurs more on a person-to-person basis than during group meetings and thus diffuses potential opposition.[65] Although business in the Middle East tends to be transacted in a highly personalized manner, the final decisions are made by the top leaders, who feel that they must impose their will for the company to be successful. In comparison, in cultures that emphasize collective harmony, such as Japan, participatory or group decision making predominates, and consensus is important. The best-known example is the bottom-up (rather than top-down) decision-making process used in most Japanese companies, described in more detail in the following Comparative Management in Focus section.

One final area of frequent incongruence concerns the relative speed of decision making. A country's culture affects how fast or slow decisions tend to be made. The relative speed may be closely associated with the level of delegation, as just discussed—but not always. The pace at which decisions are made can be very disconcerting for outsiders. North Americans and Europeans pride themselves on being decisive; managers in the Middle East, with a different sense of temporal urgency, associate the importance of the matter at hand with the length of time needed to make a decision. Without knowing this cultural attitude, a hasty American would insult an Egyptian; a quick decision, to the Egyptian, would reflect a low regard for the relationship and the deal.

Exhibit 5-9 illustrates, in summary form, how all the variables just discussed can affect the steps in the decision-making process.

EXHIBIT 5-9 Cultural Variables in the Decision-Making Process

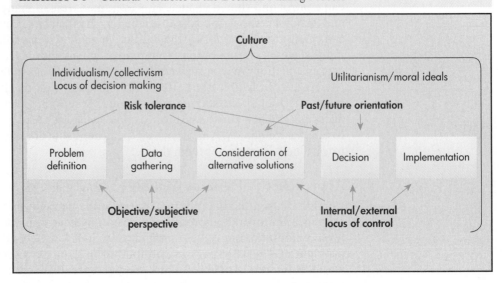

Comparative Management in Focus

Decision Making in Japanese Companies

Japanese companies are involved in joint ventures throughout the world, especially with U.S. companies. The GM–Toyota joint venture agreement process, for example, was the result of more than two years of negotiation and decision making. In this new company and in similar companies, Americans and Japanese are involved in decision making at all levels on a daily basis. The Japanese decision-making process differs greatly not only from the U.S. process but from that of many other countries—especially at the higher levels of their organizations.

An understanding of the Japanese decision-making process—and indeed of many Japanese management practices—requires an understanding of Japanese national culture. Much of the Japanese culture, and therefore the basis of Japanese working relationships, can be explained by the principle of *wa*, meaning "peace and harmony." This principle is one aspect of the value the Japanese attribute to *amae,* meaning "indulgent love," a concept probably originating in the Shinto religion, which focuses on spiritual and physical harmony. *Amae* results in *shinyo*, which refers to the mutual confidence, faith, and honor required for successful business relationships. The principle of *wa* influences the work group, the basic building block of Japanese work and management. The Japanese strongly identify with their work groups, where the emphasis is on cooperation, participative management, consensus problem solving, and decision making based on a patient, long-term perspective. Open expression of conflict is discouraged, and it is of utmost importance to avoid embarrassment or shame—to lose face—as a result of not fulfilling one's obligations. These elements of work culture generally result in a devotion to work, a collective responsibility for decisions and actions, and a high degree of employee productivity. It is this culture of collectivism and shared responsibility that underlies the Japanese *ringi* system of decision making.

In the *ringi* system, the process works from the bottom up. Americans are used to a centralized system, where major decisions are made by upper-level managers in a top-down approach typical of individualistic societies. The Japanese process, however, is dispersed throughout the organization, relying on group consensus.

The *ringi* process is one of gaining approval on a proposal by circulating documents to those concerned throughout the company. It usually comprises four steps: proposal, circulation, approval, and record.[66] Usually the person who originates the written proposal, which is called a *ringi-sho,* has already worked for some time to gain informal consensus and support for the proposal within the section and then from the department head.[67] The next step is to attain a general consensus in the company from those who would be involved in implementation. To this end, department meetings are held, and if necessary expert opinion is sought. If more information is needed, the proposal goes back to the originator, who finds and adds the required data. In this way, much time and effort—and the input of many people—go into the proposal before it becomes formal.[68]

Up to this point, the process has been an informal one to gain consensus; it is called the *nemawashi* process. Then the more formal authorization procedure begins, called the *ringi* process. The *ringi-sho* is passed up through successive layers of management for approval—the approval made official by seals. In the end, many such seals of approval are gathered, thereby ensuring collective agreement and responsibility and giving the proposal a greater chance of final approval by the president. The whole process is depicted in Exhibit 5-10.

The *ringi* system is cumbersome and very time-consuming prior to the implementation stage, although implementation is facilitated because of the widespread awareness of and support for the proposal already gained throughout the organization.

EXHIBIT 5-10   Decision-Making Procedure in Japanese Companies

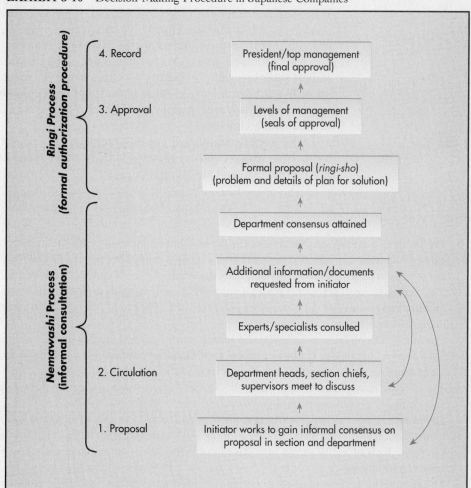

However, its slow progress is problematic when decisions are time-sensitive. This process is the opposite of the Americans' top-down decisions, which are made quite rapidly and without consultation, but which then take time to implement because unforeseen practical or support problems often arise.

Another interesting comparison is often made regarding the planning horizon (aimed at short- or long-term goals) in decision making between the American and Japanese systems. The Japanese spend considerable time in the early stages of the process defining the issue, considering what the issue is all about, and determining whether there is an actual need for a decision. They are more likely than Americans to consider an issue in relation to the overall goals and strategy of the company. In this manner, they prudently look at the "big picture" and consider alternative solutions, instead of rushing into quick decisions for immediate solutions, as Americans tend to do.[69]

Of course, in a rapidly changing environment, quick decisions are often necessary—to respond to competitors' actions, a political uprising, and so forth—and it is in such contexts that the *ringi* system sometimes falls short because of its slow response rate. The system is, in fact, designed to manage continuity and to avoid uncertainty, which is considered a threat to group cohesiveness.[70]

CONCLUSION

It is clear that competitive positioning and long-term successful operations in a global market require a working knowledge of the decision-making and negotiating processes of managers from different countries. These processes are complex and often interdependent. Although managers may make decisions that do not involve negotiating, they cannot negotiate without making decisions, however small, or they would not be negotiating. In addition, managers must understand the behavioral aspects of these processes to work effectively with people in other countries or with a culturally diverse workforce in their own countries.

With an understanding of the environment and cultural context of international management as background, we move next in Part III to planning and implementing strategy for international and global operations.

Summary of Key Points

1. The ability to negotiate successfully is one of the most important in international business. Managers must prepare for certain cultural variables that influence negotiations, including the relative emphasis on task versus interpersonal relationships, the use of general principles versus specific details, the number of people present, and the extent of their influence.

2. The negotiation process typically progresses through the stages of preparation, relationship building, exchange of task-related information, persuasion, and concessions and agreement. The process of building trusting relationships is a prerequisite to doing business in many parts of the world.

3. Culturally based differences in verbal and nonverbal negotiation behavior influence the negotiation process at every stage. Such tactics and actions include promises, threats, initial concessions, silent periods, interruptions, facial gazing, and touching; some parties resort to various dirty tricks.

4. The effective management of negotiation requires an understanding of the perspectives, values, and agendas of other parties and the use of a problem-solving approach.

5. Decision making is an important part of the negotiation process, as well as an integral part of a manager's daily routine. Culture affects the decision-making process both through a society's institutions and through individuals' risk tolerance, their objective versus subjective perspectives, their perceptions of the locus of control, and their past versus future orientations.

6. The Internet is used increasingly to support the negotiation of contracts and resolution of disputes. Web sites that provide open auctions take away the personal aspects of negotiations, though those aspects are still essential in many instances.

Discussion Questions

1. Discuss the stages in the negotiation process and how culturally based value systems influence these stages. Specifically, address the following:

   - Explain the role and relative importance of relationship building in different countries.
   - Discuss the various styles and tactics that can be involved in exchanging task-related information.
   - Describe differences in culturally based styles of persuasion.
   - Discuss the kinds of concession strategies a negotiator might anticipate in various countries.

2. Discuss the relative use of nonverbal behaviors, such as silent periods, interruptions, facial gazing, and touching, by people from various cultural backgrounds. How does this behavior affect the negotiation process in a cross-cultural context?

3. Describe what you would expect in negotiations with the Chinese and how you would handle various situations.

4. What are some of the differences in risk tolerance around the world? What is the role of risk propensity in the decision-making process?

5. Explain how objective versus subjective perspectives influences the decision-making process. What role do you think this variable has played in all the negotiations conducted and decisions made by Iraq and the United Nations?

6. Explain differences in culturally based value systems relative to the amount of control a person feels he or she has over future outcomes. How does this belief influence the decision-making process?

Experiential Exercises

Exercise 1: Multicultural Negotiations

Goal

To experience, identify, and appreciate the problems associated with negotiating with people of other cultures.

Instructions

1. Eight student volunteers will participate in the role play. Four represent a Japanese automobile manufacturer, and four represent a U.S. team that has come to sell microchips and other components to the Japanese company. The remainder of the class will observe the negotiations.

2. The eight volunteers will divide into the two groups and then separate into different rooms, if possible. At that point, they will be given instruction sheets. Neither team can have access to the other's instructions. After dividing the roles, the teams should meet for 10 to 15 minutes to develop their negotiation strategies based on their instructions.

3. While the teams are preparing, the room will be set up using a rectangular table with four seats on each side. The Japanese side will have three chairs at the table with one chair set up behind the three. The American side of the table will have four chairs side by side.

4. Following these preparations, the Japanese team will be brought in, so they may greet the Americans when they arrive. At this point, the Americans will be brought in and the role play begins. Time for the negotiations should be 20 to 30 minutes. The rest of the class will act as observers and will be expected to provide feedback during the discussion phase.

5. When the negotiations are completed, the student participants from both sides and the observers will complete their feedback questionnaires. Class discussion of the feedback questions will follow.

Feedback Questions for the Japanese Team

1. What was your biggest frustration during the negotiations?
2. What would you say the goal of the American team was?
3. What role (e.g., decider, influencer, etc.) did each member of the American team play?
   Mr. Jones
   Mr./Ms. Smith
   Mr./Ms. Nelson
   Mr./Ms. Frost
4. How would you rate the success of each of the American team members in identifying your team's needs and appealing to them?
   Mr./Ms. Jones, Vice President and Team Leader
   Mr./Ms. Smith, Manufacturing Engineer
   Mr./Ms. Nelson, Marketing Analyst
   Mr./Ms. Frost, Account Executive
5. What strategy should the American team have taken?

Feedback Questions for the American Team

1. What was your biggest frustration during the negotiations?
2. What would you say the goal of the Japanese team was?
3. How would you rate the success of each of the American team members?
   Mr. Jones, Vice President and Team Leader
   Mr./Ms. Smith, Manufacturing Engineer
   Mr./Ms. Nelson, Marketing Analyst
   Mr./Ms. Frost, Account Executive
4. What would you say the goal of the American team was?
5. What role (e.g., decider, influencer, etc.) did each member of the Japanese team play?
   Mr. Ozaka
   Mr. Nishimuro
   Mr. Sheno
   Mr. Kawazaka
6. What strategy should the American team have taken?

Feedback Questions for the Observers

1. What was your biggest frustration during the negotiations?
2. What would you say the goal of the Japanese team was?
3. How would you rate the success of each of the American team members?
   Mr./Ms. Jones, Vice President and Team Leader
   Mr./Ms. Smith, Manufacturing Engineer
   Mr./Ms. Nelson, Marketing Analyst
   Mr./Ms. Frost, Account Executive
4. What would you say the goal of the American team was?
5. What role (e.g., decider, influencer, etc.) did each member of the Japanese team play?
   Mr. Ozaka
   Mr. Nishimuro
   Mr. Sheno
   Mr. Kawazaka
6. What strategy should the American team have taken?

Exercise 2: Japanese Decision Making

Time: Two class meetings

Goal

To allow students to experience the process and results of solving a problem or initiating a project using the Japanese decision processes of *nemawashi* and *ringi*.

Preparation

Review Chapter 4 and Chapter 5. In Chapter 5, study Comparative Management in Focus: Decision Making in Japanese Companies.

   Note: Instructions for this exercise will be given by your Professor, from the Instructor's Manual.

SOURCE: E. A. Diodati, in C. Harvey and M. J. Allard, *Understanding Diversity* (New York: HarperCollins Publishers, 1995). Used with permission.

Internet Resources

Visit the Deresky Companion Website at www.prenhall.com/deresky for this chapter's Internet resources.

C a s e   S t u d y

Negotiations Between Alcatel of France and Lucent of the U.S. Finally Result in Deal in 2006

Merger negotiations between Alcatel of France, the communications equipment maker based in Paris, and Lucent Technologies, the U.S. telecommunications giant, took place in 2001. However, the finely detailed deal collapsed on May 29, 2001, after the two companies could not agree on how much control the French company would have. Lucent's executives apparently wanted the deal as a "merger of equals," rather than a takeover by Alcatel. (1)

The failed deal was regarded as a severe blow to Lucent's image. Industry watchers questioned how Lucent would be able to survive this most recent blow. Although it was not clear which company initiated the negotiations, it was reported that Lucent ended them after much of the senior management detected that the proposed deal would not be a merger of equals. (2)

In 2006, however, renewed negotiations took place, resulting in the transatlantic relationship being consummated. Shareholders in France approved the $10.7 billion merger of the telecommunications equipment makers Alcatel and Lucent on September 7, 2006. However, Alcatel investors still had concerns about the leadership and financial health of their new American partner. Alcatel's chief executive, Serge Tchuruk, tried to reassure the 1,500 shareholders gathered in Paris to back the merger, saying the company—to be called Alcatel-Lucent— is "truly global and has no equivalent today and won't in the future." (3) Mr. Tchuruk had agreed in April 2006 to pay 10.6 billion euros ($13.5 billion) for Lucent, in a deal to create the world's biggest telephone equipment maker, although industry watchers considered the bid as financially inadequate for Alcatel investors. The stock swap was valued at one Alcatel American depository share for every five Lucent shares. Tchuruk said the combined company would realize 1.4 billion euros ($1.8 billion) in cost savings over the next three years, in part by cutting 9,000 jobs, about 10 percent of the combined workforce. (4) He noted that Alcatel-Lucent's revenue would be spread almost equally across Europe, the United States and Asia, offering greater long-term stability. Alcatel does most of its business in Europe, while Lucent does the majority of its business in the United States. Lucent Shareholders also endorsed the deal.

"We are another step closer to creating the first truly global communications solutions provider with the broadest wireless, wireline and services portfolio in the industry," said the chief executive of Lucent, Patricia F. Russo, who will retain that role in the combined company.

The company has combined sales of $25 billion. (5) Amid concerns about the potential for cross-cultural conflicts, Tchuruk said that, while cultural issues could arise, "everything is under way to make sure this human factor is dealt with," he said, adding that Alcatel already operated as an international company with a wide mix of nationalities; English is the official language of the company. (6) Other industry commentators cast Alcatel-Lucent as "a Franco-American telecoms behemoth that many regard as a giant transatlantic experiment in multinational diversity." (7)

After the shareholders of both companies endorsed the deal, regulatory hurdles were cleared in both the EU and the U.S. (8)

An Alcatel-Lucent merger gives the combined company a strong position in several categories of equipment sold to the major telecommunications carriers, detailed below. (9)

Wireless telecommunications equipment
2005 TOTAL = $40.1 BILLION
Alcatel: $3.1
Lucent: $4.2
Wireline telecommunications equipment
2005 TOTAL = $20.9 BILLION
Alcatel: $3.2
Lucent: $1.4
2005 worldwide market share by telecommunications equipment sector
Wireless infrastructure
$40.1 BILLION
Alcatel: 7.7%
Lucent: 10.5%
Ericsson: 30.0%
Fiber optic (Not cables)
$8.4 BILLION
Alcatel: 15.2%
Lucent: 9.7%
Nortel Networks: 12.1%

Internet routers and other
$4.4 BILLION
Alcatel: 3.1% Cisco Systems: 57.1%
D.S.L. signal aggregators $3.7 BILLION
Alcatel: 33.2% Lucent: 7.0%
Siemens 8.7%
Equipment for carrying calls over the Internet
$2.5 BILLION
Alcatel: 2.4% Lucent: 3.4%
Nortel Networks: 21.5%
Business data networking $1.8 BILLION
Alcatel: 25.1% Lucent: 15.8%
Nortel Networks: 38.2%

REFERENCES

1. A. Sorkin and S. Romero, "Alcatel and Lucent Call Off Negotiations Toward a Merger," *New York Times*, May 30, 2001, p. C.1; S. Shiesel, "Pride and Practicalities Loom Behind Failed Lucent 'Merger'," *New York Times*, May 31, 2001, p. C.1.
2. L. H. LaBarba, "Let's Call the Whole Thing Off," *Telephony,* June 4, 2001, vol. 240, 23, pp. 14–16.
3. J. Kanter, "Shareholders in Paris Approve Merger of Alcatel and Lucent," *New York Times*, September 6, 2006, p. C.3.
4. Ibid.
5. Ibid.
6. Ibid.
7. I. Austen and V. Bajaj, "A Continental Shift," *New York Times,* March 25, 2006, p. C.1.
8. "EU Clears Proposed Alcatel-Lucent Merger," *Wall Street Journal*, July 25, 2006.
9. Data from Austen and Bajaj.

CASE QUESTIONS

1. What conditions and negotiation factors pushed forth the merger in 2006 that were not present in 2001?
2. Research the status of the merged company at the time of your reading of this case. What has happened in the industry since the merger, and how is the company faring?
3. Evaluate the comment that the merger is "a giant transatlantic experiment in multicultural diversity." What evidence is there that the company has run into cross-cultural problems since the merger took place in 2006?

IVEY

Richard Ivey School of Business
The University of Western Ontario

Part II: Comprehensive Cases

Case 4   *Nora-Sakari: A Proposed JV in Malaysia*

On Monday, July 15, 2003 Zainal Hashim, vice-chairman of Nora Holdings Sdn Bhd[1] (Nora), arrived at his office about an hour earlier than usual. As he looked out the window at the city spreading below, he thought about the Friday evening reception which he had hosted at his home in Kuala Lumpur (KL), Malaysia, for a team of negotiators from Sakari Oy[2] (Sakari) of Finland. Nora was a leading supplier of telecommunications (telecom) equipment in Malaysia while Sakari, a Finnish conglomerate, was a leader in the manufacture of cellular phone sets and switching systems. The seven-member team from Sakari was in KL to negotiate with Nora the formation of a joint venture (JV) between the two telecom companies.

This was the final negotiation which would determine whether a JV agreement would materialize. The negotiation had ended late Friday afternoon, having lasted for five consecutive days. The JV company, if established, would be set up in Malaysia to manufacture and commission digital switching exchanges to meet the needs of the telecom industry in Malaysia and in neighboring countries, particularly Indonesia and Thailand. While Nora would benefit from the JV in terms of technology transfer, the venture would pave the way for Sakari to acquire knowledge and gain access to the markets of Southeast Asia.

R. Azimah Ainuddin prepared this case under the supervision of Professor Paul Beamish solely to provide material for class discussion. The authors do not intend to illustrate either effective or ineffective handling of a managerial situation. The authors may have disguised certain names and other identifying information to protect confidentiality.

Ivey Management Services prohibits any form of reproduction, storage, or transmittal without its written permission. This material is not covered under authorization from CanCopy or any reproduction rights organization. To order copies or request permission to reproduce materials, contact Ivey Publishing, Ivey Management Services, c/o Richard Ivey School of Business, The University of Western Ontario, London, Ontario, Canada, N6A 3K7; phone (519) 661-3208; fax (519) 661-3882; e-mail cases@ivey.uwo.ca.

Copyright © 2006, Ivey Management Services Version: (A) 2006-09-07

[1]Sdn Bhd is an abbreviation for Sendirian Berhad, which means private limited company in Malaysia.
[2]Oy is an abbreviation for Osakeyhtiot, which means private limited company in Finland.

The Nora management was impressed by the Finnish capability in using high technology to enable Finland, a small country of only five million people, to have a fast-growing economy. Most successful Finnish companies were in the high-tech industries. For example, Kone was one of the world's three largest manufacturers of lifts, Vaisala was the world's major supplier of meteorological equipment, and Sakari was one of the leading telecom companies in Europe. It would be an invaluable opportunity for Nora to learn from the Finnish experience and emulate their success for Malaysia.

The opportunity emerged two and half years earlier when Peter Mattsson, president of Sakari's Asian regional office in Singapore, approached Zainal[3] to explore the possibility of forming a cooperative venture between Nora and Sakari. Mattsson said:

> *While growth in the mobile telecommunications network is expected to be about 40 percent a year in Asia in the next five years, growth in fixed networks would not be as fast, but the projects are much larger. A typical mobile network project amounts to a maximum of 50 million, but fixed network projects can be estimated in hundreds of millions. In Malaysia and Thailand, such latter projects are currently approaching contract stage. Thus it is imperative that Sakari establish its presence in this region to capture a share in the fixed network market.*

The large potential for telecom facilities was also evidenced in the low telephone penetration rates for most Southeast Asian countries. For example, in 1999, telephone penetration rates (measured by the number of telephone lines per 100 people) for Indonesia, Thailand, Malaysia, and the Philippines ranged from 3 to 20 lines per 100 people compared to the rates in developed countries such as Canada, Finland, Germany, United States, and Sweden where the rates exceeded 55 telephone lines per 100 people.

[3]The first name is used because the Malay name does not carry a family name. The first and/or middle names belong to the individual and the last name is his/her father's name.

THE TELECOM INDUSTRY IN MALAYSIA

Telekom Malaysia Bhd (TMB), the national telecom company, was given the authority by the Malaysian government to develop the country's telecom infrastructure. With a paid-up capital of RM2.4 billion,[4] it was also given the mandate to provide telecom services that were on par with those available in developed countries.

TMB announced that it would be investing in the digitalization of its networks to pave the way for offering services based on the ISDN (integrated services digitalized network) standard, and investing in international fiber optic cable networks to meet the needs of increased telecom traffic between Malaysia and the rest of the world. TMB would also facilitate the installation of more cellular telephone networks in view of the increased demand for the use of mobile phones among the business community in KL and in major towns.

As the nation's largest telecom company, TMB's operations were regulated through a 20-year license issued by the Ministry of Energy, Telecommunications and Posts. In line with the government's Vision 2020 program which targeted Malaysia to become a developed nation by the year 2020, there was a strong need for the upgrading of the telecom infrastructure in the rural areas. TMB estimated that it would spend more than RM1 billion each year on the installation of fixed networks, of which 25 percent would be allocated for the expansion of rural telecom. The objective was to increase the telephone penetration rate to over 50 percent by the year 2005.

Although TMB had become a large national telecom company, it lacked the expertise and technology to undertake massive infrastructure projects. In most cases, the local telecom companies would be invited to submit their bids for a particular contract. It was also common for these local companies to form partnerships with large multinational corporations (MNCs), mainly for technological support. For example, Pernas-NEC, a JV company between Pernas Holdings and NEC, was one of the companies that had been successful in securing large telecom contracts from the Malaysian authorities.

NORA'S SEARCH FOR A JV PARTNER

In October 2002, TMB called for tenders to bid on a five-year project worth RM2 billion for installing digital switching exchanges in various parts of the country. The project also involved replacing analog circuit switches with digital switches. Digital switches enhanced transmission capabilities of telephone lines, increasing capacity to approximately two million bits per second compared to the 9,600 bits per second on analog circuits.

Nora was interested in securing a share of the RM2 billion contract from TMB and, more importantly, in

acquiring the knowledge in switching technology from its partnership with a telecom MNC. During the initial stages, when Nora first began to consider potential partners in the bid for this contract, telecom MNCs such as Siemens, Alcatel, and Fujitsu seemed appropriate candidates. Nora had previously entered into a five-year technical assistance agreement with Siemens to manufacture telephone handsets.

Nora also had the experience of a long-term working relationship with Japanese partners which would prove valuable should a JV be formed with Fujitsu. Alcatel was another potential partner, but the main concern at Nora was that the technical standards used in the French technology were not compatible with the British standards already adopted in Malaysia. NEC and Ericsson were not considered, as they were already involved with other local competitors and were the current suppliers of digital switching exchanges to TMB. Their five-year contracts were due to expire soon.

Subsequent to Zainal's meeting with Mattsson, he decided to consider Sakari as a serious potential partner. He was briefed about Sakari's SK33, a digital switching system that was based on an open architecture, which enabled the use of standard components, standard software development tools, and standard software languages. Unlike the switching exchanges developed by NEC and Ericsson which required the purchase of components developed by the parent companies, the SK33 used components that were freely available in the open market. The system was also modular, and its software could be upgraded to provide new services and could interface easily with new equipment in the network. This was the most attractive feature of the SK33 as it would lead to the development of new switching systems.

Mattsson had also convinced Zainal and other Nora managers that although Sakari was a relatively small player in fixed networks, these networks were easily adaptable, and could cater to large exchanges in the urban areas as well as small ones for rural needs. Apparently Sakari's smaller size, compared to that of some of the other MNCs, was an added strength because Sakari was prepared to work out customized products according to Nora's needs. Large telecom companies were alleged to be less willing to provide custom-made products. Instead, they tended to offer standard products that, in some aspects, were not consistent with the needs of the customer.

Prior to the July meeting, at least 20 meetings had been held either in KL or in Helsinki to establish relationships between the two companies. It was estimated that each side had invested not less than RM3 million in promoting the relationship. Mattsson and Ilkka Junttila, Sakari's representative in KL, were the key people in bringing the two companies together. (See Exhibits C4-1 and C4-2 for brief background information on Malaysia and Finland, respectively.)

---

[4]RM is Ringgit Malaysia, the Malaysian currency. As at December 31, 2002, US$1 = RM3.80.

EXHIBIT C4-1   Malaysia: Background Information

Malaysia is centrally located in Southeast Asia. It consists of Peninsular Malaysia, bordered by Thailand in the north and Singapore in the south, and the states of Sabah and Sarawak on the island of Borneo. Malaysia has a total land area of about 330,000 square kilometers, of which 80 percent is covered with tropical rainforest. Malaysia has an equatorial climate with high humidity and high daily temperatures of about 26 degrees Celsius throughout the year.

In 2000, Malaysia's population was 22 million, of which approximately nine million made up the country's labor force. The population is relatively young, with 42 percent between the ages of 15 and 39 and only 7 percent above the age of 55. A Malaysian family has an average of four children and extended families are common. Kuala Lumpur, the capital city of Malaysia, has approximately 1.5 million inhabitants.

The population is multiracial; the largest ethnic group is the Bumiputeras (the Malays and other indigenous groups such as the Ibans in Sarawak and Kadazans in Sabah), followed by the Chinese and Indians. Bahasa Malaysia is the national language but English is widely used in business circles. Other major languages spoken included various Chinese dialects and Tamil.

Islam is the official religion but other religions (mainly Christianity, Buddhism, and Hinduism) are widely practiced. Official holidays are allocated for the celebration of Eid, Christmas, Chinese New Year, and Deepavali. All Malays are Muslims, followers of the Islamic faith.

During the period of British rule, secularism was introduced to the country, which led to the separation of the Islamic religion from daily life. In the late 1970s and 1980s, realizing the negative impact of secularism on the life of the Muslims, several groups of devout Muslims undertook efforts to reverse the process, emphasizing a dynamic and progressive approach to Islam. As a result, changes were introduced to meet the daily needs of Muslims. Islamic banking and insurance facilities were introduced and prayer rooms were provided in government offices, private companies, factories, and even in shopping complexes.

Malaysia is a parliamentary democracy under a constitutional monarchy. The Yang DiPertuan Agung (the king) is the supreme head, and appoints the head of the ruling political party to be the prime minister. In 2000 the Barisan Nasional, a coalition of several political parties representing various ethnic groups, was the ruling political party in Malaysia. Its predominance had contributed not only to the political stability and economic progress of the country in the last two decades, but also to the fast recovery from the 1997 Asian economic crisis.

The recession of the mid 1980s led to structural changes in the Malaysian economy which had been too dependent on primary commodities (rubber, tin, palm oil, and timber) and had a very narrow export base. To promote the establishment of export-oriented industries, the government directed resources to the manufacturing sector, introduced generous incentives, and relaxed foreign equity restrictions. In the meantime, heavy investments were made to modernize the country's infrastructure. These moves led to rapid economic growth in the late 1980s and early 1990s. The growth had been mostly driven by exports, particularly of electronics.

The Malaysian economy was hard hit by the 1997 Asian economic crisis. However, Malaysia was the fastest country to recover from the crisis after declining IMF assistance. It achieved this by pegging its currency to the USD, restricting outflow of money from the country, banning illegal overseas derivative trading of Malaysian securities, and setting up asset management companies to facilitate the orderly recovery of bad loans. The real GDP growth rate in 1999 and 2000 were 5.4 percent and 8.6 percent, respectively (Table C4-1).

TABLE C4-1   Malaysian Economic Performance 1999 to 2002

Economic Indicator	1999	2000	2001	2002
GDP per capita (US$)	3,596	3,680	3,678	3,814
Real GDP growth rate	5.4%	8.6%	0.4%	4.2%
Consumer price inflation	2.8%	1.6%	1.4%	1.8%
Unemployment rate	3.0%	3.0%	3.7%	3.5%

SOURCE: IMD. Various years. "The World Competitiveness Report."

Malaysia was heavily affected by the global economic downturn and the slump in the IT sector in 2001 and 2002 due to its export-based economy. GDP in 2001 grew only 0.4 percent due to an 11 percent decrease in exports. A US $1.9 billion fiscal stimulus package helped the country ward off the worst of the recession and the GDP growth rate rebounded to 4.2 percent in 2002 (Table C4-1). A relatively small foreign debt and adequate foreign exchange reserves make a crisis similar to the 1997 one unlikely. Nevertheless, the economy remains vulnerable to a more protracted slowdown in the United States and Japan, top export destinations and key sources of foreign investment.

In 2002, the manufacturing sector was the leading contributor to the economy, accounting for about 30 percent of gross domestic product (GDP). Malaysia's major trading partners are United States, Singapore, Japan, China, Taiwan, Hong Kong, and Korea.

SOURCES: Ernst & Young International. 1993. "Doing Business in Malaysia." Other online sources.

EXHIBIT C4-2 Finland: Background Information

Finland is situated in the northeast of Europe, sharing borders with Sweden, Norway, and the former Soviet Union. About 65 percent of its area of 338,000 square kilometers is covered with forest, about 15 percent lakes, and about 10 percent arable land. Finland has a temperate climate with four distinct seasons. In Helsinki, the capital city, July is the warmest month with an average midday temperature of 21 degrees Celsius, and January is the coldest month with an average midday temperature of −3 degrees Celsius.

Finland is one of the most sparsely populated countries in Europe with a 2002 population of 5.2 million, 60 percent of whom lived in the urban areas. Helsinki had a population of about 560,000 in 2002. Finland has a well-educated workforce of about 2.3 million. About half of the workforce is engaged in providing services, 30 percent in manufacturing and construction, and 8 percent in agricultural production. The small size of the population has led to scarce and expensive labor. Thus Finland had to compete by exploiting its lead in high-tech industries.

Finland's official languages are Finnish and Swedish, although only 6 percent of the population speaks Swedish. English is the most widely spoken foreign language. About 87 percent of the Finns are Lutherans and about 1 percent Finnish Orthodox.

Finland has been an independent republic since 1917, having previously been ruled by Sweden and Russia. A president is elected to a six-year term, and a 200-member, single-chamber parliament is elected every four years.

In 1991, the country experienced a bad recession triggered by a sudden drop in exports due to the collapse of the Soviet Union. During 1991–1993, the total output suffered a 10 percent contraction and the unemployment rate reached almost 20 percent. Finnish Markka experienced a steep devaluation in 1991–1992, which gave Finland cost competitiveness in the international market.

With this cost competitiveness and the recovery of Western export markets the Finnish economy underwent a rapid revival in 1993, followed by a new period of healthy growth. Since the mid 1990s the Finnish growth has mainly been bolstered by intense growth in telecommunications equipment manufacturing. The Finnish economy peaked in the year 2000 with a real GDP growth rate of 5.6 percent (Table C4-2).

Finland was one of the 11 countries that joined the Economic and Monetary Union (EMU) on January 1, 1999. Finland has been

TABLE C4-2 Finnish Economic Performance 1999 to 2002

Economic Indicator	1999	2000	2001	2002
GDP per capita (US$)	24,430	23,430	23,295	25,303
Real GDP growth rate	3.7%	5.6%	0.4%	1.6%
Consumer price inflation	1.2%	3.3%	2.6%	1.6%
Unemployment	10.3%	9.6%	9.1%	9.1%

SOURCE: IMD. Various years. "The World Competitiveness Report."

experiencing a rapidly increasing integration with Western Europe. Membership in the EMU provide the Finnish economy with an array of benefits, such as lower and stable interest rates, elimination of foreign currency risk within the Euro area, reduction of transaction costs of business and travel, and so forth. This provided Finland with a credibility that it lacked before accession and the Finnish economy has become more predictable. This will have a long-term positive effect on many facets of the economy.

Finland's economic structure is based on private ownership and free enterprise. However, the production of alcoholic beverages and spirits is retained as a government monopoly. Finland's major trading partners are Sweden, Germany, the former Soviet Union, and the United Kingdom.

Finland's standard of living is among the highest in the world. The Finns have small families with one or two children per family. They have comfortable homes in the cities and one in every three families has countryside cottages near a lake where they retreat on weekends. Taxes are high, the social security system is efficient, and poverty is virtually nonexistent.

Until recently, the stable trading relationship with the former Soviet Union and other Scandinavian countries led to few interactions between the Finns and people in other parts of the world. The Finns are described as rather reserved, obstinate, and serious people. A Finn commented, "We do not engage easily in small talk with strangers. Furthermore, we have a strong love for nature and we have the tendency to be silent as we observe our surroundings. Unfortunately, others tend to view such behavior as cold and serious." Visitors to Finland are often impressed by the efficient public transport system, the clean and beautiful city of Helsinki with orderly road networks, scenic parks and lakefronts, museums, cathedrals, and churches.

SOURCES: Ernst & Young International. 1993. "Doing Business in Finland." Other online sources.

NORA HOLDINGS SDN BHD

The Company

Nora was one of the leading companies in the telecom industry in Malaysia. It was established in 1975 with a paid-up capital of RM2 million. Last year, the company recorded a turnover of RM320 million. Nora Holdings consisted of 30 subsidiaries, including two public-listed companies: Multiphone Bhd and Nora Telecommunications Bhd. Nora had 3,081 employees, of which 513 were categorized as managerial (including 244 engineers) and 2,568 as non-managerial (including 269 engineers and technicians).

The cable business. Since the inception of the company, Nora had secured two cable-laying projects. For the latter project worth RM500 million, Nora formed a JV with two Japanese companies, Sumitomo Electric Industries Ltd (held 10 percent equity share) and Marubeni Corporation (held 5 percent equity share). Japanese partners were chosen in view of the availability of a financial package that came together with the technological assistance needed by Nora. Nora also acquired a 63 percent stake in a local cable-laying company, Selangor Cables Sdn Bhd.

The telephone business. Nora had become a household name in Malaysia as a telephone manufacturer. It started in 1980 when the company obtained a contract to supply telephone sets to the government-owned Telecom authority, TMB, which would distribute the sets to telephone subscribers on a rental basis. The contract, estimated at RM130 million, lasted for 15 years. In 1985 Nora secured licenses from Siemens and Nortel to manufacture telephone handsets and had subsequently developed Nora's own telephone sets—the N300S (single line), N300M (micro-computer controlled), and N300V (hands-free, voice-activated) models.

Upon expiry of the 15-year contract as a supplier of telephone sets to the TMB, Nora suffered a major setback when it lost a RM32 million contract to supply 600,000 N300S single line telephones. The contract was instead given to a Taiwanese manufacturer, Formula Electronics, which quoted a lower price of RM37 per handset compared to Nora's RM54. Subsequently, Nora was motivated to move towards the high-end feature phone domestic market. The company sold about 3,000 sets of feature phones per month, capturing the high-end segment of the Malaysian market.

Nora had ventured into the export market with its feature phones, but industry observers predicted that Nora still had a long way to go as an exporter. The foreign markets were very competitive and many manufacturers already had well-established brands.

The payphone business. Nora's start-up in the payphone business had turned out to be one of the company's most profitable lines of business. Other than the cable-laying contract secured in 1980, Nora had a 15-year contract to install, operate, and maintain payphones in the cities and major towns in Malaysia. In 1997, Nora started to manufacture card payphones under a license from GEC Plessey Telecommunications (GPT) of the United Kingdom. The agreement had also permitted Nora to sell the products to the neighboring countries in Southeast Asia as well as to eight other markets approved by GPT.

While the payphone revenues were estimated to be as high as RM60 million a year, a long-term and stable income stream for Nora, profit margins were only about 10 percent because of the high investment and maintenance costs.

Other businesses. Nora was also the sole Malaysian distributor for Nortel's private automatic branch exchange (PABX) and NEC's mobile telephone sets. It was also an Apple computer distributor in Malaysia and Singapore. In addition, Nora was involved in: distributing radio-related equipment; supplying equipment to the broadcasting, meteorological, civil aviation, postal, and power authorities; and manufacturing automotive parts (such as the suspension coil, springs, and piston) for the local automobile companies.

The Management

When Nora was established, Osman Jaafar, founder and chairman of Nora Holdings, managed the company with his wife, Nora Asyikin Yusof, and seven employees. Osman was known as a conservative businessman who did not like to dabble in acquisitions and mergers to make quick capital gains. He was formerly an electrical engineer who was trained in the United Kingdom and had held several senior positions at the national Telecom Department in Malaysia.

Osman subsequently recruited Zainal Hashim to fill the position of deputy managing director at Nora. Zainal held a master's degree in microwave communications from a British university and had several years of working experience as a production engineer at Pernas-NEC Sdn Bhd, a manufacturer of transmission equipment. Zainal was later promoted to the position of managing director and six years later, the vice-chairman.

Industry analysts observed that Nora's success was attributed to the complementary roles, trust, and mutual understanding between Osman and Zainal. While Osman "likes to fight for new business opportunities," Zainal preferred a low profile and concentrated on managing Nora's operations.

Industry observers also speculated that Osman, a former civil servant and an entrepreneur, was close to Malaysian politicians, notably the Prime Minister, while Zainal had been a close friend of the Finance Minister. Zainal disagreed with allegations that Nora had succeeded due to its close relationships with Malaysian politicians. However, he acknowledged that such perceptions in the industry had been beneficial to the company.

Osman and Zainal had an obsession for high-tech and made the development of research and development (R&D) skills and resources a priority in the company. About 1 percent of Nora's earnings was ploughed back into R&D activities. Although this amount was considered small by international standards, Nora planned to increase it gradually to 5 to 6 percent over the next two to three years. Zainal said:

> We believe in making improvements in small steps, similar to the Japanese kaizen principle. Over time, each small improvement could lead to a major creation. To be able to make improvements, we must learn from others. Thus we would borrow a technology from others, but eventually, we must be able to develop our own to sustain our competitiveness in the industry. As a matter of fact, Sakari's SK33 system was developed based on a technology it obtained from Alcatel.

To further enhance R&D activities at Nora, Nora Research Sdn Bhd (NRSB), a wholly-owned subsidiary, was formed, and its R&D department was absorbed into this new company. NRSB operated as an independent research company undertaking R&D activities for Nora as well as private clients in related fields. The company facilitated R&D activities with other companies as well as government organizations, research institutions, and universities. NRSB, with its staff of 40 technicians/engineers, would charge a fixed fee for basic research and a royalty for its products sold by clients.

Zainal was also active in instilling and promoting Islamic values among the Malay employees at Nora. He explained:

> Islam is a way of life and there is no such thing as Islamic management. The Islamic values, which must be reflected in the daily life of Muslims, would influence their behaviors as employers and employees. Our Malay managers, however, were often influenced by their western counterparts, who tend to stress knowledge and mental capability and often forget the effectiveness of the softer side of management which emphasizes relationships, sincerity, and consistency. I believe that one must always be sincere to be able to develop good working relationships.

SAKARI OY

Sakari was established in 1865 as a pulp and paper mill located about 200 kilometers northwest of Helsinki, the capital city of Finland. In the 1960s, Sakari started to expand into the rubber and cable industries when it merged with the Finnish Rubber Works and Finnish Cable Works. In 1973 Sakari's performance was badly affected by the oil crisis, as its businesses were largely energy-intensive.

However, in 1975, the company recovered when Aatos Olkkola took over as Sakari's president. He led Sakari into competitive businesses such as computers, consumer electronics, and cellular phones via a series of acquisitions, mergers, and alliances. Companies involved in the acquisitions included the consumer electronics division of Standard Elektrik Lorenz AG; the data systems division of L.M. Ericsson; Vantala, a Finnish manufacturer of color televisions; and Luxury, a Swedish state-owned electronics and computer concern.

In 1979, a JV between Sakari and Vantala, Sakari-Vantala, was set up to develop and manufacture mobile telephones. Sakari-Vantala had captured about 14 percent of the world's market share for mobile phones and held a 20 percent market share in Europe for its mobile phone handsets. Outside Europe, a 50–50 JV was formed with Tandy Corporation which, to date, had made significant sales in the United States, Malaysia, and Thailand.

Sakari first edged into the telecom market by selling switching systems licensed from France's Alcatel and by developing the software and systems to suit the needs of small Finnish phone companies. Sakari had avoided head-on competition with Siemens and Ericsson by not trying to enter the market for large telephone networks. Instead, Sakari had concentrated on developing dedicated telecom networks for large private users such as utility and railway companies. In Finland, Sakari held 40 percent of the market for digital exchanges. Other competitors included Ericsson (34 percent), Siemens (25 percent), and Alcatel (1 percent).

Sakari was also a niche player in the global switching market. Its SK33 switches had sold well in countries such as Sri Lanka, the United Arab Emirates, China, and the Soviet Union. A derivative of the SK33 main exchange switch called the SK33XT was subsequently developed to be used in base stations for cellular networks and personal paging systems.

Sakari attributed its emphasis on R&D as its key success factor in the telecom industry. Strong in-house R&D in core competence areas enabled the company to develop technology platforms such as its SK33 system that were reliable, flexible, widely compatible, and economical. About 17 percent of its annual sales revenue was invested into R&D and product development units in Finland, the United Kingdom, and France. Sakari's current strategy was to emphasize global operations in production and R&D. It planned to set up R&D centers in leading markets, including Southeast Asia.

Sakari was still a small company by international standards (see Exhibit C4-3 for a list of the world's major telecom equipment suppliers). It lacked a strong marketing capability and had to rely on JVs such as the one with Tandy Corporation to enter the world market, particularly the United States. In its efforts to develop

EXHIBIT C4-3   Ten Major Telecommunication Equipment Vendors

Rank	Company	Country	1998 Telecom Equipment Sales (US$ billions)
1	Lucent	USA	26.8
2	Ericsson	Sweden	21.5
3	Alcatel	France	20.9
4	Motorola	USA	20.5
5	Nortel	Canada	17.3
6	Siemens	Germany	16.8
7	Nokia	Finland	14.7
8	NEC	Japan	12.6
9	Cisco	USA	8.4
10	Hughes	USA	5.7

SOURCE: International Telecommunication Union. 1999. Top 20 Telecommunication Equipment Vendors 1998. http://www.itu.int/ITU-D/ict/statistics/at_glance/Top2098.html.

market position quickly, Sakari had to accept lower margins for its products, and often the Sakari name was not revealed on the product. In recent years, Sakari decided to emerge from its hiding place as a manufacturer's manufacturer and began marketing under the Sakari name.

In 1989 Mikko Koskinen took over as president of Sakari. Koskinen announced that telecommunications, computers, and consumer electronics would be maintained as Sakari's core business, and that he would continue Olkkola's efforts in expanding the company overseas. He believed that every European company needed global horizons to be able to meet global competition for future survival. To do so, he envisaged the setting up of alliances of varying duration, each designed for specific purposes. He said, "Sakari has become an interesting partner with which to cooperate on an equal footing in the areas of R&D, manufacturing, and marketing."

The recession in Finland which began in 1990 led Sakari's group sales to decline substantially from FIM22 billion[5] in 1990 to FIM15 billion in 1991. The losses were attributed to two main factors: weak demand for Sakari's consumer electronic products, and trade with the Soviet Union which had come to almost a complete standstill. Consequently Sakari began divesting its less profitable companies within the basic industries (metal, rubber, and paper), as well as leaving the troubled European computer market with the sale of its computer subsidiary, Sakari Macro. The company's new strategy was to focus on three main areas: telecom systems and mobile phones in a global framework, consumer electronic products in Europe, and deliveries of cables and related technology.

The company's divestment strategy led to a reduction of Sakari's employees from about 41,000 in 1989 to 29,000 in 1991. This series of major strategic moves was accompanied by major leadership succession. In June 1992, Koskinen retired as Sakari's president and was replaced by Visa Ketonen, formerly the president of Sakari Mobile Phones. Ketonen appointed Ossi Kuusisto as Sakari's vice president.

After Ketonen took over control, the Finnish economy went through a rapid revival in 1993, followed by a new period of intense growth. Since the mid 1990s the Finnish growth had been bolstered by intense growth in telecommunications equipment manufacturing as a result of an exploding global telecommunications market. Sakari capitalized on this opportunity and played a major role in the Finnish telecommunications equipment manufacturing sector.

In 2001, Sakari was Finland's largest publicly-traded industrial company and derived the majority of its total sales from exports and overseas operations. Traditionally, the company's export sales were confined to other Scandinavian countries, Western Europe, and the former Soviet Union. However, in recent years, the company made efforts and succeeded in globalizing and diversifying its operations to make the most of its high-tech capabilities. As a result, Sakari emerged as a more influential player in the international market and had gained international brand recognition. One of Sakari's strategies was to form JVs to enter new foreign markets.

THE NORA-SAKARI NEGOTIATION

Nora and Sakari had discussed the potential of forming a JV company in Malaysia for more than two years. Nora engineers were sent to Helsinki to assess the SK33

---

[5]FIM is Finnish Markka, the Finnish currency until January 1, 1999. Markka coins and notes were not withdrawn from circulation until January 1, 2002, when Finland fully converted to the Euro. As at December 31, 2000, US$1 = FIM6.31, and €1 = FIM5.95.

technology in terms of its compatibility with the Malaysian requirements, while Sakari managers travelled to KL mainly to assess both Nora's capability in manufacturing switching exchanges and the feasibility of gaining access to the Malaysian market.

In January 2003, Nora submitted its bid for TMB's RM2 billion contract to supply digital switching exchanges supporting four million telephone lines. Assuming the Nora-Sakari JV would materialize, Nora based its bid on supplying Sakari's digital switching technology. Nora competed with seven other companies short listed by TMB, all offering their partners' technology—Alcatel, Lucent, Fujitsu, Siemens, Ericsson, NEC, and Samsung. In early May, TMB announced five successful companies in the bid. They were companies using technology from Alcatel, Fujitsu, Ericsson, NEC, and Sakari. Each company was awarded a one-fifth share of the RM2 billion contract and would be responsible for delivering 800,000 telephone lines over a period of five years. Industry observers were critical of TMB's decision to select Sakari and Alcatel. Sakari was perceived to be the least capable of supplying the necessary lines to meet TMB's requirements, as it was alleged to be a small company with little international exposure. Alcatel was criticized for having the potential of supplying an obsolete technology.

The May 21 Meeting

Following the successful bid and ignoring the criticisms against Sakari, Nora and Sakari held a major meeting in Helsinki on May 21 to finalize the formation of the JV. Zainal led Nora's five-member negotiation team which comprised Nora's general manager for corporate planning division, an accountant, two engineers, and Marina Mohamed, a lawyer. One of the engineers was Salleh Lindstrom, who was of Swedish origin, a Muslim, and had worked for Nora for almost ten years.

Sakari's eight-member team was led by Kuusisto, Sakari's vice president. His team comprised Junttila, Hussein Ghazi, Aziz Majid, three engineers, and Julia Ruola (a lawyer). Ghazi was Sakari's senior manager who was of Egyptian origin and also a Muslim who had worked for Sakari for more than 20 years while Aziz, a Malay, had been Sakari's manager for more than 12 years.

The meeting went on for several days. The main issue raised at the meeting was Nora's capability in penetrating the Southeast Asian market. Other issues included Sakari's concerns over the efficiency of Malaysian workers in the JV in manufacturing the product, maintaining product quality, and ensuring prompt deliveries.

Commenting on the series of negotiations with Sakari, Zainal said that this was the most difficult negotiation he had ever experienced. Zainal was Nora's most experienced negotiator and had single-handedly represented Nora in several major negotiations for the past ten years. In the negotiation with Sakari, Zainal admitted making the mistake of approaching the negotiation by applying the approach he often used when negotiating with his counterparts from companies based in North America or the United Kingdom. He said:

> *Negotiators from the United States tend to be very open and often state their positions early and definitively. They are highly verbal and usually prepare well-planned presentations. They also often engage in small talk and "joke around" with us at the end of a negotiation. In contrast, the Sakari negotiators tend to be very serious, reserved and "cold." They are also relatively less verbal and do not convey much through their facial expressions. As a result, it was difficult for us to determine whether they are really interested in the deal or not.*

Zainal said that the negotiation on May 21 turned out to be particularly difficult when Sakari became interested in bidding a recently announced tender for a major telecom contract in the United Kingdom. Internal politics within Sakari led to the formation of two opposing "camps." One "camp" held a strong belief that there would be very high growth in the Asia-Pacific region and that the JV company in Malaysia was seen as a hub to enter these markets. Although the Malaysian government had liberalized its equity ownership restrictions and allowed the formation of wholly-owned subsidiaries, JVs were still an efficient way to enter the Malaysian market for a company that lacked local knowledge. This group was represented mostly by Sakari's managers positioned in Asia and engineers who had made several trips to Malaysia, which usually included visits to Nora's facilities. They also had the support of Sakari's vice president, Kuusisto, who was involved in most of the meetings with Nora, particularly when Zainal was present. Kuusisto had also made efforts to be present at meetings held in KL. This group also argued that Nora had already obtained the contract in Malaysia whereas the chance of getting the U.K. contract was quite low in view of the intense competition prevailing in that market.

The "camp" not in favor of the Nora-Sakari JV believed that Sakari should focus its resources on entering the United Kingdom, which could be used as a hub to penetrate the European Union (EU) market. There was also the belief that Europe was closer to home, making management easier, and that problems arising from cultural differences would be minimized. This group was also particularly concerned that Nora had the potential of copying Sakari's technology and eventually becoming a strong regional competitor. Also, because the U.K. market was relatively "familiar" and Sakari has local knowledge, Sakari could set up a wholly-owned subsidiary instead of a JV company, and consequently avoid JV-related problems such as joint control, joint profits, and leakage of technology.

Zainal felt that the lack of full support from Sakari's management led to a difficult negotiation when new misgivings arose concerning Nora's capability to deliver its part of the deal. It was apparent that the group in favor of the Nora-Sakari JV was under pressure to further justify its proposal and provide counterarguments against the U.K. proposal. A Sakari manager explained, "We are tempted to pursue both proposals since each has its own strengths, but our current resources are very limited. Thus a choice has to made, and soon."

The July 8 Meeting

Another meeting to negotiate the JV agreement was scheduled for July 8. Sakari's eight-member team arrived in KL on Sunday afternoon of July 7, and was met at the airport by the key Nora managers involved in the negotiation. Kuusisto did not accompany the Sakari team at this meeting.

The negotiation started early Monday morning at Nora's headquarters and continued for the next five days, with each day's meeting ending late in the evening. Members of the Nora team were the same members who had attended the May 21 meeting in Finland, except Zainal, who did not participate. The Sakari team was also represented by the same members in attendance at the previous meeting plus a new member, Solail Pekkarinen, Sakari's senior accountant. Unfortunately, on the third day of the negotiation, the Nora team requested that Sakari ask Pekkarinen to leave the negotiation. He was perceived as extremely arrogant and insensitive to the local culture, which tended to value modesty and diplomacy. Pekkarinen left for Helsinki the following morning.

Although Zainal had decided not to participate actively in the negotiations, he followed the process closely and was briefed by his negotiators regularly. Some of the issues which they complained were difficult to resolve had often led to heated arguments between the two negotiating teams. These included:

1. Equity ownership. In previous meetings both companies agreed to form the JV company with a paid-up capital of RM5 million. However, they disagreed on the equity share proposed by each side. Sakari proposed an equity split in the JV company of 49 percent for Sakari and 51 percent for Nora. Nora, on the other hand, proposed a 30 percent Sakari and 70 percent Nora split. Nora's proposal was based on the common practice in Malaysia as a result of historical foreign equity regulations set by the Malaysian government that allowed a maximum of 30 percent foreign equity ownership unless the company would export a certain percentage of its products. Though these regulations were liberalized by the Malaysian government effective from July 1998 and new regulations had replaced the old ones, the 30–70 foreign-Malaysian ownership divide was still commonly observed.

Equity ownership became a major issue as it was associated with control over the JV company. Sakari was concerned about its ability to control the accessibility of its technology to Nora and about decisions concerning the activities of the JV as a whole. The lack of control was perceived by Sakari as an obstacle to protecting its interests. Nora also had similar concerns about its ability to exert control over the JV because it was intended as a key part of Nora's long-term strategy to develop its own digital switching exchanges and related high-tech products.

2. Technology transfer. Sakari proposed to provide the JV company with the basic structure of the digital switch. The JV company would assemble the switching exchanges at the JV plant and subsequently install the exchanges in designated locations identified by TMB. By offering Nora only the basic structure of the switch, the core of Sakari's switching technology would still be well-protected.

On the other hand, Nora proposed that the basic structure of the switch be developed at the JV company in order to access the root of the switching technology. Based on Sakari's proposal, Nora felt that only the technical aspects in assembling and installing the exchanges would be obtained. This was perceived as another "screw-driver" form of technology transfer while the core of the technology associated with making the switches would still be unknown.

3. Royalty payment. Closely related to the issue of technology transfer was the payment of a royalty for the technology used in building the switches. Sakari proposed a royalty payment of 5 percent of the JV gross sales while Nora proposed a payment of 2 percent of net sales.

Nora considered the royalty rate of 5 percent too high because it would affect Nora's financial situation as a whole. Financial simulations prepared by Nora's managers indicated that Nora's return on investment would be less than the desired 10 percent if royalty rates exceeded 3 percent of net sales. This was because Nora had already agreed to make large additional investments in support of the JV. Nora would invest in a building which would be rented to the JV company to accommodate an office and the switching plant. Nora would also invest in another plant which would supply the JV with surface mounted devices (SMD), one of the major components needed to build the switching exchanges.

An added argument raised by the Nora negotiators in support of a 2 percent royalty was that Sakari would receive side benefits from the JV's access to Japanese technology used in the manufacture of the SMD components. Apparently the Japanese technology was more advanced than Sakari's present technology.

4. Expatriates' salaries and perks. To allay Sakari's concerns over Nora's level of efficiency, Nora suggested that

Sakari provide the necessary training for the JV technical employees. Subsequently, Sakari had agreed to provide eight engineering experts for the JV company on two types of contracts, short term and long term. Experts employed on a short-term basis would be paid a daily rate of US$1,260 plus travel/accommodation. The permanent experts would be paid a monthly salary of US$20,000. Three permanent experts would be attached to the JV company once it was established and the number would gradually be reduced to only one after two years. Five experts would be available on a short-term basis to provide specific training needs for durations of not more than three months each year.

The Nora negotiation team was appalled at the exorbitant amount proposed by the Sakari negotiators. They were surprised that the Sakari team had not surveyed the industry rates, as the Japanese and other western negotiators would normally have done. Apparently Sakari had not taken into consideration the relatively low cost of living in Malaysia compared to Finland. In 2000, though the average monthly rent for a comfortable, unfurnished three-bedroom apartment was about the same (US$660) in Helsinki and Kuala Lumpur, the cost of living was considerably lower in KL. The cost of living index (New York = 100) of a basket of goods in major cities, excluding housing, for Malaysia was only 83.75, compared to 109.84 for Finland.[6]

In response to Sakari's proposal, Nora negotiators adopted an unusual "take-it or leave-it" stance. They deemed the following proposal reasonable in view of the comparisons made with other JVs which Nora had entered into with other foreign parties:

Permanent experts' monthly salary ranges to be paid by the JV company were as follows:

1. Senior expert (7 to 10 years experience)............ RM24,300–RM27,900
2. Expert (4 to 6 years experience)............. RM22,500–RM25,200
3. Junior expert (2 to 3 years experience)............ RM20,700–RM23,400
4. Any Malaysian income taxes payable would be added to the salaries.
5. A car for personal use.
6. Annual paid vacation of five weeks.
7. Return flight tickets to home country once a year for the whole family of married persons and twice a year for singles according to Sakari's general scheme.
8. Any expenses incurred during official traveling.

Temporary experts are persons invited by the JV company for various technical assistance tasks and would not be granted residence status. They would be paid the following fees:

1. Senior expert........................RM1,350 per working day
2. Expert.............................RM1,170 per working day
3. The JV company would not reimburse the following:
   - Flight tickets between Finland (or any other country) and Malaysia.
   - Hotel or any other form of accommodation.
   - Local transportation.

In defense of their proposed rates, Sakari's negotiators argued that the rates presented by Nora were too low. Sakari suggested that Nora's negotiators take into consideration the fact that Sakari would have to subsidize the difference between the experts' present salaries and the amount paid by the JV company. A large difference would require that large amounts of subsidy payments be made to the affected employees.

5. Arbitration. Another major issue discussed in the negotiation was related to arbitration. While both parties agreed to an arbitration process in the event of future disputes, they disagreed on the location for dispute resolution. Because Nora would be the majority stakeholder in the JV company, Nora insisted that any arbitration should take place in KL. Sakari, however, insisted on Helsinki, following the norm commonly practiced by the company.

At the end of the five-day negotiation, many issues could not be resolved. While Nora could agree on certain matters after consulting Zainal, the Sakari team, representing a large private company, had to refer contentious items to the company board before it could make any decision that went beyond the limits authorized by the board.

THE DECISION

Zainal sat down at his desk, read through the minutes of the negotiation thoroughly, and was disappointed that an agreement had not yet been reached. He was concerned about the commitment Nora had made to TMB when Nora was awarded the switching contract. Nora would be expected to fulfill the contract soon but had yet to find a partner to provide the switching technology. It was foreseeable that companies such as Siemens, Samsung, and Lucent, which had failed in the bid, could still be potential partners. However, Zainal had also not rejected the possibility of a reconciliation with Sakari. He could start by contacting Kuusisto in Helsinki. But should he?

---

[6]IMD & World Economic Forum. 2001. The World Competitiveness Report.

Case 5   Allure Cruise Line*—Challenges of Strategic Growth and Organizational Effectiveness: Part 2

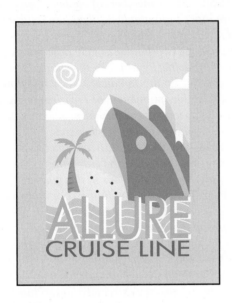

INTERVIEW WITH ALLURE CRUISE LINE EXECUTIVE

Additional interviews were conducted with several members of Allure's senior leadership team to obtain more information regarding the cruise industry and Allure's current challenges.

The following interview is from an initial meeting with Joy Prazulinni, the hotel director who lives and works onboard the Allure *Regent* ship, who shared her perspective on the challenges of life onboard the Allure ships as well as some of the current issues that need to be addressed.

OD Team Member: *"Ms. Prazulinni, what are the hotel director's responsibilities?"*

Ms. Prazulinni: *"The hotel director is responsible for all of the hotel operations within the ship. This includes housekeeping, rooms and front desk operations, purser's office, restaurant and dining rooms, all passenger entertainment, and the cruise director's area. The hotel director is one of the senior executives onboard the ship and reports to the captain."*

---

*Note: The data used to develop this case study was garnered through the managers of an existing cruise line. The name of the cruise line, as well as the individuals in the case study, and some data have been changed to protect the confidentiality of the cruise line; specific data changes can be found in Section 4 of this study.

OD Team Member: *"Describe for me the demographic makeup of your ship's crew."*

Ms. Prazulinni: *"As you know there are three vessels in the Allure fleet, but overall I'd say there are on average about 40 or so nationalities represented onboard at any one time. This fluctuates between 53 and 32, depending on people's contracts and such (as you probably know, each week when we are in our home port so many crew sign off—it's the end of their contract time—and so many crew come onboard to replace them, having just had their time off). The nationality of our crew is in constant flux."*

OD Team Member: *"That is a lot of cultures. How would you describe the communication between the managers and officers onboard?"*

Ms. Prazulinni: *"Well, for safety reasons all crew members are required to pass an English test. This is done at their hire. If a crew member doesn't meet the minimum standards, they frankly don't work for Allure or any cruise line until their English is up to the minimum. However, for many of our officers, English is their fourth or fifth language. There is also a large variety in the accents of the officers which can make it difficult for them to understand each other. The difficulty becomes even greater when they are communicating on the phone or via email.*

"As for the rest of the crew, the language communication barrier is often a challenge. We rely on our hiring agents to screen potential crew for English skills, as we logistically cannot, so there are varying levels of ability in English."

OD Team Member: *"That is a challenge. What about the food for the crew?"*

Ms. Prazulinni: *"As hotel director, I am responsible for all food service onboard, not just for our passengers but our 'internal passengers'— our crew—as well; and this is something I hear much about. It is very difficult to please all of the different tastes of the nationalities on board; we typically serve Western food for a variety of reasons (such as preparation times and available ingredients). Trying to appeal to all tastes and cultures has high costs associated* with trying to do so, but we know that there is a high impact on the morale of the crew. Every ethnic group wants attention, although they try to be understanding and make efforts. For example, we know that some cultures eat rice at every meal, so now we are serving rice three times a day in our crew mess."

OD Team Member: *"How would you describe the social life of the crew members onboard?"*

Ms. Prazulinni: *"Well, remember that the crew members are living and working together in a small space; they spend a lot of time together both, how do you say, 'on the clock' and off it as well. They socialize heavily, [laughs] and sometimes too heavily. Many of the crew are between the ages of 19 and their early 40s, and like to 'party' and socialize. Many crew members date and break up, and this causes huge conflicts since they live and work in such close proximity. If the crew members are married, we try to keep them on the same ship in the same cabin.*

"Many of the female crew members on board feel confused about the cultural differences in what is and what is not acceptable behavior between the different genders. Some cultures onboard do not feel that women are 'equal' and therefore do not treat the women as equals or in authority, especially if the woman is an officer and the man is lower in rank. While I am Italian and did not grow up in the States, I understand that the U.S. has laws against harassment. Other countries do not have such laws and therefore it is not necessarily something these men—and women— have had to learn.

"The social life has a big impact on crew morale. Crew members tend to be fatigued because of their long working hours; many experience loneliness. They live in cramped quarters and have little privacy; they feel confined. And they miss their family and friends back home. Other factors impacting morale include the food concerns, and a perceived lack of entertainment for crew onboard. The crew members have many ups and downs to their onboard existence.

"This really affects the shipboard managers: They need to create an environment to help the crew feel valued and thanked. Allure has designated an area of beach on the island leased by the company and visited on some of the itineraries. We also have parties for the crew. On the new ships, Allure would like to provide larger crew areas and more crew amenities."

OD Team Member: *"Let's go back to discussing the varied backgrounds and societal cultures onboard. Is there animosity among people from different countries onboard the ships?"*

Ms. Prazulinni: *"You can definitely see a 'brotherhood mentality' at times within the crew members. You hate to stereotype, but you do see trends among people of the same nationality. For example, members of the Filipino culture tend to be more collective, quiet, they have an 'all for one' attitude; they enjoy singing karaoke as a pastime. Many members of the Jamaican culture are more individualistic, they like loud music, dancing, party loudly, very gregarious. So you have these two fundamentally different ways of looking at life; for example, the Filipinos feel disrespected by the Jamaicans. As you know we have a larger population of French in our dining rooms so it is natural they form a 'family,' sometimes to the exclusion of other crew."*

OD Team Member: *"I've heard the term 'mafia' sometimes used onboard ships. Can you explain what that means in this context?"*

Ms. Prazulinni: *"In the dining room, most crew members are from Eastern and Western Europe. There are also Jamaican and Filipino crew members here as well, but they are assigned to separate stations of the restaurants, such as the beverage area or kitchen area. The dining rooms are extremely hierarchical with many jobs at many different levels. The leader of each of the dining rooms is the Dining Room Manager, who is supported by the head servers. Under each head server are the servers, and each server is assisted by the assistant servers. The head server needs to be a presence within the dining room and talk to all passengers, ensure that they are enjoying their experience, etc. Servers are tipped personnel and therefore make small salaries with tips being divided up among the servers and assistant servers. However, servers do make very good money, so their positions are highly sought after.*

"'Dining Room Mafia' is the terminology that the crew uses to describe what occurs in the dining room. Often the head server shows favoritism for and promotes only the crew members who are from his of her own country. Typically, Eastern and Western Europeans are in leadership positions within the dining room and food service areas.

"When the head servers are confronted, they deny that this is occurring. It is very difficult to track because the head server keeps all of the performance records. This is a persistent problem—and it is a dining room only phenomenon for some reason.

"The leadership team on board has not been able to get their arms around this problem. But unfortunately this isn't just an Allure problem: This behavior occurs across all cruise lines—culturally existent within the industry,

and dining room crew see it as a fact of life. We want this to end at Allure, and hopefully your team can help us find a solution."

OD Team Member: *"The dining room is an interesting work environment. Any other items we should know about regarding their work area?"*

Ms. Prazulinni: *"It's important to understand some of the operational constraints within the food service area. U.S. Public Health Service inspects dining room and galley areas fairly frequently. These scores are a very big deal in the cruise industry, and they're usually published in newspapers around the world. When they meet our goal scores, managers receive a bonus. The catch is that all managers within the food prep and service areas need to work well together to provide high quality experience, while keeping the cleanliness of our operation to standards."*

OD Team Member: *"I think you have answered my questions, Ms. Prazulinni. Are there any final thoughts that you may have?"*

Ms. Prazulinni: *"I really hope that your team can help us out. Allure is a wonderful organization, and our growth will be a great thing for our passengers our crew, and of course our business. In Italy we have a saying, that loosely translated in English is 'family is the foundation of your house, and your tower can only be as tall as its foundation can support.' I have been at sea for over 12 years and this has been my favorite family to work with. But like all families, we have some challenges that we want your help to overcome. We want to improve that foundation so our tower can be even higher."*

ASSIGNMENT

Cross-cultural and People Challenges

The organization is currently experiencing some morale issues among their crew and some cross-cultural challenges on board the three existing ships. These issues are beginning to have an impact on the service that is being provided to the passengers.

The senior leadership team at Allure Cruise Line is concerned that some of the current issues with the crew members onboard the ships will interfere with larger business plans that are coming soon. They realize that, if they do not address these "people issues" now, it could potentially jeopardize the success of the Mediterranean expansion project in the future.

Given the information that is presented by Joy Prazulinni, the hotel director, what does your team think are the main "people issues" onboard Allure's ships?

- Discuss some of the key factors that influence the morale of the crew. What recommendations do you have for the leaders on board to help improve the morale of the crew?
- Discuss the communication challenges on board. How could these communication issues be improved?
- What recommendations do you have for the leadership team of Allure to help improve the dissatisfaction of the crew with the variety of food that is offered in the mess hall?
- What are your impressions of Allure's policy which limits the socialization between certain crew and passengers? Since this is having a negative impact on the morale of the crew (Joy noted a "rift" between those crew who are permitted to fraternize with passengers and those who cannot), would you recommend that Allure change this policy to allow more crew to mix with the passengers, or rescind the policy so no crew can fraternize?
- Discuss some of the cross-cultural and social misunderstandings, particularly in terms of sexual harassment, among the crew members. What are your recommendations to address these serious misunderstandings?
- Discuss some the cross-cultural challenges among the Jamaican and Filipino crew members. How might this situation be improved?
- Discuss the problems with the mafias on board. What specific recommendations do you have for the leadership team of Allure to address this problem?
- Does this case study relate to the contemporary business environment? If not, why? If it does, how?

Case 6 Guanxi in Jeopardy

JOINT VENTURE NEGOTIATIONS IN CHINA[1]

Nothing like this has ever happened before. A nation with a fifth of the world's population has a bad 500 years. It is humiliated by barbarians; it lacerates itself; it sinks from torpor to anarchy. And then, in the space of a few decades, it steps forward. Its economy grows at a rate for which the word miraculous seems too modest. Its culture shows a new vitality. Its armed forces modernize. And the rest of the world watches, impressed and nervous at the same time, wondering if the new giant still seethes with resentment about the half millennium in which it was slighted.

KENNETH AUCHINCLOSS,
Newsweek[2]

INTRODUCTION

Tom Sherman was deeply perplexed as he studied the translation of a cover story from yesterday's edition of the *Beijing Daily,* the only local English newspaper. The article, titled "Motosuzhou/Electrowide, Inc.: *Guanxi* in Jeopardy," had taken him by surprise. Tom has always known that efforts in securing a joint venture with Motosuzhou, a local Chinese manufacturer, would need an enormous amount of diligence and persistence, which he thought that he and his appointed team members were portraying to their Chinese counterparts. The many sleepless nights Tom and his team worked together in planning the next day's negotiation strategies based on events that transpired with Motosuzhou the day before, coupled with the frustrations of living in a strange place and trying to cope with stark living accommodations, had ultimately accentuated the frustrations of the team.

"Why can't Motosuzhou comply with our objectives?" Tom repeatedly asked himself. The success in securing the joint venture would be a symbolic victory for a man who dedicated this entire career to Electrowide, Inc. Tom could retire from the company knowing that his last "hoorah" might have opened the door to new global

opportunities for Electrowide, Inc. After all, China was becoming an enormous window of global opportunity especially for Western firms. Several of the company's competitors were already operational in Malaysia and Hong Kong. In order to compete successfully in today's globally expanding economy, Electrowide realized it needed to quickly serve markets and that the best way to do this was to locate production in Asia. As it appeared, however, Tom was in jeopardy of returning to the United States without the joint venture agreement necessary for Electrowide's entry into the People's Republic of China.

ELECTROWIDE, INC.

Electrowide is a $5B manufacturer of a broad range of automotive electronics products. In an effort to become more proactive in today's ever increasing competitive automotive electronics market, the company is undergoing a massive structural overhaul, streamlining many of its operations and flattening levels of organizational hierarchy. The purpose of this restructuring is to grant more autonomy to the company's various product line departments with respect to operation and business planning decisions so that eventually each will be responsible for its own profit and loss statements. One of the company's key strategic objectives is to become a major, aggressive player in Asia. This is considered a major change in the company's strategic direction. As part of this rapid expansion effort, Electrowide officially opened a regional design center in Tokyo. The center has world-class engineering capabilities that enable Electrowide to develop original designs at this site. The company employs about 15,000 people in the United States and is aggressively pursuing a policy of increasing its overseas workforce.

Electrowide is looking to find an Asian partner to help manufacture and sell engine management systems that run emission-control, fuel nozzle, and ignition systems for Chinese-made vehicles. Output would be initially sold to the Chinese market with plans to export later. It is projected that the company's first manufacturing JV in China will result in at least $3M in sales its first year. The company also estimates that the JV will have a cooperative life of ten years. The company believes that the facility that its partner can provide will play a major role not only in rapidly promoting Electrowide's business growth, but in providing product development expertise in the region. According to Mike Strong, CEO, "A good part of our growth is going to come from finding the right partners in Asia."

---

[1]The concept of *guanxi* requires immediate explanation. It is pronounced as *Guaan-ji* and refers to the special relationship two people develop or already have with each other. Pye in *Chinese Negotiating Style* (Cambridge, MA: Oelgeschlager, Gunn and Hain, 1982, p. 101) describes it as "friendship with implications of a continual exchange of favors, and the relationship is continuously bound by these exchanges."

[2]Kenneth Auchincloss, "Friend or Foe," *Newsweek*, April 1, 1996, 32.

MOTOSUZHOU

Motosuzhou is an enterprise of the Beijing municipal government, from where it takes ultimate direction. Structurally, the company is a top-heavy hierarchy with a deputy director overseeing daily operations and various supervisors in charge of functional units (see Exhibit C6-1.) Decision making is top-down in nature. Approvals for RFCs (request for changes) must follow a precise, government-audited procedure.

Consequently, some decisions take several months to be approved. However, as part of modest experiments in Beijing, the company is on a selected, government-approved list along with 1,000 other companies that enable it to run its own operations free from government interference. Motosuzhou is a small company, operational since 1962. Its labor force is comprised mainly of rural employees, mostly Han Chinese. Although the company's strength is in achieving economies of scale in assembly-line manufacturing of engine control subassemblies, competition in the local market is growing.

The company's objective in teaming with a foreign enterprise is to develop a long-lasting relationship that will work in harmony with local government policies, as well as to gradually acquire technology through transfer by importing equipment and designs and adapt them to the automotive industry in China. The company's facilities and operations are such that to be inundated with new and improved technology techniques too quickly would prove devastating. Certainly, Motosuzhou does not want to fail in the eyes of the government or the community. Electrowide appeared to be keenly interested in Motosuzhou because of the American company's technical proficiency in its design of automotive subsystems. Acquisition of such knowledge would give Motosuzhou a competitive edge in the industry. Also, Motosuzhou would rely on Electrowide for financing most of the cost incurred in establishing the venture. The company is currently on a mission to educate its workforce by providing after-hour English language studies at a local university.

Motosuzhou Team

Deng Zang is 62 years old, with a B.S. in Business Administration earned from a local evening university. Deng is factory director, a position he has held for ten years. He speaks English poorly.

Ai Hwa Chew is 55 years old, a high school graduate with an accumulation of post-high school classes taken at the factory-run university. Ai Hwa was considered a member of the "delayed generation," that is, one who lost educational opportunities during the Cultural Revolution. His English is very poor, and he relies heavily on an interpreter or one of his managers when English translation is needed. Overall, Ai Hwa is considered a very serious, diligent, and competent deputy director of Supply and Distribution. He is well respected in the company.

Wang Yoo is 65 years old, with a B.S. in Accounting from Beijing University and is relatively fluent in English. He has served as the Minister of Finance for 15 years. He is a cousin of Deng Zang.

EXHIBIT C6-1   Motosuzhou Organizational Chart

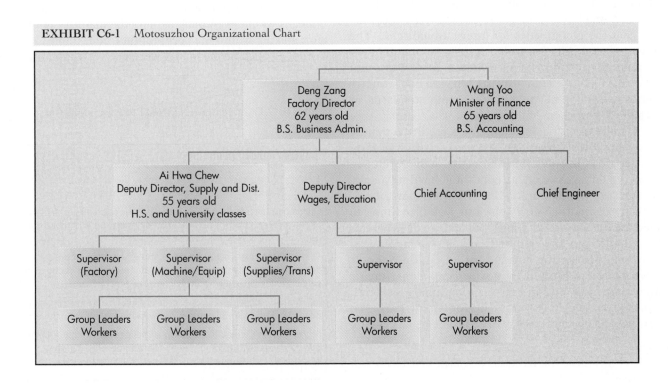

CHINA: CURRENT BUSINESS ASSESSMENT

China is presently on a course of economic liberalization. It is a country that is increasingly worried about anarchy. Gradually, more and more power is filtering to the provinces and localities. Rich coastal cities such as Shanghai and Guangzhou operate freely. City leaders establish their own economic targets, court foreign investors, and even raise internal trade barriers against the products of other parts of China. The huge rural population is leaving its ancestral villages for coastal cities, trying to find jobs in the new, growing economy. Chinese cities, in contrast to those in many developing countries, contain high proportions of workers in factories and offices and a low proportion of workers in the service sector. During the "Deng" (i.e., Deng Xiaoping, former premier of the People's Republic) years, from 1978 to 1994, China's real growth rose an average of 9 percent a year. It is predicted that by the year 2025, China's economy will be by far the largest in the world, 1.5 times the size of the U.S. economy.[3]

American firms agree that China has never been an easy place to conduct business. Many foreign investments do not succeed financially. The costs of entering the Chinese market are climbing steeply. Tax preferences for foreign investors have been scaled back. The central government is becoming more restrictive with the JVs that provincial officials used to approve quickly. The Chinese are growing tougher in their bargaining stance. There are tighter limits on certain industries such as utilities and oil refining. One wonders if this will spread to the manufacturing sector as well. The foreign impression is that the Chinese act as if they are in the "driver's seat." As China grows economically, it openly scoffs at the global rules for international trade. The government still controls decisions on imports. Furthermore, contracts in Chinese courts are not enforceable. In the courts' eyes, China is a poor country that should not be held to the same standards as wealthy nations.[4]

With respect to education, it was predicted that by the year 2000, percent of its workers and staff in coastal areas, inland cities, and moderately developed areas would have a college education, building a solid intellectual foundation for China. Furthermore, it was anticipated that university entrants would continue to increase. Because only a small percentage of graduates are admitted to universities, China has found alternative ways of meeting demand for education. Schools have been established by government departments and businesses, and in the case of China's factories, workers' colleges exist internally, providing part-time classes. Acquiring literacy is still a problem, particularly among the rural population. The difficulty of mastering written Chinese makes raising the literacy rate particularly difficult. This creates problems in the workplace. An overview of the labor force reveals that males account for slightly more than half of the workforce and occupy the great majority of leadership positions. Though traditional Chinese society is male-centered, on the whole women are better off than their counterparts decades ago.

However, discrimination still exists in hiring for urban jobs, with women offered lower wages and benefits than their male counterparts. In the mid-1980s, less than 40 percent of the labor force had more than a primary education. Skilled workers, engineers, and managerial personnel are still in short supply. Yet China ranks second to the United States as a host country for foreign investment. However, U.S. firms must forge alliances based on common interests to ensure effective market entry. If the Chinese leaders are threatened and demeaned as was the case when the United States denounces China's MFN (Most Favored Nation) status, China will surely behave in an increasingly disruptive fashion. However, if U.S. firms reach out to the Chinese, the prospects for mutual growth will be somewhat brighter. With China's vast need for the investment and technology that America has to offer, it should not be difficult to gain China's cooperation.

STAGE OF EVENTS

Recently at Electrowide, all employees received an announcement pertaining to structural redesign stemming from a year's worth of BPE (business process engineering) initiatives. The establishment of various councils would eventually assume the majority of decision making within the corporation (see Exhibit C6-2). Although specific personnel were not yet appointed to

---

[3]Robert J. Samuelson, "The Big Game," *Newsweek*, April 1, 1996, 37.
[4]Ibid., 90.

EXHIBIT C6-2 Electrowide Restructuring: Establishment of Councils

Process Councils' Definitions

Strategy Management Council: To develop Electrowide's mission, vision, values, and short-term/long-term strategic direction.

Operations Strategy Council: To lead operations transition from a product focus to a process-focused organization with common operating processes and practices.

Product Technology Council: To drive implementation of product line planning, program teams, re-use and technology centers, and to decide Electrowide's strategic enabling technologies.

Information Technology Council: To direct information technology prioritization, policy, alignment, and worldwide infrastructure.

People Process Council: To establish guidelines for selecting, developing, evaluating, and rewarding people to develop a global workforce with the necessary skill sets for Electrowide.

each process council, roles and responsibilities in addition to process definitions were established (see Exhibit C6-3). Most of the councils, however, including SMC (Strategy Management Council), were not operational. Electrowide had plans to empower the SMC with responsibilities for establishing processes and guidelines for exploring and establishing acquisitions and joint venture particularly focusing on overseas opportunities. At the same time, the corporation was on another aggressive transformation mission: to seek global pursuits at a rapidly expanding rate in order to become a $10 billion international enterprise. In consideration of a study that Electrowide conducted several months ago, China was strongly favored as a revenue gateway for the corporation. Tom was not appointed to sit on any of the newly established councils. However, considering his decades of experience in managing manufacturing operations at Electrowide, and having developed strong bonds to several top corporate executives, he was selected to lead a team to China which was commissioned to pursue a JV with Motosuzhou (see Exhibit C6-4).

Tom was assigned a two-person team to carry out this mandate but was not consulted as to its composition. He was 55 years old, with a B.S. in Mechanical Engineering from the University of Michigan. He was considered highly technical and knowledgeable about industrial operation and manufacturing techniques. His career has spanned 32 years with Electrowide. He has held various technical management positions within the company and is currently manager of Materials Resource Management, overseeing production inventory for North American Operations. His only international experience

---

EXHIBIT C6-3   Councils' Roles and Responsibilities

Strategy Management Council

■ Set policy, direction, strategy, and pace for the corporate strategy management business processes and ensure alignment with corporate objectives.

■ Manage the corporate portfolio based on strategic direction; for example, the SMC determines core competencies, makes portfolio decisions, and commissions the Ventures Council to fill gaps in core competencies.

■ Balanced scorecard metrics: revenue, earnings before tax margin, net asset turnover.

Operations Council

■ Develop operations strategy, for example, operations planning, quality systems, facilities, integrated supply management.

■ Develop the global labor strategy.

■ Lead transition from product focus to common process focus.

■ Balanced scorecard metrics: best practices of an electronics company, delivery on time.

Information Council

■ Set priority for infrastructure development.

■ Approve information technology infrastructure projects and overall IT spending.

People Council

■ Establish the strategy for right sizing, redeployment, and re-skilling of the global workforce.

■ Establish the framework for global labor strategy implementation.

■ Balanced scorecard metrics: employee satisfaction index.

EXHIBIT C6-4   Request for Approval by the Executive Committee

Electrowide, Inc.

Recommended Action:	Authorize Electrowide, Inc., to establish a joint venture with Motosuzhou.
Recommended By:	Mike Strongarm, CEO
Performance Responsibility:	Tom Sherman

Objective: To establish a joint venture between Electrowide and Motosuzhou of China to conduct manufacturing operations in China.

Electrowide, Inc., seeks to establish a joint venture entity in the Suzhou Township, Guangzhou Province, China. This request is only for the establishment of the entity. In the event that the Executive Committee does not approve this project, the newly established joint venture can be dissolved at minimal legal cost. This proposal consists of providing detailed designs, financial, and technical clout necessary to commercialize the joint venture's technology. Manufacturing cost savings will be realized through low labor costs in China. Long-term objectives will include expanding the manufacturing capabilities to include additional automotive electronic product for both export and for sale to domestic Chinese vehicle manufactures.

The Chinese government announced plans to withdraw the tax and tariff exemption for imports of capital equipment by foreign-invested companies.

We request that the Executive Committee ratify and confirm the establishment of the joint venture in order to conduct manufacturing operations in China.

Date:

_____

Approval Recommended: Mike Strongarm, CEO
Electrowide, Inc.

_____

Doyle P. Cunningham, Director of Taxes

_____

Bart C. Chang
Sr. Vice President Marketing and President, Electrowide, Inc.

_____

Suzanne A. Jenkins
Corporate Vice President and Controller

was participating in a technology transfer symposium in Canada two years ago. He plans to retire at the end of the year.

Tom requested the personnel files of his two team members. He noted that Barb Morgan was 42 years old and had a joint B.S. in Psychology and Computer Science from Johns Hopkins University in Baltimore. Barb had begun her career at Electrowide three years ago as a contractor but was hired as a permanent employee upon completion of her first year. Barb's most recent assignment in the company was project manager for an acquisition venture in Sweden. She spoke conversational Chinese as well as fluent French. Apparently, her current assignment was near completion, and she wanted to continue seeking overseas assignments partly as a means of trying to cope with her recent divorce.

Mark Porter's current assignment in Corporate Business Planning was also coming to an end, and he was eager to do some international work. He was 31 years old and had a B.S. in Finance from the University of Pennsylvania and an MBA from Duke University. He was apparently a "fast-tracker" at Electrowide, rotating among various organizational functions every 1.5 years, and had been employed with the company six years. His most recent position was that of business analyst responsible for relaying backlog data to Corporate Finance and Shareholder's Relations. According to his file, he is a type-A personality and a self-starter, focusing on excelling no matter what the cost or sacrifice.

Tom also noted that, as part of the study, Motosuzhou was investigated along with several other possible Eastern Asian partners. Such parameters as the partner's physical location in the country, the size of its labor force, and the strength of the resources that could enhance as well as reduce operational costs for Electrowide were examined. In addition, the company was dependent on finding a local manufacturing company with a strong, established network that could readily market products produced under the JV without additional expense in the effort. Furthermore, finding a local company with ties to government officials was thought to be of benefit. Early warnings about any impending government policy changes that might impact operations within the JV would be advantageous. Above all, management wanted to ensure that its corporate objectives would be achieved upon establishment of the JV. Motosuzhou seemed to fit most closely to the criteria identified in the study.

Tom envisioned that he and the rest of the team would spend the majority of their first several weeks with Motosuzhou discussing the specific details of the proposed JV. Instead, their counterparts were keenly interested in learning about their visitors' personal lives, their interests, the size of their families, and the like. Usually, the days were spent touring the city and surrounding countryside, while long hours were spent at night engaging in elaborate dinner get-togethers and

nightlife entertainment. Mark never showed much interest or appreciation of the scenery. His thoughts were usually preoccupied with how to steer the course of the next day's discussions on the details of the proposed JV. He was not one for small talk. Barb was quite affable with her Chinese hosts initially. She particularly enjoyed experiencing a night of *quyi*, for which the Motosuzhou team generously paid admission. Yet her enthusiasm diminished when she took notice that Ai Hwa and his constituents tended not to include her in conversation but rather directed their discussions and eye contact to Barb's male counterparts. One night in particular stood out in Tom's mind. As Ai Hwa Chew was making toasts to his guests thanking them for their interests in his company, he presented Tom with a sterling silver tea set. Tom felt a bit uncomfortable accepting such an expensive gift and even tried to tactfully refuse it. However, Ai Hwa stubbornly refused Tom's insistence. Tom thought that he detected irritation in Hwa's voice but decided not to apologize and prolong the uncomfortable silence that punctuated the room.

By the fourth week, Tom and his team were growing a bit restless. Habitually, they left telephone messages with Ai Hwa's secretary requesting to meet with him and his constituents. Tom even went as far as to establish specific days and times for these proposed discussions. Nothing constructive with respect to these transpired during that week. Tom's patience grew thin as he tried to force smile after smile during long dinner extravaganzas where conversation continued to remain light and disassociated from any issues pertaining to work. Mark was growing extremely impatient, and he frequently excused himself early from get-togethers, or, on occasion, refrained from attending altogether.

A change in routine finally occurred during the fifth week. Deng Zang felt the proper time had materialized when issues concerning the JV should be approached with Electrowide. He commissioned Ai Hwa to put together a formal written invitation that was subsequently hand-delivered to the hotel early in the week. Tom and his team were invited to an arranged meeting to be conducted in Ai Hwa Chew's office the morning following receipt of the letter. Although no agenda was distributed and the time and location for the meeting were changed at 11 P.M. the night before, the team managed to regain their composure in anticipation of cooperative dialogue with their potential partners. Tom had been instructed by executive staff to remain firm in its pursuit of negotiating specific roles and responsibilities that each party would assume under the JV. Electrowide was to provide and control design, financial, and technical clout necessary to commercialize the JV's technology. Conversely, Electrowide wanted Motosuzhou to provide the manufacturing plant facility, marketing functions utilizing a local sales force, as well as provide the majority of the technical labor force. Furthermore, Electrowide thought it was in its best interest to allow Motosuzhou to continue in its current managerial capacity inasmuch as Electrowide lacked the personnel proficient in Chinese. Moreover, Electrowide planned to hold a 51 percent stake in the venture, with Motosuzhou taking a 39 percent portion, and the remainder to go to the Beijing Municipal government.

Meetings continued throughout the week. Although Mark would have preferred to continue doing research in his hotel room, Tom insisted that his attendance at the meetings was crucial. As the meetings progressed, the American team's overall assessment of whether the objectives of most of their concessions were going to be met was favorable. Barb was instructed not to vocally participate in negotiations, but her keen eye played an important role. She recorded conversations at each meeting and noticed that affirmative nodding by the Chinese counterparts was apparent. Tom's team interpreted this as a sign that concessions outlined by the Electrowide team would be easily confirmed. Barb also noticed, however, that the Chinese team rarely posed specific questions about the details of the JV. The inference was that the Motosuzhou team understood the concessions and, therefore, had no concerns. The interpreter that Motosuzhou provided to the team continually assuaged any doubts about failing progress. This constant reminder renewed the team's faith that Motosuzhou was a compatible fit with Electrowide.

In about the eighth week, however, positive attitudes on the part of Tom and his team began to wane. From the start, HQ promised Tom that his maximum required length of stay would not exceed two months as the company planned at most six weeks to secure agreement for the JV. Tom would certainly miss his daughter's college graduation if negotiations persisted much longer. In addition, Barb, who was a member of the Information Technology Council, was "burning the candle at both ends" as she feverishly worked on several assignments faxed to her from HQ. Mark had contracted the Asian flu and was miserably trying to battle its nasty symptoms while trying to play Tom's right-hand man. Moreover, war games with Taiwan were growing intense, the threat of which strengthened the team's desire to repatriate as soon as possible. Ai Hwa Chew and his aides were behaving less passively. Questions particular to the concessions proposed by Electrowide were now being raised. Motosuzhou had its own objectives to pursue as commissioned by the minister of Finance, Wang Yoo. Motosuzhou knew it was in its best interest to comply with government mandates; otherwise, the company risked losing its position on the list of free-enterprise entities. Ai Hwa was skeptical about Electrowide's concessions. His assessment was that Electrowide really wanted to gain greater control for itself in the local Asian market. Nowhere in the objective statement as documented on the "Request for Approval" were marketing concessions addressed or implied. One concession Motosuzhou was adamant in winning was control of financial operations of the JV. Moreover, the Chinese company insisted that any profits earned under the JV could be invested only in China, the currency remaining in *yuan*.

Although this was a crucial point for them, Motosuzhou focused on softer issues initially. For example, Motosuzhou requested that training, consulting, and warranties would be provided to them free of charge. Ai Hwa Chew kept reminding the American team that such provisions were considered free goods in their Chinese system, and hence were perceived as indications of one's sincerity and good will. In addition, Ai Hwa Chew pointed out inconsistencies between the partner's accounting systems which created disagreement regarding allocation of manufacturing costs. Tom was alarmed, for his assessment of Motosuzhou's accounting policies was that they were in complete disarray and that the Chinese firm's management would greatly appreciate it if this function was handled by Electrowide. No formal auditing records had been kept. Ai Hwa Chew kept assuring Tom that Wang Yoo could provide auditing documentation that the state agency kept on file on all its state-run operations. However, Tom's direct request to the top Finance representative at the Ministry for copies of accounting records fell on deaf ears. Tom knew that he could not allow accounting practices to continue as they were because they would result in the reduction of Electrowide's operating margins, an outcome that violated one of Electrowide's ultimate objectives for establishing a JV. HQ also instructed Tom to remain firm on providing training instructors and training materials. However, training costs were to be a necessary expense of Motosuzhou.

To drive a further wedge in objectives, Ai Hwa Chew made it very clear that he was not comfortable continuing management practices as they currently operated. He stressed the need for more harmony in all aspects of the negotiations and JV operations. At the same time, the Executive Committee at Electrowide was enmeshed in activities to finalize formulation, appointments, and operations of each of the council organizations. Consequently, Tom found it increasingly difficult to relay concerns and seek support and approval for changes requested. In addition, the time difference made it difficult for Tom to directly communicate issues to HQ on a timely basis. Delays were not part of Electrowide's plan in securing the JV.

Tom and his team decided to take matters into their own hands. While Ai Hwa called for a few days' reprieve to honor the Chinese Winter holiday, the Electrowide team took advantage of the free days. Unknown to their potential partners, the American team sought the counsel of an American law firm located in Beijing. To circumvent the likelihood of any future misunderstandings between the two parties, Tom instructed the attorney to structure a very formal extensive contract to address every conceivable contingency.

The next morning, over breakfast, as Tom and his team were reviewing their plan of action on how to best present the contract to Ai Hwa Chew, the hotel concierge presented Tom with a Western Union telegram. Tom scanned the contents, shared the information with his team, and then tossed the telegram in the trash, thinking little of its effect on the day's negotiation activities. "Today," Tom assuredly thought, "I feel we're going to come to final agreement." As the telegram started to unfurl in the trash, its contents exposed the following: "Trade Representative Mickey Kantor was quoted as bashing Beijing over MFN status on account of China violating intellectual property issues."

Tom wanted to waste little time in presenting the contract to his counterpart. He was anxious to solidify the deal. Almost immediately upon entering Ai Hwa Chew's office, Tom handed over the legal document, which was written entirely in English. As the interpreter read the contract, Ai Hwa's eyes grew dim and his face flushed. While only one-third of the way into listening to the concessions, Ai Hwa motioned Tom and his party to the door of his office. Once outside the office, Tom and his team were quite confused. Shortly, thereafter, Ai Hwa's secretary notified the group that the day's negotiation meetings were canceled. Tom and his team left feeling a bit confused but thought that perhaps Ai Hwa needed some time alone to review the contents of the contract. Unknown to Tom, Ai Hwa was drafting a letter to the Minister of Finance requesting to meet with him. The tone of the letter was rather urgent.

The next morning, Tom spotted the article in the *Beijing Daily*. He was disappointed and at a loss as to how to make reparations.

CASE QUESTIONS

1. What are the main characteristics of Chinese culture? How do they differ from the predominant characteristics of U.S. culture? How do these differences relate to the negotiation process?
2. What are the criteria that should be used in selecting a joint venture partner? Have those criteria been met in this situation? Why, or why not?
3. Evaluate the composition of Electrowide's team and of Motosuzhou's team. Did each of the companies make appropriate choices for this negotiation? Give reasons for your answer.
4. Should Barb Morgan have been on the negotiating team? Evaluate and give your reasons.
5. What should Tom Sherman do?

APPENDIX 1: KEY ASPECTS OF CHINESE CULTURE AS THEY RELATE TO NEGOTIATIONS[5]

Guanxi: **The Value of an Ongoing Relationship**

Guanxi is the word that describes the intricate, pervasive network of personal relations that every Chinese cultivates with energy, subtlety, and imagination. *Guanxi* is the currency of getting things done and getting ahead in Chinese society. *Guanxi* is a relationship between two people containing implicit mutual obligation, assurances, and intimacy, and is the perceived value of an ongoing relationship and its future possibilities that typically govern Chinese attitudes toward long-term business. If a relationship of trust and mutual benefit is developed, an excellent foundation will be built for future business with the Chinese. Guanxi ties are also helpful in dealing with the Chinese bureaucracy as personal interpretations are used in lieu of legal interpretations.

Because of cultural differences and language barriers, visitors to China are not in a position to cultivate *guanxi* with the depth possible between two Chinese. Regardless, *guanxi* is an important aspect of interrelations in China and deserves attention so that good friendly relations may be developed. These connections are essential to getting things accomplished.[6]

FORMAL AND INFORMAL RELATIONS

At present, it is likely that the majority of social contracts foreigners have with the Chinese are on a more formal than informal level. Informality in China relates not to social pretension or artifice but to the concept of face. Great attention is paid to observance of formal, or social, behavior and attendant norms. The social level is the level of form and proper etiquette where face is far more important than fact. It is considered both gauche and rude to allow one's personal feelings and opinions to surface here to the detriment of the social ambience. It is much more important to compliment a person or to avoid an embarrassing or sensitive subject than to express an honest opinion if honesty is at the expense of another's feelings. Directness, honesty, and individualism that run counter to social conventions and basic politeness have no place on the social level; emotions and private relationships tend to be kept private in Chinese society.

---

[5]This appendix is very largely drawn from James A. Brunner's case, "Buckeye Glass Co. in China," in *International Management: A Cross-Cultural and Functional Perspective* by Kamal Fatehi (Upper Saddle River, NJ: Prentice Hall).

[6]An extremely useful new article that extends this analysis of *guanxi* is "Achieving Business Success in Confucian Societies: The Importance of Guanxi (Connections)" by Irene Y. M. Yeung and Rosalie Tung, *Organizational Dynamics* (Autumn 1996): 54–65. The article is accompanied by an excellent bibliography.

CHINESE ETIQUETTE FOR SOCIAL FUNCTIONS

Ceremonies and rules of ceremony have traditionally held a place of great importance in Chinese culture. Confucianism perpetuated and strengthened these traditions by providing the public with an identity, mask, or persona with which a person is best equipped to deal with the world with a minimum of friction. Confucianism consists of broad rules of conduct evolved to aid and guide interpersonal relations. Confucius assembled all the details of etiquette practiced at the courts of the feudal lords during the period c. 551–479 B.C. These rules of etiquette are called the *li* and have long since become a complete way of life for the Chinese.

The *li* may appear overly formalistic to Westerners at first glance. Upon closer inspection, it is apparent that the rules of etiquette play a very important role in regulating interpersonal relations. Some basic rules of behavior are as follows:

- A host should always escort a guest out to his car or other mode of transportation and watch until the guest is out of sight.
- Physical expression is minimal by Western standards. A handshake is polite, but backslapping and other enthusiastic grasping is a source of embarrassment.
- At culture functions and other performances, audience approval of performers is often subdued by American standards. Although the accepted manner of expressing approval varies between functions and age groups, applause is often polite rather than roaring and bravo-like cheers.
- A person should keep control over his temper at all times.
- One should avoid blunt, direct, or abrupt discussion, particularly when the subject is awkward; delicate hints are often used to broach such a topic.

- It is a sign of respect to allow another to take the seat of honor (left of host) or to be asked to proceed through a door first.
- The serving of tea often signals the end of an interview or meeting. However, it is also served during extended meetings to quench the thirst of the negotiators.

SMILING AND LAUGHTER

Laughter and smiling in Chinese culture represent the universal reaction to pleasure and humor. They are also a common response to negative occurrences, such as death and other misfortunes. When embarrassed or in the wrong, the Chinese frequently respond with laughter or smiling, which will persist if another person continues to speak of an embarrassing topic or does not ignore the wrong. Westerners are often confused and shocked by this behavior, which is alien to them. It is important to remember that smiling and laughter in the previously discussed situations are not exhibitions of glee, but rather are a part of the concept of face when used in response to a negative or unpleasant situation.[7]

SOURCE: This case was prepared by John Stanbury, Assistant Professor of International Business Studies at Indiana University, Kokomo, with the considerable assistance of Carole Pelteson and Duwayne Cox, MBA students. The views represented here are those of the case authors and do not necessarily reflect the views of the Society for Case Research. Authors' views are based on their own professional judgments.

The names of the organization and individuals' names and the events described in this case have been disguised to preserve anonymity.

Presented to and accepted by the Society for Case Research. All rights reserved to the authors and SCR.

---

[7]L. Pye, *Chinese Negotiating Style* (Cambridge, MA: Oelgeschlager, Gunn and Hain, 1982), 101.

CHAPTER

6

Formulating Strategy

Outline

Opening Profile: Wal-Mart Finds that Its Formula Doesn't Fit Every Culture

WIESBADEN, Germany, July 31, 2006—Three days after Wal-Mart Stores announced that it would pull out of Germany, Roland Kögel was wandering through the aisles of a somewhat threadbare Wal-Mart in a strip mall in this western German city.

"Why are they giving up now?" he asked. "They have good prices and a good variety of products."

Yet Mr. Kögel, 54, confessed that he never bought groceries at Wal-Mart. Food is cheaper at German discount chains. He also does not visit this store often, because it is on the edge of town and he does not own a car. His one purchase for the day was tucked under his arm: a neck pillow.

Shoppers like Roland Kögel help explain why Wal-Mart raised the white flag in Germany, the site of the company's first foray into Europe.

After nearly a decade of trying, Wal-Mart never cracked the country—failing to become the all-in-one shopping destination for Germans that it is for so many millions of Americans. Wal-Mart's problems are not limited to Germany. The retail giant has struggled in countries like South Korea and Japan as it discovered that its

Wal-Mart in Beijing, China.

formula for success—low prices, zealous inventory control and a large array of merchandise—did not translate to markets with their own discount chains and shoppers with different habits.

Over all, Wal-Mart is still expanding outside the United States, particularly in markets where it entered by acquiring a strong retailer. Still, given Wal-Mart's formidable record at home, the company's recent setbacks have exposed a rare vulnerability overseas.

Some of Wal-Mart's problems stem from hubris, a uniquely powerful American enterprise trying to impose its values around the world. At Wal-Mart's headquarters in Bentonville, Ark., however, the message from these missteps is now registering loud and clear.

In particular, Wal-Mart's experience in Germany, where it lost hundreds of millions of dollars since 1998, has become a sort of template for how not to expand into a country.

"It is a good, important lesson, a turning point," an international spokeswoman for Wal-Mart, Beth Keck, said. "Germany was a good example of that naïvete." She added, "We literally bought the two chains and said, 'Hey, we are in Germany, isn't this great?'"

Among other things, she said, Wal-Mart now cares less whether its foreign stores carry the name derived from its founder, Sam Walton, as the German Wal-Marts do. Seventy percent of Wal-Mart's international sales come from outlets with names like Asda in Britain, Seiyu in Japan or Bompreço in Brazil.

Wal-Mart is also trying to integrate acquisitions with more sensitivity—a process that involves issues like deciding whether to consolidate multiple foreign headquarters and how aggressively to impose Wal-Mart's corporate culture on non-American employees.

In Germany, Wal-Mart stopped requiring sales clerks to smile at customers—a practice that some male shoppers interpreted as flirting—and scrapped the morning Wal-Mart chant by staff members.

"People found these things strange; Germans just don't behave that way," said Hans-Martin Poschmann, the secretary of the Verdi union, which represents 5,000 Wal-Mart employees here.

Wal-Mart's changes came too late for Germany, but they could help it crack other markets, like China, where it already has 60 stores and 30,000 employees. Far from being chastened by its setbacks, Wal-Mart is forging ahead with an aggressive program of foreign acquisitions.

A Wal-Mart store in South Korea.

In a single week last fall, Wal-Mart completed the purchase of the Sonae chain in Brazil, bought a controlling stake in Seiyu of Japan, and became a partner in the Carcho chain in Central America. The deals added 545 stores and 50,000 employees to Wal-Mart's overseas empire.

"I'm hard pressed to name a U.S.-based general merchandise retailer that is doing better than Wal-Mart International," said Bill Dreher, who follows Wal-Mart for Deutsche Bank in New York.

Starting from scratch 14 years ago, Wal-Mart International has grown into a $63 billion business. It is the fastest-growing part of Wal-Mart, with nearly 30 percent sales growth in June, compared with the same month last year. Even subtracting one-time gains from acquisitions, it grew at nearly 12 percent, about double the rate of Wal-Mart's American stores.

Sustaining that pace is critical for Wal-Mart, because high fuel prices have helped sap the buying power of Americans. In June, store traffic in its home market declined. Wal-Mart estimated that its sales in the United States in stores open at least one year would increase only 1 percent to 3 percent in July.

Wal-Mart Germany, with 85 stores and $2.5 billion in sales, is almost a footnote for a company focused on Asia and Latin America. But the problems it encountered here have echoes elsewhere. For example, it never established comfortable relations with its German labor unions.

"They didn't understand that in Germany, companies and unions are closely connected," Mr. Poschmann said. "Bentonville didn't want to have anything to do with unions. They thought we were communists."

Ms. Keck said Wal-Mart did cultivate good relations with the leaders of the works' council, which represents the unionized work force, and changed policies in response to employee concerns.

Wal-Mart will soon get another chance to deal with organized labor, albeit of a less independent sort. In China, the state-controlled All-China Federation of Trade Unions is organizing workers in Wal-Mart's stores.

Germany also provides a lesson in the perils of buying existing chains. Wal-Mart's purchase of Wertkauf and Interspar saddled it with stores in undesirable locations. The Wiesbaden outlet is worlds away from a squeaky-clean American Wal-Mart: nearby are a couple of sex shops.

"These were some of the least attractive of the big-box retailers out there," said James Bacos, director of the retail and consumer goods practice at Mercer Management Consulting in Munich.

Compounding the problem, Wal-Mart shut down the headquarters of one of the chains, infuriating employees who opted to quit rather than move. Such a decision would have been routine in the United States, where Ms. Keck said, "moving is a big part of the Wal-Mart culture." In Germany, she said, it prompted an exodus of talented executives.

In South Korea, Wal-Mart had only 16 stores—a small presence that contributed to its decision in May to sell out to a Korean discount chain. Many Koreans have never heard of Wal-Mart. In Seoul, a sprawling area of 10 million, there is only a single store.

This lack of scale causes another problem that has afflicted Wal-Mart in several countries: its inability to compete with established discounters, like the Aldi chain in Germany and E-Mart in Korea.

The obvious lesson is to try to bulk up. In Brazil, Wal-Mart opened only 25 stores in its first decade there and struggled to compete against bigger local rivals. Then, in 2004, it bought Bompreço, giving it a presence in the country's poor, but fast-growing, northeast.

Wal-Mart did not change the names of the stores, which range from neighborhood grocers to large American-style hypermarkets. But with 295 stores in Brazil, Wal-Mart now ranks third in the market, after Carrefour of France and the market leader, Companhia Brasileira de Distribução.

Size has given Wal-Mart increased leverage with suppliers there, though analysts say the company needs even more stores to be in a position to undercut local discounters on the prices it offers customers.

At a Wal-Mart store in suburban Rio de Janeiro the other day, Ana Paula Cunha de Almeida, a 26-year-old housewife, had loaded her shopping cart with rice, beans and flour. But she was also carrying a bag from a smaller grocery store, where she had bought meat, cheese and cold cuts.

"These are always cheaper somewhere else," she said.

The grocery business has proven the most difficult for Wal-Mart to crack. Aldi, with 4,100 stores in Germany, undercuts Wal-Mart on price, while still offering high-quality food.

Even in Canada, where Wal-Mart steamrolled local department store chains when it entered the country as a nonfood retailer in 1994, the grocery trade looms as a challenge. Wal-Mart recently announced plans to build supercenters that will also sell groceries. But analysts predicted Wal-Mart would face stiff competition from Canada's largest chain, Loblaw.

Bernie Skelding, a vacationer shopping at a Wal-Mart in Huntsville, Ontario, north of Toronto, said he liked going to the store when he had a varied shopping list. But he added, "If I'm looking for food, I go to Loblaw's."

Wal-Mart's most successful markets, like Mexico, are those in which it started big. There, the company bought the country's largest and best-run retail chain, Cifra, and has never looked back. This year, Wal-Mart is spending more than $1 billion in Mexico to open 120 new stores.

Taking over Cifra "gave them a critical mass to build from," said Tufic Salem, an analyst at Credit Suisse First Boston in Mexico City. "The management stayed, and they knew the market very well."

Perhaps the most striking example of a Wal-Mart success is Asda, which was Britain's No. 1 discount chain when Wal-Mart acquired it in 1999. With sales of $26.8 billion, Asda now accounts for 43 percent of Wal-Mart's international revenue.

Wal-Mart's German experience also taught it to use local management. The company initially installed American executives, who had little feel for what German consumers wanted.

"They tried to sell packaged meat when Germans like to buy meat from the butcher," Mr. Poschmann said.

Map 6-1   Wal-Mart in the Americas

Some of Wal-Mart's missteps—selling golf clubs in Brazil, where the game is unfamiliar, or ice skates in Mexico—are so frequently mentioned, they have become the stuff of urban legend. But even more subtle differences in shopping habits have tripped up the company.

In Korea, Wal-Mart's stores originally had taller racks than those of local rivals, forcing shoppers to use ladders or stretch for items on high shelves. Wal-Mart's utilitarian design—ceilings with exposed pipes—put off shoppers used to the decorated ceilings in E-Mart stores.

Beyond the ambience, Wal-Mart's shoes-to-sausage product line does not suit the shopping habits of many non-American shoppers. They prefer daily outings to a variety of local stores that specialize in groceries, drugs or household goods, rather than shopping once a week at Wal-Mart.

"They have stacks of goods in boxes," said Lee Jin Sook, 46, a housewife sitting on a subway in Seoul. "That may be good for some American housewives who drive out in their own cars." But Koreans, she said, prefer smaller packages: "Why would you buy a box of shampoo bottles?"

"I heard Wal-Mart later tried to change their style," Ms. Lee added, "but I guess it was too late."

SOURCE: Mark Landler reported from Wiesbaden, Germany, for this article, and Michael Barbaro from Portland, Ore. Reporting was contributed by Choe Sang-Hun from Seoul, South Korea; Heather Timmons from London; Elisabeth Malkin from Mexico City; Ian Austen from Huntsville, Ontario; and Paulo Prada from Rio de Janeiro: www.nytimes.com, August 2, 2006, Copyright © The New York Times Co. used with permission.

As the opening profile on Wal-Mart illustrates, companies around the world are spending increasing amounts of money and time on global expansion in search of profitable new markets, acquisitions, and alliances, though not always with successful results. Clearly, according to the foreign direct investment (FDI) figures, shown in Exhibit 6-1, global investment is expanding, buoyed by a wave of mergers and acquisitions in the 30 of the OECD (Organization for Economic Cooperation and Development) nations. Top recipients of FDI were the United Kingdom (by far), followed by the United States and France; top investors were the Netherlands, France, and the United Kingdom.[1]

However, these figures do not tell the whole story as far as global competition is concerned. After the Boston Consulting Group, in mid-2006, identified 100 emerging-market companies that they felt have the potential to reach the top rank of global corporations in their industries, *Business Week* challenged that:

> *Multinationals from China, India, Brazil, Russia, and even Egypt are coming on strong. They're hungry—and want your customers. They're changing the global game.*

> BUSINESS WEEK,
> *July 31, 2006*[2]

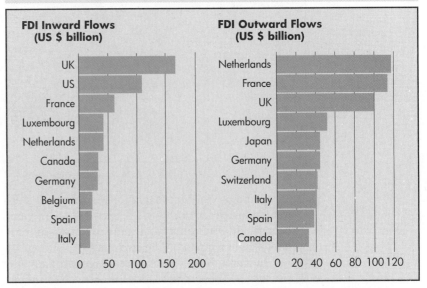

EXHIBIT 6-1 Foreign Direct Investment in OECD Countries—Top Ten Recipients and Investors in 2005

SOURCE: OECD Balance of payments statistics and OECD International Investment, April 11, 2006. Retrieved from www.oecd.org/daf/investment/statistics, August 19, 2006. Statistics: Discrepancies between quarterly and annual figures can occur.

Management consultant Ram Charan advises that we are now truly in a global game, one that he calls a "seismic change" to the competitive landscape brought about by globalization and the Internet. This first wave of emerging-nation players, he says, are taking advantage of three forces spurred on by the Internet—mobility of talent, mobility of capital, and mobility of knowledge. The strategies of companies such as America Movil of Mexico, China Mobile, Petrobras of Brazil, and Mahindra and Mahindra of India (which is penetrating Deere's market on its own U.S. turf) are to use their bases in their emerging markets—from which they have had to eke out meager profits—as "springboards to build global empires."[3] Add these new challengers to the already hyper-competitive arena of global players, and it is clear that managers need to pay close and constant attention to strategic planning. Because international opportunities are far more complex than those in domestic markets, managers must plan carefully—that is, strategically—to benefit from them. Many experienced managers are wary about expanding into politically risky areas or those countries where they find government practices to be prohibitive. This wariness was noted by the OED in June 2006, when they warned for the first time "that investment and growth were threatened by 'knee-jerk' reactions against takeovers, based on national security concerns and a sense that not all countries and their companies played by the same rules."[4]

The process by which a firm's managers evaluate the future prospects of the firm and decide on appropriate strategies to achieve long-term objectives is called **strategic planning**. The basic means by which the company competes—its choice of business or businesses in which to operate and the ways in which it differentiates itself from its competitors—is its **strategy**. Almost all successful companies engage in long-range strategic planning, and those with a global orientation position themselves to take full advantage of worldwide trends and opportunities. Multinational corporations (MNCs), in particular, report that strategic planning is essential to contend with increasing global competition and to coordinate their far-flung operations.

In reality, however, that rational strategic planning is often tempered, or changed at some point, by a more incremental, sometimes messy, process of strategic decision making by some managers. When a new CEO is hired, for example, he or she will often call for a radical change in strategy. That is why new leaders are carefully chosen, on the basis of what they are expected to do. So, although the rational strategic planning process is presented in this text because it is usually the ideal, inclusive method of determining long-term plans, managers must remember that people are making decisions, and their own personal judgments, experiences, and motivations will shape the ultimate strategic direction.

REASONS FOR GOING INTERNATIONAL

Companies of all sizes "go international" for different reasons, some reactive (or defensive) and some proactive (or aggressive). The threat of their own decreased competitiveness is the overriding reason many large companies adopt an aggressive global strategy. To remain competitive, these companies want to move fast to build strong positions in key world markets with products tailored to the common needs of 650 million customers in Europe, Latin America, and Japan. Building on their past success, companies such as IBM and Digital Equipment are plowing profits back into operations overseas. Europe is now attracting much new investment capital because of both the European Union (EU) and the opening of extensive new markets in Eastern Europe. Indeed, AOL Europe was launched as a counterpoint to AOL's declining business in the United States. The company lobbied hard to establish rules guaranteeing AOL Europe equal access to telecommunications networks.[5]

Reactive Reasons

Globalization of Competitors

One of the most common reactive reasons that prompt a company to go overseas is global competition. If left unchallenged, competitors who already have overseas operations or investments may get so entrenched in foreign markets that it becomes difficult for other companies to enter at a later time. In addition, the lower costs and market power available to these competitors operating globally may also give them an advantage domestically. Nor is this global perspective limited to industries with tangible products. Following the global expansion of banking, insurance, credit cards, and other financial services, financial exchanges are now also going global by buying or forming partnerships with exchanges in other countries, their strategies facilitated by advances in technology.[6]

Trade Barriers

Automakers from overseas first began building manufacturing plants in this country in the 1970s, largely as a defensive response to protectionist threats. But even as General Motors and Ford have been announcing thousands of job cuts, the foreign automakers [such as Toyota, Honda, Mercedes-Benz] are aggressively building new factories and expanding plants they opened not long ago.

New York Times,
June 22, 2005[7]

Although trade barriers have been lessened in recent years as a result of trade agreements, which have led to increased exports, some countries' restrictive trade barriers do provide another reactive reason that companies often switch from exporting to overseas manufacturing. Barriers such as tariffs, quotas, buy-local policies, and other restrictive trade practices can make exports to foreign markets too expensive and too impractical to be competitive. Many firms, for example, want to gain a foothold in Europe—to be regarded as insiders—to counteract trade barriers and restrictions on non–European Union (EU) firms (discussed further in the Comparative Management in Focus: Strategic Planning for the EU Market in this chapter). In part, this fear of "Fortress Europe" is caused by actions such as the EU's block exemption for the franchise industry. This exemption prohibits a franchisor, say McDonald's, from contracting with a single company, say Coca-Cola, to supply all its franchisees, as it does in the United States.

Regulations and Restrictions

Similarly, regulations and restrictions by a firm's home government may become so expensive that companies will seek out less restrictive foreign operating environments.

Avoiding such regulations prompted U.S. pharmaceutical maker SmithKline and Britain's Beecham to merge. Both thereby guaranteed that they would avoid licensing and regulatory hassles in their largest markets: Western Europe and the United States. The merged company is now an insider in both Europe and America.

Customer Demands

Operations in foreign countries frequently start as a response to customer demands or as a solution to logistical problems. Certain foreign customers, for example, may demand that their supplying company operate in their local region so that they have better control over their supplies, forcing the supplier to comply or lose the business. McDonald's is one company that asks its domestic suppliers to follow it to foreign ventures. Meat supplier OSI Industries does just that, with joint ventures in 17 countries, such as Bavaria, so that it can work with local companies making McDonald's hamburgers.[8]

Proactive Reasons

Many more companies are using their bases in the developing world as springboards to build global empires, such as Mexican cement giant Cemex, Indian drugmaker Ranbaxy, and Russia's Lukoil, which has hundreds of gas stations in New Jersey and Pennsylvania.

BUSINESS WEEK,
July 31, 2006[9]

Economies of Scale

Careful, long-term strategic planning encourages firms to go international for proactive reasons. One pressing reason for many large firms to expand overseas is to seek economies of scale—that is, to achieve world-scale volume to make the fullest use of modern capital-intensive manufacturing equipment and to amortize staggering research and development costs when facing brief product life cycles.[10] The high costs of research and development, such as in the pharmaceutical industry (for example, Ranbaxy Laboratories in India), along with the cost of keeping up with new technologies, can often be recouped only through global sales.

Growth Opportunities

. . . at the time (1989) it was prescient, giving FedEx a ten-year jump on rivals . . . but we saw the puck and skated toward it.

MICHAEL DUCKER,
VP International, FedEx Express Unit, April 3, 2006[11]

As illustrated by the above comment, companies in mature markets in developed countries experience a growth imperative to look for new opportunities in emerging markets. In this example, FedEx founder and CEO Frederick W. Smith was farsighted in predicting that Asia would become an economic juggernaut and purchased Tiger International Inc. for $895 million in 1989. Tiger was a struggling cargo hauler; however, it had the assets that Smith wanted—flying rights into major Asian airports and managers with local knowledge. This brave move rewarded FedEx with 39 percent of the China-to-U.S. air express market. Continuing to seek aggressive growth opportunities in the region, FedEx is moving its hub to Guangzhou, China, with a $150 million investment, in 2008.[12] When expansion opportunities become limited at home, firms such as McDonald's are often driven to seek expansion through new international markets. A mature product or service with restricted growth in its domestic market often has "new life" in another country, where it will be at an earlier stage of its life cycle. Avon Products, for example, has seen a decline in its U.S. market since its traditional sales and marketing strategy of "Avon Calling" (house-to-house sales) now meets with empty houses, due to the spiraling number of women who work outside the home. To make up for this loss, Avon pushed overseas to 26 emerging markets, such as Mexico, Poland, China, India, South Africa, and Vietnam (bringing its total to 100 countries in which it operates overseas). In Brazil, for instance, Josina Reis Teixeira carries her sample kit to the wooden shacks in the tiny village of Registro, just outside of São Paulo. In some markets, Avon adapted to cultural influences, such as in China, where consumers are suspicious of door-to-door salespeople. There, Avon set up showrooms (beauty boutiques) in its branch offices in major cities so that women can consult cosmeticians and sample products. Subsequently, the company's patience paid off when it was awarded a direct selling license in China in June 2006, and began recruiting over 399,000 direct sales agents.[13]

In addition, new markets abroad provide a place to invest surplus profits as well as employ underutilized resources in management, technology, and machinery. When entirely new markets open up, such as in Eastern Europe, both experienced firms and those new to international competition usually rush to take advantage of awaiting opportunities. Such was the case with the proactive stance that Unisys took in preparing for and jumping on the newly opened market opportunity in Vietnam.

Cemex, the Mexican cement giant, is one company aggressively taking advantage of growth opportunities through acquisitions, as detailed in the accompanying Management Focus. After learning his family's business from the bottom up for eighteen years, Lorenzo Zambrano became CEO and started his gutsy expansion into world markets. His strategy has been to acquire foreign companies, allow time to integrate them into Cemex and pay off the debt, and then look for the next acquisition.

Management Focus

Mexico's Cemex Continues Its Global Expansion in 2007

In October, 2006, the Mexican cement giant Cemex continued its global expansion when it made an unsolicited bid of $12.8 billion for the Rinker Group of Australia. The deal would create one of the world's largest construction materials companies.

If the transaction goes through, it would also strengthen Cemex's leading position in the American housing market, particularly in Sun Belt states like Florida and Arizona. Eighty percent of Rinker's sales come from the United States.

The acquisition would be the largest ever by a Mexican company. Over the last 15 years, Cemex's chairman, Lorenzo Zambrano, has transformed his company into a multinational company with operations on five continents. Sales in 2005 reached $15.3 billion.

The global cement and construction materials industry has been consolidating over the last few years as giants like Lafarge of France, Holcim of Switzerland and Cemex have sought to grow through acquisitions.

Daniel Altman, an analyst in New York for Bear Stearns, said: "These companies make acquisitions through all parts of the cycle. They see something they like and they buy it."

But Mr. Altman and many other analysts questioned whether Cemex had picked the right moment to make the bid. Several years of blistering growth in the United States housing market have stopped short, particularly in Florida, which accounts for about 45 percent of Rinker's overall sales.

Mr. Zambrano sought to allay investor concerns in a conference call with investors, arguing that Cemex was a long-term investor.

"Of course I am worried about the U.S. housing slowdown and the Florida residential market," he said, "but I am confident that those are manageable risks."

Mr. Zambrano, a graduate of Stanford Business School, has confounded Wall Street before with his purchases, taking on billions in debt to expand first in Spain, then in Latin America and the United States.

Last year, Cemex became the world's largest producer of ready-mix concrete when it bought RMC of Britain for $5.8 billion, giving it a strong presence in Europe.

Mr. Zambrano's gambles have paid off, as Cemex executives have cut costs and generated profit to pay down debt.

The company has also invested heavily in high technology, allowing managers at its Monterrey headquarters in northern Mexico to track global operations.

"I would give Cemex the benefit of the doubt based on the experience of the past," said Gonzalo Fernandez, an analyst with Santander Investment Securities in Mexico City.

SOURCE: E. Malkin, "Mexican Cement Company Bids for Australian Concern," Copyright New York Times Co. October 28, 2006, used with permission.
Update: In April 2007, Australia's Rinker Group Ltd. accepted a revised $14.25 billion cash offer from Cemex.

Resource Access and Cost Savings

Resource access and cost savings entice many companies to operate from overseas bases. The availability of raw materials and other resources offers both greater control over inputs and lower transportation costs. Lower labor costs (for production, service, and technical personnel), another major consideration, lead to lower unit costs and have proved a vital ingredient to competitiveness for many companies.

Sometimes just the prospect of shifting production overseas improves competitiveness at home. When Xerox Corporation started moving copier-rebuilding operations to Mexico, the union agreed to needed changes in work style and productivity to keep the jobs at home. Lower operational costs in other areas—power, transportation, and financing—frequently prove attractive.

Incentives

Governments in countries such as Poland seeking new infusions of capital, technology, and know-how willingly provide incentives—tax exemptions, tax holidays, subsidies, loans, and the use of property. Because they both decrease risk and increase profits, these incentives are attractive to foreign companies. One study surveyed 103 experienced managers concerning the relative attractiveness of various incentives for expansion into the Caribbean region (primarily Mexico, Venezuela, Colombia, Dominican Republic, and Guatemala). The results indicate the opinion of those managers about which incentives are most important; however, the most desirable mix would depend on the nature of the particular company and its operations. The first two issues reflect managers' concerns about limiting foreign exchange risk, where restrictions often change overnight and limit the ability of the firm to repatriate profits. Other concerns are those of political instability and the possibility of expropriation, and those of tax concessions.[14] Nor are those incentives limited to emerging economies. The state of Alabama, in the U.S., has spent hundreds of millions to attract the Honda, Hyundai, and Toyota plants.[15] As of July 2007, Europe's Airbus was also considering opening a plant in Alabama.

STRATEGIC FORMULATION PROCESS

Typically, the strategic formulation process is necessary both at the headquarters of the corporation and at each of the subsidiaries. One study reported, for example, that 70 percent of 56 U.S. MNC subsidiaries in Latin America and the Far East operated on planning cycles of five or more years.[16]

The global strategic formulation process, as part of overall corporate strategic management, parallels the process followed in domestic companies. However, the variables, and therefore the process itself, are far more complex because of the greater difficulty in gaining accurate and timely information, the diversity of geographic locations, and the differences in political, legal, cultural, market, and financial processes. These factors introduce a greater level of risk in strategic decisions. However, for firms that have not yet engaged in international operations (as well as for those that do), an ongoing strategic planning process with a global orientation identifies potential opportunities for (1) appropriate market expansion, (2) increased profitability, and (3) new ventures by which the firm can exploit its strategic advantages. Even in the absence of immediate opportunities, monitoring the global environment for trends and competition is important for domestic planning.

The strategic formulation process is part of the strategic management process in which most firms engage, either formally or informally. The planning modes range from a proactive, long-range format to a reactive, more seat-of-the-pants method, whereby the day-by-day decisions of key managers, in particular owner-managers, accumulate to what can be discerned retroactively as the new strategic direction.[17] The stages in the strategic management process are shown in Exhibit 6-2. In reality, these stages seldom follow such a linear format. Rather, the process is continuous and intertwined, with data and results from earlier stages providing information for the next stage.

The first phase of the strategic management process—the *planning phase*—starts with the company establishing (or clarifying) its mission and its overall objectives.

EXHIBIT 6-2   The Strategic Management Process

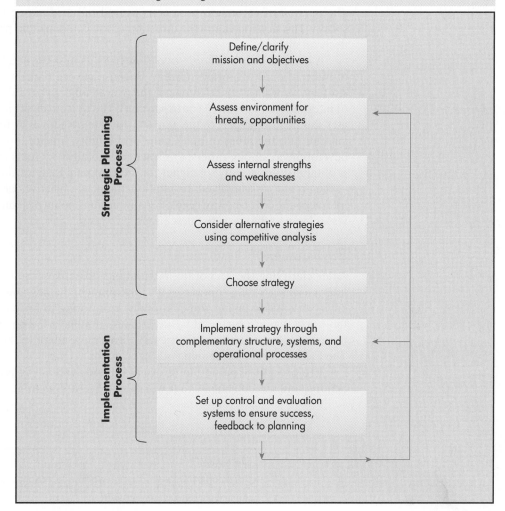

The next two steps comprise an assessment of the external environment that the firm faces in the future and an analysis of the firm's relative capabilities to deal successfully with that environment. Strategic alternatives are then considered, and plans are made based on the strategic choice. These five steps constitute the planning phase, which will be further explained in this chapter.

The second part of the strategic management process is the *implementation phase.* Successful implementation requires the establishment of the structure, systems, and processes suitable to make the strategy work. These variables, as well as functional-level strategies, are explored in detail in the remaining chapters on organizing, leading, and staffing. At this point, however, it is important to note that the strategic planning process by itself does not change the posture of the firm until the plans are implemented. In addition, feedback from the interim and long-term results of such implementation, along with continuous environmental monitoring, flows directly back into the planning process.

STEPS IN DEVELOPING INTERNATIONAL AND GLOBAL STRATEGIES

In the planning phase of strategic management—strategic formulation—managers need to carefully evaluate dynamic factors, as described in the stages that follow. However, as discussed earlier, managers seldom consecutively move through these phases; rather, changing events and variables prompt them to combine and reconsider their evaluations on an ongoing basis.

Mission and Objectives

The *mission* of an organization is its overall *raison d'être* or the function it performs in society. This mission charts the direction of the company and provides a basis for strategic decision making.

A company's overall *objectives* flow from its mission, and both guide the formulation of international corporate strategy. Because we are focusing on issues of international strategy, we will assume that one the overall objectives of the corporation is some form of international operation (or expansion). The objectives of the firm's international affiliates should also be part of the global corporate objectives. A firm's global objectives usually fall into the areas of marketing, profitability, finance, production, and research and development, among others, as shown in Exhibit 6-3. Goals for market volume and for profitability are usually set higher for international than for domestic operations because of the greater risk involved. In addition, financial objectives on the global level must take into account differing tax regulations in various countries and how to minimize overall losses from exchange rate fluctuations.

Environmental Assessment

After clarifying the corporate mission and objectives, the first major step in weighing international strategic options is the **environmental assessment**. This assessment includes environmental scanning and continuous monitoring to keep abreast of variables around the world that are pertinent to the firm and that have the potential to shape its future by posing new opportunities (or threats). Firms must adapt to their environment to survive. The focus of strategic planning is how to adapt.

The process of gathering information and forecasting relevant trends, competitive actions, and circumstances that will affect operations in geographic areas of potential

---

EXHIBIT 6-3   Global Corporate Objectives

Marketing

Total company market share—worldwide, regional, national

Annual percentage sales growth

Annual percentage market share growth

Coordination of regional markets for economies of scale

Production

Relative foreign versus domestic production volume

Economies of scale through global production integration

Quality and cost control

Introduction of cost-efficient production methods

Finance

Effective financing of overseas subsidiaries or allies

Taxation—globally minimizing tax burden

Optimum capital structure

Foreign-exchange management

Profitability

Long-term profit growth

Return on investment, equity, and assets

Annual rate of profit growth

Research and Development

Develop new products with global patents

Develop proprietary production technologies

Worldwide research and development labs

interest is called **environmental scanning**. This activity should be conducted on three levels—global , regional, and national (discussed in detail later in this chapter). Scanning should focus on the future interests of the firm and should cover the following major variables (as discussed by Phatak[18] and others):

- *Political instability.* This variable represents a volatile and uncontrollable risk to the multinational corporation, as illustrated by the upheaval in the Middle East in recent years. MNCs must carefully assess such risk because it may result in a loss of profitability or even ownership.[19]

- *Currency instability.* This variable represents another risk; inflation and fluctuations in the exchange rates of currencies can dramatically affect profitability when operating overseas. For example, both foreign and local firms got a painful reminder of this risk when Mexico devalued its peso in 1998 and the currency collapsed in Indonesia, and in 2002 Argentina was suffering the same problems.

- *Nationalism.* This variable, representing the home government's goals for independence and economic improvement, often influences foreign companies. The home government may impose restrictive policies—import controls, equity requirements, local content requirements, limitations on the repatriation of profits, and so forth. Japan, for example, protects its home markets with these kinds of restrictive policies. Other forms of nationalism may be exerted through the following: (1) pressure from national governments—exemplified by the United States putting pressure on Japan to curtail unfair competition; (2) lax patent and trademark protection laws, such as those in China in recent years, which erode a firm's proprietary technology through insufficient protection; and (3) the suitability of infrastructure, such as roads and telecommunications.

- *International competition.* Conducting a global competitor analysis is perhaps the most important task in environmental assessment and strategy formulation. The first step in analyzing the competition is to assess the relevant industry structures as they influence the competitive arena in the particular country (or region) being considered. For example, will the infrastructure support new companies in that industry? Is there room for additional competition? What is the relative supply and demand for the proposed product or service? The ultimate profit potential in the industry in that location will be determined by these kinds of factors.[20]

- *Environmental Scanning.* Managers must also specifically assess their current competitors—global and local—for the proposed market. They must ask some important questions: What are our competitors' positions, their goals and strategies, and their strengths and weaknesses, relative to those of our firm? What are the likely competitor reactions to our strategic moves?[21]

The firm can also choose varying levels of environmental scanning. To reduce risk and investment, many firms take on the role of the "follower," meaning that they limit their own investigations. Instead, they simply watch their competitors' moves and go where they go, assuming that the competitors have done their homework. Other firms go to considerable lengths to carefully gather data and examine options in the global arena.

Ideally, the firm should conduct global environmental analysis on three different levels: multinational, regional, and national. Analysis on the multinational level provides a broad assessment of significant worldwide trends—through identification, forecasting, and monitoring activities. These trends would include the political and economic developments of nations around the world, as well as global technological progress. From this information, managers can choose certain appropriate regions of the world to consider further.

Next, at the regional level, the analysis focuses in more detail on critical environmental factors to identify opportunities (and risks) for marketing the company's products, services, or technology. For example, one such regional location ripe for investigation by a firm seeking new markets is the EU.

Having zeroed in on one or more regions, the firm must, as its next step, analyze at the national level. Such an analysis explores in depth specific countries within the desired region for economic, legal, political, and cultural factors significant to the company. For example, the analysis could focus on the size and nature of the market, along with any possible operational problems, to consider how best to enter the market. In many volatile countries, continuous monitoring of such environmental factors is a vital part of ongoing strategic planning. In Peru in 1988, inflation had soared to 2,000 percent, and leftist terrorists were kidnapping or murdering business leaders. Although key managers fled and many multinational companies pulled out of Peru, Procter & Gamble remained to take advantage of a potentially large market share when competitors left.

"... you couldn't go to a better business school [than what you learn by managing here]," said Susana Elesperu de Freitas, the 34-year-old Peruvian manager of Procter & Gamble's subsidiary, who was flanked by armed bodyguards wherever she went.[22] Since then, Procter & Gamble, a consumer products company, has expanded and is now a major force in Peru.

This process of environmental scanning, from the broad global level down to the local specifics of entry planning, is illustrated in Exhibit 6-4. The first broad scan of all potential world markets results in the firm being able to eliminate from its list those markets that are closed or insignificant or do not have reasonable entry conditions. The second scan of remaining regions, and then countries, is done in greater detail—perhaps eliminating some countries based on political instability, for example. Remaining countries are then

EXHIBIT 6-4   Global Environmental Scanning and Strategic Decision-Making Process

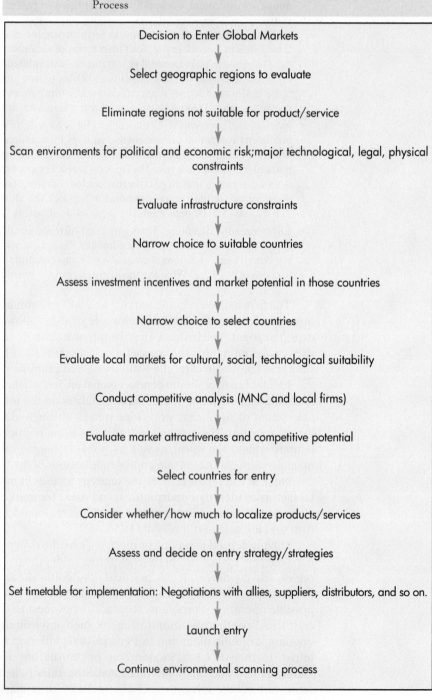

Decision to Enter Global Markets

↓

Select geographic regions to evaluate

↓

Eliminate regions not suitable for product/service

↓

Scan environments for political and economic risk; major technological, legal, physical constraints

↓

Evaluate infrastructure constraints

↓

Narrow choice to suitable countries

↓

Assess investment incentives and market potential in those countries

↓

Narrow choice to select countries

↓

Evaluate local markets for cultural, social, technological suitability

↓

Conduct competitive analysis (MNC and local firms)

↓

Evaluate market attractiveness and competitive potential

↓

Select countries for entry

↓

Consider whether/how much to localize products/services

↓

Assess and decide on entry strategy/strategies

↓

Set timetable for implementation: Negotiations with allies, suppliers, distributors, and so on.

↓

Launch entry

↓

Continue environmental scanning process

assessed for competitor strengths, suitability of products, and so on. This analysis leads to serious entry planning in selected countries; managers start to work on operational plans, such as negotiations and legal arrangements.

Sources of Environmental Information

The success of environmental scanning depends on the ability of managers to take an international perspective and to ensure that their *sources of information and business intelligence* are global. A variety of public resources are available to provide information. In the United States alone, more than 2,000 business information services are available on computer databases tailored to specific industries and regions. Other resources include corporate "clipping" services and information packages. However, internal sources of information are usually preferable—especially alert field personnel who, with firsthand observations, can provide up-to-date and relevant information for the firm. Extensively using its own internal resources, Mitsubishi Trading Company employs worldwide more than 60,000 market analysts, whose job it is to gather, analyze, and feed market information to the parent company.[23] Internal sources of information help to eliminate unreliable information from secondary sources, particularly in developing countries. As Garsombke points out, the "official" data from such countries can be misleading: "Census data can be tampered with by government officials for propaganda purposes or it may be restricted. . . . In South Korea, for instance, even official figures can be conflicting depending on the source."[24]

Internal Analysis

After the environmental assessment, the second major step in weighing international strategic options is the **internal analysis**. This analysis determines which areas of the firm's operations represent strengths or weaknesses (currently or potentially) compared to competitors, so that the firm may use that information to its strategic advantage.

The internal analysis focuses on the company's resources and operations and on global synergies. The strengths and weaknesses of the firm's financial and managerial expertise and functional capabilities are evaluated to determine what key success factors (KSFs) the company has and how well they can help the firm exploit foreign opportunities. Those factors increasingly involve superior technological capability (as with Microsoft and Intel), as well as other strategic advantages such as effective distribution channels (as with Wal-Mart), superior promotion capabilities (Disney), low-cost production and sourcing position (as with Toyota), superior patent and new product pipeline (Merck), and so on.

Using such operational strengths to advantage is exemplified by Japanese car manufacturers: Their production quality and efficiency have catapulted them into world markets. As to their global strategy, they have recognized that their sales and marketing functions have proven a competitive weakness in the European car wars, and the Japanese are working on these shortcomings. Japanese automakers—Toyota, Honda, Mazda, and so on—are following Ford and GM in seeking to become more sophisticated marketers throughout Europe.

All companies have strengths and weaknesses. Management's challenge is to identify both and take appropriate action. Many diagnostic tools are available for conducting an internal resource audit. Financial ratios, for example, may reveal an inefficient use of assets that is restricting profitability; a sales-force analysis may reveal that the sales force is an area of distinct competence for the firm. If a company is conducting this audit to determine whether to start international ventures or to improve its ongoing operations abroad, certain operational issues must be taken into account. These issues include (1) the difficulty of obtaining marketing information in many countries, (2) the often poorly developed financial markets, and (3) the complexities of exchange rates and government controls.

Competitive Analysis

At this point, the firm's managers perform a *competitive analysis* to assess the firm's capabilities and key success factors compared to those of its competitors. They must judge the relative current and potential competitive position of firms in that market and location—whether that is a global position or that for a specific country or region. Like a chess game, the firm's managers also need to consider the strategic intent of competing firms and what might be their future moves (strategies). This process enables the strategic planners to determine where the firm has **distinctive competencies** that will give it strategic advantage as well as what direction might lead the firm into a sustainable competitive advantage—that is, one that will not be immediately eroded by emulation. The result of this process will also help to identify potential problems that can be corrected or that may be significant enough to eliminate further consideration of certain strategies.[25]

This stage of strategic formulation is often called a **SWOT analysis** (Strengths, Weaknesses, Opportunities, and Threats), in which a firm's capabilities relative to those of its competitors are assessed as pertinent to the opportunities and threats in the environment for those firms. In comparing their company with potential international competitors in host markets, it is useful for managers to draw up a competitive position matrix for each potential location. For example, Exhibit 6-5 analyzes a U.S. specialty seafood firm's competitive profile in Malaysia. The U.S. firm has advantages in financial capability, future growth of resources, and sustainability, but a disadvantage in quickness. It also is at a disadvantage compared to the Korean MNC in important factors such as manufacturing capability and flexibility and adaptability. Because the other firms seem to have little **comparative advantage**, the major competitor is likely to be the Korean firm. At this point, then, the U.S. firm can focus in more detail on assessing the Korean firm's relative strengths and weaknesses.

Most companies develop their strategies around key strengths, or **distinctive competencies**. Distinctive—or "core"—competencies represent important corporate resources because, as Prahalad and Hamel explain, they are the "collective learning in the organization, especially how to coordinate diverse production skills and integrate multiple streams of technologies."[26] Core competencies—like Sony's capacity to miniaturize and Philips's optical-media expertise—are usually difficult for competitors to imitate and represent a major focus for strategic development at the corporate level.[27] Canon, for example, has used its core competency in optics to its competitive advantage throughout its diverse businesses: cameras, copiers, and semiconductor lithographic equipment.

Managers must also assess their firm's weaknesses. A company already on shaky ground financially, for example, will not be able to consider an acquisition strategy, or perhaps any growth strategy. Of course, the subjective perceptions, motivations, capabilities, and goals of the managers involved in such diagnoses frequently cloud the decision-making

EXHIBIT 6-5　Global Competitor Analysis

Comparison Criteria	A U.S. Firm Compared with Its International Competitors in Malaysian Market				
	A (U.S. MNC)	B (Korean MNC)	C (Local Malaysian Firm)	D (Japanese MNC)	E (Local Malaysian Firm)
Marketing capability	0	0	0	0	—
Manufacturing capability	0	+	0	0	0
R&D capability	0	0	0	—	0
HRM capability	0	0	0	0	0
Financial capability	+	—	0	0	—
Future growth of resources	+	0	—	0	—
Quickness	—	0	+	—	0
Flexibility/adaptability	0	+	+	0	0
Sustainability	+	0	0	0	—

Key:
+ = firm is better relative to competition.
0 = firm is same as competition.
— = firm is poorer relative to competition.
SOURCE: Diane J. Garsombke, "International Competitor Analysis," *Planning Review* 17, no. 3 (May–June 1989): 42–47.

process. The result is that because of poor judgment by key players sometimes firms embark on strategies that are contraindicated by objective information.

Strategic Decision-Making Models

We can further explain and summarize the hierarchy of the strategic decision-making process described here by means of three leading strategic models. Their roles and interactions are conceptualized in Exhibit 6-6. At the broadest level are those global, regional, and country factors and risks discussed above and in Chapter 1 that are part of those considerations in an **institution-based theory** of existing and potential risks and influences in the host area.[28] For example, firms considering operating in Russia are realizing the potential vulnerability to a changing political attitude to the market reforms and openness from recent progress since President Putin's actions to exert control over key industries. Secondly, or concurrently, the firm's competitive position in its industry can be reviewed using Michael Porter's **industry-based model** of five forces that examines the dynamics within an industry. The forces refer to the relative level of competition already in the industry, the relative ease with which new competitors may or may not enter the field, how much power the suppliers and also the buyers have within the industry, and the extent of substitute products or services that prevail.[29] These strategic models can provide the decision makers with a picture of the kinds of opportunities and threats that the firm would face in a particular region or country within its industry. This assumes, of course, that the locations that are under consideration have already been pinpointed as attractive and growing markets for the industry. However, that picture would be true for any firm within the particular industry. In other words, all firms within an industry face the same environmental and industrial factors; the difference among firms' performance is as a result of each firm's own resources, capabilities, and strategic decisions. The factors that determine a firm's unique niche or competitive advantage within that arena are a function of its own capabilities (strengths and weaknesses) as relative to those opportunities and threats which are perceived for that location; this is the **resource-based** view of the firm—when considering the unique value of the firm's competencies and that of its products or services.[30] While these models may indicate varying choices, this strategic decision-making process should enable the managers to give an overall assessment of the strategic fit between the firm and the opportunities in that location and so result in a "go/no go" decision for that point in time. Those managers may want to start the process again relative to a different location in order to compare the relative levels of strategic fit. If it is determined that there is a good strategic fit and a decision is made to enter that market/location, the next step, as indicated in Exhibit 6-6, is to consider alternative entry strategies. A discussion of these entry strategies follows after we first examine the broader picture of the overall strategic approach that a firm might take towards world markets.

Global and International Strategic Alternatives

The strategic planning process involves considering the advantages (and disadvantages) of various strategic alternatives in light of the competitive analysis. While weighing alternatives, managers must take into account the goals of their firms and the competitive status of other firms in the industry. Depending on the size of the firm, managers must consider two levels of strategic alternatives. The first level, *global strategic alternatives* (applicable primarily to MNCs), determines what overall approach to the global marketplace a firm wishes to take. The second level, *entry strategy alternatives*, applies to firms of any size; these alternatives determine what specific entry strategy is appropriate for each country in which the firm plans to operate. Entry strategy alternatives are discussed in a later section. The two main global strategic approaches to world markets—global strategy and regional, or local, strategy—are presented in the following subsections.

Approaches to World Markets

Global Strategy

In the last decade, increasing competitive pressures have forced businesses to consider global strategies—to treat the world as an undifferentiated worldwide marketplace. Such strategies are now loosely referred to as **globalization**—a term that refers to the establishment of

EXHIBIT 6-6   A Hierarchial Model of Strategic Decision Making

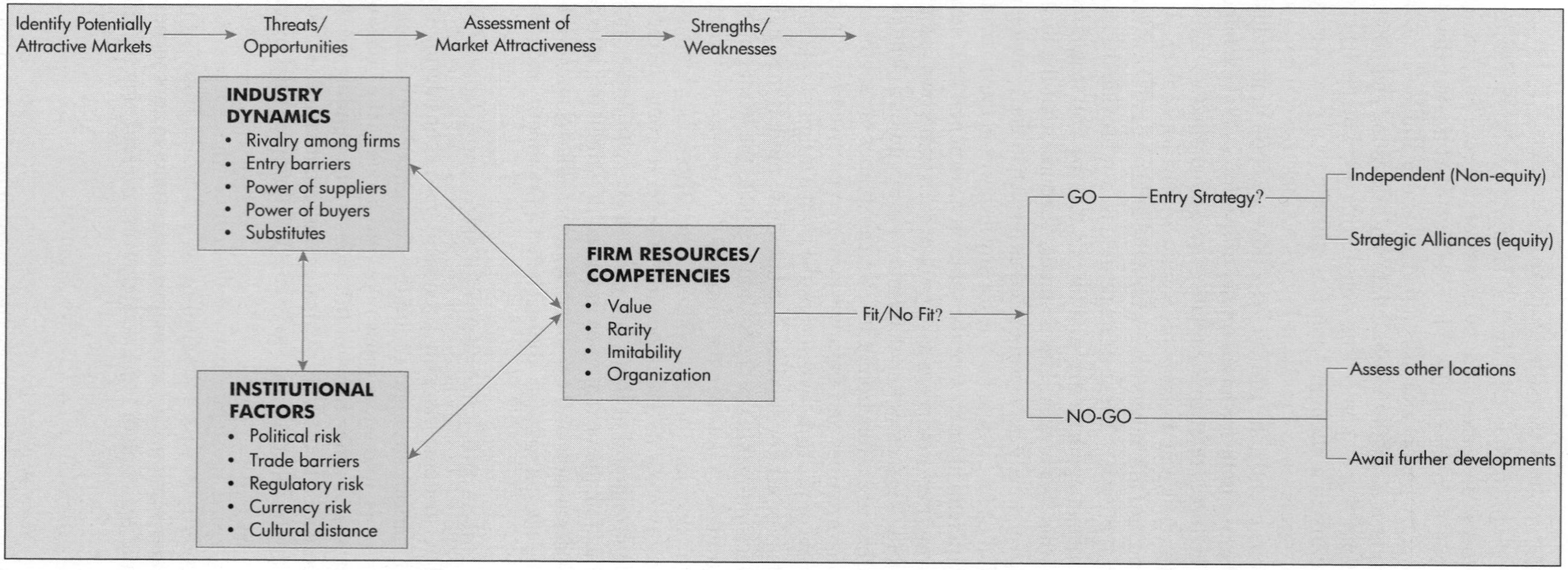

Identify Potentially → Threats/ → Assessment of → Strengths/
Attractive Markets   Opportunities   Market Attractiveness   Weaknesses

INDUSTRY DYNAMICS
- Rivalry among firms
- Entry barriers
- Power of suppliers
- Power of buyers
- Substitutes

INSTITUTIONAL FACTORS
- Political risk
- Trade barriers
- Regulatory risk
- Currency risk
- Cultural distance

FIRM RESOURCES/ COMPETENCIES
- Value
- Rarity
- Imitability
- Organization

Fit/No Fit?

GO ———— Entry Strategy?

Independent (Non-equity)

Strategic Alliances (equity)

NO-GO

Assess other locations

Await further developments

worldwide operations and the development of standardized products and marketing. Many, analysts, like Porter, have argued that globalization is a competitive imperative for firms in global industries: "In a global industry, a firm must, in some way, integrate its activities on a worldwide basis to capture the linkages among countries. This includes, but requires more than, transferring intangible assets among countries."[31] The rationale behind globalization is to compete by establishing worldwide economies of scale, offshore manufacturing, and international cash flows. The term *globalization,* therefore, is as applicable to organizational structure as it is to strategy. (Organizational structure is discussed further in Chapter 8.)

The pressures to globalize include (1) increasing competitive clout resulting from regional trading blocs; (2) declining tariffs, which encourage trading across borders and open up new markets; and (3) the information technology explosion, which makes the coordination of far-flung operations easier and also increases the commonality of consumer tastes.[32] Use of Web sites has allowed entrepreneurs, as well as established companies, to go global almost instantaneously through e-commerce—either B2B or B2C.[33] Examples are eBay, Yahoo!, Lands' End, and the ill-fated E-Toys, which met its demise in 2001. In addition, the success of Japanese companies with global strategies has set the competitive standard in many industries—most visibly in the automobile industry. Other companies, such as Caterpillar, ICI, and Sony, have fared well with global strategies.

One of the quickest and cheapest ways to develop a global strategy is through strategic alliances. Many firms are trying to go global faster by forming alliances with rivals, suppliers, and customers. The rapidly developing information technologies are spawning cross-national business alliances from short-term virtual corporations to long-term strategic partnerships. (Strategic alliances are discussed further in Chapter 7.)

A global strategy is inherently more vulnerable to environmental risk, however, than a regionalization (or "multi-local") strategy. Global organizations are difficult to manage because doing so requires the coordination of broadly divergent national cultures. It also means, say Morrison, Ricks, and Roth, that firms must lose some of their original identity— they must "denationalize operations and replace home-country loyalties with a system of common corporate values and loyalties."[34] In other words, the global strategy necessarily treats all countries similarly, regardless of their differences in cultures and systems. Problems often result, such as a lack of local flexibility and responsiveness and a neglect of the need for differentiated products. In some recent research into how U.S. companies compete, Morrison et al. discovered that many companies are finding that "globalization is no panacea, and, in fact, global imperatives are being eclipsed by an upsurge in regional pressures."[35] These researchers claim that many companies now feel that regionalization/localization is a more manageable and less risky approach, one that allows them to capitalize on local competencies as long as the parent organization and each subsidiary retain a flexible approach to each other. As discussed in the opening profile, Wal-Mart is one global company that has learned the hard way that it should have acted more "local" in some regions of the world, including Germany and South Korea, where it has had to abandon operations.

Regionalization/Localization

Nokia, Nestle, Google, and Wal-Mart have failed to adjust to the tastes of South Korean consumers. In contrast, the British retailer Tesco is a remarkable case of succeeding in localizing. Samsung Tesco is 89 percent owned by the British retail giant, but has relied heavily on local managers from Samsung. It is one of Tesco's biggest overseas success stories, generating a third of its overseas sales.

MR. NA HONG SEOK,
Analyst in Seoul, South Korea, March 23, 2006[36]

For those firms in multidomestic industries—those industries in which competitiveness is determined on a country-by-country basis rather than a global basis—regional strategies are more appropriate than globalization.[37] The **regionalization strategy [multidomestic (or multi-local) strategy]** is one in which local markets are linked together within a region, allowing more local responsiveness and specialization. Top managers within each region decide on their own investment locations, product mixes, and competitive positioning; in other words, they run their subsidiaries as quasi-independent organizations.

Since there are pressures to globalize—such as the need for economies of scale to compete on cost—there are opposing pressures to regionalize, especially for newly developed economies (NDEs) and less developed countries (LDCs). These localization pressures include unique consumer preferences resulting from cultural or national differences (perhaps something as simple as right-hand-drive cars for Japan), domestic subsidies, and new production technologies that facilitate product variation for less cost than before.[38] By "acting local," firms can focus individually in each country or region on the local market needs for product or service characteristics, distribution, customer support, and so on.

As with any management function, the strategic choice as to where a company should position itself along the globalization–regionalization continuum is contingent on the nature of the industry, the type of company, the company's goals and strengths (or weaknesses), and the nature of its subsidiaries, among many factors. In addition, each company's strategic approach should be unique in adapting to its own environment. Many firms may try to "Go Global, Act Local" to trade off the best advantages of each strategy. Matsushita is one firm with considerable expertise at being a "GLOCAL" firm (GLObal, LoCAL). Matsushita has more than 150 production and research and development (R&D) bases in 38 countries. In Malaysia, for example, where Matsushita employs 23,500 people in its 13 subsidiaries, the company diligently follows its policy of trying to keep the expatriate headcount down and train local managers—only 230 employees there are Japanese. Other Matsushita local policies are to develop local R&D to tailor products to markets, to let plants set their own rules, and to be a good corporate citizen in every country.[39]

Global Integrative Strategies

Many MNCs have developed their global operations to the point of being fully integrated—often both vertically and horizontally, including suppliers, productive facilities, marketing and distribution outlets, and contractors around the world. Dell, for example, is a globally integrated company, with worldwide sourcing and a fully integrated production and marketing system. It has factories in Ireland, Brazil, China, Malaysia, Tennessee, and Texas, and it has an assembly and delivery system from 47 locations around the world. At the same time, it has extreme flexibility. Since Dell builds computers to each order, it carries very little inventory and, therefore, can change its operations at a moment's notice. Thomas Friedman described the process that his notebook computer went through when he ordered it from Dell:

> *The notebook was co-designed in Austin, Texas, and in Taiwan. . . . The total supply chain for my computer, including suppliers of suppliers, involved about four hundred companies in North America, Europe, and primarily Asia, but with thirty key players. (It was delivered by UPS 17 days after ordering.).*

> THOMAS FRIEDMAN,
> *The World Is Flat, 2005*[40]

Although some companies move very quickly to the stage of global integration—often through merger or acquisition—many companies evolve into multinational corporations by going through the entry strategies in stages, taking varying lengths of time between stages. Typically, a company starts with simple exporting, moves to large-scale exporting with sales branches abroad (or perhaps begins licensing), then proceeds to assembly abroad (either by itself or through contract manufacturing), and eventually evolves to full production abroad with its own subsidiaries. Finally, the MNC will undertake the global integration of its foreign subsidiaries, setting up cooperative activities among them to achieve economies of scale. By this point, the MNC has usually adopted a geocentric orientation, viewing opportunities and entry strategies in the context of an interrelated global market instead of regional or national markets. In this way, alternative entry strategies are viewed on an overall portfolio basis to take maximum advantage of potential synergies and leverage arising from operations in multicountry markets.[41]

Using E-Business for Global Expansion

Companies of all sizes are increasingly looking to the Internet as a means of expanding their global operations. However, the Internet is not just about e-business:

> *The real story is that the Internet is driving global marketplace transformation and paradigm shift in how companies get things done, how they compete and how they serve their customers.*"[42]

While the benefits of e-business are many, including rapid entrance into new geographic markets (see Exhibit 6-7), less touted are the many challenges inherent in a global B2B or B2C strategy. These include cultural differences and varying business models, and governmental wrangling and border conflicts, in particular the question over which country has jurisdiction and responsibility over disputes regarding cross-border electronic transactions.[43] Potential problem areas that managers must assess in their global environmental analysis include conflicting consumer protection, intellectual property and tax laws, increasing isolationism even among democracies, language barriers, and a lack of tech-savvy legislators worldwide.[44]

Savvy global managers will realize that e-business cannot be regarded as just an extension of current businesses. It is a whole new industry in itself, complete with a different pool of competitors and entirely new sets of environmental issues. A reassessment of the environmental forces in the newly configured industry, using Michael Porter's five forces analytical model, should take account of shifts in the relative bargaining power of buyers and suppliers, the level of threat of new competitors, existing and potential substitutes, as well as a present and anticipated competitor analysis.[45] The level of e-competition will be determined by how transparent and imitable the company's business model is for its product or service as observed on its Web site.

It is clear that a competitive global B2B or B2C strategy must offer a technology solution that goes beyond basic transaction or listing service capabilities.[46] To assess the potential competitive position of the company, managers must ask themselves the following:

- Does the exchange provide a technology solution that helps industry trading partners to do business more efficiently?
- Is the exchange known to be among the top three to five within its vertical industry?
- Does the exchange offer industry-specific technology and expertise that gives it an advantage over generic exchange builders?[47]

There is no doubt that the global e-business competitive arena is a challenging one, both strategically and technologically. But many companies around the world are plunging

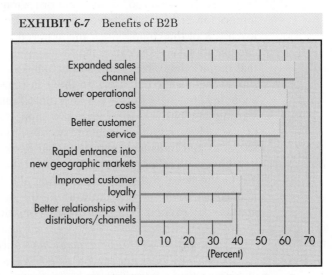

EXHIBIT 6-7   Benefits of B2B

SOURCE: Data from IDC Internet executive Advisory Council Surveys, 2001.

in, fearing that they will be left behind in this fast-developing global e-marketplace. Included are Fuji Xerox, which has formed a new e-marketplace with NEC and other leading e-commerce players, including Simitomo, Hewlett Packard Japan, Ltd., Sumisho Computer Systems, and U.S. software developer Ariba. Its site, PLEOMART (plenty of markets), is a B2B marketplace for companies to buy and sell, on the Internet, office equipment and supplies, parts, and related solutions services such as consultation, finance, and logistics services.[48] In Melbourne, Australia, the Broken Hill Proprietary Company (BHP), which specializes in natural resources and regional steel for the global market, has launched its own one-stop global e-marketplace. The site provides logistics, sample products, and supply procurements to e-business producer marketplaces. Recently, BHP has conducted a series of Internet-based "reverse" auctions, where suppliers agree on starting prices and then bid against each other to lower prices for ferro-alloys. BHP's Francis Egan, vice president for Global Supply, reports that BHP already spends about $10 billion annually on goods and services online. He says that "online auctions allow us to move readily, aggregate our buying power and leverage greater savings they also provide economies of scale and promote greater efficiency in the supply function itself."[49]

For companies like eBay, e-business is their business—services are provided over the Internet for end users and for businesses. With a unique business model, and as a young company, eBay has embarked on a global e-strategy. The company has positioned itself to be global and giant: part international swap meet, part clearinghouse for the world's manufacturers and retailers. The international e-commerce market is evolving rapidly, and executives at eBay's annual financial conference in May 2006 discussed how eBay is responding effectively to challenges. "In Europe, eBay is on track to be a bigger business than it is in the United States, while Asia remains eBay's fastest growing region with tremendous long-term potential."[50]

> *Across all of our businesses, we see greater opportunities for future growth than ever before. Each of our brands [Marketplaces, Payments and Communications] is the global leader in its space and well positioned to pursue new opportunities and accelerate growth. Together, they're working to turbo charge one another. Our multi-brand strategy is opening up entirely new vistas of opportunity for the company.*
>
> MEG WHITMAN,
> *CEO, eBay, Canada News Wire Group, May 4, 2006*[51]

E-Global or E-Local?

Although the Internet is a global medium, the company is still faced with the same set of decisions regarding how much its products or services can be "globalized" or how much they must be "localized" to national or regional markets. Local cultural expectations, differences in privacy laws, government regulations, taxes, and payment infrastructure are just a few of the complexities encountered in trying to "globalize" e-commerce. Further complications arise because the local physical infrastructure must support e-businesses that require the transportation of actual goods for distribution to other businesses in the supply chain, or to end users. In those instances, adding e-commerce to an existing "old-economy" business in those international markets is likely to be more successful than starting an e-business from scratch without the supply and distribution channels already in place. However, many technology consulting firms, such as NextLinx, provide software solutions and tools to penetrate global markets, extend their supply chains, and enable new buyer and seller relationships around the globe.

Going global with e-business, as Yahoo! has done, necessitates a coordinated effort in a number of regions around the world at the same time to gain a foothold and to grab new markets before competitors do. Certain conditions dictate the advisability of going e-global:

> *The global beachhead strategy makes sense when trade is global in scope; when the business does not involve delivering orders; and when the business model can be hijacked relatively easily by local competitors.*[52]

This strategy would work well for global B2B markets in steel, plastics, and electronic components.

The e-local, or regional strategic, approach is suited to consumer retailing and financial services, for example. Amazon and eBay have started their regional approach in Western Europe. Again, certain conditions would make this strategy more advisable:

> *[The e-local/regional approach] is preferable under three conditions: when production and consumption are regional rather than global in scope; when customer behavior and market structures differ across regions but are relatively similar within a region; and when supply-chain management is very important to success.*[53]

The selection of which region or regions to target depends on the same factors of local market dynamics and industry variables as previously discussed in this chapter. However, for e-businesses, additional variables must also be considered, such as the rate of Internet penetration and the level of development of the local telecommunications infrastructure.

One company which learned the hard way how to localize its e-business is Handango, Inc., of Hurst, Texas—a maker of smart-phone and wireless-network software. As the company vice president of marketing, Clint Patterson, said, reflecting on their move into Asian markets several years ago: "We didn't understand what purchasing methods would be popular or even what kinds of content. We didn't have a local taste. We realized we needed someone on the street to hold our hand."[54] For example, Handango found it needed a local bank account to do business in Japan, because Japanese consumers use a method called *konbini* to make online payments. This means that when they place their order online, instead of paying with a credit card, they go to a local convenience store and pay cash to a clerk, who then transfers the payment into the online vendor's account. In order to adapt to this system Handango formed an alliance with @irBitway, a local consumer-electronics Web portal, which now acts as Handango's agent in the konbini system, and also has taken over Handango's local marketing and translation.[55] Handango ran into a similar problem in Germany, finding out that Germans do not like debt and prefer to pay for their online purchases with wire transfers from their bank accounts. To get around this, the company found a local partner to interface with local banks, and then adapted its Web site to the new payment method.[56]

Entry Strategy Alternatives

For a multinational corporation (or a company considering entry into the international arena), a more specific set of strategic alternatives, often varying by targeted country, focuses on different ways to enter a foreign market. Managers need to consider how potential new markets may best be served by their company in light of the risks and the critical environmental factors associated with their entry strategies. The following sections examine the various entry and ownership strategies available to firms, including exporting, licensing, franchising, contract manufacturing, service-sector outsourcing, turnkey operations, management contracts, joint ventures, and fully owned subsidiaries set up by the firm. These alternatives are not mutually exclusive; several may be employed at the same time. They are addressed in order of ascending risk.

Exporting

Exporting is a relatively low-risk way to begin international expansion or to test out an overseas market. Little investment is involved, and fast withdrawal is relatively easy. Small firms seldom go beyond this stage, and large firms use this avenue for many of their products. Because of their comparative lack of capital resources and marketing clout, exporting is the primary entry strategy used by small businesses to compete on an international level. Jordan Toothbrush, for example, a small company with one plant in Norway and with limited resources, is dependent on good distributors. Since Jordan exports around the world, the company recognizes the importance of maintaining good distributor relations. A recent survey by Dun and Bradstreet showed that more than half of small to medium-sized businesses anticipate growth in their export sales in the next few years.[57]

An experienced firm may want to handle its exporting functions by appointing a manager or establishing an export department. Alternatively, an export management company (EMC) may be retained to take over some or all exporting functions, including dealing with host-country regulations, tariffs, duties, documentation, letters of credit, currency conversion, and so forth. Frequently, it pays to hire a specialist for a given host country.

Certain decisions need special care when managers are setting up an exporting system, particularly the choice of distributor. Many countries have regulations that make it very hard to remove a distributor who proves inefficient. Other critical environmental factors include export-import tariffs and quotas, freight costs, and distance from supplier countries.

Licensing

An international licensing agreement grants the rights to a firm in the host country to either produce or sell a product, or both. This agreement involves the transfer of rights to patents, trademarks, or technology for a specified period of time in return for a fee paid by the licensee. Anheuser-Busch, for instance, has granted licenses to produce and market Budweiser beer in England, Japan, Australia, and Israel, among other countries. Many food manufacturing MNCs license their products overseas, often under the names of local firms, and products like those of Nike and Disney can be seen around the world under various licensing agreements. Like exporting, licensing is also a relatively low-risk strategy because it requires little investment, and it can be a useful option in countries where market entry by other means is constrained by regulations or profit-repatriation restrictions.

Licensing is especially suitable for the mature phase of a product's life cycle, when competition is intense, margins decline, and production is relatively standardized.[58] It is also useful for firms with rapidly changing technologies, for those with many diverse product lines, and for small firms with few financial and managerial resources for direct investment abroad. A clear advantage of licensing is that it avoids the tariffs and quotas usually imposed on exports. The most common disadvantage is the licensor's lack of control over the licensee's activities and performance.

Critical environmental factors to consider in licensing are whether sufficient patent and trademark protection is available in the host country, the track record and quality of the licensee, the risk that the licensee may develop its competence to become a direct competitor, the licensee's market territory, and legal limits on the royalty rate structure in the host country.[59]

Franchising

Similar to licensing, **franchising** involves relatively little risk. The franchisor licenses its trademark, products and services, and operating principles to the franchisee for an initial fee and ongoing royalties. Franchises are well known in the domestic fast-food industry; McDonald's, for example, operates primarily on this basis. For a large up-front fee and considerable royalty payments, the franchisee gets the benefit of McDonald's reputation, existing clientele, marketing clout, and management expertise. The "Big M" is well recognized internationally, as are many other fast-food and hotel franchises, such as Holiday Inn. A critical consideration for the franchisor's management is quality control, which becomes more difficult with greater geographic dispersion.

Franchising can be an ideal strategy for small businesses because outlets require little investment in capital or human resources. Through franchising, an entrepreneur can use the resources of franchisees to expand; most of today's large franchises started out with this strategy. An entrepreneur can also use franchisees to enter a new business. Higher costs in entry fees and royalties are offset by the lower risk of an established product, trademark, and customer base, as well as the benefit of the franchisor's experience and techniques.[60]

Contract Manufacturing

A common means of using cheaper labor overseas is contract manufacturing, which involves contracting for the production of finished goods or component parts. These goods or components are then imported to the home country, or to other countries, for assembly or sale. Alternatively, they may be sold in the host country. If managers can ensure the reliability and quality of the local contractor and work out adequate means of capital repatriation, this strategy can be a desirable means of quick entry into a country with a low capital investment and none of the problems of local ownership. Firms like Nike use contract manufacturing around the world.

Offshoring

Offshoring is when a company moves one or all of its factories from the 'home' country to another country, as is the case with some of Toyota's factories in the U.S. Offshoring provides the company with access to foreign markets while avoiding trade barriers, as well as, frequently, an overall lower cost of production. According to the U.S. Commerce Department, approximately 90 percent of the output from U.S.-owned offshore factories is sold to foreign consumers.[61]

Service Sector Outsourcing

An increasing number of firms are outsourcing "white-collar" jobs overseas in an attempt to reduce their overall costs. Often they enter overseas markets by setting up local offices, research laboratories, call centers, and so on in order to utilize the highly skilled but lower-wage **"human capital"** that is available in countries such as India, the Philippines, and China, as well as the ability to offer global, round-the-clock service from different time zones. Some examples include the following:

> *General Electric:* 20,000 in India; big China R&D center: services in finance, IT support, R&D for medical, lighting, aircraft
>
> *Accenture:* 5,000 in the Philippines; accounting, software, back-office work
>
> *Oracle:* Doubling India staff to 4,000; software design, customer support, accounting
>
> *Conseco:* 1,700 in India, three more centers planned; insurance claim processing[62]

Overall, it seems that India has benefited in IT jobs; as noted by Bill Gates of Microsoft "India is the absolute leader in IT services offered on the world market."[63] However, as India gets more sophisticated at taking over high-skilled jobs outsourced from European and U.S. multinationals, they are starting to turn away call-center work, saying that it doesn't pay well any longer. In addition, companies are finding that salaries in India are increasing with the demand for jobs from MNCs, and with the Indian technology companies themselves growing in global clout. Outsourcing of low-end office jobs may then start to migrate to other countries such as the Philippines or South Africa.[64] In turn, both Indian and American IT service providers are opening offices in Hungary, Poland, and the Czech Republic to take advantage of the German and English-speaking workforce for European clients.

Whether the firms outsource (or "offshore") white-collar or blue-collar jobs, they must consider strategic aspects of that decision beyond immediate cost savings. According to Hewitt Associates, a global human resources consulting firm, the "global sourcing" strategy utilized by the firms it surveyed was often short-sighted:

> *Although cost reduction is the primary driver, less than half of companies analyze the tax environments of considered countries, only three-fourths measure the impact on supply chain costs, and only 34 percent assess the cost of plant or office shutdown.[65]*

Even with its increasing outsourcing of jobs, IBM has acknowledged the need to consider factors other than cost, as it started a radical revamping of its 200,000 people services workforce in 2006, saying

> *The idea is to perform work for clients where it can be done most competitively. That means not only India and China, but Tulsa, Oklahoma, and Boulder, Colorado.*

BUSINESS WEEK,
June 5, 2006.[66]

Managers are in fact broadening their strategic view of sending skilled work abroad, now using the term "transformational outsourcing" to refer to the growth opportunities provided by making better use of skilled staff in the home office which are brought about by the gains in efficiency and productivity through leveraging global talent.[67] The U.S.-based bank Wachovia Corp., for example, signed a $1.1 billion deal in 2006 with India's Genpact to outsource finance and accounting jobs but at the same time the company outsourced administration of its human-resources programs to Hewitt Associates, based in the U.S.[68] However, the risk of backlash from customers, community, and current employees necessitates careful consideration of the reasons for a company to go offshore. Managers also must consider the risk of losing control of proprietary technology and processes and decide whether to set up the company's own subsidiary offshore (a "captive" operation) instead of contracting with outside specialists. Bank of America, for example, split their strategy by opening their own subsidiary in India, but also allied with Infosys technologies and Tata Consultancy Services for 30 percent of its IT resources to be outsourced.[69]

Turnkey Operations

In a so-called **turnkey operation**, a company designs and constructs a facility abroad (such as a dam or chemical plant), trains local personnel, and then turns the key over to local management—for a fee, of course. The Italian company Fiat, for example, constructed an automobile plant in the former Soviet Union under a turnkey agreement. Critical factors for success are the availability of local supplies and labor, reliable infrastructure, and an acceptable means of repatriating profits. There may also be a critical risk exposure if the turnkey contract is with the host government, which is often the case. This situation exposes the company to risks such as contract revocation and the rescission of bank guarantees.

Management Contracts

A management contract gives a foreign company the rights to manage the daily operations of a business but not to make decisions regarding ownership, financing, or strategic and policy changes. Usually, management contracts are enacted in combination with other agreements, such as joint ventures. By itself, a management contract is a relatively low-risk entry strategy, but it is likely to be short term and provide limited income unless it leads to another more permanent position in the market.

International Joint Ventures

At a much higher level of investment and risk (though usually less risky than a wholly owned plant), joint ventures present considerable opportunities unattainable through other strategies. A joint venture involves an agreement by two or more companies to produce a product or service together. In an **international joint venture (IJV)** ownership is shared, typically by an MNC and a local partner, through agreed-upon proportions of equity. This strategy facilitates an MNC's rapid entry into new markets by means of an already established partner who has local contacts and familiarity with local operations. IJVs are a common strategy for corporate growth around the world. They also are a means to overcome trade barriers, to achieve significant economies of scale for development of a strong competitive position, to secure access to additional raw materials, to acquire managerial and technological skills, and to spread the risk associated with operating in a foreign environment.[70] Not surprisingly, larger companies are more inclined to take a high-equity stake in an IJV, to engage in global industries, and to be less vulnerable to the risk conditions in the host country.[71] The joint venture reduces the risks of expropriation and harassment by the host country. Indeed, it may be the only means of entry into certain countries, like Mexico and Japan, that stipulate proportions of local ownership and local participation.

In recent years, IJVs have made up about 20 percent of direct investments by MNCs in other countries, including such deals as that between Mittal Steel of India and Arcelor of France in 2006—creating the world's biggest steel company.[72] Many companies have set up joint ventures with European companies to gain the status of an "insider" in the

European Common Market. Most of these alliances are not just tools of convenience but are important—perhaps critical—means to compete in the global arena. To compete globally, firms have to incur, and defray, immense fixed costs—and they need partners to help them in this effort.[73]

Sometimes countries themselves need such alliances to improve economic conditions: The Russian Federation has recently opened its doors to joint ventures, seeking an infusion of capital and management expertise. IJVs are one of the many forms of strategic global alliances that are further discussed in the next chapter.

In a joint venture, the level of relative ownership and specific contributions must be worked out by the partners. The partners must share management and decision making for a successful alliance. The company seeking such a venture must maintain sufficient control, however, because without adequate control, the company's managers may be unable to implement their desired strategies. Initial partner selection and the development of a mutually beneficial working agreement are, therefore, critical to the success of a joint venture. In addition, managers must ascertain that there will be enough of a "fit" between the partners' objectives, strategies, and resources—financial, human, and technological—to make the venture work. Unfortunately, too often the need for preparation and cooperation is given insufficient attention, resulting in many such marriages ending in divorce. About 60 percent of IJVs fail, usually because of ineffective managerial decisions regarding the type of IJV, its scope, duration, and administration, as well as careless partner selection.[74]

Fully Owned Subsidiaries

In countries where a **fully owned subsidiary** is permitted, an MNC wishing total control of its operations can start its own product or service business from scratch, or it may acquire an existing firm in the host country. Philip Morris acquired the Swiss food firm Jacobs Suchard to gain an early inside track in the European Common Market and to continue its diversification away from its aging tobacco business. With this move, Philip Morris became the second U.S. company, after Mars, to ensure itself a place in Europe's food industry. Such acquisitions by MNCs allow rapid entry into a market with established products and distribution networks and provide a level of acceptability not likely to be given to a "foreign" firm. These advantages somewhat offset the greater level of risk stemming from larger capital investments, compared with other entry strategies. Examples of acquisitions to gain further growth and entry into global markets include that of the Lenovo Group of China of the IBM Personal Computing Division, creating a global business with worldwide reach;[75] and the Procter and Gamble acquisition of Gillette, which paved the way for the creation of the world's largest consumer goods company.[76]

At the highest level of risk is the strategy of starting a business from scratch in the host country—that is, establishing a new wholly owned foreign manufacturing or service company or subsidiary with products aimed at the local market or targeted for export. Japanese automobile manufacturers, such as Honda, Nissan, and Toyota, have successfully used this strategy in the United States to get around U.S. import quotas.

This strategy exposes the company to the full range of risk, to the extent of its investment in the host country. As evidenced by events in South Africa and China, political instability can be devastating to a wholly owned foreign subsidiary. Add to this risk a number of other critical environmental factors—local attitudes toward foreign ownership, currency stability and repatriation, the threat of expropriation and nationalism—and you have a high-risk entry strategy that must be carefully evaluated and monitored. There are advantages to this strategy, however, such as full control over decision making and efficiency, as well as the ability to integrate operations with overall companywide strategy.

Exhibit 6-8 summarizes the advantages and critical success factors of these entry strategies, which must be taken into account when selecting one or a combination of strategies depending on the location, the environmental factors and competitive analysis, and the overall strategy with which the company approaches world markets.

Complex situational factors face the international manager as she or he considers strategic approaches to world markets, along with which entry strategies might be

EXHIBIT 6-8 International Entry Strategies: Advantages and Critical Success Factors

Strategy	Advantages	Critical Success Factors
Exporting	Low risk	Choice of distributor
	No long-term assets	Transportation costs
	Easy market access and exit	Tariffs and quotas
Licensing	No asset ownership risk	Quality and trustworthiness of licensee
	Fast market access	Appropriability of intellectual property
	Avoids regulations and tariffs	Host-country royalty limits
Franchising	Little investment or risk	Quality control of franchisee and franchise operations
	Fast market access	
	Small business expansion	
Contract manufacturing/ offshoring	Limited cost and risk	Reliability and quality of local contractor
	Short-term commitment	Operational control and human rights issues
Service-sector outsourcing	Lower employment costs	Quality control
Turnkey operations	Access to high skills and markets	Domestic client acceptance
	Revenue from skills and technology where FDI restricted	Reliable infrastructure Sufficient local supplies and labor Repatriable profits
		Reliability of any government partner
Management contracts	Low-risk access to further strategies	Opportunity to gain longer-term position
Joint ventures	Insider access to markets	Strategic fit and complementarity of partner, markets, products
	Share costs and risk	
	Leverage partner's skill base technology, local contacts	Ability to protect technology
		Competitive advantage
		Ability to share control
		Cultural adaptability of partners
Wholly owned subsidiaries	Realize all revenues and control	Ability to assess and control economic, political, and currency risk
	Global economies of scale	
	Strategic coordination	Ability to get local acceptance
	Protect technology and skill base	Repatriability of profits
	Acquisition provides rapid market entry into established market	

appropriate, as illustrated in Comparative Management in Focus: Strategic Planning for the EU Market.

Strategic Choice

The strategic choice of one or more of the entry strategies will depend on (1) a critical evaluation of the advantages (and disadvantages) of each in relation to the firm's capabilities, (2) the critical environmental factors, and (3) the contribution that each choice would make to the overall mission and objectives of the company. Exhibit 6-8 summarized the advantages and the critical success factors for each entry strategy discussed. However, when it comes down to a choice of entry strategy or strategies for a particular company, more specific factors relating to that firm's situation must be taken into account. These include factors relating to the firm itself, the industry in

Comparative Management in Focus

Strategic Planning for the EU Market

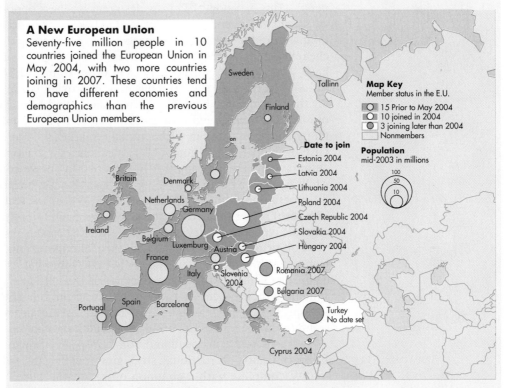

A New European Union
Seventy-five million people in 10 countries joined the European Union in May 2004, with two more countries joining in 2007. These countries tend to have different economies and demographics than the previous European Union members.

Map 6-2   A New European Union
SOURCE: *New York Times*, March 10, 2004, reprinted with permission Copyright © The New York Times Co.

Multinationals are well placed to benefit from enlargement (inclusion of the ex-communist states) because they have the greatest access to capital, technology and skills. Local entrepreneurs have flair but often lack the funds to grow. Only a handful of locally owned groups—such as Mol, the Hungarian oil group, or CEZ, the Czech electricity company—are big enough to invest abroad.

FINANCIAL TIMES,
April 27, 2004[77]

If you're investing in Hungary or Poland, you get access to the lower costs they offer, compared with, say, Germany or France or Britain. At the same time, if you're producing in Poland, you have an ability to move your goods and services around within the European Union.

MARK AMBLER,
PriceWaterhouseCoopers, London[78]

Business units [in Europe] still tend to focus on individual countries, and managerial practices still follow long-standing national patterns.

FRANCESCO CAIO,
CEO Merloni Elettrodomestici, Fabriano, Italy[79]

The addition of the eight Central and Eastern Europe (CEE) countries (the Czech Republic, Estonia, Hungary, Latvia, Lithuania, Poland, the Slovak Republic, and Slovenia), as well as Malta and Cyprus, to the EU in May 2004, and then Bulgaria and Romania in 2007, makes it a 27-nation unified market of more than 400 million people. This expanded EU provides great business opportunities, in particular for small and medium-sized enterprises (SMEs), to gain access to the EU market by taking advantage of the lower costs in the CEE compared to the rest of the EU, cheaper wages, lower corporate taxes, and educated workforces. Those countries have strengthened their economies in order to meet EU accession requirements, including privatizing state-run business, improving the infrastructure, and revamping their finance and banking systems. Manea and Pearce researched the strategies of MNEs in Central and Eastern Europe (CEE) and found that, because of uncertainty about investing in CEE, "initially market-seeking operations dominated in CEE, with little integration of CEE subsidiaries into global MNE networks."[80] The authors found that European MNEs tended to pursue country-centered strategies, while Asian MNEs invested more in exporting. They recommended that "product differentiation using CEE creative capabilities (i.e. technology and engineering expertise) rather than cost-competitiveness, may ultimately secure a more sustainable and embedded entry into MNEs' wider European (or global) networks."[81]

For firms within Europe, the euro eliminates currency risk, and so "Pan European thinking becomes not only practicable but essential."[82] The success of companies within Europe, then, depends on their efficiency in streamlining and consolidating their processes and in integrating product and marketing plans across Europe. The challenge is to balance the national and the continental view because a common currency does not bring about cultural or linguistic union.[83]

Clearly, both European and non-European companies must reconsider their European, and indeed global, strategies now that the enlarged EU has become a reality, complete with a common currency, the euro. "Foreign" managers, for example, need to develop an action program to ensure that their products have continued access to the EU and to adapt their marketing efforts to encompass the whole EU. The latter task is difficult, if not impossible, however, because the "citizen of Europe" is a myth; national cultures and tastes cannot be homogenized. With many different languages and distinctive national customs and cultures, companies trying to sell in Europe must thread their way through a maze of varying national preferences. These and other challenges lie ahead, along with numerous opportunities.

UPS is one of many firms experiencing this double-edged sword. Its managers realize that Europe is still virgin territory for service companies, and they expect revenue to grow by 15 percent a year there. However, UPS has run into many conflicts, both practical and cultural. Some of the surprises "Big Brown" experienced as it put its brown uniforms on 25,000 Europeans and sprayed brown paint on 10,000 delivery trucks around Europe include the following:

> *Indignation in France, when drivers were told they couldn't have wine with lunch; protests in Britain, when drivers' dogs were banned from delivery trucks; dismay in Spain, when it was found that the brown UPS trucks resembled the local hearses; and shock in Germany, when brown shirts were required for the first time since 1945.*[84]

Meanwhile, adventurous European businesses are spreading their wings across neighboring countries as they realize that open markets can offer as much growth and profitability as does protectionism—probably more. The Dutch willingness to surrender KLM to a holding company based in Paris is driven not only by the logic of European integration, but also by the promise of a long-overdue deregulation of the trans-Atlantic market.[85]

In one of Europe's biggest mergers, the Zeneca Group P.L.C. of Britain acquired Astra A.B. of Sweden. The resulting pharmaceutical giant was deemed necessary to fund new drug research and to compete in a market dominated by U.S. corporations. Early European mergers were dominated by British companies. But now that Continental European companies will have their shares denominated in euros, there will likely be more cross-border deals among those countries because they will be free of currency-exchange problems.[86]

Companies within the EU are gaining great advantages by competing in a continental-scale market and thereby avoiding duplication of administrative procedures, production, marketing, and distribution. The Italian company Benetton Group SPA is one such company—competing by being technologically efficient. For insiders, a single EU internal market means greater efficiencies and greater economic growth through economies of scale and the removal of barriers, with the consequent lowering of unit costs.

Companies based outside the EU enjoy the same advantages if they have a subsidiary in at least one member state, but they sometimes feel discrimination simply because they are outside what, for the member states, is a domestic market. In other words, the EU has a protectionist wall—of tariffs, quotas, local content laws, and competitive tactics—to keep out the United States and Japan. However, the EU has also created opportunities for nonmembers. Many companies, especially MNCs, start from a better position than some firms based inside the community because of (1) their superior competitiveness and research and development, (2) an existing foothold in the market, and (3) reduced operating expenses (one subsidiary for the whole EU instead of several). But European harmonized standards, while seeking to eliminate trade barriers within Europe, serve to limit access to EU markets by outside companies through the standardized specifications of products allowed to be sold in Europe. The harmonization laws set minimum standards for exports and imports that are EU-wide. However, those standards also frequently hinder European companies from efficient sourcing of raw materials or component parts from "foreign" companies.

Opinions differ about the long-term impact on U.S. firms: The EU could unify its markets, adversely affecting some U.S. industries; market access could be reduced; and demands for reciprocal market access in the United States might ensue. In November 2003, for example, when President Bush imposed tariffs on steel imports, the WTO ruled that the tariffs were illegal and authorized European and Asian nations to impose retaliatory tariffs against the United States. Not long after, President Bush was forced to reverse himself and lift the tariffs.[87]

Others feel that the new single market provides little threat to and considerable opportunity for Americans. Many U.S. firms (in anticipation of protectionism) have invested in Europe since the beginning of the Common Market in 1958, and they now feel satisfied with their current positions. Indeed, U.S. companies (GE, Dow, 3M, Hewlett-Packard) that already have well-established European presences enjoy the same free flow of goods, services, capital, and people as Europeans. It is clear, though, that the EU Competition Commissioner is keeping a keen eye on any anticompetitive tactics from abroad. In fact, in March 2004, the EU Commission ordered Microsoft to "discontinue abuses of its dominant market position."(The EU-Microsoft battle was continuing in 2007).[88] Indeed, foreign companies wishing to merge with or acquire companies in Europe, or even with companies outside of Europe, who plan to do business in the EU, need to be aware of the EU competition policies and merger control. In reviewing the failed GE-Honeywell merger, which was knocked down by the EU Commission, even though the proposed marriage was one of two U.S. companies, Anwar noted:

Under the European Merger Control Regulation (MCR) 4064/89, the
Commission can review and investigate any business concentration (mergers,

takeovers, acquisitions) that exceeds a world-wide turnover (revenues) of $4.6 billion or $250 million sales in the European region.[89]

Whereas in the U.S. those acquisitions that may create a monopoly will not be allowed, within the EU the prohibition criterion is "a business concentration that strengthens a market position and impedes competition."[90]

Nevertheless, many firms are opting for joint ventures with European partners, sacrificing their usual preference of 100 percent ownership (or majority control) to extend operations around Europe. This strategy also opens doors to markets dominated by public procurement, as with the AT&T–Philips venture to produce telecommunications equipment. But for a number of firms—both foreign and European—operating in Western Europe, at least, has become cost prohibitive. The average Western European earns more, works fewer hours, takes longer vacations, and receives more social entitlements and job protection than workers in Asia and North America. European MNCs have the highest labor and taxation costs among the TRIAD nations.[91] Siemens AG of Germany, for example, shifted almost all its semiconductor assembly work from its plants in Germany—where it was not permitted to operate around the clock or on weekends—to a plant in Singapore, where it operates twenty-four hours a day, 365 days a year, and pays $4.40 an hour for workers.[92]

Suzuki, Toyota, Nissan, and other Japanese companies are also experiencing the dilemma of operating in Europe. They are reluctant to freely pour yen into Europe, but they want to keep a foothold in the market. Suzuki, for example, found that in its Spanish plant it took five times the number of workers and cost 46 percent more to produce a Suzuki Samurai than in its Japanese plants.

which it operates, location factors, and venture-specific factors, as summarized in Exhibit 6-9.

After consideration of the factors for the firm as shown in Exhibit 6-9, as well as what is available and legal in the desired location, some entry strategies will no doubt fall out of the feasibility zone. With those options remaining, then, strategic planners need to decide which factors are more important to the firm than others. One method is to develop a weighted assessment to compare the overall impact of factors such as those in Exhibit 6-8 relative to the industry, the location, and the specific venture—on each entry strategy. Specific evaluation ratings, of course, would depend on the country conditions at a given point in time, the nature of the industry, and the focal company.

Based on a study of more than 10,000 foreign entry activities into China between 1979 and 1998, Pan and Tse concluded that managers tend to follow a hierarchy of decision-sequence in choosing an entry mode. As depicted in Exhibit 6-10, managers first decide between equity based and non-equity based. Then, equity modes are split into wholly owned operations and equity joint ventures (EJVs); non-equity modes are divided into contractual agreements and export. Pan and Tse found that the location choice—specifically the level of country risk—was the primary influence factor at the level of deciding between equity and non-equity modes. Host-country government incentives also encouraged the choice of equity mode.[93]

Gupta and Govindarajan also propose a hierarchy of decision factors but consider two initial choice levels. The first is the extent to which the firm will export or produce locally; the second is the extent of ownership control over activities that will be performed locally in the target market.[94] As shown in Exhibit 6-11, there is an array of choice combinations within those two dimensions. Gupta and Govindarajan point out that, among the many factors to take into account, alliance-based entry modes are more suitable under the following conditions:

- Physical, linguistic, and cultural distance between the home and host countries is high.
- The subsidiary would have low operational integration with the rest of the multinational operations.

EXHIBIT 6-9 Factors Affecting Choice of International Entry Mode

Factor Category	Examples
Firm factors	International experience
	Core competencies
	Core capabilities
	National culture of home country
	Corporate culture
	Firm strategy, goals, and motivation
Industry factors	Industry globalization
	Industry growth rate
	Technical intensity of industry
Location factors	Extent of scale and location economies
	Country risk
	Cultural distance
	Knowledge of local market
	Potential of local market
	Competition in local market
Venture-specific factors	Value of firm—assets risked in foreign location
	Extent to which know-how involved in venture is informal (tacit)
	Costs of making or enforcing contracts with local partners
	Size of planned foreign venture
	Intent to conduct research and development with local partners

SOURCE: Excerpted and adapted from *International Management—Concepts and Cases* by A. V. Phatak, pp. 270–275. Copyright © 1997 South-Western College Publishing, Cincinnati, Ohio, a division of International Thomson Publishing Inc.

EXHIBIT 6-10 A Hierachical Model of Choice of Entry Modes

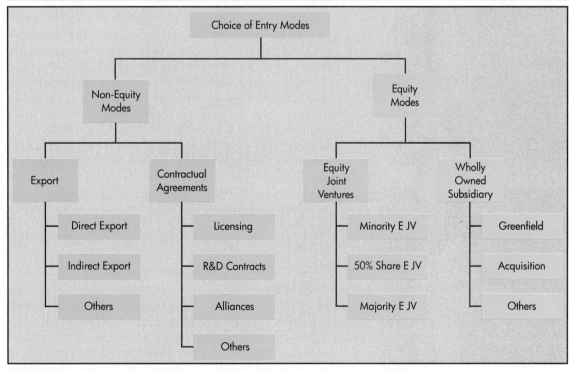

SOURCE: Yigang Pan and David K. Tse, "The Hierarchical Model of Market Entry Modes," *Journal of International Business Studies*, 31, no. 4 (4th Quarter 2000): 535–554.

EXHIBIT 6-11 Alternative Modes of Entry

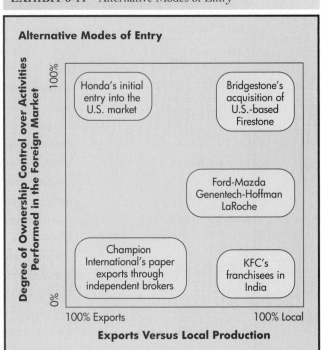

SOURCE: Anil K. Gupta and Vijay Gorindarajan, "Managing Global Expansion: A Conceptual Framework," *Business Horizons,* March/April 2000, pp. 45–54.

- The risk of asymmetric learning by the partner is low.
- The company is short of capital.
- Government regulations require local equity participation.[95]

The choice of entry strategy for McDonald's, for example, varies around the world according to the prevailing conditions in each country. With its 4,700 foreign stores, McDonald's is, according to *Fortune*, "a virtual blueprint for taking a service organization global."[96] CEO Mike Quinlan notes that, in Europe, the company prefers wholly owned subsidiaries, since European markets are similar to those in the United States and can be run similarly. Those subsidiaries in the United States both operate company-owned stores and license out franchises. Approximately 70 percent of McDonald's stores around the world are franchised. In Asia, joint ventures are preferred so as to take advantage of partners' contacts and local expertise, and their ability to negotiate with bureaucracies such as the Chinese government. Headed by billionaire Den Fujita, McDonald's has more than 1,000 stores in Japan; in China it had 23 stores in 1994, with more planned, in spite of conflicts with the Chinese government, such as when it made McDonald's move from its leased Tiananmen Square restaurant. In other markets, such as in Saudi Arabia, McDonald's prefers to limit its equity risk by licensing the name—adding strict quality standards—and keeping an option to buy later. Some of McDonald's implementation policies are presented in Chapter 7.

Timing Entry and Scheduling Expansions

As with McDonald's, international strategic formulation requires a long-term perspective. Entry strategies, therefore, need to be conceived as part of a well-designed, overall plan. In the past, many companies have decided on a particular means of entry that seemed appropriate at the time, only to find later that it was shortsighted. For instance, if a company initially chooses to license a host-country company to produce a product, then later decides that the market is large enough to warrant its own production facility, this new strategy will no longer be feasible because the local host-country company already owns the rights.[97]

The Influence of Culture on Strategic Choice

In addition, strategic choices at various levels often are influenced by cultural factors, such as a long-term versus a short-term perspective. Hofstede found that most people in such countries as China and Japan generally had a longer-term horizon than those in Canada and the United States.[98] Whereas Americans, then, might make strategic choices with a heavy emphasis on short-term profits, the Japanese are known to be more patient in sacrificing short-term results in order to build for the future with investment, research and development, and market share.

Risk orientation was also found to explain the choice between equity and non-equity modes.[99] Risk orientation relates to Hofstede's uncertainty avoidance dimension.[100] Firms from countries where, generally speaking, people tend to avoid uncertainty (for example, Latin American and African countries) tend to prefer non-equity entry modes to minimize exposure to risk. Managers from firms from low-uncertainty avoidance countries are more willing to take risks and are, therefore, more likely to adopt equity entry modes.[101]

Choice of equity versus non-equity mode has also been found to be related to level of power distance. According to Hofstede, a high power-distance country (such as Arab countries and Japan) is one where people observe interpersonal inequality and hierarchy.[102] Pan and Tse found that firms from countries tending toward high power distance are more likely to use equity modes of entry abroad.[103]

These are but a few of the examples of the relationships between culture and the choices that are made in the strategic planning and implementation phase. They serve to remind us that it is people who make those decisions and that the ways people think, feel, and act are based on their ingrained societal culture. People bring that context to work, and it influences their propensity toward or against certain types of decisions.

CONCLUSION

The process of strategic formulation for global competitiveness is a daunting task in the volatile international arena and is further complicated by the difficulties involved in acquiring timely and credible information. However, early insight into global developments provides a critical advantage in positioning a firm for future success.

When an entry strategy is selected, the international manager focuses on translating strategic plans into actual operations. Often this involves strategic alliances; always it involves functional level activities for **strategic implementation**. These subjects are covered in Chapter 7.

Summary of Key Points

1. Companies "go international" for many reasons, including reactive ones, such as international competition, trade barriers, and customer demands. Proactive reasons include seeking economies of scale, new international markets, resource access, cost savings, and local incentives.

2. International expansion and the resulting realization of a firm's strategy are the product of both rational planning and responding to emergent opportunities.

3. The steps in the rational planning process for developing an international corporate strategy comprise defining the mission and objectives of the firm, scanning the environment for threats and opportunities, assessing the internal strengths and weaknesses of the firm, considering alternative international entry strategies, and deciding on strategy. The strategic management process is completed by putting into place the operational plans necessary to implement the strategy and then setting up control and evaluation procedures.

4. Competitive analysis is an assessment of how a firm's strengths and weaknesses vis-à-vis those of its competitors affect the opportunities and threats in the international environment. Such assessment allows the firm to determine where the company has distinctive competences that will give it strategic advantage or where problem areas exist.

5. Corporate-level strategic approaches to international competitiveness include globalization and regionalization. Many MNCs have developed to the point of using an integrative global strategy. Entry and ownership strategies are exporting, licensing, franchising, contract manufacturing, offshoring, outsourcing services, turnkey operations, management contracts, joint ventures, and fully owned subsidiaries. Critical environmental and operational factors for implementation must be taken into account.

6. Companies of all sizes are increasingly looking to the Internet as a means of expanding their global operations, but localizing Internet operations is complex.

Discussion Questions

1. Discuss why companies "go international," giving specific reactive and proactive reasons.
2. Discuss the ways in which managers arrive at new strategic directions—formal and informal. Which is the best?
3. Explain the process of environmental assessment. What are the major international variables to consider in the scanning process? Discuss the levels of environmental monitoring that should be conducted. How well do you think managers conduct environmental assessment?
4. How can managers assess the potential relative competitive position of their firm in order to decide on new strategic directions?
5. Discuss the relative advantages of globalization versus regionalization.
6. What are the relative merits of the entry strategies discussed in this chapter? What is their role in an integrative global strategy?
7. Discuss the considerations in strategic choice, including the typical stages of the MNC and the need for a long-term global perspective.

Application Exercises

1. Choose a company in the microcomputer industry or a chain in the fast-food industry. In small groups, conduct a multilevel environmental analysis, describing the major variables involved, the relative impact of specific threats and opportunities, and the critical environmental factors to be considered. The group findings can then be presented to the class, allowing a specific time period for each group so that comparison and debate of different group perspectives can follow. Be prepared to state what regions or specific countries you are interested in and give your rationale.
2. In small groups, discuss among yourselves and then debate with the other groups the relative merits of the alternative entry strategies for the company and countries you chose in exercise 1. You should be able to make a specific choice and defend that decision.
3. For this exercise, research (individually or in small groups) a company with international operations and find out the kinds of entry strategies the firm has used. Present the information you find, in writing or verbally to the class, describing the nature of the company's international operations, its motivations, its entry strategies, the kinds of implementation problems the firm has run into, and how those problems have been dealt with.

Experiential Exercise

In groups of four, develop a strategic analysis for a type of company that is considering entry into Russia. Which entry strategies seem most appropriate? Share your results with the class.

Internet Resources

Visit the Deresky Companion Website at www.prenhall.com/Deresky for this chapter's Internet resources.

There's Detroit and There's Trnava: The Strategic Attraction of Eastern Europe

For Slovakia, the recent inauguration of an $890 million automobile factory was a major event. The prime minister and other government officials attended. French executives from Peugeot Citroën, which built the factory, flew into the tiny town of Trnava, where the sprawling factory is expected to employ up to 3,500 people and churn out as many as 300,000 compact cars a year. After the collapse of Communism in 1989, many foreign carmakers rushed to acquire local carmakers or build their own factories in countries like Slovakia, Poland, Hungary, Romania and the Czech Republic.

That relative trickle, though, is now a flood. The money has been pouring in, and the pace and frenzy is prompting talk of Europe's auto industry shifting from west to east.

By 2010, the Czech Republic could nearly double its production over last year, to more than a million cars. Indeed, as a whole, Eastern Europe has become Europe's backyard manufacturing center, and it could be producing 3.4 million cars annually by 2010, a 33 percent jump over 2005, according to forecasts by PricewaterhouseCoopers. Even Russia's production is expected to rise to 1.6 million cars a year from 1.2 million now.

That kind of growth can only be envied by more established carmaking countries: the United States could be making some 12.6 million cars, a 9 percent jump over last year, and Japan about 10.3 million, a mere 2 percent increase from last year.

By contrast, Britain is expected to drop to 1.5 million from 1.8 million in 2005. France is expected to stagnate at 3.6 million, compared with 3.5 million last year. Belgium was struck a blow recently when Volkswagen said it was stopping production in a plant near Brussels, eliminating 4,000 jobs. Even before Peugeot opened its Trnava plant, it announced that it was cutting 11,000 jobs, mainly in Western Europe. The move included closing a plant in Ryton, England.

This year, car production in Central and Eastern Europe, excluding Russia, is on track to exceed 2.4 million vehicles, as carmakers from Europe, Asia and the United States pour billions of dollars of fresh investment into local factories.

That may be a fraction of the 57.5 million cars made last year in the 20 top automobile-producing nations in 2005. But the explosive growth contrasts starkly to plans by many automakers to scale back employment and thus production in Western Europe and the United States. Within the last year or so, General Motors, Toyota, Volkswagen, Peugeot, Fiat, Suzuki, Hyundai and Kia have announced plans to build or expand assembly plants in the region. "Making a car is not like making a plastic bag," said Sigrid de Vries, the spokeswoman for the Association of European Automobile Manufacturers in Brussels. "You have to be close to the market and flexible, you have to be close to the customer, and this requires a certain reorganization."

The reasons for Central Europe's new wave of growth are complex. For one thing, the region, together with Russia and China, is one of the world's great untapped auto markets.

Sluggish auto industries under the old Communist regimes left many families without cars. Local governments championed local automakers, like Skoda in the Czech Republic and Dacia in Romania. They were driven to near ruin under Communism, but some of those automakers were then bought by Western carmakers after 1989, when Volkswagen acquired Skoda and Renault bought Dacia.

High gas prices in the West have also encouraged consumers to start shifting from big cars and S.U.V.'s to the kind of compact cars that are a specialty in Eastern Europe. Above all, labor here is the cheapest in the region.

Engineers in Slovakia earn half of what Western engineers make, and assembly line workers one-third to one-fifth, according to Alain Baldeyrou, Peugeot's plant manager in Trnava. If that does not sweeten the region for foreign carmakers, East European governments offer incentives, from financing some of the investment to offering a low flat-and-simple tax on employee wages and corporate profits, as in Slovakia, where all taxes are a simple 19 percent. By 2010, new investment will lift the region's production to just below that of France, which is expected to be making 3.59 million cars that same year, and more than twice that of Britain, where production will drop to 1.49 million, from 1.77 million in 2005.

"Central Europe is in the European Union, it has the advantage of a stable economy, and they want the euro," said Matt Pottle, central European automotive director for PricewaterhouseCoopers. He added that this was likely to mean far slower growth in some Western countries that now specialize in small-car production, like France and Spain.

It will also create more manufacturing jobs in the four major Central European countries, where the number has already risen to 284,507 in 2004, the last year for which figures are available, from 235,826 five years earlier; during the same time, such jobs fell slightly to 1,978,338, from 1,991,848 in Western Europe.

"Their largest challenge may be potential shortages of qualified labor," Mr. Pottle said, noting that "prices of labor are rising quite rapidly."

Within recent months, European carmakers have introduced a variety of new models that they will assemble in their Eastern European assembly plants. At the recent Paris Auto Show, Renault featured the Logan, a four-door car assembled in Romania, starting at 5,700 euros (about $7,200) in Eastern Europe.

"Today, Europe is a price market," said Stéphane Lemperier, a Renault executive, where consumers buy based on low prices. When Ford introduces an update of its successful subcompact, the Ka, which is now assembled in Valencia, Spain, the new model will be built at a factory Ford will share with the Italian automaker Fiat in Tichy, in southern Poland, where Fiat will assemble a new version of its popular Cinquecento.

But Eastern Europe is not making just cheap small cars. Volkswagen assembles its Touareg S.U.V. and the big Q7 of its Audi affiliate in Slovakia; Porsche assembles the body of its expensive Cayenne in a factory near Bratislava, and then ships them to Germany for finishing.

And the automakers are pulling their suppliers into the region as well. Peugeot officials said that steel coils for the Trnava plant now come from mills in France, Germany and Austria. But they plan to begin using Slovak steel next year after U.S. Steel brings online a $160 million hot-dip galvanizing mill, able to make 385,000 tons of automobile-grade steel sheet a year, in Kosice, in eastern Slovakia.

Seats for the Trnava plant are manufactured by Faurecia, a Peugeot-controlled company, at a suppliers' park near the main factory. Slovakia, the Czech Republic and Poland have been vying to attract suppliers for the big new assembly plant Hyundai is building at Novosice in the eastern corner of the Czech Republic, a short drive from Slovakia and Poland.

With many of the countries of Eastern Europe now in the European Union, cars from the region enter Western Europe without duties, essentially erasing the border for the automotive industry. Countries not in the union that are protectionist, like Russia, are also attracting investment of their own.

G.M. may be losing money elsewhere, but it expects to almost double its sales in Central and Eastern Europe, including Russia, within the next three years, and to expand its dealer network in the region by 80, to about 480, according to Automotive News Europe.

This summer, G.M. opened a plant near St. Petersburg to assemble the Chevrolet Captiva, a midsize S.U.V.; by 2008, G.M. hopes to bring online a $127 million plant nearby to assemble about 25,000 vehicles a year.

The decisions to move assembly plants east raise awkward questions among workers and their labor union representatives in the West. Labor union leaders in Germany, with the backing of leaders in other countries, have been pressing the European Union to limit the kinds of incentives that Eastern European countries offer automakers to settle there.

Union leaders are as irate as they are helpless. ' "It's a deliberate act of vandalism by the company," said James O'Boyle, a union leader at the Ryton plant, just north of Coventry, that is scheduled to close. Peugeot, he said, would lay off about 2,800 workers in Ryton, and though unemployment in the region is low, at about 4 percent, the auto workers would have to settle for inferior jobs.

"No doubt people can find jobs, if they take immense cuts in wages and cuts in benefits," Mr. O'Boyle said. "Some people will go on to better things, but they are a minority."

Jean-Martin Folz, Peugeot's chief executive, denied that the closing in Ryton and the expansion in Trnava reflected a repositioning of the industry eastward. "What you are observing is the economic growth of the European Union," he said, "the growth of manufacturing here." Ryton was closed, he said on the edge of the inauguration ceremony, "because it was the least profitable of our factories."

The new plant has been a boon to locals, like Stefan Bosnak, Trnava's mayor, who attended the ceremony. He said that unemployment had dropped to about 5 percent from 13 percent three years ago for the region of 70,000 people, which had a reservoir of skilled engineers left over from the Communist arms industry.

Mr. Baldeyrou, the plant manager, said wages were not the critical factor. "The share of salaries in the price of a car is about 15 percent," he said. "Materials form the greater part, not wages." And in the former Communist countries, unions pose few threats for foreign investors. Fewer than half a million of Slovakia's work force of 2.3 million are unionized, and the number is falling.

"People are doing a good job; there are good social benefits," said Ivan Stefanec, a member of Parliament from the region. "So there is no immediate need for unions."

SOURCE: John Tagliabue, "There's Detroit and There's Trnava," www.nytimes.com, November 25, 2006, Copyright The New York Times Co., reprinted with permission.

CASE QUESTIONS

1. What entry strategies are being used by the auto companies discussed in this chapter?

2. Describe and discuss the reasons the companies have for establishing manufacturing in eastern European countries. Why do those companies feel that they need to open plants in those countries? Do you agree with their reasons?

3. What is the impact of this strategy on the strategic planning of those companies that supply and service those companies?

4. What is the impact of these developments on the unions in the west?

5. What is the likely impact on the overall EU economy and growth prospects?

6. Discuss the environment for the auto industry at the time of your reading of this case. Is it true that there is a repositioning of the global auto industry? Why is that?

CHAPTER 7

Global Alliances and Strategy Implementation

Outline

Opening Profile: Spanish Companies Flex Their Acquisition Muscles

With a hot real estate market and a growing generation of internationally seasoned managers, Spanish corporations are shopping for companies in Europe and the United States, outmaneuvering many of their neighbors in Germany, France and Britain.

The 16 billion euro ($20.5 billion) takeover of the British airport company BAA by Grupo Ferrovial is the latest in a string of large purchases by Spanish companies looking beyond their border. Next, analysts and dealmakers say, could be more acquisitions in banking, as well as in construction and airport companies.

Considered Europe's sleepy corporate citizens until recently, Spanish companies completed deals worth $64.9 billion outside their own borders in 2005, up 69 percent from the year before. For the first half of 2006 they made $61.4 billion worth of deals outside the country, according to data from Thomson Financial. Because of the deals, Spanish companies are becoming global leaders in some industries, even as protectionist barriers are going up across Europe. Abertis Infraestructuras of Barcelona struck a deal in 2006 to buy Autostrade of Italy for $14.8 billion; the combination, if cleared by the Italian government, would create the world's largest toll road operator.

Telefónica became Europe's second-largest telecommunications company behind Vodafone last year, after it acquired the British mobile phone company O2 for $31.5 billion in October of 2006.

Cintra Concesiones de Infraestructuras de Transporte struck a deal to lease a United States toll road in Indiana. The move helped unleash plans for billions of dollars in privatizations of highways, marinas and public garages around the United States. Many of those deals are expected to go to Spain's infrastructure companies, including Cintra.

"Traditionally Spanish companies have invested in Latin America, because it was the natural market for language and cultural reasons," said Javier García de Enterría, a partner with the Madrid office of the law firm of Clifford Chance. In part because of increasing instability there, they are turning instead to the European market, and in some cases even looking to the United States, he said.

The long tradition of Latin American investment is actually helping Spanish companies as they look elsewhere for deals.

"Many of these companies have invested in Latin America in the last decade, and that has allowed these companies to grow in size and to develop the structures of multinational companies," said Alejandra Kindelán, the chief economist of Grupo Santander. "They know how to deal with different markets and countries," she said, and "now they can look beyond emerging markets to more mature markets."

Spanish expansion in the United States has traditionally been limited to Hispanic markets, but that is rapidly changing. In addition to Spanish companies bidding on toll road projects and highway building in the United States, the bank BBVA is on the hunt for what many expect to be a large transaction.

"As the United States gets more comfortable with the idea, you will see more and more" Spanish companies winning deals, said Luis J. Perez, a partner with the law firm of Hogan & Hartson in Miami.

Ms. Kindelán and other economists say that an important factor in Spanish companies' appetite for foreign expansion has been the adoption of the euro, which has kept interest rates low and allowed Spanish companies to borrow money much more cheaply than in the past.

The Spanish economy has been the "single biggest beneficiary" of European monetary policy, said Holger Schmieding, Bank of America's chief economist in London. The European Union's harmonization fund, which gave money to poorer nations, also provided a lift, as did European Union financing of roads and airports.

In addition, Spanish companies can hire and fire temporary workers without major restrictions, Mr. Schmieding said. That means they can downsize or can grow quickly, unlike their rivals in France or Germany. The country illustrates how "even partial labor market reforms can pay good benefits," he said.

Still, it is not clear whether Spanish companies still need the help of their European peers or are really able to outperform them.

Expansion in Europe through mergers and acquisitions is "a necessary step toward further expansion in the United States, Canada, or Asia," Mauro F. Guillen, a professor in international management at the Wharton School of the University of Pennsylvania, writes in his book "The Rise of Spanish Multinationals" published last year.

"Without the skills and managerial personnel of their European counterparts, it is likely that Spanish firms will remain strong in the 10 percent of the world represented by Spain and Latin America, and largely absent from the rest," he wrote.

But so far, some Spanish-led cross-border acquisitions in Europe have been less tricky to navigate than deals coming out of other countries.

The Grupo Santander purchase of the British bank Abbey National has had fewer visible culture clashes than comparable acquisitions, like the combination of the German bank HVB and the Italian bank Unicredito, for example. Spanish deal experts say their cross-border integration may be easier because local mangers have a more open approach than their German, Dutch or French counterparts.

"We are used to dealing with foreigners, in part because the service industry is a significant part of our culture," said Juan Gich, head of investment banking for Iberia at Lehman Brothers.

In addition, a new generation of managers, who have been educated at business schools in London, New York and Paris, bring a confident attitude to cross-border deals. "They're saying we can conquer Europe, and we can integrate," Mr. Gich said.

SOURCE: Heather Timmons and Renwick McLean, "Spanish Companies Flex Their Acquisition Muscle," www.nytimes.com, June 8 2006, Copyright © The New York Times Co., 2006, reprinted with permission.

STRATEGIC ALLIANCES

It is no longer an era in which a single company can dominate any technology or business by itself. The technology has become so advanced, and the markets so complex, that you simply can't expect to be the best at the whole process any longer.

FUMIO SATO,
CEO, Toshiba Electronics[1]

Strategic alliances are partnerships between two or more firms that decide they can better pursue their mutual goals by combining their resources—financial, managerial, technological—as well as their existing distinctive competitive advantages. Alliances—often called *cooperative strategies*—are transition mechanisms that propel the partners' strategies forward in a turbulent environment faster than would be possible for each company alone.[2] Alliances typically fall under one of three categories: joint ventures, equity strategic alliances, and non-equity strategic alliances.[3]

Joint Ventures

As discussed in Chapter 6, a **joint venture (JV)** is a new independent entity jointly created and owned by two or more parent companies. The JV form for a firm may comprise a majority JV (where the firm has more than 50 percent equity), a minority JV (less than 50 percent equity), or a 50–50 JV (where two firms have equal equity). An **IJV** is a joint venture among companies in different countries. In that case, the firm shares the profits, costs, and risks with a local partner, and benefits from the local partner's local contacts and markets. (Advantages and disadvantages of IJVs were discussed in Chapter 6). An example of a 50–50 equity IJV is that between France's PSA Peugeot-Citroen Group and Japan's Toyota at Kolin in the Czech Republic. As noted by Fujio Cho, president of the world's richest carmaker, Toyota Motors:

Each company has brought its own style, culture and way of thinking to this partnership—but our different approaches have benefited our joint venture enormously.[4]

The benefits noted by the two companies are that Toyota "gains an insight into the mindset of one of Europe's biggest indigenous carmakers and knowledge of its suppliers and their capabilities."[5] And Peugeot-Citroen can gain experience from Toyota's lean manufacturing system. The companies acknowledge that the IJV has resulted in faster development and increased production capacity, and that costs are shared without either company renouncing its independence.[6]

Equity Strategic Alliances

Two or more partners have different relative ownership shares (equity percentages) in the new venture in an equity strategic alliance. As do most global manufacturers, Toyota has equity alliances with suppliers, subassemblers, and distributors; most of these are part of Toyota's network of internal family and financial links. Another example of equity strategic alliances is TCL-Thompson Electronics. France's Thompson owns 33 percent of the combined company and China's TCL owns the remaining 67 percent.[7]

Non-equity Strategic Alliances

Agreements are carried out through contract rather than ownership sharing in a non-equity strategic alliance. Such contracts are often with a firm's suppliers, distributors, or manufacturers, or they may be for purposes of marketing and information sharing, such as with many airline partnerships. UPS, for example, is a global supply-chain manager for many companies around the world, such as Nike, which essentially do not touch their own products but contract with UPS to arrange the entire process from factory to warehouse to customer to repair, even collecting the money.[8]

Global Strategic Alliances

Working partnerships between companies (often more than two) across national boundaries and increasingly across industries are referred to as global strategic alliances. A glance at the global airline industry, for example, tells us that global alliances have become a mainstay of competitive strategy:

> *Not one airline is competing alone; each major U.S. carrier has established strategic links with non-U.S. companies. Delta is linked with Swissair, Sabena, and Austrian; American with British Airways, U.S. Airways, JAL, and Qantas; Northwest with Continental, KLM (which merged with Air France in 2003), and Alitalia; and United with SAS, Lufthansa, Air Canada, Thai, South African Airways, Varig, Singapore, Air New Zealand, and Ansett Australia.*[9]

Alliances are also sometimes formed between a company and a foreign government, or among companies and governments. The European Airbus Industrie consortium comprises France's Aerospatiale and Germany's Daimler–Benz Aerospace, each with 37.9 percent of the business; British Aerospace with 20 percent, and Spain's Construcciones Aeronauticas with 4.2 percent.

Alliances may comprise full global partnerships, which are often joint ventures in which two or more companies, while retaining their national identities, develop a common, long-term strategy aimed at world leadership. Whereas such alliances have a broad agenda, others are formed for a narrow and specific function, including production, marketing, research and development, or financing. More recently these have included electronic alliances, such as Covisint, which is redefining the entire system of car production and distribution through a common electronic marketplace. Covisint is an e-business exchange developed by DaimlerChrysler AG, Ford, General Motors, Nissan, and Renault to meet the needs of the automotive industry, and is focused on procurement, supply chain, and product development solutions.[10]

Global and Cross-Border Alliances: Motivations and Benefits

1. **To avoid import barriers, licensing requirements, and other protectionist legislation.** Japanese automotive manufacturers, for example, use alliances such as the GM–Toyota venture, or subsidiaries, to produce cars in the United States so as to avoid import quotas.
2. **To share the costs and risks of the research and development of new products and processes.** In the semiconductor industry, for example, where each new generation of memory chips is estimated to cost more than $1 billion to develop, those costs and the rapid technological evolution typically require the resources of more than one, or even two, firms. Intel, for example, has alliances with Samsung and NMB Semiconductor for technology (DRAM) development; Sun Microsystems has partners for its technology (RISC), including

N. V. Philips, Fujitsu, and Texas Instruments. Toshiba, Japan's third-largest electronics company, has more than two dozen major joint ventures and strategic alliances around the world, including partners such as Olivetti, Rhone-Poulenc, GEC Alstholm in Europe, LSI Logic in Canada, and Samsung in Korea. Fumio Sato, Toshiba's CEO, recognized long ago that a global strategy for a high-tech electronics company such as his necessitated joint ventures and strategic alliances.

3. **To gain access to specific markets, such as the EU, where regulations favor domestic companies.** Firms around the world are forming strategic alliances with European companies to bolster their chances of competing in the European Union (EU) and to gain access to markets in Eastern European countries as they open up to world business. The EU's new law, passed in November 2003, was intended to increase the opportunities for cross-border mergers and takeovers, for companies both within and outside of the EU.[11] U.S. companies protested that the law did not go far enough to open up a "fortress Europe," because hostile bids would be more difficult to pursue.[12] However, seven of the ten largest deals that Citigroup completed around the world in 2003, for example, were in Europe—including the $2 billion acquisition of British tavern chain Pubmaster.[13] Chun Joo Bum, chief executive of the Daewoo Electronics unit, acknowledges that he is seeking local partners in Europe for two reasons: (1) to provide sorely needed capital (a problem amid Asia's economic woes) and (2) to help Daewoo navigate Europe's still disparate markets, saying "I need to localize our management. It is not one market."[14]

   Market entry into some countries may only be attained through alliances—typically joint ventures. South Korea, for example, has a limit of 18 percent on foreign investment in South Korean firms.

4. **To reduce political risk while making inroads into a new market.**

   Carefully orchestrated partnerships with governments and other business groups are crucial to the [Disney] entertainment group's thrust into China and the rest of south-east Asia.

   BOB IGER,
   President and COO, Walt Disney[15]

   Hong Kong Disneyland is jointly owned by the Chinese government, which owns a 57 percent stake. Beijing is especially interested in promoting tourism through the venture, and in the employment for the 5,000 workers Disney employs directly, as well as the estimated 18,000 in related services.[16] Maytag Corporation, also determined to stay on the right side of the restrictive Chinese government while gaining market access, formed a joint venture with RSD, the Chinese appliance maker, to manufacture and market washing machines and refrigerators. Maytag also invested large amounts in jointly owned refrigeration products facilities to help RSD get into that market. Coca-Cola—a global player with large-scale alliances—is not beyond using some very small-scale alliances to be "political" in China. The company uses senior citizens in the party's neighborhood committees to sell Coke locally.

5. **To gain rapid entry into a new or consolidating industry and to take advantage of synergies.**

   Disney now has 3.5m subscribers for content services, offered through Japan's largest mobile operators.

   STEVE WADSWORTH,
   President, Internet Division, Walt Disney[17]

   Technology is rapidly providing the means for the overlapping and merging of traditional industries such as entertainment, computers, and telecommunications in new digital-based systems, creating an information superhighway. Disney's business model of cellular partnerships and content sales, for example, created Disney mobile operations in Hong Kong, Taiwan, South Korea, Singapore, and the Philippines.[18] The company uses joint venture partners such as the Hong Kong government, or licensees and distributors such as Oriental Land and NTT DoCoMo.[19]

   In many cases, technological developments are necessitating strategic alliances across industries in order for companies to gain rapid entry into areas in which they have no expertise or manufacturing capabilities. Competition is so fierce that they cannot wait to develop those resources alone. Many of these objectives, such as access to new technology and to new markets, are evident in AT&T's network of alliances around the world. Agreements with Japan's NEC, for example, gave AT&T access to new semiconductor and chip-making technologies, helping it learn how to better integrate computers with communications. Another joint venture with Zenith Electronics led to the next generation of high-definition television (HDTV).[20]

Challenges in Implementing Global Alliances

The strategy that so quietly slipped into oblivion was no less than GM's scheme for world domination . . . known as the global alliance strategy. GM's decisions to end its partnerships with Fiat Auto, Fuji Heavy Industries (parent of Subaru) and Isuzu are testimony to the strategy's failure. GM also sharply reduced its stake in longtime partner Suzuki.

AUTOMOTIVE NEWS,
May 8, 2006 [21]

Effective global alliances are usually tediously slow in the making but can be among the best mechanisms to implement strategies in global markets. In a highly competitive environment, alliances present a faster and less risky route to globalization. It is extremely complex to fashion such linkages, however, especially where many interconnecting systems are involved, forming intricate networks. Many alliances fail for complex reasons—as with the General Motors global alliance strategy noted above. Many also end up in a takeover in which one partner swallows the other. McKinsey & Company, a consulting firm, surveyed 150 companies that had been in alliances and found that 75 percent of them had been taken over by Japanese partners. Problems with shared ownership, differences in national cultures, the integration of vastly different structures and systems, the distribution of power between the companies involved, and conflicts in their relative locus of decision making and control are but a few of the organizational issues that must be worked out.

Often, the form of governance chosen for multinational firm alliances greatly influences their success, particularly in technologically intense fields such as pharmaceuticals, computers, and semiconductors. In a study of 153 new alliances, researchers found that the choice of the means of governance—whether a contractual agreement or a joint venture—depended on a desire to control information about proprietary technology.[22] Thus, joint ventures are often the chosen form for such alliances because they provide greater control and coordination in high-technology industries.

Cross-border partnerships, in particular, often become a "race to learn"—with the faster learner later dominating the alliance and rewriting its terms. In a real sense, an alliance becomes a new form of competition. In fact, according to researcher David Lei,

Perhaps the single greatest impediment managers face when seeking to learn or renew sources of competitive advantage is to realize that co-operation can represent another form of unintended competition, particularly to shape and apply new skills to future products and businesses.[23]

All too often, cross-border allies have difficulty collaborating effectively, especially in competitively sensitive areas; this creates mistrust and secrecy, which then undermine the purpose of the alliance. The difficulty that they are dealing with is the dual nature of strategic alliances—the benefits of cooperation versus the dangers of introducing new competition through sharing their knowledge and technological skills about their mutual product or the manufacturing process. Managers may fear that they will lose the competitive advantage of the firm's proprietary technology or the specific skills that their personnel possess. One example of a situation of potential loss of proprietary technology affecting entire industries became apparent in January 2004 when China announced that foreign computer and chip makers selling various wireless devices there would have to use Chinese encryption software and co-produce their products with Chinese companies from a designated list.[24]

The cumulative learning that a partner attains through the alliance could potentially be applied to other products or even other industries that are beyond the scope of the

EXHIBIT 7-1   The Dual Role of Strategic Alliances

Cooperative	Competitive
Economies of scale in tangible assets (e.g., plant and equipment).	Opportunity to learn new intangible skills from partner, often tacit or organization embedded.
Upstream–downstream division of labor among partners.	Accelerate diffusion of industry standards and new technologies to erect barriers to entry.
Fill out product line with components or end products provided by supplier.	Deny technological and learning initiative to partner via outsourcing and long-term supply arrangements.
Limit investment risk when entering new markets or uncertain technological fields via shared resources.	Encircle existing competitors and preempt the rise of new competitors with alliance partners in "proxy wars" to control market access, distribution, and access to new technologies.
Create a "critical mass" to learn and develop new technologies to protect domestic, strategic industries.	Form clusters of learning among suppliers and related firms to avoid or reduce foreign dependence for critical inputs and skills.
Assist short-term corporate restructurings by lowering exit barriers in mature or declining industries.	Alliances serve as experiential platforms to "demature" and transform existing mature industries via new components, technologies, or skills to enhance the value of future growth options.

SOURCE: David Lei, "Offensive and Defensive Uses of Alliances," in Heidi Vernon-Wortzel and L. H. Wortzel, *Strategic Management in Global Economy,* 3rd ed. (New York: John Wiley & Sons, 1997).

alliance, and therefore would hold no benefit to the partner holding the original knowledge.[25] As noted by Lei, the Japanese have far overtaken their U.S. allies in developing and applying new technologies to other uses. Examples are in the power equipment industry (e.g., Westinghouse–Mitsubishi), the office equipment industry (Kodak–Canon), and the consumer electronics industry (General Electric–Samsung). Some of the trade-offs of the duality of cross-border ventures are shown in Exhibit 7-1.

The enticing benefits of cross-border alliances often mask the many pitfalls involved. In addition to potential loss of technology and knowledge or skill base, other areas of incompatibility often arise, such as conflicting strategic goals and objectives, cultural clashes, and disputes over management and control systems. Sometimes it takes a while for such problems to evidence themselves, particularly if insufficient homework has been done in meetings between the two sides to work out the implementation details. The alliance between KLM Royal Dutch Airlines and Northwest Airlines linking their hubs in Detroit and Amsterdam, for example, resulted in a bitter feud among the top officials of both companies over methods of running an airline business—the European way or the American way—and over cultural differences between the companies, as well as a power struggle at the top over who should call the shots.[26]

Guidelines for Successful Alliances

Many difficulties arise in cross-border alliances in melding the national and corporate cultures of the parties, in overcoming language and communication barriers, and in building trust between the parties over how to share proprietary assets and management processes. Some basic guidelines, as follow, will help to minimize potential problems. However, nothing is as important as having a long "courtship" with a potential partner to establish compatibility strategically and interpersonally and set up a "prenuptial" plan with the prospective partner. Even setting up some pilot programs on a short-term basis for some of the planned combined activities can highlight areas that may become problematic.

1. Choose a partner with compatible strategic goals and objectives and with whom the alliance will result in synergies through the combined markets, technologies, and management cadre.

2. Seek alliances where complementary skills, products, and markets will result. If each partner brings distinctive skills and assets to the venture, there will be reduced potential for direct competition in end products and markets. In addition, each partner will begin the alliance in a balanced relationship.[27]

3. Work out with the partner how you will each deal with proprietary technology or competitively sensitive information—what will be shared and what will not, and how shared technology will be handled. Trust is an essential ingredient of an alliance, particularly in these areas; but this must be backed up by contractual agreements.

4. Recognize that most alliances last only a few years and will probably break up once a partner feels it has incorporated the skills and information it needs to go it alone. With this in mind, managers need to "learn thoroughly and rapidly about a partner's technology and management: transfer valuable ideas and practices promptly into one's own operations."[28]

Some of the opportunities and complexities in cross-border alliances are illustrated in the following Comparative Management in Focus on joint ventures in the Russian Federation. Such alliances are further complicated by the different history of the two parties' economic systems and the resulting business practices.

Comparative Management in Focus

Joint Ventures in the Russian Federation

Map 7-1: Russia

> *President Putin has promised improvements in the business climate, oil revenues are buoying the economy, and over-zealous tax officials are being reined in. But foreign investment in strategically important areas is subject to tight new controls. The overall picture is complicated, but Russia is a country that investors cannot afford to ignore.*[29]

Foreign companies have started to think twice about investing in international joint ventures (IJVs) in Russia since President Putin's moves to take control of key industries, including banks, newspapers, and oil assets. He has partly renationalised the Yukos oil company, Russia's biggest, after jailing its former chief Mikhail Khodorkovsky for eight years. In June 2007, he forced BP (British Petroleum) to sell the largest gas field to Gazprom, the Russian natural gas monopoly by threatening to revoke the license held by the TNK-BP joint venture.[30] All in all, investors are confused, though many are determined to take advantage of a more stable and now-convertible rouble, an underexploited natural resource potential, and a skilled, educated population of 145 million. But respondents to a survey of 158 corporate investors and non-investors in Russia in 2005 indicated that they thought that doing business in Russia was more risky and less profitable than China, India, or South-east Asia. Their main concerns were corruption and bribe-taking at all levels of the state bureaucracy and weak legislative and enforcement regimes.[31] The level of uncertainty by foreign investors is fueled by the experience of some companies in joint ventures in Russia, such as General Motors Corp.'s joint venture with Russia's biggest car maker, OAO Avtovaz. The $340 million IJV was the first between a Russian and Western automaker; GM's strategy was to partner with a local producer to make a low-cost, locally developed model. The GM venture stopped making Chevrolet Niva sport-utility vehicles on Feb. 9, 2006, after Avtovaz halted delivery of parts, demanding that GM pay more for them. Rosoboronexport, the Russian state arms trader, took control of Avtovaz from the management group that had run the company since the Soviet era. The takeover "appeared to be the start of a Kremlin drive to revive Russia's ailing auto industry—which is rapidly losing market share to Western imports and locally assembled foreign models—through direct state intervention. It would also highlight the Kremlin's tough new approach to foreign investment in industries deemed strategic."[32] Subsequent negotiations were focusing on an acceptable compromise.

In spite of the uncertainty, many companies feel that they should take advantage of the growth opportunities in Russia—the seventh biggest population in the world. Foreign direct investment (FDI) was around $17 billion in 2006, coming from companies such as Dutch brewer Heineken, Swedish retailer IKEA, and Citibank, which says its business in Russia is growing at an annual rate of 70 percent. Moscow and other major cities are experiencing a consumer boom, spurred on by rising incomes in the middle class, making Russia one of the fastest growing regions for global consumer giants such as Coca-Cola, Procter & Gamble, and Nestle.[33] They join those already taking advantage of those opportunities such as Caterpillar, IBM, GE, Ford, Hewlett-Packard, Pepsi-Co., Eastman Kodak, and AT&T, as well as thousands of smaller IJVs—primarily in software, hotels, and heavy industrial production. Many, like Bell Labs, are involved in research and development, taking advantage of the Russians' high-level education and technical capabilities.

Most large global companies—accustomed to economic upheavals in Russia—have stuck to their long-term plans.[34] Gillette, for example, which has had a joint venture with Leninets, forming Petersburg Products International (PPI), since 1990, is one that stayed and continues its commitment there. But it was not without its problems during the difficult 1998–1999 period. The effective distribution systems it had painstakingly built up collapsed, as the partners' wholesalers and retailers ran out of money and stopped their orders.

> *Overnight, the ability to invoice and receive payment disappeared. So Gillette had to rebuild the distribution system and develop financial support for its suppliers, offering them credit to be paid upon their next orders.*[35]

Gillette now employs more than 500 people throughout Russia and has built another $40 million razor blade manufacturing plant near St. Petersburg.

Overall, managers of foreign companies planning to set up business in Russia, notes Buckley, should carefully consider the following:

- Investigate whether a joint venture is the best strategy. If a lot of real estate is needed, it may be better to acquire a Russian business, because of the difficulties involved in acquiring land.
- Set up meetings with the appropriate ministry and regional authorities well in advance. Have good communication about your business needs and build local relationships.
- Be sure to be totally above board in paying all relevant taxes to avoid crossing the Russian authorities.
- Set up stricter controls and accountability systems than usual for the company.
- Communicate clearly up front that your firm does not pay bribes.
- Assign the firm's best available managers and delegate to them enough authority to act locally.
- Take advantage of local knowledge by hiring appropriate Russian managers for the venture.
- Designate considerable funds for local promotion and advertising so as to establish the corporate image with authorities and consumers.[36]

Foreign managers' alliance strategy must also take into account the goals of potential Russian partners. For example, when viewed from the perspective of Russian managers, Hitt et al. found that:

> The less stable Russian institutional environment has influenced Russian managers to focus more on the short term [than those in China], selecting partners that provide access to financial capital and complementary capabilities so as to enhance their firms' ability to weather that nation's turbulent environment.[37]

An awareness and acceptance of the motivations of Russian firms for alliances with foreign companies will aid in finding and achieving a cooperative joint venture.

STRATEGIC IMPLEMENTATION

Implementation McDonald's Style

- Form paradigm-busting arrangements with suppliers.
- Know a country's culture before you hit the beach.
- Hire locals whenever possible.
- Maximize autonomy.
- Tweak the standard menu only slightly from place to place.
- Keep pricing low to build market share. Profits will follow when economies of scale kick in.[38]

Decisions regarding global alliances and entry strategies must now be put into motion with the next stage of planning: strategic implementation. Implementation plans are detailed and pervade the entire organization because they entail setting up overall policies, administrative responsibilities, and schedules throughout the organization to enact the selected strategy and to make sure it works. In the case of a merger or IJV, this process requires compromising and blending procedures among two or more companies and is extremely complex. The importance of the implementation phase of the strategic management process cannot be overemphasized. Until they are put into operation, strategic plans remain abstract ideas: verbal or printed proposals that have no effect on the organization.

Successful implementation requires the orchestration of many variables into a cohesive system that complements the desired strategy—that is, a *system of fits* that will facilitate the actual working of the strategic plan. In this way, the structure, systems, and processes of the firm are coordinated and set into motion by a system of management by objectives (MBO), with the primary objective being the fulfillment of strategy. Managers must review the organizational structure and, if necessary, change it to facilitate the administration of the strategy and to coordinate activities in a particular location with headquarters (as discussed further in Chapter 8). In addition to ensuring the strategy–structure fit, managers must allocate resources to make the strategy work, budgeting money, facilities, equipment, people, and other support. Increasingly, that support necessitates a unified technology infrastructure in order to coordinate diverse businesses around the world and to satisfy the need for current and reliable information. An efficient technology infrastructure can provide a strategic advantage in a globally competitive environment. Jack Welch, while CEO of General Electric (he retired in late 2001), used to refer to his e-commerce initiative, saying, "It will change relationships with suppliers. Within 18 months, all our suppliers will supply us on the Internet, or they won't do business with us."[39]

An overarching factor affecting all the other variables necessary for successful implementation is that of leadership; it is people, after all, who make things happen. The firm's leaders must skillfully guide employees and processes in the desired direction. Managers with different combinations of experience, education, abilities, and personality tend to be more suited to implementing certain strategies. In an equity-sharing alliance, sorting out which top managers in each company will be in which position is a sensitive matter. Who in which company will be CEO is usually worked out as part of the initial deal in alliance agreements. This problem seems to be frequently settled these days by setting up joint CEOs, one from each company. Setting monitoring systems into place to control activities and ensure success completes, but does not end, the strategic management process. Rather, it is a continuous process, using feedback to reevaluate strategy for needed modifications and for updating and recycling plans. Of particular note here we should consider what is involved in effective management of the increasingly popular global sourcing strategy; then we will review what is involved in managing performance in international joint ventures, since they are such a common form of global alliance, and yet they are fraught with implementation challenges.

Implementing a Global Sourcing Strategy

The entry strategy of global sourcing was discussed in Chapter 6. Outsourcing abroad—alliances with firms in other countries to perform specific functions for the firm—is often in the news because of the politically charged issue of domestic jobs apparently being "lost" to others overseas. Beyond finding lower paid workers, however, the strategic view of global sourcing is developing into "transformational outsourcing"—that is, the view that, properly implemented, global sourcing can produce gains in efficiency, productivity, quality, and profitability by fully leveraging talent around the world.[40] Procter & Gamble, for example, having outsourced everything from IT infrastructure and Human Resources around the world, has announced that CEO Alan G. Lafley wants 50 percent of all new P&G products to come from other countries by 2010, compared to 20 percent now.[41] However, implementing such a strategy is more difficult than it is made to seem in the press, as many companies have encountered unexpected problems when outsourcing. Advice on implementation from experiences by companies such as Dell, IBM, and Reuters Group PLC lead us to the following guidelines:

1. **Examine your reasons for outsourcing.** Make sure that the advantages of efficiency and competitiveness will outweigh the disadvantages from your employees, customers, and community; don't outsource just because your competitors are doing it.
2. **Evaluate the best outsourcing model.** Opening your own subsidiary in the host country (a "captive" operation) may be better than contracting with an outside firm if it is crucial for you to keep control of proprietary technology and processes.
3. **Gain the cooperation of your management and staff.** Open communication and training is essential to get your domestic managers on board; uncertainty, fear, and disagreement from them can jeopardize your plans.

4. **Consult your alliance partners.** Consult with your partners and treat them with the respect that made you decide to do business with them.

5. **Invest in the alliance.** Plan to invest time and money in training in the firm's business practices, in particular those to do with quality control and customer relations.[42]

Managing Performance in International Joint Ventures

Much of the world's international business activity involves international joint ventures (IJVs), in which at least one parent is headquartered outside the venture's country of operation. IJVs require unique controls. Ignoring these specific control requisites can limit the parent company's ability to efficiently use its resources, coordinate its activities, and implement its strategy.[43]

The term **IJV control** can be defined, according to Schaan, as "the process through which a parent company ensures that the way a joint venture is managed conforms to its own interest."[44] Most of a firm's objectives can be achieved by careful attention to control features at the outset of the joint venture, such as the choice of a partner, the establishment of a strategic fit, and the design of the IJV organization.

The most important single factor determining IJV success or failure is the choice of a partner. Most problems with IJVs involve the local partner, especially in less developed countries. In spite of this fact, many firms rush the process of partner selection because they are anxious to "get on the bandwagon" in an attractive market. In this process, it is vital to establish whether the partners' strategic goals are compatible (see Chapter 6). The strategic context and the competitive environment of the proposed IJV and the parent firm will determine the relative importance of the criteria used to select a partner.[45] IJV performance is also a function of the general fit between the international strategies of the parents, the IJV strategy, and the specific performance goals that the parents adopt.[46] Research has shown that, to facilitate this fit, the partner selection process must determine the specific task-related skills and resources needed from a partner, as well as the relative priority of those needs.[47] To do this, managers must analyze their own firms and pinpoint any areas of weakness in task-related skills and resources that can be overcome with the help of the IJV partner.

Partnerships with companies in India present both positive and negative examples of IJV performance, although overall IJVs there run into considerable problems. Although India still insists on joint ventures in sectors such as telecommunications, agriculture, retailing, and insurance, it has lifted restrictions for other industries, allowing wholly-owned operations in them. However, a number of recent IJVs have done poorly, especially for the Indian partner. TVS Motor, for example, which is the third-largest motorbike manufacturer in India (a market with around 8 million bikes a year), recently bought out its Japanese partner Suzuki. From Suzuki's perspective, the only entry strategy available to the company under government regulations at the time was a joint venture. However, after a while TVS complained that it was not able to develop the company's own capabilities because "Suzuki wanted to keep its technology for itself. It was a frustrating episode."[48] On the other hand, an IJV between Indian engineering group Kirloskar with Japan's Toyota, for vehicle production, has had more positive results, with Mr. Kirloskar acknowledging that Toyota has been open in sharing ideas and improving the productivity of his firm.[49]

Organizational design is another major mechanism for factoring in a means of control when an IJV is started. Beamish et al. discuss the important issue of the strategic freedom of an IJV. This refers to the relative amount of decision-making power that a joint venture will have, compared with the parents, in choosing suppliers, product lines, customers, and so on.[50] It is also crucial to consider beforehand the relative management roles each parent will play in the IJV because such decisions result in varying levels of control for different parties. An IJV is usually easier to manage if one parent plays a dominant role and has more decision-making responsibility than the other in daily operations. Alternatively, it is easier to manage an IJV if the local general manager has considerable management control, keeping both parents out of most of the daily operations.[51]

International joint ventures are like a marriage: The more issues that can be settled before the merger, the less likely it will be to break up. Control over the stability and success of the IJV can be largely built into the initial agreement between the partners. The contract can specify who has what responsibilities and rights in a variety of circumstances, such as the contractual links of the IJV with the parents, the capitalization, and the rights and obligations regarding intellectual property. Of course, we cannot assume equal ownership of the IJV partners; where ownership is unequal, the partners will claim control and staffing choices proportionate to the ownership share. The choice of the IJV general manager, in particular, will influence the relative allocation of control because that person is responsible for running the IJV and for coordinating relationships with each of the parents.[52]

Where ownership is divided among several partners, the parents are more likely to delegate the daily operations of the IJV to the local IJV management—a move that resolves many potential disputes. In addition, the increased autonomy of the IJV tends to reduce many common human resource problems: staffing friction, blocked communication, and blurred organizational culture, to name a few, which all result from the conflicting goals and working practices of the parent companies.[53] Regardless of the number of parents, one way to avoid such potential problem situations is to provide special training to managers about the unique nature and problems of IJVs.[54]

Various studies reveal three complementary and interdependent dimensions of IJV control: (1) *the focus of IJV control*—the scope of activities over which parents exercise control; (2) the *extent, or degree, of IJV control achieved by the parents;* and (3) the *mechanisms of IJV control used by the parents.*[55]

We can conclude from two research studies—Geringer's study of 90 developed country IJVs and Schaan and Beamish's study of ten IJVs in Mexico—that parent companies tend to focus their efforts on a selected set of activities that they consider important to their strategic goals, rather than monitoring all activities.[56] Schaan also found a considerable range of mechanisms for control used by the parent firms in his study, including indirect mechanisms such as parent organizational and reporting structure, staffing policies, and close coordination with the IJV general manager (GM). Monitoring the GM typically includes indirect means, perhaps bonuses and career opportunities, and direct mechanisms, such as requiring executive committee approval for specific decisions and budgets. These studies show that a variety of mechanisms are available to parent companies to monitor and guide IJV performance.

The extent of control exercised over an IJV by its parent companies seems to be primarily determined by the decision-making autonomy that the parents delegate to the IJV management—which is largely dependent on staffing choices for the top IJV positions and thus on how much confidence the partners have in these managers. In addition, if top managers of the IJV are from the headquarters of each party, the compatibility of the managers will depend on how similar their national cultures are. This is because there are many areas of control decisions where agreement will be more likely between those of similar cultural backgrounds.[57]

Knowledge Management in IJVs

> *The most effective strategic leadership practices in the 21st century will be ones through which strategic leaders find ways for knowledge to breed still more knowledge.*[58]

Managing the performance of an IJV for the long term, as well as adding value to the parent companies, necessitates managing the knowledge flows within the IJV network. When managed correctly, "alliances serve as a source of new knowledge for the firm."[59] Sirmon et al. contend that if firms can access and "absorb" this new knowledge, it can be used to alter existing capabilities or create new ones.[60] Yet, as found by Hitt et al., "cultural differences and institutional deficits can serve as barriers to the transfer of knowledge in alliance partnerships"[61] Clearly, then, managers need to recognize that it is critical to overcome cultural and system differences in managing knowledge flows to the advantage of the alliance.

Knowledge management, then, is "the conscious and active management of creating, disseminating, evolving, and applying knowledge to strategic ends."[62] Research on eight

EXHIBIT 7-2 Knowledge Management in IJVs

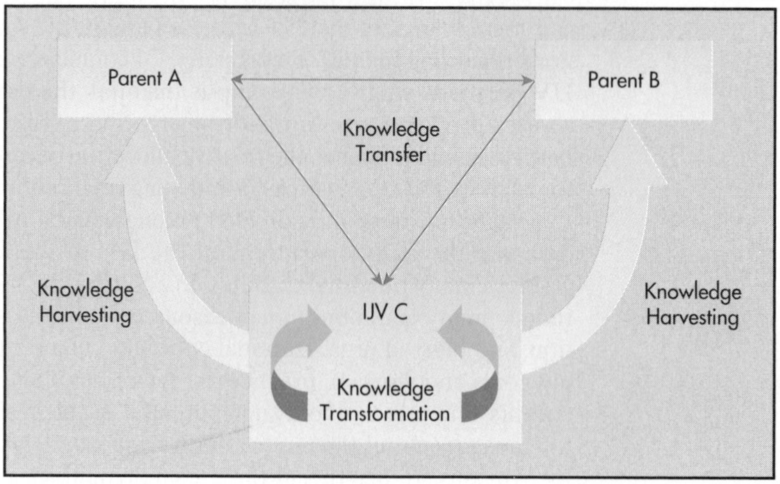

Note: Knowledge transfer usually follows the paths AB and/or BA and BC. Harvesting follows the paths CA and CB.

SOURCE: I. Berdrow and H. W. Lane, "International Joint Ventures: Creating Value Through Successful Knowledge Management," *Journal of World Business*, Vol. 38, 1, February 2003, pp. 15–30, with permission from Elsevier.

IJVs by Berdrow and Lane led them to define these processes as follows and as shown in Exhibit 7-2.

1. **transfer:** managing the flow of existing knowledge between parents and from the parents to the IJV.
2. **transformation:** managing the transformation and creation of knowledge within the IJV through its independent activities.
3. **harvest:** managing the flow of transformed and newly created knowledge from the IJV back to the parents.[63]

In particular, the sharing and development of technology among IJV partners provides the opportunity for knowledge transfer among those individuals who have internalized that information, beyond any tangible assets; the challenge is to develop and harvest that information to benefit the parents through complementary synergies. Those IJVs that were successful in meeting that challenge were found to have personal involvement by the principals of the parent company in shared goals, in the activities and decisions being made, and in encouraging joint learning and coaching.[64]

The many operational activities and issues involved in strategic implementation—such as negotiating, organizing, staffing, leading, communicating, and controlling—are the subjects of other chapters in this book. Elsewhere we include discussion of the many variables involved in strategic implementation that are specific to a particular country or region, such as goals, infrastructure, laws, technology, ways of doing business, people, and culture. In the following sections, the focus is on three pervasive influences on strategy implementation: government policy, societal culture, and the Internet.

Government Influences on Strategic Implementation

Host governments influence, in many areas, the strategic choices and implementations of foreign firms. The profitability of those firms is greatly influenced, for example, by the level of taxation in the host country and by any restrictions on profit repatriation. Other important influences are government policies on ownership by foreign firms, on labor union rules, on hiring and remuneration practices, on patent and copyright protection, and so on. For the most part, however, if the corporation's managers have done their groundwork, all these factors are known beforehand and are part of the location and entry strategy decisions. However, what hurts managers is to set up shop in a host country and then have major economic or governmental policy changes after they have made a considerable investment.

Unpredictable changes in governmental regulations can be a death knell to businesses operating abroad. Recent changes in Russia causing uncertainty for foreign investors were already discussed. Another country that is often the subject of concern for foreign firms is China. Already one of the toughest countries for mergers and acquisitions, China recently added new restrictions on foreign investors, thus prolonging the time that a number of firms have to continue to wait to find out if their deals will go through.

> *Starting in [September 2006], more deal proposals will require approval by the national Ministry of Commerce, the body that is responsible for the Xugong impasse. Acquisitions that will require the ministry's approval include companies with a well-known brand or those that could have an impact on "China's economic security".*

> FINANCIAL TIMES,
> *August 10, 2006*[65]

Caterpillar was one of the companies with rapid market growth in producing diesel engines in China in the early 1990s—construction was booming and foreign investment was flooding in. But in 1993, China—afraid that foreign investment was causing inflation—revoked tax breaks and restricted foreign investment. The tables turned on Caterpillar after that because there was not enough domestic demand for their products. While China contends it is more committed to a market economy since it joined the World Trade Organization (WTO) in November 2001, history shows that foreign firms need to be cautious about entering China.

Political change in itself can, of course, bring about sudden change in strategic implementation of alliances of foreign firms with host-country projects. This was evident in May 1998 when President Suharto of Indonesia was ousted following economic problems and currency devaluation. The new government began reviewing and canceling some of the business deals linked with the Suharto family, including two water-supply privatization projects with foreign firms—Britain's Thames Water PLC and France's Suez Lyonnaise des Eaux SA. The Suharto family had developed a considerable fortune from licensing deals, monopolies, government "contracts," and protection from taxes.[66] Alliances with the family were often the only way to gain entry for foreign companies.

Cultural Influences on Strategic Implementation

When managers are responsible for implementing alliances among partners from diverse institutional environments, such as transition and established market economies, they are faced with the critical challenge of reconciling conflicting values, practices, and systems. Research by Danis, published in 2003, shows those important differences among Hungarian managers and Western expatriates (see Exhibit 7-3).[67] Such advance knowledge can provide expatriate managers with valuable information to help them in successful local operations.

In other situations, the culture variable is often overlooked when deciding on and implementing entry strategies and alliances, particularly when we perceive the target country to be familiar to us and similar to our own. However, cultural differences can have a subtle and often negative effect. In fact, in a study of 129 U.K. cross-border acquisitions in continental Europe, Schoenberg found that 54 percent of the acquiring firms cited poor performance resulting from the implementation of their acquisitions, compared to their domestic mergers.[68] The researchers' study of those firms revealed six dimensions of national and corporate cultural differences between the management styles of the U.K. firms and the continental European firms:

- Organizational formality
- The extent of participation in decision making
- Attitude towards risk
- Systemisation of decision-making
- Managerial self-reliance
- Attitudes towards funding and gearing.[69]

EXHIBIT 7-3 Key Differences in Managerial Values, Practices, and Systems Among Hungarian Managers and Western Expatriates

Western	Hungarian	Perceived source of difference*
Key differences in values		
Extensive use of espoused values	Relative absence of espoused values	Systemic legacy
Focus on core competencies	Focus on empire building	Systemic legacy
Focus on a broad set of stakeholders	Focus on a narrow set of stakeholders	Systemic legacy
Market mentality	Production/volume mentality	Systemic legacy
Professional relationships	Personal relationships	Systemic legacy
Living to work	Working to live	Cultural and systemic legacy
Key differences in practices		
Team orientation/play by the rules	Individual orientation/beat the system	Cultural and systemic legacy
Consensual management style	Autocratic management style	Systemic legacy
High information/knowledge sharing	Low information/knowledge sharing	Systemic legacy
Plan for the future mentality	Survival mentality	Recent economic events
Key differences in managerial systems		
Market-driven technology	Volume-driven technology	Systemic legacy
Small, flat structures	Large, hierarchical structures	Systemic legacy
Formal, strategic HR systems	Informal, administrative HR systems	Systemic legacy
Transparent information systems	Opaque information systems	Systemic legacy

*Consensus of Hungarian and Western respondents.
SOURCE: Reprinted from *Journal of World Business*, August 2003, Vol. 38, No. 3. W. M. Danis, "Differences in Values, Practices, and Systems among Hungarian Managers and Western Expatriates: An Organizing Framework and Typology," pp. 224–244; with permission from Elsevier © 2003.

Among these dimensions, risk-orientation was the key factor that impacted the performance of the combined firm, because risk-taking propensity impacts managers' approach towards strategic options. Overall, risk-taking firms are likely to pursue aggressive strategies and deal well with change, whereas risk-averse companies are likely to tread more carefully and employ incremental strategies. Clearly, for companies entering into an IJV, successful implementation will depend largely on careful planning to take account of such differences, in particular that of risk-orientation, to improve organizational compatability. The greater the cultural distance between the allied firms, the more likely that problems will emerge such as conflict regarding the level of innovation and the kinds of investments each firm is willing to pursue.

Since many of Europe's largest MNCs—including Nestlé, Electrolux, Grand Metropolitan, and Rhone-Poulenc—experience increasing proportions of their revenues from their positions in the United States, and employ more than 2.9 million Americans, they have decided to shift the headquarters of some product lines to the United States. As they have done so, however, there is growing evidence that managing in the United States is not as easy as they anticipated it would be because of their perceived familiarity with the culture. Rosenzweig documents some reflections of European managers on their experiences of managing U.S. affiliates. Generally, he has found that European managers appreciate that Americans are pragmatic, open, forthright, and innovative. However, they also say that the tendency of Americans to be informal and individualistic means that their need for independence and autonomy on the job causes problems in their relationship with the head office Europeans. Americans simply do not take well to directives from a foreign-based headquarters.[70] Rosenzweig presents some comments from French managers on their activities in the United States:

French Managers Comment on Their Activities in the United States:

- "Americans see themselves as the world's leading country, and it's not easy for them to accept having a European in charge."
- "It is difficult for Americans to develop a world perspective. It's hard for them to see that what may optimize the worldwide position may not optimize the U.S. activities."

- "The horizon of Americans often goes only as far as the U.S. border. As a result, Americans often don't give equal importance to a foreign customer. If a foreign customer has a special need, the response is sometimes: 'It works here, why do they need it to be different?'"
- "It might be said that Americans are the least international of all people, because their home market is so big."[71]

Other European firms have had more successful strategic implementation in their U.S. plants by adapting to U.S. culture and management styles. When Mercedes-Benz of Germany launched its plant in Tuscaloosa, Alabama, U.S. workers and German "trainers" had doubts. Lynn Snow, who works on the door line of the Alabama plant, was skeptical whether the Germans and the Americans would mesh well. Now she proudly asserts that they work together, determined to build a quality vehicle. As Jürgen Schrempp, then CEO of Mercedes's parent, Daimler-Benz, observed, " 'Made in Germany'—we have to change that to 'Made by Mercedes,' and never mind where they are assembled."[72]

The German trainers recognized that the whole concept of building a Mercedes quality car had to be taught to the U.S. workers in a way that would appeal to them. They abandoned the typically German strict hierarchy and instead designed a plant in which any worker could stop the assembly line to correct manufacturing problems. In addition, taking their cue from Japanese rivals, they formed the workers into teams that met every day with the trainers to problem solve. Out the window went formal offices and uniforms, replaced by casual shirts with personal names on the pocket. To add to the collegiality, get-togethers for a beer after work became common. "The most important thing is to bring together the two cultures," says Andreas Renschler, who has guided the M-Class since it began in 1993. "You have to generate a kind of ownership of the plant."[73] The local community has also embraced the mutual goals, often having beer fests and including German-language stations on local cable TV.

The impact of cultural differences in management style and expectations is perhaps most noticeable and important when implementing international joint ventures, mergers, or acquisitions. The complexity of a such alliances requires that managers from each party learn to compromise to create a compatible and productive working environment, particularly when operations are integrated. Sometimes a cross-border alliance deal may in itself contradict cultural traditions, as explained in the following Management Focus: Mittal's Marriage to Arcelor Breaks the Marwari Rules.

Management Focus

Mittal's Marriage to Arcelor Breaks the Marwari Rules

The biggest steel merger in history was consummated in June 2006 during a 20-minute meeting at a hotel near the Brussels Airport after a five-month takeover battle. The combination of India's Mittal Steel and Luxembourg steelmaker Arcelor creates the world's biggest steel company. The Arcelor acquisition brings Mittal's production to over 100 million tons, creating a company with 333,000 employees on four continents.[74]

The deal did not come about easily, but Lakshmi Mittal, Mittal Steel's founder and 90 percent owner, skillfully managed opposition from two fronts—strategically and culturally.

Strategically, Mr. Mittal worked hard to overcome overwhelming hostility by Arcelor to his initial proposal. Arcelor had planned a deal with Russian steelmaker Severstal in a bid to block the Mittal acquisition.[75] But after two rejected bids from Mittal Steel, Mr. Mittal reached an agreement to acquire Arcelor in a deal valued at $33.7 billion. Mittal, his son Aditya, and a team

of negotiators gained agreement to a 2008 business plan and provided a comparison of their deal to the one from Severstal. Mittal also provided a plan for corporate governance rules to promote Arcelor's business model and a commitment that his family would vote its share to support the board's recommendations.[76] It was clear to Mr. Mittal that the Arcelor executives had an outdated view of Mittal Steel, but he spent a lot of time explaining and showing Arcelor executives how Mittal Steel operates. The Arcelor chairman, Joseph Kinsch, spent some time talking to the members of Mittal family and discussing the potential alliance. Finally a better relationship was acknowledged by both sides and the deal was sealed, with Kinsch saying "I hope it can become a love marriage between our teams."[77]

Apart from the strategic negotiations of the deal, which finally turned from hostile to friendly, there was opposition for other reasons. There was a battle from France, seemingly over a perception of losing control of a company that was already a European multinational, though there was no objection to Arcelor's effort to bring in the Russian company Severstal as a white knight.[78] In addition, critics in the French and Luxembourg governments seemed to view the takeover by a family-run company as "a betrayal of old continental European traditions to a new cost-cutting imperative of globalization."[79] A similar objection came from India, showing how growth can bring Indians into conflict with cultural traditions. The objection was that Lakshmi Mittal, Indian-born head of Mittal Steel, was breaking the Marwari rules. Mittal belongs to an ethnic goup called Marwari that "traditionally believes it is critical for companies to maintain family ownership."[80] Three of the five major steel companies in India are controlled and run by Marwari families, as well as companies in a number of other industries. Various family members run the operations of those companies, managing separate factories and strategic deals with other firms. The Marwaris, often India's most affluent families whose businesses thrived under the old protective government policies, had considerable business networks among the families, favoring doing business with them over others. As an ethnic group, they developed their own business practices:

Marwaris started business days with Hindu prayer and ended with an accounting of that day's cash flow. This practice, called partha, allowed them to respond quickly to market changes. Another, called modi, was a secret language that other Indians couldn't decipher and was used for trading data and business records.[81]

When Lakshmi Mittal, billionnaire steel tycoon—a global strategist based in London running a Dutch-registered company—launched a dramatic bid to take over Mittal Steel's chief rival, the reaction in India was one of shock. But Mittal said, "We have to put behind our family interest for the interest of the industry and the shareholders at large."[82] In giving up half of his 90 percent share of his company, to hold less than 45 percent of the combined company, he stated that he did not think his cultural traditions should deter the company from growth. In addition Arcelor-Mittal will be based in Luxembourg, not in London where Mr. Mittal lives. He will share the chairmanship and be able to appoint only one-third of the board's 18 seats. Mittal recognizes that to be globally competitive Marwari family businesses will have to change their governance policies.[83]

In China, too, strategic implementation necessitates an understanding of the pervasive cultural practice of *guanxi* in business dealings. Discussed in previous chapters, *guanxi* refers to the relationship networks that "bind millions of Chinese firms into social and business webs, largely dictating their success."[84] Tapping into this system of reciprocal social obligation is essential to get permits, information, assistance to access material and financial resources, and tax considerations. Nothing gets done without these direct or indirect connections. In fact, a new term has arisen—**guanxihu**, which refers to a bond between specially connected firms that generates preferential treatment to members of the network. Without *guanxi*, even implementing a strategy of withdrawal is difficult. Joint ventures can get hard to dissolve and as bitter as an acrimonious divorce. Problems include the forfeiture of assets and the inability to gain market access through future joint venture partners—all experienced by Audi, Chrysler, and Daimler-Benz. For example:

Audi's decision to terminate its joint venture prompted its Chinese partner, First Automobile Works, to expropriate its car design and manufacturing processes. The result was an enormously successful, unauthorized Audi clone, with a Chrysler engine and a First Automobile Works nameplate.[85]

E-commerce Impact on Strategy Implementation

With subsidiaries, suppliers, distributors, manufacturing facilities, carriers, brokers and customers all over the globe, global trade is complicated and fragmented. Shipments cross borders multiple times a day. Are they compliant with all the latest trade regulations? Are they consistently classified for each country? Can you give your buyers, customers and service providers the latest information, on demand?[86]

As indicated in this quote, global trade is extremely complicated. Deciding on a global strategy is one thing; implementing it through all the necessary parties and intermediaries around the world presents a whole new level of complexity. Because of that complexity, many firms decide to implement their global e-commerce strategy by outsourcing the necessary tasks to **e-commerce enablers**, companies that specialize in providing the technology to organize transactions and follow through with the regulatory requirements. These specialists can help companies sort through the maze of different taxes, duties, language translations, and so on specific to each country. Such services allow small and medium-sized companies to go global without the internal capabilities to carry out global e-commerce functions. One of these specialist e-commerce enablers is NextLinx, which applies technology to the wide range of services it provides for strategic implementation, allowing all trading partners to collaborate in a single online location, using the same information and processes. These kinds of Web-based services allow a company to manage an entire global trade operation, including automation of imports and exports by screening orders and generating the appropriate documentation, paying customs charges, complying with trade agreements, etc.[87]

CONCLUSION

Cross-border strategic alliances are becoming increasingly common as innovative companies seek rapid entry into foreign markets and as they try to reduce the risks of going it alone in complex environments. Those companies that do well are those that do their groundwork and pick complementary strategic partners. Too many, however, get "divorced" because "the devil is in the details"—which is what happens when "a marriage made in heaven" runs into unanticipated problems during actual strategic implementation.

Summary of Key Points

1. Strategic alliances are partnerships with other companies for specific reasons. Cross-border, or global, strategic alliances are working partnerships between companies (often more than two) across national boundaries and increasingly across industries.
2. Cross-border alliances are formed for many reasons, including market expansion, cost- and technology-sharing, avoiding protectionist legislation, and taking advantage of synergies.
3. Technological advances and the resulting blending of industries, such as those in the telecommunications and entertainment industries, are factors prompting cross-industry alliances.
4. Alliances may be short or long term; they may be full global partnerships, or they may be for more narrow and specific functions such as research and development sharing.
5. Alliances often run into trouble in the strategic implementation phase. Problems include loss of technology and knowledge skill-base to the other partner, conflicting strategic goals and objectives, cultural clashes, and disputes over management and control systems.
6. Successful alliances require compatible partners with complementary skills, products, and markets. Extensive preparation is necessary to work out how to share management control and technology and to understand each other's culture.
7. Strategic implementation—also called *functional level strategies*—is the process of setting up overall policies, administrative responsibilities, and schedules throughout the organization. Successful implementation results from setting up the structure, systems, and processes of the firm, as well as the functional activities that create a *system of fits* with the desired strategy.
8. Differences in national culture and changes in the political arena or in government regulations often have unanticipated effects on strategic implementation.
9. Strategic implementation of global trade is increasingly being facilitated by e-commerce enablers—companies that specialize in providing the software and Internet technology for complying with the specific regulations, taxes, shipping logistics, translations, and so on for each country with which their clients do business.

Discussion Questions

1. Discuss the reasons that companies embark on cross-border strategic alliances. What other motivations may prompt such alliances?
2. Why are there an increasing number of mergers with companies in different industries? Give some examples. What industry do you think will be the next for global consolidation?
3. Discuss the problems inherent in developing a cooperative alliance to enhance competitive advantage, but also incurring the risk of developing a new competitor.

4. What are the common sources of incompatibility in cross-border alliances? What can be done to minimize them?
5. Explain what is necessary for companies to successfully implement a global sourcing strategy.
6. Discuss the political and economic situation in the Russian Federation with your class. What has changed since this writing? What are the implications for foreign companies to start a joint venture there now?
7. What is involved in strategic implementation? What is meant by creating a *system of fits* with the strategic plan?
8. Explain how the host government may affect strategic implementation—in an alliance or another form of entry strategy.
9. How might the variable of national culture affect strategic implementation? Use the Mittal Steel example to highlight some of these factors.
10. Discuss the importance of knowledge management in IJVs and what can be done to enhance effectiveness of that process.

Application Exercises

1. Research some recent joint ventures with foreign companies situated in Russia. How are they doing? Bring your information to class for discussion. What is the climate for foreign investors in Russia at the time of your reading this chapter?
2. Review the opening profile featuring Spanish companies. Do some follow-up research on one of those acquisitions and report to the class about its performance.

Experiential Exercise: Partner Selection in an International Context

—BY PROFESSOR ANNE SMITH

Read the following three scenarios and think about the assigned questions before class. Although the names of the specific telecommunications firms have been disguised, each scenario is based on actual events and real companies in the telecommunications service industry.

Scenario 1: TOOLBOX and FROZEN in Mexico

By October 30, 1990, managers from TOOLBOX (A Baby Bell[1] located in the eastern United States) and FROZEN (a Canadian telecommunications service and equipment provider) had been working for months on a final bid for the Telmex privatization. In two weeks, a final bid was due to the Mexican Ministry of Finance for this privatization; TOOLBOX's consortium was competing against four other groups.

Teléfonos de México (Telmex) was a government-run and -owned telecommunications provider, which included local, long-distance, cellular, and paging services in Mexico. Yet, in late 1989, the Mexican government decided to privatize Telmex. Reasons for Telmex's privatization included its need for new technology and installation expertise and the large pent-up demand for phone service in Mexico (where only one in five households had a phone). In early 1990, managers from TOOLBOX's international subsidiary were in contact with many potential partners such as France Telecom, GTE, FROZEN, and Spain's Telefonica. By June 1990, TOOLBOX and FROZEN had chosen each other to partner and bid on the Telmex privatization. During the past six months, discussions had gone smoothly between the international managers at TOOLBOX and FROZEN. With a local Mexican partner (required by the Mexican government), the managers worked out many details related to their Telmex bid, such as who would be in charge of installations and backlog reduction, who would install new cellular equipment, who would upgrade the marketing and customer service function, and who would select and install the central office switches. A TOOLBOX international manager commented, "We got along extremely well with our neighbors to the north. Not surprisingly, given that we speak the same language, have similar business values . . . but, basically we liked their international people, which was essential for our largest international deal ever." A FROZEN international manager stated, "It was ironic that our top executive in charge of business development had been a summer intern at TOOLBOX when he was in college. So, he liked our selection of TOOLBOX for this partnering arrangement, even though he was not familiar with the current TOOLBOX top managers." By September 1990, investment bankers estimated that a winning bid would probably top $1.5 billion. On November 15, 1990, all final bids for the privatization would be due. Having worked out the operational details (contingent on a winning bid), managers from TOOLBOX and FROZEN returned to meet with their top managers one final time to get some consensus on a final bid price for Telmex.

Scenario 2: The Geneva Encounter

At the Telecom 1984 convention in Geneva, Robert and Jim (a GEMS senior vice president and a business development manager, respectively) had just finished hearing the keynote address and were wandering among the numerous exhibits. This convention, hosted every four years in Geneva, included thousands of exhibits of telecommunications services and hardware providers; tens of thousands of people attended. Though GEMS (a Baby Bell in the southwestern United States) did not have a booth at the 1984 convention, Robert and Jim were trying to learn about international telecommunications providers and activities. On the third day of the conference, Robert and Jim were standing at an exhibit of advanced wireless technologies when they struck up a conversation with another bystander who was from Israel.

"You can get lost in this convention," exclaimed Jim. Daniel from Israel agreed, "Yes, this is my first trip to the Telecom convention, and it is overwhelming . . . Tell me about GEMS. How is life freed from Ma Bell?" Robert, Jim, and Daniel continued their conversation over drinks and dinner. They learned that Daniel was an entrepreneur who was involved in many different ventures. One new venture that Daniel was pursuing was Yellow Pages directories and publishing. Daniel was delighted to meet those high-level executives from GEMS because of the Baby Bells' reputations as high-quality telephone service providers. Several months after the conference, Robert and Jim visited Daniel in Israel to discuss opportunities there. Six months later, GEMS and Daniel's firm were jointly developing software for a computerized directory publishing system in Israel. GEMS had committed people and a very small equity stake ($5 to $10 million) to this venture.

Scenario 3: LAYERS and Jack in UK Cable

In early 1990, LAYERS (another Baby Bell from the western United States) was considering investing in an existing cable television franchise in the United Kingdom. In 1984, pioneer/pilot licenses had been awarded in some cities. Many of these initial licenses were awarded to start-up companies run by entrepreneurs with minimal investment capital. Unfortunately, "the 100 percent capital allowances that were seen as vital to make the financial structuring of the cable build a commercial reality" were abolished, creating a "break in the industry's development [from 1985 to 1989] whilst many companies that were interested in UK cable were forced to reexamine their financial requirements."[2]

Jack had obtained one of these early UK cable licenses in 1984, and his investment capital was quickly consumed from installing cable coupled with slow market penetration. By 1986, his efforts toward this venture had waned. In the 1990 Broadcast Act, the government relaxed its rule for cable operators and allowed non-EC control of UK cable companies. This created incentives for current cable operators to sell an equity stake in their ventures. This allowed U.S. and Canadian telephone companies to bring desperately needed cash as well as marketing and installation expertise to these cable ventures. Aware of the impending changes, Jack was once again focusing on his cable operations. He arranged a meeting with several LAYERS international managers in November 1989, in anticipation of the changes. Turning on his charm and sales abilities, Jack explained to the LAYERS international managers the potential for UK cable television.[3] He also shared with these managers that he was willing to sell a large equity stake in his company to get it growing again. The international managers from LAYERS were impressed by Jack's enthusiasm, but they were even more intrigued by the possibility of learning about the convergence of cable and telephone services from this UK "laboratory." The LAYERS international managers decided that they would discuss this deal with their executive in charge of unregulated activities. By June 1990, LAYERS had an equity stake, estimated to be between $30 and $50 million, in Jack's UK cable venture.

SOURCE: This exercise was written by Professor Anne Smith, University of New Mexico, based on her research of the firms discussed. Copyright 1998 by Professor Anne Smith. Used with permission.

[1]Seven Baby Bells (also know as Regional Bell Operating Companies, or RBOCs for short) were created in 1984, when they were divested from AT&T. The term "Baby Bell" is really a misnomer given their large size, between $7 billion and $10 billion in revenues, at divestiture. In 1984, the Baby Bells were granted discrete territories where they offered local telephone service; these seven firms also were allowed to offer cellular service in their local service territories. From the AT&T divestiture settlement, the Baby Bells were allowed to keep the lucrative Yellow Pages and directory assistance services. Yet, these seven firms had no international activities or significant international managerial experience at divestiture.
[2]The Cable Companion, The Cable Television Association, pp. 1–12.
[3]In the UK, cable operators were allowed to offer both cable and telephone service.

Questions

Think about these questions from the perspective of the Baby Bell in each scenario:

1. In your opinion, which one of these scenarios should lead to a long-term successful international partnering relationship? Based on what criteria?
2. In your opinion, which one of these scenarios has the least chance of leading to a long-term, successful international partnering relationship? Why?

Internet Resources

Visit the Deresky Companion Website at www.prenhall.com/deresky for this chapter's Internet resources.

Case Study

Lenovo's Global Expansion

Squeezed at home, China's biggest computer maker, Lenovo, is buying IBM's money-losing PC business. But venturing abroad is fraught wih risk.

www.time.com/asia,
December 12, 2004[1]

Lenovo's eye-catching performance at home reminds investors that, had it not bought the IBM PC business 18 months ago, it probably would be a much more profitable company now.

FINANCIAL TIMES,
November 10, 2006[2]

After 13 months of negotiations, IBM decided to sell its PC division to China-based Lenovo goup (previously called Legend) and take a minority stake in its former rival; the deal was valued at $1.75 billion and was announced on December 7, 2004. Lenovo had turned down IBM's overtures in 2001; it was the biggest computer company in China. However, in 2004 the company was experiencing pressure domestically from Dell, and experiencing shrinking margins as a result of the country joining the WTO, which sent foreign rivals swarming into the country, thus depressing prices. This pressure prompted a number of Chinese companies to buy foreign firms. The same year, IBM had become concerned because its PC unit had experienced a loss of $258 million in 2003, and had debts of $500 million.[3] And so, a global alliance was born, with Lenovo paying $1.25 billion for the IBM PC unit, as well as assuming debt of $500 million, while IBM took a stake of 18.9 percent in Lenovo.[4] To cinch the deal, Lenovo's Yang Yuanqing stepped down as CEO to give that position to Steve Ward of IBM; he also compromised to move the global headquarters from Beijing to New York, stating that the new relationship must have "trust, respect, compromise."[5] The deal created the world's third-largest PC business, with worldwide headquarters (then) in Purchase, New York, and principal operations in Beijing and Raleigh, North Carolina. It employs over 19,000 people worldwide, comprising approximately half Lenovo and half IBM employees. The companies were meshing Lenovo's strong market in China and IBM's global PC client network, as well as a powerful name brand.

With the deal, Lenovo transitioned from a domestic company to a global group with 60 perent of it sales in other countries. In IBM's announcement, the company representative said that "this sale moves our PC business from an element in the IBM portfolio to a key element in IBM's network of alliances."[6]

Ten months later, Yang Yuanqing, now Lenovo's chairman, announced a restructuring that would create China's first technology multinational. The move included giving half the company's top jobs to executives of American, Australian, and Indian origin.[7] Lenovo now had a unified management structure and had integrated all major functions. Lenovo estimated that strategy would save around $200 million a year by consolidating procurement alone, additional savings were anticipated by integrating supply chains. Growth was expected to be achieved by expanding to emerging markets and also by targeting the small business maket in developed economies.[8] In running the combined company, some cultural and operational differences provided hurdles that management had to resolve. While English was made the official language in headquarters, communication difficulties still arose, as well as those practical differences due to business trasitioning many time zones and great distances. In addition, there were cross-cultural differences, as well as those arising from the way business was traditionally conducted at the two companies. Lenovo's work practices had been very rules-driven, with very specific requirements of managers and employees; IBM's work practices are known to be process-driven, where, for example, weekly conference calls would be scheduled regardless of the need.[9]

---

[1]Matthey Forney, "A Whole Lot to Swallow," www.time.com/asia, December 12, 2004.

[2]Justine Lau, "No Place Like Home," *Financial Times*, November 10, 2006.

[3]www.time.com/asia, December 12, 2004.

[4]Ibid.

[5]Steve Ward, "A Revolution Founded on Give and Take," *Financial Times,* November 10, 2005.

---

[6]www.ibm.com, December 12, 2004.

[7]Simon London, "A Global Power Made in China," *Financial Times,* November 9, 2005.

[8]Ibid.

[9]Simon London, "Your Rules and My Processes," *Financial Times,* November 10, 2005.

Because of the 12-hour time difference, conference calls are usually scheduled either very early in the morning or late at night. In addition, while most of the Lenovo managers speak English, very few IBM managers could speak Mandarin, and even language lessons did not help much in their interpretation of meaning of their Chinese colleagues.[10] The Chinese, for their part, were anxious to learn global business practices.

Subsequent pressures in the desktop business resulted in an 85 perent profit drop in the year to March 31, 2006. Lenovo laid off 1,000 employees and moved its headquarters from Purchase, New York, to Raleigh, North Carolina. Mr. Yang replaced CEO Steve Ward with William Amelio, former head of Dell in Asia.

Now, the 48-year-old CEO, who can't even say "jet lag" in Mandarin, spends his days zipping around the globe on a mission to transform Lenovo into a juggernaut with the same brand clout as Dell and Hewlett-Packard Co. Among his first-year tasks: launching a $100 million restructuring effort to push Lenovo toward profitability.

THE WALL STREET JOURNAL,
November 21, 2006[11]

Amelio decided to rotate the headquarters between Beijing, Hong Kong, Singapore, Raleigh (NC) and Paris,

and he spends most of his time visiting those offices; he lives in Singapore with his wife and four children. He works hard to reduce cross-cultural conflicts, saying that "in the U.S. and Europe, we have highly opinionated executives who like to make their voices heard. The China team tends to listen more and express themselves more thoughtfully. The Americans and Europeans need to know that if a Chinese colleague is nodding silently, it doesn't mean they're agreeing."[12]

It seems that Amelio has achieved some results. On November 10, 2006, Lenovo Group reported results for the second fiscal quarter ended September 30, 2006. Lenovo's consolidated revenue for the second quarter increased 1 percent year over year to US$3.7 billion. The company's shipments worldwide increased by approximately 10 percent, compared with the industry average of 8 percent. However, the growth was mostly in China. Yang Yuanqing, Lenovo's chairman noted that operational efficiency had improved due to the company's restructuring efforts. However, he stated that "due to slow growth in mature PC markets and intensified competition, we did face some challenges in certain segments."[13] Analysts have noted Lenovo's weak brand awareness in the U.S., but that the strong sales in China provide the company with cash flow to sustain losses in overseas markets."[14] Lenovo faces daunting challenges in world markets, in particular strong global price competition.

[10]Ibid.
[11]Jane Spencer, "To Sell PCs, Lenovo CEO Hits the Sky," *The Wall Street Journal*, November 21, 2006.

[12]Ibid.
[13]"Lenovo Reports Second Quarter FY2006/07 Results," *Business Wire Latin America*, November 10, 2006.
[14]Simon London, "A Global Power Made in China," *Financial Times*, November 9, 2005.

CASE QUESTIONS

1. Discuss in depth the reasons for this alliance, from the perspectives of both Lenovo and IBM.
2. What were the industry conditions that made the deal enticing in 2004 when it was not so in 2001?

3. What is the track record of Chinese companies going global by acquiring foreign companies?
4. Follow up on the results for Lenovo at the time of your reading this case. Present your findings to the class.

CHAPTER

Organization Structure and Control Systems

8

Outline

Opening Profile: Changing Organizational Structures of Emerging Market Companies

Rapidly changing competition and global business activities demand that companies run their worldwide operations efficiently and effectively, based on the right business models and organizational structures. Stable organizational structures and control systems are necessary to seek timely internationalization. The major variables involved in choosing the right organizational structure depend on a company's global involvement and degree of localization. In 2007, fast-growing companies from emerging markets (EMs), BRIC (Brazil, Russia, India and China), and rapidly developing economies (RDEs) continue to internationalize their operations.[1] Examples are Cemex (Mexico), CNOOC (China), Dr. Reddy's Laboratories (India), Embraer (Brazil), Gazprom (Russia), Haier Company (China), Infosys Technologies (India), Koc Holdings (Turkey), Lenovo Group (China), Tata Motors (India), and Wipro (India).[2] These emerging market companies are the first wave of highly successful firms benefiting from the globalization phenomenon.[3]

Interestingly, the expansion models sought by these new emerging market companies from Asia, Latin America, and Eastern Europe are unique and may not fit with today's mainstream multinational corporation (MNC) model because of the following three reasons: First, many emerging market companies are avoiding the traditional roadmap to internationalization and capitalizing on the "born global phenomenon," which means running their operations and opening subsidiaries worldwide from the beginning. Second, they are finding niche businesses where competition is limited. Third, they are thriving in those old-economy industries that have been abandoned by established MNCs from developed countries.

A new breed of companies is emerging in those geographic areas that have excelled in global business because of their unique organizational structures and design. Like Korean chaebols (industrial conglomerates), most emerging market companies were started as family businesses and entrepreneurial entities where ownership and control of firms resided with the families. Therefore, the control mechanism is somewhat bureaucratic and headquarters-centered. Currently, a multitude of changes are in the pipeline that will force emerging market companies to redefine their family-based governance structures and rigid control systems. The ongoing changes include simplifying firms' traditional hierarchical structures, reducing the role of family members, providing more operational powers to international subsidiaries, and redesigning organizational systems that could follow the traditional MNC-model or company-specific forms.

Major structural changes include simplifying hierarchies, reducing family ownerships, providing more powers to subsidiaries, and seeking organizational structures based on either the traditional MNC model or company-specific hybrid structures. Interestingly, many emerging market companies have been following the model of "be global, act local" in becoming good citizens and adapting their products and services. Embraer, Haier Group, Lenovo, Mittal Steel, Orsacom, and others fit in this category. In addition, overseas Chinese business networks (OCBNs) are also changing to become part of the globalization phenomenon. Increasingly, emerging market companies from Asia, Latin America, and Eastern Europe will seek internationalization in their own unique ways, leading to hybrid structures and fast-growth entities. Of course, these newly emerging MNCs will continue to be part of global integration, multidomestic synergies, and international/global/transnational strategies. Their future goals and scope of operations will determine organizational structures and global initiatives.

SOURCE: Written exclusively for this text by Syed Tariq Anwar, Professor, West Texas A&M University, January 5, 2007.

Strategic plans are abstract sets of decisions that cannot affect a company's competitive position or bottom line until they are implemented. Having decided on the strategic direction for the company, international managers must then consider two of the key variables for implementing strategy: the organizational structure and the control and coordinating mechanisms. The necessity of adapting organizational structures to facilitate changes in strategy and the competitive environment is illustrated in the opening profile describing new approaches by companies in emerging markets, some of which are now referred to as "emerging giants."[4]

ORGANIZATIONAL STRUCTURE

There is no permanent organization chart for the world. . . . It is of supreme importance to be ready at all times to take advantage of new opportunities.

ROBERT C. GOIZUETA,
(Former) Chairman and CEO, Coca-Cola Company[5]

Organizational structures must change to accommodate a firm's evolving internationalization in response to worldwide competition. Considerable research has shown that a firm's structure must be conducive to the implementation of its strategy.[6] In other words, the structure must "fit" the strategy, or it will not work. Managers are faced with how best to attain that fit in organizing the company's systems and tasks.

The design of an organization, as with any other management function, should be contingency based, taking into account the variables of that particular system at that specific point in time. Major variables include the firm's strategy, size, and appropriate technology, as well as the environment in those parts of the world in which the firm operates. Given the increased complexity of the variables involved in the international context, it is no easy task to design the most suitable organizational structure and subsystems. In fact, research shows that most international managers find it easier to determine what to do to compete globally (strategy) than to decide how to develop the organizational capability (structure) to do it.[7] Additional variables affecting structural choices—geographic dispersion as well as differences in time, language, cultural attitudes, and business practices—introduce further layers of complication. We will show how organizational structures need to, and typically do, change to accommodate strategies of increasing internationalization.

EVOLUTION AND CHANGE IN MNC ORGANIZATIONAL STRUCTURES

Historically, a firm reorganizes as it internationalizes to accommodate new strategies. The structure typically continues to change over time with growth and with increasing levels of investment or diversity and as a result of the types of entry strategy chosen. Internationalization is the process by which a firm gradually changes in response to international competition, domestic market saturation, and the desire for expansion, new markets, and diversification. As discussed in Chapter 6, a firm's managers weigh alternatives and decide on appropriate entry strategies. Perhaps the firm starts by exporting or by acting as a licensor or licensee, and then over time continues to internationalize by engaging in joint ventures or by establishing service, production, or assembly facilities or alliances abroad, moving into a global strategy. At each stage, the firm's managers redesign the organizational structure to optimize the strategy's chances to work, making changes in the firm's tasks and relationships and designating authority, responsibility, lines of communication, geographic dispersal of units, and so forth. This model of **structural evolution** has become known as the **stages model**, resulting from Stopford's research on 187 U.S. multinational corporations (MNCs).[8] Of course, many firms do not follow the stages model because they may start their internationalization at a higher level of involvement—perhaps a full-blown global joint venture without ever having exported, for example.

Even a mature MNC must make structural changes from time to time to facilitate changes in strategy—perhaps a change in strategy from globalization to regionalization (see Chapter 6) or an effort to improve efficiency or effectiveness. The reorganization of Aluminum Company of America (Alcoa), for example, split the company into smaller, more autonomous units, thereby giving more focus to growing businesses, such as automotive products, where the market for aluminum is strong. It also enabled Alcoa to link businesses with similar functions that are geographically divided—that is, to improve previously insufficient communication between Alcoa's aluminum operations in Brazil and its Australian counterparts. Alcoa, as with most MNCs, has found the need to continuously adapt its structure to accommodate global expansion and new ventures. Alcoa has a presence in 41 countries, and employed 120,000 people worldwide.[9] The typical ways in which firms organize their international activities are shown in the following list. (Larger companies often use several of these structures in different regions or parts of their organization.) After the presentation of some of these structural forms, the focus will turn to transitional organizational arrangements.

- Domestic structure plus export department
- Domestic structure plus foreign subsidiary
- International division
- Global functional structure
- Global product structure

EXHIBIT 8-1   Domestic Structure Plus Foreign Subsidary

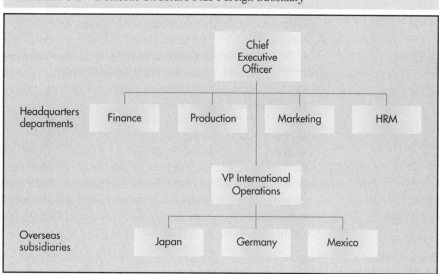

As previously stated, many firms—especially smaller ones—start their international involvement by exporting. They may simply use the services of an export management company for this, or they may reorganize into a simple *domestic structure plus export department.*

To facilitate access to and development of specific foreign markets, the firm can take a further step toward worldwide operations by reorganizing into a *domestic structure plus foreign subsidiary* in one or more countries (see Exhibit 8-1). To be effective, subsidiary managers should have a great deal of autonomy and be able to adapt and respond quickly to serve local markets. This structure works well for companies with one or a few subsidiaries located relatively close to headquarters.

With further market expansion, the firm may then decide to specialize by creating an *international division*, organized along functional, product, or geographic lines. With this structure, the various foreign subsidiaries are organized under the international division, and subsidiary managers report to its head and are typically given the title Vice President, International Division. This vice president, in turn, reports directly to the CEO of the corporation. The creation of an international division facilitates the beginning of a global strategy. It permits managers to allocate and coordinate resources for foreign activities under one roof, and thus enhances the firm's ability to respond, both reactively and proactively, to market opportunities. Some conflicts may arise among the divisions of the firm because more resources and management attention tend to get channeled toward the international division than toward the domestic divisions and because of the different orientations of various division managers.[10] Companies such as IBM and PepsiCo have international divisions called, respectively, IBM World Trade and PepsiCola International.

Integrated Global Structures

To respond to increased product diversification and to maximize benefits from both domestic and foreign operations, a firm may choose to replace its international division with an integrated global structure. This structure can be organized along functional, product, geographic, or matrix lines.[11]

The **global functional structure** is designed on the basis of the company's functions—production, marketing, finance, and so forth. Foreign operations are integrated into the activities and responsibilities of each department to gain functional specialization and economies of scale. This form of organization is primarily used by small firms with highly centralized systems. It is particularly appropriate for product lines using similar technology and for businesses with a narrow spectrum of customers. This structure results in plants that are highly integrated across products and that serve single or similar markets.[12]

Much of the advantage resulting from economies of scale and functional specialization may be lost if the managers and the work systems become too narrowly defined to have the necessary flexibility to respond to local environments. An alternative structure can be based on product lines.

For firms with diversified product lines (or services) that have different technological bases and that are aimed at dissimilar or dispersed markets, a **global product (divisional) structure** may be more strategically advantageous than a functional structure. In this structure, a single product (or product line) is represented by a separate division. Each division is headed by its own general manager, and each is responsible for its own production and sales functions. Usually, each division is a **strategic business unit** (SBU)—a self-contained business with its own functional departments and accounting systems. The advantages of this organizational form are market concentration, innovation, and responsiveness to new opportunities in a particular environment. It also facilitates diversification and rapid growth, sometimes at the expense of scale economies and functional specialization. H. J. Heinz Company CEO William R. Johnson came on board in April 1998 and decided that the company should restructure to implement a global strategy. He changed the focus of the company from a multidomestic international strategy using the global geographic area structure to a global strategy using the global product divisional structure. His goal was further growth overseas by building international operations; this structure also readily incorporated Heinz's Specialty Pet Food Division for marketing those products around the world.[13] Particularly appropriate in a dynamic and diverse environment, the global product structure is illustrated in Exhibit 8-2.

With the global product (divisional) grouping, however, ongoing difficulties in the coordination of widely dispersed operations may result. One answer to this problem, particularly for large MNCs, is to reorganize into a global geographic structure.

In the **global geographic (area) structure**—the most common form of organizing foreign operations—divisions are created to cover geographic regions (see Exhibit 8-3). Each regional manager is responsible for the operations and performance of the countries

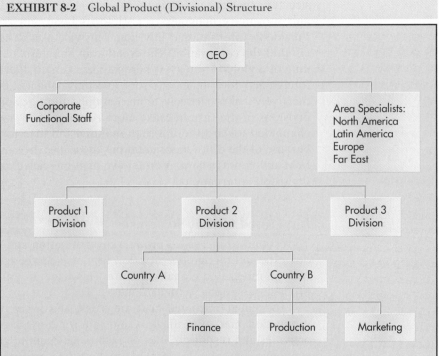

EXHIBIT 8-2   Global Product (Divisional) Structure

EXHIBIT 8-3 Global Geographic Structure

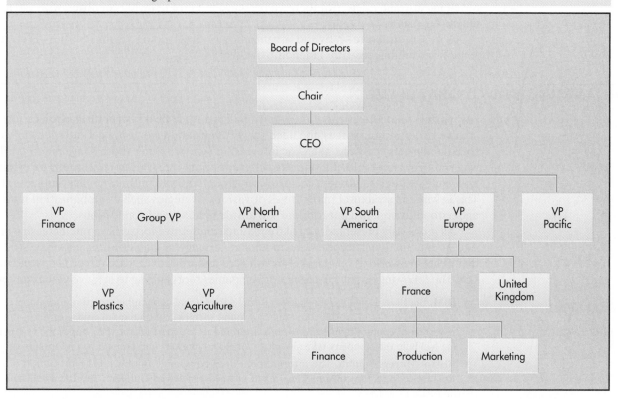

within a given region. In this way, country and regional needs and relative market knowledge take precedence over product expertise. Local managers are familiar with the cultural environment, government regulations, and business transactions. In addition, their language skills and local contacts facilitate daily transactions and responsiveness to the market and the customer. While this is a good structure for consolidating regional expertise, problems of coordination across regions may arise. With the geographic structure, the focus is on marketing, since products can be adapted to local requirements. Therefore, marketing-oriented companies, such as Nestlé and Unilever, which produce a range of products that can be marketed through similar (or common) channels of distribution to similar customers, will usually opt for this structure. Nestlé SA, for example, uses this decentralized structure, which is more typical of European companies, because "it is not Nestlé's policy to generate most of its sales in Switzerland, supplemented by a few satellite subsidiaries abroad. Nestlé strives to be an insider in every country in which it operates, not an outsider."[14] In 2005, Nestlé reinforced its global business strategy of emphasizing its brands by making its head of marketing responsible for Nestlé's seven SBUs—dairy, confectionery, beverages, ice cream, food, pet care, and food services. Those SBUs help determine the company's regional business strategy, which then shapes the local market business strategies.[15] Still Nestlé's marketing manager, Mr. Brabeck, insists that

> *There is no such thing as a global consumer, especially in a sector as psychologically and culturally loaded as food. . . . This means having a local character.*

> PETER BRABECK,
> *Nestlé Marketing Manager*[16]

Grouping a number of countries under a region doesn't always work out, however, as Ford experienced with its European Group. It soon discovered tensions among the units in Germany, Britain, and France resulting from differences in their national systems and cultures, and in particular management styles. Nevertheless, it has pursued its consolidation into five regionalized global centers for the design, manufacture, and marketing of 70 lines of cars around the world. In 2001, under Ford's CEO Jac Nasser—born in Lebanon and raised in Australia—Ford negotiated a presence in more than 200 countries, with 140 manufacturing plants.[17]

A **matrix structure**—a hybrid organization of overlapping responsibilities—is used by some firms but has recently fallen into disfavor.

ORGANIZING FOR GLOBALIZATION

No matter what the stage of internationalization, a firm's structural choices always involve two opposing forces: the need for **differentiation** (focusing on and specializing in specific markets) and the need for **integration** (coordinating those same markets). The way the firm is organized along the differentiation–integration continuum determines how well strategies—along a localization–globalization continuum—are implemented. This is why the structural imperatives of various strategies such as globalization must be understood to organize appropriate worldwide systems and connections.

As previously presented, global trends and competitive forces have put increasing pressure on multinational corporations to adopt a strategy of **globalization**, a specific strategy that treats the world as one market by using a standardized approach to products and markets. The following are two examples of companies reorganizing to achieve globalization:

- **IBM.** Big Blue decided to move away from its traditional geographic structure to a global structure based on its 14 worldwide industry groups, such as banking, retail, and insurance, shifting power from country managers to centralized industry expert teams. IBM hopes the restructuring will help the company take advantage of global markets and break down internal barriers.
- **Bristol-Meyers Squibb.** The international drug company announced the formation of new worldwide units for consumer medicine businesses such as Bufferin, and for its Clairol and hair-care products.[18]

Organizing to facilitate a globalization strategy typically involves rationalization and the development of strategic alliances. To achieve rationalization, managers choose the manufacturing location for each product based on where the best combination of cost, quality, and technology can be attained. It often involves producing different products or component parts in different countries. Typically, it also means that the product design and marketing programs are essentially the same for all end markets around the world—to achieve optimal economies of scale. The downside of this strategy is a lack of differentiation and specialization for local markets.

Organizing for global product standardization necessitates close coordination among the various countries involved. It also requires centralized global product responsibility (one manager at headquarters responsible for a specific product around the world), an especially difficult task for multiproduct companies. Henzler and Rall suggest that structural solutions to this problem can be found if companies rethink the roles of their headquarters and their national subsidiaries. Managers should center the overall control of the business at headquarters, while treating national subsidiaries as partners in managing the business—perhaps as holding companies responsible for the administration and coordination of cross-divisional activities.[19]

A problem many companies face in the future is that their structurally sophisticated global networks, built to secure cost advantages, leave them exposed to the risk of environmental volatility from all corners of the world. Such companies must restructure their global operations to reduce the environmental risk that results from multicountry sourcing and supply networks.[20] In other words, the more links in the chain, the more chances for things to go wrong. The overseas Chinese business network, a less formal, but powerful, form of transnational network alliances which minimizes much risk is described in the accompanying Comparative Management in Focus.

Organizing to "Be Global, Act Local"

In their rush to get on the globalization bandwagon, too many firms have sacrificed the ability to respond to local market structures and consumer preferences. Managers are now realizing that—depending on the type of products, markets, and so forth—a compromise

Comparative Management in Focus

The Overseas Chinese Global Network

In increasing strength, overseas Chinese businessmen from Southeast Asia are investing in China, where they possess linguistic and cultural advantages over big Western corporations. Navigating layers of government and the rituals of business etiquette is easier if you speak the language and appreciate the history.

THE NEW YORK TIMES[21]

The Chinese who left the mother country had to struggle, and that became a culture of its own. Because we have no social security, the Overseas Chinese habit is to save a lot and make a lot of friends.

LEE SHAU KEE,
*65, Real Estate Developer, Hong Kong
(net worth $6 billion)*[22]

Compared to the Japanese *keiretsu,* the emerging Chinese commonwealth is an interconnected, open system—a new market mechanism for conducting global business.[23] It is now becoming apparent to many business leaders who have finally figured out Japan's *keiretsu* that they "now need to understand a distinctively Chinese model, where tycoons cut megadeals in a flash and heads of state wheel and deal like CEOs."[24]

The "Chinese commonwealth" is a form of global network that has become the envy of Western multinationals. It is a network of entrepreneurial relationships spread across continents, though primarily in Asia. What is increasingly being referred to as the "big dragon of Greater China" includes mainland China's 1.3 billion citizens and more than 55 million overseas Chinese—most of them from Taiwan, Indonesia, Hong Kong, and Thailand. It is estimated that the overseas Chinese control $2 trillion in liquid assets and contribute about 80 percent of the capital for the People's Republic of China (PRC). If the overseas Chinese lived in one country, their GNP would exceed that of mainland China.[25] In addition, this "Bamboo Network," which transcends national boundaries, is estimated to contribute about 70 percent of the private sector in Malaysia, Thailand, Indonesia, and the Philippines."[26] Most observers believe that this China-based informal economy is the world leader in economic growth, industrial expansion, and exports. It comprises mostly mid-sized, family-run firms linked by transnational network channels. These channels for the movement of information, finance, goods, and capital help to explain the relative flexibility and efficiency of the numerous ongoing informal agreements and transactions that bind together the various parts of the Chinese-based trading area.[27] The network alliances bind together and draw from the substantial pool of financial capital and resources available in the region, including those of entrepreneurial services in Hong Kong; technology and manufacturing capability in Taiwan; outstanding communications in Singapore; and vast endowments of land, resources, and labor in mainland China.

The overseas Chinese, now models for entrepreneurship, financing, and modernization for the world, and in particular for Beijing, are refugees from China's poverty, disorder, and communism. Business became the key to survival for those Chinese emigrants faced with uncertainties, hardships, and lack of acceptance in their new lands. The uncertainties, a survivor mentality, and the cultural basis in the Confucian tradition of patriarchical authority have led to a way of doing business that is largely confined to family and trusted friends. This business mentality and approach to life has led to many self-made billionaires among the Overseas Chinese. Among them is Y. C. Wang, the Taiwanese plastics king, who had to leave school after the sixth grade but taught himself what was necessary to develop a new industry.[28] More recently, there has been a new wave of investors—overseas Chinese who are attracted by rapid growth in China, compared to slow growth in their home countries, such as Singapore and Indonesia.[29] The network of alliances of the ethnic Chinese is based on *guanxi*—personal connections—among families, business friends, and political associations, often rooted in the traditional clans. Massive amounts of cross-investment and trade are restricted primarily to families and long-standing connections, including those from the province of the PRC from which the overseas Chinese or their ancestors migrated. As examples, Chinese ties in Hong Kong have provided about 90 percent of the investment in the adjacent province of Guangong; and telephone calls from the special economic zone of Xiamen in the PRC to Taiwan now average 60,000 a month, up from 10 a month eight years ago.[30] The web of those connections has created an influential network that is the backbone of the East Asian economy.

The history, culture, and careful, personal approach to business of the overseas Chinese have led to some underlying values—Kao calls them "life-raft" values—which have shaped a distinctive business culture. These values include thrift and a very high savings level, regardless of need; extremely hard work; trust in family before anyone else; adherence to patriarchal authority; investment strictly based on kinship and affiliations; a preference for investment in tangible goods; and an ever-wary outlook on life.[31] This shared web of culture and contacts has spawned an intensely commercial and entrepreneurial network of capitalists and a dominant power in Asia. Two benefits of such a business culture are speed and patience. Because of their knowledge of and trust in their contacts, the overseas Chinese can quickly smell profits and make decisions even more quickly; a deal to buy a hotel in Asia can be completed in days, compared to months in the United States.[32] Patience to invest for the long term is an outcome of closely held ownership and management, often in a single family, so that outside shareholders are not demanding short-term profits. No doubt sharing language and cultural bonds is a vital lubricant for business, especially with people in China, where there are few firm laws on which businesspeople can rely.[33]

must be made along the globalization–regionalization continuum, and they are experimenting with various structural configurations to "be global and act local." Colgate-Palmolive's organizational structure illustrates such a compromise. The primary operating structure is geographic—that is, localized. The presidents of four major regions—North America, Europe, Latin America, and Asia Pacific—report to the COO while other developing regions such as Africa, Eastern Europe, and the Middle East report to the chief of operations of international business development. Then that person reports to the CEO of Colgate-Palmolive, who oversees the centralized coordinating operations (that is, the "globalized" aspects), for technology, finance, marketing, human resources management, and so on.[34]

Levi Strauss is another example of a company attempting to maximize the advantages of different structural configurations. First, the company has ensured its ability to respond to local needs in a different way by allowing its managers to act independently: Levi's success turns on its ability to fashion a global strategy that doesn't snuff out local initiative. It's a delicate balancing act, one that often means giving foreign managers the freedom needed to adjust their tactics to meet the changing tastes of their home markets.[35]

Second, Levi Strauss keeps centralized control of some aspects of its business but decentralizes control to its foreign operations, organized as subsidiaries. These subsidiaries are supplied by a global manufacturing network of Levi plants and contract manufacturers. This approach allows local coordination and the flexibility to respond to ever-changing fashion trends and fads in denim shading.[36]

Another company's plan to go global by acting local does not involve changing the company's basic structure. Fujitsu, a Japanese high-technology conglomerate producing computers, telecommunications equipment, and semiconductors, has found a way to internationalize by proxy. Fujitsu has substantial stakes in two foreign companies—Amdahl, a Silicon Valley maker of IBM-compatible mainframes, and International Computers Ltd. (ICL), Britain's biggest computer company—that accounts for nearly half of Fujitsu's overseas revenues. These firms are run by Westerners, who are given free reign to manage and even compete against each other. The plan is doing so well that Fujitsu is looking for similar deals in Europe. As Fujitsu's president, Takuma Yamamoto, explains, "We are doing business in a borderless economy, but there is a rising tide of nationalism, and you have to find ways to avoid conflict. That is one reason we give our partners autonomy."[37]

One well-known global consumer products company, Procter & Gamble, is succeeding with its global–local "Four Pillars" structure, as described in the accompanying Management Focus.

Management Focus

Procter & Gamble's Think Globally–Act Locally Structure

On October 10, 2006, Procter & Gamble (P&G) Chairman of the Board, President and Chief Executive, A. G. Lafley, addressed shareholders at its annual meeting saying,

"We are now focused on delivering a full decade of industry-leading top and bottom line growth. We have the strategies, strengths and the structure to continue to transform our company in the face of unrelenting change and competition."[38]

Lafley was referring to their Four Pillars structure and to their recent merger with Gillette; both are described below.

With the Gillette merger, P&G now has over 135 employees working in over 80 countries around the world. P&G touches the lives of people around the world three billion times a day with its broad portfolio of leading brands, including Pampers®, Tide®, Charmin®, Downy®, Crest®, Gillette®, and Braun®.[39]

In January 2006, Gillette India announced its merger plans with Procter & Gamble India. The plan was for the Boston-based blades and razor company to adopt P&G's organizational structure and effective July 1, 2006, relocate its headquarters from Gurgaon to P&G Plaza in Mumbai, which would house all P&G subsidiaries in India. Zubair Ahmed, head of Gillette India, stated that "even as Gillette India stays as a separate legal entity in India, P&G's organizational structure, distribution, systems and facilities will help increase our reach, cost efficiencies, speed to market and our current growth momentum."[40]

By July 1, 2006—nine months after closing the Gillette deal—P&G had completed business systems integration in 31 countries spanning five of P&G's seven geographic regions. The company is now taking orders, shipping products, receiving payments, tracking financials, and handling payroll as a single company in these countries. Systems integration is continuing in another 14 countries, including the largest region, North America. When completed, nearly 80 percent of the company's sales will have been integrated.

P&G's organizational structure is broadly divided into three heads: GBU (Global Business Unit), MDO (Market Development Organization), and GBS (Global Business Services). Gillette will move from business units based on geographic regions to GBUs based on product lines. MDOs will develop market strategies to build business based on local knowledge and GBS will bring together business activities such as accounting, human resource systems, order management, and information technology, thus making it cost-effective.[41]

Since 2001, P&G has acquired three leading companies with leading brands in Clairol, Wella, and Gillette. The acquisition of Gillette added five brands with annual sales in excess of $1 billion. Lafley said he is confident the company can deliver on a full decade of growth because of P&G's strategies and strengths, and the company's unique organizational structure. P&G's structure makes it the only consumer products company with global business unit profit centers, global market development organizations, and global shared services, all supported by innovative corporate functions. Lafley reported that he's pleased with progress on the Gillette integration, which will result in $1.0 billion to $1.2 billion in annual cost synergies before taxes and about $750 million in revenue synergy growth by 2009.[42]

P&G's organization structure is described below as given in the company's corporate information description on their Web site.[43]

P&G'S GLOBAL/LOCAL STRUCTURE

Four pillars—Global Business Units, Market Development Organizations, Global Business Services, and Corporate Functions—form the heart of P&G's organizational structure.

- Global Business Units (GBUs) build major global brands with robust business strategies.
- Market Development Organizations (MDOs) build local understanding as a foundation for marketing campaigns.
- Global Business Services (GBS) provide business technology and services that drive business success.
- Corporate Functions (CFs) work to maintain our place as a leader of our industries.

P&G approaches business knowing that we need to Think Globally (GBUs) and Act Locally (MDOs). This approach is supported by our commitment to operate efficiently (GBS) and our constant striving to be the best at what we do (CFs). This streamlined structure allows us to get to market faster.

Global Business Units

Philosophy: Think Globally

General Role: Create strong brand equities, robust strategies and ongoing innovation in products and marketing to build major global brands.

GBUs:

- Baby Care/Family Care
- Beauty Care/Feminine Care
- Fabric & Home Care
- Snacks & Beverage
- Health Care

Market Development Organizations (MDO)

Philosophy: Act Locally

General Role: Interface with customers to ensure marketing plans fully capitalize on local understanding, to seek synergy across programs to leverage Corporate scale, and to develop strong programs that change the game in our favor at point of purchase.

MDO Regions:

- North America
- Asia/India/Australia
- Northeast Asia
- Greater China
- Central-Eastern Europe/Middle East/Africa
- Western Europe
- Latin America

Global Business Services (GBS)

Philosophy: Enabling P&G to win with Customers and Consumers

General Role: Provide services and solutions that enable the Company to operate efficiently around the world, collaborate effectively with business partners, and help employees become more productive.

GBS Centers:

- GBS Americas located in Costa Rica
- GBS Asia located in Manila
- GBS Europe, Middle East & Africa located in Newcastle

Corporate Functions (CF)

Philosophy: Be the Smartest/Best

General Role: Ensure that the functional capability integrated into the rest of the company remains on the cutting edge of the industry. We want to be the thought leader within each CF.

Corporate Functions:

- Customer Business Development
- External Relations
- Finance & Acct.
- Human Resources
- Information Technology
- Legal
- Marketing
- Consumer & Market Knowledge
- Product Supply
- Research & Development
- Workplace Services

Although strategy may be the primary means to a company's competitive advantage, the burden of realizing that advantage rests on the organizational structure and design. Because of the difficulties experienced by companies trying to be "glocal" companies (global and local), researchers are suggesting new, more flexible organizational designs involving interorganizational networks and transnational design.

EMERGENT STRUCTURAL FORMS

Companies are increasingly abandoning rigid structures in an attempt to be more flexible and responsive to the dynamic global environment. Some of the ways they are adapting are by transitioning to formats known as interorganizational networks, global e-corporation network structures, and transnational corporation network structures, described as follows.

Interorganizational Networks

Whether the ever-expanding transnational linkages of an MNC consist of different companies, subsidiaries, suppliers, or individuals, they result in relational networks. These networks may adopt very different structures of their own because they operate in different local contexts within their own national environments. By regarding the MNC's overall structure as a network of interconnected relations, we can more realistically consider its organizational design imperatives at both global and local levels. Royal Philips Electronics of the Netherlands, one of the world's biggest electronics companies, has operating units in 60 countries, using a network structure. These units range from large subsidiaries, which might be among the largest companies in a country, to very small single-function operations, such as research and development or marketing divisions for one of Philips's businesses. Some have centralized control at Philips's headquarters; others are quite autonomous. For some time, Philips had fallen far behind its Japanese competitors in productivity because of missteps and seemingly endless restructurings. However, when Philips' chief executive Gerard J. Kleisterlee—a 30-year Philips veteran—took over in 2001, he again reorganized the company. He divested $850 million in less important or unprofitable businesses and shuttered a dozen factories, and outsourced manufacturing for much of the electronics and appliance manufacturing as well as chip production.[44] The restructuring seems to be working, with Philips' 2003 sales hitting EUR29 billion, including a 34 percent increase in sales in China.[45]

In yet another structural variation, Intel, in adapting to changes in the semiconductor industry, announced in early 2005 a wholesale reorganization of its businesses. Intel's executives decided that they wanted the company to focus more on what was going on outside the business, and developed a structural focus they call "Platformisation"—that is, customizing a range of chips in a combination suitable for a particular target market, as a response for the increasing need for speedy adaptation to the market.[46] As the world's biggest semiconductor maker, with 78,000 employees worldwide, the company's general description of its approach to organizing, in response to an inquiry by this author, is as follows:

> *Intel is not a very hierarchical company so a formalized organizational structure is not a particularly good representation of how the company works. At the highest level, Intel is organized into largely autonomous divisions. Intel uses matrix management and cross-functional teams including IT, knowledge management, human resources, finance, legal, change control, data warehousing, common directory information management, and cost reduction teams (to name a few) to rapidly adapt to changing conditions.*

> WWW.INTEL.COM,
> *August 19, 2006*[47]

The network of exchange relationships, say Ghoshal and Bartlett, is as representative of any MNC as it is of Philips. The network framework makes clear that the company's operating units link vastly different environmental and operational contexts based on varied economic, social, and cultural milieus. This complex linkage highlights the intricate task of a giant MNC to rationalize and coordinate its activities globally to achieve an advantageous cost position while simultaneously tailoring itself to local market conditions (to achieve benefits from differentiation).[48]

The Global E-Corporation Network Structure

The organizational structure for global e-businesses, in particular for physical products, typically involves a network of virtual e-exchanges and "bricks and mortar" services, whether those services are in-house or outsourced. This structure of functions and

EXHIBIT 8-4   The Global E-Corporation Network Structure

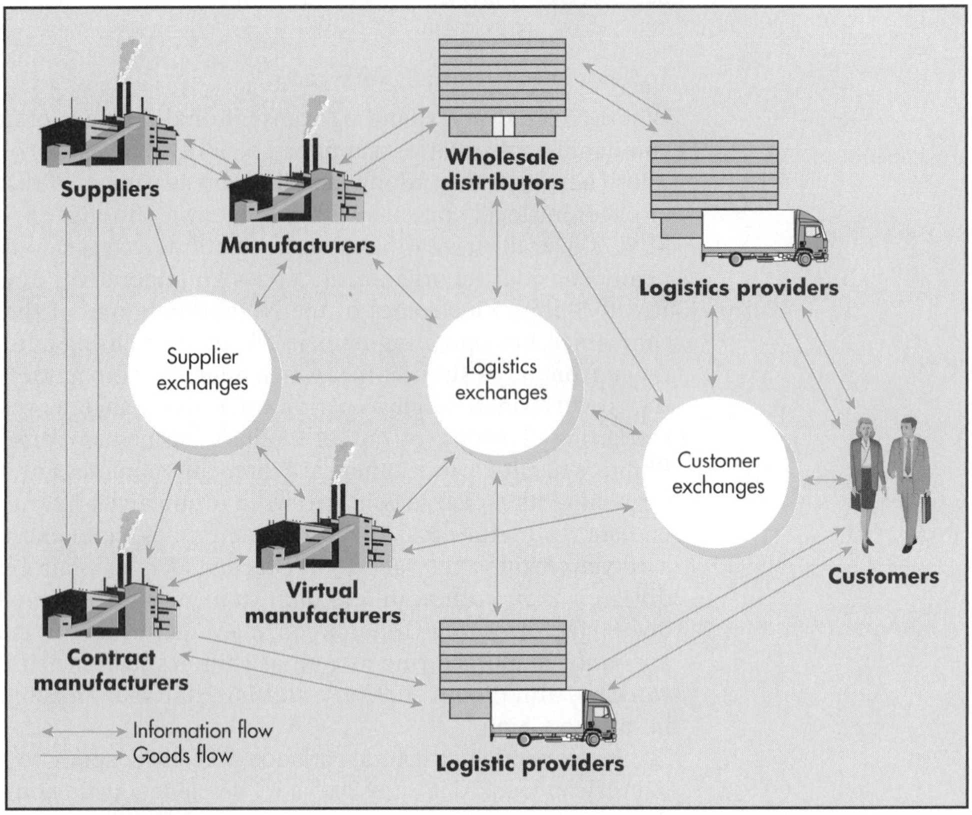

SOURCE: AMR Research.

alliances makes up a combination of electronic and physical stages of the supply chain network, as depicted in Exhibit 8-4.

As such, the network comprises some global and some local functions. Centralized e-exchanges for logistics, supplies, and customers could be housed anywhere; suppliers, manufacturers, and distributors may be in various countries, separately or together, wherever efficiencies of scale and cost may be realized. The final distribution system and the customer interaction must be tailored to the customer-location physical infrastructure and payment infrastructure, as well as local regulations and languages.[49]

The result is a global e-network of suppliers, subcontractors, manufacturers, distributors, buyers, and sellers, communicating in real time through cyberspace. This spreads efficiency throughout the chain, providing cost-effectiveness for all parties.[50] Dell Computer is an example of a company that uses the Internet to streamline its global supply systems. It has a number of factories around the world that supply custom-built PCs to customers in that region. Customers' orders are received through call centers or Dell's own Web site. The order for components then goes to its suppliers, which have to be within a 15-minute drive of its factory. The component parts are delivered to the factory, and the completed customers' orders are collected within a few hours. Dell maintains Internet connections with its suppliers and connects them with its customer database so that they have direct and real-time information about orders. Customers also can use Dell's Internet system to track their orders as they go through the chain.[51]

Dell's organizational structure to implement its business model has evolved to what is known as a virtual company, or value web, as shown in Exhibit 8-5. Dell's strategy is to conduct critical activities in-house, while outsourcing non-strategic activities.

The Transnational Corporation (TNC) Network Structure

To address the globalization–localization dilemma, firms that have evolved through the multinational form and the global company are now seeking the advantages of horizontal

EXHIBIT 8-5   Dell's Value Web Model

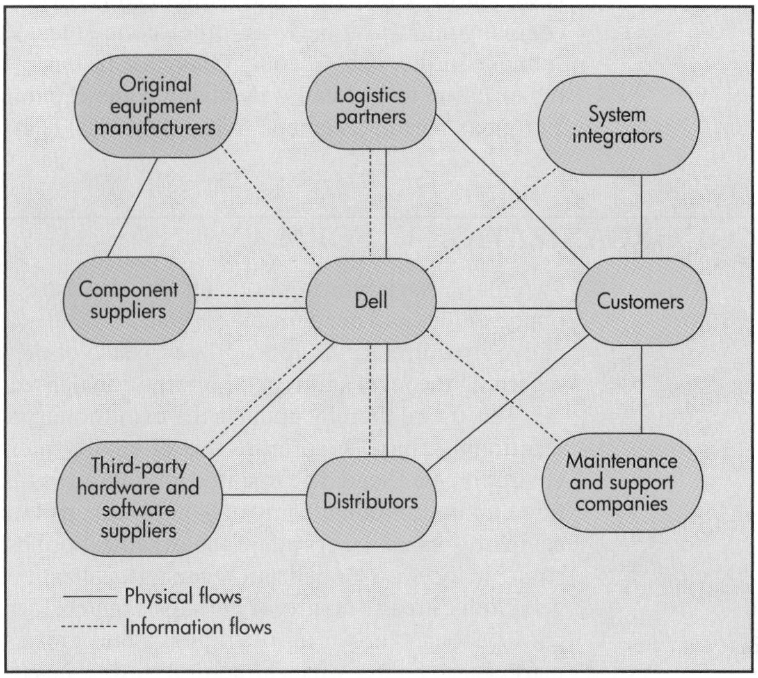

SOURCE: Adapted from Kenneth L. Kraemer and Jason Dedrick, "Dell Computer: Organization of a Global Production Network" (December 1, 2002). Globalization of IT. Paper 255, Center for Research on Information Technology and Organizations, University of California, Irvine.

organization in the pursuit of transnational capability—that is, the ability to manage across national boundaries, retaining local flexibility while achieving global integration.[52] This capability involves linking foreign operations to each other and to headquarters in a flexible way, thereby leveraging local and central capabilities. ABB (Asea Brown Boveri) is an example of such a decentralized horizontal organization. ABB operates in 140 countries with 1,000 companies, with only one management level separating the business units from top management. ABB prides itself on being a truly global company, with 11 board members representing seven nationalities. Thus, this structure is less a matter of boxes on an organizational chart and more a matter of a network of the company's units and their system of horizontal communication. This involves lateral communication across networks of units and alliances rather than in a hierarchy. The system requires the dispersal of responsibility and decision making to local subsidiaries and alliances. The effectiveness of that localized decision making depends a great deal on the ability and willingness to share current and new learning and technology across the network of units.

Whatever the names given to the organizational forms emerging to deal with global competition and logistics, the MNC organizational structure as we know it, with its hierarchical pyramid, subsidiaries, and world headquarters, is gradually evolving into a more fluid form to adapt to strategic and competitive imperatives. Facilitating this change, Kilmann points out, is the information technology explosion fueled by computers, fax machines, teleconferencing, the Internet, and so forth:

> *Competitive companies in the future will be elaborate networks of people and information, each exerting an influence on the other. [These networks will comprise] a small hub of staff connected to each other by their physical proximity, which is electronically connected to global associates who help control assets and negotiate agreements to extend the company's business influence.*[53]

In this new global web, the location of a firm's headquarters is unimportant. It may even be, says Reich, "a suite of rooms in an office park near an international airport—a communications center where many of the web's threads intersect."[54] The web is woven by decisions made by managers around the world, both decisions within the company and those between other companies. Various alliances tie together units and subunits in the web. Corning Glass, for instance, changed from its national pyramidlike organization to a global web, giving it the capability of making optical cable through its European partner, Siemens AG, and medical equipment with Ciba-Geigy.[55]

CHOICE OF ORGANIZATIONAL FORM

Two major variables in choosing the structure and design of an organization are the opportunities and need for (1) globalization and (2) localization. Exhibit 8-6 depicts alternative structural forms appropriate to each of these variables and to the strategic choices regarding the level and type of international involvement desired by the firm.

This figure thereby updates the evolutionary stages model to reflect alternative organizational responses to more recent environments and to the anticipated competitive environments ahead. The updated model shows that, as the firm progresses from a domestic to an international company—and perhaps later to a multinational and then a global company—its managers adapt the organizational structure to accommodate their relative strategic focus on globalization versus localization, choosing a global product structure, a geographic area structure, or perhaps a matrix form. The model proposes that, as the company becomes larger, more complex, and more sophisticated in its approach to world markets (no matter which structural route it has taken), it may evolve into a transnational corporation (TNC). The TNC strategy is to maximize opportunities for both efficiency and local responsiveness by adopting a transnational structure that uses alliances, networks, and horizontal design formats. The relationships between choice of global strategy and the appropriate structural variations necessary to implement each strategic choice are further illustrated in Exhibit 8-7.

EXHIBIT 8-6 Organizational Alternatives and Development for Global Companies

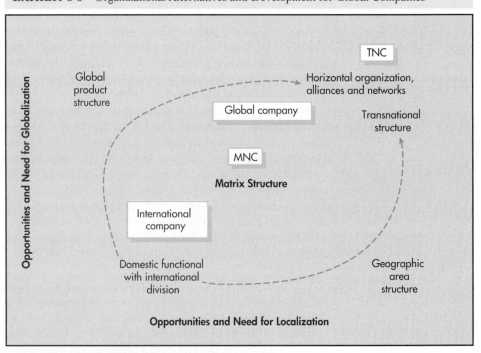

SOURCE: Based on models by R. E. White and T. A. Poynter, "Organizing for Worldwide Advantage," *Business Quarterly* 54 (Summer 1989); John M. Stopford and Louis T. Wells, Jr., *Managing the Multinational Enterprise* (New York: Basic Books, 1972); and C. A. Bartlett, "Organizing and Controlling MNCs," *Harvard Business School Case Study*, no. 9 (March 1987): 365, 375.

EXHIBIT 8-7   Global Strategy–Structure Relationships

	Multidomestic Strategy	International Strategy	Globalization Strategy	Transnational Strategy
	Low ←——→ Need for Coordination ←——→ High			
	Low ←——→ Bureaucratic Costs ←——→ High			
Centralization of authority	Decentralized to national unit	Core competencies centralized; others decentralized to national units	Centralized at optimal global location	Simultaneously centralized and decentralized
Horizontal differentiation	Global area structure	International division structure	Global product group structure	Global matrix structure "Matrix in the Mind"
Need for complex integrating mechanisms	Low	Medium	High	Very high
Organizational culture	Not important	Quite important	Important	Very important

SOURCE: C. W. L. Hill and E. R. Jones, *Strategic Management: An Integrated Approach*, 3rd ed., p. 390. Copyright © 1995 by Houghton Mifflin Company. Reprinted with Permission.

Organizational Change and Design Variables

When a company makes drastic changes in its goals, strategy, or scope of operations, it will usually also need a change in organizational structure. However, other, less obvious indications of organizational inefficiency also signal a need for structural changes: conflicts among divisions and subsidiaries over territories or customers, conflicts between overseas units and headquarters staff, complaints regarding overseas customer service, and overlapping responsibilities are some of these warning signals. Exhibit 8-8 lists some indications of the need for change in organizational design.

At persistent signs of ineffective work, a company should analyze its organizational design, systems, and work flow for the possible causes of those problems. The nature and extent of any design changes must reflect the magnitude of the problem. In choosing a new organizational design or modifying an existing structure, managers must establish a system of communication and control that will provide for effective decision making. At such times, managers need to localize decision making and integrate widely dispersed and disparate global operations.

Besides determining the behavior of the organization on a macro level (in terms of what the different divisions, subsidiaries, departments, and units are responsible for), the organizational design must determine behavior on a micro level. For example, the organizational design affects the level at which certain types of decisions will be made. Determining how many and what types of decisions can be made and by whom can have drastic consequences; both the locus and the scope of authority must be carefully considered. This centralization–decentralization variable actually represents a continuum. In the real world, companies are neither totally centralized nor totally decentralized: The level of centralization imposed is a matter of degree. Exhibit 8-9 illustrates this centralization–decentralization continuum and the different ways that decision making can be shared between headquarters and local units or subsidiaries. In general, centralized decision making is common for some functions (finance, research and development) that are organized for the entire corporation, whereas other functions (production, marketing, sales) are more appropriately decentralized. Two key issues are the speed with which the decisions have to be made and whether they primarily affect only a certain subsidiary or other parts of the company as well.

As noted, culture is another factor that complicates decisions on how much to decentralize and how to organize the work flow and the various relationships of authority and responsibility. Part IV more fully presents how cultural variables affect people's attitudes about working relationships and about who should have authority over whom. At this point, it is important merely to note that cultural variables must be taken into account

EXHIBIT 8-8   When Is Change Needed?

- A change in the size of the corporation—due to growth, consolidation, or reduction
- A change in key individuals—which may alter management objectives, interests, and abilities
- A failure to meet goals, capitalize on opportunities, or be innovative
- An inability to get things done on time
- A consistently overworked top management that spends excessive hours on the job
- A belief that costs are extravagant or that budgets are not being met
- Morale problems
- Lengthy hierarchies that inhibit the exercise of strategic control
- Planning that has become increasingly staff-driven and is thus divorced from line management
- Innovation that is stifled by too much administration and monitoring of details
- Uniform solutions that are applied to nonuniform situations. The extreme opposite of this condition—when things that should or could function in a routine manner do not—should also be heeded as a warning. In other words, management by exception has replaced standard operating procedures

The following are a few specific indicators of *international* organizational malaise:

- A shift in the operational scope—perhaps from directing export activities to controlling overseas manufacturing and marketing units, a change in the size of operations on a country, regional, or worldwide basis, or failure of foreign operations to grow in accordance with plans and expectations.
- Clashes among divisions, subsidiaries, or individuals over territories or customers in the field
- Divisive conflicts between overseas units and domestic division staff or corporate staff
- Instances wherein centralization leads to a flood of detailed data that is neither fully understood nor properly used by headquarters
- Duplication of administrative personnel and services
- Underutilization of overseas manufacturing or distribution facilities
- Duplication of sales offices and specialized sales account executives
- Proliferation of relatively small legal entities or operating units within a country or geographic area
- An increase in overseas customer service complaints
- Breakdowns in communications within and among organizations
- Unclear lines of reporting and dotted-line relationships, and ill-defined executive responsibilities

SOURCE: Business International Corporation, *New Directions in Multinational Corporate Organization* (New York: Business International Corporation, 1981).

EXHIBIT 8-9   Locus of Decision Making in an International Organization

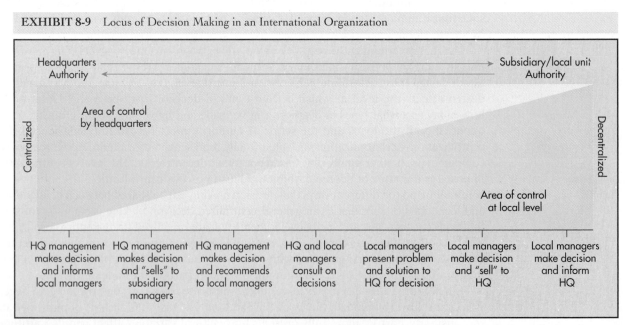

SOURCE: Based on and adapted from R. Tannenbaum and W. Schmidt; and A. G. Kefelas, *Global Business Strategy* (Cincinnati: South-Western, 1990).

when designing an organization. Delegating a high level of authority to employees in a country where workers usually regard "the boss" as the rightful person to make all the decisions is not likely to work well. Clearly, managers must think through the interactions of organizational, staffing, and cultural issues before making final decisions.

In summary, no one way to organize is best. Contingency theory applies to organizational design as much as to any other aspect of management. The best organizational structure is the one that facilitates the firm's goals and is appropriate to its industry, size, technology, and competitive environment. Structure should be fluid and dynamic—and highly adaptable to the changing needs of the company. The structure should not be allowed to get bogged down in the administrative heritage of the organization (that is, "the way we do things around here" or "what we've always done") to the point that it undermines the very processes that will enable the firm to take advantage of new opportunities.

Most likely, however, the future for MNC structure lies in a global web of networked companies. Ideally, a company tries to organize in a way that will allow it to carry out its strategic goals; the staffing is then done to mesh with those strategic goals and the way the organizational structure has been set up. In reality, however, the existing structural factors often affect strategic decisions, so the end result may be a trade-off of desired strategy with existing constraints. So, too, with staffing: "Ideal" staffing plans have to be adjusted to reflect the realities of assigning managers from various sources and the local regulations or cultural variables that make some organizing and staffing decisions more workable than others.

What may at first seem a linear management process of deciding on strategy, then on structure, and finally on staffing is actually an interdependent set of factors that must be taken into consideration and worked out as a set of decisions. Chapter 9 explores how staffing decisions are—or should be—intricately intertwined with other decisions regarding strategy, structure, and so forth. A unique set of management cadre and skills in a particular location can be a competitive advantage in itself, and so it may be a smart move to build strategic and organizational decisions around that resource rather than risk losing that advantage. The following sections present some other processes that are involved in implementing strategy and are interconnected with coordinating functions through organizational structure.

CONTROL SYSTEMS FOR GLOBAL OPERATIONS

> *The establishment of a single currency makes it possible, for the first time, to establish shared, centralized accounting and administrative systems.*
>
> FRANCESCO CAIO,
> *CEO, Merloni Elettrodomestici*[56]

To complement the organizational structure, the international manager must design efficient coordinating and reporting systems to ensure that actual performance conforms to expected organizational standards and goals. The challenge is to coordinate far-flung operations in vastly different environments with various work processes; rules; and economic, political, legal, and cultural norms. The feedback from the control process and the information systems should signal any necessary change in strategy, structure, or operations in a timely manner. Often the strategy, the coordinating processes, or both need to be changed to reflect conditions in other countries.

Monitoring Systems

The design and application of coordinating and reporting systems for foreign subsidiaries and activities can take any form that management wishes. MNCs usually employ a variety of direct and indirect coordinating and control mechanisms suitable for their organization structure. Some of the typical control methods used for the major organizational structures

EXHIBIT 8-10 Control Mechanisms in MNC Organizational Structures

Multinational Structures	Output Control	Bureaucratic Control	Decision-Making Control	Organization Control
International division structure	Most likely profit control	Must follow company policies	Some centralization possible	Treated like other divisions
Global geographic structure	Profit center most common	Some policies and procedures necessary	Local units have autonomy	Local subsidiary culture often most important
Global product structure	Unit output for supply; sales volume for sales	Tight process controls for product quality and consistency	Centralized at product division headquarters	Possible for some companies but not always necessary
Transnational network structure	Used for supplier units and some independent profit centers	Less important	Few decisions centralized at headquarters; more decisions centralized in key network nodes	Organizational culture transcends national cultures; supports sharing and learning; the most important control mechanism

SOURCE: Adapted from John B. Cullen, *Multinational Management: A Strategic Approach,* 2nd ed. (Cincinnati: South-Western, 1999), 329.

discussed here are shown in Exhibit 8-10. These are self-explanatory. For example, in the transnational network structure, decision-making control is centralized to key network nodes, greatly reducing emphasis on bureaucratic control. Output control in this exhibit refers to the assessment of a subsidiary or unit based only on the results attained. Other specific mechanisms are summarized in the next sections.

Direct Coordinating Mechanisms

Direct mechanisms that provide the basis for the overall guidance and management of foreign operations include the design of appropriate structures (discussed previously in this chapter) and the use of effective staffing practices (discussed in Chapter 9). Such decisions proactively set the stage for operations to meet goals, rather than troubleshooting deviations or problems after they have occurred. When McDonald's first opened its doors in Moscow in 1990, the biggest control problem was that of quality control for its food products. McDonald's anticipated that challenge and adopted a strategy of vertical integration for its sourcing of raw materials.[57] To control the quality, distribution, and reliability of its ingredients, McDonald's built a $40 million, 110,000-square-foot plant in a Moscow suburb to process the required beef, milk, buns, vegetables, sauces, and potatoes. In addition, the company brought the managers to Toronto, Canada, for five months of training.[58] Top management at McDonald's anticipated difficulties with the setup and daily operations of this IJV and, indeed, had been working toward the opening day for 13 years. Through careful planning for the control of crucial operational factors, they solved the sourcing, distribution, and employment problems inherent in the former Soviet Union.[59]

Other direct mechanisms are visits by head-office personnel and regular meetings. Top executives from headquarters may use periodic visits to subsidiaries to check performance, troubleshoot, and help to anticipate future problems. International Telephone and Telegraph Corporation (ITT) holds monthly management meetings at its New York headquarters. Performance data are submitted by each ITT subsidiary general manager from around the world, and problems and solutions are shared.[60] The meetings allow each general manager to keep in touch with her or his associates, with the overall mission and strategy of the organization, and with comparative performance data and new problem-solving techniques. Increasingly, the tools of technology are being applied as direct mechanisms to ensure up front that operations will be carried out as planned, in particular in countries where processes such as efficient infrastructure and goods forwarding cannot be taken for granted. An example of this is the logistics monitoring system set up by Air Express International in Latin America to minimize its many problems there.[61]

Indirect Coordinating Mechanisms

Indirect coordinating mechanisms typically include sales quotas, budgets, and other financial tools, as well as feedback reports, which give information about the sales and financial performance of the subsidiary for the last quarter or year.

Domestic companies invariably rely on budgets and financial statement analyses, but for foreign subsidiaries, financial statements and performance evaluations are complicated by *financial variables in MNC reports,* such as exchange rates, inflation levels, transfer prices, and accounting standards.

To reconcile accounting statements, MNCs usually require three different sets of financial statements from subsidiaries. One set must meet the national accounting standards and procedures prescribed by law in the host country. This set also aids management in comparing subsidiaries in the same country. A second set must be prepared according to the accounting principles and standards required by the home country. This set allows some comparison with other MNC subsidiaries. The third set of statements translates the second set of statements (with certain adjustments) into the currency of the home country for consolidation purposes, in accordance with FASB Ruling Number 52 of 1982. A foreign subsidiary's financial statements must be consolidated line by line with those of the parent company, according to International Accounting Standard Number 3, adopted in the United States.[62]

Researchers have noted comparative differences between the use of direct versus **indirect controls** among companies headquartered in different countries. One study by Egelhoff examined the practices of 50 U.S., U.K., and European MNCs over their foreign subsidiaries. It compared the use of two mechanisms—the assignment of parent-company managers to foreign subsidiaries and the use of performance reporting systems (that is, comparing behavior mechanisms with output reporting systems).[63] The results of this study show that considerable differences exist in practices across MNC nationalities. For example, says Egelhoff, U.S. MNCs monitor subsidiary outputs and rely more on frequently reported performance data than do European MNCs. The latter tend to assign more parent-company nationals to key positions in foreign subsidiaries and can count on a higher level of behavior control than their U.S. counterparts.[64]

These findings imply that the U.S. system, which measures more quantifiable aspects of a foreign subsidiary, provides the means to compare performance among subsidiaries. The European system, on the other hand, measures more qualitative aspects of a subsidiary and its environment, which vary among subsidiaries—allowing a focus on the unique situation of the subsidiary but making it difficult to compare its performance to other subsidiaries.[65]

MANAGING EFFECTIVE MONITORING SYSTEMS

Management practices, local constraints, and expectations regarding authority, time, and communication are but a few of the variables likely to affect the **appropriateness of monitoring (or control) systems**. The degree to which headquarters' practices and goals are transferable probably depends on whether top managers are from the head office, the host country, or a third country. In addition, information systems and evaluation variables must all be considered when deciding on appropriate systems.

The Appropriateness of Monitoring and Reporting Systems

One example of differences in the expectations regarding monitoring practices, and therefore in the need for coordination systems, is indicated by a study of Japanese and U.S. firms. Ueno and Sekaran state that their research shows that "the U.S. companies, compared to the Japanese companies, tend to use communication and coordination more extensively, build budget slack to a greater extent, and use long-term performance evaluations to a lesser extent."[66] Furthermore, Ueno and Sekaran conclude that those differences in reporting systems are attributable to the cultural variable of individualism in U.S. society, compared to collectivism in Japanese society. For example, U.S. managers are more likely to use formal communication and coordination processes, whereas Japanese managers use informal and implicit processes. In addition, U.S. managers, who are evaluated on individual performance, are more likely to build slack into budget calculations for a safety net than their Japanese counterparts, who are evaluated on group performance. The implications of this study are that managers around the world who understand the cultural bases for differences in control practices will be more flexible in working with those systems in other countries.

The Role of Information Systems

Reporting systems, such as those described in this chapter, require sophisticated information systems to enable them to work properly—not only for competitive purposes but also for purposes of performance evaluation. Top management must receive accurate and timely information regarding sales, production, and financial results to be able to compare actual performance with goals and to take corrective action where necessary. Most international reporting systems require information feedback at one level or another for financial, personnel, production, and marketing variables.

The specific types of functional reports, their frequency, and the amount of detail required from subsidiaries by headquarters will vary. Neghandi and Welge surveyed the types of functional reports submitted by 117 MNCs in Germany, Japan, and the United States.[67] They found that U.S. MNCs typically submit about double the number of reports than do German and Japanese MNCs, with the exception of performance reviews. German MNCs submit a few more reports than do Japanese MNCs. U.S. MNCs thus seem to monitor much more via specific functional reports than do German and Japanese MNCs. The Japanese MNCs put far less emphasis on personnel performance reviews than do the U.S. and German MNCs—a finding consistent with the Japanese culture of group decision making, consensus, and responsibility.

Unfortunately, the accuracy and timeliness of information systems are often less than perfect, especially in less developed countries, where managers typically operate under conditions of extreme uncertainty. Government information, for example, is often filtered or fabricated; other sources of data for decision making are usually limited. Employees are not used to the kinds of sophisticated information generation, analysis, and reporting systems common in developed countries. Their work norms and sense of necessity and urgency may also confound the problem. In addition, the hardware technology and the ability to manipulate and transmit data are usually limited. The **MIS adequacy** in foreign affiliates is a sticky problem for headquarters managers in their attempt to maintain efficient coordination of activities and consolidation of results. Another problem is the **noncomparability of performance data across countries**—the control problem caused by the difficulty of comparing performance data across various countries because of the variables that make that information appear different—which hinders the evaluation process.

The Internet has, of course, made the availability and use of information attainable instantaneously. Many companies are starting to supply Internet MIS systems for supply-chain management. European partners Nestlé S.A. and Danone Group, world leaders in the food industry, set up Europe's first Internet marketplace for e-procurement in the consumer goods sector, called CPGmarket.com:

> *CPGmarket.com will enhance the efficiency of logistics while at the same time reducing procurement costs for businesses producing, distributing and selling consumer goods. CPG (based on mySAP.com e-business platform) allows companies not only to buy and sell, but also to access industry information. . . . Participants will benefit from a more efficient market, reducing costs through higher transaction efficiency and simplified processes.*[68]

Evaluation Variables Across Countries

A major problem that arises when evaluating the performance of foreign affiliates is the tendency by headquarters managers to judge subsidiary managers as if all of the evaluation data were comparable across countries. Unfortunately, many variables can make the evaluation information from one country look very different from that of another country, owing to circumstances beyond the control of a subsidiary manager. For example, one country may experience considerable inflation, significant fluctuations in the price of raw materials, political uprisings, or governmental actions. These factors are beyond the manager's control and are likely to have a downward effect on profitability—and yet, that manager may, in fact, have maximized the opportunity for long-term stability and profitability compared with a manager of another subsidiary who was not faced with such adverse conditions. Other variables influencing profitability patterns include transfer pricing, currency devaluation, exchange-rate fluctuations, taxes, and expectations of contributions to local economies.

One way to ensure more meaningful performance measures is to adjust the financial statements to reflect the uncontrollable variables peculiar to each country where a subsidiary is located. This provides a basis for the true evaluation of the comparative return on investment (ROI), which is an overall control measure. Another way to provide meaningful, long-term performance standards is to take into account other nonfinancial measures. These measures include market share, productivity, sales, relations with the host-country government, public image, employee morale, union relations, and community involvement.[69]

CONCLUSION

The structure, control, and coordination *processes* are the same whether they take place in a domestic company, a multinational company with a network of foreign affiliates, or a specific IJV. It is the extent, the focus, and the mechanisms used to organize those activities that differ. More coordination is needed in global companies because of uncertain working environments and information systems and because of the variable loci of decision making. Headquarters managers must design appropriate systems to take into account those variables and to evaluate performance.

Summary of Key Points

1. An organization must be designed to facilitate the implementation of strategic goals. Other variables to consider when designing an organization's structure include environmental conditions, the size of the organization, and the appropriate technology. The geographic dispersion of operations as well as differences in time, language, and culture affect structure in the international context.

2. The design of a firm's structure reflects its international entry strategy and tends to change over time with growth and increasing levels of investment, diversity, or both.

3. Global trends are exerting increasing pressure on MNCs to achieve economies of scale through globalization. This involves rationalization and the coordination of strategic alliances.

4. MNCs can be regarded as interorganizational networks of their own dispersed operations and other strategic alliances. Such relational networks may adopt unique structures for their particular environment, while also requiring centralized coordination.

5. The transnational structure allows a company to "be global and act local" by using networks of decentralized units with horizontal communication. This permits local flexibility while achieving global integration.

6. Indications of the need for structural changes include inefficiency, conflicts among units, poor communication, and overlapping responsibilities.

7. Coordinating and monitoring systems are necessary to regulate organizational activities so that actual performance conforms to expected organizational standards and goals. MNCs use a variety of direct and indirect controls.

8. Financial monitoring and evaluation of foreign affiliates are complicated by variables such as exchange rates, levels of inflation, transfer prices, and accounting standards.

9. The design of appropriate monitoring systems must take into account local constraints, management practices and expectations, uncertain information systems, and variables in the evaluation process.

10. Two major problems in reporting for subsidiaries must be considered: (1) inadequate management information systems and (2) the noncomparability across countries of the performance data needed for evaluation purposes.

Discussion Questions

1. What variables have to be considered in designing the organizational structure for international operations? How do these variables interact, and which do you think are most important?
2. Explain the need for an MNC to "be global and act local." How can a firm design its organization to enable this?
3. What is a transnational organization? Since many large MNCs are moving toward this format, it is likely that you could at some point be working within this structure. How do you feel about that?
4. Discuss the implications of the relative centralization of authority and decision making at headquarters versus local units or subsidiaries. How would you feel about this variable if you were a subsidiary manager?
5. As an international manager, what would make you suggest restructuring your firm? What other means of direct and indirect monitoring systems do you suggest?
6. What is the role of information systems in the reporting process? Discuss the statement "Inadequate MIS systems in some foreign affiliates are a control problem for MNCs."

Application Exercises

1. If you have personal access to a company with international operations, try to conduct some interviews and find out about the personal interactions involved in working with the organization's counterparts abroad. In particular, ask questions about the nature and level of authority and decision making in overseas units compared with headquarters. What kinds of conflicts are experienced? What changes would your interviewees recommend?
2. Do some research on monitoring and reporting issues facing an MNC with subsidiaries in (1) India and (2) the former East Germany. Discuss problem areas and your recommendations to the MNC management as to how to control potential problems.
3. Find out about an IJV in the United States. Get some articles from the library, write to the company for information, and if possible visit the company and ask questions. Present your findings on the company's major control issues to the class—both at the beginning of the venture and now. What is the company doing differently in its control process compared to a typical domestic operation? Are the control procedures having the desired results? What recommendations do you have?

Experiential Exercise

In groups of four, consider a fast-food chain going into Eastern Europe. Decide on your initial level of desired international involvement and your entry strategy. Draw up an appropriate organizational design, taking into account strategic goals, relevant variables in the particular countries in which you will have operations, technology used, size of the firm, and so on. At the next class, present your organization chart and describe the operations and rationale. (You could finalize the chart on an overhead or flip chart before class begins.) What are some of the major control issues to be considered?

Internet Resources

Visit the Deresky Companion Website at prenhall.com/deresky for this chapter's Internet resources.

Case Study

Asea Brown Boveri (ABB), Sweden (2007): What Went Wrong?

Since its inception, Asea Brown Boveri (hereafter called ABB) has always attracted the business and academic community because of its unique organizational structure, consistent growth pattern, and extensive worldwide operations.[1] After the merger of Asea and Brown, Boveri and Cie (BBC), ABB had an excellent international expansion. Academics and business practitioners studying multinational corporations (MNCs) and global companies often admired ABB because of its outstanding growth, highly sophisticated management, and peculiar corporate structure.[2] ABB particularly became famous for its unique decentralized horizontal organizational system and global networking, which was based on lateral communication across the company's 1,000 entities around the globe.[3] The phrase "think global, act local" became synonymous with ABB and its former chairman, Percy Barnevik, who aggressively advocated and practiced the concept in the company.[4] ABB continues to be a global leader in the areas of power and automation technologies although the company's corporate image has been affected because of heavy losses in 2001 and 2002. In 2005 ABB's revenues surpassed $22 billion, $2 billion

more than the previous year. In 2007, the ABB Group has operations in over 100 countries, employs 107,000 people worldwide, and is listed on the stock exchanges of Zurich, Stockholm, London, Frankfurt, and New York.[5] The company is headquartered in Zurich. In the last five years, ABB has not been able to achieve the same growth and expansion because of changing markets and slow demand.

The ABB Group has over 115 years of rich history dating back to the late 1800s. The Group was formed in 1988 when Asea AB of Västerås, Sweden, and BBC Brown Boveri Limited of Baden, Switzerland, merged their operations and formed ABB (Asea Brown Boveri) Limited. Each company held 50 percent of the new entity and was headquartered in Zurich, Switzerland. The merger was highly rated by the media because of Europe's 1992 economic integration. In 1883, Ludvig Fredholm founded Elektriska Aktiebolaget in Stockholm that in 1890 merged with Wenstroms and Granstroms Elektriska Kraftbolag to form Asea (Allmanna Svenska Elektriska Aktiebolaget). In the next 50 years, Asea grew from an unknown company to an international entity having subsidiaries in Great Britain, Denmark, Finland, and Spain. The company became famous for its transmission lines, generators, transformers, locomotives, and motors.[6]

BBC was founded by Charles E. L. Brown and Walter Boveri in Baden, Switzerland, in 1891. By the early 1900s, BBC had its operations in Austria, Germany, Italy, and Norway. Like Asea, BBC manufactured power plants, turbines, transformers, hydroelectric power stations, locomotives, and other industrial products. The company invented many new technologies and set the pace for the power generation industry. Before merging with Asea, BBC was operating globally and employed 97,000 workers worldwide.[7] Under the leadership of its former chairman Percy Barnevik, the company launched a massive global expansion program because of growing demand, especially in East Asia and Eastern Europe. Between 1993 and 1998, ABB continued to grow in

SOURCE: Written exclusively for this book by Syed Tariq Anwar, Copyright © Syed Tariq Anwar. Updated by Helen Deresky in 2007.

An earlier version of this case was presented by Syed Tariq Anwar at the 2004 Academy of International Business Annual Conference, Stockholm, Sweden, July 10–13, 2004.

The material in this case is intended to be used as a basis for classroom/academic discussion rather than to illustrate either effective or ineffective handling of a managerial situation or business practices.

[1] See company Web site (www.abb.com).

[2] For more information, see *The Asian Wall Street Journal*. (1995). "U.S. power provider ABB profits from localization," (May 22), p. 4; *The Asian Wall Street Journal*. (1996). "Swiss-Swedish ABB is among Europe's leaders in looking to Asia for continued revenue growth," (March 4), p. 19; Belanger, Jacques et al. (editors). (1999). *Being local worldwide: ABB and the challenge of global management*, New York: Cornell University Press; Berggren, Christian. (1996). "Building a truly global organization? ABB and the problems of integrating a multi-domestic enterprise," *Scandinavian Journal of Management*, 12 (2), pp. 123–137.

[3] For detail, see Deresky, Helen. (2003). *International Management: Managing Across Borders and Cultures*, Upper Saddle River, New Jersey: Prentice Hall, p. 305; Kotabe, Masaaki and Kristiaan, Helsen. (2004). *Global Marketing Management*, New York: John Wiley & Sons, pp. 549–550.

[4] Burham, K. and Heimer, C. (1998). *ABB—the dancing giant*, London, UK: Financial Times/Pitman Publishing.

[5] For more information, see company Web site (www.abb.com); *Forbes*. (2004). "The world's 2000 leading companies, (April 12), pp. 144–220; *Value Line*. (2002). "Machinery industry," (August 2): p. 1331; *The Wall Street Journal*. (2003). "The great asbestos swindle," (January 6), p. A18; *The Wall Street Journal*. (2003). "How 'Europe's GE' and its star CEO tumbled to earth," (January 23), pp. A1 & A8.

[6] See company Web site (www.abb.com).

[7] See company Web site (www.abb.com).

Europe, Asia, and Latin America by seeking acquisitions, alliances, and joint ventures that helped the company to consolidate its position in world markets. The year 1998 was particularly important for ABB when it acquired Elsag Bailey Process Automation. The acquisition made ABB a major player in the global automation market.

ABB's current history and corporate profile are incomplete without discussing its two former high-ranking officers, Percy Barnevik (chairman) and Goeran Lindahl (chief executive), who left the company in 2001. Both were criticized by the world media over their generous pension payments received from ABB after departing the company. Barnevik alone received over $87 million in pension benefits. Interestingly, during the same year, ABB lost $691 million. In addition, the company's U.S. subsidiary was sued for asbestos liabilities. Since Barnevik coordinated the merger between Asea and Brown Boveri, he was highly admired by the analysts because of his corporate foresight and making ABB one of the best global companies in the world.[8] In the late 1990s, Barnevik was known as another Jack Welch (former CEO of General Electric) because of his leadership, star image, and global vision.[9] Jürgen Dormann, the current CEO who worked for Aventis, took over the company in September 2002 and has brought a multitude of structural changes to avoid bankruptcy. Although ABB lost $691 million in 2001 and $161 million in 2002, it earned a net profit of $108 million in 2003.[10]

What Went Wrong with ABB's Organizational Structure?

Global companies formulate their organizational structures on the basis of location, market coverage, competition, and product lines. Like other companies, ABB was severely impacted by the East Asian crisis. The region's currency depreciations and weaker economies had an adverse affect that brought massive reductions in the company's revenues. In addition to the East Asian crisis, ABB's own corporate blunders, complex organizational structure, and reshuffling of the top management added miseries to the company. The net result was a major financial downfall that affected the company's market value, growth, and global operations. ABB's organizational problems and missteps that led to the negative image, lost market share, and corporate retrenchment are as follows:

1. **Global diversifications and internationalization issues:** In the 1990s, ABB expanded operations and sought internationalization at a very fast pace. The company established hundreds of subsidiaries worldwide that included power/electrical equipment, oil, gas and petrochemicals, automation technologies, and other heavy industries. During the tenure of Barnevik, ABB became highly infatuated with global expansion that eventually brought losses and corporate problems.[11] ABB was famous for its unique matrix structure at the global level. In the 1970s and 1980s, many companies capitalized on the matrix structure that was thought to be highly efficient at the multidimensional and global levels.[12] In the initial stages, companies benefited because of the matrix's economies of scale, innovative operations, lateral personal communications, and transfer of resources. The weaknesses of the matrix system were found in the areas of authority and chain of command that led to ambiguity and increased costs.[13] Likewise, ABB encountered problems in its matrix structure and had difficulty materializing its goals at the global level (see Figure 1).

2. **Leadership gaps and performance issues:** In 2002, ABB started to see the impact of the East Asian crisis and weaker demand from other parts of the world. In addition, ABB's organizational structure and control system made things even worse. This resulted in major restructuring and changes in its top management. From 2000 to 2003, the Group undertook significant corporate changes that led to unloading the company's financial services and oil and gas divisions. ABB had somewhat recovered in 2004 by restructuring its power and automation technology divisions. Barnevik did an excellent job in the 1990s regarding internationalizing ABB. After a period of rapid growth, Barnevik's leadership and management style became ineffective and controversial because of ABB's far-flung operations, complex organizational structure, and widespread international subsidiaries. During Barnevik's long tenure with ABB, the company had no plan of succession. In addition, ABB's top management actively sought decentralization while keeping its global matrix structure in many markets. This impacted the company's performance, eventually leading to losses.

[8]For more discussion, see Barth, Steve. (1998). "World trade's executive of the decade," *World Trade Magazine,* (December), pp. 1–7, (www.global-insight.com); *Financial Times.* (1998). "All the power but none of the glory", (August 24), p. 7; *Financial Times.* (2001). "Foundations look shady on the house that Percy built," (September 18), p. 24.
[9]*The Economist.* (1988). "Asea-Brown Boveri! Power play," (May 28), pp. 19–22.
[10]*Business Week.* (2002). "Barnevik's fall from grace," (March 25), p. 1; *Business Week.* (2002). "Making a federal case out of overseas abuses," (November 25), p. 78.

[11]For more information, see *Financial Times.* (1997). "A multinational cadre of managers is the key," (October 8), p. 10; *Financial Times.* (2002). "How a toxic mixture of asbestos liabilities and plummeting demand poisoned an industrial powerhouse," (October 23), p. 13; *The Wall Street Journal.* (2003). "How 'Europe's GE' and its star CEO tumbled to earth," (January 23), pp. A1 & A8; *The Wall Street Journal.* (2003). "ABB U.S. unit files for chapter 11, cites asbestos claimants," (February 18), p. A19.
[12]Agthe, Klaus E. (1990). "Managing the mixed marriage," *Business Horizons,* 33 (1), pp. 37–43.
[13]For detail, see Kearney, A. T. (2002). *Waging war on complexity: How to master the matrix organizational structure*, Chicago, Illinois: A. T. Kearney, Inc.

FIGURE 1   ABB's Old Versus New Corporate Strategy and Organizational Models During the Tenures of CEOs Percy Barnevik and Jürgen Dormann (1988–2004) and Fred Kindle (2005 on)

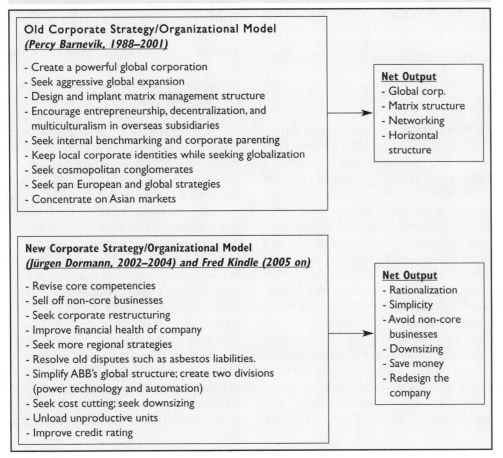

Old Corporate Strategy/Organizational Model
(Percy Barnevik, 1988–2001)

- Create a powerful global corporation
- Seek aggressive global expansion
- Design and implant matrix management structure
- Encourage entrepreneurship, decentralization, and multiculturalism in overseas subsidiaries
- Seek internal benchmarking and corporate parenting
- Keep local corporate identities while seeking globalization
- Seek cosmopolitan conglomerates
- Seek pan European and global strategies
- Concentrate on Asian markets

Net Output
- Global corp.
- Matrix structure
- Networking
- Horizontal structure

New Corporate Strategy/Organizational Model
(Jürgen Dormann, 2002–2004) and Fred Kindle (2005 on)

- Revise core competencies
- Sell off non-core businesses
- Seek corporate restructuring
- Improve financial health of company
- Seek more regional strategies
- Resolve old disputes such as asbestos liabilities.
- Simplify ABB's global structure; create two divisions (power technology and automation)
- Seek cost cutting; seek downsizing
- Unload unproductive units
- Improve credit rating

Net Output
- Rationalization
- Simplicity
- Avoid non-core businesses
- Downsizing
- Save money
- Redesign the company

SOURCES: *Business Week; The Economist; Financial Times; The Wall Street Journal* (various issues).

3. **East-Asian financial crisis:** The East Asian financial crisis was triggered by China's devaluation of the yuan and later spread to other parts of East Asia. In the 1990s, East Asia's economic health was solid and the region had started a variety of infrastructural projects. ABB was one of the major beneficiaries of the Asian development. After the crisis, large industrial conglomerates like ABB with extensive involvement in the region were unable to deal with the changing markets. Cancellations of projects that led to heavy losses and downsizing were the end result. ABB could not recover from the East Asian crisis and saw its revenues dry up in the region that led to a total loss of over $1 billion in 2001/2002.

4. **Controversy over pension benefits:** In the last few years, CEO salaries and their exorbitant pension benefits have been severely criticized by the media. Company executives from Enron, World Com, ImClone, and others have been sent to jail for mishandling company money and unethical behavior. In 2002, Barnevik became part of the controversy when it was discovered that he had received pension benefits from ABB worth $87 million. This was major negative publicity for the company when it lost over $500 million during the same period.

5. **Issues of asbestos-related liabilities:** Like other companies, ABB was also hit hard by massive asbestos claims because of the U.S. Combustion Engineering Unit the company acquired in 1990. In 2003, ABB allocated $1.2 billion to deal with these claims. In 2003, in the U.S. alone, 90,000 new asbestos claims were filed, raising the corporate liability to U.S. plaintiffs to about $200 billion. According to a survey published by Rand Institute of Civil Justice, in the coming years there could be another 2.4 million workers affected by the asbestos-related crisis, making new claims of $200 billion.[14] ABB has allocated a significant contingency fund to deal with the current and future asbestos claims. The asbestos issue was a major setback to ABB's global restructuring and recovery.

6. **Changing global competition:** Global competition in the power plants and other heavy industry has changed in the last ten years. At the time of the Asea and BBC merger, markets were booming in the Asian region. For a long

---

[14]*Fortune.* (2002). "The $200 billion miscarriage of justice," (March 4), pp. 154–170.

time, ABB maintained a strong presence in the industry because of its unique organizational structure and worldwide operations. As of 2007, there tends to be more competition in the industry and some of the large market opportunities have disappeared. Like other industries, power plants and infrastructural industries were affected by factors that ABB could not control.

What Lies Ahead?

ABB continues to make changes in its top leadership as well as in its organizational structure. As of 2005, Fred Kindle is the new CEO.[15] The company conducted a thorough evaluation of its global operations and core competencies. ABB continues to re-fetch its global growth by being more proactive in its regional growth. For example, the company seems more realistic in its core operations, and non-core assets such as oil, gas, and petrochemicals have been unloaded to deal with current financial problems. ABB has cut over 12,000 jobs worldwide to streamline the operations and continues to deal with its asbestos-related liabilities. ABB's poor performance and pension scandals forced management to concentrate on its regional operations. The company redesigned its complex organizational structure and control system based on rationalization, performance, and growth (see Figure 1). The ABB Group in 2007 comprises five divisions, replacing two core divisions by their respective business areas. They are Power Products,

Power Systems, Automation Products, Process Automation, and Robotics. When the new organizational structure was announced in September 2005, ABB's top management had devised a major restructuring plan to sell its oil, gas, and petrochemical division for $925 million.[16] In the coming years, the company will continue to reformulate its core competencies and more corporate changes are expected. Additional corporate rationalization and organizational streamlining is possible if ABB sees recovery in its global markets.

In conclusion, ABB is an interesting case study in the areas of organizational structure and control systems. Right from its inception (after the merger in 1988), ABB has been the first-mover company and a market leader in the power and oil and gas industry. Led by its former visionary chairman Barnevik, ABB was highly pragmatic and entrepreneurial in its early growth and global expansion. Regarding organizational structure and control systems, the ABB case is relevant from two areas. First, market leaders may not maintain a strong competitive edge forever. Organizational structures and control systems must conform to the markets and competition. Besides this, the design of the global organizational structure must fit the strategy and the environment. Second, very few MNCs exploit new markets by applying the same organizational structures. In the coming years, it will be interesting to see if ABB can maintain worldwide growth by following its newly devised plan or just keep shedding operations and other subsidiaries.

[15]*Financial Times.* (2004). "ABB surprises with new chief," (March 2), p. 16.

[16]www.ABB.com, accessed November 25, 2006.

CASE QUESTIONS

1. Discuss ABB's position in the global infrastructure industry.
2. Analyze and evaluate ABB's organizational structure and its control systems during the tenures of Percy Barnevik and Jürgen Dormann (see Figure 1). Also, draw a chart to discuss the company's strengths and weaknesses.
3. What specific strategies does ABB need to undertake in the coming years to be a key player in the industry? What structural changes should be made to implement those strategies?
4. What did you learn from ABB's complex organizational structure and its global operations?

Case 7 Dell's Problems in China

Dell eventually needs to reinvent its direct business approach in China if it wants to adapt to the local market.[1]

THOMAS WANG,
Analyst, Analysys International,[2] *in 2005*

There's tremendous growth in the future in China. That is clearly one of the world powers today, and it'll be more so in future. If you want to grow globally, you have to have a large presence in China.[3]

MORT TOPFER,
Former Vice Chairman, Dell Inc., in 2005

INTRODUCTION

In August 2006, David Miller, President of the Chinese operations of U.S.-based Dell Inc. (Dell), the world's leading PC manufacturer, joined Dell China's major competitor, Lenovo. In the same month, four more top executives[4] from Dell China and Dell Asia-Pacific joined Lenovo. Earlier, in December 2005, William Amelio, President, Dell Asia-Pacific and Japan, had joined Lenovo as its CEO. (Refer to Exhibit C7-1 for information on Dell's major competitors in China.)

Industry analysts attributed this exodus of top executives to differences between them and Dell's U.S. headquarters regarding the application of Dell's direct model in China. The Chinese executives wanted to change the model and bring in resellers and distributors. According to Li Chong, an analyst with Analysys International, "Lenovo is now taking a diverse approach to China's PC market, which is geographically complicated. But Dell is still insisting on the purity of its direct model."[5]

By the second quarter of the financial year 2006–07, Dell's market share in China had slipped to 7.5 percent as compared to 8.3 percent in the first quarter, while unit sales grew by 37 percent in the same period. Dell's revenues in China grew by 29 percent in the first quarter of 2006–07 and by 31 percent in the second quarter, in spite of the sluggish global sales. (Refer to Exhibit C7-2 for more information on the top PC vendors in the world in the second quarter of 2006.) Analysts were of the view that though its sales in China were increasing; Dell's business growth in China was slowing down. (Refer to Table C7-1 for market shares of desktop vendors in China in the first and second quarters of 2006–2007.)

Dell entered China in 1995, and was successful in capturing the urban markets and corporate customers. The company was able to use its direct sales model successfully in these markets. By 2004, the urban markets had reached saturation and Dell failed to gauge the increasing demand for computers from smaller towns and rural areas. Chinese companies like Lenovo, Founder, and THTF reached those markets at the right time by launching low-priced products and sprucing up their distribution networks, which Dell failed to do.

Dell was not performing well globally. In the second quarter ending August 4, 2006, Dell reported a drop of 46.4 percent in net income, which fell to US\$502 million as against US\$935 million in the corresponding quarter of the year 2005 (Refer to Table C7-2 for Dell's global quarterly revenue and income figures).

[1]Weitao Li, "Straight Talk," *China Daily,* November 28, 2005.
[2]China-based Analysys International provides data, information, and advice about the technology, media, and telecom industry in China to over 10,000 clients across the world.
[3]"Dell to Build Second China Plant," *American Statesman,* March 25, 2005.
[4]The other executives included Sotaro Amano, Corporate Director, Home and Business Sales, Dell Japan; Gerry Smith, Design Center and Display Unit, Dell Singapore; David Schmoock, Vice President Marketing, Asia Pacific and Japan; and Christopher Askew, Vice President, Dell Service Unit, Asia-Pacific and Japan.
[5]"Dell Faces Exodus of China Executives," *China Daily,* August 17, 2006.

EXHIBIT C7-1 Dell—Major Competitors in China

Lenovo Group Ltd.

Lenovo is the fourth-largest PC manufacturer in the world and the largest in China as of May 2007. Lenovo, formerly known as Legend, was incorporated in Hong Kong in 1988. Lenovo's products include desktops, laptops, servers, handheld computers, and imaging equipment. The company, which was unknown outside China, acquired IBM for US$1.25 billion in May 2005. With this acquisition, Lenovo planned to capture markets in the West. The annual revenues of the company for 2005 were projected at US$13 billion. In March 2004, Lenovo became a partner of the International Olympic Committee, undertaking to provide computer equipment for the 2008 Olympic Games in Beijing.

Founder Holdings Ltd.

Founder is an Asia-Pacific based multinational group, whose subsidiaries are located across Asia. The company's activities cover both computer software and hardware. Founder was developed by a group of individuals from Peking University in 1975. In 2004, the turnover of the company was HK$2,014 million. As against a profit of HK$7,215,000 during 2003, the company recorded a loss of HK$27,183,000 during 2004.

TCL Corporation

Founded in 1981, TCL is a leading manufacturer of electronics in China. One of the fastest-growing companies in China, the company recorded average growth of 42.65 percent for 12 years from the early 1990s. However, the company has had to bear the brunt of severe price competition and erosion. TCL's businesses include multimedia, mobile phones, personal computers, home appliances, electric lighting, and digital products. TCL recorded total revenues of RMB28.2 billion yuan and profit of RMB0.57 billion in 2003.

Tsinghua Tongfang (THTF)

THTF, supplier of IT products and solution plans, recorded total revenues of RMB9.706 billion in the financial year 2004–05. THTF's products include desktop PCs, notebook PCs, and digital and computerized peripheral products. The company is also involved in digital media systems and content, energy and environment engineering, pharmaceuticals, applied nuclear technology, and software application services.

SOURCE: Compiled from various sources.

EXHIBIT C7-2 Top Five Vendors—Worldwide PC Shipments

Vendor	Q2 2006 Shipments (Thousands)	Market Share	Q2 2005 Shipments (Thousands)	Market Share	Growth (Q2) 2006/05
Dell	9,986	19.2%	9,002	19.0%	10.9%
HP	8,272	15.9%	7,320	15.4%	13.0%
Lenovo	4,010	7.7%	3,555	7.5%	12.8%
Acer	2,796	5.4%	2,061	4.3%	35.7%
Fujitsu/ Siemens	1,775	3.4%	1,771	3.7%	0.2%
Others	25,245	48.5%	23,767	50.1%	6.2%

SOURCE: www.idc.com

TABLE C7-1 Desktop Vendors in China—Market Share (Q1 and Q2 2006)

Vendor	Q1 2006	Q2 2006
Lenovo	37.5%	35.4%
Founder	13.7%	14.1%
Tongfag	9.3%	8.9%
Dell	8.3%	7.5%
HP	4.2%	5.2%
TCL	3.1%	3.7%
Others	23.9%	25.2%

SOURCE: Analysys International

BACKGROUND NOTE

In 1983, Michael Dell was a freshman at the University of Texas, Austin. He upgraded IBM-compatible PCs in his spare time. It was not long before he realized that by buying and assembling components he could make cost-effective PCs. This led to the establishment of Dell Computer Corporation (Dell), and its incorporation on May 3, 1984. By the beginning of 1985, Dell was a US$6 million company. Its revenues grew to US$70 million by the end of fiscal 1986–87. Dell introduced support services that included a 24-hour hotline and marketing and sales support teams for its growing business.

TABLE C7-2   Dell Global—Quarterly Revenue and Income Figures
(in million US$)

	Q2 2006	Q1 2006	Q4 2005	Q3 2005	Q2 2005	Q1 2005
Net revenue	14,094	14,216	15,183	13,911	13,428	13,386
Gross margin	2,190	2,472	2,709	2,589	2,499	2,491
Operating income	605	949	1,246	1,196	1,173	1,174
Net income	502	762	1,012	944	935	934

SOURCE: www.dell.com

International forays began in 1987, when Dell ventured into the U.K. market. In 1988, Dell went public and issued 3.5 million shares at US$8.5 each. By 1990–91, Dell's sales stood at US$500 million. In the same year, Dell opened a manufacturing plant in Ireland. In order to cater to small businesses and individual customers, Dell entered the retail channel through agreements with CompUSA, Staples, Best Buy, Costco, Sam's Club, Business Depot, and PC World in the year 1991–92. Its revenues in this year were US$890 million. By 1992–93, the revenues reached US$2 billion. In 1993–94, Dell reported revenues of US$2.8 billion, placing it among the top five PC companies in the world. However, there was a cash crunch in the company, and Dell posted a loss of US$35.8 million in 1993–94, as against profit of US$50.9 million in 1991–92 and US$101.6 million in 1992–93.

At this juncture, Mort Topfer, who had earlier worked in Motorola[6] as President of Land Mobile Products, joined Dell. That was when Dell realized that the use of indirect distribution channels had not been very successful. Standard PCs sold through retail channels could not provide users the advantage of Dell's customization. Though sales through the retail channels were growing, Dell was not making any profit on these sales. In mid 1994, Dell decided to exit from the retail market and go back to its direct sales model.

After re-introducing the direct model, Dell experienced phenomenal growth and sales increased to US$3.5 billion in the fiscal 1994–95, with a 3 percent share in the U.S. market. In July 1996, Dell ventured into selling the computers through the Internet via its Web site www.dell.com. By December 1996, Dell's revenues on the Web stood at US$1 million a day. The Web site initially catered to the needs of the individual customers. Once the order was received, it was sent to a special email box. It was ensured that the order was complete and had all the required details and was then sent to the build-to-order system.[7] Under the system, Dell would begin assembling computers only after receiving all the specifications from the customer. Once the order was placed, customers could log in to check the status of their order.

By 1999, Dell commanded a 16 percent share in the U.S. market. In March 2000, Dell's stock hit a record high of US$58.13. (Refer to Exhibit C7-3 for Dell's stock price between 1996 and 2005.) In 2001, Dell emerged as the largest PC manufacturer in the world with six manufacturing facilities across the globe, including Texas; Nashville, Tennessee in North America; Eldorado do Sul in Brazil; Limerick in Ireland; Penang in Malaysia; and Xiamen in China. Dell had sales offices in 34 countries and sold its products in more than 170 countries across the world. In the year 2000–01, Dell's net revenues were US$31.89 billion, with North and South America accounting for 72 percent, Europe 20 percent, and the Asia Pacific region for 8 percent of the total revenues.

According to Michael Dell, the company branched into new markets, mainly to cater to the needs of the customers. He said, "We don't go searching for technology as if it were some new compound on the element chart that hasn't been discovered; instead, we listen to our customers. That information tells us where we should go innovate on their behalf. So you don't get a lot of these exciting products that don't actually sell very much."[8]

Dell started selling printers in March 2003 for personal and workgroup use. The printers were competitively priced. For US$139, customers could buy a combination of printer, scanner, and copier. By 2005, Dell's share in the U.S. printer market was at 12 percent, with revenues from printing and imaging products at US$1.3 billion. Dell targeted the inkjet printer segment with products priced at US$70, which was about US$20

---

[6]Motorola is a Fortune 100 global communications leader that provides seamless mobility products and solutions across broadband, embedded systems, and wireless networks. The sales during 2004 were at US$31.3 billion.

[7]Build-to-order systems enable the manufacture of any quantity of standard products on demand without forecasts, inventory, or purchasing delays.

[8]Lashinsky Adam, "Where Dell Is Going Next," *Fortune*, October 18, 2004.

EXHIBIT C7-3 Dell Stock Price (October 1996—September 2006)

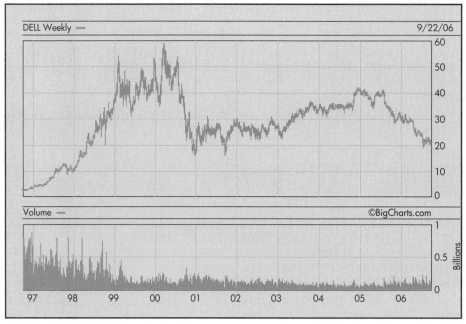

SOURCE: www.bigcharts.com

EXHIBIT C7-4 Dell—Financial Highlights (1987–1997)
(in million US$)

	1987	1988	1989	1990	1991	1992	1993	1994	1995	1996	1997
Net revenue	70	159	258	389	546	890	2,014	2,873	3,475	5,296	7,759
Gross income	16	50	81	110	182	282	450	433	738	1,067	1,666
Operating income	4	17	23	13	45	67	129	−39	249	377	714
Net income	2	9	14	5	27	51	102	−36	149	272	531

Dell—Financial Highlights (1998–2006)

	1998	1999	2000	2001	2002	2003	2004	2005	2006
Net revenue	12,327	18,243	25,265	31,888	31,168	35,404	41,444	49,205	55,908
Gross income	2,722	4,106	5,218	6,443	5,507	6,349	7,552	9,015	10,288
Operating income	1,316	2,046	2,263	2,663	1,789	2,844	3,544	4,254	4,789
Net income	944	1,460	1,666	2,177	1,246	2,122	2,645	3,323	3,825

SOURCE: www.dell.com

lower than the prevalent market rate. Dell entered into collaborations with companies like Lexmark, Fuji, Xerox, Samsung, and Kodak. According to Michael Dell, "We've got access to more intellectual property than any single competitor out there by leveraging a network of partners who have technology, but didn't necessarily have customer relationships or an understanding of what features needed to be in the products."[9] (Refer to Exhibit C7-4 for financial highlights of Dell between 1997 and 2006.)

[9]Lashinsky Adam, "Where Dell Is Going Next," *Fortune,* October 18, 2004.

DELL'S DIRECT MODEL

Dell adopted a unique model of selling PCs bypassing the conventional model of selling through the reseller channel. In the conventional model, resellers purchased PCs from the manufacturers and distributed them to the customers. Sometimes, resellers customized the PCs by installing certain components and, sometimes, the required software. Using the direct model, Dell provided consumers with tailor-made products and offered add-on products and services like PC upgradation, PC replacement, maintenance, and technical support. Through the direct model, Dell was able to reduce inventory costs and overheads. Under Dell's direct model, PCs were built according to customer specifications after receiving the order. In contrast, other vendors needed to forecast the demand for PCs and ship the products accordingly.

Dell's model called for highly complex execution, where the company needed to stack products and components to assemble the PCs at very short notice. This also called for superior manufacturing and logistics capabilities, along with information systems. Dell adopted a structure known as the virtual company or value web model, which focused on a few key strategic activities and outsourcing of non-strategic activities. (Refer to Figure C7-1 for Dell's value web model.)

The global production network of Dell was spread across the Americas, Europe, and Asia, and combined final assembly was undertaken in-house with outside suppliers and contract manufacturers. Among Dell's contract manufacturers and original design manufacturer were SCI, Solectron, Celestica, Hon Hai, Quanta, and Arima. These companies manufactured printed circuit board assemblies, sub-assemblies, and some of the final products like notebook PCs for Dell. Components and peripherals, which included disk drives, CD-ROM drives, semiconductors, add-on cards, monitors, keyboards, mouse, and speakers, were obtained from outside suppliers. The PCs were loaded with software like Microsoft or other software as required by Dell's corporate customers. Outside partners like Wang, Unisys, IBM, and BancTec provided Dell with services like system integration, installation, on-site repairs, and consulting.

On the basis of its value web model, Dell's factories stacked inventory only for five days, while most of its competitors kept 45 days of inventory. Dell's suppliers set up their warehousing space near Dell's factories. Suppliers needed to deliver items within 90 minutes. Dell started assembling the product only when it received an order for one, over the phone or through the Internet. After an order was received, it took Dell only six hours to make and ship the product. (Refer to Exhibit C7-5 for benefits of Dell's direct model

FIGURE C7-1   Dell's Value Web Model

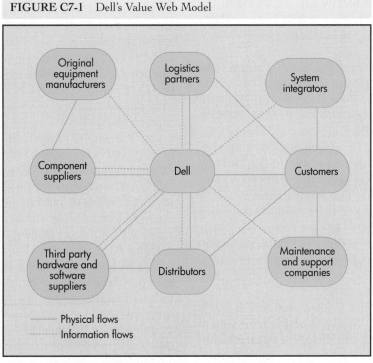

SOURCE: Adapted from Kenneth L. Kraemer and Jason Dedrick, "Dell Computer: Organization of a Global Production Network" (December 1, 2002). Globalization of IT. Paper 255, Center for Research on Information Technology and Organizations, University of California, Irvine.

EXHIBIT 7-5 Benefits of the Dell Direct Model

Most Efficient Path to the Customer: We believe that the most efficient path to the customer is through a direct relationship, with no intermediaries to add confusion and cost. We are organized around groups of customers with similar needs. This allows our teams to understand the specific needs of specific customers—without customer needs being "translated" by inefficient resellers and middlemen.

Single Point of Accountability: We recognize that technology can be complex, so we work to keep things easy for our customers. We make Dell the single point of accountability so that resources necessary to meet customer needs can be easily marshaled in support of complex challenges. Our customers tell us they want streamlined and fast access to the right resources; Direct provides just that.

Build-to-Order: We provide customers exactly what they want in their computer systems through easy custom configuration and ordering. Build-to-order means that we do not maintain months of aging and expensive inventory. As a result, we typically provide our customers with the best pricing and latest technology for features they really want.

Low-Cost Leader: We focus resources on what matters to our customers. With a highly efficient supply chain and manufacturing organization, a concentration on standards-based technology developed collaboratively with our industry partners, and a dedication to reducing costs through business process improvements, we consistently provide our customers with superior value.

Standards-Based Technology: We believe that standard technology is key to providing our customers with relevant, high-value products and services. Focusing on standards gives customers the benefit of extensive research and development from Dell and an entire industry—not from just a single company. Unlike proprietary technologies, standards give customers flexibility and choice.

SOURCE: www.dell.com

DELL IN CHINA

PC sales in China were less than one million units in 1995. By 2003, the figure had increased to over 12 million units, and in the same year China surpassed Japan to become the second-largest PC market in the world. In 1995, the market leaders in China were Compaq, AST, IBM, and Legend. Locally assembled PCs or grey market imports were very popular. By 2000, the government established standards for locally sold PCs. One of the major domestic players in the market, Legend (later Lenovo), started expanding by building a national distribution network.

Several factors influenced the growth of the computer industry in China. (Refer to Exhibit C7-6 for the details.) With the Chinese market experiencing significant growth in the mid–1990s, Dell had to enter China in order to remain competitive in Asia and gain market share. In the initial years, Dell faced many problems as tariffs on imported components were high and the government was supporting companies that set up manufacturing bases in China. The foreign firms in China depended on resellers to sell their products, as goods which were not manufactured in China could not legally be sold in mainland China. In order to obtain production licenses and market access, foreign companies operating in China needed to transfer technology and form alliances with local companies.

Dell ventured into the Chinese market in 1995, importing products from Malaysia and reselling them through Chinese retailers and distributors. Dell established a presence by opening offices in Guangzhou in 1997 and in Shanghai in 1998. Phil Kelly (Kelly), President, Dell Asia Pacific, believed that Dell needed to set up a manufacturing base in China, rather than import products from Malaysia; Dell's management in the United States was not ready to take this step. They were concerned about the costs involved, and the quality of suppliers and skills available in the Chinese market. Kelly persisted as he was convinced that Dell's direct model in China would be successful. Finally, the headquarters gave Kelly the go-ahead.

Dell decided on Xiamen (Fijian Province), and Kelly and his team successfully convinced local leaders about the benefits they would reap through their association with Dell. The Xiamen municipal government cooperated with Dell, forming a committee of six people to help Dell set up its operations. Dell found that Xiamen provided the ideal environment for investment, tax relief, and production. Dell's executives were pleased with the cooperation extended by the government in Xiamen and its low pollution levels. In 1998, Dell established a manufacturing facility, the China Customer Center (CCC), in Xiamen. Since Dell was the only multinational in Xiamen at this time, it was able to attract and retain talented workers locally. Xiamen was located across the straits of Taiwan, where most of Dell's suppliers were located, and was also close to major cities in mainland China like Beijing and Shanghai. By August 2005, the Xiamen facility shipped ten million PC units.

As its sales started improving, Dell decided to penetrate the Chinese market further. This strategy was in line with its mission—to be "the most successful computer company in the world," "delivering the best customer experiences in the markets." In its mission statement, Dell undertook to meet customer expectations of highest quality, leading technology, competitive pricing, individual and company accountability, best-in-class service and support, flexible customization capability, superior corporate citizenship, and financial stability.

EXHIBIT 7-6   Factors Influencing Growth of Computer Industry in China

In 1990, there were only 500,000 PCs in China. In 2003, China surpassed Japan to become the second-largest PC market in the world, with PC sales growing to 12 million. Between 1990 and 2000, production of computer hardware in China grew from US$1 billion to US$23 billion. The growth can be attributed to rapid economic growth in China and increased foreign investment inflows into China.

The precursor of these changes was the government policy of 1980s that required foreign companies to transfer technology in order to access the Chinese market. China has invested heavily on information infrastructure and in promoting exports. The computer policy of China was guided by the philosophy of learning from outsiders without surrendering economic and technological control.

The main factors that influenced the development of China's computer industry are

- China's domestic market with a population of over 1.3 billion and unlimited supply of low-cost labor coupled with economic growth. This presents a highly attractive proposition of China as a production platform and a market. The government required foreign investors to produce locally and enter into local partnerships or technology transfer.

- China's computer industry developed in a transitional economy with ownership structures including both capital and state ownership.

- China has built its computer industry on the base of huge science and technology capabilities that are not found in most developing countries. China's independent science and technology capabilities grew owing to the United State's technology export restrictions on it, which limited China's access to advanced technologies in computers and semiconductors.

Computer Industry Policy

In 1986, China's seventh plan initiated the development of a commercially oriented computer and electronics industry. Several multinational companies like IBM, Hewlett-Packard, Toshiba, and Compaq formed joint ventures with Chinese partners to market their own products. China discouraged the import of computers by levying high tariffs on imports—tariffs stood at 82 percent in 1992, but were reduced to 35 percent in 1993 and were done away with in a phased manner. China created export processing zones to encourage exports.

The government promoted several domestic firms without intervening in their management. One of the major players in the market, Legend (Lenovo), has developed in association with the Chinese Academy of Sciences, which is a leading government institution. Another major player, Great Wall, was a spin off of the Ministry of Electronics. Through their association with different government departments, these companies were able to access the benefits of R&D carried out by institutions supported by the Chinese government.

In the early 1990s, the share of the foreign players in the Chinese PC market was around 60 percent, and this has fallen subsequently. Regulations require foreign companies to set up domestic production and joint ventures with local companies. By 2002, the share of Chinese companies in the market was 70 percent. Chinese manufacturers were able to achieve high market shares by focusing on the middle and lower end of the market. The growing price competition among domestic manufacturers had an adverse affect on profit margins which were driven to the lowest possible limits.

China's Computer Trade Balance

(in million US$)

	1992	1993	1994	1995	1996	1997	1998	1999	2000
Exports	820	1,258	2,006	3,750	5,315	7,543	10,169	11,698	16,577
Imports	1,344	1,344	1,763	2,403	2,876	3,868	5,300	6,969	9,883
Trade balance	−524	−86	233	1,347	2,439	3,675	4,869	4,729	6,694

SOURCE: www.uscc.gov

China—PC Market Size

	Q3 2004	Q2 2005	Q3 2005
Shipment (million sets)	3.124	3.428	3.561
Market size (RMB10 billion)	1.895	1.966	2.026

SOURCE: Analysys International

SOURCE: Adapted from "China's Emergence as a Computer Industry Power: Implications for the US," by Jason Dedrick and Kenneth L Kraemer, presented before the U.S. China Economic and Security Review Commission, February 12, 2004, and other sources.

Dell laid its focus on the corporate market in China. This market segment included both large and medium businesses, government institutions, multinational companies, and small businesses, which functioned in industries like telecommunications, banking, taxation, finance, and education/research. Dell created a China-specific Web site, www.dell.com.cn, which provided a Chinese/English language interface. The Web site provided its government and corporate customers with customized Web pages and B2B services. These Web pages allowed customers to place orders from their own intranets and interact directly with the company online. Customers could also order PCs of their own specified configurations over the telephone or through the Internet.

Dell encountered problems with the term "direct sales" in China, where the Chinese equivalent was "zhi xiao." This term was generally used in China to describe illegal market schemes. To avoid any misunderstanding of the term, the company distributed brochures to its customers. These brochures highlighted the sales and manufacturing processes in Dell and replaced "zhi xiao" with a new phrase "zhi xian ding gou," meaning direct orders.

Dell adopted a simpler form of its direct model for the Chinese market. Initially Dell's products were limited to desktops targeted at corporate buyers. Then Dell set up a call center and sales team. As the penetration of credit cards in China was low, Dell could not insist on payment through the Internet in this form. Instead, it asked its delivery men to carry wireless debit card machines to enable customers to pay for the computer on delivery. In some cases, it used a cash-on-delivery system and entered into agreements with several banks to facilitate payments.

Kelly worked towards minimizing costs for Dell by hiring local talent. In the planning stages, Kelly brought in a team of Dell employees from Southeast Asia to help minimize the costs involved in setting up the factory and acquiring suppliers and support services. Once these were in place, local people were recruited for managerial positions. By 1999, all the people reporting to the production head were from China.

In addition to the direct sales approach, Dell also provided sales and technical support to its customers through a network of authorized distributors. In China, customers paid a lot of importance to "Guanxi," that is, personal relationships. Dell's decision to sell through distributors addressed the Chinese customers' need to have a personal relationship with the seller/manufacturer. China thus became the first market in the world where Dell followed a hybrid "dual system" business model.

Dell launched sales and technical support services in nine major cities, including Shanghai, Beijing, Guangzhou, Chengdu, Nanjing, and Hangzhou. Having a manufacturing plant at Xiamen helped Dell keep production costs low due to the availability of cheap labor. Since Dell did not invest heavily in intermediaries like distributors and resellers due to its direct model, it passed on the benefits of low cost to customers by offering them products at lower prices. By adopting the direct model, Dell was able to reduce channel costs. Through the direct model, Dell was also able to obtain real-time feedback and market information. To take orders over the telephone and solve the technical problems of its customers, Dell established 530 toll-free numbers across 258 cities in China. The company also advertised its products through promotional events, newspapers, and direct mails.

Through all these efforts, Dell's revenues from its Asian markets increased by 48 percent for 1999 as compared to 1998. A report from IDC stated that Dell recorded the highest growth in the Asia Pacific PC market in 1998. By 1999, China had emerged as the fifth-largest PC market in the world, and in order to consolidate its position in the market Dell introduced several new models with better configurations at lower prices. By the third quarter of 1999, Dell was ranked fifth among the top PC vendors in China.

However, with corporate clients making up 60 percent of Dell's clientele in China, Dell recognized that it was not focusing enough on individual customers or on establishing personal relationships with them. In order to cater to the individual customers, Dell launched Smart PCs in mid–2001. These PCs were competitively priced at 5000 Yuan.[10] The company was able to provide PCs at a lower cost as it was procuring components from Taiwan, where they were considerably cheaper than in China. In 2002, Dell's overall revenues in China grew by 24 percent as compared to revenues in 2001. By 2003, China had emerged as Dell's fourth-largest international market. According to Gartner,[11] in 2003, Dell was the second largest player in China.

In September 2004, Dell opened an Enterprise Command Center in Xiamen to provide high-level round-the-clock support for server and storage customers. Through these centers, teams of troubleshooters could come up with more efficient service delivery solutions. In August 2005, there were 5,500 employees in Dell China.

In fiscal 2004, Dell had a 7.2 percent share in the Chinese PC market. Dell was the second-largest player in the market in 2003 and had fallen by two places to the fourth position by 2004. The market leader Lenovo was far ahead of Dell, commanding a share of 25.1 percent. The other major players were Beijing Founder Electronics with a share of 9.9 percent, and Tsinghua Tongfang (THTF) with a share of 7.8 percent. Dell's

---

[10]US$1 = 8.0806 Yuan as of December 2, 2005.
[11]Gartner Inc. is a leading provider of research and analysis on the global information technology industry. It serves more than 10,000 clients.

TABLE C7-3   Dell in China

- One of the four focus markets across the world.
- 4th fastest-growing market for Dell worldwide.
- Revenue: Approx US$300 million per quarter.
- Ranked #8 in the China Fortune Magazine survey of Top 10 Best Employers in China.
- Ranked #11 in 2002 China's Top 200 Exporters list—Ministry of Commerce.
- Grew 63% and become the second-largest PC vendor in China in 2003.

SOURCE: Compiled from various sources.

market share dropped despite the increase in overall PC shipments in China, which rose by 29 percent in 2004 as against a 63 percent rise in 2003. Lenovo's PC shipments grew by 34 percent, Founder by 80 percent, and Tongfang (THTF) by 71 percent. HP's PC shipments grew by 38 percent. Lenovo's outstanding success could be attributed to the increase in sales to educational institutions and government organizations.

Dell's total sales in China reached 10 million units in 2005. In May 2006, the company opened a second manufacturing facility in Xiamen. The 594,000-square-foot center was expected to double Dell's production capacity in China. The center would cater to the customers in Japan, South Korea, and Hong Kong. The first facility mainly catered to the customers in mainland China. (Refer to Table C7-3 for highlights of Dell's operations in China.)

THE PROBLEMS

With the urban markets in China almost saturated, the sales of PCs were growing faster in semi-urban and rural areas. However, in these areas the use of the Internet and credit cards was not widespread. This was a major hindrance to Dell's direct model, as the model depended on pre-orders from consumers. Dell received only 10 percent of its total orders through the Internet in China, because of low Internet usage. The number of e-commerce transactions was also low owing to low credit card and Internet usage.

Dell had mainly concentrated on urban cities like Shanghai and Guangzhou. In these markets, PC penetration was higher and growth was around 2 to 3 percent a year as of 2004. In smaller cities and townships, growth was projected at 40 percent per annum. Lenovo's line of desktops had fared particularly well in these cities, helping the company capture a major chunk of the market. In contrast, Dell's direct model had not done well in these regions.

Dell's direct model was clearly unable to address the needs of the growing markets in fourth- and fifth-tier cities. Despite its efforts to make the direct model popular in these markets, logistics and management costs were very high. The logistical support system in China was not as strong as it was in the United States, and there was no nationwide equivalent to FedEx or UPS in the country. However, Dell's management still felt that consumers even in smaller cities and townships could order a Dell PC over the telephone and that its direct model would work here, too.

The key value proposition of the direct model—enabling customers to customize products—did not hold good in rural markets and in the less developed regional markets of China, as consumers were not aware of the details of the functioning of computers and about the configuration that would suit them the best. They had several queries about computers, and preferred buying from retailers who could provide them with quick service whenever they had problems with their PCs.

According to industry analysts, Dell had not made efforts to reach the rural and semi-urban market and instead concentrated on large cities in the firm belief that there was still ample room for growth in these markets. Dell did not have the infrastructure and the distribution channels to venture into China's rural markets and compete with established Chinese players like Lenovo.

The average Chinese buyer had to spend an equivalent of two months salary to buy a computer and expected to see the machine and learn more about it before they actually bought one. Unlike in developed countries, in China, buying a computer was a family decision. According to Helen Lau, analyst at Hong Kong–based Sun Hung Kai Investment Services, "I don't think these low-income people are ready to adopt this purchasing style yet. It's different in the major cities where people don't mind spending 10,000 Renminbi to buy a computer."[12] As far as marketing was concerned, analysts pointed out that in China, the cultural and economic infrastructure that supported direct marketing was not in place. *The Financial Times* of London said that there were several unofficial agents in China, who bought Dell's computers and sold them to consumers for a profit.

In August 2004, Dell pulled out of the low-end PC market in China and reduced the overall growth target in the market. On account of the high level of price competition and undercutting in the lower end brands, Dell felt it would be better for it to concentrate on the higher

---

[12]Lemon Sumner, "Dell Wants More than Satisfaction in Asia," *Computer World Hong Kong*, October 1, 2005.

end of the market. Amelio said, "What we found was happening was some of our competitors decided to get really aggressive in the consumer space. They decided they wanted to get really aggressive in the lower price bands. So we pulled out of the lower price bands and moved up into higher price bands in the consumer space. That's where we're going to hang for a bit."[13] This move was expected to push Dell down from the third to the fourth position in the Chinese market in terms of market share.

Another problem area for Dell in China was the lack of innovative products. It had not introduced any products specifically for the Chinese market or for the markets in fourth- and fifth-tier cities. There was a huge demand for less expensive and highly functional products in these markets.

Dell found itself embroiled in a controversy when a Chinese newspaper published an email by a salesperson from Dell US. In the email, the salesperson wrote, "From a IBM perspective, and please do not think I'm throwing stones. As you know Lenovo is a Chinese government owned company that recently purchased IBM's desktop/notebook business. While the US government has given its stamp of approval (no US secrets are in jeopardy) to continue to purchase these units, people must understand that every dollar they spend on these IBM systems is directly supporting/funding the Chinese government. Just something to think about."[14]

Dell China's management immediately expressed its regret over the comments and said they did not reflect the company's views. However, the Chinese media and industry analysts were put off by the comments. According to Fang Dongxing, IT Analyst on Blog.com, "Dell is the bane of China's IT hardware industry. It not only undermines the advantages of Chinese companies in cost and price, but also threatens its Chinese rivals with the strong weapons of global purchasing power and international brand recognition."[15]

THE FUTURE

China's PC shipments reached 3.56 million in the third quarter of 2005, up 10.8 percent compared to the third quarter of 2004. The market was worth RMB20.26 billion with revenue growth of 6.9 percent as compared to the corresponding quarter of the previous year. With the price of PCs going down, Chinese consumers had begun showing a preference for branded products and so small vendors were struggling to survive. With several foreign players entering the arena, the focus had shifted to

fourth- and fifth-tier cities. According to Wang Tow from Analysys International, "The concentration degree in China's PC market is increasing and channel sales become the breaking point for vendors. Some local vendors in certain areas still have some market potential to explore due to the regional protectionism, but vendors who haven't enough strength while spread their sales channels aimlessly will face severe crisis for survival."[16]

Lenovo introduced a low-cost Yuanmeng line, with starting price at US$370, in the second half of 2004, which found many takers in smaller cities. With Lenovo establishing itself in smaller cities and towns, Dell was likely to find it tough to break into these markets. It appeared to be imperative for Dell to look seriously at new and emerging markets in China, especially the low-end rural markets.

According to industry analysts, Dell needed to act fast in order to establish formidable presence in the semi-urban and rural markets in China before Lenovo occupied all the territory. A few analysts recommended that Dell should broaden its horizon to include smaller cities and towns in its expansion plans. According to Simon Ye, principal analyst at Gartner in Shanghai, "Dell is too focused on China's largest cities, where the company offers mostly high-end PCs designed for corporate customers. But these markets have become saturated and PC sales have slowed, which prompted a price war last year among vendors."[17]

Meanwhile, Dell announced that China had surpassed Japan to become its third-largest market during the third quarter ending October 2005. (The top two markets for Dell were the United States and the United Kingdom.) Making a re-entry into the budget PC market in May 2005, Dell introduced models priced at 2,999 Yuan. This move was termed as Dell's answer to Lenovo's budget PCs. In September 2006, Dell was planning to launch consumer desktop PCs with microprocessors from Advanced Micro Devices.[18] The processors were priced lower than Intel microprocessors and were widely used in China. By using these processors, Dell expected to further reduce its PC prices and reach more customers.

A few observers, however, felt that Dell did not need to act in haste to move into semi-urban and rural markets, at the cost of losing market share in urban markets. Though the growth in hardware sales in the bigger cities had slowed down, it was still growing. Dell was highly competitive in these markets and could consolidate its

[13]Fisher Ken Caesar, "AMD Trouncing Dell in China's Low-Cost Market," www.arstechnica.com, August 16, 2004.
[14]"Dell Offers Regret over Remark," *China Daily,* June 6, 2005.
[15]Vance Ashlee, "Dell Red-faced over Salesman's Lenovo Jibes," www.thregister.co.uk, June 3, 2005.

[16]Wang Jessica, "Analysys International Says China's PC Market Continued Growing to Reach RMB 20.26 Billion in Q3 2005, While Dell's Market Share Drop Down," www.analysys.com, November 30, 2005.
[17]Lemon Sumner, "Competition Heats Up for Dell in China's PC Market," www.infoworld.com, March 18, 2005.
[18]Founded in 1969, Advanced Micro Devices is a U.S.-based manufacturer of integrated circuits, and is the second largest supplier of x–86 compatible processors in the world.

position further. According to Ma, an analyst in IDC, no major overhaul was required in Dell's approach towards the Chinese market: "There's something important to remember about Dell in China: they're really not a consumer play at all, their success in China has been on the commercial side."[19] Analysts also felt that Dell's China Web site needed some revamping to cater to the local needs. The only difference between the English and Chinese Web site was the language. The use of local models and ambience would help Dell in making the site attractive to Chinese users.

Another high-potential business where Dell was losing market share was laptops. The laptop market in China was projected at 4.7 million units in 2006 as against 3.37 million units in 2005. In the second quarter of 2005, Lenovo was the market leader in this segment with a share of 29.1 percent, followed by Dell with a share of 14.3 percent and HP with 9.3 percent. Dell faced stiff competition from HP, which was regularly cutting prices. By the second quarter of 2006, HP had emerged as the second-largest player in the market with a share of 11 percent and Dell fell to the third position, though its market share grew from 9.2 percent in the first quarter to 9.4 percent by the second quarter of 2006.

Dell's failure to take advantage of the growing opportunities in the PC market in China had raised several questions about the success and applicability of its direct model in the emerging markets like China. Kevin Rollins, CEO Dell who co-designed the direct model with Michael Dell, expressed the view that "Direct Model is continually being defined, particularly in China, one of the most exciting, vibrant and rapidly growing markets in the world."[20] Though Dell had faced these problems in most of the markets in which it operated, ultimately the model proved successful. According to Helen Lau, analyst at Celestial Asia Securities Holdings based in Hong Kong, "Dell cannot be totally written off. I would like to still wait for several more quarters . . . to decide if Dell is really falling behind, Dell is a very formidable competitor."[21]

QUESTIONS FOR DISCUSSION

1. Dell has been quite successful in the urban markets in China but failed to replicate its success in semi-urban and rural markets. What measures should Dell take to strengthen its presence in the semi-urban and rural markets of China? Explain.

2. One of the reasons for Dell's success globally has been its direct model. In the light of the facts given in the case, what do you think are the advantages and disadvantages of the direct model?

3. In November 2003, Dell started selling some of its PCs and laptops through Costco. Analysts felt that this move implied that Dell had started exploring alternative channels apart from its direct model. Do you think this move is correct? What steps should Dell take to overcome the drawbacks of its direct model?

---

[19]Lemon Sumner, "Dell Wants More than Satisfaction in Asia," *Computer World Hong Kong,* October 1, 2005.

[20]Weitao Li, "Straight Talk," *China Daily,* November 28, 2005.
[21]Lemon Sumner, "Competition Heats up for Dell in China's PC Market," www.infoworld.com, March 18, 2005.

Case 8 Starbucks' International Operations—2006

Internationally, we are in our infancy.[1]

HOWARD SCHULTZ,
Chairman and Chief Global Strategist, Starbucks, March 2003

The expansion strategy internationally is not bulletproof as it is in the U.S.[2]

MITCHELL J. SPEISER
Analyst, Lehman Brothers, June 2003

Although Starbucks had a presence in 37 countries around the world by mid 2006, most of Starbucks' international operations were in trouble.[3]

WWW.STARBUCKS.COM,
October 2006

ALL'S NOT WELL WITH STARBUCKS

In March 2003, *Fortune* came out with its annual list of "Fortune 500 companies." For Howard Schultz (Schultz), Chairman of Starbucks Corp (Starbucks), this list was special as Starbucks featured in the list. It was a dream come true for the Seattle-based entrepreneur.

Though the U.S. economy was reeling under recession and many retail majors were reporting losses and applying for bankruptcy, Starbucks announced a 31 percent increase in its net earnings and a 23 percent increase in sales for the first quarter of 2003. Analysts felt that the success of Starbucks showed that a quality product speaks for itself. The fact that Starbucks spent less than 1 percent of its sales on advertising and marketing strengthened this view. In addition to being a popular brand among customers, Starbucks was also considered the best place to work due to its employee-friendly policies.[4]

However, analysts felt that the success of Starbucks was primarily due to its profitable domestic operations. It was reported that although Starbucks had a presence in 37 countries around the world by mid–2006,[5] most of Starbucks' international operations were in trouble. Although the company had managed to gain a foothold in markets like China, it faced several difficulties in countries like Germany and France. Even in Japan, which was Starbucks' biggest market outside the United States, the company had had a difficult time for several years before it managed to stabilize in 2004. Analysts pointed out that Starbucks' international operations were not as well planned as its U.S. operations. They also observed that the volatile international business environment made it difficult for the company to effectively manage its international operations

Many analysts felt that it was important for the company to focus on its international operations. With the U.S. market becoming saturated, Starbucks would be forced to look outside the United States for revenues and growth.

BACKGROUND NOTE

The history of Starbucks dates back to 1971, when Jerry Baldwin, Zev Siegl, and Gordon Bowker launched a coffee bean retailing store named Starbucks to sell specialty whole-bean coffee in Seattle. By 1981, the number of Starbucks stores increased to five and Starbucks also established a small roasting facility in Seattle. Around the same time, Howard Schultz (Schultz), who was working with Hammarplast—a Swedish housewares company that marketed coffee makers—noticed that Starbucks, a small company from Seattle, was ordering more coffee makers than anyone else. In order to find out more about the company, Schultz visited Seattle. Schultz was so impressed by the company and its founders that he offered to work for the company.

[1]Cora Daniels, "Mr. Coffee: The man behind the $4.75 Frappuccino makes the 500," *Fortune,* April 14, 2003.

[2]Stanley Holmes, Irene M. Kunii, Jack Ewing, Kerry Capell, "For Starbucks, There's No Place Like Home," *BusinessWeek,* June 9, 2003.

[3]"Company Fact Sheet—August 2006," www.starbucks.com (accessed on October 6, 2006).

[4]Starbucks was the first organization in the United States to offer stock options and health care coverage to part-time employees.

[5]"Company Fact Sheet—August 2006," www.starbucks.com (accessed on October 6, 2006).

In 1982, Schultz joined Starbucks as marketing manager, with an equity stake in the company. During his first year at Starbucks, he studied the various types of coffee and the intricacies of the coffee business. The turning point came in 1983 when Schultz was sent to Milan (Italy) for an international housewares show. There he observed that every street in the city had an espresso coffee bar, where people met and spent time. Schultz realized that Starbucks could introduce espresso coffee bars in the United States. Schultz put forward this idea to his partners. But they did not like the idea of selling espresso coffee. However, after a lot of persuasion from Schultz, they agreed to allow him to sell espresso coffee in their retail shop. The business picked up and by the weekend they were making more money by selling the beverage than by selling coffee beans. Still, when the partners refused to venture into the beverage business Schultz decided to quit the company and start out on his own.

In April 1985, Schultz opened a coffee bar, Il Giornale, in Seattle, with seed capital of $150,000 invested by Jerry Baldwin and Gordon Bowker. The rest of the capital was raised through private placement. Soon, the second and third stores were opened in Seattle and Vancouver, respectively. In 1987, when Schultz heard that Starbucks' owners were selling off six stores along with a roasting plant and the Starbucks brand name, he raised $3.8 million through private placements and bought Starbucks. As Starbucks was a more established name, Schultz decided to retain it instead of Il Giornale.

Schultz expanded Starbucks to Chicago, Los Angeles, and other major cities. But with increasing overhead expenses, the company reported a loss of $1.2 million in the year 1990. However, Schultz was confident of his business plan and continued his expansion spree. He even hired employees from companies such as PepsiCo. By 1991, the number of Starbucks' stores increased to 116 and it became the first privately owned company to offer employee stock options. In 1992, Starbucks was listed on the stock exchange at a price of $17 per share.

The strategy adopted by Starbucks was to blanket a region with its new stores. By doing so it could reduce the customers' rush in one store and also increase its revenues through new stores. This helped the company to reduce its distribution costs and the waiting period for customers in its stores, thereby increasing the number of customers. It was reported that on an average a customer visited Starbucks stores 18 times a month, a very high number compared to other American retailers. By 1993 there were around 100 Starbucks outlets. This increased to 145 by the end of 1994.

Along with serving coffee, Starbucks also sold merchandise. In 1995, it started selling CDs of its famous in-house music program. It also entered into alliances with various players such as Canadian Airlines, United Airlines, Starwood Hotel, and Barnes & Noble Inc. to serve Starbucks coffee.

Analysts attributed the success of Starbucks not only to its aggressive expansion, but also to its product innovation. Starbucks came out with new products to attract customers. For instance, in 1995, to cater to the needs of diet-conscious youngsters, it launched *Frappuccino*—a low-fat creamy iced coffee. In 1996, it launched ice cream and ice cream bars through its subsidiary Starbucks and Dreyer's Grand Ice Cream, Inc. In the same year it also entered into an agreement with PepsiCo to launch bottled Starbucks *Frappuccino*. Due to all these initiatives Starbucks recorded an average growth of 20 percent per year since 1991, and its store traffic increased to 6 to 8 percent per year by the mid–1990s.

However, in the mid–1990s, with the market reaching saturation, Starbucks could no longer depend on the U.S. market for growth. Analysts felt that to maintain its growth rates and to boost revenues, Starbucks should venture abroad. In 1995, Starbucks formed Starbucks Coffee International, its wholly owned subsidiary, to monitor the company's international expansion. In 1996, Starbucks entered Japan through a joint venture with the Sazaby's Inc. (a leading Japanese tea shop and interior-goods retailer), and over the years it expanded into Southeast Asia, Europe, and the Middle East. By mid 2006, Starbucks had more than 3,400 stores outside the United States (including company-operated stores as well as joint venture and licensed locations.) (Refer to Table C8-1 for Starbucks' international presence.)

INTERNATIONAL EXPANSION STRATEGIES

Starbucks decided to enter the Asia Pacific rim markets first.[6] Growing consumerism in the Asia Pacific countries and eagerness among the younger generation to imitate western lifestyles made these countries attractive markets for Starbucks.

Starbucks decided to enter international markets by using a three-pronged strategy—joint ventures, licensing, and wholly owned subsidiaries. (Refer to Exhibit C8-1 for the modes of entry in international markets.) Prior to entering a foreign market, Starbucks focused on studying the market conditions for its products in the country. It then decided on the local partner for its business. Initially Starbucks test marketed with a few stores that were opened in trendy places, and the company's experienced managers from Seattle handled the operations.

After successful test marketing, local baristas (brew masters) were given training for 13 weeks in Seattle. Starbucks did not compromise on its basic principles. It

---

[6]Asia Pacific rim markets consist of Japan, the Philippines, Indonesia, Thailand, Taiwan, Malaysia, Singapore, China, South Korea, North Korea, New Zealand, Australia, Vietnam, Cambodia, and Papua New Guinea.

TABLE C8-1 Starbucks' International Presence in 2006*

Country	Type Of Entry	Name Of The Partner	Year
Canada	Wholly owned subsidiary	Starbucks Coffee Canada	1996
Japan	Joint venture	Sazaby Inc.	1996
Malaysia	Licensee	Berajaya Group bhd	1998
New Zealand	Licensee	Restaurant Brands	1998
Taiwan	Joint venture	President Coffee Corp.	1998
Kuwait	Licensee	M.H. Alshaya Co., W.L.L.	1999
China			
• Beijing	Licensee	Mei Da Coffee Co., Ltd.	1999
• Hong Kong	Joint venture	Maxim's Caterers Ltd.	2000
• Shanghai	Joint venture	President (Coffee) Cayman Holdings, Ltd.	2000
Philippines	Licensee	Rustan's Coffee Corp	2000
Australia	Joint venture	Markus Hofer	2000
Israel	Joint venture	Delek Corporation**	2001
Austria	Licensee	Bon Appetit Group**	2001
Switzerland	Licensee	Bon Appetit Group**	2001
Germany	Joint venture	KarstadtQualle AG	2002
Greece	Joint venture	Marinopoulos Brothers	2002
Mexico	Joint venture	SC de Mexico	2002
Hawaii	Joint venture	Café Hawaii Partners	2002
Hong Kong	Joint venture	Maxim's Caterers Ltd	2000
Indonesia	Joint venture	PT Mitra A diperkasa	2002
Puerto Rico	Joint venture	Puerto Rico Coffee Partners LLC	2002
Lebanon	Licensee	M.H. Alshaya Co., W.L.L.	N.A.
Spain	Joint venture	Grupo Vips	2002
Cyprus	Joint venture	Marinopoulos Brothers S A,	2003
France	Joint venture	Grupo Vips	2004
Jordan	Licensee	M.H. Alshaya Co., W.L.L.	2005
Ireland	Wholly owned subsidiary	Starbucks Coffee Ireland	2005
Bahamas	Licensee	Coffee Cay Ltd.	2005

* This list is not exhaustive

** Starbucks closed its operations in Israel and bought out the stakes of its partners in Austria and Switzerland in 2003.

SOURCE: Compiled from various sources.

EXHIBIT C8-1 Modes of Entry into International Markets

There are six ways to enter a foreign market. They are exporting, turnkey projects, licensing, franchising, joint venture with a host country firm, and setting up a wholly owned subsidiary in the host country. Each mode of entry has its advantages and disadvantages. The method a company chooses depends on a variety of factors, including the nature of the particular product or service and the conditions for market penetration in the foreign target market.

Exporting

Most firms begin their global expansion with exports and later switch over to another mode. In the 1990s, the volume of exports in the world economy had increased significantly due to the decline in trade barriers. However, exporting still remains a challenge for smaller firms. Firms planning to export must identify foreign market opportunities, familiarize themselves with the mechanics of exports, and learn to deal with foreign exchange risk.

Turnkey Projects

In a turnkey project, the contractor handles every aspect of the project for a foreign client including the training of operating personnel. After the completion of the contract, the foreign client is handed the "key" to the plant that is ready for operation. Turnkey projects are common in chemical, pharmaceutical, and petroleum refining industries.

EXHIBIT C8-1 (cont.)

Licensing

Licensing is an arrangement whereby a company (licenser) grants the rights to intangible property like patents, inventions, formula, process, designs, copyrights, and trademarks to another company (licensee) for a specified period of time. The licenser receives a royalty fee from the licensee. For example, in the early 1960s, Xerox licensed its patented xerographic know-how to Fuji-Xerox. It was initially meant for ten years; but the license was extended several times. In return, Fuji-Xerox paid Xerox a royalty fee equal to 5 percent of the net sales revenue that it earned.

Franchising

Franchising is similar to licensing except that it requires long-term commitments. In franchising, the franchiser not only sells intangible property to the franchisee, but also insists that the franchisee abide by the rules of business. In some cases, the franchiser also assists the franchisee in running the business. The franchiser receives a royalty payment that is usually a percentage of the franchisee's revenues. Service companies usually opt for franchising. For example, McDonald's pursues its expansion abroad through franchising. McDonald's sets down strict rules for the franchisees to operate their restaurants. The rules extend to cooking methods, staffing policy, and design and location of the restaurants. McDonald's also organizes the supply chain and provides management training and financial assistance to the franchisees.

Joint Ventures

In contrast to licensing and franchising arrangements, joint ventures allow companies to own a stake and play a role in the management of the foreign operation. Joint ventures require more direct investment and training, management assistance, and technology transfer. Joint ventures can be equity or non-equity partnerships. Equity joint ventures are contractual arrangements with equal partners. Non-equity ventures are the ones where the host country partner has a greater stake. In some countries, a joint venture is the only way for a foreign company to set up operations.

Wholly Owned Subsidiaries

In a wholly owned subsidiary, the firm owns 100 percent of the stock of the subsidiary. Wholly owned subsidiaries can be established in a foreign country in two ways. A firm can set up new operations in the foreign country or it can acquire a firm and promote its products through that firm.

The following are the advantages and disadvantages of various entry modes.

Entry Mode	Advantage	Disadvantage
Exporting	Ability to realize location and experience curve economies	High transport costs Trade barriers
		Problems with local marketing agents
Turnkey contracts	Ability to earn returns from process technology skills in countries where FDI is restricted	Creating efficient competitors
		Lack of long-term market presence
Licensing	Low development costs and risks	Lack of control over technology
		Inability to realize location and experience curve economies
		Inability to engage in global strategic coordination
Joint ventures	Access to local partner's knowledge	Lack of control over technology
	Sharing development costs and risks	Inability to engage in global strategic coordination
	Politically acceptable	
		Inability to realize location and experience economies
Wholly owned subsidiaries	Protection of technology	High costs and risks
	Ability to engage in global strategic coordination	
	Ability to realize location and experience economies	

SOURCE: Compiled from various sources.

ensured similar coffee beverage lineups and "*No Smoking*" rules in all its stores across the globe.

When Starbucks entered into a joint venture with Sazaby Inc. to open Starbucks stores in Japan in 1996, analysts felt that Starbucks was unlikely to succeed. They even advised Starbucks to forego its principles such as *No Smoking,* and ensure that the size of the stores would not be more than 500 square feet due to the high rents in Japan. However, Starbucks stuck to its *No Smoking* principle, which attracted young Japanese women to the

Starbucks stores, and the size of the stores was 1200–1500 square feet—similar to the stores in the United States.

According to Starbucks sources, listening to its local partner also helped. Starbucks took advantage of its local partner Sazaby's knowledge about Japanese coffee-drinking habits and introduced new products such as Green Tea Frappucino, which became popular.

Starbucks entered China in 1999. The first store opened in Beijing and was operated under license by Mei Da Coffee Co., Ltd. In 2000, Starbucks entered into joint ventures with Hong Kong–based Maxim's Caterers to open stores in Hong Kong and Macau, and with President (Coffee) Cayman Holdings, Ltd. to open stores in the Shanghai region.

Starbucks was successful in attracting a young crowd in all its Asian markets, as young people in these markets were eager to imitate the American culture. It even adapted itself to the local culture to gain market acceptance. For instance, Starbucks offered curry puffs and meat buns in Asian markets as Asians generally prefer to eat something while having coffee.

Analysts felt that the strong coffee-drinking culture in Europe posed both challenges and opportunities for Starbucks. It would face tough competition from the sidewalk cafes of France, coffeehouses of Vienna, and espresso bars of Italy that had developed a strong coffee-drinking culture across the continent, exposing Europeans to the best coffee in the world. However, Starbucks executives commented that Europe used to make great coffees, but by the late 1990s the taste had gone awry. In 1998, Starbucks opened its first store in England, and soon expanded its presence to Switzerland, Germany, and Greece.

It was generally felt that though old people would stick to the existing coffee houses, the young would be attracted to Starbucks. Said Helmut Spudich, editor of *Der Standard* (a Vienna-based paper), "The coffeehouses in Vienna are nice, but they are old. Starbucks is considered hip."[7] Another important factor that could lead to the success of Starbucks in Europe was its ambience and *No Smoking* environment, unlike traditional European coffee bars. The self-service mode of operation also attracted the young crowd as it was observed that youngsters did not like to wait for the waiter to come and take orders. According to Starbucks sources, it was successful because it was not just selling coffee but an experience, which was unique only to Starbucks stores. Peter Maslen, the president of Starbucks International, said, "The coffee is good but it's just the vehicle. The romance of coffee, the occasion, the community, is what Starbucks is selling."[8]

In the Middle East, Starbucks went in for licensing (except in Israel where it had a joint venture). The Middle East license agreement with M.H. Alshaya Co., W.L.L., covered seven countries: Kuwait, Bahrain, Lebanon, UAE, Saudi Arabia, Oman, and Qatar. Respecting the culture in the Middle East, Starbucks stores offered a segregated section for ladies.

In September 2002, Starbucks announced that it would increase the number of international stores to 10,000 by 2005. However, analysts pointed out that it would be difficult for Starbucks to make profits in international markets, and they were soon to be proved right.

PROBLEMS IN INTERNATIONAL MARKETS

In the early 2000s, Starbucks faced many problems in its international operations. (Refer to Exhibit C8-2 for risks in international markets.) The volatile political environment in the Middle East created serious problems for Starbucks. In July 2002, Arab students gave a call for a boycott of American goods and services due to the alleged close relationship between the United States and Israel. The boycott targeted U.S. companies, including Starbucks, Burger King, Coca-Cola, and Estée Lauder. Starbucks topped the list of companies to be boycotted due to Schultz's alleged closeness to the Jewish community.[9]

The problem was aggravated when it was reported that, in one of his lectures to students at the University of Washington, Schultz had said, "One of my missions is to sensitize you; you should not be immune to what is happening in the world. I travel a great deal and one of the things that I see is the rise of anti-Semitism in Europe, especially France and England."[10] His address to Jewish Americans made matters worse. Schultz said, "What is going on in the Middle East is not an isolated part of the world. The rise of anti-Semitism is at an all time high since the 1930s. Palestinians aren't doing their job, they're not stopping terrorism."[11] These comments from Schultz resulted in angry protests from the Arab countries and pro-Palestinian groups across the Middle East and Europe. Analysts felt that Schultz's comments strengthened the feeling that he was acting as an Israeli mouthpiece.

Starbucks distanced itself from Schultz's comments, saying that they represented his personal beliefs and not those of the company. Schultz also denied allegations that he was anti-Palestinian and released a personal statement, saying that "My position has always been pro-peace and for the two nations to co-exist peacefully."[12] In addition to the above incidents, the U.S. declaration of war on Iraq in early 2003 made matters worse for the company. Due to increasing security threats, Starbucks closed its six stores in Israel.

---

[7]"Planet Starbucks," *BusinessWeek,* September 9, 2002.

[8]"Starbucks Jolts Europe's Coffee Houses," *Seattle Times,* May 19, 2002.

[9]In 1998, Schultz was honored with the "Israeli 50th Anniversary Tribute Award" by the Jerusalem Fund of Aish Ha-Torah (a group supporting Israel).

[10]"Starbucks: The Cup that Cheers," www.zmag.org, July 11, 2002.

[11]"Starbucks: The Cup that Cheers," www.zmag.org, July 11, 2002.

[12]"Starbucks: The Cup that Cheers," www.zmag.org, July 11, 2002.

EXHIBIT C8-2   Types of Risk in International Business

Typically a firm operating internationally is exposed to different types of risk. These can be listed as strategic, operational, political, country, technological, or environmental risks.

Strategic Risk

MNCs typically face a diverse set of risks, all of which cannot be assessed quantitatively. Michael Porter defines five forces impacting a firm's competitiveness—threat of substitutes, threat of new entrants in the industry, bargaining power of suppliers, bargaining power of customers, and the intensity of competition within the industry. A firm's strategic decisions to respond to the above-mentioned five forces are a source of risk.

Operational Risk

Operational risk arises out of factors internal to the company such as machinery breakdown, industrial strife, supply and distribution imperfections, excess or shortfall in inventory, etc. It causes a downtime in the day-to-day operations of the enterprise. Reducing costs by eliminating wastage and reducing variances and lead time by improving processes are important to bring about global efficiency. The greater the number of parts and processes involved in production, the greater the risk of not achieving the desired quality and productivity standards.

Political Risk

Political risk refers to political actions that have a negative impact on the firm's value. The process of establishing a cause-and-effect relationship between political factors and business income is called political risk analysis. Political risk is not confined to developing countries. It exists even in highly industrialized economies. While macro-political risks such as war and anti-globalization efforts affect the value of all firms in the country, micro-political risks like regulation of certain industries affect the value of a firm or firms within that industry adversely.

Country Risk

Country risk is a wider concept that encompasses economic conditions, government policies, political conditions, and security factors. The challenge of country risk analysis is in the aggregation of risk factors.

Technological Risk

Technological risk means the probability of adverse effects on business due to factors like obsolescence of an existing technology, development costs of new technology, failure of a new technology, and security concerns of electronic transactions.

Environmental Risk

Environmental risk can be of two forms. The company may incur regulators' wrath because it polluted the environment, or there may be a public outcry in the event of an environmental damage caused by the company. Environment risk management might not provide short-term gains like financial risk management does. But in the long run, it can certainly become a source of competitive advantage and also enhance the corporate image.

SOURCE: Compiled from various sources.

Starbucks also faced criticism from non-governmental organizations (NGOs), which urged the company to acquire certified coffee beans, ensuring that those coffee beans were grown and marketed under certain economic and social conditions. Starbucks also faced problems due to economic recession in countries such as Switzerland, Germany, and Japan in the early 2000s, where it experienced declining sales and revenues. Starbucks faced stiff competition, high business development costs, and resistance from customers in international markets.

By the late 1990s, Starbucks noticed that store traffic in Japan, its largest overseas market, was falling. It was observed that over a period of time, after the novelty wore off, customers opted for other stores, as they did not like the taste of Starbucks coffee. Commented a customer, "I never go to Starbucks if I can help it. The coffee tastes artificial."[13] The Starbucks sales in Japan

declined by over 17 percent in 2002. In order to boost its sales, it even introduced food items like rice and salmon wraps, and white peach muffins; however, it still failed to gain market acceptance.

In May 2003, Starbucks' Japanese business announced an annual loss of $3.9 million on revenues of $467 million.[14] Analysts felt that one of the main reasons for this was Starbucks' rapid expansion in Japan, which resulted in stores eating into each others' business.

After this, Starbucks announced that it would slow the pace at which it opened new stores in Japan. The company said it would open between 70 and 75 stores in 2003, as opposed to the 108 stores opened the previous year. "The Starbucks boom is over in Japan," said Seiichiro Samejima (Samejima), an analyst at Ichiyoshi Research Institute Inc., a stock rating company in Japan. "They continue to cannibalize their own market by

[13]"For Starbucks, There's No Place Like Home," *BusinessWeek*, June 9, 2003.

[14]"For Starbucks, There's No Place Like Home," *BusinessWeek*, June 9, 2003.

opening new stores, and the quality of their food is not yet competitive with other chains."[15]

In Europe Starbucks faced stiff competition from well-established local players who offered specialty coffee at lower prices. Reportedly, in European markets, Starbucks was perceived as an "overpriced imitator of the real thing."[16] For example, in England, the Starbucks tall latte coffee was sold at $2.93, while the same was available for $2.12 at the local coffee shop.

Even in Germany, which had the largest number of Starbucks stores in Europe, the company faced stiff competition from many local coffee shops, which imitated the "Starbucks experience." Eventually, in November 2004, Starbucks acquired the 82 percent stake held by its German partner, KarstadtQuelle AG,[17] after the latter said that it wanted to focus on its core department store businesses. At the end of 2004, Starbucks had only 35 stores in Germany. The company had announced previously that its goal was to open 200 stores in the country by the end of 2006. However, considering the slow pace of store openings, analysts were doubtful that it would achieve its goal.

Starbucks entered France, a country known for its coffee-drinking culture, in early 2004 by opening its first store in Paris. The company formed a 50-50 joint venture with Madrid-based restaurant and retail firm Grupo Vips, which was also the chain's partner in Spain. In France, Starbucks faced competition from more than 50,000 traditional French cafes where the French habitually went for their coffee. Most of these cafes served traditional strong French coffee and, unlike Starbucks, most of them allowed smoking.[18] Analysts felt that Starbucks would find it difficult to draw away customers from the smaller cafes to its Americanized coffee.

Another challenge for Starbucks in France was high real estate and labor costs. Starbucks had opened stores in high-traffic tourist areas in Paris and other parts of France, where the real estate costs were very high. Besides, the cost of labor was also higher in France than in most of Starbucks' other markets. For instance, the minimum wage in France, at $9.92 an hour, was 93 percent higher than the hourly minimum wage of $5.15 in the United States.[19]

Starbucks had to adapt itself to suit French tastes. The company modified many of its food items and introduced several new items to match the French taste. In addition to this, although the company persisted with its *No Smoking* policy within the stores, it offered pavement seating and service, where people could smoke.

In spite of this, Starbucks never really managed to take off in France. Even in 2006, two years after the first store opened in the country, it was observed that most of the people who frequented Starbucks in France were American and Asian tourists, along with a few locals looking for a change. Although Starbucks did not disclose whether or not it was profitable in France, it was widely believed that the company was not profitable. "I think it's losing a phenomenal amount of money here," said Ralph Hababou, co-founder of Columbus Cafe, a French coffee store chain and a major rival of Starbucks in France. "The cost of hiring employees and buying leases is simply too high."[20]

It was observed that Starbucks was unable to earn more revenues from its international operations due to its complex joint ventures and licensing agreements. While the company invested huge amounts in imparting training to the employees and promoting its products, it earned only a percentage share in total profits and royalty fees. It was further felt that the company did not have any control over the operational costs.

In addition to its problems in international markets, Starbucks experienced operational problems due to lack of a trained workforce and suitable real estate for its stores. Commenting on the operational hindrances faced by Starbucks, Maslen said, "If we could train the people and find the real estate, the expansion could happen tomorrow, almost. There is demand."[21]

In order to have better control over operational costs, Starbucks decided to go for new suppliers for items such as mugs. It was reported that the company was thinking of sourcing mugs from low-cost Japanese vendors rather than importing them from the United States, and planning to source its paper goods (such as plates and cups) from Southeast Asia.

Company sources also revealed that Starbucks would close its loss-making stores. However, analysts pointed out that closing the loss-making stores and adopting cost cutting would increase profitability only in the short run and not drive future growth.

In late 2005, in an effort to reestablish its presence in the lucrative Japanese market, Starbucks entered the ready-to-drink coffee segment. The company launched "Starbucks Discoveries," a ready-to-drink coffee product that was retailed through convenience stores. Starbucks Discoveries was initially launched in two flavors—Seattle, a latte, and Milano, an espresso.

Starbucks announced that its decision to enter the ready-to-drink coffee segment was based on research conducted by the company, which indicated that Asian consumers thought chilled coffee had the highest quality of all ready-to-drink coffee beverages. In addition to

---

[15]Ian Messer, "Japan's Coffee Shops Spill Over," *Bloomberg News,* May 21, 2003

[16]"For Starbucks, There's No Place Like Home," *BusinessWeek,* June 9, 2003.

[17]KarstadtQuelle AG was the largest department store in Europe. It was created in 1999 through the merger of Karstadt Warenhaus AG, which was founded in 1920, and Quelle Schickedanz AG & Co, founded in 1927.

[18]In October 2006, the French government announced that it would impose a ban on smoking in public places from February 2007, and from smoking in bars, restaurants, hotels, and night clubs by early 2008.

[19]Eric Wahlgren, "Will Europe Warm to Starbucks?" *BusinessWeek,* January 24, 2005.

[20]Rachel Tiplady, "Can Starbucks Blend into France," *BusinessWeek,* April 20, 2006.

[21]"Starbucks Jolts Europe's Coffee Houses," *Seattle Times,* May 19, 2002.

EXHIBIT C8-3   Starbucks: Annual Income Statements
(All amounts in millions of US dollars except per-share amounts)

Particulars	Sep 05	Sep 04	Sep 03	Sep 02	Sep 01	Sep 00
Revenue	6,369.3	5,294.3	4,075.5	3,288.90	2,649.00	2,169.20
Cost of goods sold	2,605.2	2,191.4	1,685.9	2,582.70	2,068.00	1,684.30
Gross profit	3,764.1	3,102.8	2,389.6	706.20	581.00	484.90
Gross profit margin (%)	59.1	58.6	58.6	21.50	21.90	22.40
SG&A expense	2,606.2	2,169.0	1,699.6	202.20	151.40	110.20
Depreciation and amortization	377.3	325.6	265.3	221.10	177.10	142.20
Operating income	780.6	608.2	424.7	282.90	252.50	232.50
Operating margin (%)	12.3	11.5	10.4	8.60	9.50	10.70
Total net income	494.5	390.6	268.3	215.10	181.20	94.60
Net profit margin (%)	7.8	7.4	6.6	6.50	6.80	4.40
Diluted EPS ($)	0.61	0.47	0.34	0.54	0.46	0.25

SOURCE: www.hoovers.com

this, most Starbucks customers in Asia believed that chilled-cup coffee was the best way for Starbucks to enter the market outside of their retail stores. The company claimed that Starbucks Discoveries was made fresh and kept refrigerated. It also had a short shelf life of 14 days—one of the shortest for similar products on the market at that time.

In February 2006, Starbucks Japan posted a profit increase of 30 percent for the previous nine months, helped by strong sales of seasonal drinks and food. The company observed that more customers were ordering food to go with their coffee, and increased the number of food items it offered. Reportedly, in early 2006, one store in Tokyo carried more than 60 different food items.

However, one market where Starbucks had managed to gain a strong foothold was China. After it opened the first store in 1999, the company had expanded to more than 200 stores by the end of 2005.[22] Analysts said that it was noteworthy that Starbucks had managed to expand in China, a tea-drinking nation. In June 2005, Starbucks increased its stake in its joint venture with Maxim's Caterers in Hong Kong from 5 to 51 percent.[23] The company also announced that it believed that China would eventually be its largest market outside the US.[24]

OUTLOOK

In fiscal year 2005, Starbucks' revenues from international operations formed 16 percent of the company's total revenues.[25] During the year, the company had opened 1,672 stores around the world, including the first ones in the Bahamas, Jordan, and Ireland.[26]

By early 2006, Starbucks had more than 11,000 stores around the world.[27] The company announced that it was looking at other new markets for expansion. It had identified India as one of the potential markets, and was targeting metros like Delhi, Mumbai, and Chennai as the entry points into the market. Starbucks also announced that it was looking at Brazil and Russia as other potential markets in 2006–2007.[28]

Analysts pointed out that Starbucks should rethink its entry strategy in international markets and focus on pricing to achieve real success. They also cautioned Starbucks against the external risks resulting from volatile political and business environments across the world. They felt that with increasing tensions between America and the rest of the world, the business environment, especially in the Middle East and Southeast Asian regions, was becoming increasingly volatile. Acknowledging the risks involved in the international markets, Schultz said, "We're not taking our success for granted. We also understand that the burden of proof at times is on us given the fact that a lot is being written and there's more sensitivity than ever before about America and American companies. These are the very early days for the growth and development of the company internationally. Clearly there's a big world out there for Starbucks to expand in."[29] Exhibit C8-3 shows Starbucks' Income Statements through 2005.

Only time can tell whether Starbucks will be able to brew its success in the international markets.

[22]Annual Report 2005, www.starbucks.com.
[23]"Starbucks: A Great Leap Forward," *Drinks Business Review,* www.drinks-business-review.com, September 22, 2005.
[24]Annual Report 2005, www.starbucks.com.
[25]Annual Report 2005, www.starbucks.com.
[26]Annual Report 2005, www.starbucks.com.
[27]"Company Timeline—August 2006," www.starbucks.com.
[28]Annual Report 2005, www.starbucks.com.
[29]"Starbucks Backlash: The Java Giant's Expansion Brews Dissent Overseas," www.globalexchange.org, April 16, 2003.

QUESTIONS FOR DISCUSSION

1. Analysts feel that MNCs can mitigate some of the risks in international markets by deciding on a suitable mode of entry into these markets. Analyze the entry strategies adopted by Starbucks for its international expansion.

2. Careful analysis and management of risks not only mitigate losses but also provide superior returns. In the light of this statement do you think Starbucks did not analyze and manage the risks involved in the different markets it entered?

3. A company faces diverse set of risks in international markets. What were the risks faced by Starbucks in its international operations? Explain how Starbucks can reduce risks in its international business.

Case 9   Note on the Global Auto Industry in 2007

The global auto industry is a behemoth and one of the most dynamic, competitive, and strategically located industries in the world. In the 1970s, the industry was dominated by 12 to 15 companies at the global level. In 2007, the industry profile reveals that modular technologies and assembly line operations have replaced the mainstream manufacturing model that prevailed in the 1970s and eighties.[1] Also, quality problems and cutthroat prices have made a few companies survive while others have seen their market shares disappear. The 1998 transnational merger of Daimler-Benz and Chrysler Corporation supports this argument where two companies sought a mega-merger to survive in the industry.

As of 2007, only two auto companies originate from North America (General Motors and Ford). Japan has two firms (Toyota and Honda) and Europe survives with four companies (DaimlerChrysler, Volkswagen, Fiat, and Renault-Nissan). A quick look at the industry shows that in early 2007, Toyota maintains a huge market value of $193 billion versus Honda's $63 billion and DaimlerChrysler's $59 billion.[2] General Motors, Ford, and other companies have been trailing behind because of their losses, high raw material prices, labor disputes, liquidity pressures, branding problems, and energy prices. At the global level, the auto industry has witnessed a major shift in its structure that has appeared in the forms of hundreds of strategic alliances and collaborative activities in research and development (R&D), distribution agreements, joint ventures, and equity stakes. The reasons behind these structural changes are the industry's evolutionary processes, competition, economies of scale in manufacturing, and consolidations.[3] In addition, rising costs and consumer demands have compelled many auto manufacturers to move assembly plants to low cost locations. Japanese auto manufacturers have survived because of their quality models and moving plants to North America.[4] In addition, consumer demand in emerging markets (EMs) has also forced large auto manufacturers to move facilities abroad to take advantage of cheaper labor and future market opportunities.[5]

The industry's new landscape has made it increasingly difficult for the auto companies to deal with issues such as worldwide integration, manufacturing efficiencies and rationalization, and other competition issues. As stated earlier, the world auto market is highly dynamic and competitive because of changing technologies, competition, and cost factors. Apart from the established brands, the product life cycles in the industry are short and unpredictable for new models. In the new product development process, future benefits sometimes elude quality standards and business models. Many auto analysts believe that in the coming years, only a handful of major auto manufacturers will survive at the global level because of future consolidations and mergers. Companies maintaining strong brand identities and quality platforms will succeed regarding their global integration initiatives. Today's auto executives face an uphill task regarding reviving their profit centers and smoothing global integration. The next four years (2007–2010) are going to be difficult in the areas of cost cutting, plant rationalizations, R&D savings, and labor relations.

In short, the industry at the global level is expected to witness a multitude of changes that could include plant closings, volatility in sales, lower profits, job cuts, and time-consuming labor negotiations. Restructuring areas aimed at bringing productivity and efficiencies could include smart and flexible manufacturing, faster

SOURCE: Written exclusively for this text by Syed Tariq Anwar, Professor, West Texas A&M University.

[1]For detail, see *The New York Times.* 2005. "Japan makes more cars elsewhere," (August 1): C1&C9; *Financial Times.* 2002. "Fitting together a modular approach," (August 15): 6; *Financial Times.* 2006. "FT—Motor industry," (September 28): 1–4.

[2]See Reuters. 2006, www.reuters.com.

[3]*The Wall Street Journal.* 2006. "Chrysler gains edge by giving new flexibility to its factories," (April 11): A1&A15.

[4]*The Wall Street Journal.* 2005. "Foreign auto makers aim to boost U.S. market share," (January 12): A1&A4.

[5]See *The New York Times.* 2006. "Detroit, far South," (July 21): C1&C4; *The Wall Street Journal.* 2006. "China's fast gains in auto parts reflect new manufacturing edge," (August 1): A1&A6; *The Wall Street Journal.* 2006. "Toyota races to rev up production for a boom in emerging markets," (November 13): A1&A15.

product development, and supplier networks.[6] Overall, the global auto industry is a classic example in the areas of global competition, industry evolutions, sustainable competitive advantage, and creative destruction. Lessons we learn from the global auto industry are that companies need to deal with changing markets, lean manufacturing, and growth constraints. Regardless of products and sectors, today's global industries are never

static; they are always on the move to stay competitive regarding changing their business models and practices.[7]

Following are two case studies demonstrating the challenges and strategies of companies in the auto industry: DaimlerChrysler and Renault-Nissan. You are encouraged to compare their history, strategies, and results leading up to the time you are reading the cases, and follow up on what has happened since with them.

---

[6]For more discussion, see The Harbour Associates. 2006. *The Harbour Report: North America 2006*, Troy, Michigan; *Standard & Poor's Industry Surveys*. 2006. "Autos & Auto Parts," (June 29): 1–38.

[7]For detail, see McGahan, Anita M. 2004. *How Industries Evolve*, Boston, Massachusetts: Harvard Business School Press; Porter, Michael E. 1998. "How competitive forces shape strategy," in Porter, Michael E. *On Competition*, Boston, Massachusetts: Harvard Business School Press: 21–38.

Case 10   Renault-Nissan: The Paradoxical Alliance

I. INTRODUCTION

It was late March 1999. As a seasoned executive of a global corporation, General Motors' vice chairman Bob Lutz knew that well over 50 percent of alliances were destined for failure—especially those taking place across such distant—and distinctive—national cultures as the French and the Japanese cultures. These thoughts were undoubtedly in his mind as he learned that the French company Renault had just bought a 36.6 percent stake in Japanese Nissan for US$5.4 billion to form an alliance between the two companies. His remark to a journalist became instant news:

> *Renault would be better off buying US$5 billion of gold bars, putting them on a ship and dumping them in the Japanese Nissan for US$5.4 billion to form an alliance between the two companies.*

Bob Lutz was not alone in his opinion. The international media, company executives, management academics, and consultants all over the world were nearly unanimous in their disapproval of the Renault-Nissan alliance. A sample of their comments gives a sense of their main concerns:

> *Much has been made of the culture clash between [the May 1998 merging partners] Daimler and Chrysler but it will be nothing compared to Nissan and Renault. At their core, they*

are both nationalistic and patriotic, and each believes its way is the right way to do things. We will have quite a teething period for the first year or two as they feel each other out.

> *Two mules don't make a race-horse.*

> *I would have preferred Renault to take 51 percent even if it meant having to assume Nissan's debt on its balance sheet. That way Renault could have become the real boss and set some firm direction, rather than having to negotiate.*

> *French taxpayers might be left footing the bill for Renault, whose top managers were perhaps blinded by the brilliance of their own vision.*

> *Even the most optimistic observers reckon that the payoff horizon—assuming that the alliance could overcome its enormous business and cultural hurdles—would be long-term, not short.*[1]

Not only did mainstream managerial theories support these concerns fully, there were also Renault and Nissan themselves. On the one hand, Renault had just been taken off the losers' league of automakers following a remarkable comeback that was turning losses of US$680 million in 1996 into combined profits of US$1.65 billion in 1998 and 1999. In addition, Renault was still recovering from a highly publicized failure to merge with Volvo in 1995. A distinctively French and European car maker, Renault had never run a global operation: In 1998 the company sold no cars in the

---

This case study was written by Piero Morosini, Adjunct Professor of Strategy and Leadership at the European School of Management and Technology. It is not intended to represent either effective or ineffective handling of a management situation. Copyright European School of Management and Technology, 2005.

[1]Ghosn, C. 2002. Global Leader Series, Speech at INSEAD, Fontainebleau, France, September 24. Also see K. Hughes, J. Barsoux, and J. Manzoni. 2003. "Redesigning Nissan (A): Carlos Ghosn Takes Charge," Fontainebleau: INSEAD Case 303-044-1, and "Redesigning Nissan (B): Leading Change," Fontainebleau: INSEAD Case 303-045-1.

United States and only 2,476 units in Japan, the world's two largest automotive markets.

On the other hand, Nissan was nearly bankrupt in 1999. Since 1991 it had been losing money and market share continuously, and car production had dropped by 600,000 units. The latter meant that Nissan's factories were running at 53 percent capacity utilization. The company's product portfolio was aging, and it had ten times the number of suppliers and four times the number of manufacturing platforms as Ford and Volkswagen, respectively. Its US$20 billion debt mountain was more comparable to that of a medium-sized developing country than that of a large automaker.

The joining companies were quite complementary in geographic scope and skills. Renault had a flair for marketing and design, and was strong in Europe and Latin America. Nissan was an engineering powerhouse with a strong market presence in Japan, North America, and Asia. However, these two companies had no history of working together. To complicate matters, in March 1999 the French state had a 44 percent controlling stake in Renault, and Nissan, as Japan's second largest automaker, was a highly emblematic symbol of that country's industrial strength. Not surprisingly, after its alliance with Nissan was publicly announced, Renault's share price fell and three separate rating agencies issued negative reviews of the company's debt.

It was on a sunny afternoon in mid-March 2004 in Paris, almost five years to the day that the Renault-Nissan alliance had been so universally written off, that Renault's president Louis Schweitzer was preparing to retire. Seated comfortably behind his office desk at Renault's headquarters, he told a journalist:

> *The future is rosy. Clearly we have the pieces in place that are required for growth . . . Renault-Nissan has been an incredible, and in many ways unexpected, success . . . Someday, maybe—I hope so—Nissan may help [Renault's re-entry into] the United States [market].*[2]

Renault's original US$5.4 billion investment in Nissan was worth US$18.4 billion in March 2004. This made Renault's 36.6 percent stake in Nissan (which Renault increased to 44.4 percent in 2003), worth more than the total market value of the French carmaker itself. Nissan's head of Europe (and former Renault executive) Patrick Pelata called it "the biggest return on investment in the history of the automotive industry." The Japanese company's profits of US$7.6 billion and 11 percent operating margins were the highest in the automotive industry. As indicated by these results, in March 2004 the Renault-Nissan alliance was universally regarded as a successful model by competitors, practitioners, and business schools around the world.

II. THE SOCIAL INITIATION STAGES OF THE ALLIANCE

In early 2004, an observer wrote:

> *The Renault-Nissan alliance was called "a marriage of desperation for both parties" when it was announced in March 1999. A more precise description, however, should have heralded a successful corporate [tinkunacuy] period turning into a long-term marriage.*[3]

This observer was referring to tinkunacuy, a Kichua word denoting an ancient conjugal practice of social initiation in Peru's Andean civilizations of millennia in age. Within certain Andean communities, whenever a young couple contemplates future marriage, they move in together for a number of months. If the experience of living together is satisfactory, they go on to marry. In any other case, the couple gives up their marriage hopes to once more become single individuals ready for tinkunacuy with another partner in the community.[4]

There is more than what meets the eye in tinkunacuy. The partners expect—and are expected by the community—to marry, and so they prepare mentally and emotionally as individuals beforehand. Then both partners give the best of each other openly, truthfully, and respectfully, to experience life together and share their dreams as a married couple. Tinkunacuy thus resolves for the Andean people the timeless paradox of building solid conjugal relationships. On the one hand, a couple gets the chance of building its shared dreams together. On the other, they get to know, take risks, and experience first-hand the practicalities and uncertainties of cooperating with each other as a couple before entering a life-long commitment.

During July to December 1998, Renault's and Nissan's top executives (joined by a selected number of managers

[2]Phelan, M. 2004. "Retiring CEO says Renault-Nissan are poised for growth," *Tribune Business News*. 17 March.

[3]Morosini, P. 2005. "Nurturing Successful Alliances Across Boundaries—Lessons from the Renault-Nissan case." In *The Handbook for Strategic Alliances*, Oded Shenkar (Ed.), Sage: 300.
[4]Tinkunacuy (which, in Peru is also called by its more Hispanicized name, servinacuy) is still practiced in a number of Andean communities within Peru. Since antiquity, tinkunacuy was assisted by phitotherapeutical contraceptive practices, and it was the man who had the formal prerogative of renouncing the subsequent step of marriage. However, in such cases he had to provide adequate compensation to his tinkunacuy partner. See Espinoza Soriano, W. 1997. *Los Incas, Economia, sociedad y estado en la era del tahuantinsuyo*, Lima, Peru: Amaru Editores. A modern, perhaps more liberal and egalitarian version of tinkunacuy-like practices was pioneered in Scandinavia during the late 1950s. It has become widespread in most Western societies ever since, not only as a social practice but also enshrined in many of these countries' codes of civil law.

from both companies) went through a six-month living experiment of working together with the aim of forging a formal alliance between the two companies. What these companies did during this period of social initiation explains much of the subsequent success of their alliance.

In June 1998 Renault's Schweitzer disregarded advice from investment bankers against a direct approach and wrote to Nissan's President Yoshikazu Hanawa proposing broad strategic cooperation. He sent a similar letter to the president of Mitsubishi Motor Cars (MMC). Unlike MMC, Hanawa's answer was quick and enthusiastic. A framework for cooperation was sketched by an internal support team in July 1998. Schweitzer and Hanawa met a dozen times over the ensuing months to learn to trust each other and imagine a future alliance between their companies. Hanawa gave an insight into the atmosphere the two leaders created during these initial stages:

> With many people around, it is difficult to tell each other the truth, that is why I decided to negotiate alone. . . . I believe the process leading up to an alliance is all about telling the truth; dishonesty only makes the process longer. . . . I was impressed with Mr. Schweitzer's courageous decision to embrace a new business opportunity."[5]

As a next step Schweitzer and Hanawa picked 100 engineers and managers from both companies to work together in joint study teams without any formal objective. Instead, these people were encouraged to drop their mental stereotypes about France and Japan and concentrate on hard business fact-finding. Free from cultural stereotypes and from following pre-conceived goals, the teams set a discovery trip of sorts in motion. Some of the executives involved in the teamwork recall the prevailing feelings:

> The kind of information that we were sharing with each other prior to the alliance agreement was a very rare case . . . since both sides had strong individual needs to make themselves stronger, the joint study took place sincerely.
>
> It was extraordinary in terms of synergies. We really believed in it. . . . Quite frankly, we were so complementary in terms of geography, products, personality . . . so we had great confidence.[6]

By working together with neither prejudices nor pre-established goals, the teams found a common ground as well as concrete opportunities for collaboration between the two companies. Armed with this hard

business data, in October 1998 Schweitzer prepared a two-page mock press release entitled "Nissan and Renault join forces." Schweitzer explained:

> We had to move closer strategically, but it could not be a simple acquisition or a merger, because a Franco-Japanese merger is no easy matter. . . . I suggested to him [Hanawa] that three people from Renault should become members of the Nissan board of directors: the COO, the vice-president product planning and the deputy chief financial officer. I only asked for those three."[7]

Hanawa observed:

> I did not agree with it [the mock press release] from the start, of course. But I was not surprised. Through our discussions, I felt that Mr. Schweitzer always had a more comprehensive view of the partnership than I did.[8]

On November 10, Renault's Schweitzer, Ghosn (who would become COO, and later, in 2000, CEO of Nissan), and Douin made a presentation to the Nissan board of directors describing the benefits of a large-scale collaboration between the two companies. The presentation drew heavily on the findings of the joint study teams. No formal commitment was yet in sight but it was decided that the work of the joint study teams would continue until December 1998.

Both Renault's Schweitzer and Nissan's Hanawa had clear ideas of what they wanted out of a strategic alliance. But they were unfamiliar to each other and had no history of working together. As in tinkunacuy, they set a living process of social initiation in motion to test their companies' ability to work cooperatively and deliver on the promise of a shared future. The process itself had useful outcomes, that is, to allow for joint discoveries, to develop the ability to share knowledge trustingly and openly, and to develop social capital in the form of valuable social networks between the two companies. The six-month social initiation process gave Renault an advantage over competitive suitors such as Ford or DaimlerChrysler. The latter companies resorted to a more conventional "due diligence" process. In other words, they carried out static analytical evaluations rather than an actual experiment of social collaboration, and focused on finding synergies based on past and current strengths, rather than on jointly imagining a shared future. It is in fact revealing to compare what Renault-Nissan's particular approach to social initiation

[5]Korine, H, K. Asakawa, and P-Y Gomes. 2002. "Partnering with the Unfamiliar: Lessons from the Case of Renault and Nissan," *Business Strategy Review* 13(2): 41-50.
[6]Ibid.

[7]Ibid.
[8]Edmonson, G. 1999. "Dangerous Liaison: Renault and Nissan," *BusinessWeek*, 29 March.

led to during the subsequent negotiation stages of their alliance, vis-à-vis what happened to some of their competitors that took a more conventional approach to initiating their own strategic alliances.

III. TWO APPROACHES TO ALLIANCE NEGOTIATION

March 1999 saw two archetypal approaches to alliance negotiation and closure at play in the automotive industry. On the one hand, DaimlerChrysler CEO Jürgen Schrempp had a two-month due diligence carried out to assess the prospect of an alliance with Nissan. Then on March 9, he met at length with his management board in a hotel in the shores of Lake Geneva. A "green team" of company managers focused on the likely benefits of an alliance with Nissan. A "red team" focused on the drawbacks. After listening to both sides, Schrempp and his management team made a decision. The next day, Schrempp flew to Tokyo and met for three hours with Nissan's Hanawa. DaimlerChrysler broke off alliance talks with Nissan after that meeting. Soon after, following a similar process, DaimlerChrysler entered into an equity alliance with Mitsubishi Motor Corporation (MMC). When signing that deal, Schrempp remarked: "They [MMC] are the ideal partner for us."

Renault's approach to negotiating an alliance with Nissan was different. In their case, both the substance and the style of their alliance negotiations were an organic result of what the two companies achieved during their social initiation stages. The level of confidence in their ability to work cooperatively, the mutual trust that had been created, and the informal pledges that had been jointly formulated played a critical role in the final outcome of the negotiations. In other words, these negotiations were not just about signing an alliance deal following a sound due diligence assessment. Rather, the prospective allies enacted a process of social commitment that codified the mutual pledges stemming from their earlier experiment of working together. This is made evident by examining the negotiations of the Renault-Nissan alliance in greater detail.

Already in August 1998 Schweitzer had proposed to Hanawa:

We have a firm and trusting relationship. To make our relationship stronger, why not think about holding each other's shares?[9]

To which Hanawa replied:

Nissan, frankly, has no money to spend on buying Renault stock.[10]

The Frenchman replied:

We can talk about this again in the future. From Renault's point of view, there is no future for us if we cannot work together with Nissan.[11]

The proposal soon became that Renault would buy a stake in Nissan. Hanawa outlined four conditions any foreign buyer had to meet: to keep the Nissan name, protect jobs, promote restructuring under the lead of Nissan, and pick a CEO from inside Nissan. Schweitzer did not object. At the same time, Hanawa told Schweitzer Nissan would need to raise US$6 billion in cash. This was well above Schweitzer's US$3 billion limit. In November 1998, Hanawa visited DaimlerChrysler's headquarters and was greeted with a proposal to invest in Nissan itself. He flew to Paris the next day to inform Schweitzer that he planned to continue negotiations with the German-American automaker. A disappointed Schweitzer remarked:

We cannot provide the amount of cash Nissan needs. If Renault cannot tie up with Nissan we will eventually be driven out of the market.[12]

However, on March 10, 1999, DaimlerChrysler's Schrempp abruptly called off alliance talks with Nissan. Hanawa considered his options. He decided to approach Ford's CEO Jacques Nasser, with whom he'd had earlier contacts. However, Schweitzer sent Hanawa a confidential note saying that there was hope that Renault could make a much larger investment in Nissan than he had proposed earlier. But Schweitzer requested that, no later than March 13, Hanawa sign a "freeze" agreement preventing Nissan from approaching other carmakers until talks with Renault were completed or called off. Hanawa flew to Paris. After inspecting the "freeze" agreement, he still could not pin down the exact amount of Renault's investment in Nissan.

"Please trust me," said Schweitzer.[13]

Hanawa signed the "freeze" agreement. On March 16, 1999, Renault board approved a US$5.4 billion investment in Nissan. The following day, Renault and Nissan announced a signed alliance agreement that closely resembled the two-page mock press release that had been written back in October 1998 during the social initiation process of the alliance. Says Schweitzer:

The decision we made during the final negotiations was not to change our position. It was an important choice on our part to say: "It's not because DaimlerChrysler is not around that we

---

[9]Ibid.
[10]Ibid.

[11]Ibid.
[12]Ibid.
[13]Ibid.

are changing our proposal." I decided not to [change the proposal] because I felt it would destroy the relationship of trust which was indispensable for us to work together.[14]

Hanawa adds:

The fact that we agreed on the terms of equal position was important for me, as dominance destroys motivation.[15]

IV. BUILDING THE GLUE TO CEMENT THE ALLIANCE

(a) Boundary-Spanning Leadership

Carlos Ghosn became COO of Nissan on July 1, 1999. From the outset, this South American of Lebanese descent and French education provided an example of boundary-spanning leadership traits at work in Nissan. At the time of his COO appointment Carlos Ghosn did not speak Japanese, but he addressed the people in Japan directly, without pre-existing mental models, cultural prejudices, or preconceptions. Said Ghosn:

I am not going [to Japan] with any preconceived ideas.[16]

Ghosn encouraged the expatriates he brought with him to Japan to do the same thing:

[In July 1999] I handpicked 17 [French executives] from Renault and brought them to Nissan. I chose people who were around 40 years old, experts in their field, very open minded and coaches, not people who wanted to play it solo. . . . [Before coming to Japan I told them:] we are not missionaries. We are not going there to teach the Japanese [about] the role of women in Japanese business. We are there to help fix Nissan, that's all. Any issue that does not contribute to that is of no concern to us.[17]

Amongst the 17 Renault expatriates that Ghosn brought to Japan were Patrick Pelata and Thierry Moulonguet, whom, as heads of Nissan product development and finance, respectively, would play a critical role in the company's revival. Once in Japan, Ghosn oversaw the reduction of Nissan's board of directors

from 37 members to 10. When Nissan's Hanawa asked him whom he wanted as Japanese members on the executive committee board, Ghosn replied:

I don't know. You choose. You know me so please, you pick them—knowing what you know of me.[18]

Immediately after this, Ghosn formed the company's boundary-spanning leadership team:

I requested that 1,500 profiles of Nissan employees be posted in headquarters to select about 200 people for nine cross-functional teams. I was looking for young mavericks who would be the backbone of the next Nissan leadership generation. Multicultural experience was not considered an absolute requirement for success, but it was a value-added. I think that the basic personal qualities of an individual can always overcome any lack of experience. It is important how you handle small frustrations. And when you have taken time to understand and accept that people don't think or act the same way in France or in Japan, then the cultural differences can become seeds for innovation as opposed to seeds for dissention.[19]

In early 2000, Nissan's new leadership cadre was in place. It was a reduced group of 200 executives not permanently housed at the company's Tokyo headquarters, as had been the case until then, but spending time there on a project-by-project basis. Together with this newly formed boundary-spanning leadership team, Carlos Ghosn began patiently crafting building blocks inside Nissan and made walk-the-talk and transparent communication his leadership trademark. As a result, the company's executive team presided over one of the fastest, most successful turnarounds ever.

(b) Company-Wide Building Blocks

One of the first things that Nissan's boundary-leadership team did was to set company-wide building blocks such as a common language in place. Said Ghosn:

I told the old guard [of Nissan managers from the outset]: You speak English. Learn it immediately if you must or you're out. But some key

---

[14]"Korine, H. et al, op. cit.

[15]Ibid.

[16]Woodruff, D. 1999. "Cultural chasm: Renault faces hurdles in bid to turn Nissan around," *Asian Wall Street Journal*, March 31: 1.

[17]Ghosn, C. 2002. Global Leader Series, Speech at INSEAD, Fontainebleau, France, September 24. Also see Hughes, K, J. Barsoux and J. Manzoni, op. cit.

[18]Ibid.

[19]See Thornton, E. 1999. "Remaking Nissan," *Business Week*, November 15: 70-74. Also see Miller, Z. and Zaun, T. 2002. "Nissan intends to return favor to a French ally," *Asian Wall Street Journal*, April 5: A1.

words were not understood in the same way by different Japanese people or even different French people. So I asked a mixed Renault-Nissan team to establish a dictionary of essential terms. The 100 or so entries included clear definitions for terms like "commitment," "authority," "objectives," "transparency" and "targets."[20]

A common language helped Nissan's work in "cross-functional" and "cross-company" teams effectively, with Renault and Nissan executives from different functions and nationalities working together to achieve challenging business objectives. Examples of the latter include "launch 22 new car models in the next three years," "improve manufacturing capacity utilization in Japan from 53 percent in 1999 to 82 percent in 2002," and "cut automotive debt in half, to US$5.8 billion net in the next three years."

Another building block Ghosn instilled in Nissan early on was to look for and encourage certain common character traits on the company's employees, especially for those who played—or were expected to assume—leadership roles. One such character trait was "walk-the-talk" behavior. Explained Ghosn:

> *What we think, what we say, and what we do must be the same. We have to be impeccable in ensuring that our words correspond to our actions. If there are discrepancies between what we profess and how we behave, that will spell disaster."*[21]

(c) The Nissan Revival Plan

Nissan's Revival Plan (NRP) was a company-wide business initiative that Ghosn introduced in July 1999 as the company's COO. The NRP had clear quantitative and qualitative targets, which required the involvement of—and had a strong effect on—most of Nissan's component areas, and which had a strong emotional impact on the company executives in charge of implementing it. On the brink of complete financial and market collapse, the plan aimed to radically strengthen the company's "common glue" around the mission of revival. Some of the main strategic goals in the plan read:

- *Return to profitability during the year March 2000 to March 2001. The [annual] net income after tax of the Nissan Group will be positive.*
- *An [annual] operating margin superior to 4.5 percent of sales during the year March 2002 to March 2003.*

- *A 50 percent decrease in net debt, from $12.6 billion today to $6.3 billion by March 2003.*
- *Reduce purchasing costs by 20 percent by March 2003.*
- *Reduce 21,000 jobs (from 148,000 to 127,000) by March 2003.*[22]

When Ghosn unveiled the plan at the Tokyo Motor Show in October 18, 1999, few people believed Nissan would achieve its ambitious goals. A Japanese analyst captured the prevailing mood:

> *It is impossible for Japanese managers to carry out such a drastic restructuring program.*[23]

Nissan's stock, already at record lows at the time of the October 1999 Tokyo Motor Show, fell a further 5 percent less than two weeks following the NRP announcement. However, Nissan achieved—and in many cases exceeded—all of the NRP's stated goals contrary to every expectation. When asked how Nissan managed to do this, Ghosn often responded that "cross-functional teams" were a key ingredient for success. Many of these teams had already been in place during the social initiation stages of the alliance, and were utilized to design the NRP without resorting to outsiders such as consultants or industry experts. At the October 18 Tokyo Motor show Ghosn had explained:

> *How did we elaborate the Nissan Revival Plan? On July 5 we established nine cross-functional teams. Each one was led by two Executive Committee members and headed by a pilot. Team members were selected by the leaders and the pilot from the company's managerial ranks. The composition had to be cross-functional and international. It is not top-down. It is not bottom-up. It is both. Each team had one topic. One goal: Make proposals to develop the business and reduce costs. One deadline: This morning's Board meeting for final decisions. One rule: No sacred cows, no taboos, no constraints. One belief: The solutions to Nissan's problems are inside the company. Only one issue is non-negotiable. The return to profit.*[24]

Not all of the NRP involved painful, restructuring goals. There was also room for dreams. When announcing it October 18, 1999, Ghosn had concluded by saying:

---

[20]See: Wickens, M. 2002. "Nissan saviour a comic-book hero," *Toronto Star*, March 16, WH25.

[21]Emerson, V. 2001. "An interview with Carlos Ghosn," *Journal of World Business*, Spring 2001: 3–11.

[22]Ghosn, C. 1999. "We don't have a choice" (speech transcript), *Automotive News*, November 8: 36–44.

[23]Hirano, K. 1999. "Tokyo stocks close mixed in thin trading," *Japanese Economic Newswire*, October 19: 1.

[24]Ghosn, C. 1999. "We don't have a choice" (speech transcript) *Automotive News*, November 8: 36–44.

I know and I measure how much effort, how much sacrifice and how much pain we will have to endure for the success of the NRP. But believe me, we don't have a choice and it will be worth it. We all shared a dream; a dream of a reconstructed and revived company, a dream of a thoughtful and bold Nissan on track to perform profitable growth in a balanced alliance with Renault to create a major global player in the world car industry. This dream today becomes a vision with the NRP. This vision will become a reality as long as every single Nissan employee will share it with us.[25]

Rather than one-sided restructuring, the key to the success of the NRP was product development. At the very heart of the plan was the company's commitment to launch 22 entirely new car models over the ensuing three years, something that very few automotive companies had attempted to do before. This was the task of a dedicated cross-functional team, and the reason behind many of the company's new hires and investments since 1999. Isuzu Motors star designer Shiro Nakamura was recruited in September 1999 to restore allure to Nissan's tarnished brand image vis-à-vis the customers. This had meant heavy discounts on Nissan's car models compared to competitors with better brand reputations. Already in 2000, all of Nissan's design teams scattered worldwide under Nissan's regional engineering functions were unified under Nakamura's leadership. R&D investments rose from 3.7 percent of net sales in 1998 to 5 percent. A significant amount of the increased budget went to support the recruitment of 1,000 new engineers for leading-edge projects such as fuel-cell powered cars.

Moreover, in 1999 Ghosn approved a US$930 million new assembly plant in central Mississippi to supply the key U.S. market—representing one-third of Nissan's sales—with new pickup trucks, minivans, and sport-utility models starting from mid-2003. In May 2000, Nissan also announced a US$300 million investment to produce new Nissan car models in Brazil, an effort headed by a former Renault executive. Explained Ghosn:

People need to know what the prize is, what are they aiming for, what are the benefits or the advantage to them of changing some established tradition. When this is clearly spelled out, people will be motivated to follow. . . . [We are like] a Formula One pilot, [who is] constantly using the accelerator and the brakes. He uses them at the same time to go to the max. We are at the same time accelerating and braking.[26]

Braking and accelerating at the same time also proved useful in dealing with Nissan's army of 5,000 auto-parts suppliers and 600 dealers, all of which had long-standing cross-shareholding ties with Nissan. This system, called keiretsu, had a long tradition in Japanese capitalism. It had provided an environment of mutual loyalty, stability, and low-risk that had nurtured the growth of most of Japan's large corporations since the mid-19th century. However, keiretsu's intrinsic lack of flexibility was proving to be one of its most serious shortcomings within the rapidly changing global business milieu of the 21st century. In the case of Nissan, keiretsu meant that even though many of the company's networks of suppliers and dealers had overgrown costs and low productivity compared to their competitors, they were kept in place because of long-dated shareholding ties. When unveiling the NRP, Ghosn made it clear to journalists, dealers, and suppliers that maintaining keiretsu was not amongst the company's objectives:

With the exception of four companies, none is considered to be indispensable for the future. This means we will be unwinding most of our shareholdings strictly on the basis of a cost/benefit analysis. . . . Our objective is to free all capital resources from non-strategic, non-core assets and to invest more in our core business while at the same time significantly reducing our debt.[27]

The day after the unveiling of the NRP, Nissan's suppliers and dealers were given a deadline of January 2000 to submit bids for new contracts that would be in line with the restructuring targets that had been announced. It was made clear that not all of the bids would be accepted—but it was equally transparent that the selected companies would gain a much greater access to Nissan's business.

Company-wide business initiatives such as the NRP became a continuous feature of Nissan, driving its leadership cohesiveness and competitive performance across functional and cultural boundaries. Thus in 2001, after the NRP's goals had been achieved and the company revived, Nissan launched "180," another company-wide business initiative where "1" stands for one million additional car units sold, "8" denotes an 8 percent margin, and "0" stands for zero debt, all to be achieved by 2005. As the goals of "180" were being met before schedule, in June 2004 Ghosn started to publicize "Value Up," yet another company-wide business initiative that was going to turn Nissan and Renault's brands and product portfolio into higher value-added items in the consumer's minds. The

[25]Ibid.
[26]Emerson, V, op. cit. Also see Shirouzu, N, White, J. B., and Zaun, T. 2000. "A revival at Nissan shows there's hope for Japan Inc.," *Asian Wall Street Journal*, November 17: 1.

[27]Ghosn, C., 1999, "We don't have a choice," (speech transcript) *Automotive News*, November 8: 36-44.

cross-functional teams became a permanent supporting feature in all of Nissan's company-wide business initiatives. Said Ghosn:

> In my experience, executives in a company rarely reach across boundaries. Working together in cross-functional teams helps managers to think in new ways, challenge existing practices, explaining the necessity for change and projecting difficult messages across the entire company.[28]

(d) Building Glue between Renault and Nissan

The implementation stages of the Renault-Nissan alliance did not only contemplate French executives helping Nissan strengthen its "common glue." Parallel to this process, the social amalgamation process between Renault and Nissan themselves continued gradually and inexorably. An example of this was given by the knowledge interactions between the two companies that took place over the 1999–2004 period via the so-called "cross-company teams." Explained Ghosn:

> The experience of the Mexico regional "cross-company team" is a good example of cooperation between Renault and Nissan! [In early 1999] Nissan was suffering from overcapacity in the Mexican market. Renault had abandoned this market since 1986. Putting managers from both companies together meant that they immediately recognized the synergy opportunity. In just five months they put together a plan for producing Renault cars in Nissan plants. A year later, in December 2000, the first Renault models rolled off the production lines. The improvement in Nissan's manufacturing position has been dramatic. At the Cuernavaca plant, capacity utilization went from 56% to nearly 100% by January 2002. And this greatly accelerated Renault's re-entry into Mexico. What's more, Renault could use Nissan's local dealers as distributors.[29]

"Cross-company teams" provided an approach that allowed Renault and Nissan to go through a social initiation experience first, and to then move into more formal frameworks of collaboration and knowledge exchanges on a case-by-case basis. This social approach was found to be so effective in nurturing collaboration between Renault and Nissan, that all other formal aspects—i.e.,

legal, structural, organizational—were made secondary to it. Observed Ghosn:

> At a certain point in negotiations between the two companies [back in July 1998], there was a discussion about how they would work together. Renault's negotiators assumed that the best way forward would be to set up a series of joint ventures, and they wanted to discuss all legal issues surrounding a joint venture: who contributes what and how much, how the output is shared and so forth. The Nissan team pushed back; they wanted to explore management and business issues, not legal technicalities. As a result, negotiations were stalled. . . . I recommended abandoning the joint venture approach. If you want people to work together, the last thing you need is a legal structure that gets in the way. My solution was to introduce informal cross-company teams (CCTs). Some teams focused on specific aspects of automobile manufacturing and delivery. . . . Others focused on a [geographic] region. . . . All told, we created 11 such cross-company teams. . . . Through these teams, Renault and Nissan managers have found many ways to leverage the strengths of both companies."[30]

(e) Communication Rituals

From the outset, Ghosn instilled a culture of extremely transparent, open, precise, and factual communications, both inside Nissan and with outside parties such as the media. In 2002, Ghosn reflected back upon what Nissan's leadership set out to do in this area:

> If you want to mobilize 130,000 people, in different cultures and different countries, you have to be precise, you have to be factual, and you have to base everything you say on hard evidence that people can measure.[31]

In 2001, Thierry Moulonguet—a former Renault executive who became Nissan's VP of Finance in June 1999—characterized this new approach to communications further:

> With Carlos Ghosn the rules of the game are simple and clear. That was perfectly understood by the young generation of Japanese managers. He is very approachable. Anyone can send him an e-mail, he looks at all of them. He reacts in an open and straightforward way.[32]

[28]Ghosn, C. 2002. *Global Leader Series*, Speech at INSEAD, Fontainebleau, France, September 24. Also see Hughes, K. et al., op. cit.
[29]Ghosn, C. 2002. "Saving the business without losing the company," *Harvard Business Review*, Jan: 3-11.

[30]Ibid.
[31]Ghosn, C. 2002. *Global Leader Series*, Speech at INSEAD, Fontainebleau, France, September 24. Also see Hughes, K. et al., op. cit.
[32]Hauter, F. 2001. "Carlos Ghosn: "En situation de crise, la transparence s'impose," *Le Figaro Enterprises*, July 2: 28–29.

A year later, addressing an audience of business school students, Ghosn provided additional arguments supporting the need for total clarity in communications:

> If people don't know the priority, don't understand the strategy, don't know where they're going, don't know what is the critical objective, you're heading for trouble. Confusion is the first sign of trouble. It's [the leader's] duty to clarify the environment, to make sure there is the maximum light in the company.[33]

Nissan's new culture of transparent and factual communications was instilled by its top leaders' habit of "walking-the-talk." In other words, it was made alive within the company through their top leaders' daily behavior, interactions, and practices. In 2001, Ghosn's response to a journalist summarized this approach. Asked how much time he spent in communications, he replied:

> Even in brainstorming sessions, even when we elaborate strategy, you communicate all the time.[34]

Some of these daily events and practices became powerful and visible rituals that made the new walk-the-talk approach to communications come alive within the company. For example, in order to communicate his conviction that the solutions to Nissan's problems were inside the company, Ghosn would make surprise visits to Nissan's research facilities and production plants, gathering input from senior managers and line workers alike. The decision to make English Nissan's common, official language was backed up with intensive language courses for all the company's employees, regardless of level. In spite of the company's critical state in 1999, Ghosn also started the practice of inviting the media to Nissan's annual shareholder meetings and gave them complete freedom to report what they saw. He explained the rationale behind this new transparency:

> [People say] you cannot criticize your own company, but if you don't look at reality as it is, even being harsh at yourself, you'll never fix it.[35]

Ghosn's reactions to critical observations by journalists and other similar outsiders often puzzled them. Far from being defensive, Ghosn would talk candidly about the company's shortcomings while pointing the way out of them. For instance, a journalist who in 1999 expressed disbelief that Nissan lacked even the most basic competitive marketing data received the following reply from Ghosn:

> You laugh, [but] it's real. We had no substantial analysis, segment by segment [of] what was going on.[36]

His choice to communicate the NRP to the outside world at the same time that Nissan employees were learning about it, in the Tokyo Motor Show on October 18, 1999, was a powerful sign of the company's determination to establish transparent, reliable goals and achieve them in a no-nonsense fashion. Ghosn explained:

> Credibility has two legs . . . the first is performance, but [we have nothing to show at the start]; the second leg of credibility is transparency—what I think, what I say, what I do is the same thing. So we have to be extremely transparent.[37]

Supporting this, following the public announcement of Nissan's revival plan (NRP) in October 1999, Ghosn stuck to its ambitious goals even though these were regarded as unrealistic by an overwhelming majority of competitors, industry experts, the international media, and most qualified observers. Said Ghosn:

> The big risk is that if you announce ambitious [goals], people will not believe you. They'll say, "He said 100 percent, but if he gets 50 percent he'll be happy." . . . Well, we want 100, and we're going to get 100. If we don't get it next year [2000], that's it. We will resign.[38]

Instilling this new culture of transparent communications was not easy. In 1999, Ghosn had found a rather compartmentalized culture within Nissan that prevented the flow of communications across the company's various functions, borders, and hierarchical lines. He observed:

> Country organizations were not talking to each other, people were not talking to each other. I want to destroy this spirit.[39]

The "cross-functional teams" were crucial to turn the prevailing culture into a more open spirit that fostered cross-boundary communications. But there were other organizational changes that provided further support to the new culture. In late March 2000, Ghosn—in one of the few unilateral decisions he made since his arrival in

[33]Ghosn, C. 2002. *Global Leader Series*, Speech at INSEAD, Fontainebleau, France, September 24. Also see Hughes, K. et al., op. cit.
[34]Nuss, E. 2001. "Why should we change? The Nissan Revival Plan," INSEAD-*The Business Link*, 3: 18-22.
[35]Ghosn, C. 2002. *Global Leader Series*, Speech at INSEAD, Fontainebleau, France, September 24. Also see Hughes, K. et al., op. cit.

[36]Shirouzu, N. et al., op. cit.
[37]Ghosn, C. 2002. Global Leader Series, Speech at INSEAD, Fontainebleau, France, September 24. Also see Hughes, K. et al., op. cit.
[38]Peterson, T. 2000. "Nissan's Carlos Ghosn: 'No Ifs, No Ands, No Buts," *BusinessWeek*, 18 January.
[39]Burt, T. and A. Harney. 1999. "Le cost-killer makes his move," *Financial Times*, 9 November: 19.

Japan—replaced the company's divisional presidencies in North America and Europe with four cross-functional management teams that met monthly. He remarked:

> Each time you have a regional president, you start to have problems of communication and retention of information, either from headquarters to the region or from the region to the headquarters. We don't want that. This is a killer for the global performance of the company.[40]

(f) Cross-Boundary Rotations

Nissan used personnel and career growth policies effectively in order to break boundaries, rotate key executives around, and create a truly global leadership cadre inside the company. For example, a new stock option plan for all of Nissan's managers worldwide was put into place in July 1999. It helped in moving key development, design, and purchasing executives to centralized, global locations that facilitated cross-functional knowledge interactions. To support this further, a new global promotion and compensation system was rolled out in 2000. Based on the employees' profit contribution, it broke an old tradition of incentives based on seniority at Nissan and throughout corporate Japan. Nissan also established and led a Nomination Advisory Committee to review promotion recommendations. Since 2000, no leadership promotions have been made at Nissan without a performance review by this Committee, which used a performance rather than seniority criterion to endorse its recommendations.

However, preparing the mindsets and attitudes of its employees was a key step that *preceded* the rollout of Nissan's sweeping changes in personnel, career growth, and incentives policies. Ghosn had made this clear when unveiling the NRP in October 1999:

> Performance-based career advancement will be established at the latest by the end of 2000 to make sure we act in a coherent manner across the company. Concretely, some of the changes will not be implemented before ensuring that the people in charge have changed their attitude, and that the clear performance indicators for which they are accountable exist.[41]

Preparing mindsets and molding attitudes was made challenging due to the magnitude of the changes involved. One Nissan manager commented:

> There is a schism [inside Nissan]. We've told those who are resisting the changes that they have one year to change their attitude.[42]

At first Nissan employees were disoriented by the changes and complained:

> We attend meetings late into the night, and the next morning we are requested to come in at 6 am. If this goes on for days and days, it just won't work, unless we get paid more.[43]

However, Carlos Ghosn was unwavering and demanded total commitment to the implementation of these changes by Nissan's boundary-spanning leadership cadre. Already by December 1999, he told the press:

> There is a group in the company who still think this will blow over, though their number grows smaller by the day.[44]

Nissan's new global promotion criterion put into place in 2000—based on performance—was ruthlessly showcased in March 2001. On that date, Nissan announced a series of high-profile casualties affecting executives who had failed to meet their targets repeatedly, including one company vice president and twenty subsidiary presidents. Said Ghosn:

> Accountability has to start at the top [otherwise] it is very difficult to push a company at all levels [and] make sure everybody is committed to the subject.[45]

However, the benefits of the new personnel and career growth policies were showcased in other ways as well. Challenging long-dated boundaries of gender, in 2001 a high-profile female Japanese executive was hired from JP Morgan Securities to head Nissan's communications department, becoming the first woman ever to lead a function within the company. The move grabbed widespread attention from the Japanese media, who commented that up until then ambitious Japanese female executives had had to switch from domestic to foreign-owned companies in order to make progress in their careers. Boundaries of age and seniority were also challenged by Nissan's new policies. In 2000, Nissan executives in their early forties had for the first time been promoted to very senior positions based on their profit-contribution performance rather than their seniority. Likewise, many of the best-performing heads of Nissan's cross-functional teams were promoted rapidly. Said one of them:

[40]Ghosn, C. 2002. "Saving the business without losing the company," *Harvard Business Review,* Jan: 3–11.

[41]Ghosn, C. 1999. "We don't have a choice," (Speech Transcript), *Automotive News*, 8 November: 36–44.

[42]Larimer, T. 2001. "Rebirth of the Z," *Time*, January 15: 18–20.

[43]Kawato, N. and H. Ikematsu. 2000. "Feelings mixed on 'Ghosn reform," *The Daily Yomiuri*, 27 January: 18.

[44]Taylor, A. 1999. "The man who vows to change Japan Inc.," *Fortune*, 20 December: 73–77.

[45]Nuss, E. 2001. "Why should we change? The Nissan Revival Plan," *INSEAD—The Business Link* 3: 18–22.

In the old system everyone could be promoted, so there was no pressure. . . . For many employees it was a good system but for those with good skills, it was no good. If I [had] been replaced by a younger man in the past I would have been shocked. But now I don't think I would care, because clearly the person has better skills than mine.[46]

V. CONCLUSION

As he contemplated retirement in his Paris office in March 2004, Renault's president made statements that mystified most outsiders who came to visit him. This did not seem to trouble Schweitzer. Looking back at the Renault-Nissan alliance he simply said:

We did not try to forge a common culture. . . . We never talked about an alliance of equals.[47]

Anyone hearing his declarations without knowing much about the alliance would probably predict a corporate disaster story. But Renault-Nissan was exactly the opposite. Not only had this alliance been the largest corporate marriage between a Western and an Eastern partner to that date, but it also was one of the very few examples of successful international alliances in any major global industry. Nevertheless, to most people this marriage had looked as odd as could possibly be imagined, and its chances of success hopelessly slim from the outset.

This feeling of oddity would intensify after learning *how* the Renault-Nissan alliance attained success. This in itself countered much of the prevailing theories—but then the perplexing facts of this alliance were far too compelling to be ignored. Not forging a common culture did not prevent Renault and Nissan from nurturing a strong "common glue" between themselves. Even if these companies did not talk about an alliance of equals, they nevertheless created an environment of genuine trust, loyalty, and reciprocity. Although neither of them were particularly strong industry players—Nissan actually being nearly bankrupt at the time of the alliance—these two companies managed to forge a top-performing global partnership in less than five years. Most surprisingly, French and Japanese managers cooperated effectively across national and corporate cultural divides that most pundits could only characterize as gaping.

March 2004 marked the end of an era for the Renault-Nissan alliance. Both companies announced they would share a single CEO starting in 2005 in the person of Carlos Ghosn, a former Renault executive whom, as Nissan's CEO, had presided over the company's remarkable revival since May 1999. Renault and Nissan jointly announced financial results for the first time in 2004. Their combined US$109 billion in sales and US$4 billion in profits catapulted both companies from the bottom of the automakers' leagues to the world's fifth largest car manufacturer and one of the most profitable.

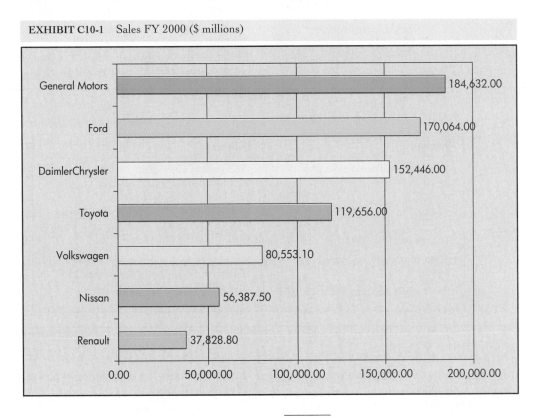

EXHIBIT C10-1 Sales FY 2000 ($ millions)

Company	Sales
General Motors	184,632.00
Ford	170,064.00
DaimlerChrysler	152,446.00
Toyota	119,656.00
Volkswagen	80,553.10
Nissan	56,387.50
Renault	37,828.80

[46]Ibison, D. 2001. "Nissan puts merit before service," *Irish Times*, July 27: 63.

[47]de Saint-Seine, S. 2004. *Automotive News Europe*, 9–7: 10.

EXHIBIT C10-2   Cross-Functional Teams: Focus and Objectives

Cross-Functional Team	Team Review Focus	Objectives Based on Review
Business Development	Profitable growth New product opportunities Brand identity Product development lead time	Launch 22 new models by 2002 Introduce a minicar model by 2002 in Japan
Purchasing	Supplier relationships Product specifications and standards	Cut number of suppliers in half Reduce costs by 20% over three years
Manufacturing and Logistics	Manufacturing efficiency and cost effectiveness	Close three assembly plants in Japan Close two power-train plants in Japan Improve capacity utilization in Japan from 53% in 1999 to 82% in 2002
Research and Development	R&D capacity	Move to a globally integrated organization Increase output efficiency by 20% per project
Sales and Marketing	Advertising structure Distribution structure Dealer organization Incentives	Move to a single global advertising agency Reduce SG&A costs by 20% Reduce distribution subsidiaries by 20% in Japan Close 10% of retail outlets in Japan Create prefecture business centers or common back offices
General and Administrative	Fixed overhead costs	Reduce SG&A costs by 20% Reduce global head count by 21,000
Finance and Cost	Shareholdings and other noncore assets Financial planning structure Working capital	Dispose of noncore assets Cut automotive debt in half to $5.8 billion net Reduce inventories
Phaseout of Products and Parts Complexity Management	Manufacturing efficiency and cost effectiveness	Reduce number of plants in Japan from seven to four by 2002 Reduce number of platforms in Japan from 24 to 15 by 2002 Reduce by 50% the variation in parts (e.g., due to differences in engines or destination) for each model
Organization	Organizational structure Employee incentive and pay packages	Create regional management committees Empower program directors Implement performance-oriented compensation and bonus packages, including stock options

EXHIBIT C10-3   Nissan Revival Plan

Promised	Delivered
• Positive annual net income after tax by 2000–2001	($6.5) billion 1999–2000 $2.7 billion 2000–2001 $2.7 billion 2001–2002 $4.1 billion in March 2002 to March 2003
• Annual operating margin of 4.5 percent of sales by 2002–2003	10.8 percent by March 2002 to March 2003
• 50% reduction in net debt to $6.3 billion by March 2003	Net debt of $6.6 billion in September 2001 18 percent reduction by September 2001
• Eliminate 21,000 jobs by March 2003	19,900 job cuts by September 2001

QUESTIONS FOR DISCUSSION

1. What are the key reasons behind Nissan's performance during the 1999–2006 period?
2. Did Renault's and Nissan's decision to form a strategic alliance make sense? Why/why not?
3. Why was Renault-Nissan's announcement of their strategic alliance greeted with such unanimous pessimism by the international business media and market analysts?

The instructor and the students will examine:

a. What are the key success factors of alliances according to the management literature? According to your own experience?

b. How did the Renault-Nissan alliance stand against these success factors?

c. What were the real risks that Renault and Nissan faced when entering this alliance?

4. What were Carlos Ghosn's key challenges to successfully implementing the Renault-Nissan alliance?

5. What did Ghosn actually do during the first couple of years from his appointment as Nissan's COO? The instructor and the students will look at:

a. What were Carlos Ghosn's first steps? Why?

b. How (and using which criteria) did Carlos Ghosn choose his key leadership cadre at Nissan? What did the profiles of his French and Japanese managers look like? Why was he set on those particular profiles?

c. How was the Nissan Revival Plan implemented? Why were the cross-functional teams so successful in implementing the plan (and afterwards as well)?

d. How would you describe Carlos Ghosn's approach to managing Renault's and Nissan's profound corporate and national cultural differences?

6. What has happened since 1999? Do you think the alliance is successful at the time of your reading the case? What is its position now in the global auto industry?

7. What are the three most important lessons that you learned from this case? Why?

Case 11   *DaimlerChrysler AG: A Decade of Global Strategic Challenges Leads to Divorce in 2007*

Today you can eliminate that hyphen because we are taking further steps to make DaimlerChrysler truly one company everywhere in the world: no hyphens, no spaces.

DIETER ZETSCHE,
CEO of DaimlerChrysler, January 25, 2006[1]

Cerberus Takes Over Majority Interest in Chrysler Group and Related Financial Services Business for EUR 5.5 Billion ($7.4 billion) from DaimlerChrysler

WWW.DAIMLERCHRYSLER.COM,
May14, 2007.

As this book goes to press, there is news about the majority takeover of Chrysler by Cerebus, detailed at the end of this case. It is evident that much has happened, in the year covered between the two quotes above, to dash the hopes for global domination of the auto industry by DaimlerChrysler.

As you read this case trace the evolution of Daimler's international strategies and the performance of the joint venture with Chrysler; analyze the events and results. Include an update as of the time of your reading the case. What went wrong? What roles have other auto companies, such as Toyota, played in this saga? What lies ahead? (Include in your reading the previous "Note on the Auto Industry" and the "Renault–Nissan" case).

In 1998, the news of the merger of Daimler-Benz AG and Chrysler Corporation was received by the global auto industry with great jubilation and fanfare. Highly publicized in its global strategy, future outlook, and corporate brand, the merger created a transnational corporation that combined two global auto manufacturers. At the time of the merger, both firms had their business operations on every continent of the world. After the merger, the new company was called DaimlerChrysler with revenues of over $154 billion and a profit of $5.6 billion; there were over 441,000 workers worldwide. During the same year, DaimlerChrysler's market share stood at 7.4 percent in the global auto industry (see Tables C11-1 and C11-2).[2] Interestingly, the merger was considered highly unusual since it was initiated by a German company. Historically, mergers in the European Union (EU) were often discouraged by businesses and regulatory agencies because of Europe's foreign direct investment

SOURCE: Written exclusively for this text by Syed Tariq Anwar, Professor, West Texas A&M University.
[1]*Financial Times.* 2006. "Zetsche Delivers a Slick New Model," (January 25):

[2]For detail, see *The Wall Street Journal.* 1998. "Eaton: DaimlerChrysler Will be 'Transnational'," (August 31): B8. Also see Marjorie, Sorge and Mark Phelan.1998. "The Deal of the Century," *Automotive Industries,* (June): 46–69; *The Wall Street Journal.* 1998. "There are no German or U.S. Companies, Only Successful Ones," (May 7): A1&11.

TABLE C11-1 Chronology of DaimlerChrysler Merger: Pre and Post-Merger Phases and Developments (1998–2007)

Phase I. Pre-Merger Period and Developments (1998):

January 12, 1998:	Jürgen Schrempp (Chairman, Daimler-Benz) proposed to Robert Eaton (Chairman, Chrysler Corp.) for a possible merger while visiting an auto show in Detroit.
February 12–18, 1999:	Both companies' representatives and advisors met to discuss the merger issues and its feasibility.
March 2, 1998:	Both Chairmen (Schrempp and Eaton) met in Lausanne, Switzerland, to chalk out future plans.
March–April, 1998:	Working teams from both companies discussed and outlined details of the merger.
April 23–May 6, 1998:	Working teams from both companies finalized the merger agreement and other documentation.
May 6, 1998:	Both companies signed the merger agreement in London, UK.
May 7, 1998:	Merger agreement is announced in the press.
July 23, 1998:	EU's European Commission approved the DaimlerChrysler merger.
July 31, 1998:	U.S.'s Free Trade Commission approved the merger plan.
August 6, 1998:	DaimlerChrysler announced plans to list its share as Aglobal stock@ instead of ADRs.*
September 18, 1998:	Chrysler shareholders approved the merger with 97.5 percent Ayes@ votes.
September 18, 1998:	Daimler-Benz shareholders approved the merger with 99.9 percent Ayes@ votes.
November 6, 1998:	To qualify for pooling-of-interests accounting treatment, Chrysler issued 23.5 million shares.
November 9, 1998:	Daimler-Benz receives 98 percent of stock for its exchange offer.
November 17, 1998:	DaimlerChrysler stock started trading on 21 stock exchanges worldwide under the symbol DCX.

Phase II. Post-Merger Period and Developments (2000–2004):

2000:	DaimlerChrysler took a $1.9 billion (37.1%) stake in Mitsubishi Motors Corp. (MMC). Kirk Kerkorian, a Las Vegas casino owner and Chrysler's biggest individual shareholder filed a $2 billion law suit against DaimlerChrysler citing a $1 billion loss after the merger.
2001:	Chrysler reported losing $1.4 billion euros; U.S. management team is removed by DaimlerChrysler.
2002:	As a head of Chrysler, Dieter Zetsche tries to fix the company but many hurdles remain.
April 2003:	Chrysler Group's turnaround did not work and lost $1 billion because of weak sales, overcapacity, and old factories; MMC also lost money.
August 2003:	DaimlerChrysler agreed to pay $300 million to Kerkorian to settle $2 billion class action lawsuit but continues to fight Tracinda Investment Group's $2 billion suit of post-merger losses and other liabilities.
Dec. 2003/Jan. 2004:	Schrempp appeared in a Delaware court to testify in the lawsuit brought by Tracinda Investment Group against DaimlerChrysler. Schrempp says that "the deal was a merger of equals."
April 2004:	Despite losses in 2004, DaimlerChrysler's supervisory board supports Schrempp; the company refuses to retract from its global strategy; DaimlerChrysler and Hyundai opened talks about their troubled alliance.
May 3, 2004:	DaimlerChrysler and Beijing Automotive Industry Holding Company Ltd. (BAIC) announced the production of Mercedes-Benz C-Class and E-Class cars in Beijing, China. The project's annual capacity will be 25,000 cars per year.
May 2004:	Daimler refused to inject capital into the troubled Mitsubishi Motors Corp. DaimlerChrysler announced selling its 10.5 percent stake in Hyundai Motor Company; also announced realigning its strategic alliance.

Phase III. Strategic Realignment and Changes (2005–2006):

Early 2005:	DaimlerChrysler continues to face problems in its sales and management structure although Chrysler earns $1.9 billion because of new models; leadership challenges are the main problems.
March–April 2005:	DaimlerChrysler recalls 1.3 million Mercedes cars for quality-related issues. This was the largest recall in the company history; Mercedes loses $1.1 billion in the first quarter.
July 2005:	Schrempp steps down from the CEO job and leaves behind a multitude of problems for the company.
	A high-profile and turnaround expert from the company's Chrysler Division Dieter Zetsche becomes the new CEO of the company; Deutsche Bank reduces its ownership in the company from 10.4 percent to 6.9 percent by selling 35 million shares; the bank's sale brings in $360 million.

TABLE C11-1   (cont.)

August–December 2005:	DaimlerChrysler brings changes to its sales and management structure.
Late 2005 to early 2006:	DaimlerChrysler faces quality problems in its Mercedes-Benz brand.
March–July 2006:	DaimlerChrysler decides to keep its smart car. Earnings double.
July–September 2006:	Zetsche starts a nationwide media blitz under the title "Dear Dr. Z" and promises a fresh start in quality and customer support.
August 2006:	DaimlerChrysler was ordered to pay 230 million euros to investors in a law suit.
October 2006:	Like other auto manufacturers, DaimlerChrysler also reports losses in its North American operations; the company's turnaround is not there yet; cuts production; other issues in cost containment include high gasoline prices and healthcare; inventories pile up.
November–December 2006:	Bloated inventory, inflexible unions, and slow sales continue to be one of the major problem for the company; may lose money again in 2006.October 2006.
May 2007:	After many months of speculation, Daimler decides selling its majority stake in Chrysler to Cerberus Capital Management LP, a New York-based private equity group for $7.8 billion. Daimler still maintains 20 percent stake in Chrysler (for more details, see postscript).
May 14, 2007:	Company announces that Cerberus Capital Management, L.P. will take a 80.1% equity interest in new company Chrysler Holding, LLC; Daimler to hold 19.9%.
Fall 2007:	DaimlerChrysler becomes Daimler AG, subject to agreement of new structure at shareholders' meeting.

Note: * ADR: American Depository Receipts.

SOURCES: DaimlerChrysler, AG. (History/Group Archives & Investor Relations), www.daimlerchrysler.com; Anwar, Syed T. 2006. DaimlerChrysler AG: The Making of a New Transnational Corporation, in Deresky, Helen. *International Management: Managing Across Borders and Cultures*, 5th edition, Upper Saddle River, New Jersey: Prentice Hall, pp. 330–342; *Business Week*; *The Economist*; *Financial Times*; *The Wall Street Journal* (various issues).

TABLE C11-2   DaimlerChrysler: Pre- and Post-merger Financial and Corporate Data (1997 and 2006)

A. Financial Data (1997)	Daimler-Benz	Chrysler
Revenues:	$71.5 billion	$61.1 billion
Profit:	4.6	2.8
Assets:	76.1	60.4
Stockholders' Equity:	19.5	11.3
Market Capitalization:	86.8	35.9
Employees:	300,000	121,000
Unit Sales:	1.1 million	2.9 million
Fortune Global 500 Rank in 1998:	17	25

B. Financial Data (2006)	DaimlerChrysler
Revenues:	$190.00 billion
Profit:	4.70 billion
Current Assets:	142.22 billion
Market Capitalization:	59.04 billion
Fortune Global 500 Rank in 2006:	7
Fortune's Most Admired Company Rank:	Not included among the first 50 companies
Total Employees:	365,451

C. The Board of Management (as of December 2006)

Dr. Dieter Zetsche, Chairman of the Board of Management (*appointed until 2010*)
Günther Fleig, Human Resources & Labor Relations Director (*appointed until 2009*)
Dr. Rüdiger Grube, Corporate Development (*appointed until 2010*)
Thomas W. LaSorda, Chrysler Group (*appointed until 2012*)
Andreas Renschler, Truck Group (*appointed until 2010*)
Eric Ridenour, Chief Operating Officer (COO) Chrysler Group (*appointed until 2008*)
Thomas W. Sidlik, Global Procurement & Supply (*appointed until 2008*), Chrysler Corp.
Bodo Uebberm, Finance & Controlling, Financial Services (*appointed until 2011*)
Dr. Thomas Weber, Group Research & Mercedes Car Group Development (*appointed until 2010*)

SOURCES: Company Web site (www.daimlerchrysler.com); Reuters (www.reuters.com).

(FDI) barriers.[3] In 1999, the *Wall Street Journal* noted on the European corporate mergers:

> *Many of the biggest deals were negotiated in government offices or between scions of the establishment. Interlocking shareholdings shielded management from the sanctions of the market. Size counted more than profits. Hostile takeovers simply weren't done.*[4]

To stockholders, the news of the DaimlerChrysler merger was particularly appealing since the company was to become the third largest auto manufacturer after General Motors and Ford.[5] Since 1997, both companies had looked for merger partners but were unable to find the right firms that could bring complementary assets and value-added activities. Though perceived as an unlikely marriage because of branding mismatch, the auto industry welcomed the merger in 1999.[6] The Harbour Associates, an industry research firm, commented:

> *Clearly the story of the year was the fusion of Daimler-Benz and Chrysler Corporation— resulting in the world's fifth-largest producer of*

vehicles. *The announcement sent shock waves through the industry.—Aside from the culture shock, there was also the sentimental fallout. Without question, the Big Three entity is gone forever.*[7]

The DaimlerChrysler merger displayed two distinct features regarding its place in the auto industry. First, Daimler-Benz's Mercedes brand ranked as one of most visible luxury brands. Second, in the case of Chrysler, the company's strength lied in its low end/sub-compact cars and trucks and was one of the Big Three auto manufacturers in North America. In 1998, Chrysler's product lines included cars, minivans, Jeep, and sub-compact utility vehicles. The company was particularly known for its money making mini vans, Jeep, and Dodge trucks.

Before the merger, both companies had encountered a multitude of problems in their global operations and markets. In the case of Chrysler, the only alternative for future growth and survival was to merge with another auto company. Both companies had investigated the prospects of a merger with Fiat, Honda, BMW, and Renault. Because of diverse market segments, branding incompatibilities, and strong corporate cultures, no progress was achieved.

TABLE C11-3   DaimlerChrysler's Brands and Businesses (as of December 2006)

A. Mercedes Car Group: • Maybach • Mercedes-Benz • C-Smart B. Chrysler Group: • Dodge • Chrysler • Jeep C. DaimlerChrysler Truck Group: • Mercedes-Benz • Freightliner • Fuso • Sterling Trucks • Western Star Trucks • Thomas Built Buses	D. Commercial Vehicles: • Mercedes-Benz • Freightliner • Fuso • Sterling Trucks • Western Star Trucks • Thomas Built Buses • Setra • Orion E. Components: • Detroit Diesel • Mercedes-Benz F. Financial Services: • DaimlerChrysler Financial Services • DaimlerChrysler Bank

SOURCE: DaimlerChrysler Web site. <www.daimlerchrysler.com>, (data retrieved on December 2, 2006).

[3]For more discussion, see Anwar, S. 2005. "EU's Competition Policy and the GE-Honeywell Merger Fiasco: Transatlantic Divergence and Consumer and Regulatory Issues," *Thunderbird International Business Review,* 47(5): 601–626; Anwar, 2003, op. cit.; Blasko, Matej, Jeffry M. Netter and Joseph F. Sinkey. 2000. "Value Creation and Challenges of an International Transaction: The DaimlerChrysler Merger," *International Review of Financial Analysis,* 9(1): 77–102; Karolyi, G. Andrew. 2003. "DaimlerChrysler AG, the First Truly Global Share," *Journal of Corporate Finance,* 9: 409–430; Neubauer, Fred, Ulrich Steger and Georg Radler. 2000. "The Daimler/Chrysler Merger: The Involvement of the Boards," *Corporate Governance,* 8(4): 376–387.

[4]*The Wall Street Journal.* 1999. "Europe Marks a Year of Serious Flirtation with the Free Markets," (December 30): A1.
[5]See *The New York Times.* 1998a. "Daimler-Benz Will Acquire Chrysler in $36 Billion Deal that will Reshape Industry," (May 7), pp. 1&C4; *The Economist.* 1998. "A New Kind of Car Company," (May 9): 61–62; *The Wall Street Journal.* 1998b. "Chrysler Might Merge with Daimler-Benz—or be Taken Over," (May 6): A1&8.
[6]Harbour & Associates, Inc. 1999. *The Harbour Report 1999: North America,* Troy, Michigan: Harbour & Associates, Inc., p. 3; *The Wall Street Journal.* 1998. "Chrysler Approves Deal with Daimler-Benz; Big Questions Remain," (May 7): A1&1.
[7]Harbour & Associates, Inc. 1999, op. cit.

Despite the fact that the merger was welcomed by auto analysts and consumers, there were concerns regarding both companies' future growth potential, changing global segments, and incompatible governance issues.[8]

BRIEF HISTORY OF THE COMPANIES

Business history reveals that Gottlieb Daimler and Karl Benz were the early pioneers in building the motor carriage and two-cylinder V-engine in Germany. Daimler and Benz's early successes helped them establish the auto brand in the growth stage of the industry. In 1924, Benz and Cie and Daimler-Motoren-Gesellschaft merged and formed what today is known as Daimler-Benz. After the 1980s, the company became the largest conglomerate in Germany and was highly rated for its luxury cars in the auto industry. Unlike other German multinational corporations (MNC), Daimler-Benz mostly remained in Europe because of its rigid corporate culture and regional strategies. Ewing describes this phenomenon that has been unique to German and other European companies in the post-war environment:

> *Devastated spiritually and physically, many of Germany's big companies became defensive and risk-averse. In postwar Germany, they created webs of cross-holdings and reciprocal board memberships. The incestuous system functioned well during the cold war. But it could not cope with the global competition that accelerated after the 1989 fall of the Berlin Wall and, more recently, the introduction of the euro.[9]*

Chrysler was founded in 1925 by Walter P. Chrysler, who had worked for Buick Motor Company. Unlike Daimler-Benz, Chrysler manufactured cars for the masses and particularly targeted the mainstream American consumer. Between 1941 and 1960, Chrysler introduced many new auto models and took credit for bringing forth new technologies and innovations in North America. As the third largest auto manufacturer, Chrysler always remained behind GM and Ford and was rated as one of the "late movers" in the industry. In the early 1980s, the company was on the verge of bankruptcy but was rescued by the U.S. government. In the early 1990s, Chrysler vehicles started to get good ratings from analysts but continued to remain behind other manufacturers in quality and consumer satisfaction. When Daimler-Benz proposed the merger in January 1998, Chrysler's Board saw a major opportunity for future survival and access to new markets. In the next four months, both companies negotiated extensively

and closed the deal in May 1998 (see Tables C11-1 and C11-2).

After the merger, DaimlerChrysler management sought an organizational structure that was adaptable and ready to combine two different corporate cultures, eventually creating a transnational corporation. The companies were particularly careful not to create a structure that could have jeopardized their global strategy during the transitionary period. In the first 12 months, both companies faced many challenges regarding reorganization, and above all, how best to combine Daimler-Benz's highly hierarchical and rigid management structure with Chrysler's informal corporate practices. DaimlerChrysler's new organizational structure particularly took into consideration German and American business systems and appointed two co-chairmen, Jürgen Schrempp from Daimler-Benz and Chrysler's Robert E. Eaton.[10]

Reasons for the Merger

As stated earlier, the DaimlerChrysler merger was heavily influenced by the 1990s' global competition in the auto industry. The industry was facing some daunting issues such as downsizing, cost issues, low profits, and lackluster consumer demand. The top eight manufacturers from North America, Japan, and Europe were heavily burdened with debt, unions' demands, and high cost issues because of labor contracts and healthcare insurance. Daimler-Benz and Chrysler saw the merger as a unique opportunity to streamline their operations worldwide. Other factors included joint research and development (R&D) opportunities, access to emerging markets, and rationalization in manufacturing.[11] The major factors that contributed to the merger are discussed as follows:[12]

1. Company-specific cost issues: In the 1990s, Chrysler was known as a low-cost producer and its product and development departments were known for speed and delivery. Most of the changes were the result of Chrysler's legendary CEO Lee Iacocca, who ran the company in the early 1980s. Daimler-Benz, on the other hand, was a quality leader in the global luxury segments. Although, Daimler-Benz's product development and manufacturing cost remained high and often lagged behind in bringing new products to the market, the company never lost it luxury appeal among the consumers. Both companies saw the opportunity to combine their operations, aiming at sharing R&D know-how and joint sales. The merger proposal envisioned over $1.2 billion savings in the areas of collaboration and product development.

[8]Anwar. 2003, op. cit.

[9]Ewing, Jack. 2000. "The Show of Muscle Isn't So Scary," *Business Week,* (January 10): p. 24.

[10]Sorge, Marjorie & Mark Phelan.1998. "The Deal of the Century," *Automotive Industries,* (June): 47.

[11]For detail, see *The Wall Street Journal.* 1999. "Daimler Faces Big Test in Small-Car Market," (November 29): C14; Cliffe, Sarah. 1999. "Can This Merger be Saved?" *Harvard Business Review,* 77(1): 29–44; *The Economist.* 1999. "How to Make Mergers Work," (January 9): 15–16.

[12]For detail, see Anwar. 2003, op. cit.

2. Supplier networks and value chains: In Chrysler's post-restructuring period, the company created a good supplier network and outsourcing activities in its value chains.[13] This attracted Daimler-Benz, which had encountered difficulties in its supply chain areas. The company also wanted to use Chrysler's suppliers in its small-car and future sub-compact models where the company lacked expertise and manufacturing facilities.

3. Compatibility in diesel engine technology: At the time of the merger, Daimler-Benz and Chrysler were considered good manufacturers in diesel technology and were willing to share their know-how in the post-merger period. The diesel engine technology in the sub-compact segments was particularly attractive to Chrysler since it was a low-cost manufacturer in the industry.

4. Issues of dealer networks: Historically, Daimler-Benz had a strong dealer network in Europe, Latin America, and North America. On the other hand, Chrysler's dealer network remained inadequate in Europe. The company had limited visibility in the European markets for a long time while General Motors and Ford were well established in the same market. This was appealing to Chrysler because of its mini vans, Jeep, and other sub-compact brands. Both companies wanted to use each other's dealer networks in Europe and Latin America as well.

5. The euro and Europe's single market: Business environment in the European markets played a major contributing factor behind the merger. Cross-border mergers were on the rise because of Europe's single market, corporate consolidations, and above all, availability of corporate bonds and high-yield debt markets. Companies in Europe and North America wanted to capitalize on these changes to seek expansion.

6. Post-NAFTA Synergies: In the early 1990s, with the passage of the NAFTA (North American Free Trade Agreement) Treaty, the United States started to attract FDI from Europe because of future corporate expansion and growth potential. Under NAFTA's rules-of-origin, foreign companies were mandated to invest in auto transplants in North America.[14] To Daimler-Benz, merging with another auto producer was a viable option to comply with NAFTA's rules-of-origin. Earlier, the same rules also prompted the company to start manufacturing its model M-series in Tuscaloosa, Alabama, for the North America market. Merging with Chrysler was seen even more promising since it showed additional growth prospects in North America.

7. Daimler-Benz's difficulties in corporate restructuring: As Germany's premier corporation, Daimler-Benz was in a strong position regarding its sales and profits and continued to increase its market share from core businesses (automotive and vehicles) in the 1980s. In 1985, the company's profits increased by 52 percent to $577 million. In the late 1980s, the company saw its sales declining and encountered problems in aerospace, computers, and household appliances.[15] In the coming years, the company had to seek major downsizing and laid off thousands of employees. During the same period, the company's profit fell by 30 percent.[16] In the 1990s, Daimler-Benz sought major corporate restructuring and survived by unloading unprofitable non-core operations. This helped the company to streamline operations but future growth did not look promising. Selected options available to the company included a merger or other FDI activities in world markets. Daimler-Benz preferred a merger to FDI activities. Eventually, in 1998, a merger with Chrysler was proposed to capitalize on the North American market. Other contributing factors that encouraged the merger included NAFTA-related market and healthy business conditions in Europe.

8. Auto industry and globalization: In the Cold War era, markets in the developed countries and emerging markets started to take off because of globalization, FDI, and strong consumer demand. Daimler-Benz realized that it was critical to expand globally not only by exporting products but also by getting involved beyond the German market. This encouraged the company to seek FDI beyond its European hub. Also, a merger partner was deemed necessary in this process because of costs and supply chain issues.

9. Brand portfolios and manufacturing synergies: Daimler-Benz and Chrysler's core products were in the automotive sectors. At the time of the merger, Daimler-Benz earned 80 percent of its revenues from cars and commercial vehicles. Chrysler was even more dependent on its automotive products. The new company's brand portfolio looked so promising that in just a few months both partners were ready to form a new entity. The major reason for the merger was to save money by eliminating corporate duplication and using the same manufacturing platforms worldwide. Except in a few segments, the companies had minimum overlap in their brand portfolios. At the time of the merger, Daimler-Benz had a great luxury brand and commercial vehicles and trucks while Chrysler concentrated on low-end market.

10. German corporate culture and governance issues: In the post–World War period, German companies developed a unique corporate structure that was based on hierarchical system, cross-shareholdings, and inward looking/Pan-European strategies. In the post–Cold War

[13]Hartley, Janet, Bertie M. Greer and Seungwook Park. 2002. "Chrysler Leverages Its Suppliers' Improvement Suggestions," *Interfaces*, 32(4): 20–27.

[14]For NAFTA's rules-of-origin, see Anwar, Syed T. 1996. "The Impact of NAFTA on Canada's Automobile Industry: Issues and Analysis," *World Competition*, 19(3): 115–136. For M-series and its development, see Haasen, Adolf. 1999. "M-Class: The Making of a New Daimler-Benz," *Organizational Dynamics*, 27(4): 74–78.

[15]The companies included Dornier, MTU, and AEG.
[16]*Financial Times*. 1993. "Daimler-Benz Profits to Fall by up to 30 Percent," (April 17): 1.

period, Europe was engulfed in competition, expansion, and above all, FDI from North America. This forced German companies to seek a different corporate model based on global expansion and openness. Daimler-Benz was influenced by the changes that encouraged the company to expand globally, especially in North America.[17]

POST-MERGER PROBLEMS

Table C11-1 presents pre- and post-merger developments of the company. The merger can be discussed in three phases—phase I (1998), phase II (2000–2004), and phase III (2005–2006). The post-merger environment (phases II and III, 2000–2006) reveals that DaimlerChrysler did not experience smooth sailing, encountering a multitude of unanticipated problems. This resulted in setbacks that raised questions about the company's future viability. More discussion on these problems is presented below.

1. Cross-cultural problems and "the merger of equals" issue: In the auto industry, Daimler-Benz was viewed as a conservative and rigid company regarding its corporate bureaucracy, product development, and quality standards—a corporate culture reflective of Germany's national culture. On the other hand, Chrysler's corporate culture was typical American—informal, outward oriented, and somewhat less rigid in its operations and more risk-taking. Daimler-Benz lacked exposure to the American way of management and business practices. The cultural mismatch eventually created problems in the areas of future planning, supervisory board, research and development, expatriate management, executive salaries, and labor relations.[18] In the post–World War II era, the German system was developed on the basis of a hierarchical structure that encouraged seniority, consensus building, and above all, the supervisory boards' powers in the day-to-day operations. In the first few years, some of Chrysler's operations in the United States took a downturn because of management shakeups, disagreements on joint vision, collective strategies, production, and branding issues. Since DaimlerChrysler was made into a

transnational company, dealing with two national cultures with distinct business practices was a daunting task. Neither of the companies' executives was ready for the changes that were to take place in the transnational structure. Since Chrysler was an independent organization before the merger, American managers disliked Daimler-Benz's control and majority ownership, especially seeing the new entity's headquarters moving to Germany.[19] Some managers resented moving to Stuttgart because of uprooting their families and the American way of life, and they resented the dominance of the Germans in the merged company. Language problems were cited as another hurdle in the assimilation process. On the other hand, the German managers balked at the much higher salaries of Chrysler's managers.

After the merger, Daimler-Benz controlled 51 percent of the company and moved the headquarters to Stuttgart. In addition, DaimlerChrysler's shareholders fretted over the loss of shareholder value that instigated a $9 billion lawsuit and two other class action suits by Chrysler's largest individual investor, Kirk Kerkorian. The investor claimed a $1 billion loss because of the company's poor performance in the stock market. In 1999, DaimlerChrysler shares were trading at $108. In 2002, the stock dropped down to $35, losing billions of dollars of shareholder value. Kerkorian blamed DaimlerChrysler's management for the merger's problems On the other hand, in a federal court in 2003, Schrempp strongly defended the company position and its $36 billion deal as a "merger of equals."[20] In short, both companies' top managements did not anticipate dealing with so many problems in the areas of cultural assimilation, executive departures, disappearing shareholder value, and weak demand for Chrysler products. Eventually, this resulted in a major distraction for the company. In 2006, DaimlerChrysler continued to struggle with global integration in the areas of manufacturing, low profits, and corporate assimilation.

2. Competition and market structure of the global auto industry: Today's auto industry is an integral part of the developed world and is highly competitive and global in its markets and product development. The industry is continuously impacted by production costs, labor issues, and energy (gasoline) prices (see Tables C11-4,

[17]For more discussion, see Broadbeck, Felix C., Michael Frese and Mansour Javidan. 2002. "Leadership Made in Germany: Low on Compassion, High on Performance," *Academy of Management Executive,* 16(1): 16–30; *Financial Times.* 2002. "Is Germany's Model Finding Its Level?" (September 5): 7; Kogut, Bruce and Gordon Walker. 2001. "The Small World of Germany and the Durability of National Networks," *American Sociological Review,* 66(3): 317–335; Peck, Simon I. and Winfried Ruigrok. 2000. "Hiding Behind the Flag? Prospects for Change in German Corporate Governance," *European Management Journal,* 18(4): 420–430; Tuschke, Anja and Wm. Gerard Sanders. 2003. "Antecedents and Consequences of Corporate Governance Reform: The Case of Germany," *Strategic Management Journal,* 24: 631–649; *The Wall Street Journal,* 2002. "Behind the Crisis in Germany, a Past that Is Crippling," (December 6): A1&12.

[18]Anwar, 2003. op. cit.; also see *Financial Times.* 1999. "Two Tribes on the Same Trail," (August 31): 10.

[19]For more discussion on this topic, see Sorge, Marjorie and Mark Phelan. 1998. "The Deal of the Century," *Automotive Industries,* (June): 47; *Financial Times.* 1998. "Culture Crucial to Synergy Equation," (May 8): 22; *The Wall Street Journal.* 1998. "For Daimler-Benz, a Cultural Road Test," (May 8): B1; *Business Week.* 1998. "A Secret Weapon for German Reform," (October 12): 138; *The Wall Street Journal.* 1999. "DaimlerChrysler's Transfer Woes," (August 24): B1; *The Wall Street Journal.* 1999. "DaimlerChrysler Readies Management Recall," (September 15): A25.

[20]*Financial Times.* 2003. "Schrempp Says Chrysler Was Merger of Equals," (December 10): 17; *Financial Times.* 2004. "The Battle of Daimler Chrysler," (January 2): 5.

TABLE C11-4 Auto Assembly Plants in North America: Selected Manufacturing and Labor Productivity Data (1998)

Company	1998 Annual Capacity	1998 Actual Production	1998 Utilization	1998 Hours Per Vehicle (HPV)*	1998 Workers Per Vehicle (WPV)*
Auto Alliance (Michigan)**	268,464	167,607	62%	25.70	3.07
BMW (Alabama)	65,800	54,802	83	NA	NA
CAMI (Canada)	26,352	54,819	24	41.60	3.34
DaimlerChrysler (14 plants)	2,906,480	2,906,366	100	33.86	3.27
Ford (22 plants)	4,429,280	4,298,784	97	24.87	3.04
General Motors (29 plants)	6,272,808	4,945,990	79	32.58	3.24
Honda (4 plants)	947,120	881,694	93	21.41	2.49
Mercedes (Alabama)	80,088	68,732	86	NA	NA
Mitsubishi (Illinois)	259,440	157,139	61	NA	NA
Nissan Motors (3 plants)	792,232	498,631	63	19.20***	2.45***
NUMMI (California)****	387,318	361,897	93	21.78	2.69
Subaru-Isuzu (Indiana)	248,160	216,198	87	NA	NA
Toyota Motor (4 plants)	667,400	647,030	97	21.63	2.48
Volkswagen (Mexico)	391,040	338,959	87	NA	NA

Notes: * HPV and WPV data may not include all assembly plants; ** Mazda and Ford; *** Nissan Smyrna plant only;
**** NUMMI (New United Motors Manufacturing, Inc.; Joint Venture of GM and Toyota); NA: Not available.

SOURCE: Adapted in part from Harbour & Associates. 1999. *The Harbour Report 1999: North America*, Troy, Michigan: Harbour & Associates, Inc.

TABLE C11-5 Auto Assembly Plants in North America: Selected Manufacturing and Labor Productivity Data (2004–2005)

Company	2005 Annual Capacity	2005 Actual Production	2005 Utilization	2004 Utilization	2005 Total Hours Per Vehicle (HPV)*	2004 Total Hours Per Vehicle (HPV)*
Auto Alliance (Michigan)**	257,523	272,499	106%	52%	25.43	29.59
BMW (South Carolina)	160,176	124,816	78	90	NA	NA
CAMI (Canada)	165,252	190,031	115	88	19.48	23.88
DaimlerChrysler (13 plants)	2,848,200	2,678,937	94	90	23.73	25.17
Ford (23 plants)	3,948,774	3,107,698	79	86	23.77	24.48
General Motors (29 plants)	5,123,337	4,567,916	89	85	22.65	23.28
Honda (7 plants)	1,482,530	1,348,896	91	87	21.43	20.62
Mercedes (Alabama)	169,200	95,558	56	74	NA	NA
Mitsubishi (Illinois)	234,248	87,637	37	48	26.48	29.89
Nissan Motors (6 plants)	1,265,992	1,198,720	95	87	18.93	18.29
NUMMI (California)***	388,822	417,380	107	99	20.59	21.78
Subaru-Isuzu (Indiana)	248,160	118,991	48	48	NA	NA
Toyota Motor (6 plants)	1,123,074	1,190,036	106	107	21.33	19.46

Notes: *HPV data may not include all assembly plants; ** Mazda and Ford; *** NUMMI (New United Motors Manufacturing, Inc.; Joint Venture of GM and Toyota); NA: Not available.

SOURCE: Adapted in part from Harbour & Associates. 2006. *The Harbour Report 2006: North America*, Troy, Michigan: Harbour & Associates, Inc.

C11-5, C11-6, and C11-7).[21] The industry's impact is visible in almost every sector of national economies.[22] In some markets, the competitive environment is further complicated by national subsidies, tariff barriers, and

cash rebates.[23] To launch a new auto model, it takes an investment of $500 million to $1 billion. Sourcing/outsourcing strategies are used by the automakers to control cost and logistical problems. Auto plants are located on the basis of markets and suppliers' networks. The major players in the industry include General Motors, Ford, Toyota, Honda, Nissan, Volkswagen, and others.

[21]See *Value Line.* 2004. "Auto and Truck Industry," (March 5): 101–109; *Standard & Poor's Industry Surveys.* 2003. "Industry Surveys: Autos and Auto Parts," (December 25): 1–29; *The Wall Street Journal.* 2004. "U.S. Car Makers Lose Market Share," (January 6): A3.
[22]Anwar. 2003. op. cit.

[23]*The Wall Street Journal.* 2004. "Detroit's Challenge: Weaning Buyers from Years of Deals," (January 6): A1&A2.

TABLE C11-6   Major Global Auto Manufacturers: Selected 10-Year Financial Data (1997–2006)

Company	1997	1998	1999	2000	2001	2002	2003	2004	2005	2006
DaimlerChrysler:										
Revenues ($ mill)	127,131	154,615	151,035	152,446	136,072	156,838	171,870	179,339	177,394	190,000
Net profit ($ mill)	7,279.0	6,448.0	5,173.0	3,338.0	(589.2)	5,114.0	(526.0)	3,338.0	4,043.0	4,070.0
Pretax profit per vehicle ($)*	1,336	1,470	1,497	170	1,679	226	(496)	357	487	NA
Earnings per share ($)	7.15	6.54	6.25	3.26	(0.59)	5.22	(0.55)	3.01	3.97	4.00
Net Profit Margin (%)	5.7	4.2	3.4	2.2	NA	3.3	NA	1.7	2.3	2.1
Ford:										
Revenues ($ mill)	153,627	144,416	162,558	170,064	162,412	163,420	165,066	171,652	177,089	162,115
Net profit ($ mill)	6,920.0	6,570.0	7,237.0	4,823.0	(5,453)	284.0	921.0	4,220.5	2,440.0	(2,530)
Pretax profit per vehicle ($)*	901	854	1034	709	(1,293)	(211)	(291)	(23)	(495)	NA
Earnings per share ($)	5.62	5.28	5.86	3.22	(3.02)	0.15	0.45	2.13	1.25	(1.35)
Net Profit Margin (%)	4.5	4.5	4.5	2.8	NA	0.2	0.6	2.5	1.4	NA
General Motors:										
Revenues ($ mill)	173,168	161,315	176,558	184,632	177,260	186,763	185,524	193,517	192,604	206,750
Net profit ($ mill)	5,972.0	3,662.0	5,576.0	4,452.0	601.0	1,736.0	3,862.0	3,630.0	(3,417.0)	2,405
Pretax profit per vehicle ($)*	32	315	853	388	73	267	(50)	(51)	(1,772)	NA
Earnings per share ($)	7.89	5.24	8.53	6.68	1.77	3.35	5.03	6.40	(6.05)	4.25
Net Profit Margin (%)	3.4	2.3	3.2	2.4	0.3	0.9	1.5	1.9	NA	1.2
Honda:										
Revenues ($ mill)	45,111	51,688	57,536	52,170	55,357	66,429	77,232	80,549	84,345	92,645
Net profit ($ mill)	1,959.6	2,430.4	2,475.8	1,874.4	2,727.0	3,555.5	4,393.4	4,527.4	5,082.0	4,930
Pretax profit per vehicle ($)*	1,040	993	1,440	1,294	1,345	1,406	1,392	1,353	1,641	NA
Earnings per ADR ($)*	1.01	1.30	1.27	0.96	1.40	1.83	2.30	2.42	2.76	2.70
Net Profit Margin (%)	4.3	4.9	4.3	3.6	4.9	5.4	5.8	5.6	6.0	5.3
Nissan:										
Revenues ($ mill)	49,358	54,583	56,388	49,110	46,588	56,905	65,600	80,152	80,584	83,750
Net profit ($ mill)	382.0	(229.9)	(6,456)	2,670	2,799.0	4,126.4	4,447.4	4,787.7	4,563.3	4,500
Pretax profit per vehicle ($)*	301	(66)	(17)	(2,782)	1,105	1,975	2,013	1,930	2,030	NA
Earnings per ADR ($)*	0.30	(0.18)	(3.25)	1.26	1.39	1.95	2.16	2.32	2.22	2.20
Net Profit Margin (%)	0.8	NA	NA	5.4	6.0	7.3	6.8	6.0	5.7	5.4
Toyota:										
Revenues ($ mill)	87,807	105,832	119,656	106,030	107,443	128,965	163,638	172,749	182,930	189,000
Net profit ($ mill)	3,416.1	3,747.0	4,540.0	5,447.0	4,177.0	6,247.0	10,995	10,907	12,918	14,500
Pretax profit per vehicle ($)*	1,239	1,348	1,234	1,464	1,477	1,814	2,118	1,916	2,098	NA
Earnings per ADR ($)*	1.79	1.98	2.02	2.92	2.28	3.52	6.39	6.66	7.38	8.05
Net Profit Margin (%)	3.9	3.35	3.8	5.1	3.9	4.8	6.7	6.3	7.1	7.1

Notes: *Earnings per ADR (American Depository Receipts); NA:– not available; * Pretax profit per vehicle is for worldwide operations.
SOURCES: *The Harbour Report* – North America, 1997–2006 (various issues); *Value Line,* 1997–2006 (various issues).

TABLE C11-7   Top 15 Global Auto and Truck Manufacturers Ranked by Market Capitalization (December 2006)

Company (*Country*)	Market Capitalization	Revenue	Revenue Growth	Gross Margin	Net Profit Margin	Employees
1. Toyota (*Japan*)	$193.01 bill.	$195.83 bill	13.4%	19.6%	6.5%	285,977
2. Honda (*Japan*)	63.59	91.48	14.5	28.6	4.9	144,785
3. DaimlerChrysler (*Germany*)	59.04	203.20	5.4	16.9	2.5	365,451
4. Nissan (*Japan*)	53.20	na	15.4	na	na	163,686
5. Volkswagen (*Germany*)	41.24	136.58	7.1	13.6	0.8	344,902
6. AB Volvo (*Sweden*)	26.53	36.67	14.0	22.3	6.3	82,652
7. Fiat (*Italy*)	23.97	68.16	2.0	15.4	1.5	173,932
8. General Motors (*US*)	16.79	206.70	−0.5	14.9	−4.8	335,000
9. PACCAR (*US*)	15.99	15.86	23.4	16.2	9.0	21,900
10. Ford (*US*)	15.18	166.13	2.7	4.9	−4.0	300,000
11. Tata Motors (*India*)	7.23	na	21.3	na	na	33,536
12. Oshkosh Truck (*US*)	3.56	3.42	15.8	17.7	5.9	9,387
13. Navistar (*US*)	2.27	11.59	28.2	16.0	2.5	14,800
14. Brilliance China Auto. (*China*)	0.617*	0.896*	−16.4	6.6	−13.0	8,911
15. Rush Enterprises (*US*)	0.458*	2.23*	70.3	14.7	2.5	2,507

Notes: *–Million; na: not available.
SOURCE: Reuters www.reuters.com, (data retrieved on December 2, 2006).

Toyota is considered the most efficient manufacturer in quality and consumer satisfaction (see Tables C11-5, C11-6, and C11-7).[24] Like other producers, DaimlerChrysler wants to become a major global player but has been unable to realize its goals. *Financial Times* accurately commented:

> At DaimlerChrysler, there were fears within the company about the pace at which Mr. Schrempp was driving his concept of 'Welt AG'—a global car maker—at a time when the group's core Mercedes brand needed defending in the face of competitors challenging its traditions of quality and luxury."[25]

The industry's cut-throat competition and quality issues continue to be a problem for the company in 2007. Ultimately, it is a hindrance in the company's global strategy.

[24]For more discussion on auto companies, see Anwar. 2003, op. cit; *Business Week*. 2003. "BMW: Will Panke's High-Speed Approach Hurt the Brand?" (June 9): 57–60; *The Economist*. 2004. "Cadillac Comeback," (January 24): 61–63; *Financial Times*. 2004. "Toyota Leads Japanese Conquest of Europe," (March 2): 7; Harbour & Associates, *Inc.* 2003, op. cit; *The Wall Street Journal*, 2004. "At Ford, High Volume Takes Backseat to Profits, (May 7): A1&A12; *The Wall Street Journal*.2004 "Toyota's Earnings More than Doubled," (May 12): A3&A6; *The Wall Street Journal*.2004 "As VW Tries to Sell Pricier Cars, Everyman Image Holds It Back," (May 13): A1&A8.
[25]*Financial Times*. 2004. "German Chiefs Watch Their Backs as They Eye the World," (May 14): 14.

3. Lackluster demand in the auto industry: The global auto industry is always impacted by weak consumer confidence that is a reflection of countries' economic health. The East Asian crisis impacted DaimlerChrysler's sales. Furthermore, the European and North American markets did not help either because of the economic slowdown and unemployment problems.

4. Production and manufacturing glitches: At the time of the merger, Daimler-Benz and Chrysler wanted to streamline their manufacturing by using the same platforms. The idea looked good on paper but companies had a hard time operationalizing this strategy worldwide because of logistical problems, mismatch of manufacturing and production methods, and cost issues. Costs were hard to contain and in the North American sub-compact market Chrysler lagged in sales and market share (see Table C11-8).

5. Incompatible brand portfolios: At the time of the merger, Daimler-Benz and Chrysler had a major plan to combine their brand portfolios, but it never really happened because of the mismatch of brand portfolios. Daimler-Benz targeted the upscale market while Chrysler mostly pursued low-end/sub-compact markets in North America. Although both companies cooperated in product development and supplier network, tangible benefits were seen to be limited in the post-merger period (see Table C11-8).

6. DaimlerChrysler's stalled Asian strategy: To make a strong foothold in Asia, DaimlerChrysler took a 37.1 percent ($1.9 billion) stake in Mitsubishi Motors Corporation in 2000. At that time, the investment and the alliance looked viable because of Asia's booming

TABLE C11-8   DaimlerChrysler Compared with Top Six Auto Manufacturers: Strengths, Weaknesses and Current/Future Plans (as of December 2006)

DaimlerChrysler	General Motors	Ford	Volkswagen	Toyota	Honda	Nissan
Sales: $203.2 bil* Mkt.Cap: $59.0 bil	Sales: $206.7 bil Mkt.Cap: $59.0 bil	Sales: $166.1 bil. Mkt.Cap: $15.1 bil	Sales: $136.5 bil. Mkt.Cap: $41.2 bil	Sales: $195.8 bil Mkt.Cap: $193 bil	Sales: $91.4 bil Mkt.Cap: $63.5 bil	Sales: NA Mkt.Cap: $53.2 bil
Strengths: • Established brand; and is the fourth largest automaker; good market coverage in over 100 countries; sells luxury as well as sub-compact vehicles • Established distribution and sales network; major conglomerate • Major manufacturer of utility trucks in North America **Weaknesses:** • The merger of DaimlerChrysler has not created a viable synergy to increase market share and productivity • Has been unable to deal with two corporate cultures (American and German) in the integration process • Quality and branding issues remain to be resolved; Chrysler brand has not done well in sub-compact cars • Chrysler cars do not get good	**Strengths:** • Established brand in the U.S.; also the largest automaker in the world • Major player in global markets with excellent brand variety; largest exporter of vehicles from the U.S. • Maintains a good manufacturing and distribution system worldwide • GM's global operations have improved since 2001 **Weaknesses:** • Market share has been weakening; big losses in 2006 • Slow to change because of its company size; big organization with a massive bureaucratic structure, cost, and expensive labor contracts • Product development cost is high • Brand Portfolio is diverse	**Strengths:** • Ford is the third largest automaker in the world • Maintains visible brands and supplier network • Big player in utility trucks **Weaknesses:** • Ford is having major problems in 2006; to fix the problems, hired a new CEO in 2006 • Quality issues are haunting the company • Distribution system is weak in overseas markets • Losing market share in North America; Toyota has surpassed Ford in sales **Current/Future Plans:** • Reorganization is being undertaken to address quality issues and market expansion • Profit is preferred over high volume strategy	**Strengths:** • Good brand recognition; strong worldwide sales • Strong presence in Europe and Latin American • Excellent distribution network in Europe **Weaknesses:** • Key models in the sub-compact segments are aging • Suffers from cost over-runs • Limited brand visibility in North America, especially in the sub-compact market; dealer network is weak • Limited product offerings and brand portfolio • Sales and marketing outside of Europe is weak **Current/Future Plans:** • New models have been scarce • Volkswagen does not attract a mass market outside of Europe	**Strengths:** • In 2007, Toyota may surpass GM in sales • Aggressively expanding in global markets worldwide • Maintains outstanding manufacturing plants worldwide; Toyota production system (TPS) continues to be the worldwide benchmark in quality • Toyota products are rated highly in North America and other parts of the world • Low cost manufacturer in many categories; hybrid cars are the leader in North America • Overseas expansion is on productive **Weaknesses:** • Corporate culture is somewhat myopic • Product designs continue to be unappealing and may need an overhaul	**Strengths:** • Established manufacturer • Quality standards are well known • Strong brand visibility in Asia and North America • Low-cost auto manufacturer; highly focused in R[D and product development] maintains good economies of scale • Expanding in North America and Asia. **Weaknesses:** • Honda has a limited presence in some markets of Europe and Latin America. • Beyond the sub-compact markets, Honda's product portfolio lacks variety • Limited diversification and expansion **Current/Future Plans:** • Future expansion is possible in North America and Europe	**Strengths:** • Nissan has made a tremendous recovery under the leadership of Carlos Ghosn • Nissan brand has been reinvigorated by Renault; in 2006, one of the most visible brands in the world • Many new products have been introduced • Quality has improved; turnaround strategy has been working • Renault-Nissan alliance has cut costs and gained market share since 2003 • Overhauled Nissan's corporate culture and business practices **Weaknesses:** • Still lacks marketing charisma to compete with Toyota • Limited product portfolio in global markets **Current/Future Plans:** • Global reorganization is on track; new

(continued)

TABLE C11-8   (cont.)

DaimlerChrysler	General Motors	Ford	Volkswagen	Toyota	Honda	Nissan
Sales: $203.2 bil* **Mkt.Cap: $59.0 bil**	**Sales: $206.7 bil** **Mkt.Cap: $59.0 bil**	**Sales: $166.1 bil.** **Mkt.Cap: $15.1 bil**	**Sales: $136.5 bil.** **Mkt.Cap: $41.2 bil**	**Sales: $195.8 bil** **Mkt.Cap: $193 bil**	**Sales: $91.4 bil** **Mkt.Cap: $63.5 bil**	**Sales: NA** **Mkt.Cap: $53.2 bil**
ratings in North America • In 2006, the company's global strategy has somewhat stalled; alliances with Mitsubishi and Hyundai are unproductive **Current/Future Plans:** • Reorganization regarding global operations and manufacturing may take place in the coming years • More cost cutting will be coming in the coming years	**Current/Future Plans:** • Asia-Pacific business has improved • Will target new markets, especially the Chinese market • Hybrid models will be built in future • More emphasis is placed on flexible manufacturing • Continue to overhaul its small car segments • Will be bring new models in 2007–2008	• Hybrid car is in the pipeline • Ford is switching to Flexible production systems • Concentrating more on sub-compacts	**Current/Future Plans:** • Reorganization is in progress; product development issues are being addressed • Plan on expanding in the Chinese market • Entry into the high-end market will continue in the coming years	• Limited market share in the European luxury segments **Current/Future Plans:** • Continues to expand worldwide; will be a major player in the coming years • Overseas manufacturing is a major part of Toyota's global strategy	• Also getting into other segments (small 6-seater executive jet/ commuter plane)	models are in the pipeline • Making big efforts in product development; also will be manufacturing cars in China

Notes: *2006 sales and market capitalization.

SOURCES: (1). Anwar, Syed T. 2006. "DaimlerChrysler AG in 2004: Global Strategy Gone Sour," in Deresky, Helen. *International Management: Managing Across Borders and Cultures*, 5th edition, Upper Saddle River, New Jersey; Prentice Hall, pp. 330–342; Harbour & Associates, Inc. 2006. *The Harbour Report: North America 2006.* Troy, Michigan: Harbour & Associates, Inc.; *Automotive Industries; Business Week; The Economist; Financial Times; Value Line; The Wall Street Journal* (various issues).

sub-compact markets. Though an underdog from Japan, Mitsubishi was not a strong player in North America. In 2004, the company lost over $200 million because of limited product lines and other marketing issues. DaimlerChrysler refused to inject capital into troubled Mitsubishi. In addition, in May 2004, DaimlerChrysler announced selling a 10.5 percent stake in Hyundai Motor Company and realigned its strategic alliance with the Korean partner. During the same month, to enter into China, DaimlerChrysler and Beijing Automotive Industry Holding Company Limited announced the production of Mercedes-Benz's C and E-Class cars in China. The project's annual capacity was expected to produce 25,000 cars per year. Though DaimlerChrysler's China venture looks viable in the long term, it will take time to have the project matured.[26]

WHAT LIES AHEAD?

In 2005, DaimlerChrysler faced problems in its sales and management structure, although Chrysler had earned $1.9 billion because of new models. Leadership challenges and quality issues continued to haunt the company. In early 2005, the company recalled 1.3 million Mercedes cars for poor quality and manufacturing glitches. This was the largest recall in the company's history. During this process, Mercedes losses mounted to $1.1 billion in the first quarter of 2005 (see Table C11-1). Within these circumstances and as expected, in July 2005, Schrempp stepped down from the CEO position and handed the power to Chrysler's U.S. head Dieter Zetsche.[27] During the same period, Deutsche Bank reduced its ownership in the company from 10.4 percent to 6.9 percent by selling 35 million shares. This amounted to $360 million (see Table C11-1).

In the fall of 2006, Zetsche initiated major structural changes in the company's management structure and operations and had an influence in appointing a younger group of executives to the board of management (see Table C11-2). Zetsche's major restructuring initiatives and corporate changes included job cuts, plant closings, using smart and flexible manufacturing, and value pricing strategies in North America. In the coming years, Zetsche faces the following challenges in the company overhaul and reorganization: (1) brand image of Mercedes, (2) dealing with labor unions, (3) fixing its

Asian strategy, and (4) re-aligning the merger and getting tangible results and synergies.[28]

According to DaimlerChrysler, the company's post-merger period was based on global strategy by con-centrating on four competitive areas: global presence, strong brands, broad product range, and technology leadership.[29] The company has been successful in global markets and is a force to be reckoned with because of a well-diversified brand portfolio (passenger cars and commercial vehicles), but sales have been declining. Of course, this is an industry-wide phenomenon. The company maintains strong brands and a broad product portfolio but lags in market share, quality in sub-compact segments, and global integration. In the coming years, the company's management faces an uphill task regarding reviving its profits and smooth global integration.[30] In the next four years (2007–2010), if DaimlerChrysler achieves its global objectives in the areas of cost cutting, worldwide integration, rationalization, and R&D savings, the merger will definitely be rated as a *cause celebre* achievement. If all goes well, the company will be credited for making a transatlantic corporation. On the other hand, as of 2007, it remains a question mark regarding the merger's viability and long-term prospects.[31] It was speculated that Daimler could de-merge from Chrysler.[32] According to a management guru Hamel, mega-mergers are always a problem in the business world regarding creating value and integrating companies' cultures.[33] On the other hand and within the changing circumstances and DaimlerChrysler's strategies in 2006, *The Economist* correctly observed:[34]

> *Without Daimler, Chrysler would be in liquidation; and without Chrysler, Mercedes would be confined to a limited future of narrowing horizons, as rivals encroached on the luxury market. Strategic mergers may sometimes be necessary, even if they are mighty hard to pull off.*

Postscript

In May 2007, Daimler decided to sell its 80 percent stake in Chrysler to an influential New York-based private

---

[26]For more discussion, see *Business Week*. 2004. "A Shaky Automotive Menage A Trois," (May 10): 40–41; *Financial Times*. 2004. "DaimlerChrysler to Sell Its $1 billion Hyundai Stake," (May 4): 17; *The Wall Street Journal*. 2004. "Mitsubishi Motors to Review Products, Overhaul Its Culture," (May 3): A12; *The Wall Street Journal*. 2004. "DaimlerChrysler Agrees to Sell Its 10% Stake in Hyundai Motor," (May 12): A6.
[27]For detail, see *Financial Times*. 2006. "Chrysler Aims for Shift from Big-Three Image," (June 29): 20; *Financial Times*. 2006." Zetsche Takes on New Chrysler Promotion Task," (July 1): 10; *The Wall Street Journal*. 2006."Schrempp to Leave Daimler, His Merger a Mixed Legacy," (July 29): A1&A8.

[28]For detail, see *Business Week*. 2005. "Dark Days at Daimler," (August 15): 30–38; *Business Week*. (2006). "Mercedes Gets Back up to Speed," (November 13): 46–47; *The Wall Street Journal*. 2006. "Daimler to Tout Ties to Mercedes in Chrysler Ads," (June 15): A9.
[29]See company Web site (www.daimlerchrysler.com).
[30]*The Wall Street Journal*. 2006. "Daimler CEO Defends Strategy, Reign," (May 6): A3.
[31]Anwar. 2003. op.cit.
[32]*The New York Times*. 2006. "Daimler Minus Chrysler = Pure Speculation," (October 26): C1&C13.
[33]Hamel, Gary. 2004. "When Dinosaurs Mate," *The Wall Street Journal*, (January 22): A12.
[34]*The Economist*. 2006. "In Tandem (at last)," (April 1): 52. For more information on Cerberus, see: HYPERLINK "http://www.cerberus.com" www.cerberus.com; Thornton, Emily. 2005. What's Biggerthan CISCO, Coke, or McDonald's? *Business Week*, (October 3): 101–110.

equity firm Cerberus Capital Management LP for $7.8 billion. The Wall Street Journal called this break-up "Chrysler's private bailout". Financial Times commented: "Mistakes about the scale of synergies and the role of big egos contributed to the break-up."

As discussed in the case, the DaimlerChrysler merger was hailed as the "merger of equals". At a news conference in May 2007, Dieter Zetsche stated: "we have found the best solution for Chrysler and for Daimler." After the de-merger, Daimler will continue to maintain 20 percent ownership in Chrysler. Interestingly, Daimler paid $36 billion to acquire Chrysler in 1998. Recently, the auto industry had been speculating the de-merger of DaimlerChrysler. During the de-merger talks, companies that showed interest in buying Chrysler included Magna International, Blackstone Group, and Centerbridge Capital Partners. Kirk Kerkorian, a billionaire from Las Vegas was equally interested in buying Chrysler for $4.5 billion.

In conclusion, Daimler sold Chrysler to Cerberus for the following reasons:

(1) Cerberus' offer of $7.8 billion was better than other bidders. In addition, Cerberus owned 51 percent of General Motors' financing unit as well as other automotive-related assets such as GDX Automotive, Blue Bird, NABI, North American Bus Industries, and Transamerica Leasing. Cerberus' pending deals include Collins & Aikman, Delphi and Tower Automotive.

(2) Cerberus agreed to assume the responsibility of Chrysler's pension and health care liabilities which exceeded $18 billion in 2007.

(3) Cerberus is known for breaking up its acquired assets. It is expected that Cerberus will seek a major restructuring in the next coming years to make Chrysler a profitable corporation.

(4) Cerberus may force United Auto Workers Union (UAW) to accept its terms for future reorganization and restructuring in the areas of pension and healthcare benefits and future product lines.

The Wall Street Journal. 2007. Chrysler's Private Bailout, (May 15): A16. *Financial Times. 2007.* Divorce on earth puts to a carmaking dream, (May 15): 20.
USA Today. 2007. Unprecedented Auto Deal, (May 15): 1B.
For more discussion on the de-merger of DaimlerChrysler, see: Bruner, Robert F. 2005. *Deals from Hell: M&As Lessons that Rise Above the Ashes,* New York: John Wiley & Sons; Ingrassia, Paul. 2007. DaimlerChrysler: The Divorce, *The Wall Street Journal,* (February 21): A17; *The Wall Street Journal. 2007.* Cerberus Finds Luster in Detroit,

(May 15): C1&C2; *Financial Times.* 2007. Daimler Chief Looks Ahead at the Long Road Ahead, (May 29): 19; *Financial Times.* 2007. ,How to Make Peace Between Two Warring Cultures (May 23): 14; *The New York Times.* 2007. Cerberus Goes Where no Firm has Gone Before, (May 15): C1&C6; Benner, Katie and Adam Lashinsky. 2007. The Dog that Ate Detroit, Fortune, (June 11): 21–22; Welch, David and Nanette Byrnes. 2007. A Deal that could Save Detroit, *Business Week,* (May 28): 30–33; *The Economist.* 2007. Divorced, (May 19): 67–68; *European Industrial Relations Review.* 2006. Agreement on Restructuring at DaimlerChrysler, (August): 8.

QUESTIONS FOR DISCUSSION

1. What were your expectations (prior to the developments in 2007) of the DaimlerChrysler merger and its future prospects in the global auto industry? (see Table C11-1).

2. Analyze and evaluate Daimler-Benz and Chrysler Corporation's strengths and weaknesses in 1998.

3. Evaluate the short-term and long-term global strategies does DaimlerChrysler took in its attempt to gain market share in the global automotive industry?

4. What did you learn from DaimlerChrysler's post-merger problems and blunders?

5. Compare and contrast DaimlerChrysler with other global auto manufacturers (GM, Ford, Toyota, Honda, Volkswagen, Nissan, etc.) regarding their global strategies and competition issues (see Table C11-8).

6. Evaluate Dieter Zetsche's strategies and reorganization in 2006. Also, analyze DaimlerChrysler's brands in the world auto markets as of end 2006.

7. Analyze what led up to the breakup of DaimlerChrysler in 2007. Evaluate the agreement with Cerebus. What lies ahead for Daimler AG, and for Chrysler?

FIGURE C11-1   Sales of Selected Auto Manufacturers and Pre-tax Profit per
Vehicle: 1997–2006

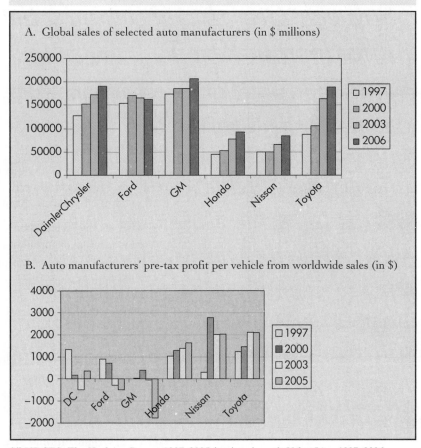

A. Global sales of selected auto manufacturers (in $ millions)

B. Auto manufacturers' pre-tax profit per vehicle from worldwide sales (in $)

SOURCES: *The Harbour Report*, 1997–2005 (various issues); *Value Line*, 1997–2006
(various issues).

Case 12   Allure Cruise Line*—Challenges of Strategic Growth and Organizational Effectiveness: Part 3

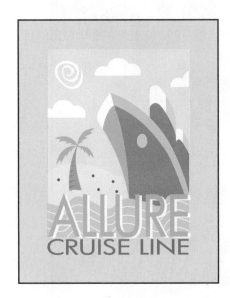

THE CHALLENGES FOR ALLURE CRUISE LINE

Now that you have familiarized yourself with the dynamics of the cruise industry in Part 1 and with some of the background, challenges, and specific goals of Allure Cruise Line in Part 2, there are several key decisions that Allure Cruise Line is currently facing in terms of their strategic growth. These are discussed and outlined below.

ASSIGNMENT: STRATEGIC GROWTH CHALLENGE

The senior leadership team at Allure Cruise Line has hired your consulting team to help them facilitate the expansion of their business to the Mediterranean. They would like to develop new itineraries and add two new ships to their fleet during the next five years.

*Note: The data used to develop this case study was garnered through managers of an existing cruise line. The name of the cruise line, as well as the individuals in the case study, and some data have been changed to protect the confidentiality of the cruise line; specific data changes can be found in Section 4 of this study.

These goals for your team can be organized by the following:

GOAL 1: Strategy

You primary role is to help the leadership team with their strategic development. The team needs your help answering the following questions:

- What are the organization's strengths and weaknesses?
- What external opportunities and threats exist?
- How feasible is the expansion to the Mediterranean?
- What options does Allure have in terms of growth strategies it can pursue?
- Which strategy/strategies might be most effective? Why?
- How will Allure penetrate these markets?
- Who will be Allure's main competitors in this market?
- How will Allure distinguish itself from its competitors in these markets?
- How will it position itself differently?

GOAL 2: Organizational Structure and Processes

In addition to the development of some recommendations regarding Allure's business strategy, the senior leadership team would also like your team to help them determine how to most effectively structure their organization now that it is expanding internationally.

- How would the European side of Allure's business be structured with relation to its American side of the business? How would you see the two businesses relating to each other?
- Where will decisions be made for each?
- What will the leadership and reporting structures potentially look like?
- What control systems would need to be put into place?
- What other types of processes might also need to be put in place?

CHAPTER

9

Staffing, Training, and Compensation for Global Operations

Outline

Opening Profile: Training: The "Toyota Way" Is Translated for a New Generation of Foreign Managers

TOYOTA CITY, Japan, Febuary 17, 2007—It does not occupy much space on the office wall, but Latondra Newton calls it the hardest thing for Toyota's new American employees to accept: those colored bar charts against a white bulletin board, in plain view for all to see.

No, they are not representing the company's progress toward goals. Rather, they are the work targets of individual workers, visibly charting their successes or failures to meet those targets.

This is part of the Toyota Way. The idea is not to humiliate, but to alert co-workers and enlist their help in finding solutions. It took a while for Ms. Newton, a general manager at Toyota's North American manufacturing subsidiary, to take this fully to heart. But now she is a convert.

"For Americans and anyone, it can be a shock to the system to be actually expected to make problems visible," said Ms. Newton, a 38-year-old Indiana native who joined Toyota after college 15 years ago and now works at the North

American headquarters in Erlanger, Ky. "Other corporate environments tend to hide problems from bosses."

Toyota's corporate culture has transformed it from a small manufacturer into a market-gobbling giant famous for quality circles and giving workers control over production lines. For years, aspiring factory leaders have come here to attend Toyota's select technical high school, the Toyota Technical Skills Academy in Toyota City.

But Toyota—on course to become the world's largest automaker—needs to sharpen its game to meet even larger challenges, including raising quality in the face of rapid overseas expansion and its largest recalls in history.

The nerve center for that task is a nondescript cluster of buildings in the lakeside town of Mikkabi, an hour away from the humble-looking headquarters of Toyota, in Toyota City.

It is the Toyota Institute, charged with preparing executives to enter the leadership class at Toyota by inculcating in them some of the most prized management secrets in corporate Japan. The institute sends off its executives to offices around the world as missionaries of sorts for the Toyota Way. The institute does not quite aspire to be Japan's answer to General Electric's famed Crotonville training center in Ossining, N.Y., which spawned a generation of top executives across American industry. But it is Toyota's best effort to avoid corporate short-sightedness and to keep the company true to its original mission of winning customers with quality cars, even as it comes under intensifying scrutiny.

"There is a sense of danger," said Koki Konishi, a Toyota general manager who heads the institute. "We must prevent the Toyota Way from getting more and more diluted as Toyota grows overseas."

It used to be enough for the culture to be transmitted by word of mouth among Toyota's Japanese employees, on factory floors and around cafeteria tables. But Toyota outgrew these informal teaching methods and created the institute, which is so secretive the company would not allow a reporter to visit it, let alone sit in on any classes. Mr. Konishi said Toyota was building similar centers in the United States, in Kentucky, and in Thailand.

"Before, when everyone was Japanese, we didn't have to make these things explicit," Mr. Konishi said. "Now we have to set the Toyota Way down on paper and teach it."

"Mutual ownership of problems," is one slogan. Other tenets include "genchi genbutsu," or solving problems at the source instead of behind desks, and the "kaizen mind," an unending sense of crisis behind the company's constant drive to improve.

The whole company prizes visibility. To nurture a sense of shared purpose, Toyota has open offices—often without even cubicle partitions between desks.

Dissemination of the Toyota Way overseas, however, can be spotty, executives and analysts warn. Toyota prides itself on pampering customers, but analysts are reporting weak or uneven service at Toyota sales subsidiaries, particularly in emerging markets like China and India.

Worse, some executives like Mr. Konishi complain of managers at Toyota factories who have not adhered to some of the company's most basic creeds, like allowing workers to stop factory lines when they spot defects. Empowering factory workers has long been central to Toyota's quality control.

And analysts say Toyota's recent and embarrassing surge in vehicle recalls was partly a failure by Toyota to spread its obsession for craftsmanship among its growing ranks of overseas factory workers and managers.

"If Toyota can't infuse its philosophy into its workers, these quality problems will keep happening," said Hirofumi Yokoi, a former Toyota accountant who is now an auto analyst at CSM Worldwide in Tokyo. "The institute was founded because Toyota is afraid of growing too fast and losing control. It's still too early to know if it will work."

For Toyota's 26 board members—all Japanese salarymen raised on the founder's ways and with an average age of 62—the adjustment to its recent emergence as a global leader will not be easy. It was not until 2001 that the company first set the Toyota Way down in writing, at the orders of Fujio Cho, the president at the time who helped orchestrate Toyota's rapid overseas growth. The company established the institute a year later.

In the last decade, as Toyota has expanded into a vast international group, it has often exported its manufacturing and management methods to 200,000 workers at 27 plants overseas without always taking the time to explain the ideas behind them, analysts and executives say.

So now, with only a third of its total workers employed at its 18 plants in Japan, much of Toyota's sprawling global empire does not always march to the same tune, these executives and analysts warn.

"Toyota is growing more quickly than the company's ability to transplant its culture to foreign markets," said Takaki Nakanishi, an auto analyst at JPMorgan Securities in Tokyo. "This is a huge issue for Toyota, one of the biggest it will face in coming years."

Ms. Newton, a general manager in charge of training and employee development in North America, can testify to that. She said that while new American hires often had difficulty at first with some tenets of the Toyota Way, they quickly caught on.

Ms. Newton includes herself in that group. At first, she confessed, she did not embrace some of these practices, especially the white bulletin board, which she said she overlooked at first as "wallpaper" because she did not look at it closely. But Ms. Newton said the institute—which has already trained about 700 foreign executives—changed her. There, she says, Toyota tackles the problem of cultural education with the same intensity that it applies to building drive trains and transmissions.

After arriving at Mikkabi last September, she and her 40 classmates from the United States, New Zealand, Singapore and Japan were immediately plunged into a week of 12- to 14-hour days, starting with lectures about the Toyota Way from the company's president, Katsuaki Watanabe; Mr. Cho; and other Japanese executives. Each day was focused on a specific core concept, with students discussing the meanings in their own words.

Ms. Newton says the students often worked late into the night on group presentations summarizing the Toyota Way and how to apply it to actual problems back at their home offices. One tenet that she studied was "drive and dedication," a practice of always seeking out problems and then solving them by breaking them into smaller, more manageable pieces. The class also discussed other slogans, like "effective consensus building" and "respect for people."

After an additional week at the Wharton School of the University of Pennsylvania, she spent five months in Kentucky on an independent project about teaching Toyota culture to generations that would enter the company around 2020. She says she flew to Japan in December to give a 10-minute presentation to Toyota's president, Mr. Watanabe.

Toyota's culture, she said, is still grounded in a Japanese-oriented brand of group-think. But in some cases, Toyota has also adapted it to fit American culture, she said, dropping group calisthenics at American factories, for example, although that is still common at Japanese plants.

She said she understood the Toyota Way better after learning from people who had lived it their entire professional lives. She now uses the wall chart as a critical motivating tool for managing her employees.

"When I saw folks in high ranks, like Mr. Watanabe, and how consistent and dedicated they were, I knew they were true believers" in the Toyota Way, Ms. Newton said. "Now, I'm a true believer, too."

[In the new millennium], the caliber of the people will be the only source of competitive advantage.

ALLAN HALCROW,
Personnel Journal[1]

Of the top 100 UK firms surveyed by Cendant International Assignment Services, 63 reported failed foreign assignments.

www.FT.com[2]

This chapter's opening profile describes how Toyota trains its host-country managers to use the Japanese management methods and the "Toyota way." Other challenges for companies around the world include the increasing trend of outsourcing employees as service and professional jobs have now joined manufacturing jobs in the category of "boundaryless" human capital (discussed in previous chapters). Clearly this is a complex issue for international human resource (IHR) managers as they seek to support strategic mandates (see Chapter 6). Global firms are finding that their practices of outsourcing skilled and professional jobs have implications for their human resource practices at home and around the world. Consequently, a firm such as Infosys, one of India's top outsourcing companies, also experiences complex human resource challenges involved in recruiting, training, and compensating increasingly sophisticated employees in its attempt to meet the escalating demand for its services. It is clear, then, that a vital component of implementing global strategy is *international human resource management* (IHRM). IHRM is increasingly being recognized as a major determinant of success or failure in international business. In a highly competitive global economy, where the other factors of production—capital, technology, raw materials, and information—are increasingly able to be duplicated, "the caliber of the people in an organization will be the only source of sustainable competitive advantage available to U.S. companies."[3] Corporations operating overseas need to pay careful attention to this most critical resource—one that also provides control over other resources.

The IHRM function comprises varied responsibilities involved in managing human resources in global corporations, including recruiting and selecting employees, providing preparation and training, and setting up appropriate compensation and performance management programs. Of particular importance is the management of **expatriates**—employees assigned to a country other than their own. An overview of those functions is provided here, while further IHRM challenges in developing a global management cadre and working within host-country practices and laws are discussed in the following chapter.

At the first level of planning, decisions are required on the staffing policy suitable for a particular kind of business, its global strategy, and its geographic locations. Key issues involve the difficulty of control in geographically dispersed operations, the need for local decision making independent of the home office, and the suitability of managers from alternate sources.

The interdependence of strategy, structure, and staffing is particularly worth noting. Ideally, the desired strategy of the firm should dictate the organizational structure and staffing modes considered most effective for implementing that strategy. In reality, however, there is usually considerable interdependence among those functions. Existing structural constraints often affect strategic decisions; similarly, staffing constraints or unique sets of competences in management come into play in organizational and sometimes strategic decisions. It is thus important to achieve a system of fits among those variables that facilitates strategic implementation.

STAFFING FOR GLOBAL OPERATIONS

> *We found the most successful formula is to hire people in-country and then bring them to our U.S. headquarters to get acquainted and have them interact with our organization.*
>
> STUART MATHISON,
> *Vice President for Strategic Planning, Sprint International*[4]

Depending on the firm's primary strategic orientation and stage of internationalization, as well as situational factors, managerial staffing abroad falls into one or more of the following staffing modes—ethnocentric, polycentric, regiocentric, and global approaches. When the company is at the internationalization stage of strategic expansion, and has a centralized structure, it will likely use an **ethnocentric staffing approach** to fill key managerial positions with people from headquarters—that is, **parent-country nationals (PCNs)**. Among the advantages of this approach, PCNs are familiar with company goals, products, technology, policies, and procedures—and they know how to get things accomplished through headquarters. This policy is also likely to be used where a company notes the inadequacy of local managerial skills and determines a high need to maintain close communication and coordination with headquarters.

Frequently, companies use PCNs for the top management positions in the foreign subsidiary—in particular, the chief executive officer (CEO) and the chief financial officer (CFO)—to maintain close control. PCNs are usually preferable when a high level of technical capability is required. They are also chosen for new international ventures requiring managerial experience in the parent company and where there is a concern for loyalty to the company rather than to the host country—in cases, for example, where proprietary technology is used extensively.

Disadvantages of the ethnocentric approach include (1) the lack of opportunities or development for local managers, thereby decreasing their morale and their loyalty to the subsidiary; and (2) the poor adaptation and lack of effectiveness of expatriates in foreign countries. Procter & Gamble, for example, routinely appointed managers from its headquarters for foreign assignments for many years. After several unfortunate experiences in Japan, the firm realized that such a practice was insensitive to local cultures and also underutilized its pool of high-potential non-American managers.[5] Furthermore, an ethnocentric recruiting approach does not enable the company to take advantage of its worldwide pool of management skill. This approach also serves to perpetuate particular personnel selections and other decision-making processes because the same types of people are making the same types of decisions.

With a **polycentric staffing approach**, local managers—**host-country nationals (HCNs)**—are hired to fill key positions in their own country. This approach is more likely to be effective when implementing a multinational strategy. If a company wants to "act local," staffing with HCNs has obvious advantages. These managers are naturally familiar with the local culture, language, and ways of doing business, and they already have many contacts in place. In addition, HCNs are more likely to be accepted by people both inside and outside the subsidiary, and they provide role models for other upwardly mobile personnel.

With regard to cost, it is usually less expensive for a company to hire a local manager than to transfer one from headquarters, frequently with a family and often at a higher rate of pay. Transferring from headquarters is a particularly expensive policy when it turns out that the manager and her or his family do not adjust and have to be prematurely transferred home. Rather than building their own facilities, some companies acquire foreign firms as a means of obtaining qualified local personnel. Local managers also tend to be instrumental in staving off or more effectively dealing with problems in sensitive political situations. Some countries, in fact, have legal requirements that a specific proportion of the firm's top managers must be citizens of that country.

One disadvantage of a polycentric staffing policy is the difficulty of coordinating activities and goals between the subsidiary and the parent company, including the potentially conflicting loyalties of the local manager. Poor coordination among subsidiaries of a multinational firm could constrain strategic options. An additional drawback of this policy is that the headquarters managers of multinational firms will not gain the overseas experience necessary for any higher positions in the firm that require the understanding and coordination of subsidiary operations.

In the **global staffing approach**, the best managers are recruited from within or outside of the company, regardless of nationality. This practice—recruiting **third country nationals (TCNs)**—has been used for some time by many European multinationals. A global staffing approach has several important advantages. First, this policy provides a greater pool of qualified and willing applicants from which to choose, which, in time, results in further development of a global executive cadre. As discussed further in Chapter 10, the skills and experiences that those managers use and transfer throughout the company result in a pool of shared learning that is necessary for the company to compete globally. Second, where third country nationals are used to manage subsidiaries, they usually bring more cultural flexibility and adaptability to a situation, as well as bilingual or multilingual skills, than parent-country nationals, especially if they are from a similar cultural background as the host-country coworkers and are accustomed to moving around. In addition, when TCNs are placed in key positions, they are perceived by employees as acceptable compromises between headquarters and local managers and thus appointing them works to reduce resentment. Third, it can be more cost-effective to transfer and pay managers from some countries than from others because their pay scale and benefits packages are lower. Indeed, those firms with a truly global staffing orientation are phasing out the entire ethnocentric concept of a home or host country. In fact, as globalization increases, terms such as *TCNs*, *HCNs*, and *expatriates* are becoming less common, because of the kind of situation where a manager may leave her native Ireland to take a job in England, then be assigned to Switzerland, then to China, and so on, without returning to Ireland As part of that focus, the term **transpatriate** is increasingly replacing the term *expatriate*. Firms such as Philips, Heinz, Unilever, IBM, and ABB have a global staffing approach, which makes them highly visible and seems to indicate a trend.

Overall, firms still tend to use expatriates in key positions in host countries that have a less familiar culture and also in less-developed economies. Clearly, this situation arises out of concern about uncertainty and the ability to control implementation of the corporation's goals. However, given the generally accepted consensus that staffing, along with structure and systems, must "fit" the desired strategy, firms desiring a truly global posture should adopt a global staffing approach. That is easier said than done. As shown in Exhibit 9-1, such an approach requires the firm to overcome barriers such as the availability and willingness of high-quality managers to transfer frequently around the world, dual-career constraints, time and cost constraints, conflicting requirements of host governments, and ineffective human resource management policies.

In a **regiocentric staffing approach**, recruiting is done on a regional basis—say within Latin America for a position in Chile. This staffing approach can produce a specific mix of PCNs, HCNs, and TCNs, according to the needs of the company or the product strategy.

What factors influence the choice of staffing policy? Among them are the strategy and organizational structure of the firm, as well as the factors related to the particular subsidiary (such as the duration of the particular foreign operation, the types of technology used, and the production and marketing techniques necessary). Factors related to the host country also play a part (such as the level of economic and technological development, political stability, regulations regarding ownership and staffing, and the sociocultural setting).[6] As a practical matter, however, the choice often depends on the availability of qualified managers in the host country. Most MNCs use a greater proportion of PCNs (also called expatriates) in top management positions, staffing middle and lower management positions with increasing proportions of HCNs ("inpatriates") as one moves down the organizational hierarchy. The choice of staffing policy has a considerable influence on organizational variables in the subsidiary, such as the locus of decision-making authority, the methods of

EXHIBIT 9-1   Maintaining a Globalization Momentum

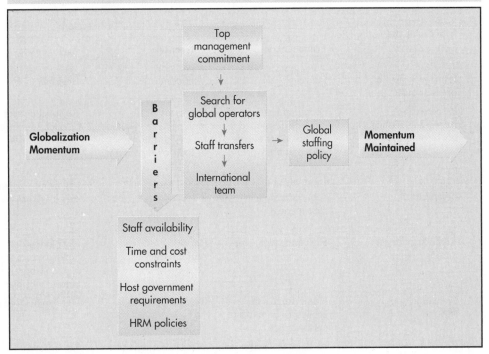

SOURCE: Adapted from D. Welch, "HRM Implications of Globalization," *Journal of General Management* 19, no. 4 (Summer 1994): 52–69.

communication, and the perpetuation of human resource management practices. These variables are illustrated in Exhibit 9-2. The conclusions drawn by the researchers some time ago are still valid today. The ethnocentric staffing approach, for example, usually results in a higher level of authority and decision making in headquarters compared to the polycentric approach.[7]

A study by Rochelle Kopp found that ethnocentric staffing and policies are associated with a higher incidence of international human resource management problems.[8] In addition, Kopp found that Japanese firms scored considerably lower than European and American firms in their practice of implementing policies such as preparing local nationals for advancement and keeping inventory of their managers around the world for development purposes. As a result of these ethnocentric practices, Japanese firms seem to experience various IHRM problems, such as high turnover of local employees, more than European and American firms.

Without exception, all phases of IHRM should support the desired strategy of the firm. In the staffing phase, having the right people in the right places at the right times is a key ingredient to success in international operations. An effective managerial cadre can be a distinct competitive advantage for a firm.

The initial phase of setting up criteria for global selection, then, is to consider which overall staffing approach or approaches would most likely support the company's strategy, as previously discussed—such as HCNs for localization, the (multilocal) strategic approach, and transpatriates for a global strategy. These are typically just starting points using idealized criteria, however. In reality, other factors creep into the process, such as host-country regulations, stage of internationalization, and—most often—who is both suitable and available for the position. It is also vital to integrate long-term strategic goals into the selection and development process, especially when rapid global expansion is intended. Insufficient projection of staffing needs for global assignments will likely result in constrained strategic opportunities because of a shortage of experienced managers suitable to place in those positions.

A more flexible approach to maximizing managerial talent, regardless of the source, would certainly consider more closely whether the position could be suitably filled by a

EXHIBIT 9-2   Relationships Among Strategic Mode, Organizational Variables, and Staffing Orientation

Aspects of the Enterprise	Orientation			
	Ethnocentric	**Polycentric**	**Regiocentric**	**Global**
Primary strategic orientation/stage	International	Multidomestic	Regional	Transnational
Perpetuation (recruiting, staffing, development)	People of home country developed for key positions everywhere in the world	People of local nationality developed for key positions in their own country	Regional people developed for key positions anywhere in the region	Best people everywhere in the world developed for key positions everywhere in the world
Complexity of organization	Complex in home country; simple in subsidiaries	Varied and independent	Highly interdependent on a regional basis	"Global Web": complex, independent, worldwide alliances/network
Authority; decision making	High in headquarters	Relatively low in headquarters	High in regional headquarters and/or high collaboration among subsidiaries	Collaboration of headquarters and subsidiaries around the world
Evaluation and control	Home standards applied to people and performance	Determined locally	Determined regionally	Globally integrated
Rewards	High in headquarters; low in subsidiaries	Wide variation; can be high or low rewards for subsidiary performance	Rewards for contribution to regional objectives	Rewards to international and local executives for reaching local and worldwide objectives based on global company goals
Communication; information flow	High volume of orders, commands, advice to subsidiaries	Little to and from headquarters; little among subsidiaries	Little to and from corporate headquarters, but may be high to and from regional headquarters and among countries	Horizontal; network relations; "virtual" teams
Geographic identification	Nationality of owner	Nationality of host country	Regional company	Truly global company, but identifying with national interests ("glocal")

SOURCE: Updated and adapted by H. Deresky in 2007, from original work by D. A. Heenan and H. V. Perlmutter. *Multinational Organization Development* (Reading, MA: Addison-Wesley, 1979), 18–19.

host-country national, as put forth by Tung, based on her research.[9] This contingency model of selection and training depends on the variables of the particular assignment, such as length of stay, similarity to the candidate's own culture, and level of interaction with local managers in that job. Tung concludes that the more rigorous the selection and training process, the lower the failure rate.

The selection process is set up as a decision tree in which the progression to the next stage of selection or the type of orientation training depends on the assessment of critical factors regarding the job or the candidate at each decision point. The simplest selection process involves choosing a local national because minimal training is necessary regarding the culture or ways of doing business locally. However, to be successful, local managers often require additional training in the MNC company-wide processes, technology, and corporate culture. If the position cannot be filled by a local national, yet the job requires a high level of interaction with the local community, careful screening of candidates from other countries and a vigorous training program are necessary.

Most MNCs tend to start their operations in a particular region by selecting primarily from their own pool of managers. Over time, and with increasing internationalization, they tend to move to a predominantly polycentric or regiocentric policy because of (1) increasing pressure (explicit or implicit) from local governments to hire locals (or sometimes legal restraints on the use of expatriates) and (2) the greater costs of expatriate staffing, particularly when the company has to pay taxes for the parent-company employee in both countries.[10] In addition, in recent years, MNCs have noted an improvement in the level of managerial and technical competence in many countries, negating the chief reason for using a primarily ethnocentric policy in the past. One researcher's comment represents a growing attitude: "All things being equal, a local national who speaks the language, understands the culture and the political system, and is often a member of the local elite should be more effective than an expatriate alien."[11] However, concerns about the need to maintain strategic control over subsidiaries and to develop managers with a global perspective remain a source of debate about staffing policies among human resource management professionals.[12] A globally oriented company such as ABB (Asea Brown Boveri), for example, has 500 roving transpatriates who are moved every two to three years, thus developing a considerable management cadre with global experience.[13]

For MNCs based in Europe and Asia, human resource policies at all levels of the organization are greatly influenced by the home-country culture and policies. For Japanese subsidiaries in Singapore, Malaysia, and India, for example, promotion from within and expectations of long-term loyalty to and by the firm are culture-based practices transferable to subsidiaries. At Matsushita, however, selection criteria for staffing seem to be similar to those of Western companies. Its candidates are selected on the basis of a set of characteristics the firm calls SMILE: specialty (required skill, knowledge), management ability (particularly motivational ability), international flexibility (adaptability), language facility, and endeavor (perseverance in the face of difficulty).[14]

MANAGING EXPATRIATES

An important responsibility of IHR managers is that of managing expatriates—those employees who they assign to positions in other countries—whether from the headquarters country or third countries. Most multinationals underestimate the importance of the human resource planning function in the selection, training, acculturation, and evaluation of expatriates. Yet the increasing significance of this resource is evidenced by the numbers. About 80 percent of mid- and large-sized U.S. companies send managers abroad and most plan to increase that number.[15]

While the number of employers sending staff abroad is on the rise, only half actually have policies in place to govern these assignments, research shows.

> *Of the 200 MNCs surveyed by HR consultancy Mercer, 44 percent have increased the number of international assignments in the past two years, but only 56 percent of those companies said they have strategies in place to help ensure their success.*

> PERSONNEL TODAY,
> *May 23, 2006*[16]

Expatriate Selection

The selection of personnel for overseas assignments is a complex process. The criteria for selection are based on the same success factors as in the domestic setting, but additional criteria must be considered, related to the specific circumstances of each international position. Unfortunately, many personnel directors have a long-standing, ingrained practice of selecting potential expatriates simply on the basis of their domestic track records and their technical expertise.[17] The need to ascertain whether potential expatriates have the necessary cross-cultural awareness and interpersonal skills for the position is too often overlooked. It is also important to assess whether the candidate's personal and family situation is such that everyone is likely to adapt to the local culture. Studies have shown there are five categories of success for expatriate managers: job factors, relational dimensions such as cultural empathy and flexibility, motivational state, family situation, and language skills. However, deciding before the expatriate goes on assignment whether he or she will be successful in those dimensions poses considerable problems for recruitment and selection purposes. Whereas language skills, for example, may be easy to ascertain, characteristics such as flexibility and cultural adjustment—widely acknowledged as most vital for expatriates—are difficult to judge before-hand. Human Resource managers wish for ways to prejudge such capabilities of candidates for assignments in order to avoid the many problems and considerable expense that can lead to expatriate failure (discussed further in this chapter and the next).

In order to address the problem of predicting how well an expatriate will perform on an overseas assignment, Tye and Chen studied factors that HR managers used as predictors of expatriate success. They found that the greatest predictive value was in the expatriate characteristics of stress tolerance and extraversion, and less on domestic work experience, gender, or even international experience. The results indicate that a manager who is extraverted (sociable, talkative) and who has a high tolerance for stress (typically experienced in new, different contexts such as in a "foreign" country) is more likely to be able to adjust to the new environment, the new job, and interacting with diverse people than those without those characteristics. HR selection procedures, then, often include seeking out managers with those characteristics because they know there will be a greater chance for successful job performance, and a lesser turnover likelihood.[18]

These expatriate success factors are based on studies of American expatriates. One could argue that the requisite skills are the same for managers from any country—and particularly so for third country nationals. A study of expatriates in China, for example, found that expatriate success factors included performance management, training, organizational support, willingness to relocate, and strength of the relationship between the expatriate and the firm.[19]

Expatriate Performance Management

While 89 percent of companies formally assess a candidate's job skills prior to a foreign posting, less than half go through the same process for cultural suitability. Even fewer gauge whether the family will cope.[20]

Deciding on a staffing policy and selecting suitable managers are logical first steps, but they do not alone ensure success. When staffing overseas assignments with expatriates, for example, many other reasons, besides poor selection, contribute to *expatriate failure* among U.S. multinationals. A large percentage of these failures can be attributed to poor preparation and planning for the entry and reentry transitions of the manager and his or her family. One important variable, for example, often given insufficient attention in the selection, preparation, and support phases, is the suitability and adjustment of the spouse. The inability of the spouse to adjust to the new environment has been found to be a major—in fact, the most frequently cited—reason for expatriate failure in U.S. and European companies.[21] In the 2005 Global Relocation Trends Survey (issued jointly by the GMAC Global Relocation Services and the National Foreign Trade Council), 67 percent of respondents cited family concerns as the main cause for assignment failure. They cited spouse dissatisfaction as the primary reason, which they attributed to cultural adjustment problems and lack of career opportunities in the host country.[22] Yet only about half of those companies studied had included the spouse in the interviewing process. In addition, although research shows that human relational skills are critical for overseas work (a fact acknowledged by the companies in a study by Tung), most of the U.S. firms surveyed failed to include this factor in their assessment of candidates.[23] The following is a synthesis of the factors frequently mentioned by researchers and firms as the major causes of expatriate failure:

- Selection based on headquarters criteria rather than assignment needs
- Inadequate preparation, training, and orientation prior to assignment
- Alienation or lack of support from headquarters
- Inability to adapt to local culture and working environment
- Problems with spouse and children—poor adaptation, family unhappiness

- Insufficient compensation and financial support
- Poor programs for career support and repatriation

After careful selection based on the specific assignment and the long-term plans of both the organization and the candidates, plans must be made for the preparation, training, and development of expatriate managers. In the following sections we discuss training and development and then compensation. However, it is useful to note that these should be components of an integrated performance management program, specific to expatriates, which includes goal setting, training, performance appraisal, and performance-related compensation. Hsi-An Shih et al. conducted a study in which they interviewed expatriates and human resource professionals in global information technology companies headquartered in five different countries. These were Applied Materials (American) with 16,000 employees in 13 countries, Hitachi High Technologies (Japanese) with 470,000 employees in 23 countries, Philips Electronics (Dutch) with 192,000 employees in 60 countries, Samsung (Korean) with 173,000 employees in 20 countries, and Winbond Electronics (Taiwanese) with 47,000 employees in six countries. Hsi-An Shih et al. found that those companies used standardized forms from headquarters, rather than tailoring them to the host environment; as such they reflected the company culture but not the local culture in which those expatriates were operating. There also was lack of on-the-job training from those companies.[24] The differences in procedures for goal setting, performance appraisal, training, and performance-related pay among those five companies are detailed in Exhibit 9-3.

EXHIBIT 9-3   Expatriate Performance Management from MNEs of Five National Origins

Company	Goal setting	Performance appraisal	Training and development	Performance-related pay
AMT (American)	Short-term: sending unit's general manager Long term: host country's general manager	Annual performance appraisal Short-term, ordinary position engineer: – 1st self rater – 2nd departmental general manager in home country Long-term, managerial position engineer: – 1st self rater – 2nd product line general manager in host country as well as client – 3rd department general manager in home country Open feedback interview exist	Applied global university Seldom take training programs while on assignment No clear connection between performance result and career development	Clear link between performance and compensation Cash bonuses and stock options
Hitachi (Japanese)	Self-setting, then finalized by host-country manager	Annually for managerial purposes, biannually for development purposes; – 1st self rater – 2nd immediate supervisor in host country – 3rd departmental general manager in home country – 4th final, jointly decided by host country supervisor and departmental general manager in home country One-way feedback discussion	Orientation Language training Seldom take training programs while on assignment Can apply to host location supervisor No clear connection between performance result and career development	Link between performance and compensation not clear Seniority-based pay system Cash bonuses

(continued)

EXHIBIT 9-3   (cont.)

Company	Goal setting	Performance appraisal	Training and development	Performance-related pay
Philips (Dutch)	Self-setting, then finalized by host-country manager	Biannual performance appraisal; – 1st self rater – 2nd immediate supervisor in home country Open feedback in interview	Orientation Seldom take training programs while on assignment No clear connection between performance result and career development	Clear link between performance and compensation Cash bonuses and stock options
Samsung (Korean)	Self-setting, then finalized by host-country manager	Biannually for managerial purposes, annually for development purposes; – 1st self-rater – 2nd immediate supervisor in host country – 3rd departmental general manager in home country Open feedback in interview	Orientation Language training Can apply to host location supervisor No clear connection between performance result and career development	Clear link between performance and compensation Senior managers: cash bonuses and stock options Ordinary expatriates; cash bonuses
Windbond (Taiwanese)	Self-setting, then finalized by host-country manager	Biannual performance appraisal; – 1st self-rater – 2nd immediate supervisor in host country – 3rd next level supervisor (usually host-country general manager) – 4th divisional general manager in home country Feedback depends on manager	Orientation Seldom take training programs while on assignment Can apply to host location supervisor No clear connection between performance result and career development	Clear link between performance and compensation Cash bonuses and stock options

SOURCE: His-An Shih, Yun-Hwa Chiang, In-Sook Kim, "Expatriate Performance Management from MNEs of Different National Origins," *International Journal of Manpower*," Bradford: 2005, Vol. 26, 2, p. 161–162, reprinted with permission of Emerald Group Publishing Ltd.

EXPATRIATE TRAINING AND DEVELOPMENT

It is clear that preparation and training for cross-cultural interactions are critical. The 2005 Global Relocation Trends Survey revealed that attrition rates for expatriates were more than double the rate of non-expatriates. They found that 21 percent of expatriates left their companies during the assignments, and another 23 percent left within a year of returning from the assignment.[25] Moreover, about half of those remain longer in their overseas assignment function at a low level of effectiveness. The direct cost alone of a failed expatriate assignment is estimated to be from $200,000 to $1.2 million. The indirect costs may be far greater, depending on the expatriate's position. Relations with the host-country government and customers may be damaged, resulting in a loss of market share and a poor reception for future PCNs.

Both cross-cultural adjustment problems and practical differences in everyday living present challenges for expatriates and their families. Examples are evident from a survey of expatriates when they ranked the countries that presented the most challenging assignments to them, along with some pet peeves from their experiences:

China: a continuing problem for expatriates; one complained that at his welcome banquet he was served duck tongue and pigeon head.

Brazil: Expatriates stress that cell phones are essential because home phones don't work.

India: Returning executives complain that the pervasiveness of poverty and street children is overwhelming.

Indonesia: Here you need to plan ahead financially because landlords typically demand rent two to three years in advance.

Japan: Expatriates and their families remain concerned that, although there is excellent medical care, the Japanese doctors reveal little to their patients.

After these five countries, expatriates rank Russia, Mexico, Saudi Arabia, South Korea, and France as challenging.[26]

Even though cross-cultural training has proved to be of high value in making the assignment a success, as indicated by 73 percent of the respondents in the 2005 Global Relocation Survey, only 20 percent of companies had formal cross-cultural training for expatriates.[27] Much of the rationale for this lack of training is an assumption that managerial skills and processes are universal. In a simplistic way, a manager's domestic track record is used as the major selection criterion for an overseas assignment.

In most countries, however, the success of the expatriate is not left so much to chance. Foreign companies provide considerably more training and preparation for expatriates than U.S. companies. Therefore, it is not hard to understand why Japanese expatriates experience significantly fewer incidences of failure than their U.S. counterparts, although this may be partially because fewer families accompany Japanese assignees. Japanese multinationals typically have recall rates of below 5 percent, signifying that they send abroad managers who are far better prepared and more adept at working and flourishing in a foreign environment.[28] While this success is largely attributable to training programs, it is also a result of intelligent planning by the human resource management staff in most Japanese organizations, as reported by Tung.[29] This planning begins with a careful selection process for overseas assignments, based on the long-term knowledge of executives and their families. An effective selection process, of course, will eliminate many potential "failures" from the start. Another factor is the longer duration of overseas assignments, averaging almost five years, which allows the Japanese expatriate more time to adjust initially and then to function at full capacity. In addition, Japanese expatriates receive considerable support from headquarters and sometimes even from local divisions set up for that purpose. At NEC Corporation, for example, part of the Japanese giant's globalization strategy is its permanent boot camp, with its elaborate training exercises to prepare NEC managers and their families for overseas battle.[30]

The demands on expatriate managers have always been as much a result of the multiple relationships that they have to maintain as they are of the differences in the host-country environment. Those relations include family relations; internal relations with people in the corporation, both locally and globally, especially with headquarters; external relations (suppliers, distributors, allies, customers, local community, etc.); and relations with the host government. It is important to pinpoint any potential problems that an expatriate may experience with those relationships so that these problems may be addressed during predeparture training. Problem recognition is the first stage in a comprehensive plan for developing expatriates (see Exhibit 9-3.). The three areas critical to preparation are cultural training, language instruction, and familiarity with everyday matters.[31] In the model shown in Exhibit 9-4, various development methods are used to address these areas during predeparture training, postarrival training, and reentry training. These methods continue to be valid and used by many organizations. Two-way feedback between the executive and the trainers at each stage helps to tailor the level and kinds of training to the individual manager. The desired goal is the increased effectiveness of the expatriate as a result of familiarity with local conditions, cultural awareness, and an appreciation of his or her family's needs in the host country.

Cross-cultural Training

Training in language and practical affairs is quite straightforward, but cros
is not; it is complex and deals with deep-rooted behaviors. The ac
cultural training should result in the expatriate learning both

EXHIBIT 9-4 IHRM Process to Maximize Effectiveness of Expatriate Assignments

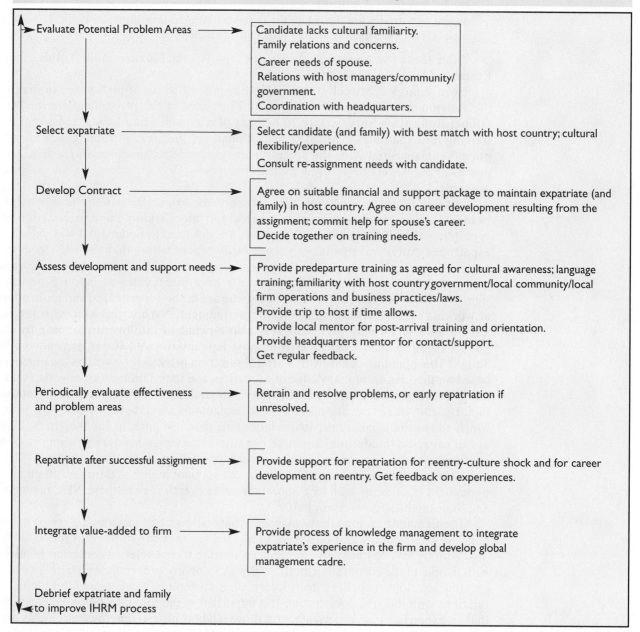

Evaluate Potential Problem Areas →
- Candidate lacks cultural familiarity.
- Family relations and concerns.
- Career needs of spouse.
- Relations with host managers/community/government.
- Coordination with headquarters.

Select expatriate →
- Select candidate (and family) with best match with host country; cultural flexibility/experience.
- Consult re-assignment needs with candidate.

Develop Contract →
- Agree on suitable financial and support package to maintain expatriate (and family) in host country. Agree on career development resulting from the assignment; commit help for spouse's career.
- Decide together on training needs.

Assess development and support needs →
- Provide predeparture training as agreed for cultural awareness; language training; familiarity with host country government/local community/local firm operations and business practices/laws.
- Provide trip to host if time allows.
- Provide local mentor for post-arrival training and orientation.
- Provide headquarters mentor for contact/support.
- Get regular feedback.

Periodically evaluate effectiveness and problem areas →
- Retrain and resolve problems, or early repatriation if unresolved.

Repatriate after successful assignment →
- Provide support for repatriation for reentry-culture shock and for career development on reentry. Get feedback on experiences.

Integrate value-added to firm →
- Provide process of knowledge management to integrate expatriate's experience in the firm and develop global management cadre.

Debrief expatriate and family to improve IHRM process

improve interactions with host-country individuals by reducing misunderstandings and inappropriate behaviors. Black and Mendenhall suggest that trainers should apply social learning theory to this process by using the behavioral science techniques of incentives and rehearsal until the trainee internalizes the desired behaviors and reproduces them.[32] The result is a state of adjustment, representing the ability to effectively interact with host nationals.

Culture Shock

The goal of this training is to ease the adjustment to the new environment by reducing **culture shock**—a state of disorientation and anxiety about not knowing how to behave in an unfamiliar culture. The cause of culture shock is the trauma people experience in new and different cultures, where they lose the familiar signs and cues that they had used to interact in daily life and where they must learn to cope with a vast array of new cultural cues and expectations.[33] The symptoms of culture shock range from mild to deep-seated psychological panic or crisis. The inability to work effectively, stress within the family, and hostility toward host nationals are the common dysfunctional results of culture shock—often leading to the manager giving up and going home.

It is helpful to recognize the stages of culture shock to understand what is happening. Culture shock usually progresses through four stages, as described by Oberg: (1) *honeymoon*, when positive attitudes and expectations, excitement, and a tourist feeling prevail (which may last up to several weeks); (2) *irritation and hostility*, the crisis stage when cultural differences result in problems at work, at home, and in daily living—expatriates and family members feel homesick and disoriented, lashing out at everyone (many never get past this stage); (3) *gradual adjustment*, a period of recovery in which the "patient" gradually becomes able to understand and predict patterns of behavior, use the language, and deal with daily activities, and the family starts to accept their new life; and (4) *biculturalism*, the stage in which the manager and family members grow to accept and appreciate local people and practices and are able to function effectively in two cultures.[34] Many never get to the fourth stage—operating acceptably at the third stage—but those who do report that their assignment is positive and growth oriented.

Subculture Shock

Similar to culture shock, though usually less extreme, is the experience of **subculture shock**. This occurs when a manager is transferred to another part of the country where there are cultural differences—essentially from what she or he perceives to be a "majority" culture to a "minority" one. The shock comes from feeling like an "immigrant" in one's own country and being unprepared for such differences. For instance, someone going from New York to Texas will experience considerable differences in attitudes and lifestyle between those two states. These differences exist even within Texas, with cultures that range from roaming ranches and high technology to Bible-belt attitudes and laws and to areas with a mostly Mexican heritage.[35]

Training Techniques

Many training techniques are available to assist overseas assignees in the adjustment process. These techniques are classified by Tung as (1) *area studies*, that is, documentary programs about the country's geography, economics, sociopolitical history, and so forth; (2) *culture assimilators*, which expose trainees to the kinds of situations they are likely to encounter that are critical to successful interactions; (3) *language training*; (4) *sensitivity training*; and (5) *field experiences*—exposure to people from other cultures within the trainee's own country.[36] Tung recommends using these training methods in a complementary fashion, giving the trainee increasing levels of personal involvement as she or he progresses through each method. Documentary and interpersonal approaches have been found to be comparable, with the most effective intercultural training occurring when trainees become aware of the differences between their own cultures and the ones they are planning to enter.[37]

Similarly categorizing training methods, Ronen suggests specific techniques, such as workshops and sensitivity training, including a field experience called the *host-family surrogate*, where the MNC pays for and places an expatriate family with a host family as part of an immersion and familiarization program.[38]

Most training programs take place in the expatriate's own country prior to leaving. Although this is certainly a convenience, the impact of host-country (or in-country) programs can be far greater than those conducted at home because crucial skills, such as overcoming cultural differences in intercultural relationships, can actually be experienced during in-country training rather than simply discussed.[39] Some MNCs are beginning to recognize that there is no substitute for on-the-job training (OJT) in the early stages of the careers of those managers they hope to develop into senior-level global managers. Colgate-Palmolive—whose overseas sales represent two-thirds of its $6 billion in yearly revenue—is one company whose management development programs adhere to this philosophy. After training at headquarters, Colgate employees

---

EXHIBIT 9-5   *Corporate Programs to Develop Global Managers*

- ABB (Asea Brown Boveri) rotates about 500 managers around the world to different countries every two to three years in order to develop a management cadre of transpatriates to support their global strategy.
- PepsiCo has an orientation program for its foreign managers, which brings them to the United States for one-year assignments in bottling division plants.
- British Telecom uses informal mentoring techniques to induct employees into the ways of their assigned country; existing expatriate workers talk to prospective assignees about the cultural factors to expect (www.FT.com).
- Honda of America Manufacturing gives its U.S. supervisors and managers extensive preparation in Japanese language, culture, and lifestyle and then sends them to the parent company in Tokyo for up to three years.
- General Electric likes its engineers and managers to have a global perspective whether or not they are slated to go abroad. The company gives regular language and cross-cultural training for them so that they are equipped to conduct business with people around the world (www.GE.com).

---

become associate product managers in the United States or abroad—and, according to John R. Garrison, manager of recruitment and development at Colgate, they must earn their stripes by being prepared to country-hop every few years. In fact, says Garrison, "That's the definition of a global manager: one who has seen several environments firsthand."[40] Exhibit 9-5 shows some other global management development programs for junior employees.

The importance of developing a global orientation in one's career development is illustrated by the advice offered to potential applicants to Citibank given on their Web site, as described in the accompanying Management Focus: Citibank Gives Advice on Career Planning. Citibank is now part of Citigroup—a global financial and insurance institution—since the merger of Citicorp and Travelers Insurance in 1998.

Management Focus

Citibank Gives Advice on Career Planning

BE MOBILE: TO GET SOMEWHERE, YOU HAVE TO GO PLACES!

As Citibank continues to expand globally, there is a growing need for a cadre of professionals with the global perspective to lead the organization. Two-thirds of Citibank's current management team have already had international experience. While living and working in other countries are probably the most direct ways to gain a global perspective, there are alternate routes to accomplish this objective. These are well worth exploring if your road to career growth lies over Citibank's global horizons.

A GLOBAL MOVE IS A GOOD CAREER MOVE

Expatriate assignments offer an extraordinary opportunity for experience, learning, and personal and career enrichment. Our goal is to have each expatriate assignment fulfill a business need and to provide each person who accepts an expatriate assignment with professional as well as personal growth opportunities.

SOME CAREER ADVANTAGES OFFERED BY AN EXPATRIATE ASSIGNMENT

- Develop a global business outlook and an understanding of how to leverage the bank's global position.
- Gain the broader perspective through working in different cultures, geographies, businesses, and functions.
- Interact with a wide range of customers and work with globally focused managers and colleagues, so you can stretch beyond your current environment and add breadth and depth to your work experience.
- Apply your solutions to truly unique problems within different cultures and environments.
- Take on new challenges that stretch and develop your skills by requiring you to take educated risks.

OTHER WAYS TO GAIN A GLOBAL PERSPECTIVE

While advantageous for some, international assignments aren't right for everyone. Only you and those close to you can decide if you want to live and work in a different country, and if so, at which point in time. If success on your career path requires international experience and you are unable to take on an international assignment at this time for any reason, there are other ways to gain global exposure. These might include short-term assignments in other locations, jobs that involve cross-border interaction, or a task force made up of a global team.

SOURCE: www.Citibank.com

Integrating Training with Global Orientation

In continuing our discussion of "strategic fit," it is important to remember that training programs, like staffing approaches, be designed with the company's strategy in mind. Although it is probably impractical to break down those programs into a lot of variations, it is feasible to at least consider the relative level or stage of globalization that the firm has reached because obvious major differences would be appropriate, for example, from the initial export stage to the full global stage. Exhibit 9-6 suggests levels of rigor and types of training content appropriate for the firm's managers, as well as those for host-country nationals, for four globalization stages—export, multidomestic, multinational, and global. It is noteworthy, for example, that the training of host-country nationals for a global firm has a considerably higher level of scope and rigor than that for the other stages and borders on the standards for the firm's expatriates.

As a further area for managerial preparation for global orientation—in addition to training plans for expatriates and for HCNs separately—there is a particular need to anticipate potential problems with the interaction of expatriates and local staff. In a 2003 study of expatriates and local staff (inpatriates) in Central and Eastern European joint ventures and subsidiaries, Peterson found that managers reported a number of behaviors by expatriates that helped them to integrate with local staff, but also some which were hindrances (see Exhibit 9-7).[41] Clearly, this kind of feedback from MNC managers in the field can provide the basis for expatriate training and also help HCNs to anticipate and work with the expatriates in order to meet joint strategic objectives.

EXHIBIT 9-6   Stage of Globalization and Training Design Issues

Export Stage	MNC Stage
Training Need: Low to moderate	*Training Need:* High moderate to high
Content: Emphasis should be on interpersonal skills, local culture, customer values, and business behavior.	*Content:* Emphasis should be on interpersonal skills, two-way technology, transfer, corporate value transfer, international strategy, stress management, local culture, and business practices.
Host-Country Nationals: Train to understand parent-country products and policies.	*Host-Country Nationals:* Train in technical areas, product and service systems, and corporate culture.
MDC Stage	**Global Stage**
Training Need: Moderate to high	*Training Need:* High
Content: Emphasis should be on interpersonal skills, local culture, technology transfer, stress management, and business practices and laws.	*Content:* Emphasis should be on global corporate operations and systems, corporate culture transfer, customers, global competitors, and international strategy.
Host-Country Nationals: Train to familiarize with production and service procedures.	*Host-Country Nationals:* Train for proficiency in global organization production and efficiency systems, corporate culture, business systems, and global conduct policies.

SOURCE: Adapted from J. S. Black, Mark. E. Mendenhall, Hal B. Gregersen, and Linda K. Stroh, *Globalizing People Through International Assignments* (Reading, MA: Addison Wesley Longman, 1999).

EXHIBIT 9-7 Factors That Help or Hinder the Integration of Expatriate Staff with Local Staff

Factors Helping	Factors Hindering
Forming close working relationships	Not using team concept
Learning local language	Not learning local language
Transferring technical/business knowledge	Arrogance
Ability to integrate into local life	Spouse and family problems in adjusting
Professionalism in behavior	Being autocratic
Cultural sensitivity	Low level of delegating by expatriate
Willingness to learn	Expatriate not being talented
Providing model of competitiveness	Lack of cultural sensitivity
Adaptability	Reluctance to change and adapt
Team-building skills	We–they mentality
Introducing effective management control system	Too short expatriate assignment to nation
Focus on service dimension	"Home-country" mentality
Teaching locals about market economy	Poor cross-cultural mentality
Marketing know-how	Lack of curiosity
Friendliness/openness	Acting like back home
Deep financial knowledge	Different way of thinking than local staff
Self-confidence	
Strong work ethic	
Previous assignments in the region	
Treating local staff with respect	
Listening skills	
Acceptance of local culture	

SOURCE: Reprinted from *Journal of World Business*, 38, R. B. Peterson, "The Use of Expatriates and Inpatriates in Central and Eastern Europe Since the Wall Came Down," 55–69, 2003, with permission from Elsevier.

Compensating Expatriates

> *If you're an expatriate working alongside another expatriate and you're being treated differently, it creates a lot of dissension.*

CHRISTOPHER TICE,
Manager, Global Expatriate Operations, DuPont Inc.[42]

The significance of an appropriate compensation and benefits package to attract, retain, and motivate international employees cannot be overemphasized. Compensation is a crucial link between strategy and its successful implementation: There must be a fit between compensation and the goals for which the firm wants managers to aim. So that they will not feel exploited, MNC employees need to perceive equity and goodwill in their compensation and benefits, whether they are PCNs, HCNs, or TCNs. The premature return of expatriates or the unwillingness of managers to take overseas assignments can often be traced to their knowledge that the assignment is detrimental to them financially and usually to their career progression. One company which recognizes the need for a reasonable degree of standardization in its treatment of expatriates is DuPont. The company has centralized programs for its approximately 400 international relocations in its Global Transfer Center of Expertise, so its expatriates know that everyone is getting the same package. The company seems to be on the cutting edge, however, since a recent study by Mercer Human Resource Consulting found that "25 percent of multinational corporations do not have a benefits policy for globally mobile employees; 30 percent have no formal governance procedures, and 11 percent have never reviewed their policies."[43]

From the firm's perspective, the high cost of maintaining appropriate compensation packages for expatriates has led many companies—Colgate-Palmolive, Chase Manhattan Bank, Digital Equipment, General Motors, and General Electric among them—to find ways to cut the cost of PCN assignments as much as possible. "Transfer a $100,000-a-year American executive to London—and suddenly he [or she] costs the employer $300,000," explains the *Wall Street Journal*. "Move him to Stockholm or Tokyo, and he [or she] easily becomes a million-dollar [manager]."[44]

Firms try to cut overall costs of assignments by either extending the expatriate's tour, since turnover is expensive—especially when there is an accompanying family to move—or to assign expatriates to a much shorter tour as an unaccompanied assignment.[45]

Designing and maintaining an appropriate compensation package is more complex than it would seem because of the need to consider and reconcile parent- and host-country financial, legal, and customary practices. The problem is that although little variation in typical executive salaries at the level of base compensation exists around the world, a wide variation in net spendable income is often present. U.S. executives may receive more in cash and stock, but they have to spend more for what foreign companies provide, such as cars, vacations, and entertainment allowances. In addition, the manager's purchasing power with that net income is affected by the relative cost of living. The cost of living is considerably higher in most of Europe than in the United States. In designing compensation and benefit packages for PCNs, then, the challenge to IHRM professionals is to maintain a standard of living for expatriates equivalent to their colleagues at home, plus compensating them for any additional costs incurred. This policy is referred to as "keeping the expatriate whole."[46]

To ensure that expatriates do not lose out through their overseas assignment, the **balance sheet approach** is often used to equalize the standard of living between the host country and the home country and to add some compensation for inconvenience or qualitative loss.[47] However, recently some companies have begun to base their compensation package on a goal of achieving a standard of living comparable to that of host-country managers, which does help resolve some of the problems of pay differentials.

In fairness, the MNC is obliged to make up additional costs that the expatriate would incur for taxes, housing, and goods and services. The tax differential is complex and expensive for the company, and MNCs generally use a policy of tax equalization: The company pays any taxes due on any type of additional compensation that the expatriate receives for the assignment; the expatriate pays in taxes only what she or he would pay at home. The burden of foreign taxes can be lessened, however, by efficient tax planning—a fact often overlooked by small firms. The timing and methods of paying people determine what foreign taxes are incurred. For example, a company can save on taxes by renting an apartment for the employee instead of providing a cash housing allowance. All in all, MNCs have to weigh the many aspects of a complete compensation package, especially at high management levels, to effect a tax equalization policy. The total cost to the company can vary greatly by location; for example:

> *Expatriates in Germany may incur twice the income tax they would in the U.S., and they are taxed on their housing and cost-of-living allowances as well. This financial snowball effect is a great incentive to make sure we really need to fill the position with an expatriate.*
>
> JOHN DE LEON,
> *Vice President IHRM, CH2MHill, 2003*[48]

Managing PCN compensation is a complex challenge for companies with overseas operations. All components of the compensation package must be considered in light of both home- and host-country legalities and practices. Those components include:

Salary: Local salary buying power and currency translation, as compared with home salary; bonuses or incentives for dislocation

Taxes: Equalize any differential effects of taxes as a result of expatriate's assignment

Allowances: Relocation expenses; cost-of-living adjustments; housing allowance for assignment and allowance to maintain house at home; trips home for expatriate and family; private education for children

Benefits: Health insurance; stock options

Most important, to be strategically competitive, the compensation package must be comparatively attractive to the kinds of managers the company wishes to hire or relocate. Some of those managers will, of course, be local managers in the host country. This, too, is a complex situation requiring competitive compensation policies that can attract, motivate, and retain the best local managerial talent. In many countries, however, it is a considerable challenge to develop compensation packages appropriate to the local situation and culture, while also recognizing the differences between local salaries and those expected by expatriates or transpatriates (that difference itself often being a source of competitive advantage).

TRAINING AND COMPENSATING HOST-COUNTRY NATIONALS

Training HCNs

> *We found that the key human resource role of the MNC [in Central and Eastern Europe] was to expose the local staff to a market economy; to instill world standards of performance; and provide training and functional expertise.*

RICHARD PETERSON[49]

The continuous training and development of HCNs and TCNs for management positions is also important to the long-term success of multinational corporations. As part of a long-term staffing policy for a subsidiary, the ongoing development of HCNs will facilitate the transition to an indigenization policy. Furthermore, multinational companies like to have well-trained managers with broad international experience available to take charge in many intercultural settings, whether at home or abroad, and, increasingly in developing countries. Kimberly-Clark, for example, with over 60,000 employees around the world, has steadily increased its talent development and training programs in all countries, but more recently has focused on developing markets. "In Latin America, the average employee has gone from receiving practically no training time to about 38 hours each year. By contrast, workers in Europe now receive 40 hours per year—eight hours more than in 1996."[50]

Many multinationals, in particular "chains," wish to train their local managers and workers to bridge the divide between the firm's successful corporate culture and practices, on the one hand, with the local culture and work practices on the other. One example of how to do this in China is the Starbucks firm, featured in the Management Focus: Success! Starbucks' Java Style Helps to Recruit, Train, and Retain Local Managers in Beijing.

Many HCNs are, of course, receiving excellent training in global business and Internet technology within their home corporations. For example, Kim In Kyung, twenty-four, has a job involving world travel and high technology with Samsung Electronics Company of Seoul, South Korea. Part of Samsung's strategy is to promote its new Internet focus, and this strategy has landed the farmer's daughter a $100,000 job. Her situation reflects Seoul's sizzling tech boom, where IT comprises 11 percent of its $400 billion economy and is expected to reach 20 percent by 2010.[51]

Whether in home corporations, MNC subsidiaries, or joint ventures in any country, managerial training to facilitate e-business adoption is competitively taking on increasing importance in order to take advantage of new strategic opportunities. While large companies are well ahead on the curve for information and communication technologies (ICT), there is considerable need for small and medium-sized enterprises (SMEs) to adopt such knowledge-creating capabilities. Managerial training in ICT is particularly critical for firms in new economy and emerging markets, and, in the aggregate, can provide leverage for rapid economic growth in regions such as Eastern Europe. Research in 2003 by Damaskopoulos and Evgeniou addressed these needs by surveying more than 900 SME managers in Slovenia, Poland, Romania, Bulgaria, and Cyprus. While most managers recognized the opportunities in implementing e-business strategies, they also noted the urgent need of training in order to take advantage of

Success! Starbucks' Java Style Helps to Recruit, Train, and Retain Local Managers in Beijing

Starbucks in Shanghai's historic Yu Yuan Garden area is one of the first Starbucks in China; it opened in 2000.

SOURCE: Shanghai China Store Front. Exterior shot of retail store in international market. CSR FY05 Annual Report; compliments of Starbucks Inc., November 2006, used with permission.

When we first started, people didn't know who we were and it was rough finding sites. Now landlords are coming to us.

DAVID SUN,
President of Beijing Mei Da Coffee Company (former Starbucks' partner for Northern China) (The Economist, October 6, 2001)

Starbucks Coffee International opened its 34th retailer in Beijing on July 16, 2003, in the Zhongguancun area known as "China's Silicon Valley," making it the 70th café in China's mainland.

INFO-PROD (MIDDLE EAST) LTD.,
July 2003

As we see from the above quotes, Starbucks has achieved a remarkable penetration rate in China, given that it is a country of devoted tea drinkers who do not take readily to the taste of coffee.

Starbucks is no stranger to training leaders from around the world into the Starbucks style (the company has more than 12,000 coffee shops in Europe, Latin America, North America, the Middle East, and the Pacific Rim. If the Company meets its projections and establishes locations in Brazil, Russia, India and Egypt by the end of calendar 2007, Starbucks will have a presence in 40 countries outside the United States. The plan is to have 20,000 locations in the U.S. and 20,000 locations overseas. As of May, 2007, Starbucks has 13,000 locations in 37 countries, and is focusing on expanding in China. Company managers nevertheless have had quite a challenge in recruiting, motivating, and retaining managers for its Beijing outlets. Starbucks' primary challenge

has been to recruit good managers in a country where the demand for local managers by foreign companies expanding there is far greater than the supply of managers with any experience in capitalist-style companies. Chinese recruits have stressed that they are looking for opportunity to get training and to advance in global companies rather than for money. They know that managers with experience in Western organizations can always get a job. The brand's pop-culture reputation is also an attraction to young Beijingers.

In order to expose the recruits to java-style culture as well as to train them for management, Starbucks brings them to Seattle, Washington, for three months to give them a taste of the West Coast lifestyle and the company's informal culture, such as Western-style backyard barbecues. Then they are exposed to the art of cappuccino-making at a real store before dawn and concocting dozens of fancy coffees. They get the same intensive training as anyone else anywhere in the world. One recruit, Mr. Wang, who worked in a large Beijing hotel before finding out how to make a triple grand latte, said that he enjoys the casual atmosphere and respect. The training and culture are very different from what one would expect at a traditional state-owned company in China, where the work is strictly defined and has no challenge for employees.

Starbucks has found that motivating their managers in Beijing is multifaceted. They know that people won't switch jobs for money alone. They want to work for a company that gives them an opportunity to learn. They also want to have a good working environment and a company with a strong reputation. The recruits have expressed their need for trust and participation in an environment where local nationals are traditionally not expected to exercise initiative or authority. In all, what seems to motivate them more than anything else is their dignity.

SOURCES: www.Starbucks.com Press Release, October 11, 2006; J. Adamy, "Starbucks Raises New-Stores Goal, Enters iTunes Deal," *Wall Street Journal,* October 6, 2006; "China: Starbucks Opens New Outlet in Beijing," *Info-Prod (Middle East) Ltd.,* July 20, 2003; "Coffee with Your Tea? Starbucks in China," *The Economist,* October 6, 2001.

those opportunities. Exhibit 9-8 shows, in order of priority, the training needs and issues as perceived by those SME managers. Some of these factors are at the firm level, while other issues relate to the market and regulatory levels, such as the need to increase security for commercial activity on the Internet.[52] Such findings highlight the need to recognize the strategy-staffing-training link, and the importance to the overall growth of emerging economies.

In another common scenario also requiring the management of a mixture of executives and employees, American and European MNCs presently employ Asians as well as Arab locals in their plants and offices in Saudi Arabia, bringing together three cultures: well-educated Asian managers living in a Middle Eastern, highly traditional society who are employed by a firm reflecting Western technology and culture. This kind of situation requires training to help all parties effectively integrate multiple sets of culturally based values, expectations, and work habits.

Compensating HCNs

How do firms deal with the question of what is appropriate compensation for host-country nationals, given local norms and the competitive needs of the firm? According to a survey of 90 MNCs by Mercer Human Resource Consulting in 2005:

EXHIBIT 9-8   SME Managers in Eastern Europe: Training Priorities for E-Business Development

Addressing security and privacy concerns
Developing a business plan
Developing an e-business strategy
Understanding of electronic payment methods
Financing e-business initiatives
Personalization and customer relationship management on the Internet
Sourcing e-business solutions and expertise
Developing the right partnerships for e-business
Training in technology management
Implementation of e-business strategy
Learning how to collect marketing intelligence online
Crafting the right business model for the Internet
Developing marketing strategies for the Internet
Collecting marketing intelligence online
Opportunities and pitfalls of online advertising
Understanding mobile commerce
Devising a sustainable revenue model
Understanding business-to-business marketplaces and virtual value chains

SOURCE: Reprinted from Panagiotis Damaskopoulos and Theodoros Evgeniou, "Adoption of New Economy Practices by SMEs in Eastern Europe," *European Management Journal,* 21, 2, 133–145, 2003. With permission from Elsevier.

Eighty-five percent of multinationals have a global pay strategy in place, and the remaining 15 percent plan to introduce one by 2007. These global strategies consistently include policies on positioning pay relative to the market, short-term and long-term incentive design and methodologies for job grading. More than half incorporate fixed guidelines.

WORKFORCE MANAGEMENT,
April 10, 2006[53]

Of course, no one set of solutions can be applicable in any country. Many variables apply—including local market factors and pay scales, government involvement in benefits, the role of unions, the cost of living, and so on. In Eastern Europe, for example, Hungarians, Poles, and Czechs spend 35 to 40 percent of their disposable income on food and utilities, which may run as high as 75 percent in the Russian Federation.[54] Therefore, East European managers must have cash for about 65 to 80 percent of their base pay, compared to about 40 percent for U.S. managers (the rest being long-term incentives, benefits, and perks). In addition, they still expect the many social benefits provided by the "old government." To be competitive, MNCs can focus on providing goods and services that are either not available at all or are extremely expensive in Eastern Europe. Such upscale perks can be used to atttract high-skilled workers.

Nestlé Bulgaria offers a company car and a cellular phone to new recruits. . . . Fuel prices are about $2 per gallon and cell phones cost $1,200 a year—equivalent to half a year's salary.[55]

In Japan, companies are revamping their HRM policies to compete in a global economy, in response to a decade-long economic slump. The traditional lifetime employment and guaranteed tidy pension are giving way to the more Western practices of competing for jobs, of basing pay on performance rather than seniority, and of making people responsible for their own retirement fund decisions.[56]

In China, too, change is underway. University graduates may now seek their own jobs rather than be assigned to state-owned companies, though nepotism is still common. In a study of HRM practices in China, Bjorkman and Lu found that a key concern of Western managers in China was the compensation of the HCNs. In Beijing and Shanghai, top Chinese managers have seen their salaries increase by 30 to 50 percent in the last few years. They have also received considerable fringe benefits, such as housing, company cars, pensions, and overseas training. The difficulty, too, was that in Western–Chinese joint ventures, the Chinese partner opposed pay increases.[57] Yet when trying to introduce performance-based pay, the Western companies ran into considerable opposition and usually gave up, using salary increases instead. Setting up some kind of housing scheme, such as investing in apartments, seemed to be one way that foreign-owned firms were able to compete for good managers. Those managers were, understandably, maximizing their job opportunities now that they did not have to get permission to leave the Chinese state-owned companies.[58]

According to Citigroup, it is also imperative to make clear what benefits, as well as salary, come with a position because of the way compensation is perceived and regulated around the world.[59] In Latin America, for example, an employee's pay and title are associated with what type of car they can receive.

Comparative Management in Focus

IHRM Practices in Australia, Canada, China, Indonesia, Japan, Latin America, Mexico, South Korea, Taiwan, and the United States

In a comparative long-term study of how the major IHRM functions are performed around the world, a team of 37 researchers in ten locations, led by Mary Ann von Glinow, studied how and in what environments various organizations conducted those functions. Exhibit 9-9 is a summary of their findings from their "Best

International Human Resource Management Practices Project." For the practice of compensation, for example, the first column shows those practices the researchers found to be universal within the cultures studied. The second column shows countries or regions where those practices are similar. The third column shows where those practices were specific to certain countries. For the practice of selection, for example, a major tool in Korea is the employment test, whereas in Taiwan the job interview is considered the most important criterion. Korea and Taiwan also "cluster" in de-emphasizing proven work experience; whereas the Anglo cluster showed the job interview, technical skill, and work experience to be the most important selection criteria. Those "universals" found for the selection function, were "getting along with others" and "fit with the corporate values."[60]

EXHIBIT 9-9   Trends in International Human Resource Management Practices Across Selected Countries and Regions

Practice	Universals Derived ETICS "Best Practices"	Regional or Country Clusters	Country Specific
Compensation	Pay incentives should not comprise too much of an employee's compensation package. Compensation should be based on individual job performance. There should be a reduced emphasis on seniority. Benefits should comprise an important part of a compensation package.	Seniority-based pay, pay based on group/team or organizational goals, and pay based on future goals—all are used to a larger extent in the Asian and Latin countries now.	U.S. and Canada has less use of pay incentives than expected. China and Taiwan had above-average use of pay incentives, and wanted more based on individual contributions.
Selection	"Getting along with others", and "Fit with the Corporate Values" signals a shift in selection from "West meets East."	Selection practices were remarkably similar among the Anglo countries. Specifically, job interview, technical skill, and work experience are the most important selection criteria. How well the person fits the company's values replace work experience as one of the top selection criteria for future selection practices. Selection practices are quite similar in Korea, Japan, and Taiwan. Specifically, proven work experience is de-emphasized as a selection practice in these countries. In the Anglo and Latin American countries, allowing subordinates to express themselves is perceived as an important future appraisal practice.	In Japan, a heavy emphasis is placed on a person's potential (thus hiring new graduates) and his/her ability to get along with others. A relatively low weight was given to job-related skills, and experience as a selection criterion. In Korea, employment tests are considered crucial and are used to a large extent as a selection tool, as well as hiring new graduates. Koreans de-emphasize experience. In Taiwan, the job interview is considered the most important criterion in the selection process.
Performance appraisal	In all countries, "should-be" scores were higher on every purpose, suggesting that the purposes of PA have fallen short in every country. All countries indicated that a greater emphasis be placed on development and documentation in future PA practices. In particular,	In contrast, in the Asian countries expression is used to a low extent, particularly in Korea. In the Latin American countries, the administrative purposes of performance appraisal are considered important in future practice.	In Taiwan, the administrative purposes of performance appraisal are considered important in future practice.

EXHIBIT 9-9   (cont.)

Practice	Universals Derived ETICS "Best Practices"	Regional or Country Clusters	Country Specific
	recognizing subordinates, evaluating their goal acheivement, planning their development activities, and (ways to) improving their performance are considered the most important appraisal practices for the future.		
T&D	In most countries, T&D practices are used to improve employees' technical skills. There is a growing trend toward using T&D for team building and "soft management practices."	In the Anglo countries, the softer T&D practices such as team building, understanding business practices and corporate culture, and the pro-active T&D practices such as preparation for future assignment and cross-training are used moderately; however, a significant increase in these practices is desired. In the Latin countries, an increase in the extent to which all T&D practices are used is desired.	In Mexico, T&D as a reward to employees is considered a highly desirable practice. In the U.S. and Korea, preparing employees for future job assignments is used to a lesser extent. U.S. is using outsourcing more. In the Asian countries, most T&D practices are used moderately and are consistently considered satisfactory. In Japan, remedying past performance is used to a small extent, however, a significant increase in this practice is desired. In Korea, team building is used extensively and emphasized in all T&D practices.
Relation to business strategy	Across most countries, the HRM practices most closely linked to organizational capability are training and development and performance appraisal.	In the Asian countries, linkages were indicated between both low cost and differentiation strategies and HRM practices.	In Mexico, no linkages were indicated between organizational capability and HRM practices.
Status of HRM function			In Japan and Taiwan few linkages were indicated between organizational capability and HRM practices. Status of HRM was highest in Australia and lowest in Indonesia.

Source: Mary Ann Von Gilnow, Ellen A. Drost, and Mary B. Teagarden (2002). "Converging on IHRM Best Practices: Lessons Learned from a Globally Distributed Consortium on Theory and Practice," *Human Resource Management*, 41, 1, pp. 133–135. Reprinted with permission of John Wiley and Sons, Inc.

CONCLUSION

The effectiveness of managers at foreign locations is crucial to the success of the firm's operations, particularly because of the lack of proximity to, and control by, headquarters executives. The ability of expatriates to initiate and maintain cooperative relationships with local people and agencies will determine the long-term success, even the viability, of the operation. In a real sense, a company's global cadre represents its most valuable resource. Proactive management of that resource by headquarters will result in having the right people in the right place at the right time, appropriately trained, prepared, and supported. MNCs using these IHRM practices can anticipate the effective management of the foreign operation, the fostering of expatriates' careers, and ultimately, the enhanced success of the corporation.

Summary of Key Points

1. Global human resource management is a vital component of implementing global strategy and is increasingly being recognized as a major determinant of success or failure in international business.
2. The main staffing alternatives for global operations are the ethnocentric, polycentric, regiocentric, and global approaches. Each approach has its appropriate uses, according to its advantages and disadvantages, and, in particular, the firm's strategy.
3. The causes of expatriate failure include the following: poor selection based on inappropriate criteria, inadequate preparation before assignment, alienation from headquarters, inability of manager or family to adapt to local environment, inadequate compensation package, and poor programs for career support and repatriation.
4. The three major areas critical to expatriate preparation are cultural training, language instruction, and familiarity with everyday matters.
5. Common training techniques for potential expatriates include area studies, culture assimilators, language training, sensitivity training, and field experiences.
6. Appropriate and attractive compensation packages must be designed by IHRM staffs to sustain a competitive global expatriate staff. Compensation packages for host-country managers must be designed to fit the local culture and situation, as well as the firm's objectives.

Discussion Questions

1. What are the major alternative staffing approaches for international operations? Explain the relative advantages of each and the conditions under which you would choose one approach over another.
2. Why is the HRM role so much more complex, and important, in the international context?
3. Explain the common causes of expatriate failure. What are the major success factors for expatriates? Explain the role and importance of each.
4. What are the common training techniques for managers going overseas? How should these vary as appropriate to the level of globalization of the firm?
5. Explain the balance sheet approach to international compensation packages. Why is this approach so important? Discuss the pros and cons of aligning the expatriate compensation package with the host-country colleagues compared to the home-country colleagues.
6. Discuss the importance of a complete program for expatriate performance management. What are the typical components for such a program?

Application Exercises

1. Make a list of the reasons you would want to accept a foreign assignment and a list of reasons you would want to reject it. Do they depend on the location? Compare your list with a classmate and discuss your reasons.
2. Research a company with operations in several countries and ascertain the staffing policy used for those countries. Find out what kinds of training and preparation are provided for expatriates and what kinds of results the company is experiencing with expatriate training.

Experiential Exercise

This can be done in groups or individually. After the exercise, discuss your proposals with the rest of the class.

You are the expatriate general manager of a British company's subsidiary in Brazil, an automobile component parts manufacturer. You and your family have been in Brazil for seven years, and now you are being reassigned and replaced with another expatriate—Ian Fleming. Ian is bringing his family—Helen, an instructor in computer science, who hopes to find a position; a son, age twelve; and a daughter, age fourteen. None of them has lived abroad before. Ian has asked you what he and his family should expect in the new assignment. Remembering all the problems you and your family experienced in the first couple of years of your assignment in Brazil, you want to facilitate their adjustment and have decided to do two things:

1. Write a letter to Ian, telling him what to expect—both on the job and in the community. Tell him about some of the cross-cultural conflicts he may run into with his coworkers and employees, and how he should handle them.
2. Set up some arrangements and support systems for the family and design a support package for them, with a letter to each family member telling them what to expect.

Internet Resources

Visit the Deresky Companion Website at www.prenhall.com/deresky for this chapter's Internet resources.

Fred Bailey in Japan: An Innocent Abroad

Fred Bailey gazed out the window of his 24th-floor office at the tranquil beauty of the Imperial Palace amid the hustle and bustle of downtown Tokyo. It had been only six months since Fred had arrived with his wife and two children for this three-year assignment as the director of Kline & Associates' Tokyo office. Kline & Associates was a large multinational consulting firm with offices in 19 countries worldwide. Fred was now trying to decide whether he should simply pack up and tell headquarters that he was coming home or whether he should try to convince his wife, and himself, that they should stay and finish the assignment. Given how excited they all were about the assignment to begin with, it was a mystery to Fred how things had gotten to this point. As Fred watched the swans glide across the water in the moat surrounding the Imperial Palace, he reflected on the past seven months.

Seven months ago, Dave Steiner, the managing partner of the main office in Boston, asked Fred to lunch to discuss business. To Fred's surprise, the business they discussed was not about the major project that he and his team had just finished; instead, it was about a very big promotion and career move. Fred was offered the position of managing director of the firm's relatively new Tokyo office, which had a staff of 40, including seven Americans. Most of the Americans in the Tokyo office were either associate consultants or research analysts. Fred would be in charge of the whole office and would report to a senior partner. Steiner implied to Fred that if this assignment went as well as his past projects, it would be the last step before becoming a partner in the firm.

When Fred told his wife about the unbelievable opportunity, he was shocked at her less than enthusiastic response. His wife, Jennifer (or Jenny as Fred called her), thought that it would be rather difficult to have the children live and go to school in a foreign country for three years, especially when Christine, the oldest, would be starting middle school next year. Besides, now that the kids were in school, Jenny was thinking about going back to work, at least part time. Jenny had a degree in fashion merchandising from a well-known private university and had worked as an assistant buyer for a large women's clothing store before having the two girls.

Fred explained that the career opportunity was just too good to pass up and that the company's overseas package would make living overseas terrific. The company would pay all the expenses to move whatever the Baileys wanted to take with them. The company had a very nice house in an expensive district of Tokyo that would be provided rent free, and the company would rent their house in Boston during their absence. Moreover, the firm would provide a car and driver, education expenses for the children to attend private schools, and a cost-of-living adjustment and overseas compensation that would nearly triple Fred's gross annual salary. After two days of consideration and discussion, Fred told Steiner he would accept the assignment.

The current Tokyo office managing director was a partner in the firm but had been in the new Tokyo office for less than a year when he was transferred to head a long-established office in England. Because the transfer to England was taking place right away, Fred and his family had about three weeks to prepare for the move. Between transferring responsibilities at the office to Bob Newcome, who was being promoted to Fred's position, and getting furniture and the like ready to be moved, neither Fred nor his family had much time to really find out much about Japan, other than what was in the encyclopedia.

When the Baileys arrived in Japan, they were greeted at the airport by one of the young Japanese associate consultants and the senior American expatriate. Fred and his family were quite tired from the long trip, and the two-hour ride to Tokyo was a rather quiet one. After a few days of just settling in, Fred spent his first full day at the office.

Fred's first order of business was to have a general meeting with all the employees of associate consultant rank and higher. Although Fred didn't notice it at the time, all the Japanese staff sat together and all the Americans sat together. After Fred introduced himself and his general idea about the potential and future directions of the Tokyo office, he called on a few individuals to get their ideas about how the things for which they were responsible would likely fit into his overall plan. From the Americans, Fred got a mixture of opinions with specific reasons about why certain things might or might not fit well. From the Japanese, he got very vague answers. When Fred pushed to get more specific information, he was surprised to find that a couple of the Japanese simply made a sucking sound as they breathed and said that it was "difficult to say." Fred sensed the meeting was not achieving his objectives, so he thanked everyone for coming and said he looked forward to their all working together to make the Tokyo office the fastest-growing office in the company.

After they had been in Japan about a month, Fred's wife complained to him about the difficulty she had getting certain everyday products like maple syrup, peanut butter, and good-quality beef. She said that when she could get it at one of the specialty stores it cost three to four times what it would cost in the States. She also complained that since the washer and dryer were much too small, she had to spend extra money by sending things out to be dry-cleaned. On top of all that, unless she went to the American Club in downtown Tokyo, she never had anyone to talk to. After all, Fred was gone 10 to 16 hours a day. Unfortunately, while Jenny talked, Fred was preoccupied, thinking about a big upcoming meeting between his firm and a significant prospective client, a top-100 Japanese multinational company.

The next day, Fred, along with the lead U.S. consultant for the potential contract, Ralph Webster, and one of the Japanese associate consultants, Kenichi Kurokawa, who spoke perfect English, met with a team from the Japanese firm. The Japanese team consisted of four members: the vice president of administration, the director of international personnel, and two staff specialists. After shaking hands and a few awkward bows, Fred said that he knew the Japanese gentlemen were busy and he didn't want to waste their time, so he would get right to the point. Fred then had the other American lay out their firm's proposal for the project and what the project would cost. After the presentation, Fred asked the Japanese what their reaction to the proposal was. The Japanese did not respond immediately, so Fred launched into his summary version of the proposal, thinking that the translation might have been insufficient. Again, the Japanese had only the vaguest of responses to his direct questions.

The recollection of the frustration of that meeting was enough to shake Fred back to reality. The reality was that in the five months since that first meeting little progress had been made and the contract between the firms was yet to be signed. "I can never seem to get a direct response from Japanese," he thought to himself. This feeling of frustration led him to remember a related incident that happened about a month after this first meeting with this client.

Fred had decided that the reason not much progress was being made with the client was that he and his group just didn't know enough about the client to package the proposal in a way that was appealing to the client. Consequently, he called in Ralph Webster, the senior American associated with the proposal, and asked him to develop a report on the client so that the proposal could be reevaluated and changed where necessary. Jointly, they decided that one of the more promising Japanese research associates, Tashiro Watanabe, would be the best person to take the lead on this report. To impress upon Tashiro the importance of this task and the great potential they saw in him, they decided to have the young Japanese associate meet with both Fred and Ralph. In the meeting, Fred and Ralph laid out the nature and importance of the task, at which point Fred leaned forward in his chair and said to Tashiro, "You can see that this is an important assignment and that we are placing a lot of confidence in you by giving it to you. We need the report by this time next week so that we can revise and represent our proposal. Can you do it?" After a somewhat pregnant pause, Tashiro responded hesitantly, "I'm not sure what to say." At that point, Fred

smiled, got up from his chair, walked over to the young Japanese associate, extended his hand, and said, "Hey, there's nothing to say. We're just giving you the opportunity you deserve."

The day before the report was due, Fred asked Ralph how the report was coming. Ralph said that, since he had heard nothing from Tashiro, he assumed everything was under control but that he would double-check. Ralph later ran into one of the U.S. research associates, John Maynard. Ralph knew that John was hired for Japan because of his Japanese language ability and that, unlike any of the other Americans, John often went out after work with some of the Japanese research associates, including Tashiro. So Ralph asked John if he knew how Tashiro was coming on the report. John then recounted that at the office the previous night Tashiro had asked if Americans sometimes fired employees for being late with reports. John had sensed that this was more than a hypothetical question and asked Tashiro why he wanted to know. Tashiro did not respond immediately, and since it was 8:30 in the evening, John suggested they go out for a drink. At first Tashiro resisted, but then John assured him that they would grab a drink at a nearby bar and come right back. At the bar, John got Tashiro to open up.

Tashiro explained the nature of the report that he had been requested to produce. He continued to explain that, even though he had worked long into the night every night to complete the report, it was just impossible and that he had doubted from the beginning whether he could complete the report in a week.

At this point, Ralph asked John, "Why didn't he say something in the first place?" Ralph didn't wait to hear whether or not John had an answer to this question. He headed straight to Tashiro's desk.

Ralph chewed out Tashiro and then went to Fred, explaining that the report would not be ready and that Tashiro, from the start, didn't think it could be. "Then why didn't he say something?" Fred asked. No one had any answers, and the whole episode left everyone more suspect and uncomfortable with each other.

Other incidents, big and small, had made the last two months especially frustrating, but Fred was too tired to remember them all. To Fred it seemed that working with Japanese both inside and outside the firm was like working with people from another planet. Fred felt he couldn't communicate with them, and he never could figure out what they were thinking. It drove him crazy.

On top of all this, Jennifer laid a bombshell on him. She wanted to go home, and yesterday was not soon enough. Even though the kids seemed to be doing all right, Jennifer was tired of Japan—tired of begin stared at, of not understanding anybody or being understood, of not being able to find what she wanted at the store, of not being able to drive and read the road signs, of not having anything to watch on television, of not being involved in anything. She wanted to go home and could not think of any reason why they shouldn't. After all, she reasoned, they owed nothing to the company because the company had led them to believe this was just another assignment, like the two years they spent in San Francisco, and it was anything but that!

Fred looked out the window once more, wishing that somehow everything could be fixed, or turned back, or something. The traffic below was backed up. Though the traffic lights changed, the cars and trucks didn't seem to be moving. Fortunately, beneath the ground, one of the world's most advanced, efficient, and clean subway systems moved hundreds of thousands of people about the city and to their homes.

CASE QUESTIONS

1. You are Fred. What should you do now?
2. Turn back the clock to when Fred was offered the position in Tokyo. What, if anything, should have been done differently, and by whom?

SOURCE: J. Stewart Black, in *International Human Resource Management*, eds. M. Mendenhall and Gary Oddou (Boston: PWS-Kent, 1991).

CHAPTER

10

Developing a Global Management Cadre

Outline

Opening Profile: Foreign from the Start

By Philip Shearer, Group President, Clinique, Estée Lauder, NY: (Written with Abby Ellin)

My mother was French, my father British, and I was born in Morocco. Life there was a dream: we lived on the sea; we went to the beach. It was a great combination of the easy life and hard work. It was also extraordinarily romantic, and when I say I met my wife in high school in Casablanca, everyone thinks of Humphrey Bogart.

At the same time, you learned what it was like to live in a developing country. You learned about humility and the notion that nothing is easy for everyone.

When you're born and raised in a country like this, you also know you won't stay forever; you're a foreigner. In the 1960's and early 70's the energy was in North America, so after graduating from college in France I came to the United States for business school at Cornell.

From there, I worked at a pharmaceutical company in Minneapolis. Then I worked in France, Mexico, Britain, Japan, and again in the United States for companies like L'Oréal and the Elizabeth Arden division of Eli Lilly.

You learn common themes when you live all over the world. Most important: You have to remain yourself. People will trust you and relate to you whatever your culture is, provided you are trustworthy and credible.

Still, you have to get used to other cultures. In Mexico, when you drive around the country, you ask for directions and you say, "Is such and such a place far away?" Depending on whom you ask the answer could be, "Yes, very far." On a bus, it is, "Not so far." If the person is in a car, the reply is, "Next door."

In Japan, where I lived when I was working for Elizabeth Arden, when you have a meeting the most important person will sit the farthest from the door. So, we had this lunch where I was with my boss, who then became the most important person in the room. But he said, "I don't believe in all this; I'm going to sit in the middle of the table." That created total chaos.

Americans show off a little more than people in other parts of the world; it's the cowboy culture. But in the end, you have to deliver. And that's the same all over the world.

Growing up in Morocco certainly helped my career. For example, I learned to drive at 10. My father taught me on the side of the road. After that, I caught the driving bug. I wanted to go to racing school but my father said he would pay only for college, so that's where I went.

I later went to racing school in Britain. My claim to fame is that I was the North American Ferrari Challenge champion in 2001.

Car racing is a little macho, but I am also obsessed with beauty products. A few nights ago my wife and I had dinner with a friend of mine who also races. He told me how he had just found this magical shaving cream that he absolutely loves. It turns out it is one of my products. I told him if you want your shave to be more sensual and smooth, you need to use the "post-shave healer," too. We were eating sushi, and our wives looked at us in surprise.

Not too long ago, I became an American citizen. I went from the beach of Casablanca to the corporate world of New York City. Who would have thought?

SOURCE: www.nytimes.com, September 21, 2003. Reprinted by permission of *The New York Times* Copyright 2003. The New York Times Co.

A crucial factor in global competitiveness is the ability of the firm to maximize its global human resources in the long term. In the globalized economy, the knowledge and management resources, as well as skilled and non-skilled employee resources, required for the firm to succeed are no longer concentrated in a single region but are distributed around the world. There are various categories of those resources—both people and processes—that IHR managers and others must develop and maintain; in particular it is essential for them to:

1. Maximize long-term retention and use of international cadre through career management so that the company can develop a top management team with global experience.
2. Develop effective global management teams.
3. Understand, value, and promote the role of women and minorities in international management in order to maximize those underutilized resources.
4. Work with the host-country labor relations system to effect strategic implementation and employee productivity.

EXPATRIATE CAREER MANAGEMENT

> *Nearly 80 percent of FTSE 100 chief executives in 2005 had had overseas assignments, compared with only 42 percent in 1996.*
>
> HEIDRICK & STRUGGLES, *2006*
> (*International Headhunting Firm*)[1]

It is clear from the above quote that the road to the top necessitates that managers have overseas experience. For the firm the ability to develop a top management team, globally experienced, depends largely on the success of expatriates' assignments, and that depends on the ability to well manage the transitions for the expatriate and any accompanying family members.

Preparation, Adaptation, and Repatriation

Effective human resource management of a company's global cadre does not end with the overseas assignment. It ends with the successful repatriation of the executive into company headquarters. A study by Heidrick & Struggles, the international headhunting firm, revealed that international experience has become much more important to get to the top of FTSE (London Stock Exchange) 100 companies than a decade ago. "Chief executives such as Mark Tucker at Prudential, who has experience in the U.S. and Asia, and Unilever's Patrick Cescau, who has worked in Europe, Asia and the U.S., are becoming the norm in top companies."[2] Clearly, those executives and their companies have paid careful attention to what is necessary for successful assignments, career management, and repatriation of their experiences and skills. Such firms realize that long-term, proactive management of such critical resources should begin with the end of the current assignment in mind—that is, it should begin with plans for the repatriation of the executive as part of his or her career path. The management of the reentry phase of the career cycle is as vital as the management of the cross-cultural entry and training. Otherwise, the long-term benefits of that executive's international experience may be negated.[3] Shortsightedly, many companies do little to minimize the potential effects of **reverse culture shock** (return shock). In fact, a survey of companies belonging to the American Society of Personnel Administration International (ASPAI) revealed that only 31 percent had formal repatriation programs for executives and only 35 percent of those included spouses. In addition, only 22 percent of those had conducted the programs prior to the executive's departure for the assignment.[4] Those U.S. companies without programs had various explanations: a lack of expertise in repatriation training, the cost of the programs, or a lack of a perceived need for such training.

The long-term implications of ineffective repatriation practices are clear—few good managers will be willing to take international assignments because they will see what happened to their colleagues. If a certain manager lost out on promotion opportunities while overseas and is now, in fact, worse off than before he or she left, the only people willing to take on foreign assignments in the future will be those who have not been able to succeed on the home front or those who think that a stint abroad will be like a vacation. Research has shown that employees commonly see overseas assignments as negative career moves in many U.S. multinational companies.[5] In contrast, such moves are seen as positive in most European, Japanese, and Australian companies because they consider international experience necessary for advancement to top management.

In a recent study of dual-career couples, "the perceived impact of the international assignment upon returning to the U.S." was one of the most important issues stated by managers regarding their willingness to relocate overseas.[6]

Reverse culture shock occurs primarily because of the difficulty of reintegrating into the organization but also because, generally speaking, the longer a person is away, the more difficult it is to get back into the swing of things. Not only might the manager have been overlooked and lost in the shuffle of reorganization, but her or his whole family might have lost social contacts or jobs and feel out of step with their contemporaries. These feelings of alienation from what has always been perceived as "home"—because of the loss of contact with family, friends, and daily life—delay the resocialization process. Such a reaction is particularly serious if the family's overall financial situation has been hurt by the assignment and if the spouse's career has also been kept "on hold" while he or she was abroad.

For companies to maximize the long-term use of their global cadre, they need to make sure that the foreign assignment and the reintegration process are positive experiences. This means careful career planning, support while overseas, and use of the increased experience and skills of returned managers to benefit the home office. Research into the practices of successful U.S., European, Japanese, and Australian multinational corporations (MNCs) indicates the use of one or more of the following support systems, as recommended by Tung, for a successful repatriation program:

- A mentor program to monitor the expatriate's career path while abroad and upon repatriation.
- As an alternative to the mentor program, the establishment of a special organizational unit for the purposes of career planning and continuing guidance for the expatriate.
- A system of supplying information and maintaining contacts with the expatriate so that he or she may continue to feel a part of the home organization.[7]

The Role of the Expatriate Spouse

We began to realize that the entire effectiveness of the assignment could be compromised by ignoring the spouse.

STEVE FORD,
Corporation Relocations, Hewlett-Packard[8]

Many companies are beginning to recognize the importance of providing support for spouses and children—in particular because both spouses are often corporate fast trackers and demand that both sets of needs be included on the bargaining table. The 2005 Global Relocation Trends Survey found that 81 percent of married expatriates were accompanied by their spouses. However, while 60 percent of the spouses were employed before the assignment, only 21 percent were employed during the assignment.[9] Firms often use informal means, such as intercompany networking, to help find the trailing spouse a position in the same location. They know that, with the increasing number of dual-career couples (65 percent in the United States), if the spouse does not find a position the manager will very likely turn down the assignment. They decline because they cannot afford to lose the income or because the spouse's career may be delayed entirely if he or she is out of the workforce for a few years. As women continue to move up the corporate ladder, the accompanying ("trailing") spouse is often male—estimated at more than 25 percent.[10] Companies such as Hewlett-Packard, Shell, Medtronic, and Monsanto offer a variety of options to address the dual-career dilemma.

At Procter & Gamble, employees and spouses destined for China are sent to Beijing for two months of language training and cultural familiarization. Nissho Iwai, a Japanese trading company, gets together managers and spouses who are leaving Japan with foreign managers and spouses who are on their way there. In addition, the firm provides a year of language training and information and services for Japanese children to attend schools abroad. Recent research on 321 American expatriate spouses around the world shows that effective cross-cultural adjustment by spouses is more likely (1) when firms seek the spouse's opinion about the international assignment and the expected standard of living and (2) when the spouse initiates his or her own predeparture training (thereby supplementing the minimal training given by most firms).[11]

Expatriate Retention

Managers returning from expatriate assignments are two to three times more likely to leave the company within a year because attention has not been paid to their careers and the way they fit back into the corporate structure back home.

www.FT.com[12]

Support services provide timely help for the manager and, therefore, are part of the effective management of an overseas assignment. The overall transition process

EXHIBIT 10-1   The Expatriate Transition Process

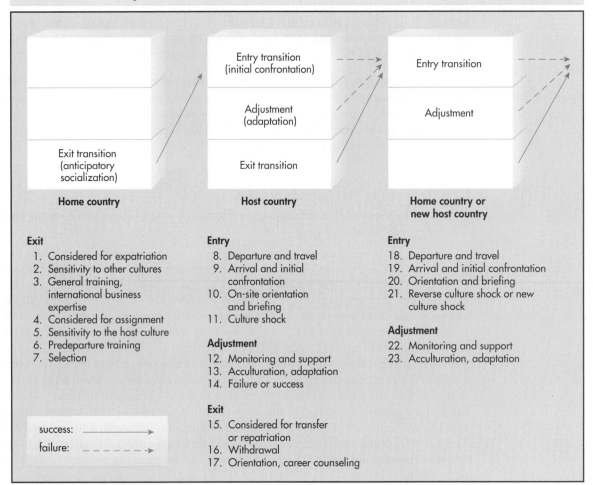

SOURCE: P. Asheghian and B. Ebrahimi, *International Business* (New York: Harper Collins, 1990), 470.

experienced by the company's international management cadre over time is shown in Exhibit 10-1. It comprises three phases of transition and adjustment that must be managed for successful socialization to a new culture and resocialization back to the old culture. These phases are (1) the exit transition from the home country, the success of which will be determined largely by the quality of preparation the expatriate has received; (2) the entry transition to the host country, in which successful acculturation (or early exit) will depend largely on monitoring and support; and (3) the entry transition back to the home country or to a new host country, in which the level of reverse culture shock and the ease of re-acculturation will depend on previous stages of preparation and support.[13]

A company may derive many potential benefits from carefully managing the careers of its expatriates. By helping managers make the right moves for their careers, the company will be able to retain people with increasing global experience and skills. But from the individual manager's perspective, most people understand that no one can better look out for one's interests than oneself. With that in mind, managers must ask themselves, and their superiors, what role each overseas stint will play in career advancement and what proactive role each will play in one's own career. Retaining the returning expatriate within the company (assuming he or she has been effective) is vitally important in order to gain the knowledge and benefit from the assignment. Yet, as discussed earlier, the attrition rate for expatriates is about double that of non-expatriates. Researchers in the 2005 Global Relocation trends Survey found the reasons for this to be that:

- Expatriates are more marketable and receive more attractive offers from other employers.
- Expatriates find that their compensation packages on overseas assignments are more generous than at home and go from one company to another to take advantage of that.
- Expatriates feel unappreciated and dissatisfied both during and after the assignment and leave the company.[14]

It is essential, therefore, that the company pay careful attention to maintaining and retaining the expatriate by managing both the assignment and the repatriation of the expatriate and the family.

THE ROLE OF REPATRIATION IN DEVELOPING A GLOBAL MANAGEMENT CADRE

In the international assignment, both the manager and the company can benefit from the enhanced skills and experience gained by the expatriate. Many returning executives report an improvement in their managerial skills and self-confidence. Some of these acquired skills, as reported by Adler, include the following:

- **Managerial skills, not technical skills:** learning how to deal with a wide range of people, to adapt to their cultures through compromise, and not to be a dictator.
- **Tolerance for ambiguity:** making decisions with less information and more uncertainty about the process and the outcome.
- **Multiple perspectives:** learning to understand situations from the perspective of local employees and businesspeople.
- **Ability to work with and manage others:** learning patience and tolerance—realizing that managers abroad are in the minority among local people; learning to communicate more with others and empathize with them.[15]

In addition to the managerial and cross-cultural skills acquired by expatriates, the company benefits from the knowledge and experience those managers gain about how to do business overseas, and about new technology, local marketing, and competitive information. The company should position itself to benefit from that enhanced management knowledge if it wants to develop a globally oriented and experienced management cadre—an essential ingredient for global competitiveness—in particular where there is a high degree of shared learning among the organization's global managers. If the company cannot retain good returning managers, then their potential shared knowledge is not only lost but also conveyed to another organization that hires that person. This can be very detrimental to the company's competitive stance. Some companies are becoming quite savvy about how to use technology to utilize shared knowledge to develop their global management cadre, to better service their customers, and—as a side benefit—to store the knowledge and expertise of their managers around the world in case they leave the company. That knowledge, it can be argued, is an asset in which the company has invested large amounts of resources. One such savvy company is Booz-Allen & Hamilton, which instituted a Knowledge On-Line (KOL) intranet as a means to enhance knowledge sharing among its employees worldwide and to improve client service. By using its intranet to link islands of information separated by geography and platform-specific applications, the renowned consulting firm has enabled its 2,000 private sector consultants to collect and share firm-wide their best thoughts and expertise.[16]

Black and Gregersen's research of 750 U.S., European, and Japanese companies concluded that those companies that reported a high degree of job satisfaction and strong performance, and that experienced limited turnover, used the following practices when making international assignments:

- They focus on knowledge creation and global leadership development.
- They assign overseas posts to people whose technical skills are matched or exceeded by their cross-cultural abilities.
- They end expatriate assignments with a deliberate repatriation process.[17]

A successful repatriation program, then, starts before the assignment. The company's top management must set up a culture that conveys the message that the organization regards international assignments as an integral part of continuing career development and advancement, and that it values the skills of the returnees. The company's objectives should be reflected in its long-range plans, commitment, and compensation on behalf of the expatriate. GE sets a model for effective expatriate career management. With its 500 expatriates worldwide, it takes care to select only the best managers for overseas jobs and then commits to placing them in specific positions upon reentry.[18] A study of the international human resource management (IHRM) policies of British multinationals indicates that careful planning for foreign assignments pays off. Farsighted policies, along with selection criteria based more on the adaptability of the manager and her or his family to the culture than on technical skills, apparently account for the low expatriate failure rate—estimated at less than 5 percent.[19]

GLOBAL MANAGEMENT TEAMS

MNCs realize it is essential to maximize their human assets in the form of global management teams so they can share resources and manage the transnational transfer of knowledge. The term **global management teams** describes collections of managers in or from several countries who must rely on group collaboration if each member is to experience optimum success and goal achievement.[20] Whirlpool International, for example, is a U.S.–Dutch joint venture, with administrative headquarters in Comerio, Italy, where it is managed by a Swede and a six-person management team from Sweden, Italy, Holland, the United States, Belgium, and Germany. To achieve the individual and collective goals of the team members, international teams must "provide the means to communicate corporate culture, develop a global perspective, coordinate and integrate the global enterprise, and be responsive to local market needs."[21] The role and importance of international teams increase as the firm progresses in its scope of international activity. Similarly, the manner in which multicultural interaction affects the firm's operations depends on its level of international involvement, its environment, and its strategy. In domestic firms, the effects of cross-cultural teams are limited to internal operations and some external contacts. In international firms that export products and produce some goods overseas, multicultural teams and cultural diversity play important roles in the relationships between buyers, sellers, and other intermediaries at the boundary of the organization. For multinational firms, the role of multicultural teams again becomes internal to the company; the teams consist of culturally diverse managers and technical people who are located around the world and are also working together within subsidiaries. The team's ability to work effectively together is crucial to the company's success. In addition, technology facilitates effective and efficient teamwork around the world. This was found by the Timberland U.K. sales conference planning team. In the past, the company's large sales conferences were cumbersome to organize because their offices were in France, Germany, Spain, Italy, and the United Kingdom. Then the team started using the British Telecom (BT) Conference Call system for the arrangements, which saved them much travel and expense. The company subsequently adopted the BT Conference Call system for the executive team's country meetings.[22] Teleconferencing and videoconferencing are now much of the way of life for global businesses. However, research indicates that face-to-face meetings are the best way to kick off a virtual team project so that the members can agree on goals and schedules and who is responsible for what. IBM project teams start with all members in a personal meeting to help to build an understanding of the other members' cultures and set up a trusting relationship.[23]

For global organizations and alliances, the same cross-cultural interactions hold as in MNCs, and, in addition, considerably more interaction takes place with the external environment at all levels of the organization. Therefore, global teamwork is vital, as are the pockets of cross-cultural teamwork and interactions that occur at many boundaries.[24] For the global company, worldwide competition and markets necessitate global teams for strategy development, both for the organization as a whole and for the local units to respond to their markets.

Global management teams play a vital role in global organizations.

As shown in Exhibit 10-2, when a firm responds to its global environment with a global strategy and then organizes with a networked "glocal" structure (see Chapter 8), various types of cross-border teams are necessary for global integration and local differentiation. These include teams between and among headquarters and subsidiaries; transnational project teams, often operating on a "virtual" basis; and teams coordinating alliances outside the organization. In joint ventures, in particular, multicultural teams work at all levels of strategic planning and implementation, as well as on the production and assembly floor.

"Virtual" Transnational Teams

> *Virtual groups, whose members interact through computer-mediated communication systems (such as desktop video conferencing systems, e-mail, group support systems, internets, and intranets), are linked together across time, space, and organizational boundaries.*[25]

Increasingly, advances in communication now facilitate **virtual global teams**, a horizontal networked structure, with people around the world conducting meetings

EXHIBIT 10-2   Global Teams in the Modern Global Enterprise

Global Environment	Global Strategy	Networked Global Organization	Global Teams
Global MNC and local competition; technological developments; varied markets, cultures; government policies, political and economic risk	Optimizing global resources for competitive advantage	Global coordination and integration; local responsiveness; organizational structure; systems; personnel policies and reward systems that support cooperation	"Virtual" global teams; cosmopolitan headquarters' teams; strategic development teams; headquarters' subsidiary teams; technology transfer teams; coalition (joint venture) teams

SOURCE: Adapted from T. Gross, E. Turner, and L. Cederholm, "Building Teams for Global Operations," *Management Review* (June 1987): 34.

EXHIBIT 10-3   Operational Challenges for Global Virtual Teams

Geographic Dispersal:	The complexity of scheduling communications such as teleconferences and videoconferences across multiple time zones, holidays, and so on.
	Lack of face-to-face meetings to establish trust or for cross-interaction processes such as brainstorming.
Cultural Differences:	Variations in attitudes and expectations toward time, planning, scheduling, risk taking, money, relationship building, and so on.
	Differences in goal sets and work styles arising out of such variables as individualism/collectivism, the relative value of work compared with other life factors; variable sets of assumptions, norms, patterns of behavior.
Language and Communications:	Translation difficulties, or at least variations in accents, semantics, terminology, or local jargon.
	Lack of personal and physical contact, which greatly inhibits trust and relationship building in many countries; the social dynamics change.
	Lack of visibility of nonverbal cues makes interpretation difficult and creates two-way noise in the communication process.
Technology:	Variations in availability, speed, acceptability, cost of equipment necessary for meetings and communications through computer-aided systems.
	Variable skill levels and willingness to interact through virtual media.

and exchanging information via the Internet, enabling the organization to capitalize on 24-hour productivity. In this way, too, knowledge is shared across business units and across cultures.[26] The advantages and cost savings of virtual global teams are frequently offset by their challenges—including cultural misunderstandings and the logistics of differences in time and space, as shown in Exhibit 10–3. Group members must build their teams while bearing in mind the group diversity and the need for careful communication.[27]

A survey of 440 training and development professionals across a variety of industries was conducted by Rosen, Furst, and Blackburn. The respondents indicated which training techniques for virtual teams were more effective than others, and reported which of those programs were most needed in the future. The results are shown in Exhibit 10-4. On the top of the list considered very valuable, for example, was "Training on how to lead a virtual team meeting" and "Leader training on how to coach and mentor team members virtually," as well as "how to monitor team progress, diagnose problems and take corrective action."[28]

Managing Transnational Teams

The ability to develop and lead effective transnational teams (whether they interact "virtually," physically, or, as is most often the case, a mixture of both) is essential in light of the increasing proliferation of foreign subsidiaries, joint ventures, and other transnational alliances. As noted by David Dotlich of Honeywell Bull. (HBI), an international computer firm, effective international teamwork is essential because cross-cultural "double-talk, double agendas, double priorities, and double interests can present crippling business risks when your storefront stretches for 6000 miles."[29] HBI represents a joint venture of NEC (Japan), Campagnie de Machines Bull (France), and Honeywell (United States). To coordinate this joint venture, HBI considered it important to have transnational teams for front-end involvement in strategic planning, engineering, design, production, and marketing. Dotlich notes that HBI's primary corporate question is how to integrate a diverse pool of cultural values, traditions, and norms in order to be competitive.[30]

EXHIBIT 10-4   Virtual Training Future Needs as Reported by 325+ Respondents (Number and Percentage of Respondents Indicating That Each Need Will Be "Very Valuable" or "Extremely Valuable" in the Future)

Virtual Team Training Module	Percentage seeing this module as very valuable	Percentage seeing this module as extremely valuable	Total percentage very and extremely valuable
Training on how to lead a virtual team meeting	40.2	31.3	71.5
Leader training on how to coach and mentor team members virtually	39.0	30.5	69.5
Training on how to monitor team progress, diagnose team problems, and take corrective actions	41.7	26.4	68.1
Training to use communications technologies	36.7	27.8	64.5
Leader training on how to manage team boundaries, negotiate member time commitments with local managers, and stay in touch with team sponsors	37.0	27.5	64.5
Training on how to establish trust and resolve conflicts in virtual teams	35.0	26.1	61.1
Communications skills training—cultural sensitivity, etc.	35.8	22.6	58.4
Team-building training for new virtual teams	33.0	24.2	57.2
Training to select the appropriate technologies to fit team tasks	36.5	20.6	57.1
Leader training on how to evaluate and reward individual contributions on the virtual team	38.3	17.8	56.1
Training on how to select virtual team members, establish a virtual team charter, and assign virtual team roles	32.1	21.4	53.5
Realistic preview of virtual team challenges	40.8	12.0	52.8
Training on what qualities to look for in prospective virtual team members and leaders	32.6	18.5	51.1

SOURCE: B. Rosen, S. Furst, and R. Blackburn, "Training for Virtual Teams: An Investigation of Current Practices and Future Needs," *Human Resources Management*, Summer 2006, 45, 2, pp. 229–247, reprinted with permission of John Wiley and Sons, Inc., Copyright John Wiley, 2006.

Teams comprising people located in far-flung operations are faced with often-conflicting goals of achieving greater efficiency across those operations, responding to local differences, and facilitating organizational learning across boundaries; conflicts arise based on cultural differences, local work norms and environments, and varied time zones. A recent study by Joshi et al. of a 30-member team of human resource (HR) managers in six countries in the Asia–Pacific region showed that network analysis of the various interactions among team members can reveal when and where negative cross-cultural conflicts occur and so provide MNC top management with information for conflict resolution so that a higher level of synergy may be attained among the group members. The advantages of synergy include a greater opportunity for global competition (by being able to share experiences, technology, and a pool of international managers) and a greater opportunity for cross-cultural understanding and exposure to different viewpoints. The disadvantages include problems resulting from differences in language, communication, and varying managerial styles; complex decision-making processes; fewer promotional opportunities; personality conflicts, often resulting from stereotyping and prejudice; and greater complexity in the workplace.[31] In the Joshi study, the greatest conflict, and therefore lack of synergy, was not, as one would expect, resulting from the headquarters–subsidiary power divide. Rather, the critical conflicts radiated from the Country A subsidiary and Country B subsidiary, given the required communication and workflow patterns between them. (Country names were kept confidential so that individuals in the study would not be identified.)

What are other ways that management can ascertain how well its international teams are performing and what areas need to be improved? The following criteria for evaluating the success of such teams have been proposed by Indrei Ratiu of the Intercultural Management Association in Paris:

- Do members work together with a common purpose? Is this purpose spelled out, and do all feel it is worth fighting for?
- Has the team developed a common language or procedure? Does it have a common way of doing things, a process for holding meetings?
- Does the team build on what works, learning to identify the positive actions before being overwhelmed by the negatives?
- Does the team attempt to spell out matters within the limits of the cultural differences involved, delimiting the mystery level by directness and openness regardless of the cultural origins of participants?
- Do the members recognize the impact of their own cultural programming on individual and group behavior? Do they deal with, not avoid, their differences in order to create synergy?
- Does the team have fun? (Within successful multicultural groups, the cultural differences become a source of continuing surprise, discovery, and amusement rather than irritation or frustration.)[32]

The actual level of success of global teams seems disappointing as reported by MNC managers of 70 global teams in a recent study by Govindarajan and Gupta. Of those managers, 82 percent said their teams fell short of their intended goals, and one-third of the teams rated their performance as largely unsuccessful. In recognizing the areas needing better team management, 58 of those executives in the study ranked five key tasks based on their level of importance and also on how difficult it is to accomplish that task. The results are shown in Exhibit 10-5. The researchers concluded from their study that the ability to cultivate trust among team members is critical to the success of global business teams if they want to minimize conflict and encourage cooperation.[33]

Following are some general recommendations the researchers make for improving global teamwork:

- Cultivating a culture of trust: One way to do this is by scheduling face-to-face meetings early on, even if later meetings will be "virtual."
- Rotating meeting locations: This develops global exposure for all team members and also legitimizes each person's position.

EXHIBIT 10-5 Managing Global Business Teams

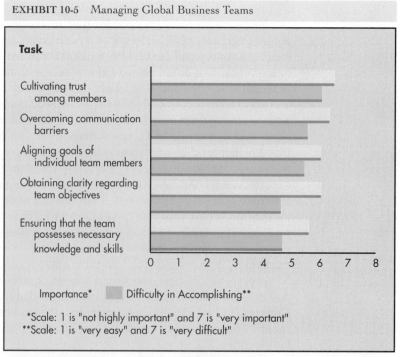

SOURCE: Adapted from V. Govindarajan and A. K. Gupta, "Building an Effective Global Business Team," *MIT Sloan Management Review*, Summer 2001, v42, i4, 63.

- Rotating and diffusing team leadership
- Linking rewards to team performance
- Building social networks among managers from different countries[34]

What other techniques do managers actually use to deal with the challenge of achieving cross-cultural collaboration in multinational horizontal projects? A comparative study of European project groups in several countries by Sylvie Chevrier, published in 2003, revealed three main strategies:[35]

- **Drawing upon individual tolerance and self-control:** In this R&D consortium, the Swiss manager treated all team members the same, ignoring cultural differences, and the team members coexisted with patience and compromise. Many of the members said they were used to multinational projects and just tried to focus on technical issues.
- **Trial-and-error processes coupled with personal relationships:** This is a specific strategy in which the project manager sets up social events to facilitate the team members getting acquainted with one another. Then, they discover, through trial and error, what procedures will be acceptable to the group.
- **Setting up transnational cultures:** Here the managers used the common professional, or occupational, culture, such as the engineering profession, to bring the disparate members together within a common understanding and process.

The managers in the study admitted their solutions were not perfect, but met their needs as best they could in the situation. Chevrie suggests that, where possible, a "cultural mediator" should be used who helps team members interpret and understand one another and come to an agreement about processes to achieve organizational goals.[36]

THE ROLE OF WOMEN IN INTERNATIONAL MANAGEMENT

The world's expatriate workforce is becoming increasingly female. Women accounted for 23 percent of international assignees in 2005, up 5 percent from the 2004 Global Relocation Trends Survey.

BUSINESS WIRE,
March 13, 2006[37]

The 2006 ranking by *Fortune* magazine of the most powerful women in business lists Indra Rising as number one. She is Pepsi's new CEO, the Indian-born strategist and former CFO and president. The article also includes a separate list called "Global Power 50" (a selection of those are listed in Exhibit 10-6). The *Fortune* surveyors conclude that "with seven new entrants, and strong showings from Europe and Asia, our international list shows that business is opening up to women—fast."[38]

However, while women's advancement in global companies is impressive, it is still true that where there are limitations on managerial opportunities for women in their own country—some more than others—there are even more limitations on their opportunities for expatriate assignments. Research on expatriate assignments continues to show that females are disproportionately underrepresented in expatriate assignments.[39]

Opportunities for indigenous female employees to move up the managerial ladder in a given culture depend on the values and expectations regarding the role of women in that society. In Japan, for example, the workplace has traditionally been a male domain as far as managerial careers are concerned (although rapid changes are now taking place). To the older generation, a working married woman represented a loss of face to the husband because it implied that he was not able to support her. Women were usually only allowed clerical positions, under the assumption that they would leave to raise a family and perhaps later return to part-time work. Employers, thus, made little effort to train them for upper level positions.[40] As a result, very few women workers have been in supervisory or managerial posts—thus limiting the short-term upward mobility of women through the managerial ranks.[41]

The younger generation and increased global competitiveness have brought some changes to traditional values regarding women's roles in Japan. More than 60 percent of

EXHIBIT 10-6   Women in Top Business Positions Around the Globe

Patricia Russo, Chairman and CEO Alcatel Lucent, France

Anne Lauvergeon, Executive Chairman, Areva, France

Linda Cook, Executive Director, Gas & Power, Royal Dutch Shell, The Netherlands

Marjorie Scardino, CEO Pearson, Britain

Xie Qihua, Chairman, Baosteel Group, China

Marina Berlusconi, Chairman, Fininvest, Italy

Ana Patricia Botin, Executive Chairman, Banesto, Spain

Mary Ma, Chief Financial Officer, Lenovo, China

Güler Sabanci, Chairman and Managing Director, Sabanci Holding, Turkey

Ho Ching, Executive Director and CEO, Temasek Holdings, Singapore

Annika Falkengren, Ceo and President, SEB, Sweden

Maria Aramburuzabala De Garza, Vice Chairman, Grupo Modelo, Mexico

Vivienne Cox, Executive Vice President, BP, Britain

Maria Ramos, CEO Transnet, South Africa

Gulzhan Moldazhanova, CEO Basic Element, Russia

Theresa Gattung, CEO, Telecom New Zealand, New Zealand

Tomoyo Nonaka, Chairman, Sanyo Electric, Japan

Galia Maor, CEO and President, Bank Leumi, Israel

Lubna Olayan, CEO Olayan Financial Group, Saudi Arabia

Chandra Kochhar, Deputy Managing Director, ICICI Bank, India.

SOURCE: Adapted from selections of "The Global Power 50," *Fortune,* October 16, 2006; and the Web sites of the listed companies.

Japanese women are now employed, including half of Japanese mothers. But how and when these cultural changes will affect the number of Japanese women in managerial positions remains to be seen. As shown in Exhibit 10-7, as of 2003, Japanese women represented only 8.9 percent of managerial workers.[42] One can understand the problems Japanese women face when trying to enter and progress in managerial careers when we review the experiences of Yuko Suzuki (see Management Focus: Japan's Neglected Resource—Female Workers).

EXHIBIT 10-7   How Women Fare: A Comparison of Professional Women in Japan to Those in Other Industrialized Countries.

Women as a percentage of . . .					
	All Workers	**Managerial Workers**	**Civil Service Workers** General	Managerial	**National Parliament/Congress**
Japan	41.0%	8.9%	20.2%	1.4%	7.3%
United States	46.6	46.0	49.3	23.1	14.3
Sweden	48.0	30.5	43.0	51.0	45.3
Germany	44.0	26.9	39.0	9.5	32.2
Britain	44.9	30.0	49.1	17.2	17.9

SOURCE: The Cabinet Office of Japan: International Labor Organization; Inter-Parliamentary Union. www.NYTimes.com, July 24, 2003. Reprinted with permission Copyright 2003 The New York Times Co.

Management Focus

Japan's Neglected Resource—Female Workers

When Yuko Suzuki went into business for herself after the advertising company she worked for went bankrupt, no amount of talk she had heard about the hardships facing professional women here prepared her for the humiliations ahead.

As an independent saleswoman, she found that customers merely pretended to listen to her. Time and again when she finished a presentation, men would ask who her boss was. Eventually she hired a man to go along with her, because merely having a man by her side—even a virtual dummy—increased her sales significantly, if not her morale.

"If I brought a man along, the customers would only establish eye contact with him, even though I was the representative of the company, and doing the talking," she said. "It was very uncomfortable."

Japan has tried all sorts of remedies to pull itself out of a 13-year economic slump, from huge public works projects to bailouts of failing companies. Many experts have concluded that the expanding the role of women in professional life could provide a far bigger stimulus than any scheme tried so far.

But it often seems that the Japanese would rather let their economy stagnate than send their women up the corporate ladder. Resistance to expanding women's professional roles remains high in a country where the economic status of women trails far behind that of women in other advanced economies.

"Japan is still a developing country in terms of gender equality," Mariko Bando, an aide to Prime Minister Junichiro Koizumi, recently told reporters. This year the World Economic Forum ranked Japan 69th of 75 member nations in empowering its women.

While 40 percent of Japanese women work, a figure that reflects their rapid, recent entry into the job market, they hold only about 9 percent of managerial positions, compared with about 45 percent in the United States, according to the government and the International Labor Organization. Women's wages, meanwhile, are about 65 percent of those of their male counterparts, one of the largest gaps in the industrial world.

Japanese labor economists and others say it is no wonder, then, that Japan, which looked like a world beater 20 years ago, is struggling to compete economically today. With women sidelined from the career track, Japan is effectively fighting with one hand tied behind its back.

"Japan has gone as far as it can go with a social model that consists of men filling all of the economic, management and political roles," said Eiko Shinotsuka, assistant dean of Ochanomizu University and the first woman to serve on the board of the Bank of Japan.

"People have spoken of the dawn of a women's age here before," she said, "but that was always in relatively good times economically, and the country was able to avoid social change. We've never had such a long economic crisis as this one, though, and people are beginning to recognize that the place of women in our society is an important factor."

By tradition Japanese companies hire men almost exclusively to fill career positions, reserving shorter-term work, mostly clerical tasks and tea serving, for women, who are widely known in such jobs here as office ladies, or simply O.L.'s.

Ms. Suzuki, who went into business for herself, is the exception. These days Ms. Suzuki, an impeccably groomed 32-year-old who dresses in crisp suits and speaks at a rapid, confident clip, is the proud owner of her own company, a short-term office suite rental business in one of Tokyo's smartest quarters. "I am the only professional out of all of my girlhood friends," she said. "The rest are housewives or regular office ladies, and they all say that what has happened to me is unbelievable."

Whatever a woman's qualifications, breaking into the career track requires overcoming entrenched biases, not least the feeling among managers that childbearing is an insupportable disruption.

That is so even though the country faces a steep population decline and keeping women sidelined has had economic costs. Women's relative lack of economic participation may be shaving 0.6 percent off annual growth, a study presented to the Labor Ministry estimated last year.

Meanwhile, at companies where women make up 40 to 50 percent of the staff, average profits are double those where women account for 10 percent or less, the Economy Ministry reported last month.

A recent issue of *Weekly Women* magazine nonetheless recounted the stories of women who said they had been illegally dismissed because of pregnancy or had sought abortions for fear of being dismissed.

"I reported to my boss that I was pregnant and would like to take off for a medical check," Masumi Honda, a 33-year-old mother was quoted as saying. "When I came home from the hospital, I was shocked that he had just left a message saying that I needn't bother coming to work any more."

Other women say the intense competitive pressure in the workplace can lead to resentment, even in progressive companies, against mothers who avail themselves of child care leave or flexible work hours.

One woman, who abandoned a career in marketing after similar experiences in two companies, recounted taking leave for three days to look after a sick child.

"After that I was not included in new projects," said the woman, who spoke on condition that she not be identified, "and after that I felt they saw me as an unreliable person. I finally decided that if I work in a company, I must understand the company's spirit, which means I couldn't feel comfortable taking maternal benefits."

The growing sense of urgency in official circles about these issues is driven largely by the projections of a population decline that could cause huge labor shortages over the next half-century and possibly even economic collapse. So far, though, government efforts to expand women's place in the economy have been modest and halting.

An advisory panel appointed by Prime Minister Koizumi recommended recently that the public and private sectors aim to have at least 30 percent of managerial positions filled by women by 2020. These days there is growing talk of affirmative action in Japan.

But changing mind-sets will be difficult. Earlier this year, former Prime Minister Yoshiro Mori, a member of a government commission charged with finding solutions to the population crisis, was widely quoted as saying the main reason for Japan's falling birthrate was the overeducation of its women.

Mr. Koizumi's top aide, Yasuo Fukuda, was recently quoted as saying that often women who are raped deserve it, while a legislator from the governing party said, approvingly, that the men who carried out such acts were virile and "good specimens." The latter comment came last month at a seminar about the falling birthrate.

While senior politicians bemoan overeducation as the cause of Japan's population problems, women unsurprisingly cite other reasons that make it difficult for them to have children and also play a bigger role in the country's economic life.

Foremost is the lack of day care, which for many forces stark choices between motherhood and career. There are also the working hours of many offices, which extend deep into the evening and sometimes all but require social drinking afterward.

Haruko Takachi, 37, a postal manager, is luckier than most. Her child was accepted into a 20-student nursery school opened last year by the Ministry of Education.

It is the only public nursery school available for the 38,000 government employees who work in Kasumigaseki, central Tokyo's administrative district. Unlike most private nurseries, which close earlier, the school remains open until 10 p.m.

"I work until 8 in the evening, but there are plenty of times when I work much later," she said. "That's just the social reality in Japan. There are some other women in my milieu, but most of them have just one child and don't plan for more."

Ms. Suzuki, who founded her own business, has been married for several years and has no children. She regards day care as just a small piece of what is needed in Japan. Men and women, she says, must rethink gender roles—an idea that she hesitantly concludes makes her a feminist.

"Men are really intimidated by professional women in Japan," she said. "But this is still a society where even when it looks like a woman has some authority, the men usually manage to stay on top."

Overall, more managerial opportunities are available for American women than for women in most other countries. However, even for American women, who now fill more than 46 percent of the managerial positions at home, commensurate opportunities are still limited to them abroad. While in the 1990s less than 3 percent of German expatriates were women, this figure has steadily increased to 10 percent in 2002.[43] However, opportunities for women at the top ranks in Germany remain very limited. In a Deutsche Bank lecture in May 2004, statistics were discussed that showed that, although women accounted for 47 percent of the total labor force, only 3.7 percent of senior managers in Germany are women.

> More than any other European economy, Germany has stunted the development of its female business community. None of the DAX index of Germany's top companies has a woman on the board.
>
> THE FINANCIAL TIMES,
> *June 15, 2004*[44]

The reasons for the different opportunities for women among various countries can often be traced to the cultural expectations of the host countries—the same cultural values that keep women in these countries from the managerial ranks. In Germany, for example, the disparity in opportunities for women can be traced in part to the lifestyles and laws. For example, children attend school only in the mornings, which restricts the ability for both parents to work. Cultural expectations may also contribute to different opportunities for women at the top levels between northern and southern Europe.

> *The North-South Divide in Europe, Inc. . . . Women are far more likely to serve on the boards of Scandinavia's biggest companies than Italy's or Spain's, and attitudes to their promotion remain deeply split.*

> THE FINANCIAL TIMES,
> *June 14, 2004*[45]

While top boardrooms in Spain and Italy remain almost exclusively male, women occupy 22 percent of board seats in the largest companies in Norway and 20 percent in Sweden. While this phenomenon can be attributed to complex social and cultural issues, firms ought to be aware of the effects on their bottom line. Research by Catalyst, published in 2004, showed that—of the 353 Fortune 500 companies they surveyed—the quartile with the largest proportion of women in top management had a return on equity of 35.1 percent higher than the quartile with the lowest female representation.[46]

The lack of expatriates who are female or represent other minority groups does not reflect their lack of desire to take overseas assignments. Indeed, studies indicate women's strong willingness to work abroad and their considerable success on their assignments. For example, Adler's major study of North American women working as expatriate managers in countries around the world showed that they are, for the most part, successful.[47]

The most difficult job seems to be getting the assignment in the first place. North American executives are reluctant to send women and minorities abroad because they assume they will be subject to the same culturally based biases as at home, or they assume a lack of understanding and acceptance, particularly in certain countries. Research on 52 female expatriate managers, for example, shows this assumption to be highly questionable. Adler showed, first and foremost, that foreigners are seen as foreigners; furthermore, a woman who is a foreigner (a *gaijin* in Japan) is not expected to act like a local woman. According to Adler and Izraeli, "Asians see female expatriates as foreigners who happen to be women, not as women who happen to be foreigners." The other women in the study echoed this view. One woman based in Hong Kong noted, " 'It doesn't make any difference if you are blue, green, purple, or a frog. If you have the best product at the best price, they'll buy."[48]

Women and minorities represent a significant resource for overseas assignments—whether as expatriates or as host-country nationals—a resource that is underutilized by U.S. companies. Adler studied this phenomenon regarding women and recommends that businesses (1) avoid assuming that a female executive will fail because of the way she will be received or because of problems experienced by female spouses; (2) avoid assuming that a woman will not want to go overseas; and (3) give female managers every chance to succeed by giving them the titles, status, and recognition appropriate to the position—as well as sufficient time to be effective.[49]

WORKING WITHIN LOCAL LABOR RELATIONS SYSTEMS

> *If you have to close a plant in Italy, in France, in Spain or in Germany, you have to discuss the possibility with the state, the local communities, the trade unions; everybody feels entitled to intervene . . . even the Church.*

> JACOB BITTORELLI,
> *Former Deputy Chairman of Pirelli*[50]

An important variable in implementing strategy and maximizing host-country human resources for productivity is that of the labor relations environment and system within which the managers of a multinational enterprise (MNE) will operate in a foreign country. Differences in economic, political, and legal systems result in considerable variation in labor relations systems across countries. In addition, European businesses continue to be undermined by their poor labor relations and by inflexible regulations. As a result, businesses have to move jobs overseas to cut labor costs, resulting from a refusal of unions to grant any reduction in employment protection or benefits in order to keep the jobs at home. In addition, non-European firms wishing to operate in Europe have to carefully weigh the labor relations systems and their potential effect on strategic and operational decisions. However, some change may be on the horizon to provide relief to businesses in Europe as some unions grant concessions to firms in order to keep their jobs. Recently, unions in Germany, France, and Italy have been losing their battle to derail labor-market reforms by the governments in those countries who are increasingly concerned that excess regulation and benefits to workers are smothering growth opportunities.[51]

The term **labor relations** refers to the process through which managers and workers determine their workplace relationships. This process may be through verbal agreement and job descriptions, or through a union's written labor contract, which has been reached through negotiation in **collective bargaining** between workers and managers. The labor contract determines rights regarding workers' pay, benefits, job duties, firing procedures, retirement, layoffs, and so on.

The prevailing labor relations system in a country is important to the international manager because it can constrain the strategic choices and operational activities of a firm operating there. The three main dimensions of the labor–management relationship that the manager will consider are (1) the participation of labor in the affairs of the firm, especially as this affects performance and well-being; (2) the role and impact of unions in the relationship; and (3) specific human resource policies in terms of recruitment, training, and compensation.[52] Constraints take the form of (1) wage levels that are set by union contracts and leave the foreign firm little flexibility to be globally competitive, (2) limits on the ability of the foreign firm to vary employment levels when necessary, and (3) limitations on the global integration of operations of the foreign firm because of incompatibility and the potential for industrial conflict.[53]

Organized Labor Around the World

The percentage of the workforce in trade unions in industrialized countries has declined in the last decade, most notably in Europe. In the U.S., union membership fell from a third in 1950 to about 12 percent in 2006.[54] According to the Bureau of Labor Statistics, there were 17 labor strikes in the U.S. involving 171,000 workers in 2004, considerably less than in 1994 when there were 322,000 workers in 45 strikes.[55] This global trend is attributable to various factors, including an increase in the proportion of white-collar and service workers as proportionate to manufacturing workers, a rising proportion of temporary and part-time workers, offshoring of jobs to gain lower wage costs, and a reduced belief in unions in the younger generations.[56] However, the numbers do not show the nature of the system in each country. In most countries, a single dominant industrial relations system applies to almost all workers. Both Canada and the United States have two systems—one for the organized and one for the unorganized. Each, according to Adams, has "different rights and duties of the parties, terms and conditions of employment, and structures and processes of decision making." Basically, in North America, an agent represents unionized employees, whereas unorganized employees can only bargain individually, usually with little capability to affect major strategic decisions or policies or conditions of employment.[57]

The traditional trade union structures in Western industrialized societies have been in *industrial unions*, representing all grades of employees in a specific industry, and *craft unions*, based on certain occupational skills. More recently, the structure has been conglomerate unions, representing members in several industries—for example, the metal workers unions in Europe, which cut across industries, and general unions, which are open to most employees within a country.[58] The system of union representation varies among countries. In the United States, most unions are national and represent specific groups of workers—for example, truck drivers or airline pilots—so a company may have to deal with several different national unions. A single U.S. firm—rather than an association of firms representing a worker classification—engages in its own negotiations. In Japan, on the other hand, it is common for a union to represent all workers in a company. In recent years, company unions in Japan have increasingly coordinated their activities, leading to some lengthy strikes.

Industrial labor relations systems across countries can only be understood in the context of the variables in their environment and the sources of origins of unions. These include government regulation of unions, economic and unemployment factors, technological issues, and the influence of religious organizations. Any of the basic processes or concepts of labor unions, therefore, may vary across countries, depending on where and how the parties have their power and achieve their objectives, such as through parliamentary action in Sweden. For example, collective bargaining in the United States and Canada refers to negotiations between a labor union local and management. However, in Europe collective bargaining takes place between the employer's organization and a trade union at the industry level.[59] This difference means that North America's decentralized, plant-level, collective agreements are more detailed than Europe's industry-wide agreements because of the complexity of negotiating myriad details in multi-employer bargaining. In Germany and Austria, for example, such details are delegated to works councils by legal mandate.[60]

The resulting agreements from bargaining also vary around the world. A written, legally binding agreement for a specific period, common in Northern Europe and North America, is less prevalent in Southern Europe and Britain. In Britain, France, and Italy, bargaining is frequently informal and results in a verbal agreement valid only until one party wishes to renegotiate.[61]

Other variables of the collective bargaining process are the objectives of the bargaining and the enforceability of collective agreements. Because of these differences, managers in MNEs overseas realize that they must adapt their labor relations policies to local conditions and regulations. They also need to bear in mind that, while U.S. union membership has declined by about 50 percent in the last 20 years, in Europe, overall, membership is still quite high, particularly in Italy and the United Kingdom—though it, too, has been falling but from much higher levels.

Most Europeans are covered by collective agreements, whereas most Americans are not. Unions in Europe are part of a national cooperative culture between government, unions, and management, and they hold more power than in the United States. Increasing privatization will make governments less vulnerable to this kind of pressure. It is also interesting to note that some labor courts in Europe deal separately with employment matters from unions and works councils. In Japan, labor militancy has long been dead, since labor and management agreed 40 years ago on a deal for industrial peace in exchange for job security. Unions in Japan have little official clout, especially in the midst of the Japanese recession.

In addition, not much can be negotiated, since wage rates, working hours, job security, health benefits, overtime work, insurance, and the like are legislated. Local working conditions and employment issues are all that are left to negotiate. In addition, the managers and labor union representatives are usually the same people, a fact that serves to limit confrontation, as well as does the cultural norm of maintaining harmonious relationships. In the industrialized world, tumbling trade barriers are also reducing the power of trade unions because competitive multinational companies have more freedom to choose alternative productive and sourcing locations. Most new union workers—about 75 percent—will be in emerging nations, like China and Mexico, where wages are low and unions are scarce.

In China, for example, in a surprising move, the government has passed a new law that will grant power to labor unions, in spite of protests by foreign companies with factories there (see the accompanying Management Focus). The order was in response to a sharp rise in labor tension and protests about poor working conditions and industrial accidents.[62] The All-China Federation of Trade Unions claimed that foreign employers often force workers to work overtime, pay no heed to labor-safety regulations, and deliberately find fault with the workers as an excuse to cut their wages or fine them.

China Drafts Law to Empower Unions and End Labor Abuse

SHANGHAI, Oct. 12, 2006—China is planning to adopt a new law that seeks to crack down on sweatshops and protect workers' rights by giving labor unions real power for the first time since it introduced market forces in the 1980s.

The move, which underscores the government's growing concern about the widening income gap and threats of social unrest, is setting off a battle with American and other foreign corporations that have lobbied against it by hinting that they may build fewer factories here.

The proposed rules are being considered after the Chinese Communist Party endorsed a new doctrine that will put greater emphasis on tackling the severe side effects of the country's remarkable growth.

Whether the foreign corporations will follow through on their warnings is unclear because of the many advantages of being in China—even with restrictions and higher costs that may stem from the new law. It could go into effect as early as next May.

It would apply to all companies in China, but its emphasis is on foreign-owned companies and the suppliers to those companies.

The conflict with the foreign corporations is significant partly because it comes at a time when labor, energy and land costs are rising in this country, all indications that doing business in China is likely to get much more expensive in the coming years.

But it is not clear how effectively such a new labor law would be carried out through this vast land because local officials have tended to ignore directives from the central government or seek ways around them.

China's economy has become one of the most robust in the world since the emphasis on free markets in the 80s encouraged millions of young workers to labor for low wages at companies that made cheap exports. As a result, foreign investment has poured into China.

Some of the world's big companies have expressed concern that the new rules would revive some aspects of socialism and borrow too heavily from labor laws in union-friendly countries like France and Germany.

The Chinese government proposal, for example, would make it more difficult to lay off workers, a condition that some companies contend would be so onerous that they might slow their investments in China.

"This is really two steps backward after three steps forward," said Kenneth Tung, Asia-Pacific director of legal affairs at the Goodyear Tire and Rubber Company in Hong Kong and a legal adviser to the American Chamber of Commerce here.

The proposed law is being debated after Wal-Mart Stores, the world's biggest retailer, was forced to accept unions in its Chinese outlets.

State-controlled unions here have not wielded much power in the past, but after years of reports of worker abuse, the government seems determined to give its union new powers to negotiate worker contracts, safety protection and workplace ground rules.

Hoping to head off some of the rules, representatives of some American companies are waging an intense lobbying campaign to persuade the Chinese government to revise or abandon the proposed law.

The skirmish has pitted the American Chamber of Commerce—which represents corporations including Dell, Ford, General Electric, Microsoft and Nike—against labor activists and the All-China Federation of Trade Unions, the Communist Party's official union organization.

The workers' advocates say that the proposed labor rules—and more important, enforcement powers—are long overdue, and they accuse the American businesses of favoring a system that has led to widespread labor abuse.

On Friday, Global Labor Strategies, a group that supports labor rights policies, is expected to release a report in New York and Boston denouncing American corporations for opposing legislation that would give Chinese workers stronger rights.

"You have big corporations opposing basically modest reforms," said Tim Costello, an official of the group and a longtime labor union advocate. "This flies in the face of the idea that globalization and corporations will raise standards around the world."

China's Labor Ministry declined to comment Thursday, saying the law is still in the drafting stages. Several American corporations also declined to comment on the case, saying it was a delicate matter and referring calls to the American Chamber of Commerce.

But Andreas Lauffs, a Hong Kong-based lawyer who runs the China employment-law practice at the international law firm of Baker & McKenzie, said some American companies considered the proposed rules too costly and restrictive.

Mr. Lauffs said the new rules would give unions collective-bargaining power and control over certain factory rules, and they would also make it difficult to fire employees for poor performance.

"You could hire a sales manager, give him a quota and he doesn't sell anything, and you couldn't get rid of him," Mr. Lauffs said. "It's not easy to get rid of someone now, but under these rules it would be impossible."

It is not clear what the final law will look like, and only an updated draft is expected soon. But specialists say the trend suggests that there may be new challenges ahead for foreign companies doing business in this country.

Under China's "iron rice bowl" system of the 1950s and 60s, all workers were protected by the government or by state-owned companies, which often supplied housing and local health coverage.

But by the 1980s, when the old Maoist model had given way to economic restructuring and the beginning of an emphasis on market forces, China began eliminating many of those protections—giving rise to mass layoffs, unemployment, huge gaps in income and pervasive labor abuse.

The worst off have been migrant workers, most of them exiles from the poorest provinces who travel far from home to live in cramped company dormitories while working long hours under poor conditions.

Migrant workers in virtually every city complain about abuses like having their pay withheld or being forced to work without a contract.

"I don't know about the labor law," said Zhang Yin, an 18-year-old migrant who washes dishes in Shanghai. "During the three months I've been here, my boss has delayed the salary payment twice. I want to quit."

Having grown increasingly concerned about the nation's widening income gap and fearing social unrest, officials in Beijing now seem determined to improve worker protection. In recent years, more and more factory workers have gone to court or taken to the streets to protest poor working conditions and overdue pay.

"The government is concerned because social turmoil can happen at any moment," says Liu Cheng, a professor of law at Shanghai Normal University and an adviser to the authorities on drafting the proposed law. "The government stresses social stability, so it needs to solve existing problems in the society."

In a surprisingly democratic move, China asked for public comment on the draft law last spring and received more than 190,000 responses, mostly from labor activists. The American Chamber of Commerce sent in a lengthy response with objections to the proposals. The European Chamber of Commerce also responded.

The law would impose heavy fines on companies that do not comply. And the state-controlled union—the only legal union in China—would gain greater power through new collective-bargaining rights or pursuing worker grievances and establishing work rules. One provision in the proposed law reads, "Labor unions or employee representatives have the right, following bargaining conducted on an equal basis, to execute with employers collective contracts on such matters as labor compensation, working hours, rest, leave, work safety and hygiene, insurance, benefits, etc."

If approved and strictly enforced, specialists say the new laws would strikingly alter the country's vast labor market and significantly push up the wages of everyday workers.

"If you really abide by the Chinese labor laws," said Anita Chan, an expert on labor issues in this country and a visiting fellow at the Australian National University, "migrant-worker wages would go up by 50 percent or more."

Until now, though, existing Chinese labor laws have gone largely unenforced, which has further complicated the debate here. Opponents of the proposed law argue that enforcing existing labor laws would be enough to solve the country's nagging problems. Advocates respond that adopting new laws would set the stage for stricter enforcement.

Even lawyers working for multinational corporations seem to agree that there is an epidemic of cheating.

Mr. Liu, the Shanghai lawyer who advised the government on the draft proposal, says many companies avoid existing laws by using employment agencies to hire workers. He says the new law will do more to protect workers from such abuse by holding companies accountable.

"The principle is not to raise the labor standard dramatically," he said, "but to raise the cost of violating the law. The current labor law is a paper tiger and is a disadvantage to those who obey it. If you don't obey the law, you won't be punished." (Update: This law was passed in July 2007)

SOURCE: David Barboza, www.nytimes.com, October 12, 2006. Copyright The New York Times Co. Reprinted with permission.

Convergence Versus Divergence in Labor Systems

The world trade union movement is poised to follow the lead of transnational companies, by extending its reach and throwing off the shackles of national boundaries. Unions are about to go global.[63]

The merger of two of the world's largest labor unions to lobby for common labor standards in multinational companies confirms the movement towards convergence in global labor systems. The partnership between the International Confederation of Free Trade Unions (ICFTU), representing 215 national groups in developed economies, and the

World Confederation of Labor, based in Brussels, with 144 member groups in Europe and Africa, provides union support for 200 million workers.[64] Political changes, external competitive forces, increased open trade, and frequent moves of MNCs around the world are forces working toward convergence in labor systems. **Convergence** occurs as the migration of management and workplace practices around the world reduce workplace disparities from one country to another. This occurs primarily as MNCs seek consistency and coordination among their foreign subsidiaries and as they act as catalysts for change by "exporting" new forms of work organization and industrial relations practices.[65] It also occurs as harmonization is sought, such as for the EC countries, and as competitive pressures in free-trade zones, such as the NAFTA countries, eventually bring about demands for some equalization of benefits for workers.[66] It would appear that economic globalization is leading to labor transnationalism and will bring about changes in labor rights and democracy around the world.[67] In East European societies in transition to market economies, for example, newly structured industrial relations systems are being created. Trends in industrial relations, such as the flattening of organizations and the decline in the role of trade unions, are viewed by many as global developments that point to convergence in labor systems.[68]

Other pressures toward convergence of labor relations practices around the world come from the activities and monitoring of labor conditions worldwide by various organizations. One of these organizations is the International Labor Organization (ILO)—comprising union, employer, and government representation—whose mission is to ensure that humane conditions of labor are maintained. Other associations of unions in different countries include various international trade secretariats representing workers in specific industries. These include the International Confederation of Free Trade Unions (ICFTU) and the World Confederation of Labor (WCL). The activities and communication channels of these associations provide unions and firms with information about differences in labor conditions around the world.[69] One result of their efforts to provide awareness and changes in labor conditions was the pressure they brought to bear on MNCs operating in South Africa in the late 1980s. The result was the exodus of foreign companies and the eventual repeal of apartheid laws. Now there is a rapidly growing labor union movement there, thanks to the pro-union African National Congress. The AFL-CIO opened an office in Johannesburg and assists the South African unions.[70]

Political and cultural shifts are also behind the new labor law in South Korea, as the country moves from a system founded on paternalism and authoritarianism to one based on more liberal values.[71]

Although forces for convergence are found in labor relations systems around the world, as discussed previously, for the most part, MNCs still adapt their practices largely to the traditions of national industrial relations systems, with considerable pressure to do so. Those companies, in fact, act more like local employers, subject to local and country regulations and practices. Although the reasons for continued divergence in systems seem fewer, they are very strong: Not the least of these reasons are political ideology and the overall social structure and history of industrial practices. In the European Union (EU), where states are required to maintain parity in wage rates and benefits under the Social Charter of the Maastricht Treaty, a powerful defense of cultural identity and social systems still exists, with considerable resistance by unions to comply with those requirements. Managers in those MNCs also recognize that a considerable gap often exists between the labor laws and the enforcement of those laws—in particular in less developed countries. Exhibit 10-8 shows the major forces for and against convergence in labor relations systems.

The NAFTA and Labor Relations in Mexico

About 40 percent of the total workforce in Mexico is unionized, with about 80 percent of workers in industrial organizations that employ more than 25 workers unionized. However, government control over union activities is very strong, and although some strikes occur, union control over members remains rather weak.[72] MNCs are required by government regulation to hire Mexican nationals for at least 90 percent of their

EXHIBIT 10-8   Trends in Global Labor Relations Systems

Forces for Global Convergence ← Current System →	Forces to Maintain or Establish Divergent Systems
Global competitiveness	National labor relations systems and traditions
MNC presence or consolidation initiatives	Social systems
Political change	Local regulations and practices
New market economies	Political ideology
Free-trade zones: harmonization	Cultural norms
(EU), competitive forces (NAFTA)	
Technological standardization, IT	
Declining role of unions	
Agencies monitoring world labor practices	

workforce; preference must be given to Mexicans and to union personnel. In reality, however, the government permits hiring exceptions.

Currently, the only labor issues that are subject to a formal traditional review under the NAFTA labor side pact are minimum wages, child labor, and safety issues. Foreign firms, such as Honeywell, operating in Mexico are faced with pressures from various stakeholders in their dealings with unions. In fact, in early 1998, AFL-CIO president John Sweeney flew to Mexico to try to develop coordinated cross-border organizing and bargaining strategies. Although no deals were made at that time, the seeds were sown in the direction of more open union activity and benefits for employees.

Many foreign firms set up production in Mexico at least in part for the lower wages and overall cost of operating there—utilizing the advantages of the NAFTA—and the Mexican government wants to continue to attract that investment, as it has for many years before NAFTA. Mexican workers claim that some of the large U.S. companies in Mexico violate basic labor rights and cooperate with pro-government labor leaders in Mexico to break up independent unions. Workers there believe that MNCs routinely use blacklists, physical intimidation, and economic pressure against union organization and independent labor groups that oppose Mexican government policies or the pro-government Confederation of Mexican Workers (CTM). GE, for example, has been accused of firing 11 employees in its Juarez plant who were involved in organizing a campaign for the Authentic Labor Front, Mexico's only independent labor group. The company was also accused of blacklisting union activists and circulating the list to some employers. In February 1994, formal complaints were filed with the Department of Labor, National Administration Office (NAO), by two U.S. unions—the Teamsters and the United Electrical, Radio, and Machine Workers Union. (U.S. unions have an interest in increasing wages and benefits in Mexico to offset some of the reasons that American companies take productive facilities there, along with U.S. jobs.) The NAO—set up by the NAFTA to monitor labor policies in the United States, Mexico, and Canada—reviewed complaints that GE may have violated Mexican labor law. That office later ruled that those claims against GE were unsubstantiated; they also ruled that neither the NAO nor its Mexican counterpart could punish other nations for failing to address union-organization rights, although they could issue formal complaints.[73]

This incident illustrates the complexities of labor relations when a firm operates in other countries—particularly with linkages and interdependence among those countries, such as through the NAFTA or the EC. Of interest are the differences among NAFTA nations in labor law in the private sector. For example, while the minimum wage in Mexico is far less than that in Canada or the United States, a number of costly benefits for Mexican workers are required, such as 15 days of pay for a Christmas bonus and 90 days of severance pay. For comparison, the following Comparative Management in Focus examines labor relations in Germany.

Comparative Management in Focus

Labor Relations in Germany

This is really a paradigm change. Traditionally, collective bargaining was focused at the industry level. Now companies and the workplace level [bargaining unit]are much more important.

DETLEF WETZEL,
Head of IG Metall, January 6, 2006[74]

DaimlerChrysler employees at Mercedes factories in Germany agreed to smaller raises and increased hours after the carmaker threatened to shed 6,000 jobs, adding to pressure for a longer workweek nationwide.[75]

Germany's **codetermination** law *(mitbestimmung)* is coming under pressure from German companies dealing with global competition, and as a result of global trends of outsourcing, industrial restructuring and the expansion of the service sector.[76] That pressure is increasingly taking the form of concession bargaining to keep jobs at home. Still some companies, tired of restrictions on their strategic decisions and necessary job cuts, are sidestepping those restrictions by registering as public limited companies in the United Kingdom.[77]

Mitbestimmung refers to the participation of labor in the management of a firm. The law mandates representation for unions and salaried employees on the supervisory boards of all companies with more than 2,000 employees and "works councils" of employees at every work site. Those companies with 2,000 or more staff have to give employees half the votes; those with 500 employees or more have to give a third of supervisory board seats to union representatives.[78] Unions are well integrated into managerial decision making and can make a positive contribution to corporate competitiveness and restructuring; this seems different from the traditional adversarial relationship of unions and management in the United States. However, the fact is that firms, in the form of affiliated organizations of companies, have to contend with negotiating with powerful industry-wide unions. Employment conditions that would be negotiated privately in the United States, for example, are subject to federal mandates in Germany—a model unique in Europe. The average metalworker, for example, earns around $2,500 a month, works a 35-hour week, and has six weeks of annual vacation. Germans on average work fewer hours than those in any other country than the Netherlands.[79] Under pressure from global competition, German unions have incurred huge membership losses in the last decade—7 million members, 40 percent fewer than in 1990; 20 percent of employees in Germany are union members, compared to 29 percent in the United Kingdom and 75 percent in Denmark.[80] As a result, the unions are now more willing to make concessions and trade flexibility for increased job security. This was the case in 2005 when the German engineering group Linde decided to build a factory in eastern Europe to take advantage of lower wages there. However, Linde reversed the decision after the IG Metall trade union local decided to match the savings by working longer hours and taking less pay.[81]

Union membership in Germany is voluntary, usually with one union for each major industry, and union power traditionally has been quite strong. Negotiated contracts with firms by the employers' federation stand to be accepted by firms that are members of the federation, or used as a guide for other firms. These contracts, therefore, result in setting the pay scale for about 90 percent of the country's workers.[82]

The union works councils play an active role in hiring, firing, training, and reassignment during times of reorganization and change.[83] Because of the depth of works council penetration into personnel and work organization matters, as required by law, their role has been described by some as "co-manager of the internal labor market."[84] This situation has considerable implications for how managers of MNCs plan to operate in Germany. IG Metall, for example, which is Germany's largest metalworking union with 2.6 million workers, has traditionally negotiated guidelines regarding pay, hours, and working conditions on a regional basis. Then, works councils use those guidelines to make local agreements. In 2006 the bargaining role started to devolve to the local unit. IG Metall's proactive role on change illustrates the evolving role of unions by leading management thinking instead of reacting to it. In addition, management and workers tend to work together because of the unions' structure. Indeed, such institutional accord is a powerful factor in changing deeply ingrained cultural traits.

Codetermination has clearly helped to modify German managerial style from authoritarian to something more akin to humanitarian without, it should be noted, altering its capacity for efficiency and effectiveness.[85] This system compares to the lack of integration and active roles for unions in the U.S. auto industry—for example, conditions that limit opportunities for change.

DaimlerChrysler (still the company's name as of June 2007), the German-American company headquartered in Germany, includes a works council in its decision making, as mandated by German law. This means that the company's labor representatives pay close attention to U.S. attitudes, which may lead to changes in the tone of the collective bargaining processes. The two-tiered system of a supervisory and a management board will remain. DaimlerChrysler was one of several companies to exert pressure in 2004 to bring down the high labor costs and taxes in Germany, under the threat of moving its plants elsewhere to remain globally competitive. With the DaimlerChrysler company accounting for about 13 percent of the DAX index of 30 German blue-chip stocks, U.S. shareholders and managers in the company hold some power to bring about change and reduce operating costs in the company—and perhaps eventually in the country. Pay for German production workers has been among the highest in the world, about 150 percent of that in the United States and about ten times that in Mexico. German workers also have the highest number of paid vacation days in the world and prefer short workdays. However, in July 2004, Jürgen Peters, chairman of Germany's powerful IG Metall engineering trade union, announced the agreement with DaimlerChrysler to accept smaller raises and increased working hours after the company threatened to move 6,000 jobs elsewhere.[86] The agreement followed one by 4,000 Siemens employees in June 2004 to extend their work week.

Foreign companies operating in Germany also have to be aware that termination costs are very high—including severance pay, retraining costs, time to find another job, and so on—and that is assuming the company is successful in terminating the employee in the first place, which is very difficult to do in Europe. This was brought home to Colgate-Palmolive when it tried to close its factory in Hamburg in 1996. The company offered the 500 employees an average of $40,000 each, but the union would not accept, and eventually Colgate had to pay a much higher (undisclosed) amount.

The German model, according to Rudiger Soltwedel of the Institute for the World Economy at Kiel, holds that competition should be based on factors other than cost.[87] Thus, the higher wage level in Germany should be offset by higher-value goods like luxury cars and machine tools, which have been the hallmark of Germany's products. To the extent that the West German unions have established the high-wage, high-skill, and high-value-added production pattern, they have also become dependent on the continued presence of that pattern.[88] In recognition of that dependency, German auto firms are in the process of remaking themselves after the Japanese model—reducing supplies and cutting costs so they can compete on a global scale. However, this social contract, which has underpinned Germany's manufacturing success, is fraying at the edges as Germany's economy weakens under the $100 billion cost of absorbing East Germany and under competitive EU pressures.[89]

Conflicting opinions over the value of codetermination are increasingly evident, as business practices become increasingly subject to EU policies. A major concern was that firms from other countries which were considering cross-border mergers would be discouraged by the EU statute, which would oblige them to incorporate codetermination if the new company includes significant German interests.

CONCLUSION

The role of the IHRM department has expanded to meet the strategic needs of the company to develop a competitive global management cadre. Maximizing human resources around the world requires attention to the many categories and combinations of those people, including expatriates, host-country managers, third country nationals, female and minority resources, global teams, and local employees. Competitive global companies need top managers with global experience and understanding. To that end, attention must be paid to the needs of expatriates before, during, and after their assignments in order to maximize their long-term contributions to the company.

Summary of Key Points

1. Expatriate career management necessitates plans for retention of expatriates during and after their assignments. Support programs for expatriates should include information from and contact with the home organization, as well as career guidance and support after the overseas assignment.
2. The expatriate's spouse plays a crucial role in the potential retention and effectiveness of the manager in host locations. Companies should ensure the spouse's interest in the assignment, include him or her in the predeparture training, and provide career and family support during the assignment and upon return.
3. Global management teams offer greater opportunities for competition—by sharing experiences, technology, and international managers—and greater opportunities for cross-cultural understanding and exposure to different viewpoints. Disadvantages can result from communication and cross-cultural conflicts and greater complexity in the workplace.
4. Women and minorities represent an underutilized resource in international management. A major reason for this situation is the assumption that culturally based biases may limit the opportunities and success of females and minorities.
5. The labor relations environment, system, and processes vary around the world and affect how the international manager must plan strategy and maximize the productivity of local human resources.
6. Labor unions around the world are becoming increasingly interdependent because of the operations of MNCs worldwide, the outsourcing of jobs around the world, and the "leveling of the playing field" for jobs.

Discussion Questions

1. What steps can the company's IHRM department take to maximize the effectiveness of the expatriate's assignment and the long-term benefit to the company?
2. Discuss the role of reverse culture shock in the repatriation process. What can companies do to avoid this problem? What kinds of skills do managers learn from a foreign assignment, and how can the company benefit from them? What is the role of repatriation in the company's global competitive situation?
3. What are the reasons for the small numbers of female expatriates? What more can companies do to use women and minorities as a resource for international management?
4. Discuss the role of international management teams relative to the level of a company's global involvement. Give some examples of the kinds of teams that might be necessary and what issues they would face.
5. Discuss the reasons behind the growing convergence and interdependence of labor unions around the world.

Application Exercise

Interview one or more managers who have held positions overseas. Try to find a man and a woman. Ask them about their experiences both in the working environment and in the foreign country generally. How did they and their families adapt? How did they find the stage of reentry to headquarters, and what were the effects of the assignment on their career progression? What differences do you notice, if any, between the experiences of the male and the female expatriates?

Experiential Exercise

Form groups of six students, divided into two teams, one representing union members from a German company and the other representing union members from a Mexican company. These companies have recently merged in a joint venture, with the subsidiary to be located in Mexico. These union workers, all line supervisors, will be working together in Mexico. You are to negotiate six major points of agreement regarding union representation, bargaining rights, and worker participation in management, as discussed in this chapter. Present your findings to the other groups in the class and discuss. (It may help to read the Comparative Management in Focus on Motivation in Mexico in Ch.11.)

Internet Resources

Visit the Deresky Companion Website at www.prenhall.com/deresky for this chapter's Internet resources.

Avon in Global Markets in 2007: Managing and Developing a Global Workforce

I was recently in Turkey, where only 10 percent of the population has Internet access at home. Yet almost 95 percent of our sales in Turkey are submitted online—our representatives go to Internet cafes.

We're also increasing investments in key geographies, like China, where we've rapidly built a sales force of 188,000 since we received our national direct-selling license in March, 2006. (As of March, 2007, this number had risen to 399,000).

ANDREA JUNG,
CEO, Avon Products., October 2006[1]

Avon Products, Inc. (hereafter called Avon) is the largest direct seller of personal care products and is the brand to be reckoned with. The company targets young as well as middle-aged customers in over 100 countries. In 2006, Avon has over 5 million independent representatives worldwide. The company is one of the well-established brands in the $90 billion toiletries/cosmetics and household nondurables industry.[2] In 1999, Andrea Jung was named the first female CEO of the company. Since taking charge, Jung has reinvigorated the company and implemented many timely changes in the U.S. and global markets. It is no longer the same company that faced sluggish sales and debt problems in the 1980s.[3] In 2005, Avon's revenues surpassed $8.15 billion and profit was $847.6 million. Approximately 70 percent of the company's revenues come from selling its products in international markets. According to *Fortune* magazine's 2004 annual business rankings, the company is one of the most admired companies in the area of household nondurables and personal products and consistently receives good ratings from the industry (see Table 1 and Figure 1). Regarding brand identity, corporate reputation, and sales network, Avon is truly a global brand for the masses. In addition, in the area of minority recruitment, Avon always receives good ratings by the analysts.[4]

Right from its inception, direct selling has been Avon's major strength in the U.S. and global markets. Other companies (Mary Kay and Amway) that capitalized on the direct selling model equally excel in their target markets and have made phenomenal expansion overseas.[5] In global markets, Avon's major competitors include Procter & Gamble, Johnson & Johnson, Pfizer, Sara Lee, Gillette, Wyeth, Estée Lauder, L'Oreal, and Unilever.[6] Avon also sells through catalogs, mall kiosks, and a Web-based store. Beyond its personal care products and cosmetics, the company has expanded in other areas that include fragrances, toiletries, jewelry, apparel, and home furnishings. Avon's products/brand names include Avon Color, Avon Skincare, Avon Bath & Body, Avon Hair Care, Avon Wellness, Avon Fragrance, beComing, and Mark.[7]

Managing and Developing a Global Workforce

In global business, a company's workforce and salespeople are the main representatives, taking orders and dealing with customers on a daily basis in consumer and industrial markets. Becoming aware of intercultural differences and getting the appropriate training play an important role in the development of a productive sales force. Areas that are important in the development of a good workforce include cultural sensitivity, motivation, ethical standards, relationship building, and organizational skills.[8] Standard international human resource training encompasses areas that deal with hiring and firing, absenteeism, team building, and creating good leadership skills. In addition, valuing workplace diversity and providing equal opportunity is important to the

[1]Andrea Jung, "Now is the time to invest," *Fortune,* October 16, 2006.
[2]See Company Web site (www.avon.com); *Standard & Poor's Industry Surveys.* (2003). "Industry surveys: Household nondurables," (December 18), pp. 1–25.
[3]*Business Week.* (1991). "Despite the face-lift, Avon is sagging," (December 2), pp. 101–102; *The Economist.* (1996). "Scents and sensibility," (July 13), pp. 57–58.
[4]For more detail, see *Fortune.* (2004). *Fortune Global 500,* (April 5), pp. F1–F72; *Fortune.* (2004). "America's most admired companies," (March 8), p. 112.

[5]In 2003, Mary Kay's worldwide revenues surpassed $1.2 billion and maintained operations in 30 countries. Amway, on the other hand, had operations in eighty countries and its sales totaled $4.5 billion. For more information, see www.marykay.com; www.amway.com.
[6]For detail, see: Hoover's.com (www.hoover.com); *Standard & Poor's Industry Surveys.* (2003). "Industry surveys: Household nondurables," (December 18), pp. 1–25.
[7]For more detail, see Company Web site (www.avon.com).
[8]Kotabe, Masaaki and Kristiaan Helsen. (2004).*Global Marketing Management*, 3rd edition, New York: John Wiley & Sons, pp. 452–476.

TABLE 1 Avon Products, Inc.: Selected Company Data

A. Company data (2006):

Senior Management:

Chairman and CEO:	Andrea Jung
Senior VP and Global Brand President:	Geralyn R. Breig
Executive VP, Global Sales Strategy:	Brian C. Connolly
Executive VP & CFO:	Charles Cramb

Financial Data (2005 Annual Report):

Sales:	$8.15 bil. (up 5% from 2004)
Net income:	$847.6 mil.
Assets:	$4.76 bil.

Company type: Public (listed on NYSE)

Global Segments Selected Results: (Figures in millions)

Total Revenue & Operating Profit	**2005**	
	Total Revenue	Operating Profit
North America		
U.S.	$2,140.7	$ 314.6
Other	369.8	38.9
Total	2,510.5	353.5
International		
Europe	2,291.4	458.9
Latin America	2,272.6	516.0
Asia Pacific	1,075.1	141.5
Total	5,639.1	1,116.4
Total from operations	8,149.6	1,469.9
Global expenses	–	(320.9)
Total	$8,149.6	$1,149.0

Other Data and Rankings:

Independent sales representatives:	Over 5 million in 2006
Ranking in *Fortune* 500 (2004):	275 (based on sales)
Ranking in *Fortune's* "most admired companies" (household/personal products; 2004):	3 (score: 6.59 out of 10)

B. Major competitors of Avon:

Total global cosmetics/beauty industry: $90 billion

Major competitors: Procter & Gamble, Johnson & Johnson, Pfizer, Sara Lee, Gillette Company, Wyeth, Estée Lauder, Tommy Hilfiger, L'Oreal, and Unilever.

SOURCES: Company Web site, October 18, 2006 (www.avon.com); Hoover's.com (www.hoovers.com);. "The 100 top brands," (August 4), pp. 72–78; *Forbes.* (2004), "The world's 2000 leading companies, (April 12), pp. 144–22; *Fortune.* (2004), "America most admired companies," (March 8), p. 112; *Fortune.* (2004). "Industry surveys: Household nondurables," (December 18), pp. 1–25; *Value Line.* (2004), "Avon Products," (April 2), p. 821.

company.[9] No matter what HR programs pursued by companies, commitment on the part of top management is critical in developing the workforce. The jobs of salespeople and company representatives become even more critical with door-to-door selling and diverse markets. Organizing the workforce in the new markets and dealing with a variety of industrial labor relations around the world can be a daunting task. Equally important areas are hiring, training, and, above all, retaining the best employees (see Table 2). In the case of Avon, effective management of its global workforce is crucial to the company's strategy since it maintains over 5 million independent representatives and approximately 46,000 associates in over a hundred countries

[9]Deresky, Helen. (2003). *International Management: Managing across Borders and Cultures,* 4th edition, Upper Saddle River, New Jersey: Prentice Hall, pp. 415–441.

FIGURE 1 Avon's Global Operations in 2006

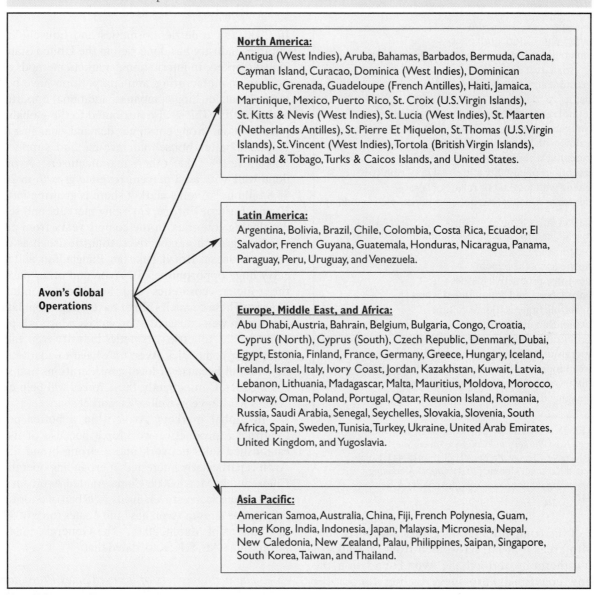

North America:
Antigua (West Indies), Aruba, Bahamas, Barbados, Bermuda, Canada, Cayman Island, Curacao, Dominica (West Indies), Dominican Republic, Grenada, Guadeloupe (French Antilles), Haiti, Jamaica, Martinique, Mexico, Puerto Rico, St. Croix (U.S. Virgin Islands), St. Kitts & Nevis (West Indies), St. Lucia (West Indies), St. Maarten (Netherlands Antilles), St. Pierre Et Miquelon, St. Thomas (U.S. Virgin Islands), St. Vincent (West Indies), Tortola (British Virgin Islands), Trinidad & Tobago, Turks & Caicos Islands, and United States.

Latin America:
Argentina, Bolivia, Brazil, Chile, Colombia, Costa Rica, Ecuador, El Salvador, French Guyana, Guatemala, Honduras, Nicaragua, Panama, Paraguay, Peru, Uruguay, and Venezuela.

Avon's Global Operations

Europe, Middle East, and Africa:
Abu Dhabi, Austria, Bahrain, Belgium, Bulgaria, Congo, Croatia, Cyprus (North), Cyprus (South), Czech Republic, Denmark, Dubai, Egypt, Estonia, Finland, France, Germany, Greece, Hungary, Iceland, Ireland, Israel, Italy, Ivory Coast, Jordan, Kazakhstan, Kuwait, Latvia, Lebanon, Lithuania, Madagascar, Malta, Mauritius, Moldova, Morocco, Norway, Oman, Poland, Portugal, Qatar, Reunion Island, Romania, Russia, Saudi Arabia, Senegal, Seychelles, Slovakia, Slovenia, South Africa, Spain, Sweden, Tunisia, Turkey, Ukraine, United Arab Emirates, United Kingdom, and Yugoslavia.

Asia Pacific:
American Samoa, Australia, China, Fiji, French Polynesia, Guam, Hong Kong, India, Indonesia, Japan, Malaysia, Micronesia, Nepal, New Caledonia, New Zealand, Palau, Philippines, Saipan, Singapore, South Korea, Taiwan, and Thailand.

SOURCE: Company Web site (www.avon.com).

(see Figure 1). In international business, consumer companies cannot operate efficiently without having the best and [most] well-trained workforce. Like other companies, Avon runs leadership programs and on-the-job training seminars on a regular basis. The company particularly maintains high standards in four areas that affect the sales force productivity and future retention (i.e., compensation, fringe benefits, professional development, and workforce environment). Avon's five values and principles include trust, respect, belief, humility, and integrity. Interestingly, Avon has also been one of the first-movers in workforce diversity and minority recruitment in the United States and over 86 percent of management positions in the company are held by women. The company conspicuously follows

what it preaches in its corporate philosophy. Avon's vision states:

To be the company that best understands and satisfies the product, service and self-fulfillment needs of women—globally.[10]

In addition, 7 of the company's Executive Team of 16 members are female.[11] In international markets the majority of the company staff and independent representatives are females, making the company a good employer and a role model in women's well-being and employment opportunities. Of course, the

---
[10]See Company Web site (www.avon.com).
[11]See Company Web site (www.avon.com).

TABLE 2 Human Resource Issues of Market Entry and Workforce Management

Pre-market entry/short-term issues:
- Availability of local management and workforce
- Expatriate recruiting
- Recruitment methods and selection
- Sales force training
- Cultural sensitivity/cross-cultural training
- Cost issues
- Dealing with labor relations/laws
- Intercultural considerations
- Perceptions of equality and equal opportunity issues
- Dealing with local labor relations/laws
- Sales force strategy (territorial, product, and customer)

Post-market entry/long-term issues:
- Job training/professional development
- Retention
- Knowledge management
- Sales force productivity issues
- Control, trust, and commitment issues
- Implanting organizational culture
- Relationship marketing
- Acculturation/adaptation issues
- Supervision/mentoring (motivation and ethical perceptions)
- Building global/local management teams
- Managing diversity/multiculturalism

SOURCES: Deresky, Helen. (2006). *International Management: Managing across Borders and Cultures*, 5th edition, Upper Saddle River, New Jersey: Prentice Hall, pp. 415–441; Kotabe, Masaaki and Kristiaan Helsen. (2004). *Global Marketing Management*, 3rd edition, New York: John Wiley & Sons, pp. 452–476.

nature of the company's product lines and operations deal with areas that attract women from all walks of life.[12] Furthermore, through the Avon Foundation, the company generously provides funding for cancer research, education, and other charitable programs. The company has been one of the major supporters of women's issues in North America and overseas. This creates commitment, harmony, and a supportive work environment that has been beneficial to the company. Avon foundation's projects include breast cancer programs in the areas of education, outreach and support services, screening, diagnostic and treatment services, and medical research and clinical care. Besides this, the company supports various programs in women's empowerment and in the arts and humanities.[13]

Future Growth and Workforce Development in Multicultural Markets

In 2006, the toiletries/cosmetics and household non-durables industry has done well in the United States and global markets. In international markets, methods of production, manufacturing, and competition have become truly global, fetching companies additional opportunities and growth.[14] This is also attributed to the globalization phenomenon, strong consumer demand, changing demographics, better household income, and supply chain efficiencies.[15] Like other manufacturers, Avon has done well, with an 8 percent revenue growth in 2006 to $8.8 billion.[16] Avon's market share is growing in China, Russia, Eastern Europe, emerging markets, and selected developing countries. In the coming years, from population and growth perspectives, countries such as China, India, Indonesia, Brazil, Pakistan, Bangladesh, and Russia carry huge opportunities for Avon and other players in the toiletries/cosmetics and household nondurables industry. These countries either have a large population or maintain a well-educated middle class, which is a prerequisite for the toiletries/cosmetics industry (see Table 3). Like other companies, Avon may have to adapt its business model because of local considerations and supply chain issues. Consequently, these forces will help expand Avon's workforce as well as its market share.

In global markets, Avon is in a better position to attract a productive workforce because of its well-established sales network and a strong brand identity. Avon is particularly interested in expanding operations in China, and in March 2006 China granted Avon a national direct selling license, reversing its 1998 ban of door-to-door selling.[17] as a result Avon has built a sales force of 399,000 in China as of March, 2007[18] The General Manager of Avon China, Mr. S. K. Kao, stated that:

> *The high numbers of licensed Sales Promoters in such a short time reflects the great appeal of the Avon earnings opportunity in the Chinese market, enhancing our confidence in the future of our business in China. We are very pleased that nearly 90 percent of our Beauty Boutiques have qualified to act as Service Centers under the government's regulations, indicating that our Beauty Boutique owners want to be involved in direct selling.*

S. K. KAO,
General Manager, Avon China[19]

---

[12]For a good discussion on this topic, see Martin, Joanne, Kathleen Knopoff, and Christine Beckman. (2001). "An alternative to bureaucratic impersonality and emotional labor: Bounded emotionality at the Body Shop," *Administrative Science Quarterly*, Vol. 43, pp. 429–469.
[13]For more detail see Company Web site (www.avon.com).

[14]Mytelka, Lynn K. (2000). "Local systems of innovation in a globalized world economy," *Industry and Innovation*, Vol. 7, No. 1, pp. 15–32.
[15]Ghemawat, Pankaj. (2003). "Globalization: The strategy of differences," *HBS Working Knowledge,* (November 10), pp. 1–4 (www.hbswk.hbs.edu).
[16]www.avon.com, March 22, 2007.
[17]Andrea Jung, "Now is the time to invest," *Fortune*, October 16, 2006.
[18]Nanette Byrnes, "Avon: More than cosmetic changes," *Business Week*, March 12, 2007.
[19]www.avon.com, July 17, 2006.

TABLE 3   Most Populous Countries and Per Capita GDP

Rank/Country	Population (2003)	Projected Population (2025)	Per Capita GDP (2003)
1. China	1,288.7 mil.	1,454.7 mil.	$1,090 (exchange rate based)
2. India	1,068.6	1,363.0	480
3. United States	291.5	351.1	32,000
4. Indonesia	220.5	281.9	796
5. Brazil	176.5	211.2	2,820
6. Pakistan	149.1	249.7	2,100 (PPP)
7. Bangladesh	146.7	208.3	389
8. Russia	145.5	136.9	2,320

(PPP) – Purchasing power parity.

SOURCES: *Standard & Poor's Industry Surveys.* (2003). Industry surveys: Household non-durables, (December 18), pp. 1–25; Bureau of Public Affairs. (2004). "Background Notes," *U.S. Department of State,* (www.state.gov/r/pa/ei/bgn/).

Because of shorter life cycles and a rising middle class, new products and markets are the key to success in the emerging markets. According to Jung,

> *India is the other top priority [after China]. Right now we have about 60,000 representatives in India. . . . India has more than 300 million women between ages 15 and 64, and a rising middle class. . . . a market creation waiting to happen.*

> ANDREA JUNG,
> *October 16, 2006*[20]

Since the company continues to grow in international markets, it will keep hiring and training the new workforce in its door-to-door selling model. The company's distribution strategies may have to be adapted to the local needs because of working women or other cultural and logistical considerations and include mail, phone, fax, retail outlets, and Web sites.[21] One priority for training Avon's international representatives is to move faster to get the representatives online. Ms. Jung says that Avon's IT team has developed a global Internet platform, and that she has put a top strategist on the case.[22] Market entry issues and workforce management will have a big impact on Avon's future expansion in international markets. In conclusion, Avon definitely carries a significant advantage over its rivals because of a well-organized and trained sales force, and above all, 5 million independent representatives in global markets.

[20]*Fortune*, October 16, 2006.

[21]Ibid.
[22]Ibid.

CASE QUESTIONS

1. Evaluate Avon's operations in global markets regarding the use of international cadre development and building company associates and independent representatives.

2. Since 70 percent of Avon's revenues are generated outside the United States, what recommendations would you provide to the company regarding dealing with a culturally diverse workforce and a multicultural marketplace in the coming years?

3. In the coming years, Avon's future global expansion is contingent on hiring and retaining the best workforce and salespeople in global markets. What training and cross-cultural practices would you recommend to the company to deal with this area?

4. China is expected to be a major market for Avon. If you were to advise Avon, how would you develop a competitive IHR plan for the company?

5. What is the role of IT in Avon's markets, in particular in developing areas? What are the implications for training its representatives?

6. What do you think are Avon's prospects in India, given that the per capita spending on beauty there is only $1, compared to between $100 and $200 in developed markets?

SOURCE: Updated and adapted by Helen Deresky, March 2007, from a case written exclusively for this book by Syed Tariq Anwar, 2004. The material in this case is intended to be used as a basis for classroom/academic discussion rather than to illustrate either effective or ineffective handling of a managerial situation or business practices.

CHAPTER

11

Motivating and Leading

Outline

Opening Profile: Fujitsu Uses Pay Cuts as a Motivational Tool

TOKYO: Taking a page from Japan's human resource handbook, Fujitsu will cut the salaries of around 14,000 managers to motivate them—and their subordinates—to work harder.

Fujitsu, one of the world's largest makers of computer and telecommunications equipment, hopes to return to a profit soon for the first time in three years. The company is betting that the pay cuts will push managers to rally rank-and-file workers in the remaining months of the fiscal year, which ends March 31.

The pay cuts will be "several percent" from each paycheck and will start at the section chief level and go up, a spokeswoman for Fujitsu, Yuri Momomoto, said. The cuts will take effect from now to March. If Fujitsu meets its goal of 30 billion yen ($281.6 million) in profit for the year, the managers might have their full salaries restored, Ms. Momomoto said.

The pay cuts are not meant to meet any particular financial goal, she said, but rather to build a sense of urgency and team spirit. While the step might seem counterintuitive to American sensibilities, in Japan it makes sense. Workers here often feel a strong kinship to their employers, especially in times of crisis. Under this logic, employees will work harder if they see their managers making sacrifices for the sake of the group.

Top executives in Japan often volunteer to take temporary pay cuts when a company performs poorly or is embroiled in scandal, even if the executives are not directly responsible.

In Fujitsu's case, by forcing all managers, regardless of rank or division, to take pay cuts, the company can distribute the pain evenly and avoid blaming any one group for the company's shortcomings.

By cutting salaries, Fujitsu can also avoid eliminating jobs, a process that is complicated by Japan's labor laws.

SOURCE: www.nytimes.com, January 27, 2004, Copyright © 2004 The New York Times Co., used with permission.

Motivating

The Westerners can't understand that we need the fork on our neck, not all these nice words and baby techniques. The Technique is the fork.

RUSSIAN MIDDLE MANAGER[1]

After managers set up a firm's operations by planning strategy, organizing the work and responsibilities, and staffing those operations, they turn their attention to everyday activities. This ongoing behavior of individual people carrying out various daily tasks enables the firm to accomplish its objectives. Getting those people to perform their jobs efficiently and effectively is at the heart of the manager's challenge.

Motivation—and therefore appropriate leadership style—is affected by many powerful variables (societal, cultural, and political). When considering the Japanese culture, for example, discussed throughout this book, it is not surprising to find that Fujitsu uses some motivational techniques very different from those in the West, as illustrated in the opening profile. Clearly Fujitsu's decision to cut pay is based on the Japanese tradition of "sink or swim" with co-workers and employer.

Our objective in this chapter is to consider motivation and leadership in the context of diverse cultural milieus. We need to know what, if any, differences exist in the societal factors that elicit and maintain behaviors leading to high employee productivity and job satisfaction. Are effective motivational and leadership techniques universal or culture based?

CROSS-CULTURAL RESEARCH ON MOTIVATION

Motivation is very much a function of the context of a person's work and personal life. That context is greatly influenced by cultural variables, which affect the attitudes and behaviors of individuals (and groups) on the job. The framework of this context was described in Chapter 3 and illustrated in Exhibit 3-1. In applying Hofstede's research on the cultural dimensions of individualism—uncertainty avoidance, masculinity, and power distance, for example—we can make some generalized assumptions about motivation, such as the following:

- High uncertainty avoidance suggests the need for job security, whereas people with low uncertainty avoidance would probably be motivated by more risky opportunities for variety and fast-track advancement.
- High power distance suggests motivators in the relationship between subordinates and a boss, whereas low power distance implies that people would be more motivated by teamwork and relations with peers.
- High individualism suggests people would be motivated by opportunities for individual advancement and autonomy; collectivism (low individualism) suggests that motivation will more likely work through appeals to group goals and support.
- High masculinity suggests that most people would be more comfortable with the traditional division of work and roles; in a more feminine culture, the boundaries could be looser, motivating people through more flexible roles and work networks.

Misjudging the importance of these cultural variables in the workplace may result not only in a failure to motivate but also in demotivation. Rieger and Wong-Rieger present the following example:

> *In Thailand, the introduction of an individual merit bonus plan, which runs counter to the societal norm of group cooperation, may result in a decline rather than an increase in productivity from employees who refuse to openly compete with each other.*[2]

In considering what motivates people, we have to understand their needs, goals, value systems, and expectations. No matter what their nationality or cultural background, people are driven to fulfill needs and to achieve goals. But what are those needs, what goals do they want to achieve, and what can motivate that drive to satisfy their goals?

The Meaning of Work

Because the focus in this text is on the needs that affect the working environment, it is important to understand first what work means to people from different backgrounds. For most people, the basic meaning of work is tied to economic necessity (money for food, housing, and so forth) for the individual and for society. However, the additional connotations of work are more subjective, especially about what work provides other than money—achievement, honor, social contacts, and so on.

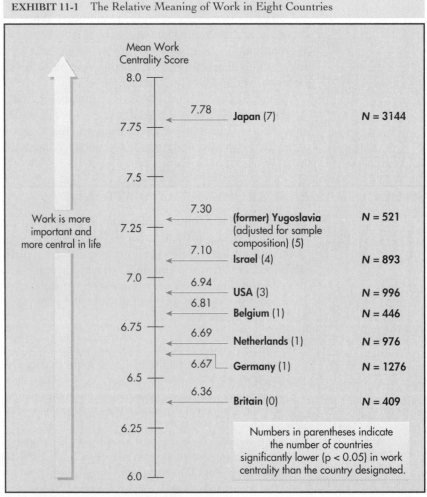

EXHIBIT 11-1   The Relative Meaning of Work in Eight Countries

SOURCE: MOW International Research Team, *The Meaning of Working: An International Perspective* (London: Academic Press, 1985).

Another way to view work, however, is through its relationship to the rest of a person's life. The Thais call work *ngan,* which is the same as the Thai word for "play," and they tend to introduce periods of play in their workdays. On the other hand, most people in China, Germany, and the United States have a more serious attitude toward work. Especially in work-oriented China, seven-day work weeks with long hours and few days off are common. A study of average work hours in various countries conducted by Steers found that Koreans worked longer hours and took fewer vacation days than workers in Thailand, Hong Kong, Taiwan, Singapore, India, Japan, and Indonesia.[3] The study concluded that the Koreans' hard work was attributable to loyalty to the company, group-oriented achievement, and emphasis on group harmony and business relationships.

Studies on the meaning of work in eight countries were carried out by George England and a group of researchers who are called the Meaning of Work (MOW) International Research Team.[4] Their research sought to determine a person's idea of the relative importance of work compared to that of leisure, community, religion, and family. They called this concept of work **work centrality**, defined as "the degree of general importance that working has in the life of an individual at any given point in time." The mean score on the work centrality index for the eight countries studied is shown in Exhibit 11-1. Clearly the Japanese hold work to be very important in their lives.

The obvious general implication from these findings is that the higher the mean work centrality score, the more motivated and committed the workers will be. Of even more importance to managers (as an aid to understanding culture-based differences in motivation) are the specific reasons for valuing work. What kinds of needs does the working environment satisfy, and how does that psychological contract differ among populations?

The MOW research team provided some excellent insights into this question when it asked people in the eight countries to what extent they regarded work as satisfying six different functions: Work (1) provides a needed income, (2) is interesting and satisfying, (3) provides contacts with others, (4) facilitates a way to serve society, (5) keeps one occupied, and (6) gives status and prestige. The results are shown in Exhibit 11-2. Note the similarities of some of these functions with Maslow's need categories and Herzberg's categories of motivators and maintenance factors. Clearly, these studies can help international

EXHIBIT 11-2   The Perceived Utility of the Functions of Work (Mean Number of Points)

Country	N	Working provides you with an income that is needed	Working is basically interesting and satisfying to you	Working permits you to have interesting contacts with other people	Working is a useful way for you to serve society	Working keeps you occupied	Working gives you status and prestige
Japan	3,180	45.4	13.4	14.7	9.3	11.5*	5.6‡
Germany	1,264	40.5	16.7	13.1	7.4	11.8	10.1
Belgium	447	35.5	21.3	17.3	10.2	8.7	6.9
Britain	471	34.4	17.9	15.3	10.5	11.0	10.9
Yugoslavia	522	34.1	19.8	9.8	15.1	11.7	9.3
United States	989	33.1	16.8	15.3	11.5	11.3	11.9
Israel	940	31.1	26.2	11.1	13.6	9.4	8.5
Netherlands	979	26.2	23.5	17.9	16.7	10.6	4.9
All countries combined	8,792	35.0†	19.5	14.3	11.8	10.8	8.5

*Working keeps you occupied was translated in Japan in such a manner that there is real question about how similar its meaning was to that intended.

†The combined totals weight each country equally regardless of sample size.

‡The mean points assigned by a country to the six functions add to approximately 100 points.

SOURCE: Meaning of Work International Research Team, *The Meaning of Working: An International Perspective* (London: Academic Press, 1985).

managers to anticipate what attitudes people have toward their work, what aspects of work in their life context are meaningful to them, and therefore what approach the manager should take in setting up motivation and incentive plans.

In addition to the differences among countries within each category—such as the higher level of interest and satisfaction derived from work by the Israelis as compared with the Germans—it is interesting to note the within-country differences. Although income was the most important factor for all countries, it apparently has a far greater importance than any other factor in Japan. In other countries, such as the Netherlands, the relative importance of different factors was more evenly distributed.

The broader implications of such comparisons about what work means to people are derived from considering the total cultural context. The low rating given by the Japanese to the status and prestige found in work, for instance, suggests that those needs are more fully satisfied elsewhere in their lives, such as within the family and community. In the Middle East, religion plays a major role in all aspects of life, including work. The Islamic work ethic is a commitment toward fulfillment, and so business motives are held in the highest regard.[5] The origin of the Islamic work ethic is in the Muslim holy book, the Qur'an, and the words of the Prophet Mohammed:

> *On the day of judgment, the honest Muslim merchant will stand side by side with the martyrs.*
>
> MOHAMMED

Muslims feel that work is a virtue and an obligation to establish equilibrium in one's individual and social life. The Arab worker is defined by his or her level of commitment to family, and work is perceived as the determining factor in the ability to enjoy social and family life.[6] A study of 117 managers in Saudi Arabia by Ali found that Arab managers are highly committed to the Islamic work ethic and that there is a moderate tendency toward individualism.[7]

Exhibit 11-3 shows the results of the study and gives more insight into the Islamic work ethic. Another study by Kuroda and Suzuki found that Arabs are serious about their work and that favoritism, give-and-take, and paternalism have no place in the Arab workplace. They contrasted this attitude to that of the Japanese and Americans, who consider friendship to be an integral part of the workplace.[8]

Other variables affect the perceived meaning of work and how it satisfies various needs, such as the relative wealth of a country.[9] When people have a high standard of living, work can take on a meaning different from simply providing the basic economic necessities of life. Economic differences among countries were found to explain variations in attitudes toward work in a study by Furnham et al. of over 12,000 young people from 41 countries on all five continents. Specifically, the researchers found that young people in Far East and Middle Eastern countries reported the highest competitiveness and acquisitiveness for money, while those from North America and South America scored highest on work ethics and "mastery" (that is, continuing to struggle to master something).[10] Such studies show the complexity of the underlying reasons for differences in attitudes toward work—cultural, economic, and so on—which must be taken into account when considering what needs and motivations people bring to the workplace. All in all, research shows a considerable cultural variability affecting how work meets employees' needs.

The Needs Hierarchy in the International Context

How can a manager know what motivates people in a specific country? Certainly, by drawing on the experiences of others who have worked there and also by inferring the likely type of motivational structure present by studying what is known about the culture in that region. In addition, some research and comparative studies about needs in specific countries are available and can provide another piece of the puzzle.

Some researchers have used Maslow's hierarchy of needs to study motivation in other countries. A classic study by Haire, Ghiselli, and Porter surveyed 3,641 managers in

EXHIBIT 11-3   The Islamic Work Ethic: Responses by Saudi Arabian Managers

Item	Mean*
Islamic Work Ethic	
1. Laziness is a vice.	4.66
2. Dedication to work is a virtue.	4.62
3. Good work benefits both one's self and others.	4.57
4. Justice and generosity in the workplace are necessary conditions for society's welfare.	4.59
5. Producing more than enough to meet one's personal needs contributes to the prosperity of society as a whole.	3.71
6. One should carry work out to the best of one's ability.	4.70
7. Work is not an end in itself but a means to foster personal growth and social relations.	3.97
8. Life has no meaning without work.	4.47
9. More leisure time is good for society.	3.08
10. Human relations in organizations should be emphasized and encouraged.	3.89
11. Work enables man to control nature.	4.06
12. Creative work is a source of happiness and accomplishment.	4.60
13. Any man who works is more likely to get ahead in life.	3.92
14. Work gives one the chance to be independent.	4.35
15. A successful man is the one who meets deadlines at work.	4.17
16. One should constantly work hard to meet responsibilities.	4.25
17. The value of work is derived from the accompanying intention rather than its results.	3.16

*On scale of 1–5 (5 highest)

SOURCE: Adapted from Abbas J. Ali, "The Islamic Work Ethic in Arabia," *Journal of Psychology* 126 (5) (1992): 507–519 (513).

14 countries. They concluded that Maslow's needs, in particular the upper level ones, are important at the managerial level, although the managers reported that the degree to which their needs were fulfilled did not live up to their expectations.[11]

In a similar study, Ronen investigated whether work-related values and needs are similar across nationalities and whether the motivation categories of Maslow and Herzberg apply universally. Studying trained, nonmanagerial male employees (in Germany, Canada, France, Japan, and the United Kingdom), he found that such similarities do exist and that there are common clusters of needs and goals across nationalities. These clusters include (1) job goals, such as working area, work time, physical working conditions, fringe benefits, and job security; (2) relationships with co-workers and supervisors; and (3) work challenges and opportunities for using skills.[12] Ronen concludes that need clusters are constant across nationalities and that Maslow's need hierarchy is confirmed by those clusters. In addition, he claims that Herzberg's categories are confirmed by the cross-national need clusters in his study.

People's opinions of how best to satisfy their needs vary across cultures also. As shown in Exhibit 11-4, priorities vary regarding sources of job-related satisfaction. For example, China, Israel, and Korea gave the highest score to "achievement" as satisfying self-actualization needs, whereas the first choice was an "interesting job" for Germany, Holland, and the United States.

One clear conclusion is that managers around the world have similar needs but show differing levels of satisfaction of those needs derived from their jobs. Variables other than culture may be at play, however. One of these variables may be the country's stage of economic development. With regard to the transitioning economy in Russia, for example, a study by Elenkov found that Russian managers stress security and belongingness needs as opposed to higher-order needs.[13] Whatever the reason, many companies that have started operations in other countries have experienced differences in the apparent needs of the local employees and how they expect work to be recognized. Mazda, of Japan, experienced this problem in its Michigan plant. Japanese firms tend to confer recognition in the form of plaques, attention, and applause, and Japanese workers are likely to be insulted by material incentives because such rewards imply that they would work harder to achieve them than

EXHIBIT 11-4   Comparative Job Motivational Components

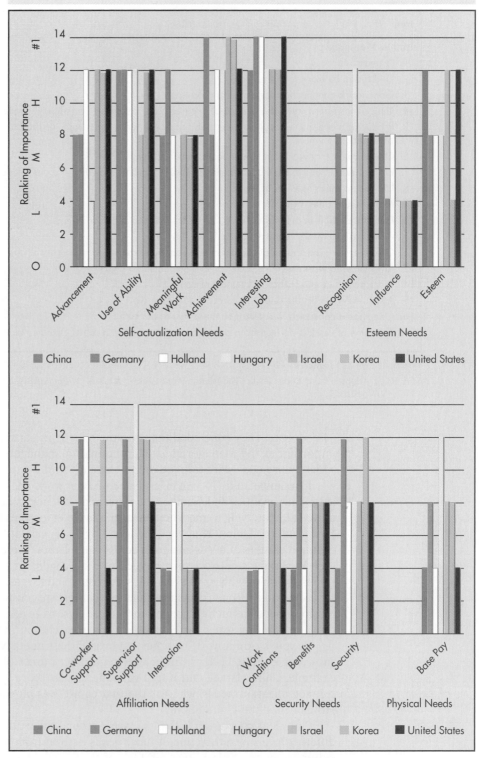

SOURCE: Adapted from data from D. Elizur, L. Borg, R. Hunt, and L. M. Beck, "The Structure of Work Values: A Cross-Cultural Comparison," *Journal of Organizational Behavior* 12 (1991): 21–28.

they otherwise would. Instead, Japanese firms focus on groupwide or companywide goals, compared with the American emphasis on individual goals, achievement, and reward.

When considering the cross-cultural applicability of Maslow's theory, then, it is not the needs that are in question as much as the ordering of those needs in the hierarchy. The hierarchy reflects the Western culture where Maslow conducted his study, and different hierarchies might better reflect other cultures. For example, Eastern cultures focus on the needs of society rather than on the needs of individuals. Nevis proposes that a hierarchy more accurately reflecting the needs of the Chinese would comprise four levels: (1) belonging, (2) physiological needs, (3) safety, and (4) self-actualization in the service of society.[14] It is difficult to observe or measure the individual needs of a Chinese person because, from childhood, these are intermeshed with the needs of society. Clearly, however, along with culture, the political beliefs at work in China dominate many facets of motivation. As the backbone of the industrial system, cadres (managers and technicians) and workers are given exact and detailed prescriptions of what is expected of them as members of a factory, workshop, or work unit. This results in conformity at the expense of creativity. Workers are accountable to their group, which is a powerful motivator. Because being "unemployed" is not an option in China, it is important for employees to maintain themselves as cooperating members of the work group.[15] Money is also a motivator, stemming from the historical political insecurity and economic disasters that have perpetuated the need for a high level of savings.[16] A Gallup opinion poll cited in the 1998 *World Competitiveness Yearbook* found that a priority among Chinese is to "work hard and get rich," compared to Europeans and Americans, who value self-achievement over wealth.[17]

The Intrinsic–Extrinsic Dichotomy in the International Context

The intrinsic–extrinsic dichotomy is another useful model (researched by a number of authors) for considering motivation in the workplace. Herzberg's research, for example, found two sets of needs: (1) motivational factors (intrinsic) and (2) maintenance factors (extrinsic).

Results from others' research using Herzberg's model provide some insight into motivation in different countries and help us to determine whether the intrinsic–extrinsic dichotomy is generalizable across cultures. Research on managers in Greece and on workers in general in an Israeli kibbutz indicate that all these people are motivated more by the nature of the work itself; dissatisfactions resulted from the conditions surrounding the work.[18] Another study in Zambia generally found the same dichotomy. Work motivation was found to result from the intrinsic factors of the opportunity for growth and the nature of the work and, to some extent, physical provisions. Factors that produced dissatisfaction and were not motivators were extrinsic—relations with others, fairness in organizational practices, and personal problems.[19]

In addition to research on single countries, Herzberg's theory has been used to compare different countries on the basis of job factors and job satisfaction. A study of MBA candidates from the United States, Australia, Canada, and Singapore, for example, indicated that Herzberg's motivational factors were more important to these prospective managers than hygiene factors.[20] In a broader study of managers from Canada, the United Kingdom, France, and Japan to determine the relative importance of job factors to them and how satisfied they were with those factors, Kanungo and Wright drew a number of interesting conclusions. Interpreting their results, we can draw some overall conclusions: The managers indicated that internally mediated factors (intrinsic, job content factors) were more important than organizationally controlled factors (extrinsic, job context factors). However, they found differences across countries, in particular between the United Kingdom and France, in how much importance the managers placed on job outcomes and also in their relative levels of satisfaction with those outcomes.[21] As a practical application of their research results, Kanungo and Wright suggest the following implications for motivation in the workplace:

> *Efforts to improve managerial performance in the UK should focus on job content rather than on job context. . . . Job enrichment programs are more likely to improve performance in an intrinsically oriented society such as Britain, where satisfaction tends to be derived from the job itself, than in France, where job context factors, such as security and fringe benefits, are more highly valued.[22]*

To answer common questions about whether Japanese-style management practices—work groups, quality circles, and long-term employment—make a difference to commitment and job satisfaction, Lincoln studied 8,302 workers in 106 factories in the United States and Japan (though not specifically using Herzberg's factors). He concluded that those practices had similar positive or negative effects on work attitudes in both countries. However, while the level of commitment to the company was essentially the same in both samples, the Japanese indicated a lower level of job satisfaction.[23]

The lower level of satisfaction is contrary to popular expectations because of the well-known Japanese environment of teamwork, productivity, long-term employment, and dedication to the company. However, previous research has also found a lower level of job satisfaction in Japan.[24] Lower work satisfaction indicates a higher level of motivation to fulfill personal and company goals (that is, to do better), compared to a lower level of motivation indicated by complacency. As Lincoln points out, however, these research findings could be the result of another cultural variable introducing a measurement bias: The Japanese tendency to "color their evaluations of nearly everything with a large dose of pessimism, humility and understatement" in their persistent quest to do better.[25] This underscores the need to consider carefully all the cultural variables involved in observing or managing motivation.

Although more cross-cultural research on motivation is needed, one can draw the tentative conclusion that managers around the world are motivated more by intrinsic than by extrinsic factors. Considerable doubt remains, however, about the universality of Herzberg's or Maslow's theories because it is not possible to take into account all of the relevant cultural variables when researching motivation. Different factors have different meanings within the entire cultural context and must be considered on a situation-by-situation basis. The need to consider the entire national and cultural context is shown in the Comparative Management in Focus: Motivation in Mexico, which highlights motivational issues for Mexican workers and indicates the importance to them of what Herzberg calls maintenance factors. As you read, consider whether this situation supports or refutes Herzberg's theory.

Comparative Management in Focus

Motivation in Mexico

In Mexico, everything is a personal matter; but a lot of managers don't get it. To get anything done here, the manager has to be more of an instructor, teacher, or father figure than a boss.

ROBERT HOSKINS,
Manager, Leviton Manufacturing, Juarez

It is particularly important for an aspiring international manager to become familiar with Mexican factory workers because of the increasing volume of manufacturing that is being outsourced there.[26]

To understand the cultural milieu in Mexico, we can draw on research that concludes that Latin American societies, including Mexico, rank high on power distance (the acknowledgment of hierarchical authority) and on uncertainty avoidance (a preference for security and formality over risk). In addition, they rank low on individualism, preferring collectivism, which values the good of the group, family, or country over individual achievement.[27] In Mexico, the family is of central importance; loyalty and commitment to family and friends frequently determine employment, promotion, or special treatment for contracts. Unfortunately, it is this admirable cultural norm that often results in motivation and productivity problems on the job by contributing to very high absenteeism and turnover, especially in the *maquiladoras*. This high turnover and absenteeism are costly to employers, thereby offsetting the advantage of relatively low labor cost per hour. "Family reasons" (taking care of sick relatives or elderly parents) are the most common reasons given for absenteeism and for failing to return to work.[28] Workers often simply do not come back to work after vacations or holidays. For many Mexican males, the value of work lies primarily in its ability to fulfill their culturally imposed responsibilities as head of household and breadwinner rather than to seek individual achievement.[29] Machismo (sharp role differentiation based on gender) and prestige are important characteristics of the Mexican culture.

As a people, speaking very generally, Mexicans are very proud and patriotic; *respeto* (respect) is important to them, and a slight against personal dignity is regarded as a grave provocation.[30] Mexican workers expect to be treated in the same respectful manner that they use toward one another. As noted by one U.S. expatriate, foreign managers must adapt to Mexico's "softer culture"; Mexican workers "need more communication, more relationship-building, and more reassurance than employees in the U.S."[31] The Mexican people are very warm and have a leisurely attitude toward time; face-to-face interaction is best for any kind of business, with time allowed for socializing and appreciating the Mexicans' cultural artifacts, buildings, and so forth. Taking time to celebrate a worker's birthday, for instance, will show that you are a *simpático* boss and will increase workers' loyalty and effort. The workers' expectations of small considerations that seem inconsequential to U.S. managers should not be discounted. In one *maquiladora,* when the company stopped providing the annual Halloween candy, the employees filed a grievance to the state Arbitration Board—Junta de Conciliación y Arbitraje.

Most managers in Mexico find that the management style that works best there is authoritative and paternal. Paternalism is expected; the manager is regarded as *el patrón* (pronounced pah-trone), or the father figure, whose role it is to take care of the workers as an extended family.[32] Employees expect managers to be the authority; they are the "elite"—power rests with the owner or manager and other prominent community leaders. For the most part, if not told to do something, the workers will not do it, nor will they question the boss or make any decisions for the boss.[33] Nevertheless, employees perceive the manager as a person, not as a concept or a function, and success often depends on the ability of a foreign manager to adopt a personalized management style, such as by greeting all workers as they arrive for their shifts.

Generally speaking, many Mexican factory workers doubt their ability to personally influence the outcome of their lives. They are apt to attribute events to the will of God, or to luck, timing, or relationships with higher authority figures. For many, decisions are made on the basis of ideals, emotions, and intuition rather than objective information. However, individualism and materialism are increasingly evident, particularly among the upwardly mobile high-tech and professional Mexican employees.

Corrective discipline and motivation must occur through training examples, cooperation, and, if necessary, subtle shaming. As a disciplinary measure, it is a mistake to directly insult a Mexican; an outright insult implies an insult to the whole family. As a motivation, one must appeal to the pride of the Mexican employees and avoid causing them to feel humiliated. Given that, "getting ahead" is often associated more with outside forces than with one's own actions; the motivation and reward system becomes difficult to structure in the usual ways. Past experiences have indicated that, for the most part, motivation through participative decision making is not as effective as motivation through the more traditional and expected autocratic methods. With careful implementation, however, the mutual respect and caring that the Mexican people have for one another can lead to the positive team spirit needed for the team structure to be used successfully by companies, such as GM in its highest-quality plant in the world in Ramos Arizpe, near Saltillo, Mexico.[34] Although a study by Nicholls, Lane, and Brechu concluded cultural constraints are considerable when it comes to using self-managing teams in Mexico, the Mexican executives surveyed suggested that the relative success depends on the implementation. The conflicts are between the norms of behavior in self-managed teams typical of U.S. and Canadian culture (such as initiative and self-leadership, bottom-up decision making), and typical values in Mexican business culture (such as resistance to change, adherence to status roles, and top-down hierarchical structure). These differences in work-role norms seem to create a behavioral impasse, at least initially, when it comes to the potential for setting up self-managed teams.[35]

Although self-managed teams require individual leaders to take risks by spearheading team initiatives, those behaviors, according to the survey of Mexican executives, "are in sharp contrast to the behavioral norms of the paternalistic and hierarchical tradition of managers and workers in the Mexican work place." The workers expect the managers to give instructions and make decisions.[36] The business culture in Mexico is also attributable to prevailing economic conditions in Mexico of low levels of education, training, and technical skills. The Mexican executives surveyed gave some suggestions for implementing work teams and cautioned that the process of implementation will take a long time. They suggested the following:

- Foster a culture of individual responsibility among team members.
- Anticipate the impact of changes in power distribution.
- Provide leadership from the top throughout the implementation process.
- Provide adequate training to prepare workers for teamwork.
- Develop motivation and harmony through clear expectations.
- Encourage an environment of shared responsibility.[37]

For the most part, Mexican workers expect that authority will not be abused but rather that it will follow the family model in which everyone works together in a dignified manner according to their designated roles.[38] Any event that may break this harmony, or seems to confront authority, will likely be covered up. This may result in a supervisor hiding defective work, for example, or, as in the case of a steel conveyor plant in Puebla, a total worker walkout rather than using the grievance process.[39] Contributing to these kinds of problems is the need to save face for oneself and to respect others' place and honor. Public criticism is regarded as humiliating. Employees like an atmosphere of formality and respect. They typically use flattery and call people by their titles rather than their names to maintain an atmosphere of regard for status and respect.

A context of continuing economic problems and a relatively low standard of living for most workers help explain why Maslow's higher-order needs (self-actualization, achievement, status) are generally not very high on most Mexican workers' lists of needs. In discussing compensation, Mariah de Forest, who consults for American firms in Mexico, suggests the following:

> *Rather than an impersonal wage scale, Mexican workers tend to think in terms of payment now for services rendered now. A daily incentive system with automatic payouts for production exceeding quotas, as well as daily/monthly attendance bonuses, works well.*[40]

As a result of economic reforms and the peso devaluation, money is now a pressing motivational factor for most employees. Since workers highly value the enjoyment of life, many companies in Mexico provide recreation facilities—a picnic area, a soccer field, and so forth. Bonuses are expected regardless of productivity. In fact, it is the law to give Christmas bonuses of 15 days of pay to each worker. Fringe benefits are also important to Mexicans; because most Mexican workers are poor, the company provides the only source of such benefits for them. In particular, benefits that help to manage family-related issues are positive motivators for employees at least to turn up for work. To this end, companies often provide on-site health care facilities for workers and their families, nurseries, free meals, and even small loans in crisis situations.[41] In addition, those companies that understand the local infrastructure problems often provide a company bus to minimize the pervasive problems of absenteeism and tardiness.

The foregoing statements are broad generalizations about Mexican factory workers. Increasing numbers of American managers are in Mexico because the NAFTA has encouraged more U.S. businesses to move operations there. For firms on U.S. soil, managers may employ many Mexican-Americans in an intercultural setting. As the second-largest and fastest-growing ethnic group in the United States, Mexican-Americans represent an important subculture requiring management attention as they take an increasing proportion of the jobs there. Yet, they remain the least assimilated ethnic group in the majority mainstream, partially from economic or occupational causes and partially from choice.[42]

Research shows that little conclusive information is available to answer a manager's direct question of exactly how to motivate in any particular culture. The reason is that we cannot assume the universal applicability of the motivational theories, or even concepts, that have been used to research differences among cultures. Furthermore, the entire motivational context must be taken into account. For example, Western firms entering markets in Eastern Europe invariably run into difficulties in motivating their local staffs. Those workers have been accustomed to working under entirely different circumstances and usually do not trust foreign managers. Typically, then, the work systems and responsibilities must be highly structured because workers in Eastern Europe are not likely to use their own judgment in making decisions and because managerial skills are not developed.[43]

A principal rule in the [Russian] workplace is "Superiors know better."

SNEJINA MICHAILOVA[44]

A study by Michailova found that most Russian employees are still used to the management style that prevailed in a centrally planned economic system. This context resulted in vertically managed hierarchies, one-man authority, and anti-individualism. The employees in the study experienced conflict when faced with different managerial styles from their Russian and Western managers in joint venture situations. Those employees were in traditional industries, were on average 45 years old, and were more motivated by the authoritarianism of their Russian managers than the attempts at empowerment by their Western managers. More importantly, the conflicting motivational techniques left them in a "double bind," as shown in Exhibit 11-5.

In sum, motivation is situational, and savvy managers use all they know about the relevant culture or subculture—consulting frequently with local people—to infer the best means of motivating in that context. Furthermore, tactful managers consciously avoid an ethnocentric attitude in which they make assumptions about a person's goals, motivation, or work habits based on their own frames of reference, and they do not make negative value judgments about a person's level of motivation because it differs from their own.

Many cultural variables affect people's sense of what is attainable, and thus affect motivation. How much control people believe they have over their environment and their destiny—whether they believe that they can control certain events, and not just be at the mercy of external forces—is one example. Although Americans typically feel a strong internal locus of control, others attribute results to, for example, the will of God (in the case of Muslims) or to the good fortune of being born in the right social class or family (in the case of many Latin Americans). For example, whereas Americans feel that hard work will get the job done, many Hong Kong Chinese believe that outcomes are determined by *joss,* or luck. Clearly, then, managers must use persuasive strategies to motivate employees when they do not readily connect their personal work behaviors with outcomes or productivity.

EXHIBIT 11-5   Conflicting Motivational Techniques in Western–Russian Joint Ventures

Western Managers to Russian Employees	Russian Managers to Russian Employees
Take initiative and come with suggestions	Do what you are supposed to do and obey the established rules
Learn from the mistakes and don't repeat them	Mistakes are not allowed and should be punished
Be longer term and future oriented	Concentrate on here and now (and don't forget how it was before)
Think of the company as an integrated entity	Act according to your own job description and don't interfere in other people's job

SOURCE: Reprinted from S. Michailova, "When Common Sense Becomes Uncommon: Participation and Empowerment in Russian Companies with Western Participation," *Journal of World Business* 37 (2002) 180–187, with permission from Elsevier.

EXHIBIT 11-6 The Role of Culture in Job Motivation

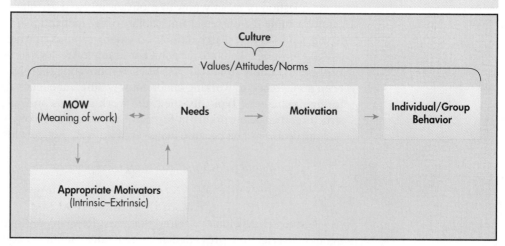

The role of culture in the motivational process is shown in Exhibit 11-6. An employee's needs are determined largely by the cultural context of values and attitudes—along with the national variables—in which he or she lives and works. Those needs then determine the meaning of work for that employee. The manager's understanding of what work means in that employee's life can then lead to the design of a culturally appropriate job context and reward system to guide individual and group employee job behavior to meet mutual goals.

Reward Systems

Incentives and rewards are an integral part of motivation in a corporation. Recognizing and understanding different motivational patterns across cultures leads to the design of appropriate reward systems. In the United States, there are common patterns of rewards, varying among levels of the company and types of occupations and based on experience and research with Americans. Rewards usually fall into five categories: financial, social status, job content, career, and professional.[45] The relative emphasis on one or more of these five categories varies from country to country. In Japan, for example, reward systems are based primarily on seniority, and much emphasis is put on the bonus system. In addition, distinction is made there between the regular workforce and the temporary workforce, which usually comprises women expected to leave when they start a family. As is usually the case, the regular workforce receives considerably more rewards than the temporary workforce in pay and benefits and the allocation of interesting jobs.[46] For the regular workforce, the emphasis is on the employee's long-term effectiveness in terms of behavior, personality, and group output. Rewarding the individual is frowned on in Japan because it encourages competition rather than the desired group cooperation. Therefore, specific cash incentives are usually limited. In Taiwan, recognition and affection are important; company departments compete for praise from top management at their annual celebration.

In contrast, the entire reward system in China is very different from that of most countries. The low wage rates are compensated for by free housing, schools, and medical care. While egalitarianism still seems to prevail, the recent free-enterprise reform movements have encouraged *duo lao, duo de* ("more work, more pay"). One important incentive is training, which gives workers more power. One approach used in the past—and one that seems quite negative to Americans—is best illustrated by the example of a plaque award labeled "Ms. Wong—Employee of the Month." While Westerners would assume that Ms. Wong had excelled as an employee, actually this award given in a Chinese retail store was for the worst employee; the plaque was designed to shame and embarrass her.[47] Younger Chinese in areas changing to a more market-based economy have seen a shift toward equity-based rewards, no doubt resulting from a gradual shift in work values.[48]

No doubt culture plays a significant role in determining the appropriate incentive and reward systems around the world. Employees in collectivist cultures such as Japan, Korea, and Taiwan would not respond well to the typical American merit-based reward system to motivate employees because that would go against the traditional value system and would disrupt the harmony and corporate culture.

Leading

Le patron, der Chef, and the Boss.

DDI,
Leaders on Leadership Survey, 2006[49]

This section on leadership (and the above quote) prompts consideration of the following questions: To what extent, and how, do leadership styles and practices around the world vary? What are the forces perpetuating that divergence? Where, and why, will that divergence continue to be the strongest? Is there any evidence for convergence of leadership styles and practices around the world? What are the forces leading to that convergence, and how and where will this convergence occur in the future? What implications do these questions have for cross-cultural leaders?

The task of helping employees realize their highest potential in the workplace is the essence of leadership. The goal of every leader is to achieve the organization's objectives while achieving those of each employee. Today's global managers realize that increased competition requires them to be open to change and to rethink their old culturally conditioned modes of leadership.

THE GLOBAL LEADER'S ROLE AND ENVIRONMENT

The greatest competitive advantage global companies in the twenty-first century can have is effective global leaders. Yet this competitive challenge is not easy to meet. People tend to rise to leadership positions by proving themselves able to lead in their home-country corporate culture and meeting the generally accepted behaviors of that national culture. However, global leaders must broaden their horizons—both strategically and cross-culturally—and develop a more flexible model of leadership that can be applied anywhere—one that is adaptable to locational situations around the world.[50] From their recent research involving 125 global leaders in 50 companies, Morrison, Gregersen, and Black concluded that effective leaders must have global business and organizational savvy. They explain global business savvy as the ability to recognize global market opportunities for a company and having a vision of doing business worldwide. Global organizational savvy requires an intimate knowledge of a company's resources and capabilities in order to capture global markets, as well as an understanding of each subsidiary's product lines and how the people and business operate on the local level. Morrison, Gregersen, and Black outline four personal development strategies through which companies and managers can meet these requirements of effective global leadership: travel, teamwork, training, and transfers (the four "T's").[51]

Travel, of course, exposes managers to various cultures, economies, political systems, and markets. Working on global teams teaches managers to operate on an interpersonal level while dealing with business decision-making processes that are embraced by differences in cultural norms and business models. Although formal training seminars also play an important role, most of the global leaders interviewed said that the most influential developmental experience in their lives was the international assignment. Increasingly, global companies are requiring that their managers who will progress to top management positions must have overseas assignment experience.[52] The benefits accruing to the organization depend on how effectively the assignment and repatriation are handled, as discussed in Chapter 10.

Effective global leadership involves the ability to inspire and influence the thinking, attitudes, and behavior of people anywhere in the world.[53] The importance of the leadership role cannot be overemphasized because the leader's interactions strongly influence the motivation and behavior of employees, and ultimately, the entire climate of the organization. The cumulative effects of one or more weak managers can have a significant negative impact on the ability of the organization to meet its objectives.

Managers on international assignments try to maximize leadership effectiveness by juggling several important, and sometimes conflicting, roles as (1) a representative of the parent firm, (2) the manager of the local firm, (3) a resident of the local community, (4) a citizen of either the host country or of another country, (5) a member of a profession, and (6) a member of a family.[54]

The leader's role comprises the interaction of two sets of variables—the content and the context of leadership. The content of leadership comprises the attributes of the leader and the decisions to be made; the context of leadership comprises all those variables related to the particular situation.[55] The increased number of variables (political, economic, and cultural) in the context of the managerial job abroad requires astute leadership. Some of the variables in the content and context of the leader's role in foreign settings are shown in Exhibit 11-7. The multicultural leader's role thus blends leadership, communication, motivational, and other managerial skills within unique and ever-changing environments. We will examine the contingent nature of such leadership throughout this section.

The E-Business Effect on Leadership

An additional factor—technology—is becoming increasingly pervasive in its ability to influence the global leader's role and environment and will, perhaps, contribute to a lessening of the differences in motivation and leadership around the world. More and more

EXHIBIT 11-7   Factors Affecting Leadership Abroad

Content	
Attributes of the Person	**Characteristics of Decisions Situation**
Job position knowledge, experience, expectations	Degree of complexity, uncertainty, and risk
Longevity in company, country, functional area	In-country information needs and availability
Intelligence and cultural learning or change ability	Articulation of assumptions and expectations
Personality as demonstrated in values,	Scope and potential impact on performance
beliefs, attitudes toward foreign situations	Nature of business partners
Multiple memberships in work and professional groups	Authority and autonomy required
Decision and personal work style	Required level of participation and acceptance by employees, partners, and government
	Linkage to other decisions
	Past management legacy
	Openness to public scrutiny and responsibility

Context	
Attributes of the Job or Position	**Characteristics of the Firm and Business Environment**
Longevity and past success of former role occupants in the position	Firm structure: size, location, technology, tasks, reporting, and communication patterns
Technical requirements of the job	Firm process: decision making, staffing control
Relative authority or power	system, reward system, information system, means
Physical location (e.g., home office, field office)	of coordination, integration, and conflict resolution
Need for coordination, cooperation, and integration with other units	Firm outputs: products, services, public image, corporate culture, local history, and community relations
Resource availability	Business environment: social-cultural, political-economic, and technological aspects of a country or market
Foreign peer group relations	

SOURCE: R. H. Mason and R. S. Spich, *Management: An International Perspective* (Homewood, IL: Irwin, 1987), 186.

often, companies like Italtel Spa are using technology such as the intranet to share knowledge and product information throughout their global operations. In the case of Italtel, this required wide delegation and empowerment of their employees so that they could decentralize.

Individual managers are realizing that the Internet is changing their leadership styles and interactions with employees, as well as their strategic leadership of their organizations. They have to adapt to the hyperspeed environment of e-business, as well as to the need for visionary leadership in a whole new set of competitive industry dynamics. Some of these new-age leadership issues are discussed in the Management Focus: Leadership in a Digital World.

Management Focus

Leadership in a Digital World

What does leadership mean in a digital world in which organizations are flexible and fluid and the pace of change is extremely rapid? What's it like to lead in an e-business organization? Jomei Chang of Vitria Technology describes it as follows: "There's no place to hide. [The Internet] forces you to be on your toes every minute, every second." Is leadership in e-businesses really all that different from traditional organizations? Managers who've worked in both think it is. How? Three differences seem to be most evident: the speed at which decisions must be made, the importance of being flexible, and the need to create a vision of the future.

Making Decisions Fast.   Managers in all organizations never have all the data they want when making decisions, but the problem is multiplied in e-business. The situation is changing rapidly and the competition is intense. For example, Meg Whitman, president and CEO of eBay, says, "We're growing at 40 percent to 50 percent per quarter. That pace absolutely changes the leadership challenge. Every three months we become a different company. In one year, we went from 30 employees to 140, and from 100,000 registered users to 2.2 million. At Hasbro [where she was previously an executive], we would set a yearlong strategy, and then we would simply execute against it. At eBay, we constantly revisit the strategy—and revise the tactics."

Leaders in e-businesses see themselves as sprinters and their contemporaries in traditional businesses as long-distance runners. They frequently use the term "Internet time," which is a reference to a rapidly speeded-up working environment. "Every [e-business] leader today has to unlearn one lesson that was drilled into each one of them: You gather data so that you can make considered decisions. You can't do that on Internet time."

Maintaining Flexibility.   In addition to speed, leaders in e-businesses need to be highly flexible. They have to be able to roll with the ups and downs. They need to be able to redirect their group or organization when they find that something doesn't work. They have to encourage experimentation. This is what Mark Cuban, president and co-founder of Broadcast.com, had to say about the importance of being flexible. "When we started, we thought advertising would be the core of our business. We were wrong. We thought that the way to define our network was to distribute servers all over the country. We were wrong. We've had to recalibrate again and again—and we'll have to keep doing it in the future."

Focusing on the Vision.   Although visionary leadership is important in every organization, in a hyperspeed environment, people require more from their leaders. The rules, policies, and regulations that characterize more traditional organizations provide direction and reduce uncertainty for employees. Such formalized guidelines typically don't exist in e-businesses, and it becomes the responsibility of the leaders to provide direction through their vision. For instance, David Pottruck, co-CEO of Charles Schwab, gathered nearly 100 of the company's senior managers at the southern end of the Golden Gate Bridge. He handed each a jacket inscribed with the phrase "Crossing the Chasm" and led them across the bridge in a symbolic march to kick off his plan to turn Schwab into a full-fledged Internet brokerage. Getting people to buy into the vision may require even more radical actions. For instance, when Isao Okawa, chairman of Sega Enterprises, decided to remake his company into an e-business, his management team resisted—that is, until he defied Japan's consensus-charged, lifetime-employment culture by announcing that those who resisted the change would be fired, risking shame. Not so amazingly, resistance to the change vanished overnight.

SOURCE: S. P. Robbins and M. Coulter, *Management,* 7th ed. (Upper Saddle River, NJ: Prentice Hall), 2001, used with permission.

CROSS-CULTURAL RESEARCH ON LEADERSHIP

Numerous leadership theories focus in various ways on individual traits, leader behavior, interaction patterns, role relationships, follower perceptions, influence over followers, influence on task goals, and influence on organizational culture.[56] Here it is important to understand how the variable of societal culture fits into these theories and what implications can be drawn for international managers as they seek to provide leadership around the world. Although the functions of leadership are similar across cultures, anthropological studies, such as those by Margaret Mead, indicate that while leadership is a universal phenomenon, what makes effective leadership varies across cultures.[57]

In addition to research studies that indicate variations in leadership profiles, the generally accepted image that people in different countries have about what they expect and admire in their leaders tends to become a norm over time, forming an idealized role for these leaders. Industry leaders in France and Italy, for example, are highly regarded for their social prominence and political power. In Latin American countries, leaders are respected as total persons and leaders in society, with appreciation for the arts being important. In Germany, polish, decisiveness, and a wide general knowledge are respected, with their leaders granted a lot of formality by everyone. Foreigners are often surprised at the informal off-the-job lifestyles of executives in the United States and would be surprised to see them pushing a lawn mower, for example.[58]

Most research on U.S. leadership styles describes managerial behaviors on, essentially, the same dimension, variously termed *autocratic* versus *democratic, participative* versus *directive, relations-oriented* versus *task-oriented,* or *initiating structure* versus *consideration continuum.*[59] These studies were developed in the West, and conclusions regarding employee responses largely reflect the opinions of U.S. workers. The democratic, or participative, leadership style has been recommended as the one more likely to have positive results with most U.S. employees.

CONTINGENCY LEADERSHIP: THE CULTURE VARIABLE

Modern leadership theory recognizes that no single leadership style works well in all situations.[60] A considerable amount of research, directly or indirectly, supports the notion of cultural contingency in leadership. This means that, as a result of culture-based norms and beliefs about how people in various roles should behave, what is expected of leaders, what influence they have, and what kind of status they are given vary from nation to nation. Clearly, this has implications for what kind of leadership style a manager should expect to adopt when going abroad.

The GLOBE Project

Recent research by the Global Leadership and Organizational Behavior Effectiveness (GLOBE) research program comprised a network of 170 social scientists and management scholars from 62 countries for the purpose of understanding the impact of cultural variables on leadership and organizational processes. Using both quantitative and qualitative methodologies to collect data from 18,000 managers in those countries, representing the majority of the world's population, the researchers wanted to find out which leadership behaviors are universally accepted and which are culturally contingent. Not unexpectedly, they found that the positive leadership behaviors generally accepted anywhere are behaviors such as being trustworthy, encouraging, an effective bargainer, a skilled administrator and communicator, and a team builder; the negatively regarded traits included being uncooperative, egocentric, ruthless, and dictatorial.[61] Those leadership styles and behaviors found to be culturally contingent are charismatic, team-oriented, self-protective, participative, humane, and autonomous.

The results for some of those countries researched are shown in Exhibit 11-8. The first column *(N)* is the sample size within that country. The scores for each country on those leadership dimensions are based on a scale from 1 (the opinion that those leadership behaviors would not be regarded favorably) to 7 (that those behaviors would

EXHIBIT 11-8   Culturally Contingent Beliefs Regarding Effective Leadership Styles

Country	N	Charisma	Team	Self-Protective	Participative	Humane	Autonomous
Argentina	154	5.98	5.99	3.46	5.89	4.70	4.55
Australia	345	6.09	5.81	3.05	5.71	5.09	3.95
Austria	169	6.03	5.74	3.07	6.00	4.93	4.47
Brazil	264	6.01	6.17	3.50	6.06	4.84	2.27
Canada (English-speaking)	257	6.16	5.84	2.96	6.09	5.20	3.65
China	160	5.57	5.57	3.80	5.05	5.18	4.07
Denmark	327	6.01	5.70	2.82	5.80	4.23	3.79
Egypt	201	5.57	5.55	4.21	4.69	5.14	4.49
England	168	6.01	5.71	3.04	5.57	4.90	3.92
Germany [Former FRG (WEST)]	414	5.84	5.49	2.97	5.88	4.44	4.30
Germany [Former GDR (EAST)]	44	5.87	5.51	3.33	5.70	4.60	4.35
Greece	234	6.02	6.12	3.49	5.81	5.16	3.98
Hong Kong	171	5.67	5.58	3.68	4.87	4.89	4.38
Hungary	186	5.91	5.91	3.24	5.23	4.73	3.23
India	231	5.85	5.72	3.78	4.99	5.26	3.85
Indonesia	365	6.15	5.92	4.13	4.61	5.43	4.19
Ireland	157	6.08	5.82	3.01	5.64	5.06	3.95
Israel	543	6.23	5.91	3.64	4.96	4.68	4.26
Italy	269	5.99	5.87	3.26	5.47	4.37	3.62
Japan	197	5.49	5.56	3.61	5.08	4.68	3.67
Malaysia	125	5.89	5.80	3.50	5.12	5.24	4.03
Mexico	327	5.66	5.75	3.86	4.64	4.71	3.86
Netherlands	289	5.98	5.75	2.87	5.75	4.81	3.53
Nigeria	419	5.77	5.65	3.90	5.19	5.48	3.62
Philippines	287	6.33	6.06	3.33	5.40	5.53	3.75
Poland	283	5.67	5.98	3.53	5.05	4.56	4.34
Portugal	80	5.75	5.92	3.11	5.48	4.62	3.19
Russia	301	5.66	5.63	3.69	4.67	4.08	4.63
Singapore	224	5.95	5.77	3.32	5.30	5.24	3.87
South Africa (Black sample)	241	5.16	5.23	3.63	5.05	4.79	3.94
South Africa (White sample)	183	5.99	5.80	3.20	5.62	5.33	3.74
South Korea	233	5.53	5.53	3.68	4.93	4.87	4.21
Spain	370	5.90	5.93	3.39	5.11	4.66	3.54
Sweden	1,790	5.84	5.75	2.82	5.54	4.73	3.97
Switzerland (German)	321	5.93	5.61	2.93	5.94	4.76	4.13
Taiwan	237	5.58	5.69	4.28	4.73	5.35	4.01
Thailand	449	5.78	5.76	3.91	5.30	5.09	4.28
Turkey	301	5.96	6.01	3.58	5.09	4.90	3.83
USA	399	6.12	5.80	3.16	5.93	5.21	3.75
Venezuela	142	5.72	5.62	3.82	4.89	4.85	3.39

Scale 1 to 7 in order of how important those behaviors are considered for effective leadership (7 = highest).
SOURCE: Selected data from Den Hartog, R. House, et al. (GLOBE Project) *Leadership Quarterly*, 10, no. 2 (1999).

substantially facilitate effective leadership). Note that reading from top to bottom on a single dimension allows comparison among those countries on that dimension. For example, being a participative leader is regarded as more important in Canada, Brazil, and Austria than it is in Egypt, Hong Kong, Indonesia, and Mexico. In addition, reading from left to right for a particular country on all dimensions allows development of an effective leadership style profile for that country. In Brazil, for example, one can conclude that an effective leader is expected to be very charismatic, team-oriented and participative, and relatively humane but not autonomous.

The charismatic leader shown in this research is someone who is, for example, a visionary, an inspiration to subordinates, and performance-oriented. A team-oriented leader is someone who exhibits diplomatic, integrative, and collaborative behaviors toward the team. The self-protective dimension describes a leader who is self-centered, conflictual, and status conscious. The participative leader is one who delegates decision making and encourages subordinates to take responsibility. Humane leaders are those who are compassionate to their employees. An autonomous leader is, as expected, an individualist, so countries that ranked participation as important tended to rank autonomy in leadership as relatively unimportant. In Egypt, participation and autonomy were ranked about equally.[62]

This broad, path-breaking research by the GLOBE researchers can be very helpful to managers going abroad, enabling them to exercise culturally appropriate leadership styles. In another stage of this ongoing research project, interviews with managers from various countries led the researchers, headed by Robert House, to conclude that the status and influence of leaders vary a great deal across countries or regions according to the prevailing cultural forces. Whereas Americans, Arabs, Asians, the English, Eastern Europeans, the French, Germans, Latin Americans, and Russians tend to glorify leaders in both the political and organizational arenas; those in the Netherlands, Scandinavia, and Germanic Switzerland have very different views of leadership.[63] Following are some sample comments made by managers from various countries:

- Americans appreciate two kinds of leaders. They seek empowerment from leaders who grant autonomy and delegate authority to subordinates. They also respect the bold, forceful, confident, and risk-taking leader, as personified by John Wayne.
- The Dutch place emphasis on egalitarianism and are skeptical about the value of leadership. Terms like *leader* and *manager* carry a stigma. If a father is employed as a manager, Dutch children will not admit it to their schoolmates.
- Arabs worship their leaders—as long as they are in power!
- Iranians seek power and strength in their leaders.
- Malaysians expect their leaders to behave in a manner that is humble, modest, and dignified.
- The French expect leaders to be "cultivated"—highly educated in the arts and in mathematics.[64]

Subsequently, further conclusions were drawn from the GLOBE results by Javidan et al. as to which leadership variables are found to be universally effective, which are found to be universal impediments to effectiveness, and which are considered to be culturally contingent attributes. Their findings are listed in Exhibit 11-9, with the corresponding GLOBE dimension in parentheses.

Other research also provides insight on the relative level of preference for autocratic versus participative leadership styles. For example, Hofstede's four cultural dimensions (discussed in Chapter 3) provide a good starting point to study leader–subordinate expectations and relationships. We can assume, for example, that employees in countries that rank high on power distance (India, Mexico, the Philippines) are more likely to prefer an autocratic leadership style and some paternalism because they are more comfortable with a clear distinction between managers and subordinates rather than with a blurring of decision-making responsibility.

Employees in countries that rank low on power distance (Sweden and Israel) are more likely to prefer a consultative, participative leadership style, and they expect superiors to adhere to that style. Hofstede, in fact, concludes that participative management approaches recommended by many American researchers can be counterproductive in certain cultures.[65] The crucial fact to grasp about leadership in any culture, he points out,

EXHIBIT 11-9   Cultural Views of Leadership Effectiveness

Behaviors and Traits Universally Considered Facilitators of Leadership Effectiveness

- Trustworthiness (integrity)
- Visionary (charismatic–visionary)
- Inspirational and motivating (charismatic–inspirational)
- Communicative (team builder)

Behaviors and Traits Universally Considered Impediments to Leadership Effectiveness

- Being a loner and asocial (self-protective)
- Non-cooperative (malevolent)
- Dictatorial (autocratic)

Culturally Contingent Endorsement of Leader Attributes

- Individualistic (autonomous)
- Status-conscious (status-conscious)
- Risk-taking (charismatic III: self-sacrificial)

SOURCE: Adapted from Mansour Javidan; Peter W Dorfman; Mary Sully de Luque; Robert J House, "In the Eye of the Beholder: Cross Cultural Lessons in Leadership from Project GLOBE," *The Academy of Management Perspectives,* vol. 20, no. 1, 2006, p. 75.

EXHIBIT 11-10   Subordinateship for Three Levels of Power Distance

Small Power Distance	Medium Power Distance (United States)	Large Power Distance
Subordinates have weak dependence needs.	Subordinates have medium dependence needs.	Subordinates have strong dependence needs.
Superiors have weak dependence needs toward their superiors.	Superiors have medium dependence needs toward their superiors.	Superiors have strong dependence needs toward their superiors.
Subordinates expect superiors to consult them and may rebel or strike if superiors are not seen as staying within their legitimate role.	Subordinates expect superiors to consult them but will accept autocratic behavior as well.	Subordinates expect superiors to act autocratically.
Ideal superior to most is a loyal democrat.	Ideal superior to most is a resourceful democrat.	Ideal superior to most is a benevolent autocrat or paternalist.
Laws and rules apply to all, and privileges for superiors are not considered acceptable.	Laws and rules apply to all, but a certain level of privilege for superiors is considered normal.	Everybody expects superiors to enjoy privileges; laws and rules differ for superiors and subordinates.
Status symbols are frowned upon and will easily come under attack from subordinates.	Status symbols for superiors contribute moderately to their authority and will be accepted by subordinates.	State symbols are very important and contribute strongly to the superior's authority with the subordinates.

SOURCE: Reprinted from *Organizational Dynamics* (Summer 1980): 42–63. Geert Hofstede, "Motivation, Leadership, and Organization: Do American Theories Apply Abroad?" Copyright 1980, with permission from Elsevier.

is that it is a complement to subordinateship (employee attitudes toward leaders). In other words, perhaps we concentrate too much on leaders and their unlikely ability to change styles at will. Much depends on subordinates and their cultural conditioning, and it is that subordinateship to which the leader must respond.[66] Hofstede points out that his research reflects the values of subordinates, not the values of superiors. His descriptions of the types of subordinateship a leader can expect in societies with three different levels of power distance are shown in Exhibit 11-10.

In another part of his research, Hofstede ranked the relative presence of autocratic norms in the following countries, from lowest to highest: Germany, France, Belgium, Japan, Italy, the United States, the Netherlands, Britain, and India. India ranked much higher than the others on autocracy.[67]

Expectations about managerial authority versus participation were also among the managerial behaviors and philosophies studied by Laurent, a French researcher. In a study conducted in nine Western European countries, the United States, Indonesia, and Japan, he concluded that national origin significantly affects the perception of what is effective management.[68] For example, Americans and Germans subscribe more to participation than do Italians and Japanese; Indonesians are more comfortable with a strict autocratic structure. Managers in Sweden, the Netherlands, the United States, Denmark, and Great Britain believe that employees should participate in problem solving rather than simply be "fed" all the answers by managers, compared with managers in those countries on the higher end of this scale, such as Italy, Indonesia, and Japan. Laurent's findings about Japan, however, seem to contradict common knowledge about Japan's very participative decision-making culture. In fact, research by Hampden-Turner and Trompenaars places Japan as second highest, after Sweden, in the extent to which leaders delegate authority.[69] Findings regarding the other countries are similar—shown in Exhibit 11-11. However, participative leadership should not mean a lack of initiative or responsibility.

Other classic studies indicate cross-cultural differences in the expectations of leadership behavior. Haire, Ghiselli, and Porter surveyed more than 3,000 managers in 14 countries. They found that, although managers around the world consistently favored delegation and participation, those managers also had a low appreciation of the capacity and willingness of subordinates to take an active role in the management process.[70]

EXHIBIT 11-11 Comparative Leadership Dimensions: Participation and Initiative

Managerial Initiative, Managers' Sense of Drive and Responsibility		Extent to Which Leaders Delegate Authority	
0 = low; 100 = high		0 = low; 100 = high	
USA	73.67	Sweden	75.51
Sweden	72.29	Japan	69.27
Japan	72.20	Norway	68.50
Finland	69.58	USA	66.23
Korea	67.86	Singapore	65.37
Netherlands	67.11	Denmark	64.65
Singapore	66.34	Canada	64.38
Switzerland	65.71	Finland	62.92
Belgium/Lux	65.47	Switzerland	62.20
Ireland	64.76	Netherlands	61.33
France	64.64	Australia	61.22
Austria	62.56	Germany	60.85
Denmark	62.79	New Zealand	60.54
Italy	62.40	Ireland	59.53
Australia	62.04	UK	58.95
Canada	61.56	Belgium/Lux	54.55
Spain	61.55	Austria	54.29
New Zealand	59.46	France	53.62
Greece	58.50	Italy	46.80
UK	58.25	Spain	44.31
Norway	54.50	Portugal	42.56
Portugal	49.74	Greece	37.95

SOURCE: C. Hampden-Turner and A. Trompenaars, *The Seven Cultures of Capitalism* (New York: Doubleday, 1993).

In addition, several studies of individual countries or areas conclude that a participative leadership style is frequently inappropriate. Managers in Malaysia, Indonesia, Thailand, and the Philippines were found to prefer autocratic leadership, whereas those in Singapore and Hong Kong are less autocratic.[71] Similarly, the Turks have been found to prefer authoritarian leadership, as do the Thais.[72]

In the Middle East, in particular, little delegation occurs. A successful company there must have strong managers who make all the decisions and who go unquestioned. Much emphasis is placed on the use of power through social contacts and family influence, and the chain of command must be rigidly followed.[73] A comparison of these and other management dimensions between Middle Eastern and Western managers is shown in Exhibit 11-12.

The effects of participative leadership can vary even in one location when the employees are from different cultural backgrounds—from which we can conclude that a subordinate's culture is usually a more powerful variable than other factors in the environment.

Research that supports this conclusion includes a study conducted in Saudi Arabia that found participative leadership to be more effective with U.S. workers than with Asian and African employees, and a study in a U.S. plant that found that participative leadership resulted in greater satisfaction and communication among U.S. employees than among Mexican employees.[74]

Exhibit 11-13 depicts an integrative model of the leadership process that pulls together the variables described in this book and in the research on culture, leadership, and motivation—and shows the powerful contingency of culture as it affects the leadership role. Reading from left to right, Exhibit 11-13 presents culture from the broad environmental factors to the outcomes affected by the entire leadership situation. As shown, the broad context in which the manager operates necessitates adjustments in leadership style to all those variables relating to the work and task environment and the people involved. Cultural variables (values, work norms, the locus of control, and so forth),

EXHIBIT 11-12   Comparison of Middle Eastern and Western Management Practices

Managerial Function	Middle Eastern Stereotype	Western Stereotype
Organizational design	Highly bureaucratic, overcentralized with power and authority at the top. Vague relationships. Ambiguous and unpredictable organization environments.	Less bureaucratic, more delegation of authority. Relatively decentralized structure.
Patterns of decision making	Ad hoc planning, decisions made at the highest level of management. Unwillingness to take high risk inherent in decision making.	Sophisticated planning techniques, modern tools of decision making, elaborate management information systems.
Performance evaluation and control	Informal control mechanisms, routine checks on performance. Lack of vigorous performance evaluation systems.	Fairly advanced control systems focusing on cost reduction and organizational effectiveness.
Manpower policies	Heavy reliance on personal contacts and getting individuals from the "right social origin" to fill major positions.	Sound personnel management policies. Candidates' qualifications are usually the basis for selection decisions.
Leadership	Highly authoritarian tone, rigid instructions. Too many management directives.	Less emphasis on leader's personality, considerable weight on leader's style and performance.
Communication	The tone depends on the communicants. Social position, power, and family influence are ever-present factors. Chain of command must be followed rigidly. People relate to each other tightly and specifically. Friendships are intense and binding.	Stress usually on equality and a minimization of differences. People relate to each other loosely and generally. Friendships not intense and binding.
Management methods	Generally old and outdated.	Generally modern and more scientific.

EXHIBIT 11-13   The Culture Contingency in the Leadership Process: An Integrative Model

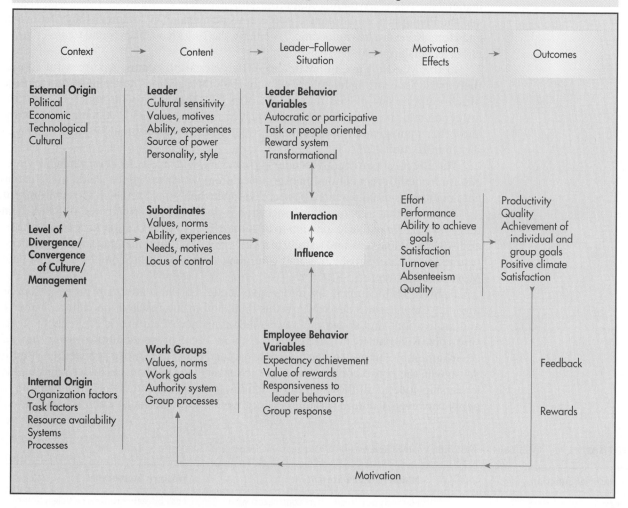

as they affect everyone involved—leader, subordinates, and work groups—then shape the content of the immediate leadership situation.

The leader–follower interaction is then further shaped by the leader's choice of behaviors (autocratic, participative, and so on) and by the employees' attitudes toward the leader and the incentives. Motivation effects—various levels of effort, performance, and satisfaction—result from these interactions, on an individual and a group level. These effects determine the outcomes for the company (productivity, quality) and for the employees (satisfaction, positive climate). The results and rewards from those outcomes then act as feedback (positive or negative) into the cycle of the motivation and leadership process.

Clearly, then, international managers should take seriously the culture contingency in their application of the contingency theory of leadership: They must adjust their leadership behaviors according to the context, norms, attitudes, and other variables in that society. One example of the complexity of the leadership situation involving obvious contextual as well as cultural factors can be seen in the results of a study of how Russian employees responded to the participative management practices of North American managers. It was found that the performance of the Russian workers decreased, which the researchers attributed to a history of employee ideas being ignored by Russian managers, as well as cultural value differences.[75] To gain more insight into comparative leadership situations, the Comparative Management in Focus: Leadership in the EU highlights the diverse leadership contexts and cultures among the countries of the EU, challenging the concept of "the EU business leader."

As noted, leadership refers not just to the manager–subordinate relationship, but also to the important task of running the whole company, division, or unit for which a manager

Comparative Management in Focus

Leadership in the EU

Research results label French captains of industry as "autocrats,"
Germans as "democrats," and British as "meritocrats."

DDI,
International Human Resources Consultants,
January 9, 2006[76]

Is "the EU business leader" a myth or reality? The European Union now comprises a 27-nation unified market of over 400 million people. Can a businessperson have an effective leadership style across such diverse contexts and people? Not according to a survey of 200 chief executives in France, Germany, and the United Kingdom. Steve Newhall, managing director of DDI Europe, an International Human Resources Consultancy, notes that "the danger for any leader is only being able to operate within one of these styles. If you take an autocratic style into a culture that expects a more democratic or meritocratic style, the chances are that you will trip up."[77]

Perhaps some people can lead well in firms that stretch across countries in the EU. But, consider the complexity in its many forms: different histories and languages, government systems, business practices, educational systems, religions, organizations, and, not the least, national cultures. We have already examined, in this book, the many dimensions of culture along which societies differ and which determine how people behave on the job—their attitudes towards work and their superiors, their perspectives on time and scheduling, their level of motivation, and so on. In addition, countries in the EU are fiercely defensive of any incursions on national culture and identity. Given those factors, the prospect of convergence of leadership styles across the EU countries seems dim. On the other hand, argue Kets de Vries and Korotov:

> *Can European organizations afford* not *to have some form of*
> *European leadership? Can an organization remain Belgian, or Polish,*
> *or Italian and* not *include a "toolset" of European capabilities?*[78]

The strategic argument for convergence of leadership styles for EU business executives is that, while the Japanese or Americans, for example, can succeed with their predominantly "local" leadership style, it is not a good option for executives in most EU companies. For them, retaining "national styles and processes" will not lead to those companies being competitive in the EU and global markets because of the blending of labor, goods, and services, and processes across the EU countries. Rather, EU leaders need an "EU style" which will work across their markets.[79]

With that lofty goal in sight—whether one considers that goal desirable or undesirable—research shows that differences in leadership style still dominate. The DDI survey on leadership in 2006 asked 200 executives what they liked or disliked about being a leader. It was found that, for example, the French are three times more likely than the British and eight times more likely than the Germans to regard being in a position of power as important.[80] In other words, there are differences in attitude towards being a leader and making decisions. Whereas French leaders like to make decisions unilaterally, German executives indicated their concern about the responsibility of their decisions; leaders in the United Kingdom seemed less troubled about their decisions.[81]

Research on the German culture, for example, tells us that German leaders most likely will evidence high assertiveness and high individualism, but low humane orientation.[82] Their primary focus is on structured tasks and performance, and less on relationships. While very organized, based on technical expertise, they have been criticized for lack of innovation as leaders.[83] These conclusions about French leaders are supported by Javidan et al., who found that:

> *To French managers, people in positions of leadership should not be expected to be sensitive or empathetic, or to worry about another's status because such attributes would weaken a leader's resolve and impede decision making. Leaders should make decisions without being distracted by other considerations.*

> JAVIDAN,
> *Dorfman, de Luque, and House, 2006*[84]

The status of leaders in France is known to be based on position and the educational institutions that they attended—known as the "grand ecoles." Title and position are attained through this elite status and thus are paramount over advancement through skills or training. French leadership style is very hierarchical and autocratic. French managers do not typically use a participative leadership style.[85]

We also see a predominantly autocratic style in the United Kingdom. Top positions of leadership are usually attained through the "old boy network" as a function of the tripartite class system that still permeates British society (upper-, middle-, and "working"-class). In this respect, leadership is based on traits, not skills, and there tends to be a highly cynical attitude throughout this style.[86]

These brief glimpses of leadership style in three of the EU countries indicate the difficulty, at least for now, of being an EU leader. Clearly, however, any leaders in positions where they deal with people and processes in several EU countries need to consider the context and cultures where they are operating and try to be flexible with their leadership style.

is responsible. When that is a global responsibility, it is vital to be able to adapt one's leadership style to the local context on many levels. Nancy McKinstry, an American leader in Europe, is very sensitive to that imperative. Since she moved to Europe, charged with the task of turning around the troubled Wolters Kluwer, the Dutch publishing group, she "has had plenty of experience of the way national and cultural differences can both bedevil and enliven business."[87] One immediate difference she noticed is that she is one of few women in senior management in Holland. That fact, added to the focus of the Dutch media on the executive as a person and the views of the employees, rather than the focus on the company as in the United States, was surprising to her. As she continues her restructuring plan, Ms. McKinstry (whose physician husband commutes every two weeks between his hospital job in New York and his family in Amsterdam) has found that there is a misconception that she is going to apply an American, bottom-line leadership style. However, she says:

> *There isn't that one-size-fits-all approach, not even within Europe. . . . If you have a product or a customer problem in France, there might be an approach that works extremely well. But if you took that same approach and tried to solve the exact same problem in Holland, you might fail.*[88]

> NANCY MCKINSTRY,
> *Chairman and CEO, Wolters Kluwer Publishing Group, Holland,*
> *July 15, 2004*[89]

Ms. McKinstry explains that in southern Europe, there's far more nuance to what people are saying compared to northern Europe, and in particular compared to the U.S. direct, optimistic style. She finds that they often don't want to say "No" to her, even though they may not be able to achieve what she is asking them. Her leadership approach is to listen hard and say "How are you going to go about meeting this goal?"[90]

CONCLUSION

Because leadership and motivation entail constant interactions with others (employees, peers, superiors, outside contacts), cultural influences on these critical management functions are very strong. Certainly, other powerful variables are intricately involved in the international management context, particularly those of economics and politics. Effective leaders carefully examine the entire context and develop sensitivity to others' values and expectations regarding personal and group interactions, performance, and outcomes—and then act accordingly.

Summary of Key Points

1. Motivation and leadership are factors in the successful implementation of desired strategy. However, while many of the basic principles are universal, much of the actual content and process are culture-contingent—a function of an individual's needs, value systems, and environmental context.

2. One problem in using content theories for cross-cultural research, such as those created by Maslow and Herzberg, is the assumption of their universal application. Because they were developed in the United States, even the concepts, such as achievement or esteem, may have different meanings in other societies, resulting in a noncomparable basis of research.

3. Implicit in motivating an employee is an understanding of which of the employee's needs are satisfied by work. Studies on the "meaning of work" indicate considerable cross-cultural differences.

4. A reexamination of motivation relative to Hofstede's dimensions of power distance, uncertainty avoidance, individualism, and masculinity provides another perspective on the cultural contexts that can influence motivational structures.

5. Incentives and reward systems must be designed to reflect the motivational structure and relative cultural emphasis on five categories of rewards: financial, social status, job content, career, and professional.

6. Effective leadership is crucial to the ability of a company to achieve its goals. The challenge is to decide what is effective leadership in different international or mixed-culture situations.

7. The perception of what makes a good leader—both traits and behaviors—varies a great deal from one society to another. The recent GLOBE leadership study across 62 countries provides considerable insight into culturally appropriate leadership behaviors.

8. Contingency theory is applicable to cross-cultural leadership situations because of the vast number of cultural and national variables that can affect the dynamics of the leadership context. These include leader–subordinate and group relations, which are affected by cultural expectations, values, needs, attitudes, perceptions of risk, and loci of control.

9. Joint ventures with other countries present a common but complex situation in which leaders must work together to anticipate and address cross-cultural problems.

Discussion Questions

1. Discuss the concept of work centrality and its implications for motivation. Use specific country examples and discuss the relative meaning of work in those countries.

2. What are the implications for motivation of Hofstede's research findings on the dimensions of power distance, uncertainty avoidance, individualism, and masculinity?

3. Explain what is meant by the need to design culturally appropriate reward systems. Give some examples.

4. Develop a cultural profile for workers in Mexico and discuss how you would motivate them.

5. Describe the variables of content and context in the leadership situation. What additional variables are involved in cross-cultural leadership?

6. Explain the theory of contingency leadership and discuss the role of culture in that theory.

7. How can we use Hofstede's four dimensions—power distance, uncertainty avoidance, individualism, and masculinity—to gain insight into leader–subordinate relationships around the world? Give some specific examples.

8. Describe the autocratic versus democratic leadership dimension. Discuss the cultural contingency in this dimension and give some examples of research findings indicating differences among countries.

9. Discuss how you would develop a profile of an effective leader from the research results from the GLOBE project. Give an example.

10. Can there be an effective "EU Leader?" Is this a realistic prospect? Discuss the factors involved with this concept.

Application Exercises

1. Using the material on motivation in this chapter, design a suitable organizational reward system for the workers in your company's plant in Mexico.

2. Choose a country and do some research (and conduct interviews, if possible) to create a cultural profile. Focus on factors affecting behavior in the workplace. Integrate any findings regarding motivation or work attitudes and behaviors. Decide on the type of approach to motivation you would take and the kinds of incentive and reward systems you would set up as manager of a subsidiary in that country. Use the theories on motivation discussed in this chapter to infer motivational structures relative to that society. Then decide what type of leadership style and process you would use. What major contingencies did you take into account?

3. Try to interview several people from a specific ethnic subculture in a company or in your college regarding values, needs, expectations in the workplace, and so on. Sketch a motivational profile of this subculture and present it to your class for discussion.

Experiential Exercises

1. Bill Higgins had served as the manager of a large U.S. timber company located in a rather remote rain forest in a South American country. Since it began its logging operations in the 1950s, a major problem facing the company has been the recruitment of labor. The only nearby source of labor is the sparsely populated local Indian group in the area. Bill's company has been in direct competition for laborers with a German company operating in the same region. In an attempt to attract the required number of laborers, Bill's company invested heavily in new housing and offered considerably higher wages than the German company, as well as a guaranteed 40-hour work week. Yet the majority of the available workers continued to work for the German company, despite its substandard housing and minimum hourly wage. Bill finally brought in several U.S. anthropologists who had worked among the local Indians. The answer to Bill's labor recruitment problem was quite simple, but it required looking at the values of the Indian labor force rather than simply building facilities that would appeal to the typical U.S. laborer.

   What did the anthropologists tell Bill?

   SOURCE: Gary P. Ferraro, *The Cultural Dimensions of International Business,* 2nd ed. (Upper Saddle River, NJ: Prentice Hall, 1994).

2. Meet with another student, preferably one whom you know well. Talk with that person and draw up a list of leadership skills you perceive him or her to possess. Then consider your research and readings regarding cross-cultural leadership. Name two countries where you think the student would be an effective leader and two where you think there would be conflict. Discuss those areas of conflict. Then reverse the procedure to find out more about yourself. Share with the class, if you wish.

Internet Resources

Visit the Deresky Companion Website at www.prenhall.com/deresky for this chapter's Internet resources.

Sir Richard Branson: Global Leader in 2007—Planes, Trains, Resorts, and Space Travel

Sir Richard Branson, long considered king of the über-stretch, has successfully wrapped his core Virgin brand (which began as a student magazine and small mail order record company in the 1970s) around everything from wine to bridal to travel and financial services. No matter what type of business it is, the autographed Virgin identity and/or signature red and white colors are prominently incorporated within the business unit's visual identity.

DE MESA, ALYCIA,
www.brandchannel.com[1]

In today's competitive world, running a global company requires strong leadership skills based on creative thinking, sound judgment, and visionary attitude. Clearly, there is no doubt that Sir Richard is visionary, as his Virgin Galactic company plans to take passengers into space in 2008 for $200,000 each. It is also clear that his vision has global breadth, as he seals a string of deals in Asia to expand Virgin's global presence, such as a joint-venture agreement in telecommunications in China.[2] Increasingly, it also entails being a down-to-earth good corporate citizen. In that regard, also, Sir Richard Branson, serial entrepreneur, has demonstrated his commitment to the world.

With his usual promotional flair and with former President Bill Clinton at his side, Sir Richard Branson announced last week that over the next decade he would put $3 billion in personal profits toward development of energy sources that do not contribute to global warming.

WALL STREET JOURNAL,
September 22, 2006[3]

What makes Sir Richard a good leader—both strategically and personally? Motivating company employees who may be located in far-flung corners of the world can be a daunting task. Companies may have powerful brands, but weaker leadership can impinge smooth operations. In any company, corporate leadership requires two important areas: content leadership (leader's attributes and decision making skills) and context leadership (variables

dealing with a particular situation).[4] Corporate leadership in global business becomes even more complex when companies enter into other markets. Global managers understand that the magic formula for success is how to adapt their organizational skills to local cultures. This may include changing corporate and functional strategies on a regular basis. The challenge of working and dealing with people in the international environment can be a complex task. Virgin Group's Chairman, President, and CEO Sir Richard Branson is a good example, who in many categories fits well with the qualities needed to be a role model in global leadership. As a founder of the group, he continues to inspire and lead Virgin and has made the company one of the top global brands. Under the leadership of Sir Branson, Virgin Group has over 200 companies in more than 30 countries, selling books, music, colas, and mobile phones, and aggressively competing in large industries such as airlines, trains, resorts, finance, and intergalactic travel. In 2007, Virgin is an $8 billion successful empire and employs 36,000 workers all over the world (see Table 1).[5] Virgin's success can be attributed to Sir Branson's charismatic personality and down-to-earth leadership style, often using common sense strategies and openness. Often called flamboyant and charismatic, Sir Branson is a highly effective leader and tough negotiator. His outward-oriented approach was a big plus in the establishment of the company. Media often called him a "walking billboard" and a "one man brand." As a tireless worker, Sir Branson has converted Virgin into a top-tier brand in Europe and other parts of the world.[6] One analyst commented:

Yet Branson himself is the opposite of elitist, his company is one of the least hierarchical one could come across. To the annoyance of his senior managers, Branson seems to pay as much attention to a chat with a clerk in the airline's mailroom as to a memorandum from his marketing director. Letters from his staff are always read first.... He manages and motivates his staff by example. Branson is highly energetic.[7]

[1]de Mesa, Alycia, "How Far Can a Brand Stretch?" BrandChannel.com, February 23, 2004, p. 1.
[2]Sundeep, Tucker, "Today Shanghai, Tomorrow the Universe," *Financial Times,* December 12, 2005.
[3]S. Beatty, "Giving Back: Branson's Big Green Investment," *Wall Street Journal,* September 22, 2006, p. W2.

[4]Deresky, Helen. (2006). *International Management: Managing Across Borders and Cultures,* 5ed, Upper Saddle River, New Jersey: Prentice Hall, p. 305.
[5]For more detail, see *Hoover's Online* (2004). "Virgin Group, Ltd.," (April), p. 1, (www.hoover.com).
[6]For more detail, see BrandChannel.com, "Brand of the Year 2003," (www.brandchannel.com); *Financial Times.* (2002). "Mature, Experienced Virgin Seeks Out Bright City Lights," (May 7), p. 24.
[7]Jackson, Tim. (1996). *Richard Branson—Virgin King: Inside Richard Branson's Business Empire,* Rocklin, California: Prima Publishing, pp. 6–7.

TABLE 1   Virgin Group: Company Data and Selected Brands

A. Company data (2006)

Chairman:	Sir Richard Branson
CEO:	Stephen Murphy
Company type:	Private
Sales:	$8.00 billion (estimated)
Sales growth:	7.7%
Total employees:	36,000 (estimated)

B: Selected companies and brands in 2006

Virgin Atlantic Airways	Virgin Mobile Australia
Virgin Blue Airlines	Virgin Mobile
Virgin Trains	Virgin Drinks
Virgin Balloon Flights	Train.com
Virgin Mobile	Limited Edition by Virgin
Virgin Active	Virgin Credit Card
Virgin V2 Music	Virgin Cola
V.Shop	Virgin Publishing
Virgin Bride	Virgin Net
Virgin Wines	Virgin Energy
Virgin Cosmetics	Virgin Cars
Virgin One	Virgin Direct
London Broncos	VirginMoney.com
The Roof Gardens	Virgin Rapido
Virgin Express	Strom Model Agency
Virgin Holidays	Virgin Student.com
Virgin Pulse	Virgin Vacations
Virgin Megastores	Virgin Galactic

SOURCES: Company Web site (www.virgin.com); Adbrand.net (www.mind-advertising.com); Hoover's.com (www.hoover.com).

Another analyst observed:

In the modern world of business, Richard Branson is an anomaly. In an era dominated by strategists, he is an opportunist. Through his company, the Virgin Group, he has created a unique business phenomenon. Never before has a single brand been so successfully deployed across such a diverse range of goods and services.[8]

From the corporate perspective, Sir Branson is famous for his team-building skills and consultative approach in day-to-day business. On many occasions, he quietly but firmly initiated new ventures from scratch and built them into large and profitable entities (see Table 1). Virgin Atlantic Airways, the flagship of the group, fits in this category, having started as a small entity and later becoming a huge success. As a company's main spokesperson, Sir Branson is always "visible" and does not miss any opportu-

nity to promote the Virgin brand, often seeking "daring personal exploits."[9] For example, on many occasions, Sir Branson attempted daredevil stunts and balloon rides across the globe to get free publicity for the company. At the micro level, Sir Branson is highly involved with the management for corporate growth and expansion. At the macro level, Sir Branson personally gets involved in the risky yet profitable ventures that the company starts. Virgin Group avoids large acquisitions and aggressively develops smaller companies for future growth in new industries. For this reason, Virgin's corporate culture keeps Sir Branson busy and well informed about the company's global operations.

Customer service is Sir Branson's utmost priority. It is one of the reasons that in customer service, Virgin

---

[8]Dearlove, Des. (1999). *Business the Richard Branson Way: 10 Secrets of the World's Greatest Brand-Builder,* New York: American Management Association., p. 1.

[9]De Vries, Manfred and F. R. Kets. (1998). "Charisma in Action: The Transformational Abilities of Virgin's Richard Branson and ABB's Percy Barnevik," *Organizational Dynamics,* (Winter), p. 9. For a good discussion on global leadership, see: Dalton, Maxine, et al. (2002). *Success for the New Global Manager: How to Work Across Distances, Countries, and Cultures,* San Francisco, California: Jossey-Bass; McCall, Morgan and George P. Hollenbeck. (2002). *Developing Global Executives,* Boston, Massachusetts: Harvard Business School Press.

Atlantic Airways is among the top brands in the airline industry. To be a successful corporate leader, one has to deal with the day-to-day activities of their companies. Sir Branson is good at leading his $8 billion empire in a variety of industries and markets where environments are dynamic and changing (see Table 1). Sir Branson's Virgin is one of the highly rated companies in the areas of airlines, resorts, auto rentals, mobile phones, and other products.[10] Virgin Mobile's operations are booming in the United Kingdom and have entered into the U.S. by making a joint venture with Sprint. In Australia, Virgin Blue, a low-cost airline, is doing well. In conclusion, Sir Branson has created an umbrella of companies where cooperation rather than intra-company competition is encouraged. Although Virgin Group does face problems in some of its new ventures and markets, the company as a whole is a classic case in the areas of global leadership—in fact, one could say "outerworld leadership" with his latest venture into space travel, Virgin Galactic LLC. Sir Branson's common sense leadership skills and strategies are a great asset to Virgin. The company's Web site accurately affirms this corporate philosophy that states:

> *Our companies are part of a family rather than a hierarchy. They are empowered to run their own affairs, yet other companies help one another, and solutions to problems come from all kinds of sources. In a sense, we are a community, with shared ideas, values, interests, and goals. The proof of our success is real and tangible.[11]*

[10]*The Wall Street Journal.* (2004). "Virgin Atlantic Plans to Boost Fleet, Routes and Work Force," (March 24), p. D8.

[11]See Company Web site (www.virgin.com).

CASE QUESTIONS

1. Discuss the key components of Sir Richard Branson's leadership style and his motivational skills.
2. Analyze and discuss the transformation and future prospects of the company in global markets under the leadership of Sir Richard Branson. Do you agree with his overall strategy?
3. What do you think of Sir Richard's pledge towards renewable energy sources? Is this all about charity alone?

SOURCE: Written especially for this book by Syed Tariq Anwar, updated by Helen Deresky in 2007.

The material in this case is intended to be used as a basis for classroom/academic discussion rather than to illustrate either effective or ineffective handling of a managerial situation or business practices.

Case 13   Infosys' Global Delivery Model

The Global Delivery Model that has been at the heart of our execution is more than just a way of getting work done offshore. It is a genuine business innovation that delivers a superior value proposition at higher quality and lower cost. By leveraging global resources and global strengths, it creates a new degree of freedom.[1]

NANDAN NILEKANI,
President, CEO and Managing Director, Infosys, 2006

Infosys can obtain skilled labor at better rates than its customers can in their own region and the focus of the GDM is maximizing skill while minimizing cost.[2]

ZAPTHINK,
Massachusetts-based IT Market Intelligence Firm, 2005

THE "LEADER"

In February 2006, Gartner,[3] a research firm focused on technology industries, published its "Magic Quadrant for Offshore Application Services, 2006." This report assessed 30 leading offshore application service providers. For its magic quadrant, Gartner evaluated service providers on the basis of parameters such as completeness of vision and their ability to execute.[4] India-based Infosys Technologies (Infosys) was placed in the "leaders" quadrant, signifying clear vision of the market direction and building competencies to sustain its leadership position in the market. (Refer to Exhibit C13-1 for the criteria used in the Magic Quadrant, and Exhibit C13-2 for traits of the companies placed in the "Leaders" quadrant.)

Gartner's magic quadrant analyzed the competencies of the service providers based on their Global Delivery Model (GDM). Gartner said that Infosys' "strong management capability relative to the other pure-play offshore providers" was one of the key demonstrated capabilities of the company. S. Gopalakrishnan (Gopalakrishnan), Chief Operating Officer and Deputy Managing Director of Infosys, said, "I am happy to see Infosys being recognized as a leader in this Offshore Application Services Magic Quadrant, the first time that Gartner has published one to focus on this area. This is an important indicator for the mainstream acceptance of GDM by clients."[5]

GDM provided a superior value proposition at higher quality and lower cost. The companies adopting this model leveraged their own global resources and strengths to achieve higher profitability. Infosys used GDM as a strategic outsourcing tool; using it, the company could take the work to the place where it could be best performed at lowest cost with minimum risk. For a GDM to be efficient, the work had to be broken into logical components and distributed to locations where they could generate maximum value. By using GDM, Infosys delivered the highest process and quality standards, while leveraging differences in cost, quality, and skill sets of manpower in different locations. The ultimate objective was to pass on these benefits to its clients.

The major part of Infosys' revenues was derived from GDM-based application services. The company

[1]"Scripting a Success Story," *India Now,* January 19, 2006.
[2]"India's Best Managed Company," *Business Today,* March 27, 2005.
[3]Gartner Inc. is a leading provider of research and analysis on the global IT, computer hardware, software, communications, and related technology industries. The company, operating in three segments—research, consulting and events—serves more than 10,000 clients. In 2005, the revenues of the company were at US$989 million, operating income was at US$69.3 million and net loss was at US$2.4 million.
[4]The criteria under ability to execute were product/service, overall viability, sales execution/pricing, market responsiveness, track record, marketing execution, customer experience, and operations.

[5]"Infosys Recognized in the 'Leader' Quadrant in Offshore Applications Services Magic Quadrant," www.infosys.com, February 25, 2006.

EXHIBIT C13-1 Magic Quadrant—Criteria

Market Definition/Description

■ Application outsourcing including multi-year agreements to buy ongoing services from external service providers. The services include people, tools, methodologies, and processes for supporting software applications.

■ Project-based contracts that need to be executed in a specified time and include purchase of application–related services for design, development, integration, or implementation.

■ Staff augmentation contracts to provide technical workers to take care of the client's application-related tasks.

Inclusion/Exclusion Criteria

■ Offshore application service revenue obtained mainly from North America, Western Europe, and the United Kingdom.

■ Company revenue of more than US$100 million, with total offshore application services revenue of at least 25 percent of the minimum total revenue.

■ Market interest and visibility.

Evaluation Criteria

■ Ability to execute the application service as described in the proposal. This includes a combination of tools, methodology, techniques, verticals, process expertise, etc. Should execute according to the needs of the client constantly.

■ Completeness of vision to deliver the services required by the client. The parameters include knowledge of the markets, customers, and the customers of the customers. Knowledge of key market trends, discipline and focus, focus on the future, investments in R&D, alliances, and partnerships.

SOURCE: Adapted from Gartner—*Magic Quadrant for Offshore Application Services, 2006.*

EXHIBIT C13-2 Traits of Companies in "Leaders" Quadrant

■ Excellence in services based on GDM.
■ Offshore application engagements of considerable scale and size.
■ Offshore services as a key element of revenue growth.
■ Focus on building brand awareness in offshore application delivery.
■ Presence in more than one of the key markets (USA, UK, and Western Europe).
■ Investment in and commitment to promote offshore application services.
■ Multi-country strategy for global delivery.

SOURCE: Gartner—*Magic Quadrant for Offshore Application Services, 2006.*

had decided to enhance its GDM capabilities by applying it to new services and adding in new global delivery locations. Commenting on the GDM, Manjari Raman, a Boston based management writer said, "What made Infosys' GDM disruptive was its framework for distributed project management—the ability to deploy multi-location, multi-time-zone teams to execute projects efficiently and at low cost."[6]

---

[6]Manjari Raman, "Can Infosys Be a Disruptive Innovator?" *Business Standard*, April 17, 2006.

BACKGROUND NOTE

Infosys was incorporated as Infosys Consultants Private Limited[7] on July 2, 1981, by a group of seven professionals.[8] From the beginning, Infosys relied heavily on overseas projects. One of the founders, Narayana Murthy, stayed in India, while the others went to the United States to carry out on-site programming for corporate clients. One of Infosys' first clients was the U.S.-based sports shoe manufacturer Reebok.

Infosys hired its first set of employees in 1982 from the Indian Institute of Technology, Chennai. These employees were provided training and were sent abroad for on-site projects. After its revenues started increasing, Infosys started spending more on training and product development. The company's revenues in 1982 were Rs1.2 million.

At this time, computers were not manufactured in India. A task like importing a computer required a license and the process would take several months. Infosys did not have the required space to install many

---

[7]In June 1992, the company's name was changed to Infosys Technologies Limited.

[8]The group comprised Narayana Murthy, Nandan Nilekani, S. Gopalakrishnan, K. Dinesh, SB Shibulal, NS Raghavan, and Ashok Arora. Ashok Arora left Infosys in 1983 to join a U.S.-based software company.

computers, so the computers it purchased were installed in the premises of one of its customers, where the new employees were trained. Products like proprietary banking software were then developed at the site. At this time, Infosys focused on acquiring domain knowledge in segments like retailing, finance, distribution, and telecommunications.

When Infosys was incorporated, it started out as a body shopper, acting as an intermediary for placing Indian software professionals in the United States. In the mid–1980s, around 90 percent of the total revenues of the company were derived from body shopping projects in the United States. The company was able to obtain several contracts as it was offering services at costs that were much lower than any U.S. company. At that time, the company's main advantage was high-quality manpower at a lower cost.

By the late 1980s, Infosys started providing on-site services. In order to execute the IT projects, it would station its people at the client's location and they would then develop software to meet their requirements. This was an expensive proposition. Local talent, especially in locations in the United States where Infosys was executing projects, was not readily available and was very expensive. For the most part, the company would place Indian employees at the clients' location, which was again a costly proposition.

In order to take advantage of the low-cost workforce in India, Infosys opened a software development center in Bangalore in 1993. It convinced its clients that their IT projects could be completed in India. By doing projects in India, Infosys gained two advantages—a cost advantage due to lower manpower outlay, and a new advantage in terms of developing the company's own technical and managerial skills for such projects. Soon, Infosys started obtaining several offshore development contracts to write customized software in India to be installed at the client's sites abroad.

By the late 1990s, Infosys had moved from competing on low wages to focus on developing intellectual property. Drawing on the knowledge and experience it obtained by developing software for varied clients, Infosys introduced generic products in the areas of banking, telecom, and retail. Small modifications could be made to these products to meet the needs of particular clients. Infosys started emphasizing the quality of its software in order to differentiate itself from other IT companies. In 1998, Infosys received CMM[9] Level 4 certification. Through adherence to CMM, Infosys was able to formalize its development processes.

With its expertise in many areas and its focus on quality, Infosys was able to bag many big IT projects, some of which were contracted on a fixed time and fixed price basis. Infosys guaranteed its clients software products of high quality, and having established itself as a firm with much better capabilities than its competitors, the company charged higher prices for its services.

The next step was developing mission-critical software, which Infosys did for clients like Nortel, Reebok, and Nordstrom. By 1999, Infosys had more than 110 customers, including multinational giants like Nestlé, Apple, and Gap. At this point, Infosys felt the need for development centers that were not too far from the client's location, where tasks of strategic importance could be carried out. For this purpose, Infosys opened two centers close to its clients' locations in Fremont, California, and Boston, Massachusetts, in October 1999. In January 2000, Infosys opened its first software development center outside India, in Toronto, Canada. In mid-2000, the company opened another center in London. (Refer to Exhibit C13-3 for some Infosys milestones.)

EXHIBIT C13-3   Infosys—Milestones

Year	Events
1981	Infosys incorporated
1987	First international office in the United States
1993	Completed IPO
1995	Set up development centers across India
1996	Set up first office in Europe in Milton, Keynes, UK
1997	Set up office in Toronto
1999	Annual revenue of US$100 million Listed in NASDAQ
	Opened offices in Germany, Sweden, Belgium, Australia
	Set up two development centers in the United States
2000	Annual revenue of US$200 million
	New office in Hong Kong
	Global development centers in Canada
	Three development centers in the United States
2001	Annual revenue of over US$400 million
	Offices in UAE and Argentina
	Development center in Japan
2002	Revenue touched US$0.5 billion
	Offices in the Netherlands, Singapore, and Switzerland
2004	Revenue crossed US$1 billion
2006	Revenue crossed US$2 billion

SOURCE: Adapted from www.infosys.com.

---

[9]Capability Maturity Model (CMM) is a set of instructions followed by an organization to gain control over the software development process. At CMM Level 4, the performance of a process is controlled through quantitative techniques.

TABLE C13-1 Infosys—Evolution of Global Delivery Model

Until 1996	Application development and maintenance
	Software re-engineering
1997–2000	Technology consulting
	Technology-enabled BPR
	Enterprise solutions
2001–2005	Business process management
	IT outsourcing
	Systems integration
2006	Management consulting

SOURCE: Adapted from S Gopalakrishnan, Infosys—*Operational Highlights, 2005–06.*

TABLE C13-2 New Services—Percentage of Revenue

Year	New Services %
2001	22.8%
2002	24.9%
2003	29.6%
2004	35.4%
2005	37.7%
2006	41.1%

SOURCE: S Gopalakrishnan, *Operational Highlights, 2005–06.*

In the initial years, GDM at Infosys was deployed only for application development. With the advancement of technology in communications, the scope of GDM widened to include new services like package implementation, independent validation, infrastructure management, business process management, testing, consulting, and systems integration. Some of the services that Infosys made a part of GDM were enterprise solutions and business consulting in 1999, independent validation in 2001, and infrastructure management and systems integration in 2002. (Refer to Table C13-1 for the evolution of GDM in Infosys.) With new services being added to GDM every year, the share of new services as a percentage of total revenues kept growing. (Refer to Table C13-2 for the details of revenue obtained from new services.)

THE GLOBAL DELIVERY MODEL

In the GDM, large-scale software development projects were divided into different categories. Falling under the first category were the tasks that were to be carried out at the location of the client. Under the second category were the tasks, which needed to be carried out closer to the client. The third category consisted of tasks that could be done in remote locations, where process-driven technology centers with highly skilled manpower were easily available. (Refer to Exhibit C13-4 for details of the tasks carried out on-site, near-site, and at offshore locations.)

The work on projects was carried out 24 hours a day, with teams at different locations across the world working round-the-clock on the project. Nandan Nilekani,

EXHIBIT C13-4 Project Components—On-site, Near-site, Offshore

	On-site	Near-site	Offshore
Strategy and Roadmap Definition	Client interaction, Interviews, Reviews, Program leadership Goal setting	Analysis and synthesis	Background research Thought leadership, Information support
Development and Integration	Architecture requirements, Change management, Implementation	Requirement analysis, High-level design, Prototype building, Implementation support	Detailed design, Code development, Testing, Integration
Systems Integration and Package Implementation	Client interaction, Process mapping, Solution definition, Architecture change, Program management	Prototype building, High-level design, Implementation support	Custom components, Integration interfaces, Report building
ITO, BPO, and AMO	First-level support, Facilities support, Program management	Near-site support centers, Service redundancy	Large offshore centers, Core service delivery

SOURCE: www.infosys.com

President, CEO, and Managing Director of Infosys, commented, "The work can be moved anywhere. This allows for a degree of freedom in the way a business is conducted. The work can be moved depending on where it would be cheaper to do so, or to a place that has unutilized capacity, or special skills. This is the kind of innovation (GDM) for which we are taking credit for."[10]

In GDM, teams spread across different global locations and carried out tasks in a coordinated manner, with adequate support from seamless communication systems and process guidelines. Infosys used global development centers (GDCs) to carry out the activities related to software development. Infosys had two types of GDCs—proximity development centers (PDC) and offshore development centers (ODC).

The PDCs, or near-shore centers, were useful especially for clients, who were reluctant to move their entire project offshore, but at the same time wanted to reduce the high costs for on-site development. Near-shore facilities were useful for large mission-critical projects, which demanded round-the-clock responsiveness and local language capabilities. In the near-shore model, some of the risks associated with the offshore model, like lack of control, language and cultural barriers, inadequate infrastructure, and geopolitical risks, could be avoided. According to Gopalakrishnan, "The global delivery model works on the concept of meritocracy of locations and under this model, near-shore destinations become just another location in the entire global network."[11]

The ODCs carried out tasks like designing, coding, testing, documentation, maintenance, fixing bugs, warranty support, etc. The ODCs were located mainly in India with only one ODC located in Canada.

Each project team was organized into modules, with each module dealing with one aspect of the project. Instead of carrying out the project sequentially, Infosys deployed the resources and activities simultaneously. The teams also interacted with each other and had a general idea about the tasks carried out by other modules.

Before any project began, the team was decided and roles were assigned to each of the team members. The required competencies and the actual competencies of each of the members were listed. Team members were given some training to fill these gaps.

After the project was complete, project teams deliberated on what went right and what went wrong in the course of the project. Every project had a closure report, which had details about the duration of the project, resources employed, deviations that occurred, and reasons for the deviations. All the employees were required to fill in a worksheet every day, which helped the project managers assess the project status. Using the combined database of the team members, the project managers could determine the time and cost required to complete the project.

For the success of GDM, knowledge and specifications had to be captured, and these had to be communicated to the off-site developers; later, the results would have to be reintegrated into the client's system at the on-site location. The major components of GDM were knowledge capture/playback, daily handoffs, quality control, continuous improvement, mobilizing and demobilizing staff as required, distribution of staff between on-site and off-site locations, recruiting and training the right kind of people, billing for cross-border teams, and connectivity of the locations. (Refer to Exhibit C13-5 for the advantages of GDM.)

Infosys gave utmost importance to recruitment, training, deploying, and retaining the right kind of people. Candidates with high analytical ability and ability to learn were selected. Other traits that were deemed necessary were attitude and willingness to work in teams. On the selection process at Infosys, *Fortune* wrote, "Securing a position at Infosys is more competitive than gaining admission to Harvard. Last year, the company had more than 1.3 million applicants for full-time positions and hired only 1% of them (Harvard College by comparison accepted 9% of applicants)."[12]

Infosys was one of the companies inducted into the Global Most Admired Knowledge Enterprises (MAKE)[13] hall of fame in 2005. From the early 1990s, Infosys began transforming the knowledge of its individual employees into an organization-wide resource. The employees shared their knowledge of different issues and experiences on

---

EXHIBIT C13-5 Advantages of Global Delivery Model

- Access to a large pool of highly talented professionals.
- 24-hour execution capability with operations spread across different time zones.
- Expedite large projects by simultaneously processing the project components.
- Enhanced security through physical and operational separation of clients' projects.
- Cost competitiveness across geographic regions.
- Uninterrupted services through built-in redundancies.
- Knowledge management system, through which solutions could be reused.

SOURCE: http://sec.edgar-online.com

---

[10]"Global Delivery Is Infy's Mantra," *Financial Express,* April 23, 2004.

[11]"Nearshore: India Software Inc. Moves Closer for Comfort," *Express Computer Online,* May 3, 2004.

[12]Julie Schlosser, "Infosys U," *Fortune,* March 20, 2006.

[13]Conducted by KNOW Network, in association with Teleos. KNOW is a global community of knowledge-driven organizations that aims at sharing knowledge management practices. Teleos is an independent knowledge management and intellectual capital research firm.

topics like technology and software development with employees in other countries—and this was called the Bodies of Knowledge (BOK). In a few years, as communications technology developed rapidly, Infosys launched Sparsh, a corporate intranet that was a repository of all the BOKs. Sparsh was launched in 1996. Taking the effort further, a company-wide KM program was initiated in 1999, with a centralized portal called KShop.

Infosys developed a KM tool called People Knowledge Map, which had contact information of the individuals who were experts in specific areas. Employees working on a particular project could contact them in need. Infosys also used CMM to prevent the occurrence of defects, and to quantify and modify its software development process. Project managers working on a particular project could access the knowledge repository to find a solution for any problem they were facing.

In order to ensure the quality of IT services it provided, Infosys benchmarked against international quality standards like ISO 9000, CMM, and the Malcolm Baldrige framework. Infosys also used Six Sigma cross-functional mapping to ensure improvement. As Infosys used SEI CMM, it could provide its clients with accurate budgeting and superior productivity and was successful in meeting the goals set for schedule, cost, quality, etc. Infosys strove to meet stringent quality requirements in its projects by using quality processes throughout the life of the project. At every stage of the project from conceptualization to closure, detailed checklists, standards, guidelines, and templates were used to illustrate every aspect of the project.[14]

By 2006, as a part of GDM, Infosys had 38 global delivery centers. About 20 of these centers were in India and the rest in North America, Asia-Pacific, and Europe. In India, five GDCs were located in Bangalore, three each in Chennai and Pune, and two each in Bhubaneswar and Mangalore. One GDC each was located in Hyderabad, Chandigarh, Mohali, Thiruvananthapuram, and Mysore. (Refer to Exhibit C13-6 for details of GDCs located outside India.)

Apart from the GDCs, Infosys had marketing offices located across the globe. As of 2006, 14 of the total 37 marketing offices were in the United States, five in India, three in Germany, two each in Switzerland and Australia, and one each in Canada, UAE, Czech Republic, Japan, Hong Kong, Belgium, Sweden, France, China, the Netherlands, and Italy.

GDM—MAKING THE MODEL WORK

For an offshore development project, a team from Infosys visited the client in order to determine the requirements of the project. After obtaining the

---

EXHIBIT C13-6 Infosys—GDCs Located Outside India

Bridgewater, New Jersey, USA

Boston, Massachusetts, USA

Chicago, Illinois, USA

Fremont, California, USA

Phoenix, Arizona, USA

Plano, Texas, USA

Charlotte, North Carolina, USA

Houston, Texas, USA

Milton Keynes, UK

London (Canary Wharf, Level 14), UK

London (Canary Wharf, Level 15), UK

Masarykova, Brno, Czech Republic

Toronto, Canada[*]

Sydney, Australia

Melbourne, Australia

Tokyo, Japan

Shanghai, China

Mauritus

[*]ODC; others are proximity centers.

SOURCE: SEC Filing Infosys.

required specifications, some of the team members stayed back with the client to coordinate and determine any changes that the client demanded in the project, while the project managers returned to the GDCs. At the clients' location, there was an on-site coordinator who communicated with the PDCs and ODCs regularly.

The work was then distributed to PDCs and ODCs. At the GDCs, project managers supervised a large team of IT professionals who developed and implemented solutions as required by the client. As and when required, some members of the teams visited the client's site. The three-way allocation of manpower among the client site, PDCs, and ODCs required close coordination.

Every week, client meetings were conducted and a status report was prepared to gauge the progress of the project. This was a part of CMM and was successfully used in GDM at Infosys. The weekly meetings were real-time meetings, usually conducted every Friday. The agenda of the meeting included review of status reports and discussion on issues related to the project. Key personnel representing the client and Infosys participated in the meeting through an audio conference facility.

The status reports were derived from the mandates of CMM and were presented every week. Infosys followed a strict mechanism for status reports, and used standard templates for the reports. The status reports of the project were delivered to the client and also to all the members involved in the project in the PDCs and ODCs. The clients' systems were linked to the facilities at Infosys in order to carry out simultaneous processing. Irrespective

---

[14]The aspects of the project were requirements analysis, change management, configuration management, tailoring, defect estimation, and schedule estimation.

of the location of the project, the project managers had full control of the project through this model.

To ensure seamless communication between the development centers and the clients, Infosys used the services of several service providers along with a mix of satellite and fiber optic links with facilities for alternate routing. In India, Infosys used the services of two telecom carriers to provide high-speed links to connect the GDCs. Internationally, multiple satellite links were used to connect GDCs with network hubs in other parts of the world. In 2005, some top executives were provided with IP phones. Instant messaging was used to communicate across Infosys campuses in India. Video conferencing was used for executive level discussions and training. Infosys established a business continuity and disaster recovery center in Mauritius.

In the year 2004, 68.1 percent of the total billed person months[15] for Infosys was from GDCs located in India, while the balance was carried out at clients' locations and at GDCs outside India. In 2006, 72.3 percent of the total billed person months originated from GDCs in India.

EXPANDING GDM

In 2003, Infosys launched GDM Plus, an enhanced service delivery model that was a combination of more services and excellence in execution. Infosys defined GDM Plus as an integrated delivery model that encompassed vertical solutions, an expanded vertical footprint, and execution excellence. According to Infosys, GDM Plus was its strategic response to changing market conditions and the competitive landscape to deliver high volumes to customers. Execution excellence was to be achieved through business solutions, technology, domain expertise, quality, operational efficiency, and people development.

In order to avoid the risk of predatory pricing by its competitors, Infosys made efforts to move up the value chain by offering high-end services like enterprise solutions and independent testing. In April 2004, the company established Infosys Consulting Inc., a wholly owned subsidiary of Infosys, in Texas, USA. By providing IT and consultancy services, the company wanted greater involvement in its clients' projects and aimed at building brand differentiation. This was particularly necessary in the light of the growing presence of Chinese firms in the IT services industry. According to Michael Guilbault, Senior Analyst, Technology Business Research,[16] "The combined offering of IT services and consultancy has helped Infosys move up the value chain by increasing its involvement in high-level projects

associated with Sarbanes-Oxley compliance,[17] the Anti-Money Laundering Act,[18] and the Patriot Act[19]."[20]

Infosys on its part felt that moving into consultancy was a business model innovation, after it had firmly established itself in back-end tasks like code writing and systems integration. According to Nilekani, "It's like Wal-Mart getting into groceries or Dell getting into printers. On top of our global delivery model, we're adding these new capabilities at the point of customer contact."[21]

THE BENEFITS

According to analysts, GDM was cited as one of the key factors behind the rapid growth of Infosys' revenues. In a span of 25 years, the company grew to generate revenues of US$2 billion in 2005–2006. Infosys' revenues grew almost four-fold in the past four years. (Refer to Exhibit C13-7 for five-year revenues of Infosys.) The company continued attracting a talented workforce in India and other countries. The number of employees of Infosys grew to 52,700 as of March 2006 against 10,700 in 2002.

In the fiscal year 2005–2006, Infosys derived more than 40 percent of its revenues through new GDM-based services like package implementation, independent validation, business process management, infrastructure management, and systems integration. The GDM enabled Infosys to achieve round-the-clock execution of projects. This ensured that large projects could be delivered by the company on time as it was able to process the project components very efficiently. Infosys reused its solutions at appropriate places, and through this, it gained considerable cost advantages.

There were several benefits that accrued to clients through the GDM. These benefits could be as high as 35 percent reductions in cost and 75 percent reductions in time to market for various products. Infosys customized its delivery model according to the requirements of clients, so projects were executed with greater flexibility.

The scope of GDM was not limited to just setting up resource bases across the world. GDM also involved use of technology processes and systems that had been

---

[15]A person month is a metric denoting the amount of work one person can do in a period of one month.
[16]Technology Business Research (TBR) provides information and insights into computer, software, telecom, and professional service industries.

[17]The Sarbanes-Oxley Act 2002 is a U.S. federal law that was passed after several major accounting scandals were reported in the United States. The legislation established higher standards for U.S. public company boards, management, and accounting firms.
[18]The International Money Laundering Abatement and Financial Anti-Terrorism Act of 2001 facilitates prevention, detection, and prosecution of international money laundering and financing terrorism.
[19]The Uniting and Strengthening America by Providing Appropriate Tools Required to Intercept and Obstruct Terrorism Act, popularly known as The USA Patriot Act, was passed in response to the September 11, 2001, terrorist attacks in the United States. The act extends the authority of federal officials to fight terrorist attacks in the United States and other countries. The Act also gave the Secretary of the Treasury regulatory powers in order to combat corruption in U.S. financial institutions.
[20]Balaka Baruah Aggarwal, "A Quiver Full of Arrows," *Dataquest,* November 24, 2005.
[21]John Heilemann, "In Through the Outsourcing Door," *Business 2.0,* November 2004.

EXHIBIT C13-7 Infosys—Five-Year Financial Highlights (U.S. GAAP)
(In US$ Millions)

Particulars	2005–06	2004–05	2003–04	2002–03	2001–02
Revenues	2,152	1,592	1,063	754	545
Cost of revenues	1,244	904	603	417	294
Gross profit	908	688	460	337	251
Operating Expenses					
Selling and marketing	136	103	77	56	27
General and administrative	173	127	82	58	44
Amortization of stock compensation			1	2	2
Amortization of intangible assets		2	7	2	
Total Operating Expenses	309	232	167	118	73
Operating income	599	456	293	219	178
Gain on sale of long-term investment		11			
Other income, net	31	24	28	18	14
Income before income taxes and minority interest	630	491	321	237	192
Provision for income taxes	70	72	51	42	28
Income before minority interest	560	419	270	195	164
Minority interest	5				
Net Income	**555**	**419**	**270**	**195**	**164**

SOURCE: www.infosys.com

developed over the years, capability of execution, and quality of manpower. Infosys had been continuously upgrading all these resources, making the model unique and difficult for others to replicate. According to Nilekani, "We will take a lead in leveraging the GDM to help clients derive maximum strategic benefit. The game has changed for those who develop traditional solutions without the strength of global delivery. The new paradigm of strategic global outsourcing will provide the flexibility to select what to outsource, when to outsource, and how to leverage global delivery throughout the value chain."[22]

THE ROAD AHEAD

Realizing the potential of GDM, several other Indian IT companies also began providing offshore services. Indian companies could charge a premium of 10 to 20 percent for their offshore services. But with these services becoming mainstream, there was competition among major players and customers became less willing to pay a premium. It was not long before multinationals also entered the fray. Several MNCs like Accenture,[23]

IBM Global Services,[24] and Electronic Data Systems[25] have started operating from India and began offering the same offshore rates as Indian companies.

But Infosys remained confident that consultants and companies abroad could not match their GDM capabilities. They would need to build the model from scratch, by retrenching the manpower in their countries and hiring equally talented employees in other locations with cost advantages. The multinationals would need to redesign their operations in order to replicate Infosys' GDM, which would be a difficult task. According to Nilekani, "We are adding the garnish to a growing base, and the balance sheet grows to absorb this. The problem for them is the opposite: their revenues decline if they change their model, as they move work from on-site to offshore. You know the internal problems of an organization that is doing that?"[26]

[22]"Infy Seeks RBI Nod for Higher Forward Cover," *Deccan Herald,* April 23, 2004.
[23]U.S.-based Accenture Limited is involved in management consulting, technology services, and outsourcing. The annual revenue of the company as of August 2005 was US$17.09 billion with net income of US$840.5 million.
[24]IBM Global Services, the technology services and consulting division of U.S.-based IBM, is the largest business technology and services provider in the world. IBM Global Services served customers spread across 150 countries.
[25]U.S.-based Electronic Data Systems, which was spun off from General Motors in 1996, is the largest independent systems management and services firm in the United States. The revenues of the company in 2005 were US$19.75 billion.
[26]Mitu Jaishankar, "Interview—Damned if I Do and Damned if I Don't," *Businessworld,* August 16, 2004.

The entry of multinationals in India also put pressure on Infosys in terms of retaining talented manpower. The multinationals started hiring experienced people from Infosys and other top Indian IT companies by offering them salaries that were 40 to 50 percent higher. In order to counter this threat, Infosys increased salaries during 2003 and also made structural changes to follow a role-based structure, according to which the reward depended on the performance. Under the role-based structure, employees could be a part of different streams in the organization such as the project management stream, technical stream, program management stream, customer interface stream, and domain consulting stream. In each of these streams, there were key roles that would determine the career path of the employee. Infosys followed a variable salary structure. For the top management, 50 percent of salary was variable, 30 percent was variable for the middle level, and 10 percent was variable for the junior level. Of the variable pay, 70 percent was linked to the company's performance, while the rest was for group and individual performance.

Apart from multinationals, Infosys faced stiff competition from other Indian IT companies that were adopting new structures. According to Azim Premji, Chairman of Wipro Technologies,[27] "I think, our structure is superior to the Infosys global delivery model. Frankly, I have not fully understood the Infosys global delivery model. Also, you must appreciate that Infosys is still struggling in trying to establish a verticalized structure."[28]

Industry analysts expressed fears that Infosys and its GDM was heavily dependent on business from U.S.-based companies. The IT spending of U.S. companies was decreasing and was expected to reduce further, and outsourcing was being severely criticized by some sections in the United States. This could put the

TABLE C13-3   Infosys—Percentage Revenues by Geographic Area

Countries	2006	2005	2004
North America	64.8	65.2	71.2
Europe	24.5	22.3	19.2
India	1.8	1.9	1.3
Rest of the World	8.9	10.6	8.3

SOURCE: Infosys, *Annual Report, 2005–06.*

company in a tight spot, owing to its over dependence on the U.S. market. (Refer to Table C13-3 for Infosys' revenues by geographic area.) In anticipation of this, Infosys was widening its markets and was making efforts to reduce its dependence on the United States.

Another challenge that Infosys faced was growing competition from countries like China and the Philippines, which had joined the IT bandwagon and were putting up a strong challenge to Indian companies by offering lower wages and more facilities. More than offshore or onshore business models, companies providing a combination of both would stay ahead of the competition. Such companies would provide low-cost and high-value-added custom-built services, organization-specific solutions, and global delivery networks that could optimize cost and quality, providing maximum benefits to clients. According to Clayton M Christensen,[29] "Right now Infosys is at the top of its game. But, in five years, you can bet that Infosys will begin to see some maturity in its core business. At that stage, it will want to find another growth business that is becoming very large. If Infosys wants to have such a business five years from now, it has to start it today. If it waits until the numbers look bad, that will be too late."[30]

QUESTIONS FOR DISCUSSION

1. Examine and comment on the factors that compelled Infosys to develop its own model for delivering IT services. Explain the working of Infosys' GDM in detail.

2. According to Nandan Nilekani, "The Global Delivery Model is a genuine business innovation that delivers a superior value proposition at higher quality and lower cost." In the light of this statement, explain how GDM is a source of competitive advantage to Infosys. What are the possible disadvantages of GDM? With several Indian and multinational IT companies joining the GDM bandwagon, how can Infosys differentiate its IT services? What changes can you propose in the GDM to adapt it to the changing business environment in the near future?

3. According to ZapThink, "Infosys can obtain skilled labor at better rates than its customers can in their own region and the focus of the GDM is maximizing skill while minimizing cost." In the light of this statement, explain how Infosys' focus on GDM has ensured that the skills of the company's workforce are maximized while minimizing their costs.

---

[27]Wipro Technologies is an India-based global IT services company with 30 offices spread across the world. For the financial year 2005–2006, the revenues of Wipro were US$2.36 billion and profits were US$460 million.

[28]"Our Structure Is Superior than Infosys: Azim Premji," www.indiainfo.com, July 22, 2005.

[29]Clayton M Christensen is a professor at Harvard Business School and the author of two books, *The Innovator's Dilemma and The Innovator's Solution.*

[30]Manjari Raman, "Can Infosys Be a Disruptive Innovator?" *Business Standard,* April 17, 2006.

Case 14 A First-Time Expatriate's Experience in a Joint Venture in China

THE LONG TRIP HOME

James Randolf was traveling back to his home state of Illinois from his assignment in China for the last time. He and his wife were about three hours into the long flight when she fell asleep, her head propped up by the airline pillow against the cabin wall. James was exhausted, but for the first time in many days he had the luxury of reflecting on what had just happened in their lives.

He was neither angry nor bitter, but the disruption of the last few weeks was certainly unanticipated and in many ways unfortunate. He had fully expected to complete his three-year assignment as the highest ranking U.S. manager of his company's joint venture (JV) near Shanghai. Now, after only 13 months, the assignment was over, and a manager from the regional office in Singapore held the post. Sure, the JV will survive, he thought, but how far had the relationship that he had been nurturing between the two partnered companies been set back? His Chinese partners were perplexed by his company's actions and visibly affected by the departure of their friend and colleague.

Was this an error in judgment resulting from Controls' relative inexperience as a multinational company and a partner in international joint ventures, James wondered? Or, had something else caused the shift in policy which resulted in the earlier-than-planned recall of several of the corporation's expatriates from their assignments? There had always been plans to reduce the number of expatriates at any particular location over time, but recently the carefully planned timetables seem to have been abandoned. Next week, James had to turn in his report covering the entire work assignment. How frank should he be? What detail should he include in his report? To whom should he send copies? There had been rumors that many senior managers were being asked to take early retirement. James did not really want to retire but could hardly contain his dissatisfaction as to how things had turned out. Maybe it would be better to take the offer, if it was forthcoming, and try to find some consulting that would make the best use of his wide spectrum of technical and managerial experience which now included an expatriate assignment in what was considered to be one of the most difficult locations in the world.

James reflected with satisfaction on his accomplishment of the initial primary objectives, which were to establish a manufacturing and marketing presence. In fact, he was quite pleased with his success at putting many things in place [that] would allow the operation to prosper. The various departments within the joint venture were now cooperating and coordinating, and the relationships he had established were truly the evidence of this achievement. He would like to have seen the operations become more efficient, however.

The worklife that awaited him upon his return was a matter of considerable concern. Reports from the expatriates who preceded him in the last few months indicated that there were no established plans to utilize their talents, and often early retirement was strongly encouraged by management. Beyond the obligatory physical examinations and debriefings, he had been told there was little for them to do. Many of the recalled expatriates found themselves occupying desks in Personnel waiting for responses about potential job opportunities.

He gazed at his wife, Lily, now settled into comfortable slumber. At least she had had a pretty good experience. She was born in Shanghai but left China in 1949. The country was then in the middle of a revolution, but, aside from her memory of her parents appearing extremely anxious to leave, she remembered little else about the issues surrounding their emigration to the United States. Most of her perceptions about "what it was like" in China came from U.S. television coverage, some fact, some fiction.

As the plane droned on into the night, James thought back to how this experience began.

This case was prepared by Dr. John Stanbury, Assistant Professor of International Business at Indiana University, Kokomo, with enormous assistance from Rina Dangarwala and John King, MBA students. It is not intended to illustrate either effective or ineffective handling of a managerial situation. The views represented here are those of the case author and do not necessarily reflect those of the Society for Case Research. The author's view is based on his own professional judgments.

The names of the organization, and the industry in which it operates, and individuals' names and the events described in this case have been disguised to preserve anonymity.

Presented to and accepted by the Society for Case Research. All rights reserved to the author and SCR.

THE COMPANY

Controls' world headquarters were in Chicago, Illinois. It had operations in several countries in Europe, Asia, and South America, but, with the exception of several *maquiladoras*, all of its expansion had occurred very recently. Its first involvement in joint ventures began only three years ago. As an in-house supplier to "Filtration, Inc.," a huge Chicago-based international manufacturing conglomerate, specializing in the design and production of temperature control and filtration systems, it had been shielded from significant competition, and most of its product lines of various electronic control mechanisms had been produced in North America. Ten years ago, however, Controls became a subsidiary of Filtration, Inc. and was given a charter to pursue business beyond that transacted with its parent. At the same time, the rules for acquiring in-house business changed as well. Controls now bid for Filtration, Inc.'s business against many of the world's best producers of this equipment. The need to utilize cheaper labor and to be located closer to key prospective customers drove the company to expand internationally at a rate that only a few years earlier would have been completely outside its corporate comfort zone.

A JV in China would provide Controls with an opportunity to gain a foothold in this untapped market for temperature control systems. This could pave the way for a greater thrust into the expanding Chinese economy. If the JV was successful, it could also lead to the establishment of plants to manufacture various products for the entire Asia/Pacific market.

The corporation's involvement in the joint venture seemed less planned than its other expansion efforts. The Freezer and Cooler Controls Business Unit (one of Controls' key business units), headquartered in Lakeland, Minnesota, sent a team of four, consisting of two engineers and two representatives from the Finance and Business Planning Departments, to investigate the possibility of partnering with a yet-to-be-identified Chinese electronics assembly operation. The team was not given an adequate budget and was limited to a visit of one month. Not being experienced international negotiators, they were only able to identify one potential partner, a Chinese state-owned firm. They quickly realized that they did not have time to conclude negotiations, and returned to HQ without having met their objective. After debriefing them upon their return to the United States, the corporation's planners decided that the Chinese JV presented a good opportunity and sent another team to continue these negotiations. Eventually, an agreement was reached with the Chinese state-owned firm. Exhibit C14-1 shows the organizational relationships between Filtration, Inc. and its subsidiaries.

HOW IT ALL BEGAN

James had always been intrigued by the idea of securing an international assignment. His interest heightened on the day that Controls, Inc. announced its intentions to expand the business through establishing a more international presence. By age 51, James had worked in managerial positions in Engineering, Quality Control, Customer Support, and Program Management for the last 15 of his 23 years with the company, but always in positions geographically based in Pauley, Illinois. He frequently mentioned the idea of working on an international assignment to his superiors during performance reviews and in a variety of other

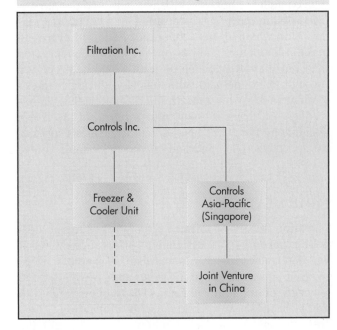

EXHIBIT C14-1   Filtration Inc. Organization Chart

settings. He did not mentally target any specific country, but preferred an assignment in the Pacific Rim due to his lifelong desire to gain an even deeper understanding of his wife's cultural heritage.

Finally, two years ago, he was able to discuss his interests with the corporation's International Human Resource manager. During this interview he was told of the hardships of functioning as an expatriate. There could be a language problem as well as difficulties caused by the remoteness from home office. He remained interested.

A year later, James was first considered for a position that required venture development in Tokyo. At one point he was even told he had been chosen for that position. With little explanation, the company instead announced the selection of a younger, more "politically" connected "fast-tracker."

When, a few months later, a discussion about the position in China was first broached by Personnel, it was almost in the context of it being a consolation prize. The position, however, appeared to be one for which James was even better suited and one which would be challenging enough to "test the mettle" of any manager in the company. The assignment was to "manage a joint venture manufacturing facility" located on Chongming Dao Island, about 25 miles north of Shanghai. The strategic objective of the JV was market entry into China.

Soon thereafter, in mid-August of 1992, James was asked to go immediately to Lakeland to meet one-on-one with Joe Whistler, the director of the Freezer and Cooler Controls Business Unit to discuss the JV. The negotiating team was still in China in the process of "finalizing" the JV agreement with the Chongming Electro-Assembly Company, a state-owned electronic device assembly operation. The corporation felt that there was a dire need to put someone on site. Joe asked if he could leave next week! James indicated that he was interested in accepting the position and that he was willing to do whatever the corporation required of him to make it happen as soon as possible. It was understood that a formal offer for the position would be processed through Personnel and communicated through James's management. When this trip didn't materialize, James wondered if this was going to be a repeat of the Tokyo assignment. Finally, in late September, James's supervisor approached him and said, "if you still want it, you've got the prize."

ORIENTATION

Filtration, Inc. has a defined set of procedures to deal with expatriate work assignment orientation. When it was determined that James was a strong candidate to go overseas, it was arranged for James and his wife to go to Chicago for orientation training. The training began with a day-long session conducted by Filtration, Inc.'s International personnel function. James thought the training was exceptionally well done. Filtration, Inc. brought in experts to discuss pay, benefits, moving arrangements, and a multitude of other issues dealing with working for the corporation in an international assignment. Part of the orientation process was a "look-see trip," the normal length of which was seven days. The trip was quickly arranged to begin two weeks later. The Randolfs were extremely excited. This would be Lily's first trip back to China. They even extended the duration of the trip to ten days to do some investigation on their own time.

There was a considerable mix-up in the planning of the "look-see" trip. Although the Personnel Department in Pauley wanted to arrange the entire trip, Controls' Asia-Pacific regional office in Singapore insisted it was better for them to handle it locally. The Randolfs were supposed to have a rental car available upon arrival but discovered that no arrangements had been made, and so they were forced to secure their own car. Their itinerary indicated that they had reservations at the Shanghai Inn, but they soon discovered that no reservations had been made there either.

In Shanghai they went sightseeing on their own for three days. Afterward, they were scheduled for seven days of official activities. They spent the following two days with an on-site consultant who was on retainer from the JV, and who showed the potential expatriates around the city. Her tour consisted of what she perceived a typical American might most like to see.

The wife of an expatriate herself, the consultant didn't speak Shanghainese or any other Chinese dialects. Travel with her was somewhat of a nightmare. As opposed to discussing the planned locations with the Chinese driver at the beginning of a day, she directed the trip one step at a time. She would show

the driver a card on which was written the address of the next location and say "[G]o here now." This approach caused considerable delays due to the inefficiencies of [traversing] the city numerous times and touring in a disorderly sequence. They were shown American-style shopping, American-style restaurants, and potential living accommodations. The Randolfs were told that leasing a good apartment commonly required a "kickback."

After visiting the JV's factory near Shanghai they traveled to the regional headquarters, Controls Asia-Pacific, in Singapore to participate in an extensive orientation workshop. Again, the topics included compensation policies and other matters of interest to potential expatriates, this time from the perspective of Controls, Inc. James and Lily both noted a significant contrast in dealings with the regional Controls, Inc. personnel staff as opposed to the "first rate" Filtration, Inc. International Human Resources people. The former was by far a less polished and informed operation. Even as they departed Singapore for the United States, they were still unsure that the move was right for them. They spent the next several days reflecting on the trip and discussing their decision. They were discouraged by the lack of maintenance apparent in the factory, which was clearly inferior to U.S. standards. Things were dirty, and little effort was expended on environmental controls. The days seemed awfully gray. However, they had quickly become enamored with the Shanghai people and this became a key factor in their ultimate decision to accept the position. As the result of their interactions with the Chinese partners and Shanghai area residents, James and Lily truly felt the promise of exciting, new, deep, long-lasting relationships.

Once they were firmly committed to the assignment, they attended a two-day orientation on living and working in China. This was provided by Prudential Relocation Services Inc. in Boulder, Colorado, and was tailored to the needs and desires of the participants. Optional curriculum tracks included the history, culture, political climate, business climate, and the people of the region. James focused his training on a business-related curriculum which was taught by professors from a local university. Additionally, whenever an expatriate returned from China to the home office on home leave, James was given an opportunity to interface with him. Exhibit C14-2 summarizes the key characteristics of Chinese culture and management.

Between November (1992) and January (1993), James worked an exhausting schedule, alternating two-week periods in Pauley and at the JV in China, where lodging and meals were provided in a hotel. During this time his wife, Lily, remained in Lakewood preparing for their permanent relocation to China. Also, Filtration, Inc. held scheduled, intensive Mandarin language courses in Chicago, which James planned to attend, but due to his

Culture

One of the strong cultural beliefs among the Chinese is that their culture is the oldest and the best. It is the center of the universe, the *Zhong guo*—center country. They believe themselves to be totally self-sufficient. In Chinese, the character of the word China means "middle kingdom," thus implying that everyone other than themselves is beneath them.

Concept of Face and Time

The concept of face is of paramount importance in China. It is a person's most precious possession. Without it, one cannot function in China. It is earned by fulfilling one's duties and other obligations. Face often requires little effort, but merely an attention to courtesy in relationships with others. Face involves a high degree of self-control, social consciousness, and concern for others. In Chinese society, display of temper, sulking, loss of self-control, or frustration create further loss of face rather than drawing respect.

Despite having invented the clock, the Chinese never define or segment time in the way that it is approached in the West. Even today, for the Chinese, time simply flows from one day to another. If a job is not completed today, they will carry it forward to the next day or the day after next. This is a manifestation of the concept of polychronic (non-linear) time. In Western cultures, people see time as monochronic (linear).

An important cultural difference between the West and China is the Chinese custom of giving precedence to form and process in completing a task over the task itself, an approach which is typically more time-consuming.

Behavior

Chinese behavior is influenced by their brutal history. This has created a careful people. They give consideration to the repercussions of every move or decision that they make.

An important aspect of behavior involves the way the Chinese think. They think about thinking and relationships, whereas the Westerner would think in linear patterns of cause and effect.

Another aspect, which confuses the Westerner, is the willingness to discuss endless possibilities even when things look hopeless.

A Chinese philosophy that relates to interacting with Westerners can be stated: Whereas a Westerner will try to tell you everything he knows in a conversation, a Chinese will listen to learn everything the Westerner knows, so that, at the end of the day, he would know both what he knew and what the Westerner knew.

Gift Giving

The Chinese are conditioned to express appreciation in tangible ways, such as by giving gifts and other favors. They regard the Westerner's frequent use of "thank you" as a glib and insincere way of passing off obligations to return favors. When they do someone a favor, they expect appreciation to be expressed in some very concrete way. If all you choose to do is say "thanks," it should be very specific and sincere, and then stop. The Chinese do not like gushy thanks. Gift giving in China is a highly developed art. Although it has greatly diminished today (there is a law forbidding government officials from accepting gifts of any kind or value), the practice remains a vital aspect of creating and nurturing relationships with people.

Living as a Foreign Guest in the People's Republic of China

Foreigners, who have gone to the People's Republic of China in the last decade to help the Chinese, have been given preferential treatment. Their quarters are often far more modern than those of a typical Chinese. The expatriate is given perquisites in excess of those available to all but the top officials, fed with highest quality food, and paid salaries many times higher than paid to their Chinese counterpart of the same status. They are sheltered from the harsh realities of Chinese life and are recipients of enormous courtesy and care.

There are three main reasons for this preferential treatment. First, as a poverty-stricken nation, the Chinese need to attract and retain foreigners to help them achieve a higher standard of living by increasing their economic and technical level. Second, the Chinese believe that people from the developed nations are so used to modern comforts that they would not be able to function competently without them. Finally, there is simple pride. They want their country to be thought of favorably.

Social

Generally, the sociocultural behavior of the Chinese differs greatly from that of Western societies. Family is very important to them, and obligation to them takes precedence when it conflicts with work responsibilities. Those outside the family are treated with indifference and sometimes with contempt. Decision making evolves from the opinion and support of the family. The highest respect is given to elders and ancestors. The reverence for authority and order explains why the Chinese are so careful about getting consensus from everyone. An important ideal that is fostered by the family is harmony.

The Chinese do not believe in the concept of privacy. This absence of individuality and freedom is a way of life in China.

Laws Made to Be Broken

Due to their history of being encumbered by rules and taboos, the Chinese have developed a perverse and seemingly contradictory attitude toward laws and regulations. They tend to ignore them and break them to suit their purpose, as long as they think they can get away with it. A significant proportion of public Chinese behavior is based on political expediency, and not on their true feelings. Since their public, official behavior is more of a survival technique than anything else, they do not feel guilty about ignoring or subverting the system. It is something they do naturally as a way of getting by.

Importance of Human Resources Management in Organizations in China

The labor environment in China is influenced by six major factors. They are National Economic Plans, the Four Modernization Programs, Political Leadership, Chinese Cultural Values, Labor Unions, and the Special Economic Zones—that is, SEZs. The SEZs were created specially for the conduct of the joint ventures with overseas countries. The main characteristics of the SEZs that are found in a joint venture are their dominating influence on matters pertaining to the employment wage system, organizational structure, management roles, and decision making.

One of the most interesting aspects of Chinese HRM is the unmistakable influence of some of the traditional cultural values

(continued)

EXHIBIT C14-2 (cont.)

such as *guanxi* (relationship), *renqing* (favor), *mianzi* (face), and *bao* (reciprocation) in recruitment and selection, training and development, and placement and promotion.

There is a definite political element involved in the behavior of Chinese Personnel managers; those who are more party-oriented base their decisions on party policies rather than for the good of the company.

Maintaining Personnel Files and Their Implications
Chinese-style personnel management generally does not forgive or forget any real or imagined past transgressions by employees under their jurisdiction. Any past mistakes or offenses committed by the employee are duly recorded in the employee's file and are often used against that person.

To hire someone from another company, the other company must release the prospective employee's file. This contains the employee's work record and entitles him or her to benefits accorded to workers in the state sector. If the employer is not willing to release the file and the employee leaves, he or she loses the benefits, a risk few Chinese are willing to take. Many foreign companies have been able to complete transfers only after compensating the other company. The average payoff has been about 1,000 yuan (in 1992), a very modest amount in $US but one-half of one month's salary for a translator.

The Chinese can be said to be ethnocentric, that is, the belief that one's own national or regional management practices are superior. This can carry over into the review and acceptance of an employee's file from other provinces. The employee's previous place of employment can impact his future job prospects. In this case, the Shanghainese would look with disfavor on an employee file (and therefore the individual) from the poorer, less sophisticated Chongming Dao area.

A related culture difference is that a foreign manager would examine an employee's file from the perspective of performance, whereas a Chinese manager would review the file to learn of an individual's seniority and to see if there is a history of causing dissention.

Rank
There are no official class distinctions in China, but rank among businesspeople and government bureaucrats is very important. It is very important that you know the rank of the individual you are likely to deal with and your response should be consistent with the rank. Connections and rank gain one access to the *tequari* or special privileges. If the top official is accompanied by the second in rank, all the discussion should be directed toward the top official and the second in rank might as well not be present.

Manufacturing and Quality Control in China
In general, the Chinese have only a rudimentary understanding of quality concepts. They almost always carry out 100 percent inspections to "control" quality. Because the Chinese have become accustomed to inferior quality goods, producing goods of high quality is often not perceived by workers to be important. Those items that do not pass quality control are offered to the employees free of charge.

There is great variety in the quality of technology used in China. For the most part the technological level resembles that of the United States in the 1950s. There is scant computerization. Materials handling is done manually. Machinery is bulky and frequently needs repair.

Scheduling of work is almost nonexistent, though work itself is assigned to groups. A typical manufacturing operation is very labor-intensive, and in most cases there is an excessively large workforce. Production planning is usually based on the number of hours to be worked rather than on the number of units to be manufactured.

Infrastructure
China's economy suffers from weak infrastructure. Electricity is unavailable at times (especially if the firm has exceeded its quota). Roads need repairs, train shipments are more often than not late, factory allocations of raw materials are (occasionally) routed to other units, and the communication systems can be considered a nightmare.

Additional Note
Neither Geert Hofstede's original study (Hofstede, 1980) nor his later work (Hofstede and Bond, 1988) included China as a country of analysis. However, Hong Kong and Taiwan were included in both instances. The results were similar for Power Distance (Large), Individualism (Low), Uncertainty Avoidance (Low), and Confucianism (High), differing only in Masculinity (Hong Kong, high, and Taiwan, low). We would therefore expect top-down decision making, centralized authority, little participative management, tolerance of uncertainty, and authority vested only in the most senior employees. This confirms the events described in the case.

---

work schedule he was unable to take advantage of the opportunity. Finally, in January, James attended the language school for a week. Fortunately, he and Lily already spoke some Cantonese, another Chinese dialect. After James was finally on-site full-time in February, he hired a language tutor to supplement this training. The orientation procedure concluded with a checklist of things that James and Controls were to accomplish after the commencement of his on-site assignment. While all of these checklist items were eventually accomplished,

priorities on the job didn't allow them to be completed in a very timely manner.

WORKPLACE ORIENTATIONS

Mandarin, China's official language, was spoken at the factory. In regions where Mandarin is not the primary language of the people, it is the language most commonly used in industry and trade, and in dealing with the government. Most residents were not proficient in

Mandarin, although the oldest members of the population had learned it only after they had completed their formal education, if at all. Mandarin became China's official language when the alphabet was standardized in 1955. Away from the workplace, people preferred to speak Shanghainese or Chongming Dao's own similar dialect.

Chongming Dao, the actual site of the factory, was situated in the Chuang Yangtze River. At approximately 50 miles long and 18 miles wide, it is China's third largest island. Its population is approximately one million people. The residents were perceived by the Shanghainese to be poor, backward farmers.

James found that he was able to maintain residencies in Shanghai and in Chongming Dao, although all the Chinese workers, including managers, lived close to their place of work. The trip from downtown Shanghai to the plant took more than two hours. First there was a half-hour trip to the site of the ferry departure, then came a 20-minute ferry ride, followed by another 20 minutes of travel by car. Work days at the factory were scheduled from Tuesdays through Saturdays. As is common in China, the schedules were centrally planned to alternate with those of other factories in a manner which conserved power consumption.

The Chinese partner had warehouses and a business center on the island, which, in addition to the factory, became part of the JV. The people worked under conditions that would be totally unacceptable to most American workers. There were no temperature or humidity controls. In the winter the plant was so cold that workers wore up to six layers of clothing. In contrast, summers were very hot and humid. None of the machinery had safety guards. Tools were generally either nonexistent or inadequate. Lighting was also very poor.

The Chinese factory's workforce was primarily young women. This was in contrast to the Chinese partner's factories that James had visited, where most of the workers were men who appeared to be over the age of 40. The plant's organization and operation fostered considerable inefficiencies. There were not process controls to prevent errors and scrap. The only visible methods of quality control were extensive amounts of 100 percent testing and inspection performed after the product was completely assembled. The layout of the plant was awkward. There were numerous little rooms and no large expansive production areas. Operations were not laid out sequentially or even in a line. The typical mode of operations was to have numerous workers working elbow to elbow around the perimeter of a large table.

Material movement was most commonly performed by dragging large tubs of materials across the floor. Storage was disorderly and bins were generally not stacked, due to a lack of shelving. Consequently, containers of parts, partially assembled products, scrap materials, and finished assemblies could be found anywhere and everywhere. Instead of scheduling plant output, the system scheduled only the number of man-hours to be expended. This lack of direction caused a considerable amount of confusion and inefficiency. It was really more of a way of accounting for the use of the excessive labor force that existed in the factory and in the area. James often commented that he could produce as much or more output with only the number of Quality Control (QC) operators that were in the plant. By his estimates, the JV employed three times as many people as were needed. James did not think that he could change this immediately but felt that he could convince the Chinese management that this practice needs to be changed eventually.

ADAPTING TO LIFE IN CHINA

Beyond some terrific people in the Personnel Department in Pauley, who could help with specific employment-related issues, James quickly came to realize that there would be little operational support from the home office. His links back to his corporation came more from Filtration, Inc. than from Controls. Filtration, Inc. at least sent a monthly package of news clippings, executive briefs, and memos that had been specifically prepared for expatriates. The package allowed James to keep up somewhat on what was happening in the larger corporate setting.

Filtration, Inc. had a couple of dozen employees in Shanghai. It was their role to establish and implement a joint venture that the parent had negotiated with a different Chinese manufacturer than the one with which Controls had partnered. As part of this team, there were also a few representatives from Controls, Inc. They were all co-located in a small office building in downtown Shanghai. It was in this corporate office environment that James found a great deal of support, a lot of helpful advice, and his unofficial mentor, a Filtration, Inc. manager who had spent four years in China. At the time, James wondered why he hadn't visited this office during his orientation trip.

The help that James received from Controls, Inc.'s subsidiary, Controls Asia-Pacific, was often ineffective and inconsistent. Nagging policies and obligatory paperwork were typical characteristics of their assistance. There were ongoing problems finding and retaining a qualified translator for James. In the agreement, the JV was responsible for providing each expatriate with a translator. Controls Asia-Pacific was responsible for the wage structure at the JV. The Personnel Department in Singapore established a maximum wage rate for the translator position at 2,000 yuan. This rate was fair for the area, but there were few high-quality translators available. When an area translator was identified, he would often be lost to another multinational company in the area who offered a salary of 3,000 yuan. To attract translators from Shanghai would require a wage comparable to the wages one would receive in Shanghai, and 2,000 yuan was significantly lower than that paid in the city.

Another aspect of employment in China which merited consideration was the movement of one's "personnel file" from a former employer to the present one. This is the rough equivalent of changing one's residency to another state in the United States. The reputation and perception of Chongming Dao was that of a rural community. This would have a negative impact on transferring a translator's file back to Shanghai in the future. Singapore didn't understand the economics and implications of this situation and refused to increase the wage rate to a level that would entice qualified translators to accept the position. James, as a result, was without a qualified translator for significant periods during his time in China. The impact on his ability to function in that setting was therefore also significant, resulting in less being accomplished than if Singapore had been more flexible.

The residence in Shanghai was available because the JV had committed to a two-year lease of an executive apartment on the 22nd floor of the Shanghai Inn. These accommodations were quite nice and offered most of the comforts of home. The hotel complex included a supermarket, exercise facilities, a theater, and several restaurants, including Shanghai's Hard Rock Cafe. The three-bedroom apartment, which James measured to be around 1,500 square feet, was converted into a two-bedroom apartment to his specifications. Amenities included cable TV with five English language channels. Accommodations on the island were significantly rougher. The original plan was for James to temporarily stay at the government's guest house on the factory grounds, until a 12-unit housing compound was constructed in the immediate vicinity. The small rooms, intense heat, and fierce mosquitoes at the guest house proved to be unbearable and, by June, James decided to make other arrangements. These entailed staying in a hotel 17 miles away with the two other expatriates from Controls, Inc. to manage the JV. Although the building was new, the quality of the construction was quite poor, which seemed to be common in China. The costs associated with constructing their compound were, by this time, estimated to be much larger than expected. Eventually, a solution was reached to fix up certain aspects of the guest house and retain it as the long-term island living arrangements for them. After this, Lily always traveled with him to and from the factory.

ADAPTING TO THE WORK

In addition to James, there were three other Controls, Inc. expatriates assigned to the JV. The director of Engineering and the director of Manufacturing were on assignment from the United States. The director of Finance was from Singapore. Each of these individuals had dual roles, that of heading up their respective departments, and the assignment to bring to the JV new technology associated with their departments. The Finance director had the particularly challenging assignment of introducing a new accounting system to the JV, one that was compatible with the Controls, Inc. system. The existing system, installed by the Chinese partner, was not designed to report profits and losses, irrelevant concepts in the formerly state-owned company.

The other expatriates occasionally complained of not getting good cooperation from the Chinese workers. James never encountered this problem, as he always communicated his requests directly to the workers.

One of the first problematic situations that evolved related to differences between expatriate conditions of employment for Filtration, Inc. and Controls, Inc. employees. Most Filtration employees enjoyed a per diem of US$95, but Controls employees were limited to US$50 per day. Additionally, the Filtration, Inc.'s visitation policies were more liberal in terms of allowing college-age children to visit their expatriate parents.

ONGOING NEGOTIATIONS

In China, a JV contract is a "nice framework" from which to begin the real negotiation process. The Controls JV negotiating team viewed the contract as a conclusion to negotiations and returned to the United States in late December of 1992. James soon discovered that the process of negotiations would be ongoing. On almost a daily basis, some element of the agreement was adjusted or augmented with new understanding.

A misconception held by the Controls negotiating team related to the ease of obtaining appropriate governmental approvals. There were various annexes and subcontracts which were yet to be finalized and approved when they departed. Some of these approvals were required from government officials with whom they had had very little interface. The impact of this miscalculation was that production in the JV didn't commence on January 1, 1993, as anticipated. Instead it took until August 1, 1993 to get the operation going.

One of the most serious issues affecting the operation of the JV which directly impacted James' effectiveness was the JV's organization structure which was negotiated by the Controls team. The organization chart for the JV is shown in Exhibit C14-3. Controls perceived the position of Chairman (COB) of the Board of Directors to be of greater importance in operating the company than that of managing director, thinking that they could "run the company" from that position.

EXHIBIT C14-3   *Controls' Joint Venture in China: Organization Chart*

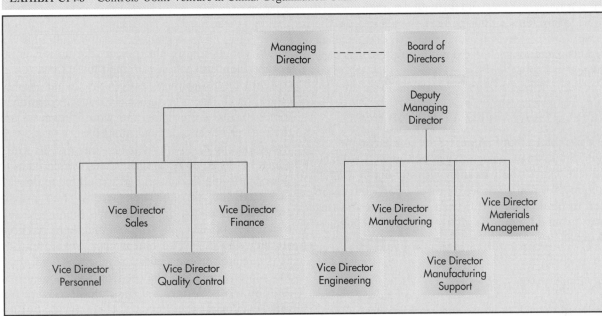

Consequently, when the organization chart was drawn up, Controls conceded the position of managing director to the Chinese partner in exchange for the right to appoint the COB for the first three of the five years. James noted that in Chinese JVs negotiated by Filtration, Inc., the U.S. partner always secured the position of managing director.

OBSERVATIONS OF CHINESE MANAGEMENT METHODS

James observed that when Chinese managers were dealing with subordinates, decision making was very top-down. This resulted in virtually all decisions of any consequence being made by the managing director. James was extremely fortunate that the managing director appointed by the Chinese partner was willing to share his power. He and the managing director developed an excellent relationship, which James consciously worked on in the firm belief that this was the key to business success in China. Toward the end of his time at the JV, James was frequently left in charge of running the factory while the managing director was visiting outside friends of influence, customers, and potential customers. The only other manager who shared this distinction was the director of Personnel.

The Personnel Department, in this JV, as in the state-owned Chinese companies, was unusually powerful when compared to most U.S. companies that James was familiar with. They maintained the all-important employment files and were very connected to the Communist Party.

OBSERVATIONS OF CHINESE MANAGEMENT TEAM

Chinese managers at the JV were considerably more educated than the workers. They had matriculated at various universities and graduated with degrees in Engineering, Management, and the like. In one case, the manager's experience and education came from his time as a career-soldier in the Army.

INTERACTIONS WITH THE CHINESE GOVERNMENT

Prior to the formation of the JV, the secretary for the Communist Party and the managing director were coequals when it came to "running the Chongming Electro-Assembly Company." About 325 of the 1,819 employees at the JV were communists. After James's arrival, there was always a question as to what would happen to the party office, which was located adjacent to the managing director's office. In many ways the party served a function similar to that of labor unions in the United States. It represented the workers and entered into discussions related to labor relations issues. The Communist Party could be viewed as a different channel to deal with issues, and James quickly recognized it as an ally.

James's only personal experience with a government bureau was while getting his residency papers established. The rules he encountered were extremely inflexible, everything had to be just right, and no copies were allowed as the Bureau required originals. The Bureau office, which was the size of a walk-in closet in the

United States, was extremely crowded and the process required forcing one's way up through the lines to get to the table where female police officers would process the paperwork. After it was all over, he noticed that they had spelled his name wrong. He did not return to correct the mistake.

INTERACTION WITH THE UNION

The JV also had a labor union, but by comparison to the United States, the organization was extremely weak and superficial. James's only dealing with the union related to a request for donations for a retirees' party the union wanted to hold. Since the JV had no retirees, and this was new ground for him, he referred them to the managing director.

GETTING IT TOGETHER

James loved to walk the floor and see what was happening in the factory. His position gave him the authority to direct actions to be taken, but often he did not have to use this authority in that way. The Chinese workers seemed to be influenced by his every action. If he would make a point to pick up trash in the parking lot, the next day he would observe that the trash had all been cleaned up. Another example was when he straightened some papers in the pigeon holes of a filing system. The next day every stack of papers was perfectly arranged. He felt that there was never a time where he walked the floor and it didn't pay off in some way. He found Chinese workers to be very attentive to detail.

He was often tested by the Chinese managers and workers alike, as is not uncommon in other parts of the world. He perceived that they would test his commitment, leadership, and his decision-making ability. They would determine how far this manager could be pushed. These tests provided him with the opportunity to do the right thing. A case in point was when a drunken salesperson accosted a woman in a nightclub. James took him to a private place and severely chastised him.

During his assignment, he remained cognizant of the fact that one of his jobs was to make the managing director look good. This required him to fire a translator on the spot when the translator remarked that anyone who wanted to stay in China was stupid.

He had great admiration for the Chinese workers at the JV. They proved to be very cooperative people. They had a great deal of pride and were very loyal to their company and the industry in which they worked. James often commented that, with informed leadership, Chinese workers would be as good as workers anywhere in the world.

What James liked best, however, was his interactions with the Chinese people. Every day brought him a new experience.

OBSERVATIONS ABOUT THE CHINESE PEOPLE

Most of the Chinese people were not communists. They would rather ignore the political situation going on around them and get on with their lives. They were eager to learn anything they could about what Westerners could teach them. Almost without exception, they looked up to Americans and would begin to imitate them after a while. James found it very gratifying. He was also delighted with their treatment of his wife, Lily, which bordered on reverence. James wondered as to the reasons for this. Perhaps it had something to do with the fact that she, through her parents, had previously escaped communist oppression and found a better life, which symbolized to the Chinese that there was hope for all. James never saw a Chinese man leering at a woman, as is common in the United States. In China, sexuality was a private matter. They tended to live a simpler life than do most Westerners. Their children were treated with reverence, even doted on. Their chaotic traffic jams seemed always to be dealt with very calmly. James never observed swearing or anger, as is common in the United States. James also found that the Chinese have an attitude that they know more than Westerners do, but that this never manifested itself in a boastful way. The attitude was more that at some point in time, Westerners would come around to their way of thinking. It was almost as though they played the role of a wiser urban patriarch guiding his young country cousin during the latter's first visit to the city. See Exhibit C14-2 for more information on Chinese culture and management.

ACTIVITIES AWAY FROM THE JOB

James and Lily had a different social life than that enjoyed in the United States. They spent hours walking and talking. Occasionally, when they were in Shanghai they had the opportunities to see shows. They saw the acrobats, went to symphony concerts and ballet, even joining crowds when Foster Beer brought Australian bands to perform in a Shanghai park.

The concerns Lily had expressed prior to expatriating disappeared as she made friends and became integrated into the social fabric of the area. Because her appearance was indistinguishable from the indigenous Shanghai-area people, she was more readily accepted and learned more about local happenings than most Westerners. At one point, two months after their arrival, Lily was hospitalized with a lung infection. Even this was resolved satisfactorily. She particularly noted that the skill level of the medical practitioners seemed to be very good, from the diagnosis to the way they painlessly took blood samples. Overall she found it easy to occupy her time. She was a traditional wife, who had not worked full time since her children were born and never had difficulty occupying the time in her life as she was a woman who was compelled to learn about everything and everybody. She spent much of her time traveling with James to and from the site, and when he was working she sought out the people and assisted at a mission nearby as she had some experience in nursing, having earned her nursing degree before marrying James.

The Randolfs preferred to eat food with fresh ingredients and were happy away from the "supermarket" society, so Lily also spent a lot of time shopping. They felt that they were able to eat quite well in China.

James and Lily learned as much of the local Shanghai dialect as they could. In spite of never becoming fully proficient, the fact that they attempted to speak it greatly pleased the local residents. They spent much of their spare time interacting with the people of the area.

Sometimes Filtration, Inc. would put on a social affair for the expatriates in Shanghai. James and Lily were always invited. While on the island, however, they always ate at the restaurant in the factory. Contrary to what they were told at their orientation training, they found the Chinese to be gregarious and fun-loving during meals. Meals were used as an opportunity to build relationships and share experiences.

JAMES'S RECALL AND DEPARTURE

Then one day, early in February 1994, James received the call from Singapore, which proved to be the most disappointing news he had heard during his entire China experience. Controls had chosen to recall him back to home office. He was directed to train his replacement and return home within the month.

Things had been going very well for several months now, and he was accomplishing a great many things. There was still so much he planned to do, including to convince the Chinese JV partner that they needed to reduce the number of workers significantly.

While he and Lily handled the news and the return arrangements with a great deal of dignity, there was a great sense of disbelief and sadness associated with the recall. Jimmy Chao, his replacement, arrived two weeks later. Jimmy was a Singaporean engineer whose experience was limited to supervising production at one of Controls' factories in that country. James spent as much time getting him up to speed as was possible. Jimmy was 18 years younger than James, quite cocky, and very opinionated and aggressive. While James provided all the coaching that he could, Jimmy was bound to do things his way.

The scene at the ferry when they departed the island for the last time was incredible. Many of the workers and all of the managers supplied by the Chinese partner were there to see them off. Many tokens of appreciation and affection were exchanged.

The plane droned inexorably on. James had, by this point in the trip, "rerun the tapes" of his whole experience over and over in his mind, and again thought about how blessed he felt to have had the experience at all: "What recommendations should I make in my report and during my debriefings? If I really think they are heading for the 'ditch,' it is my responsibility to steer them away from it. Oh well, these questions will have to wait until another day. It is time to get some sleep. I wonder what the temperature is in Pauley?"

QUESTIONS FOR DISCUSSION

1. Critique the apparent expatriate selection process used by Controls, Inc.
2. Comment on the orientation programs that James undertook.
3. What other concerns do you have about Controls' HRM strategy? What changes would you recommend to Controls' management? Or its parent?
4. Was James Randolf a good choice for this position? Justify your arguments.
5. Which of the following is the most appropriate course of action for Controls, Inc. (the subsidiary)?
   a. To continue with their present, haphazard, unplanned approach, and learn through experience and inevitable mistakes?
   b. To hire, at considerable expense, a seasoned international HRM specialist, such as a VP from another firm in the "auto" industry?
   c. To move more slowly and ensure that all involved in the formulation and implementation of International Human Resources Strategy are well trained in the field before undertaking these responsibilities?

6. What are the consequences of poorly managed expatriate management programs, especially in large organizations trying to significantly increase the percentage of total revenue earned from international and foreign activities, and their international market share?
7. What were some of the aspects of the Chinese business environment (including culture) that James had to deal with? Comment on his effectiveness as a manager in a JV in China.
8. What reasons can you give to legitimately explain his removal and replacement? How would you assess his replacement? Do you think that he will be successful? Why or why not?
9. What should James include in his report? How frank should he be? What recommendations should he make? To whom should he send copies?

NOTES

Hendryx, Steven R. "The China Trade: Making the Deal Work." *Harvard Business Review* (July–August 1986): 75–84.

Hofstede, Geert. *Cultures' Consequences: International Differences in Work Related Values,* Beverly Hills, CA: Sage Publications, 1980.

———, and Bond, Michael H. "The Confucius Connection: From Cultural Roots to Economic Growth." *Organizational Dynamics* (Spring 1988): 5–21.

Hu, Wenzhong, and Grove, Cornelius. *Encountering the Chinese: A Guide for the Americans.* Yarmouth, ME: Intercultural Press, Inc., 1993.

Kumar, Saha Sudhir. "Managing Human Resources in China." *Canadian Journal of Administrative Science* 10, no. 2 (Summer 1991): 167–177.

Macleod, Roderick. *How to Do Business with the Chinese.* New York: Bantam Books, 1988.

Wall, Jr., James J. "Managers in the People's Republic of China." *Academy of Management Executives* 4, no. 2 (1990): 19–32.

Yeung, Irene Y. M., and Tung, Rosalie L. "Achieving Business Success in Confucian Societies: The Importance of Guanxi." *Organizational Dynamics* (Autumn 1996): 54–65.

Case 15   Allure Cruise Line*—Challenges of Strategic Growth and Organizational Effectiveness: Part 4

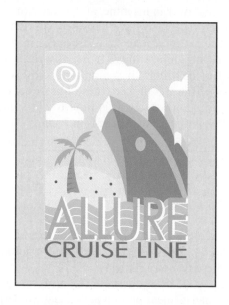

INTERVIEW WITH ALLURE CRUISE LINE EXECUTIVE

Additional interviews were conducted with several members of Allure's senior leadership team to obtain more information regarding the cruise industry and Allure's current human resources challenges.

---

*Note: The data used to develop this case study was garnered through the managers of an existing cruise line. The name of the cruise line, as well as the individuals in the case study, and some data have been changed to protect the confidentiality of the cruise line; specific data changes can be found at the end of this case.

Simon Wadsworth, Vice President of Human Resources for Allure, provided this perspective of the human resource function within the cruise industry, and specifically for Allure Cruise Line:

"The management of people within the cruise industry has often been perceived as more challenging than any land-based organization for a variety of reasons. For example, there are many legal and political ramifications to being a company headquartered in one country, operating in another country (or countries), and hiring workers from over 40 nations to work for you. We need to deal with visa policies of different countries for these 40-plus nations. Sometimes we have identified people around the world who would be great crew members for Allure; however, because of various reasons including security restrictions and challenges obtaining the appropriate visas, we are unable to hire them and bring them onboard with us. These ramifications also affect crew movement, as to when crew can be moved and the routes crew members will take coming and going from their work. The senior folks on the ships have two- to four-month contracts (e.g., Greek crew members work two months on, one off). This presents a challenge with leadership continuity.

"Our recruitment efforts occur in over 40 nations around the globe. This allows Allure to capitalize on crew member expertise. Certain countries have better schooling for specific jobs.

We go where we are permitted to go to recruit, and we strive for a good balance among various ethnic and demographic variables—we need a diverse population. For example, in the dining room, we want more mature, older, predominantly male individuals who are more service oriented (most are from European countries, such as France). Currently, recruiting firms help us to find new crew members. We have working relationships with them which allows them to offer certain packages to potential crew members within certain parameters. Allure focuses on finding and retaining mature crew members whose interest is service and their job—not focused on, say, the crew bar or preoccupied with what is happening on shore. We employ the efforts of various hiring agencies throughout the world to help with our hiring efforts.

"Like many cruise lines, Allure uses hiring agents in many countries to do the recruiting of new crew members. These agents screen out candidates and then provide us with general crew as well as a viable candidate pool for management. Then Allure recruiters interview the identified management candidates. We think our managers are very important so this is a little different than most other lines: Other cruise lines depend completely on the procurement allies to do the recruiting, hiring, and sometimes some training as well.

"The cost of our labor is pretty significant in the overall operation: about 65 percent of the total. There are high fixed costs with our labor. We are currently doing a competitive compensation study right now. We know that Allure is still doing well since the 9/11 and subsequent worldwide issues, but not as well as the company would like to be. We do know for a fact that our tipped personnel (servers, housekeepers) are paid very well—our passengers can be very generous.

"One of the challenging things we are concerned with as we look to expanding our fleet is the potential of cannibalizing our own crew. There are many questions we need to consider: How will we address the issue of the crew wanting to move to the new ships? How many crew will we allow to transfer (we'll definitely need enough experienced crew to stay on current ships but also provide support to the new operation). One of the big problems will be the significant differences between new and old ships: the 'new and 'cool' vessel will have better crew spaces and new itineraries. We know that too many crew members will want to move, so how will we select who will stay and who will go? How will we address the morale issues of those who do not move? These are some of the concerns we have

around recruitment and crew member movement for our new business objectives.

"After we recruit and hire our crew, we of course need to train them. Currently, all new crew members are flown straight to the ship and initially learn about expectations, safety, policies, and procedures when they board. We do offer continuous education onboard the ships in a variety of topic areas, including safety and customer service.

"When our crew first arrives onboard on their first day, they have safety training classes and are assigned a safety role and trained on it. They also have some up-front training on the company culture, expectations of passengers, basic safety training, regulations, rules, and sign in and paperwork, which is completed during their on-the-job training. At the beginning of their training, they are assigned to a buddy, and they start working right away. There is no space onboard to house crew who are in training but not working. Their OJT Buddy takes them on tour (we are now considering a pay differential for time doing training), goes over standards in dining room, set up of room, housekeeping hours, time of shows, etc. By the second voyage, the crew member is expected to be fully functional.

"Ideally the crew members re-sign when their contract comes up for renewal and are able to hit the ground running with little to no training—less of an impact on the operation and higher productivity. Compensation-wise, crew members receive a finishing bonus and re-signing bonus.

"Keep in mind that, if we were training crew onshore, Allure must cover all costs of transportation, meals, and lodging, so it is a lot less expensive to do the training onboard. Also, the crew members are able to still be productive and work in the operation, even if they are learning as they go.

"There are some opportunities for cross-training for transfer from one position to another, but typically their contracts will not be rewritten. We try and control the turnover since the environment is already unstable enough."

"Allure's captain's team was offered input on the type of training they needed and would like: This is very rare and does not typically occur on other cruise lines. It is difficult for officers to be away from the operations for so long so the training is done onboard in two- to three-hour modules. A corporate trainer from the home office in Miami typically facilitates the training, and it is scheduled during port days.

"So often, not only with trying to develop our managers but for many things, the challenge comes with the frequent changes in our

managers. The leadership style onboard changes every month on many cruise lines—on Allure, it changes every three months. Officers sign contracts for up to three- to six-months and typically renew their contracts after taking a two-month break. In general, the officers give one month's notice if they are leaving, and the Captain will give several months notice."

"Our crew is very diverse in terms of ethnography, background, culture, and many other variables. You could think of it as a 'small United Nations' onboard. The pro's to this situation are that it brings the best of different cultures, like living abroad. Our passengers absolutely love this diversity and have come to expect it. Conversely, with this diversity comes many challenges, most notably communication and culture. While all crew members are required to speak English for safety issues (all crew members must pass an English test), for the majority of the crew, English is not their first language. Clothing is not usually an issue, as the crew members have uniforms and are not allowed to wear any extra adornments on them.

"Even though we do our best to retain our crew members, of course there is turnover. The industry wide turnover rate is 35 percent annually (across the board at all levels within the shipboard organization). We're proud to say that Allure's turnover rate is around 31 percent. The turnover that occurs in the senior staff often occurs because they are offered one-month on/one-month off contracts from other cruise lines. While our turnover is better than the industry standard, we would still like to find ways to reduce it. We know that several factors impact turnover: (1) many crew members stay because they say it "feels like family" . . . how can we foster this? (2) the amount of developmental training has been shown to improve retention; (3) of course pay impacts retention efforts; (4) the benefits we offer—not just health care and bonuses, but shipboard benefits such as length of breaks between contracts and contract lengths overall impact retention; (5) crew amenities (e.g., Allure does not have larger cabins and Internet access in the crew cabins and instead of having individual sleeping quarters, rooms accommodate two or four).

"The crew works very hard while onboard our ships. Our itineraries run from 3 days to 14 days, and in many instances, crew members do not get a day off. Typically crew members work 75- to 110-hour weeks and are on call 24-7, seven days a week. This is typical for any cruise organization. The typical crew member lives within what we sometimes refer to as 'split scheduling'—

crew members will have some hours off in the middle of the day but work mornings and evenings. They sometimes may have only two hours off between shifts, can close at 2 a.m. and then have to open at 6 a.m. Again, this is typical for any cruise organization. If we were to try to increase the amount of time off they have, we would need to increase the labor we have, and we have no space for extra crew. Now this does not apply to positions within the bridge and engine crew, as the STCW (i.e., Standards of Training, Certification, and Watchkeeping) and maritime law restrict the number of hours they can work without rest due to potential safety issues.

"When it comes to crew duties, there are two organizational structures in place, and the two lay on top of each other. Each crew member has his or her normal position, the role for which they were hired. Then each crew member also has an extra role (a safety role) that they play on the ship (e.g., captain of the lifeboat or fire brigade). For some of these extra roles, the crew members need and receive extra training and/or certification.

"Regarding leadership onboard our vessels, the executive leadership team onboard consists of the captain/master and his three senior officers who report directly to him: the staff captain (second in charge), the hotel director, and the senior engineer. These leaders make up the 'captains team' and are the companies' leadership while the ship is out to sea.

"These leaders and all shipboard managers have Operating Procedures (OPs) for everything on the ship and any situation that can occur (e.g., for critical situations, like an incident of tuberculosis onboard, the individual would need to be helicoptered off the ship). The Captain has final say on all decisions on board.

"Not only do hierarchical differences exist between the crew and officers, but they also exist among the crew. There are some lower crew who are ranked higher than others, based on their jobs, seniority, etc. Those who are ranked higher will typically get bigger rooms and less people with whom they have to share the room.

"So, taking into account these variables of working and living so closely together, you can understand why the challenges with having the crew members live in an enclosed area with each other 24-7 can be many. Crew members live and work with each other 12, 15, 18 hours a day. Consider the ship to be like a big dormitory; and shipboard Human Resources plays the role of the hall monitor. There is a need to have strong policies and procedures, many rules for everything to ensure justness and fairness. For example: no food is allowed in the cabins, for *cleanliness reasons. Every cabin is inspected weekly (for cleanliness, food, fire safety, etc.).*

"When the crew members aren't working, they have several areas just for their recreational use. These include (1) a small crew bar/lounge with a small dance floor, (2) crew mess hall, (3) the officers' mess hall, and (4) a crew gym. Also, crew members can use passenger areas (e.g., movie theater) when they are not being used. However, general crew members are not allowed to walk around the ship on their time off. Certain officers may socialize with passengers, and may use the passenger areas when not on duty.

"Since there are so many rules and regulations—all established for various reasons—we do have a strict discipline system onboard. After five offenses, the crew member is out of a job and is sent home. An example of one of our many rules and regulations is that the majority of the crew members cannot socialize with passengers onboard. Mostly mid-level officers and above are permitted to socialize with passengers (that's about 60 or so officers). But our general crew members are not and that can cause problems between the ranks. If a crew member who is not permitted to fraternize with passengers does so, disciplinary action would be taken immediately.

"Our discipline policy is handled by the staff captain. Depending on the infraction, we have a 'five strikes and you're out' mentality here. Upon the fifth strike, we hold a Captain's review: this is the morning of our day at the home port, when the crew member can plead his or her case to the Captain, and he decides if the crew member stays or goes, based upon the evidence. There is no brig on the ship, so the crew member is confined to cabin until we reach port if it is decided they are terminated. They are met at the port by a member of our corporate human resources team and escorted by HR to the airport—need to get them out of the country ASAP.

"Other means of evaluation for performance includes a review of the Captain's performance yearly by our Vice President of Operations (currently Rebecca Brandon), and the senior leaders onboard have annual reviews of performance as well. Business metrics are used to evaluate the managers' performance in addition to their own personal performance. These include our crew turnover, attrition, retention figures, the crew re-sign rate, our USPH (sanitation/cleanliness) scores, our Environment scores, and our Safety scores. The crew performance reviews are more complicated to accomplish due to the high level of attrition."

"Besides the stressors of living and working in the same place, other unique variables that can

impact a crew member's daily life include something as simple as the weather. For example: weather changes can affect itineraries. The ships may have to stay at sea or go to other ports. This can affect the workload of the crew. Or, if many crew members get sick at once, this can affect the level of service we provide to our passengers. If a crew member is sick, he or she needs to go to the crew infirmary. Only the doctor decides if you are sick and 'not fit for duty.' Crew members cannot just 'call in sick.'

"Some of the issues that we need to consider when looking at expanding our operation include the development of a labor strategy for the new ships—how will we staff these vessels? Also, it is sometimes difficult to find high-quality crew members. We expect to need an additional 1,000 new crew members to run the ships. Will we move some of the current crew to the new ship? What will the passenger-to-crew ratios be? How will we maximize retention? And finally, where will we train the new crew members?"

THE CHALLENGES FOR ALLURE CRUISE LINE (CONTINUED)

In addition to the strategic growth challenges that Allure Cruise Line is currently facing, they are also experiencing some human resource and leadership issues onboard. The challenges are discussed and outlined below.

ASSIGNMENT – HUMAN RESOURCE AND LEADERSHIP CHALLENGE

GOAL 3: People Strategy

As you help the leadership team of Allure develop the business and organizational strategies for their organization, they are also looking to your team to help them address some of the human resource management and people issues associated with this expansion.

As part of the expansion process, Allure is planning on sending a management team abroad as expatriates to:

- Oversee the startup of the expansion and the addition of the new ships in the Mediterranean, and
- Prepare for the staffing and the training of the crew (and all other HR functions) on the new ships.

The leadership team needs help determining and planning the following:

- How do they select which managers to include on the team they will send abroad?
- Will they hire host-country nationals in Europe to help?
- How do they prepare these managers for the challenges they might encounter in Europe?

- How do they prepare this team to work as a global team potentially with managers from other countries?
- How do they prepare the managers to negotiate the deals that the expansion will require?

In addition, consider these issues:

- How do they help these managers plan for the HR functions necessary to staff and run the new ship?
- Will the HR functions and how they are set up need to look different for the Mediterranean side of the business?
- How and where will they recruit new crew members?
- What staffing approach should they adopt?
- Should some of the current Allure crew members be moved to the new ships?
- If so, how will the crew members who will be moved to the new ships be selected? How will the transfer decisions be made?
- Where will the training of the new crew take place?

FINAL COMPREHENSIVE ASSIGNMENT

Now that you have completed the four parts of the Allure Case, you and your team should prepare a formal presentation and proposal for the senior leadership team of Allure in which you present your analysis of their organization and your subsequent recommendation in which you address the key concerns and questions of the team.

Your proposal and presentation should cover the following:

- The results of your SWOT analysis.
- Your proposed recommendations regarding:
  - Whether Allure Cruise Line should expand to the Mediterranean
  - The implementation of the expansion.

- The preparation of the team who will negotiate and set up the new business.
- The human resource challenges and key decisions involved in the expansion.

Please be sure to address all of the key questions posed to you by the leadership team of Allure.

DATA MODIFIED IN CASE STUDY TO PROTECT THE IDENTITY OF THE BUSINESS

As noted earlier, this case study is based upon very real situations for a cruise business today. While the names and some of the facts have been changed to preserve the confidentiality of the business in question, it should be noted that the business scenario itself is indeed a situation that not only this organization but also many cruise lines are facing in today's business climate. Specifically, the following data has been modified for this case study:

- The name of the cruise line
- The names of interviewed executives
- The number of ships in the fleet
- The founding date of the cruise line
- The *Vision* and *Mission* of the cruise line
- The number of crew and number of officers onboard each ship
- The overall organizational structure of the cruise line

To date, the cruise line on which this case study is based has not made a decision regarding the addition of new ships nor the expansion of its respective fleets to the Mediterranean.

Integrative Term Project

This project requires research, imagination, and logic in applying the content of this course and book.

In groups of three to five students, create an imaginary company that you have been operating in the domestic arena for some time. Your group represents top management, and you have decided it is time to go international.

- Describe your company and its operations, relative size, and so forth. Give reasons for your decision to go international.
- Decide on an appropriate country in which to operate, and give your rationale for this choice.
- State your planned entry strategy, and give your reasons for this strategy.
- Describe the environment in which you will operate and the critical operational factors that you must consider and how they will affect your company.
- Give a cultural profile of the local area in which you will be operating. What are the workers going to be like? What kind of reception do you anticipate from local governments, suppliers, distributors, and so on?
- Draw up an organization chart showing the company and its overseas operations, and describe why you have chosen this structure.
- Decide on the staffing policy you will use for top-level managers, and give your rationale for this policy.
- Describe the kinds of leadership and motivational systems you think would be most effective in this environment. Give your rationale.
- Discuss the kinds of communication problems your managers might face in the host-country working environment. How should they prepare for and deal with them?
- Explain any special control issues that concern you for this overseas operation. How do you plan to deal with them?

Identify the concerns of the host country and the local community regarding your operations there. What plans do you have to deal with their concerns and to ensure a long-term cooperative relationship?

Wal-Mart: Managing Globalization in 2007

INTRODUCTION

In 2006, Wal-Mart, the largest retail chain in the world was also the world's largest company with a turnover of $312.4 billion.[1] Wal-Mart's globalization had started in 1991, when it opened a Sam's Club near Mexico City. In 1993, Wal-Mart International was set up to oversee the growing opportunities for the company worldwide. Since then, the overseas operations enjoyed rapid growth and consumer acceptance.

Wal-Mart's approach to competing in overseas markets had evolved over time. When it entered a foreign country, Wal-Mart adjusted to the local regulatory framework and customer tastes. The retailer made necessary modifications such as merchandise offerings. However, Wal-Mart did not change three main ingredients: Brand names (Wal-Mart and Sam's Club), 'Every Day Low Price' (EDLP) strategy (see Exhibits 1 and 2 at end of case), and high ethical standards. Brand names had been an important asset while entering foreign countries and establishing an initial market. Wal-Mart extended EDLP to overseas markets both to make supply chain management more effective and to gain the trust of customers. Despite the difficulties involved, Wal-Mart had also held steadfast to its high ethical standards.

Wal-Mart believed customers were alike across the world, regardless of how different their countries looked. As a senior executive put it,[2]

> Over the years many said that we would not be able to serve customers west of the Mississippi, outside of the South, in metropolitan areas or outside of the United States. Frankly, we find the

customers want the same things. Regardless of where we are, customers want to be treated well, want to have a good assortment of products to choose from; and they want the merchandise at a great price. The most amazing fact is that our associates around the world embrace and protect this culture that they have built over the last thirty-five years.

In 2005, Wal-Mart acquired a 33.3 percent interest in Central American Retail Holding Company (CARHCO), a 360-store supermarket operation, extending its presence to Costa Rica, El Salvador, Guatemala, Honduras, and Nicaragua. It also acquired a majority interest in Seiyu Ltd., a leading Japanese retailer. As of late 2006, Wal-Mart International employed more than 450,000 associates in Argentina, Brazil, Canada, China, Costa Rica, El Salvador, Guatemala, Honduras, Japan, Mexico, Nicaragua, Puerto Rico, and the United Kingdom. Overseas sales accounted for 20.1 percent of the company's fiscal 2006 sales (see Exhibits 3 and 4 for store breakdown).

GLOBAL EXPANSION

For Wal-Mart's founder, Sam Walton, going global had not been a top priority. When Walton traveled overseas, he sometimes articulated the need to serve international customers. He realized that by providing goods at low prices, Wal-Mart could raise the standard of living of people around the world just as it had done in the United States. But, senior managers could not recall Walton going into details and identifying specific countries where Wal-Marts could be set up.

It was after Walton's death that Wal-Mart's globalization program accelerated. Walton's successors realized that waiting too long to get into foreign countries would give competitors a lead that would be difficult to close. On the other hand, moving fast would give Wal-Mart the necessary time to learn the complexities of international business and to correct its mistakes before others joined the fray.

But Wal-Mart realized that going overseas was no easy task. The globalization efforts of many retailers had failed. In the United States, retailers could leverage their purchasing power, reputation, and economies of scale, but these capabilities were hard to replicate in overseas markets.

In 1993, David Glass and Rob Walton asked Bob Martin, the Chief Information Officer, to take over as president and CEO of Wal-Mart's newly created

This case was written by A V Vedpuriswar, Icfai Knowledge Center, and updated by Shirisha Regani, Icfai Center for Management Research. It was compiled from published sources, and is intended to be used as a basis for class discussion rather than to illustrate either effective or ineffective handling of a management situation.

[1] Annual Report 2006, www.walmart.com.
[2] Slater, Robert. "The Wal-Mart Decade: How a New Generation of Leaders Turned Sam Walton's Legacy into the World's #1 Company," *Penguin Group*, 2003, pp.133–134.

TABLE 1   Impressive Sales Growth between
1995 and 1999

1995	$1.5 billion
1996	$3.7 billion
1997	$5 billion
1998	$7.5 billion

SOURCE: Compiled from the Annual Reports (1995–1998) of Wal-Mart.

international division. At the time, the international operation had only one Sam's Club in Mexico. Martin was asked to build the international operations and make them contribute one-third of the company's growth within five years.

Martin decided to move fast into neighboring countries. Sam's Clubs were set up in Mexico and later in Argentina and Brazil. A plan was devised to enter China and Indonesia, and later Japan, which was a truly unique retail market in terms of consumer tastes, relationships between suppliers and retailers, and logistics systems. Martin also firmed up plans to enter Europe.

By 1997, Wal-Mart's international sales had crossed $5 billion. The international division was profitable that year, with Canada and Puerto Rico showing excellent results.

In June 1999, when Martin stepped down, the international division had become a $17 billion operation. Martin was replaced by John Menzer, who had joined Wal-Mart four years earlier as CFO. Menzer recalled:[3]

> The international division was very much a start-up in Wal-Mart, We were viewed as something that had potential, but international was still such a small part of the overall business. We were bouncing around a little bit and trying a number of different things, from acquisitions to joint ventures to "greenfield" development (building a business from the ground up, from a base of zero, as Wal-Mart essentially did in South America).

Menzer believed in a disciplined approach to global expansion. He realized that new overseas markets took at least three years to become profitable, and five years to post an acceptable return. Accordingly, Menzer adopted a more cautious approach, taking his time to do proper market research. At any given time, he examined several entry strategies, including potential companies for acquisition, before taking the plunge. Gradually, Wal-Mart entered several countries around the world.

Wal-Mart had been skeptical initially about the ease of replicating the domestic operation abroad. But as its international program grew, the retailer sensed a great

opportunity. Wal-Mart executives quickly adjusted their management and negotiation style in foreign countries. Senior officials realized they could not simply seek a meeting with the prime minister of a country and ask for permission to set up stores. When he met the President of China in October 2002, CEO Lee Scott did not ask for approval for building more stores. But he gave the President a detailed report on Wal-Mart's operations and programs for future development. He hoped this would enable his colleagues in China to tell local officials that the President was aware of and appreciated what Wal-Mart was doing in the country.

As Wal-Mart extended its global presence, the company's U.S. operations had picked up new ideas from countries across the world:

- The gravity wall: a Brazilian concept, in which fixtures were fed from behind an interior wall, enabling employees to stock fast-moving merchandise—such as sodas, diapers, paper goods—without getting in the way of customers.
- Selling shoes: A Canadian shoe program which presented shoes in a new way by leaving them in the boxes and displaying them by style rather than size.
- Selling bike racks: The drawer-style bike rack in Canada that enabled customers to look at and handle bikes more easily.
- Displaying wine: Wine racking in Mexico, a new version of fixtures for displaying and selling wine.
- Food layout: The unique food assortment and layout of the food area in Mexico.
- Selling apparel: George, a line of fashion apparel that had been developed in the UK.

MEXICO

In 1998, Wal-Mart acquired a controlling interest in Mexico's largest retailer, Cifra, which operated stores throughout the country, ranging from the largest chain of sit-down restaurants to a soft lines (apparel, home furnishings, fabric) department store. In 2000, Wal-Mart changed Cifra's name to Wal-Mart de Mexico.

Wal-Mart de Mexico operated under different formats—Wal-Mart Supercenter, Bodega, Sam's Club, Superama Supermarkets, Suburbia clothing stores, and Vips restaurants. These stores served different segments of the population. In 2004, Wal-Mart operated 640 retail, restaurant, and supermarket outlets in the country, with plans for more in the future. Wal-Mart was Mexico's largest private employer, reportedly accounting for 2 percent of Mexico's GDP at that time. Some economists even went so far as to claim that Wal-Mart's cost-cutting measures had driven down the rate of inflation in the country.

Wal-Mart modified its products to suit the tastes of local consumers. Its stores sold meat, cheese, and produce appropriate to the local diet. The company also had a Mexican bakery in all its stores. Promotions were geared to the Mexican consumer. On weekends the stores sported

[3]Slater, Robert. "The Wal-Mart Decade: How a New Generation of Leaders Turned Sam Walton's Legacy into the World's #1 Company," *Penguin Group*, 2003, pp.133–134.

a festive atmosphere with loud music, children's games, and girls distributing free product samples.

Wal-Mart's entry into Mexico had not been completely smooth. There had been start-up problems. For instance, in Mexico City, Wal-Mart initially sold tennis balls, which because of the high altitude did not bounce properly. The retailer also provided huge parking lots in a country where many shoppers traveled by bus. Wal-Mart solved the tennis ball problem and introduced shuttle buses to drop customers off at the front door. Initially, American managers stocked shelves with oversize lawn mowers and swimming pool accessories—items that Mexican shoppers looked at with curiosity but did not buy. Wal-Mart quickly realized its mistakes, and employed Mexicans to take care of product decisions to respond quickly to market needs.

On one occasion, Cifra decided to deviate from Wal-Mart's key EDLP [every day low price] strategy by putting certain items on sale. When Wal-Mart learned of this deviation, it moved swiftly, closing the store for a day and rolling back 6,000 items to the EDLP framework. For a while, customers assumed that discount sales would resume. When that did not happen, the customers embraced EDLP once again.

Since Wal-Mart had more purchasing power than the next 17 largest Latin American retailers combined, it was able to negotiate price discounts from its suppliers and generate economies of scale. It aggressively advertised that a basket of goods from Wal-Mart was cheaper than that from any other store. Executives declared that when Wal-Mart came to town, the cost of living in that town declined—in fact, they figured they saved the Mexican consumer $51 million[4] in 2002 because of their lower prices.

At the end of 2005, Wal-Mart operated a total of 807 stores in Mexico, including 107 Super centers and 71 SAMS CLUBS. The company employed more than 112,000 associates across the country.

ARGENTINA

Wal-Mart Argentina had started its operations in August 1995, with the opening of a Sam's Club in Avellaneda, in the Greater Buenos Aires area.

Like in Mexico, there were start-up problems. Wal-Mart experienced heavy crowds in Buenos Aires. But the aisles were too narrow for the unexpectedly large customer traffic. Certain cuts of meat that appealed to Argentines were missing. The jewelry department did not have the simple gold and silver items that the locals liked. Later, the aisles were widened, specialized cuts of meat added, and the jewelry line revised to emphasize simple gold and silver pieces.

In recent times, Argentina had been struggling due to political and economic instability. The economy began to slump in 1999 and crashed in 2002. That was the year

the peso was devalued by 270 percent in a matter of months with double-digit inflation following close behind. Consumer spending fell as shoppers spent the little money they had on bare necessities. It took a while before Wal-Mart and other chains felt confident enough to begin any serious growth, because of the high poverty and unemployment levels in the country. (In 2004, it was estimated that more than 57 percent of the population lived below the poverty level, and the unemployment rate was around 19.1 percent.)

At the end of 2005, Wal-Mart operated 11 Supercenters and one distribution center in the provinces of Buenos Aires, Cordoba, Entre Rios, Santa Fe, Mendoza, and Neuquen. The company employed over 4,000 associates in Argentina.

BRAZIL

Wal-Mart began operations in Brazil in May 1995, when a Sam's Club opened in São Caetano do Sul, metropolitan area of São Paulo.

The global retailer, Carrefour, which had opened hypermarkets in Brazil in 1975, proved to be a stiff competitor. Carrefour built a hypermarket right next to Wal-Mart's first São Paulo Supercenter. The store sold twice what Wal-Mart did. The 500-unit Companhia Brasileira de Distribuicao was another major rival.

In March 2004, Wal-Mart Brazil announced the acquisition of Bompreco, a retail chain with 118 units, from Dutch retailer Royal Ahold for $300 million. Bompreco was the leading supermarket and hypermarket chain in Brazil's northeast, present in nine states across the region. Bompreco operated a number of different formats including Bompreco hypermarkets ranging in size between 4,000 and 12,500 sq mt and offering 45,000 lines, and Bompreco supermarkets with a sales area of up to 3,200 sq mt and offering around 10,000 lines. Bompreco also operated mini-markets and Balaio discount stores, as well as a small number of "Hiper Magazine" stores. Wal-Mart merged the Bompreco stores with the 25 units Wal-Mart already had in Brazil, elevating the chain to the number three position. But the existing management was retained.

Wal-Mart Brazil President Vincent Trius, a Spaniard, remarked:[5]

> We've learned through the years to adapt to the local market. New stores in Brazil and Argentina devote twice as much selling space to food as the U.S. stores and now have one entrance, instead of two, to reduce confusion— and theft. Country heads are fluent speakers of either Spanish or Portuguese.

In late 2005, Wal-Mart acquired the retail operations of Sonae Distribuição Brasil S.A. (Sonae), located in Southern

[4]Simeon Tegel, "Every Day Higher Sales: Wal-Mart Wunderkind Walmex Shows Them How It's Done in a Down Economy—The Giant 2004," *Latin Trade*, August 2003.

[5]Dolan, Kerry A. "Latin America: Bumps in Brazil," *Forbes*, April 12, 2004, pp. 78–80.

Brazil, for $720 million, adding 140 new hypermarkets, supermarkets, and wholesale stores in the country.

In addition to the Sonae's stores, as of December 2005, Wal-Mart Brazil operated 22 Wal-Mart Supercenters, 15 Sam's Clubs, and 2 Todo Dias and 116 Balaio discount stores. Employing about 28,000 associates, Wal-Mart was the sixth-largest retailer in the country.

CANADA

In 1994, Wal-Mart purchased all 122 Canadian Woolco discount stores. This operation too did not get off to the right start. Indeed, for the first three years (1995–97) Wal-Mart Canada showed major losses. But things started improving subsequently. In 1996, Canada generated an operating profit in the second year of operation. Only three years after Wal-Mart acquired the Woolco Stores, it became Canada's highest-volume discount retailer. It broke even for the first time.

Wal-Mart Canada quickly overtook rivals like Eaton's, Zellers, and the Bay. Wal-Mart's low pricing and its ability to strip costs from the supply chain impressed analysts. Suppliers had to deliver at Wal-Mart distribution centers within 15 to 30 minutes of the given schedule. Otherwise, they faced fines. Wal-Mart used its bargaining power to extract price concessions from suppliers.

In 2002, with total sales estimated at $5.76 billion, a store base of 207 outlets, and additional expansion plans on the horizon, Wal-Mart was Canada's largest retailer. The Canadian subsidiary was its parent chain's No. 3 international unit behind the United Kingdom and Mexico. Wal-Mart Canada had reported eight years of continuous growth of sales and profits.

At the end of 2005, Wal-Mart operated 272 discount department stores and 6 Sam's Clubs and employed more than 60,000 associates across Canada. Each discount store housed more than 70,000 products and a wide range of specialty services.

INDONESIA

Wal-Mart had entered Indonesia, attracted by the potential of the world's fourth most populous country. The retailer faced numerous challenges in a country where foreign retailers operated under tight restrictions. Wal-Mart teamed up with Lippo Group, the most powerful Indonesian conglomerate outside the Suharto family. Through a license with Lippo's Multipolar unit, Wal-Mart got its first supercenter up and running in August 1996, followed by a second unit in January 1997. Wal-Mart was paid by Multipolar on a fee for services basis.

In Indonesia, the bulk of the shopping was done in tiny stores. But the middle class, fond of status symbols, broad selection, and good values, flocked on the weekends to the attractive malls that were increasing in Jakarta.

At Wal-Mart Supercenters, shoppers responded positively to categories like deli foods—with 1,000 roasted chickens selling each weekend day—and bakery goods,

framed art, home storage, small appliances, prerecorded music, H&BC, toys, intimates, and bodywear. Although they came at a premium, they were popular. Less popular categories included cosmetics, children's apparel, greeting cards, automotive accessories and white goods. Import tariffs were very high. There were the usual "sweetheart" deals between manufacturers and established retailers. Wall-Mart found it difficult to cut distribution costs.

While Indonesians worked hard, they did not like to challenge the status-quo. Wal-Mart encouraged all associates to embrace the idea of empowerment to make suggestions, to take ownership of the store. The amiable conversion of Indonesian associates to the Wal-Mart culture gave the chain a pronounced edge in customer service.

Despite all these initiatives, things suddenly changed for the worse for Wal-Mart. Multipolar, which was also the Indonesian franchisee of J.C.Penney, surprised just about everyone when it announced in December 1996 that it would acquire a controlling stake in Matahari, the leading retailer in Indonesia. Wal-Mart was taken aback by Multipolar's action.

Growing distrust with its local partner and the specter of political unrest progressively forced Wal-Mart to withdraw from Indonesia in 1998.

Multipolar sued Wal-Mart in February 1999, for $200m, alleging that the American retailer had mismanaged its two stores in Indonesia and misrepresented Multipolar's financing obligations. Multipolar contended that it had to invest $28.9 million instead of $20 million. The lawsuit also stated:[6]

> *Wal-Mart's level of expertise, especially that of the foreigners who managed the super centre, is low. It is also ignorant of the different tastes of consumers in Indonesia.*

CHINA

Wal-Mart entered China in August 1996 with the opening of its first Supercenter and Sam's Club in Shenzhen. Wal-Mart focused on providing quality merchandise at low prices. The retailer introduced advanced retail techniques and concepts to improve operational efficiency and customer service. Wal-Mart also procured large volumes of merchandise from China through its Global Procurement Center located in Shenzhen for export to other countries. In 2005, Wal-Mart bought more than $12 billion in merchandise, nearly 10 percent of all Chinese exports to the United States.

Despite all these initiatives, Wal-Mart's Chinese operations did not take off as fast as expected. Wal-Mart encountered problems such as supply chain fragmentation and inadequate infrastructure. Wal-Mart and other foreign retailers had to offer a 35 percent stake in each store to a Chinese joint venture partner and were restricted to a territory of approximately 40 cities each.

---

[6]"Foreigners Exit," *Country Monitor,* 10th March 1999, p. 10.

Fortunately for Wal-Mart after December 2004, as part of China's admission to the WTO, the government decided to allow foreign retailers to own their own stores outright in any city they chose, provided they could obtain government building permits.

Meanwhile, competition was intensifying. Metro, the German retail chain with $60 billion in global revenue, had announced its plans to invest $700 million to add 40 Chinese stores to the 18 it already had. Carrefour had moved its global purchasing center to China and was rapidly adding to its 43 stores there. A bigger threat to Wal-Mart was Du Sha, one of China's richest entrepreneurs, who operated a privately run hypermarket chain, the Home World Group, in northern China. He planned to increase the number of stores from 26 to 150 in the next four years, investing $750 million.

Non-tariff trade barriers often in the guise of geographical limitations, quality or safety standards, or a cap on the number of stores a company could open were among the most frequently discussed topics within China's retail sector. As China complied with WTO terms and lowered its import tariffs, it looked for ways to protect its huge domestic market. For instance, difficult testing and labeling laws had been introduced in the country.

China's banking, finance, insurance, and taxation structures were bureaucratic and cumbersome. Regional fragmentation of finance regulation, tax laws, and other institutional arrangements created problems. For instance, a company with joint ventures in several locations supplied by one supplier had to make a separate payment from each venture to the supplier. Wal-Mart worked with the Chinese government to set up a holding company to consolidate joint venture distribution and finance.

The requirement for "chops"[7] on official documents further complicated matters. As there was no widely accepted way for such chops to be electronically authenticated or transmitted, hard copy documents were needed. This meant more manpower and greater possibilities of human error.

In western countries, less-than-truck-load (LTL) service providers or express parcel delivery were available. In the United States, such services handled anything from a single carton to a full shipment in a 53-cubic-foot trailer. Shipments could also be tracked effectively. Such services were relatively undeveloped in China. Urgent or exception delivery, just-in-time inventory management, catalogue or mail order sales, and Internet sales were made possible around the world by such transport services. Although some service providers in China such as China Post or China Rail could arrange for such shipments, the choice of service providers was limited, and tracking, pickup, and delivery were unreliable. But in a promising sign for retailers, several joint ventures between Chinese state-owned transport firms and foreign freight or parcel companies were being established.

Wal-Mart continued to educate its suppliers to help them streamline their operations and reduce costs so that both parties benefited. Sometimes these issues required the company's participation in the debate on liberalization and standardization. Wal-Mart became actively involved in government relations and started talking directly with Chinese government officials at both local and national levels and through trade groups in both the United States and China.

In December 2005, Wal-Mart had 46 Supercenters, 3 Sam's Clubs, and 2 Neighborhood Markets in China, together employing more than 27,000 associates. However, at the end of 2006, Wal-Mart was laying the groundwork to become the biggest foreign chain in China with the $1 billion purchase of a major retailer—a Taiwanese-owned supermarket chain called Trust-Mart—which would more than double its presence in China.

SOUTH KOREA

In 1997, regulations governing foreign retailers in South Korea were liberalized. Wal-Mart entered Korea in July 1998 by acquiring a majority stake in Makro. Wal-Mart purchased four former Korea Makro stores and also opened six new Wal-Mart stores: three in the capital, Seoul, and one in Taejon.

The South Korean operations initially experienced difficulties with regard to the merchandise mix. Stores were also too far from city centers. A joint U.S./Korean academic study of Wal-Mart's operations found that shoppers were not "impressed" by what they experienced. The general perception was that Wal-Mart had chosen bad locations, set prices too high, and had a poor selection of merchandise. South Korean housewives did not go a long distance to shop or purchase food lacking freshness.

By the spring of 1999, the stores were remodeled from the Makro warehouse club format to Wal-Mart's supercenter format. The retailer designed the Supercenter concept to save customers time and money and also offered a unique shopping experience based on the EDLP philosophy. Supercenters featured the traditional 36 general merchandise departments. The grocery areas offered a bakery, delicatessen, frozen food section, meat, and dairy as well as fresh produce departments. In July 1999, the names on the stores were changed and a fifth unit in the Kangnam area of the capital city Seoul was opened. Sales at the remodeled stores improved dramatically. In 2000, the trend continued with a same-store sales increase in excess of 20 percent. Wal-Mart added its sixth store in 2000, and in 2001 doubled the store count as it took advantage of store sites acquired in the deal with Makro.

With a relatively high standard of living and high rates of automobile ownership, customer counts and average transaction size were high in Korea. People were

---

[7]In China, seals in the form of ivory chops used with ink were developed. Chops made from various materials are used to this day by Asian companies to authenticate agreements and other documents.

used to shopping in cars and did not like pedaling home on a bicycle as many customers in China did. This well-developed nation of 48 million potential customers had a population density of 1,263.97 occupants per square mile, with an average per capita GDP of nearly $10,000 (U.S.). Wal-Mart was initially optimistic about South Korea.

Lee Scott, remarked:[8]

> *I think the discount store market will continue to grow in the Korean market, as more customers experience the value.*

In 2005, Wal-Mart Korea operated 16 stores, averaging 180,000 sq ft each, in Incheon, Ilsan, Gusung, Daejon, Kangnam, Daegu (Siji, Bisan, Sungseo), Hwajung, and Ulsan (Joongang), Busan (Seomyun), Bucheon (Jung-dong), Incheon (Geyang), Anyang (Pyeongchon), Masan, and Pohang, and employed over 3,700 associates.

In May 2006, Wal-Mart announced that it would sell all 16 of its South Korean stores to Shinsegae, a leader department store and hypermarket chain operator in the country, in a deal valued at $882 million.[9] Shinsegae announced that it would operate the Wal-Mart stores under its successful E-Mart brand. E-Mart was one of the most successful discount store chains in South Korea, accounting for a market share of nearly 30 percent in its segment before the Wal-Mart acquisition.[10]

Although Wal-Mart had been optimistic about its potential in the country, it was compelled to change its views and it had not been able to make an impact on the South Korean retail scene. Wal-Mart's exit from South Korea was reportedly prompted by its inability to localize operations in the country, and its tardiness in opening stores. In April 2006, Carrefour had also announced that it would withdraw from South Korea. Both Wal-Mart and Carrefour announced that they would like to concentrate on their Chinese operations after exiting South Korea.

JAPAN

In Japan, Wal-Mart decided the best entry strategy was to join hands with a local partner. Accordingly, in 2002, Wal-Mart paid $46.5 million for a 6.1 percent interest in Seiyu, Japan's fourth-largest supermarket chain. Wal-Mart retained an option to increase its stake by 2007. In December 2002, Wal-Mart announced it was exercising in full the first in a series of options it had received earlier that year, to raise its stake in Seiyu to 34 percent.

In April 2004, Seiyu opened a new store in a fishing village 62 miles west of Tokyo that featured one instead of multiple floors, wide aisles, and a long row of cash registers. The store was seen as a test of the Wal-Mart-style layout, designs, brands, and supply systems in Japan.

Streamlining operations and the supply chain remained a major challenge in Japan. Wal-Mart also faced challenges in implementing its Retail Link system. Most suppliers had yet to institute the technology needed to communicate efficiently with Wal-Mart's order and replenishment system. Retailer-supplier relations had traditionally been based on personal ties that often went back several generations. Switching to impersonal electronic relations needed a major cultural adjustment.

But Jeff McAllister, COO of Wal-Mart Japan, said in a statement in 2004 that 36 of Seiyu's 403 stores had started using Wal-Mart systems, including one that allowed suppliers to monitor product sales.

At the end of 2005, Wal-Mart held a 53.56 percent stake in Seiyu, operated 405 supermarkets in Japan, and employed over 35,000 associates.[11]

GERMANY

Wal-Mart's experience in Germany (the third-biggest retail market after America and Japan), a country with 80 million people and the largest economy in Europe, had not been entirely happy. In December 1997, Wal-Mart purchased the German Wertkauf group of 21 stores. A year later, Wal-Mart added 74 Interspar hypermarkets, which were similar to Wal-Mart's Supercenters. The Wertkauf stores did business worth $1.2 billion in 1998. For buying Wertkauf and Interspar, Wal-Mart spent $1.6 billion.

Wal-Mart spent months remodeling the stores by widening the aisles, improving the lighting, and adding checkout counters. Wal-Mart hired additional staff and exposed them to the company's corporate culture. Only on August 31, 1999, did it open its flagship Supercenter in Dortmund.

Wal-Mart found the competition in Germany much tougher than anything it normally confronted abroad. The country had a large number of discounters, like Aldi, a countrywide chain of no-frills, no-service stores. Margins were low and costs high. Labor laws and tough unions made wage cutting difficult.

Unlike in the United States, German stores closed on Saturday afternoons and reopened only on Monday morning. German customers were used to bagging their own groceries. This affected Wal-Mart's productivity and slowed down the checkout lines. German consumers also did not show much enthusiasm towards the company's EDLP approach. Wal-Mart's expatriate managers initially suffered from a massive clash of cultures, which was not helped by their refusal to learn to speak German. Many

[8]Scardino, Emily. "Mass Merchant Breaks New Ground in Profitable South Korea Market," *DSN Retailing Today*, December 13, 2004, pp. 69–71.

[9]Choe Sang-Hun, "Wal-Mart Selling Stores and Leaving South Korea," *International Herald Tribune*, May 23, 2006.

[10]Choe Sang-Hun, "Wal-Mart Selling Stores and Leaving South Korea," *International Herald Tribune*, May 23, 2006.

[11]http://72.14.235.104/search?q=cache:O81Py_v8lKoJ:www.union-network.org/unisite/Sectors/Commerce/Multinationals/Wal-Mart_Report_UNI_Commerce_Dec_2005.pdf

people saw Wal-Mart as a very unattractive company to work for because of relatively low pay and an ultra-frugal policy on managers' business expenses.

Wal-Mart opened its stores two hours earlier than the nine o'clock standard. But tough zoning laws made it next to impossible to build new stores. Only in 2001 did Wal-Mart finally open two stores built from scratch.

Meanwhile, Wal-Mart made various attempts to adapt to German ways. It offered baked soft pretzels and open-faced sandwiches with sausage and butter. The pictures on the Wal-Mart brand of pet food were changed. A terrier replaced the English setter. Customers were given the option of packing their purchases. The Germans had at first been alarmed to find greeters talking to them when they entered the stores. Later, Wal-Mart's greeters spoke more quietly, and respectfully. Instead of approaching customers, greeters simply waited on the side.

Menzer admitted that Germany represented Wal-Mart's biggest challenge,[12]

> We are trying to put in our distribution, technology and operating expertise in a market that is slow to change—slow to adapt to technology and distribution.

Lee Scott also acknowledged[13] that things had not gone smoothly for Wal-Mart in Europe's largest economy, but blamed it on the company, not the German economy or the German people.

> "We got confused on what's important, and so we went out and we remodeled stores—and spent a lot of money doing things that wasn't what the customers wanted from us." But he was confident about the long term prospects: "We'll be successful because we reprioritized what our efforts are and understanding that market, understanding the German consumer and understanding Wal-Mart stores."[14]

As of January 31, 2005, Wal-Mart operated 91 Supercenters in Germany, employing more than 12,000 associates across the country. During the year it closed three stores, and in December 2005, the number of Supercenters stood at 88.

In July 2006, Wal-Mart announced that it would sell its operations in Germany to Metro AG, which operated rival stores Real Hypermarkets. The actual value of the deal was not disclosed, but Wal-Mart reportedly took a major hit in exiting the German market, as Metro paid almost $100 million less than the value of Wal-Mart's

real estate, merchandise, and other physical assets.[15] Wal-Mart's retreat from Germany was estimated to cost a total of $1 billion.[16] The company's inability to adapt to the German culture and business methods was cited to be the reason for the exit. (At the time of the exit, Wal-Mart had 85 Supercenters in Germany).[17]

THE UNITED KINGDOM

In the United Kingdom (UK), Wal-Mart had acquired ASDA, a profitable chain in 1999. ASDA had been formed in 1965 by a group of farmers from Yorkshire. Wal-Mart had kept an eye on ASDA for some time before seeking to purchase it.

Chairman Rob Walton recalled:[18]

> They had a great management team, a similar culture, and their philosophy on retailing was almost identical to ours.

ASDA's culture resembled that of Wal-Mart in many ways. Employees were called "colleagues," like Wal-Mart's "associates." They wore a badge and called each other by first name. ASDA was used to price rollbacks and people greeters, "permanently low prices forever" and "Smiley" faces.

Wal-Mart had not shown any urgency about entering the UK. It was only when another company offered to purchase ASDA early in the spring of 2000 that Wal-Mart moved quickly to finalize its $10.8 billion deal to acquire the 232-store supermarket chain. This was Wal-Mart's largest acquisition ever. ASDA, which already had a strong business competing on price, overtook the struggling J. Sainsbury to become the second-biggest supermarket chain after Tesco.

Wal-Mart realized it had a lot to learn from ASDA about selling food. ASDA, on the other hand, believed that it would be able to gain insights from Wal-Mart about merchandising. The average Wal-Mart Supercenter was 180,000 sq ft and did about 30 percent of its sales in groceries. In sharp contrast, the average ASDA store had only 65,000 sq ft and did 60 percent of its sales in groceries. But though Supercenters were three times larger, some ASDA stores did as much in sales as the average Supercenter. ASDA's sales per sq foot were the highest in Wal-Mart. That was not only because ASDA had a much larger food business but also because the UK had far fewer grocery stores per capita.

---

[12]Slater, Robert. "The Wal-Mart Decade: How a New Generation of Leaders Turned Sam Walton's Legacy into the World's #1 Company," *Penguin Group,* 2003, p. 138.

[13]Appearing on CNBC in March 2002.

[14]Slater, Robert. "The Wal-Mart Decade: How a New Generation of Leaders Turned Sam Walton's Legacy into the World's #1 Company," *Penguin Group,* 2003, p. 141.

[15]Kate Norton, "Wal-Mart's German Retreat," *BusinessWeek,* July 28, 2006.

[16]"World's Biggest Retailer Wal-Mart Closes Up Shop in Germany," http://www.dw-world.de/dw/article/ (accessed on November 20, 2006).

[17]Kate Norton, "Wal-Mart's German Retreat," *BusinessWeek,* July 28, 2006.

[18]Slater, Robert. "The Wal-Mart Decade: How a New Generation of Leaders Turned Sam Walton's Legacy into the World's #1 Company," *Penguin Group,* 2003, p. 141.

In 2000, Wal-Mart officials announced plans to spend more than $100 million over the next five years to open 50 stores in the new 25,000-sq-foot ASDA "fresh" format, which stressed fresh foods and prepared meals. Two new ASDA Supercenters modeled after the Wal-Mart ones were also in the planning stages.

ASDA's operations were improved by adding general merchandise and ramping up its food and apparel offerings, and by bringing in Wal-Mart's state of the art inventory and logistics systems. Sales per square foot in these UK units reached $2,000 in 2004, four times higher than at a Sam's Club.

In December 2005, Wal-Mart had 273 ASDA Super Centers, 21 ASDA/Wal-Mart Supercenters, 10 GEORGE stores, and 5 ASDA Living stores and 4 ASDA Small Town stores in the UK. The company employed more than 150,000 people in the UK.

THE ROAD AHEAD

Scott had publicly stated that over the next few years sales from the overseas division would grow to a third of earnings and sales growth. While Wal-Mart had kept its specific plans tightly under wraps, rumors floated about the company's growth strategy, which, analysts believed, would come from acquisitions. Some of the names that came up as potential targets of Wal-Mart's acquisition plans were the Esselunga chain in Italy; France's Auchan, Carrefour, Cora, or Casino chains; Poland's Casino Géant stores; Spain's Mercadona; and Japan's Daiei or Aeon chains. It was also reported that Wal-Mart might look at an acquisition in India.

Wal-Mart reportedly considered India to be a market with great potential. During 2005 and early 2006, the company had lobbied with the Indian government for access to the booming Indian retail sector. However, India's unfavorable foreign direct investment (FDI) regulations had hindered its entry. (In India, FDI regulations barred foreign companies from directly entering the retail sector. Because of this, foreign companies seeking to enter the retail industry need to tie-up with a domestic partner.) In 2006, the regulations were relaxed a little to allow "single brand" foreign retailers to own 51 percent of their operations in India, but this did not apply to Wal-Mart, which sold multiple brands.

Analysts said that it would not be very easy for Wal-Mart to enter India and make its presence felt, as several Indian companies like Reliance Retail and the Future Group's Pantaloon Retail India Ltd. had made ambitious plans for the segment by 2006. Foreign retailers would also have to contend with resistance from various groups in the interest of the mom-and-pop stores that formed a large part of the retail sector in India until the early 2000s. Although as of mid 2006, Wal-Mart had not made any of its plans for India public, it was reported that it was considering a variety of investment structures with Indian partners, although it would "prefer a controlling interest."[19]

In the Philippines, regulations had been eased to allow foreign investment. It was reported that Wal-Mart had been scouting for locations around the capital city of Manila. But political instability was a cause for concern. Moreover, rival Makro had been established there for several years.

A meeting in Russia of 40 Wal-Mart managers to discuss logistical matters and consumer shopping patterns was reported in April 2004. An acquisition or partnering in Russia would enable Wal-Mart to make a quick entry into a market that seemed to have reached the takeoff stage.

Meanwhile, Wal-Mart continued to face various challenges as it globalized. Technical constraints, logistics, and transportation were not the only problems. Wal-Mart also had to integrate its corporate culture into its international operations. Wal-Mart had to export the greeters, the cheers, the Sam Walton quotations and photographs, the focus on customers and EDLP, and all the other elements that went into the culture.

In the fiscal year ended January 2006, Wal-Mart International's sales increased by 11.4 % from $56.2 billion to $62.7 billion.[20] Wal-Mart International planned to open more than 200 stores in the fiscal year ended January 2007 (see Exhibits 5 and 6).

Wal-Mart's results from globalization had been mixed. Though the retailer had performed well in Canada, Mexico, and the UK, it struggled in many of its overseas markets. Germany and South Korea, in particular, had been unhappy experiences.

Would Wal-Mart conquer the globe as McDonald's had done? Could it improve the profitability of its struggling subsidiaries? Would Wal-Mart be able to leverage effectively its core strengths in overseas markets?

---

[19]John Elliot, "Why There Are no Indian Wal-Marts," *Fortune*, May 25, 2006.
[20]Annual Report 2006.

QUESTIONS FOR DISCUSSION

1. Discuss Wal-Mart's global expansion strategy. How, in your opinion, did those strategies contribute to the retail chain's international success?
2. Wal-Mart's inability to localize operations to adapt to local culture and business methods were cited as reasons for its exit from South Korea and Germany in 2006. Is this relevant only to particular markets?

What were the ways in which the company could have continued its operations? Comment with reference to the retail industry.

3. Do some research to find out how Wal-Mart is doing in its international operations at the time of your reading of this case.

EXHIBIT I Pricing Philosophy

Walton always knew he wanted to be in the retailing business. He started his career by running a Ben Franklin franchise store and learned about buying, pricing and passing good deals on to customers. He gave credit to a manufacturer's agent from New York, Harry Weiner, with his first real lesson about pricing:

"Harry was selling ladies' panties for $2 a dozen. We'd been buying similar panties from Ben Franklin for $2.50 a dozen and selling them at three pair for $1. Well, at Harry's price of $2, we could put them out at four for $1 and make a great promotion for our store. Here's the simple lesson we learned . . . say I bought an item for 80 cents. I found that by pricing it at $1.00, I could sell three times more of it than by pricing it at $1.20. I might make only half the profit per item, but because I was selling three times as many, the overall profit was much greater. Simple enough. But this is really the essence of discounting: by cutting your price, you can boost your sales to a point where you earn far more at the cheaper retail than you would have by selling the item at the higher price. In retailer language, you can lower your markup but earn more because of the increased volume."

Sam's adherence to this pricing philosophy was unshakable, as one of Wal-Mart's first store managers recalls: "Sam wouldn't let us hedge on a price at all. Say the list price was $1.98, but we had paid only 50 cents. Initially, I would say, 'Well, it's originally $1.98, so why don't we sell it for $1.25?' And, he'd say, 'No. We paid 50 cents for it. Mark it up 30%, and that's it. No matter what you pay for it, if we get a great deal, pass it on to the customer.' And of course that's what we did."

The three of the pricing philosophies followed at Wal-Mart were:

- **Every Day Low Price (EDLP)** Because you work hard for every dollar, you deserve the lowest price we can offer every time you make a purchase. You deserve our Every Day Low Price. It's not a sale; it's a great price you can count on every day to make your dollar go further at Wal-Mart.

- **Rollback** This is our ongoing commitment to pass even more savings on to you by lowering our Every Day Low Prices whenever we can. When our costs get rolled back, it allows us to lower our prices for you. Just look for the Rollback smiley face throughout the store. You'll smile too.

- **Special Buy** When you see items with the Special Buy logo, you'll know you're getting an exceptional value. It may be an item we carry every day that includes an additional amount of the same product or another product for a limited time. Or, it could be an item we carry while supplies last, at a very special price.

SOURCE: www.walmart.com

EXHIBIT II The Wal-Mart Cheer

Give me a W!
Give me an A!
Give me an L!
Give me a Squiggly!
Give me an M!
Give me an A!
Give me an R!
Give me a T!
What's that spell?
Wal-Mart!
Whose Wal-Mart is it?
My Wal-Mart!
Who's number one?
The Customer! Always!

Walton was visiting a tennis ball factory in Korea, where the workers did a company cheer and calisthenics together every morning. He liked the idea and could not wait to get back home to try it with his associates. He said, "My feeling is that just because we work so hard, we don't have to go around with long faces all the time—while we're doing all of this work, we like to have a good time. It's sort of a 'whistle while you work' philosophy, and we not only have a heck of a good time with it, we work better because of it. We do have fun, we do work hard, and we always remember whom we're doing it for—the customer." That was how the Wal-Mart cheer originated.

SOURCE: www.walmart.com

EXHIBIT III　Stores Breakdown – January 2006

Country	Discount Stores	Super Centers	Sam's Clubs	Neighborhood Markets
Argentina	0	11	0	0
Brazil	255	23	15	2
Canada	272	0	6	0
China	0	51	3	2
Germany	0	88	0	0
Japan	2	96	0	300
South Korea	0	16	0	0
Mexico	599	105	70	0
Puerto Rico	9	5	9	31
United Kingdom	294	21	0	0
International Totals	**1,431**	**416**	**103**	**335**
Grand Totals	**2,640**	**2,396**	**670**	**435**

- Brazil includes 2 Todo Dias, 116 Bompreço, and 139 Sonae.
- Japan includes 2 general merchandise only; 96 general merchandise, apparel, and food stores; and 300 supermarkets. Japan excludes 45 Wakana units, which are take-out restaurants generally less than 1,000 square feet in size.
- Mexico includes 187 Bodegas, 16 Mi Bodegas, 1 Mi Bodega Express, 1 Mercamas, 53 Suburbias, 55 Superamas, 286 Vips, and does not include Vips franchises.
- Puerto Rico includes 31 Amigos.
- United Kingdom includes 236 ASDA stores, 10 George stores, 5 ASDA Living, and 43 ASDA small stores.

SOURCE: Annual Report 2006.

EXHIBIT VI　Wal-Mart's Store Count

As of January 31, 2006	
Total number of stores in US	3,856
Total number of international stores	2,285
Total number of stores	6,141
Total Sales	$62.7 Billion

SOURCE: Annual Report 2006.

EXHIBIT V　Wal-Mart's Operations
(In millions of US dollars)

Fiscal Year Ended January 31, 2006	Wal-Mart Stores	Sam's Club	International	Other	Consolidated
Revenues from external customers	209,910	39,798	62,719	-	312,427
Intercompany real estate charge (income)	3,454	547	-	(4,001)	-
Depreciation and amortization	1,922	296	1,043	1,456	4,717
Operating Income (loss)	15,324	1,385	3,330	(1,509)	18,530
Interest expense, net					(1,172)
Income from continuing operations before income taxes and minority interest					17,538
Total assets of continuing operations	32,809	5,686	51,581	48,111	138,187

(continued)

EXHIBIT V (cont.)

Fiscal Year Ended January 31, 2005	Wal-Mart Stores	Sam's Club	International	Other	Consolidated
Revenues from external customers	191,826	37,119	56,277	-	285,222
Intercompany real estate charge (income)	2,754	513	-	(3,267)	-
Depreciation and amortization	1,561	274	919	1,510	4,264
Operating Income (loss)	14,163	1,280	2,988	(1,340)	17,091
Interest expense, net					(986)
Income from continuing operations before income taxes and minority interest					16,105
Total assets of continuing operations	29,489	5,685	40,981	43,999	120,154

Fiscal Year Ended January 31, 2004	Wal-Mart Stores	Sam's Club	International	Other	Consolidated
Revenues from external customers	174,220	34,537	47,572	-	256,329
Intercompany real estate charge (income)	2,468	484	-	(2,952)	-
Depreciation and amortization	1,482	249	810	1,311	3,852
Operating Income (loss)	12,916	1,126	2,370	(1,387)	15,025
Interest expense, net					(832)
Income from continuing operations before income taxes and minority interest					14,193
Total assets of continuing operations	27,028	4,751	35,230	38,396	105,405

SOURCE: Annual Report 2006.

EXHIBIT VI	Financial Highlights Fiscal Years Ended January 31 (in millions except per share data)					
	2006	**2005**	**2004**	**2003**	**2002**	**2001**
Net Sales	$312,427	$285,222	$256,329	$229,616	$204,011	$180,787
Cost of Sales	$240,391	$219,793	$198,747	$178,299	$159,097	$140,720
Net Income	$11,231	$10,267	$9,054	$7,955	$6,592	$6,235
Diluted Earnings per Share	$2.68	$2.41	$2.07	$1.79	$1.47	$1.39
Long-term Debt	$26,429	$20,087	$17,102	$16,597	$15,676	$12,489
Return on Assets	8.9%	9.3%	9.2%	9.2%	8.4%	8.6%
Return on Shareholders' equity	22.5%	22.1%	21.3%	20.9%	19.4%	21.3%

SOURCE: Annual Report 2006.

Glossary

affective appeals Negotiation appeals based on emotions and subjective feelings.

appropriability of technology The ability of an innovating firm to protect its technology from competitors and to obtain economic benefits from that technology.

attribution The process in which a person looks for an explanation of another person's behavior.

axiomatic appeals Negotiation appeals based on the ideals generally accepted in a society.

B2B Business-to-business electronic transactions.

B2C Business-to-consumer electronic transactions.

balance sheet approach An approach to the compensation of expatriates that equalizes the standard of living between the host and home countries, plus compensation for inconvenience.

chaebol South Korea's large industrial conglomerates of financially linked, and often family-linked, companies that do business among themselves whenever possible—for example, Daewoo.

codetermination *(mitbestimmung)* The participation of labor in the management of a firm.

collective bargaining In the United States, for example, negotiations between a labor union local and management; in Sweden and Germany, for example, negotiations between the employer's organization and a trade union at the industry level.

collectivism The tendency of a society toward tight social frameworks, emotional dependence on belonging to an organization, and a strong belief in group decisions.

communication The process of sharing meaning by transmitting messages through media such as words, behavior, or material artifacts.

comparative advantage A mutual benefit in the exchange of goods between countries, where each country exports those products in which it is relatively more efficient in production than other countries.

competitive advantage of nations The existence of conditions that give a country an advantage in a specific industry or in producing a particular good or service.

context in cultures (low to high) Low-context cultures, such as Germany, tend to use explicit means of communication in words and readily available information; high-context cultures, such as those in the Middle East, use more implicit means of communication, in which information is embedded in the nonverbal context and understanding of the people.

contract An agreement by the parties concerned to establish a set of rules to govern a business transaction.

control system appropriateness The use of control systems that are individually tailored to the practices and expectations of the host-country personnel.

convergence (of management styles, techniques, and so forth) The phenomenon of increasing similarity of leadership styles resulting from a blending of cultures and business practices through international institutions, as opposed to the **divergence** of leadership styles necessary for different cultures and practices.

core competencies Important corporate resources or skills that bring competitive advantages.

corporate social responsibility (CSR) The level of responsibility that a company takes regarding the potential social and economic effects of the company's decisions; as well as its ability to contribute towards society.

creeping expropriation A government's gradual and subtle action against foreign firms.

creeping incrementalism A process of increasing commitment of resources to one or more geographic regions.

cultural noise Cultural variables that undermine the communications of intended meaning.

cultural savvy A working knowledge of the cultural variables affecting management decisions.

cultural sensitivity (cultural empathy) A sense of awareness and caring about the culture of other people.

culture The shared values, understandings, assumptions, and goals that over time are passed on and imposed by members of a group or society.

culture shock A state of disorientation and anxiety that results from not knowing how to behave in an unfamiliar culture.

culture-specific reward systems Motivational and compensation approaches that reflect different motivational patterns across cultures.

degree of enforcement The relative degree of enforcement, in a particular country, of the law regarding business behavior, which therefore determines the lower limit of permissible behavior.

differentiation Focusing on and specializing in specific markets.

direct control The control of foreign subsidiaries and operations through the use of appropriate international staffing and structure policies and meetings with home-country executives (as compared with **indirect control**).

distinctive competencies Strengths that allow companies to outperform rivals.

domestic multiculturalism The diverse makeup of the workforce comprising people from several different cultures in the home (domestic) company.

e-business The integration of systems, processes, organizations, value chains, and entire markets using Internet-based and related technologies and concepts.

e-commerce The selling of goods or services over the Internet.

e-commerce enablers Fulfillment specialists who provide other companies with services such as Web site translation.

economic risk The level of uncertainty about the ability of a country to meet its financial obligations.

environmental assessment The continuous process of gathering and evaluating information about variables and events around the world that may pose threats or opportunities to the firm.

environmental scanning The process of gathering information and forecasting relevant trends, competitive actions, and circumstances that will affect operations in geographic areas of potential interest.

ethical relativism An approach to social responsibility in which a country adopts the moral code of its host country.

ethnocentric approach An approach in which a company applies the morality used in its home country, regardless of the host country's system of ethics.

ethnocentric staffing approach An approach that fills key managerial positions abroad with persons from headquarters—that is, with parent-country nationals (PCNs).

ethnocentrism The belief that the management techniques used in one's own country are best no matter where or with whom they are applied.

expatriate One who works and lives in a foreign country but remains a citizen of the country where the employing organization is headquartered.

expressive-oriented conflict Conflict that is handled indirectly and implicitly, without clear delineation of the situation by the person handling it.

expropriation The seizure, with inadequate or no compensation, by a local government of the foreign-owned assets of an MNC.

Foreign Corrupt Practices Act A 1977 law that prohibits most questionable payments by U.S. companies to officials of foreign governments to gain business advantages.

foreign direct investment (FDI) Multinational firm's ownership, in part or in whole, of an operation in another country.

franchising An international entry strategy by which a firm (the franchiser) licenses its trademark, products, or services and operating principles to the franchisee in a host country for an initial fee and ongoing royalties.

fully owned subsidiary An overseas operation started or bought by a firm that has total ownership and control; starting or buying such an operation is often used as an entry strategy.

generalizabilty of leadership styles The ability (or lack of ability) to generalize leadership theory, research results, and effective leadership practices from one country to another.

geocentric staffing approach A staffing approach in which the best managers are recruited throughout the company or outside the company, regardless of nationality—often, third-country nationals (TCNs) are recruited.

global corporate culture An integration of the business environments in which firms currently operate, resulting from a dissolution of traditional boundaries and from increasing links among MNCs.

global functional structure Operations are integrated into the activities and responsibilities of each department to gain functional specialization and economies of scale.

globalism Global competition characterized by networks of international linkages that bind countries, institutions, and people in an interdependent global economy and a one-world market.

global geographic (area) structure Divisions are created to cover geographic regions; each regional manager is responsible for operations and performance of the countries within a given region.

globalization The global strategy of the integration of worldwide operations and the development of standardized products and marketing approaches.

global management The process of developing strategies, designing and operating systems, and working with people around the world to ensure sustained competitive advantage.

global management team Collection of managers in or from several countries who must rely on group collaboration if each member is to experience optimum success and goal achievement.

global product (divisional) structure A single product (or product line) is represented by a separate division; each division is headed by its own general manager; each is responsible for its own production and sales functions.

global staffing approach Staff recruited from within or outside of the company, regardless of nationality.

global strategic alliances Working partnerships that are formed around MNCs across national boundaries and often across industries.

governmentalism The tendency of a government to use its policy-setting role to favor national interests rather than relying on market forces.

guanxi The intricate, pervasive network of personal relations that every Chinese person carefully cultivates.

guanxihu A bond between specially connected firms, which generates preferential treatment to members of the network.

haptic Characterized by a predilection for the sense of touch.

high-contact culture One in which people prefer to stand close, touch a great deal, and experience a "close" sensory involvement.

high-context communication One in which people convey messages indirectly and implicitly.

horizontal organization (dynamic network) A structural approach that enables the flexibility to be global and act local through horizontal coordination, shared power, and decision making across international units and teams.

host-country national (HCN) A worker who is indigenous to the local country where the plant is located.

human capital Those direct or subcontracted employees whose labor becomes part of the firm's value-added product or service. MNCs are increasingly offshoring (outsourcing) that asset around the world in order to lower the cost of human capital.

IJV control How a parent company ensures that the way a joint venture is managed conforms to its own interest.

indirect control The control of foreign operations through the use of reports, budgets, financial controls, and so forth. *See also* **direct control**.

individualism The tendency of people to look after themselves and their immediate families only and to value democracy, individual initiative, and personal achievement.

information privacy The right to control information about oneself.

information technology (IT) Electronic systems to convey information.

instrumental-oriented conflict An approach to conflict in which parties tend to negotiate on the basis of factual information and logical analysis.

integration Coordination of markets.

intercultural communication Type of communication that occurs when a member of one culture sends a message to a receiver who is a member of another culture.

internal analysis Determines which areas of a firm's operations represent strengths or weaknesses (currently or potentially) compared to competitors.

internal versus external locus of control Beliefs regarding whether a person controls his own fate and events or they are controlled by external forces.

international business The profit-related activities conducted across national boundaries.

international business ethics The business conduct or morals of MNCs in their relationships to all individuals and entities with whom they come in contact when conducting business overseas.

international codes of conduct The codes of conduct of four major international institutions that provide some consistent guidelines for multinational enterprises relative to their moral approach to business behavior around the world.

international competitor analysis The process of assessing the competitive positions, goals, strategies, strengths, and weaknesses of competitors relative to one's own firm.

internationalization The process by which a firm gradually changes in response to the imperatives of international competition, domestic market saturation, desire for expansion, new markets, and diversification.

international joint venture (IJV) An overseas business owned and controlled by two or more partners; starting such a venture is often used as an entry strategy.

international management The process of planning, organizing, leading, and controlling in a multicultural or cross-cultural environment.

international management teams Collections of managers from several countries who must rely on group collaboration if each member is to achieve success.

international social responsibility The expectation that MNCs should be concerned about the social and economic effects of their decisions regarding activities in other countries.

keiretsu Large Japanese conglomerates of financially linked, and often family-linked, groups of companies, such as Mitsubishi, that do business among themselves whenever possible.

kibun Feelings and attitudes (Korean word).

kinesic behavior Communication through posture, gestures, facial expressions, and eye contact.

knowledge management The process by which the firm integrates and benefits from the experiences and skills learned by its employees, for example, when repatriating managers from the host country.

labor relations The process through which managers and workers determine their workplace relationships.

licensing An international entry strategy by which a firm grants the rights to a firm in the host country to produce or sell a product.

locus of decision making The relative level of decentralization in an organization—that is, the level at which decisions of varying importance can be made—ranging from all decisions made at headquarters to all made at the local subsidiary.

love-hate relationship An expression describing a common attitude of host governments toward MNC investment in their country—they love the economic growth that the MNC brings but hate the incursions on their independence and sovereignty.

low-contact culture Cultures that prefer much less sensory involvement, standing farther apart and touching far less; a "distant" style of body language.

low-context communication One in which people convey messages directly and explicitly.

macropolitical risk event An event that affects all foreign firms doing business in a country or region.

managing environmental interdependence The process by which international managers accept and enact their role in the preservation of ecological balance on the earth.

managing interdependence The effective management of a long-term MNC subsidiary–host-country relationship through cooperation and consideration for host concerns.

maquiladoras U.S. manufacturing or assembly facilities operating just south of the U.S.–Mexico border under special tax considerations.

masculinity The degree to which traditionally "masculine" values—assertiveness, materialism, and the like—prevail in a society.

material culture *See* **object language**.

matrix structure A hybrid organization of overlapping responsibilities.

micropolitical risk event An event that affects one industry or company or only a few companies.

MIS adequacy The ability to gather timely and accurate information necessary for international management, especially in less developed countries.

monochronic cultures Those cultures in which time is experienced and used in a linear way; there is a past, present, and future, and time is treated as something to be spent, saved, wasted, and so on. *See also* **polychronic cultures**.

moral idealism The relative emphasis on long-term, ethical, and moral criteria for decisions versus short-term, cost-benefit criteria. *See also* **utilitarianism**.

moral universalism A moral standard toward social responsibility accepted by all cultures.

multicultural leader A person who is effective in inspiring and influencing the thinking, attitudes, and behavior of people from various cultural backgrounds.

multidomestic strategy Emphasizing local markets, allowing more local responsiveness and specialization.

multinational corporation (MNC) A corporation that engages in production or service activities through its own affiliates in several countries, maintains control over the policies of those affiliates, and manages from a global perspective.

nationalism The practice by a country of rallying public opinion in favor of national goals and against foreign influences.

nationalization The forced sale of an MNC's assets to local buyers with some compensation to the firm, perhaps leaving a minority ownership with the MNC; often involves the takeover of an entire industry, such as the oil industry.

negotiation The process by which two or more parties meet to try to reach agreement regarding conflicting interests.

noise Anything that serves to undermine the communication of the intended meaning.

noncomparability of performance data across countries The control problem caused by the difficulty of comparing performance data across various countries because of the variables that make that information appear different.

nontask sounding (*nemawashi*) General, polite conversation and informal communication before meetings.

nonverbal communication (body language) The transfer of meaning through the use of body language, time, and space.

objective–subjective decision-making approach The relative level of rationality and objectivity used in making decisions versus the level of subjective factors, such as emotions and ideals.

object language (material culture) How we communicate through material artifacts, whether architecture, office design and furniture, clothing, cars, or cosmetics.

offshoring The use of manufacturing workers located in countries other than that in which the firm is domiciled. (Commonly referred to as "sending jobs overseas.")

openness Traits such as open-mindedness, tolerance for ambiguity, and extrovertedness.

open systems model The view that all factors inside and outside a firm—environment, organization, and management—work together as a dynamic, interdependent system.

outsourcing The use of professional, skilled, service-sector workers located in countries other than that in which the firm is domiciled.

paralanguage How something is said rather than the content—the rate of speech, the tone and inflection of voice, other noises, laughing, or yawning.

parent-country national (PCN) An employee in or from the firm's home country.

parochialism The expectation that "foreigners" should automatically fall into host-country patterns of behavior.

political risk The potential for governmental actions or politically motivated events to occur in a country that will adversely affect the long-run profitability or value of a firm.

polycentric staffing approach An MNC policy of using local host-country nationals (HCNs) to fill key positions in the host country.

polychronic cultures Those cultures that welcome the simultaneous occurrence of many things and emphasize involvement with people over specific time commitments or compartmentalized activities. *See also* **monochronic cultures**.

posturing General discussion that sets the tone for negotiation meetings.

power distance The extent to which subordinates accept unequal power and a hierarchical system in a company.

privatization The sale of government-owned operations to private investors.

projective cognitive similarity The assumption that others perceive, judge, think, and reason in the same way.

protectionism A country's use of tariff and nontariff barriers to partially or completely close its borders to various imported products that would compete with domestic products.

proxemics The distance between people (personal space) with which a person feels comfortable.

questionable payments Business payments that raise significant ethical issues about appropriate moral behavior in either a host nation or other nations.

regiocentric staffing approach An approach in which recruiting for international managers is done on a regional basis and may comprise a specific mix of PCNs, HCNs, and TCNs.

regionalization strategy The global corporate strategy that links markets within regions and allows managers in each region to formulate their own regional strategy and cooperate as quasi-independent subsidiaries.

regulatory environment The many laws and courts of the nation in which an international manager works.

relationship building The process of getting to know one's contacts in a host country and building mutual trust before embarking on business discussions and transactions.

repatriation The process of the reintegration of expatriates into the headquarters organization and career ladder as well as into the social environment.

resilience Traits such as having an internal locus of control, persistence, a tolerance of ambiguity, and resourcefulness.

reverse culture shock A state of disorientation and anxiety that results from returning to one's own culture.

ringi system "Bottom-up" decision-making process used in Japanese organizations.

self-reference criterion An unconscious reference to one's own cultural values; understanding and relating to others only from one's own cultural frame of reference.

separation The retention of distinct identities by minority groups unwilling or unable to adapt to the dominant culture.

stages model *See* **structural evolution**.

stereotyping The assumption that every member of a society or subculture has the same characteristics or traits, without regard to individual differences.

strategic alliances (global) Working partnerships between MNCs across national boundaries and often across industries.

strategic business unit (SBU) A self-contained business within a company with its own functional departments and accounting systems.

strategic freedom of an IJV The relative amount of control that an international joint venture will have, compared with the parents, in choosing suppliers, product lines, customers, and so on.

strategic implementation The process by which strategic plans are realized through the establishment of a *system of fits* throughout an organization with the desired strategy—for example, in organizational structure, staffing, and operations.

strategic planning The process by which a firm's managers consider the future prospects for their company and evaluate and decide on strategy to achieve long-term objectives.

strategy The basic means by which a company competes: the choice of business or businesses in which it operates and how it differentiates itself from its competitors in those businesses.

structural evolution (stages model) The stages of change in an organizational structure that follow the evolution of the internationalization process.

subculture shock A state of disorientation and anxiety that results from the unfamiliar circumstances and behaviors encountered when exposed to a different cultural group in a country than one the person is familiar with.

subsidiary A business incorporated in a foreign country in which the parent corporation holds an ownership position.

SWOT analysis An assessment of a firm's capabilities (**s**trengths and **w**eaknesses) relative to those of its competitors as pertinent to the **o**pportunities and **t**hreats in the environment for those firms.

synergy The greater level of effectiveness that can result from combined group effort than from the total of each individual's efforts alone.

technoglobalism A phenomenon in which the rapid developments in information and communication technologies (ICTs) are propelling globalization and vice versa.

terrorism The use of, or threat to use, violence for ideological or political purposes.

transnational corporations (TNCs) Multinational corporations that are truly globalizing by viewing the world as one market and crossing boundaries for whatever functions or resources are most efficiently available; structural coordination reflects the ability to integrate globally while retaining local flexibility; typically owned and managed by nationals from different countries.

transpatriate A term similar to expatriates but referring to managers who may be from any country other than that in which the firm is domiciled, and who tends to work in several countries over time—that is, who has no true corporate "home."

turnkey operation When a company designs and constructs a facility abroad, trains local personnel, and turns the key over to local management for a fee.

uncertainty avoidance The extent to which people feel threatened by ambiguous situations; in a company, this results in formal rules and processes to provide more security.

utilitarianism The relative emphasis on short-term cost-benefit (utilitarian) criteria for decisions versus those of long-term, ethical, and moral concerns. *See also* **moral idealism**.

values A person or group's ideas and convictions about what is important, good or bad, right or wrong.

virtual global teams Employees in various locations around the world who coordinate their work and decisions through teleconferencing, email, and so on.

work centrality The degree of general importance that working has in the life of an individual at any given time.

workforce diversity The phenomenon of increasing ethnic diversity in the workforce in the United States and many other countries because of diverse populations and joint ventures; this results in intercultural working environments in domestic companies.

works council In Germany, an employee group that shares plant-level responsibility with managers.

World Trade Organization (WTO) A formal structure for continued negotiations to reduce trade barriers and settling trade disputes.

Endnotes

Chapter 1

1. Thomas L. Friedman, *The World Is Flat* (New York: Farrar, Straus and Giroux, 2005), p. 5.
2. Ibid, p. 7.
3. Adapted from unknown source, March 2006.
4. www.imf.gov, May 21, 2006.
5. P. Stephens, "A Perilous Collision Between Nationalism and Globalisation," *Financial Times,* March 3, 2006.
6. J. Sapsford and Norihiko Shirouzu, "Mom, Apple Pie and . . . Toyota?" *The Wall Street Journal,* May 11, 2006.
7. Nanette Byrnes, "Avon: More Than Cosmetic Changes," *Business Week*, March 12, 2007.
8. J. L. Levere, "A Small Company, a Global Approach," www.nytimes.com, January 1, 2004.
9. P. Drucker, Interview, in *Fortune,* January 12, 2004.
10. www.wikipedia.org, May 21, 2006.
11. George Parker and Quentin Peel, "A Fractured Europe," *Financial Times,* September 17, 2003, p. 15.
12. U.S. National Intelligence Council, quoted in *Financial Times,* March 3, 2006.
13. J. Edwards, "East Asia is An Economic Dynamo," *Financial Times,* January 6, 2004, p. 13.
14. FT Summer School, "China: Rough But Ready for Outsiders," *Financial Times,* August 26, 2003, p. 7
15. "As Families Splurge, Chinese Savings Take a Hit," *The Wall Street Journal,* May 2, 2006, pp. A1, A12.
16. Friedman, p. 114.
17. "Worrying about China," www.businessweek.com, January 19, 2004.
18. M. Wolf, "What India Must Do to Catch Up with and Possibly Outpace China," *Financial Times,* February 15, 2006, p. 13.
19. H. Kumar, "South Asia Looks to Sign Free Trade Pact," www.nytimes.com, December 31, 2003.
20. www.wikipedia.org, May 27, 2006.
21. www.worldbank.org, May 27, 2006.
22. Geri Smith, "Look Who's Pumping out Engineers," *Business Week*, May 22, 2006, pp. 42–43.
23. www.wola.org/economic/cafta/htm, May 13, 2006.
24. Stefan Wagstyl, "Doubts about Russia Cloud Overall Outlook," *Financial Times,* May 16, 2006, Special report p. 1.
25. Andrew Jack, "Foreign investment in limbo as Putin's Team Backtracks," *Financial Times,* May 1, 2006, p. 3.
26. N. Itano, "South African Companies Fill a Void," www.nytimes.com, November 4, 2003.
27. Friedman, p. 6.
28. Steve Hamm, "Big Blue Shift," *Business Week*, June 5, 2006, pp. 108–110.
29. *Forrester research report,* November 2002.
30. J. Fox, "Where Your Job is Going," *Fortune,* November 24, 2003, pp. 84–87.
31. www.FT.com, March 31, 2006.
32. "Outsourcing: Make way for China," www.businessweek.com, July 29, 2003.
33. B. Weiner, "What Executives Should Know About Political Risks," *Management Review* (January 1991): 19–22.
34. David Luhnow and Jose de Cordoba, "Bolivia's President Morales Orders Nationalization of Natural Gas," *The Wall Street Journal,* May 2, 2006, pp. A1, A15.
35. Ibid.
36. E. F. Micklous, "Tracking the Growth and Prevalence of International Terrorism," in *Managing Terrorism: Strategies for the Corporate Executive,* eds. P. J. Montana and G. S. Roukis (Westport, CT: Quorum Books, 1983), p. 3.
37. Robock and Simmonds, *International Business and Multinational Enterprises,* 4ed (Homewood, Il: Irwin, 1989), p. 378.
38. G. M. Taoka and D. R. Beeman, *International Business* (New York: HarperCollins, 1991), p. 112.
39. Ibid.
40. W. Shreeve, "Be Prepared for Political Changes Abroad," *Harvard Business Review* (July–August 1984): 111–118.
41. C. Schnitzer, M. L. Liebrenz, and K. W. Kubin, *International Business* (Cincinnati, OH: South-Western, 1985), pp. 45–47
42. Erol, "An Exploratory Model of Political Risk Assessment and the Decision Process of Foreign Direct Investment," *International Studies of Management and Organization* (Summer 1985): 75–90.
43. Ibid.
44. Morrison, W. Conaway, and J. Bouress, *Dun & Bradstreet's Guide to Doing Business Around the World* (Upper Saddle River, NJ: Prentice Hall, 1997).
45. Schnitzer, Liebrenz, and Kubin, pp. 45–47.
46. P. Smith Ring, S. A. Lenway, and M. Govekar, "Management of the Political Imperative in International Business," *Strategic Management Journal* 11 (1990): 141–151.
47. Taoka and Beeman, p. 112
48. Ibid.
49. Overseas Private Investment Corporation, *Investment Insurance Handbook*, 4, 2000.
50. Schnitzer, Liebrenz, and Kubin, pp. 45–47.
51. B. O'Reilly, "Business Copes with Terrorism," *Fortune*, January 6, 2004, p. 48.
52. *The Wall Street Journal*, December 29, 2000, p. 3.
53. F. John Mathis, "International Risk Analysis," in *Global Business Management in the 1990s,* ed. R. T. Moran (Washington, DC: Beacham, 1990), pp. 33–44.
54. Joseph Kahn, "Dispute Leaves U.S. Executive in Chinese Legal Netherworld," www.nytimes.com, November 1, 2005.
55. Ibid.
56. P. Hui-Ho Cheng, "A Business Risk in China: Jail," *Asian Wall Street Journal*, April 22, 1994, p.12
57. Rahul Jacob, "Asian Infrastructure: the biggest bet on earth, *Fortune*, October 31, 1994, pp.139–146.
58. R. J. Radway, "Foreign Contract Agreements," in *Global Business Management in the 1990s,* ed. R. T. Moran (Washington, DC: Beacham, 1990), pp. 93–103.

59. S. P. Robbins and R. Stuart-Kotze, *Management* (Scarborough, Ontario: Prentice Hall Canada, 1990), pp. 4–11.

60. Ibid.

61. "Lacking Roads, Village Building Information Highway," *The Wall Street Journal*, December 29, 2001, p. 7.

62. B. Delong, "Globalisation Means We Share Jobs as Well as Goods," *Financial Times*, August 27, 2003, p. 13.

63. Friedman, p.176.

64. Sylvia Ostry, "Technological Productivity and the Multinational Enterprise," *Journal of International Business Studies* 29, 1 (1st quarter, 1998): 85–99.

65. Ibid.

66. Jack Goldsmith and Tim Wu, *Who Controls the Internet? Illusions of a Borderless World.* (London: Oxford University Press, 2006).

67. *Financial Times*, May 17, 2006.

68. Hans Dieter Zimmerman, "E-Business," www.businessmedia.org, June 13, 2000.

69. J. Rajesh, "Five E-Business Trends," Net.Columns, www.indialine.com, February 18, 1999.

70. "Europe's borderless market: the Net," www.businessweek.com, May 17, 2003.

71. "E-Management," *The Economist,* November 11, 2000, pp. 32–34.

72. "E-commerce Report, *New York Times*, March 26, 2001, pp. 7–8.

73. S. Mohanbir, M. Sumant, "Go Global," *Business 2.0,* May 2000, pp. 178–213.

74. A. Chen and M. Hicks, "Going global? Avoid culture clashes," *PC Week*, April 3, 2000, pp. 9–10.

Chapter 2

1. A. Maitland, "No Hiding Place for the Irresponsible Business," *Financial Times Special Report*, September 29, 2003, p. 4.

2. John A. Quelch and James E. Austin, "Should Multinationals Invest in Africa?" *Sloan Management Review* (Spring 1993): 107–119.

3. Milton Friedman, *Capitalism and Freedom* (Chicago: University of Chicago Press, 1962).

4. T. Donaldson, "Defining the Value of Doing Good Business," *Financial Times*, June 3, 2005, p. 2.

5. John Dobson, "The Role of Ethics in Global Corporate Culture," *Journal of Business Ethics* 9 (1990): 481–488.

6. T. Donaldson, June 3, 2005.

7. Ibid.

8. N. Bowie, "The Moral Obligations of Multinational Corporations," in *Problems of International Justice*, ed. LuperFay (New York: Westview Press: 1987), pp. 97–113.

9. A. C. Wicks, "Norman Bowie and Richard Rorty on Multinationals: Does Business Ethics Need 'Metaphysical Comfort'?" *Journal of Business Ethics* 9 (1990): 191–200.

10. Ibid.

11. Peter Burrows, "Stalking High-Tech Sweatshops," *Business Week,* June 19, 2006, p. 63.

12. Joanna Ramey, "Clinton Urges Industry to Enlist in the War Against Sweatshops," www.labordepartment.com, April 15, 1997.

13. Jem Bendell, "Nike Says Time to Team Up," *The Journal of Corporate Citizenship*, Autumn 2005 i19 p. 10(3).

14. J. Carlton, "Ties with China Will Be Severed by Levi Strauss," *The Wall Street Journal*, May 5, 1993, p. A3.

15. *Business Week*, June 19, 2006, p. 63.

16. "The Should-list to Discuss with Mr. Hu: China, America and Human Rights," *The Economist (U.S.)*, April 22, 2006, Vol. 376, Issue 8474, p. 12.

17. Peter Marsh, "Foreign Makers Find Advantages on More Familiar Turf," *Financial Times*, May 8, 2006.

18. *Asian Wall Street Journal*, April 8, 2004.

19. Steven Greenhouse, "A.F.L.-C.I.O. Files a Trade Complaint against China's Labor Practices," *New York Times*, June 9, 2006.

20. Howard W. French, "Despite Web Crackdown, Prevailing Winds Are Free," *New York Times*, February 6, 2006.

21. Ibid.

22. Ibid.

23. B. Einhorn and B. Eglin, "The Great Firewall of China," *Business Week*, January 23, 2006, p. 63.

24. John Gapper, "Google Is Putting its Own Freedoms at Risk in China," *Financial Times*, January 20, 2006.

25. R. Waters, M. Dickie, and S. Kirchgaessner, "Evildoers? How the West's Net Vanguard Toils Behind the Great Firewall of China," *Financial Times*, February 15, 2006, p. 11.

26. M. Dickie, "Amnesty Accuses Web Groups over Human rights in China," *Financial Times*, July 20, 2006.

27. "Sweatshop Police," *Business Week*, October 20, 1997, pp. 30–32.

28. Kathleen A. Getz, "International Codes of Conduct: An Analysis of Ethical Reasoning," *Journal of Business Ethics* 9 (1990): 567–577.

29. Alison Maitland, "How Ethics Codes Can Be Made to Work," *Financial Times*, March 7, 2005, p. 9.

30. Swee Hoon Ang, "The Power of Money: A Cross-Cultural Analysis of Business-Related Beliefs," *Journal of World Business* 35, no. 1 (Spring 2000): 43.

31. C. J. Robertson and W. F. Crittenden, "Mapping Moral Philosophies: Strategic Implications for Multinational Firms," *Strategic Management Journal* 24 (2003): 385–392.

32. A. Singer, "Ethics—Are Standards Lower Overseas?" *Across the Board* (September 1991): 31–34.

33. Ibid.

34. www.TransparencyInternational.org, December 9, 2005.

35. Ibid.

36. Reena SenGupta, "Trouble at Home for Overseas Bribes," *Financial Times*, February 2, 2006, p. 9.

37. G. R. Laczniak and J. Naor, "Global Ethics: Wrestling with the Corporate Conscience," *Business*, July–August–September 1985, p. 152.

38. "How to Respond When Only Bribe Money Talks," *Financial Times*, July 11, 2005.

39. J. T. Noonan, Jr., *Bribes* (New York: Macmillan, 1984), p. ii.

40. SenGupta.

41. Ibid.

42. T. L. Carson, "Bribery and Implicit Agreements: A Reply to Philips," *Journal of Business Ethics* 6 (1987): 123–125.

43. M. Philips, "Bribery," *Ethics* 94 (July 1984): 50.

44. Laczniak and Naor.

45. L. H. Newton and M. M. Ford, *Taking Sides* (Guilford, CT: Dushkin, 1990).

46. Ibid.

47. M. E. Shannon, "Coping with Extortion and Bribery," in *Multinational Managers and Host Government Interactions*, ed. Lee A Tavis (South Bend, IN: University of Notre Dame Press, 1988).

48. Laczniak and Naor.

49. Sadahei Kusumoto, "We're Not in Honshu Anymore," *Across the Board* (June 1989): 49–50.

50. Ibid.

51. P. W. Beamish et al., *International Management* (Homewood, IL: Irwin, 1991).

52. Adapted from Asheghian and Ebrahimi, *International Business* (NY: Harper and Row, 1990).

53. R. H. Mason and R. S. Spich, *Management: An International Perspective* (Homewood, IL: Irwin, 1987).

54. Ibid.

55. Simcha Ronen, *Comparative and Multinational Management* (New York: John Wiley and Sons, 1986), pp. 502–503.

56. R. T. De George, *Competing with Integrity in International Business* (New York: Oxford University Press, 1993), pp. 3–4.

57. B. Ward and R. Dubois, *Only One Earth* (New York: Ballantine Books, 1972).

58. Ronen.

59. S. Tifft. "Who Gets the Garbage," *Time*, July 4, 1988, pp. 42–43.

60. Jang B. Singh and V. C. Lakhan, "Business Ethics and the International Trade in Hazardous Wastes," *Journal of Business Ethics* 8 (1989): 889–899.

61. R. A. Peterson and M. H. Sauber, "International Marketing Ethics: Is There a Need for a Code?" Paper presented at the International Studies Association Southwest, Houston, TX, March 16–19, 1984.

62. M. Reza Vaghefi, S. K. Paulson, and W. H. Tomlinson, *International Business Theory and Practice* (New York: Taylor and Francis, 1991), 249–250.

63. T. E. Graedel and B. R. Allenby, *Industrial Ecology* (Upper Saddle River, NJ: Prentice Hall, 1995).

64. M. Sharfman, Book Review of Graedel and Allenby, *Academy of Management Review* 20, no. 4 (1995): 1,090–1,107.

65. Ronen, 1986.

66. P. Asheghian and B. Ebrahimi, *International Business* (NY: Harper and Row, 1990), pp. 640–641.

Chapter 3

1. David A. Ricks, *Big Business Blunders: Mistakes in Multinational Marketing* (Homewood, IL: Dow Jones–Irwin, 1983).

2. Carla Joinson, "Why HR Managers Need to Think Globally," *HR Magazine* (April 1998): 2–7.

3. Ibid.

4. J. Stewart Black and Mark Mendenhall, "Cross-Cultural Training Effectiveness: A Review and a Theoretical Framework for Future Research," *Academy of Management Review* 15, no. 1 (1990): 113–136.

5. Adapted from Bernard Wysocki, Jr., "Global Reach: Cross-Border Alliances Become Favorite Way to Crack New Markets," *The Wall Street Journal,* March 26, 1990, pp. A1, A4.

6. Geert Hofstede, *Culture's Consequences: International Differences in Work-Related Values* (Beverly Hills, CA: Sage Publications, 1980), p. 25; E. T. Hall, *The Silent Language* (Greenwich, CT: Fawcett, 1959). For a more detailed definition of the culture of a society, see A. L. Kroeber and C. Kluckholhn, "A Critical Review of Concepts and Definitions," in *Peabody Museum Papers* 47, no. 1 (Cambridge, MA: Harvard University Press, 1952), p. 181.

7. David Dressler and Donald Carns, *Sociology, The Study of Human Interaction* (New York: Knopf, 1969), pp. 56–57.

8. K. David, "Organizational Processes for Intercultural Management," paper presented at the Strategic Management Association, San Francisco, CA, 1989.

9. *The Wall Street Journal*, February 20, 2001; and *The Wall Street Journal*, February 2, 1990, p. A15.

10. Lane Kelley, Arthur Whatley, and Reginald Worthley, "Assessing the Effects of Culture on Managerial Attitudes: A Three-Culture Test," *Journal of International Business Studies* (Summer 1987): 17–31.

11. J. D. Child, "Culture, Contingency and Capitalism in the Cross-National Study of Organizations," in *Research in Organizational Behavior,* ed. L. L. Cummings and B. M. Shaw (Greenwich, CT: JAI Publishers, 1981), pp. 303–356.

12. Jangho Lee, T. W. Roehl, and Soonkyoo Choe, "What Makes Management Style Similar and Distinct Across Borders? Growth Experience and Culture in Korean and Japanese Firms," *Journal of International Business Studies* 31, no. 4 (4th Quarter 2000): 631–652.

13. James A. Lee, "Cultural Analysis in Overseas Operations," *Harvard Business Review* (March–April 1966).

14. E. T. Hall, "The Silent Language in Overseas Business," *Harvard Business Review* (May–June 1960).

15. "American Culture Is Often a Puzzle for Foreign Managers in the U.S.," *The Wall Street Journal*, February 12, 1986, p. 34.

16. "One Big Market," *The Wall Street Journal*, February 6, 1989, p. 16.

17. D. A. Ralston, Yu Kai-Ceng, Xun Wang, R. H. Terpstra, and He Wei, "An Analysis of Managerial Work Values Across the Six Regions of China," paper presented at the Academy of International Business, Boston, November 1994.

18. Philip R. Harris and Robert T. Moran, *Managing Cultural Differences* (Houston, TX: Gulf Publishing, 1987).

19. K. David, "Field Research," in *The Cultural Environment of International Business*, 3rd ed., ed. V. Terpstra and K. David (Cincinnati, OH: South-Western, 1991), p. 176.

20. "Sharia Loosens Its Grip," *Euromoney* (May 1987): 137–138.

21. Mansour Javidan and Robert J. House, "Cultural Acumen for the Global Manager: Lessons from Project GLOBE," *Organizational Dynamics* (Spring 2001): 289–305.

22. V. Gupta, P. J. Hanges, and P. Dorfman, "Cultural Clusters: Methodology and Findings," *Journal of World Business,* 37 (2002): 11–15.

23. Ibid.

24. Geert Hofstede, *Cultures and Organizations: Software of the Mind* (New York: McGraw-Hill, 1997), pp. 79–108.

25. Elizabeth Weldon and Elisa L. Mustari, "Felt Dispensability in Groups of Coactors: The Effects of Shared Responsibility on Cognitive Effort" (unpublished

manuscript, Kellogg Graduate School of Management, Northwestern University).

26. P. Christopher Earley, "Social Loafing and Collectivism: A Comparison of the United States and the People's Republic of China," *Administrative Science Quarterly* 34 (1989): 565–581.

27. H. K. Steensma, L. Marino, and K. M. Weaver, "Attitudes towards Cooperative Strategies: A Cross-Cultural Analysis of Entrepreneurs," *Journal of International Business Studies* 31, no. 4 (4th Quarter 2000): 591–609.

28. G. Hofstede, *Culture's Consequences: Comparing Values, Behaviors, Institutions, and Organizations Across Nations*, 2nd ed (Thousand Oaks, CA: Sage, 2001), pp. 500–502.

29. F. Trompenaars, *Riding the Waves of Culture* (London: Nicholas Brealey, 1993).

30. L. Hoeklin, *Managing Cultural Differences: Strategies for Competitive Advantage* (New York: The Economist Intelligence Unit/Addison-Wesley, 1995).

31. Ross A. Webber, *Culture and Management, Text and Reading in Comparative Management* (Homewood, IL: Irwin, 1969), p. 186.

32. Hwang Kyu-june at Hanaro Company, Broadband Service Provider, quoted in Andrew Ward, "Love Affair Starts to Grip South Korea's Internet Generation," *Financial Times*, October 14, 2003, p. 6.

33. Ward, p. 6

34. Ibid.

35. H. Jeff Smith, "Information Privacy and Marketing: What the U.S. Should (and Shouldn't) Learn from Europe," *California Management Review* 43, no. 2 (Winter 2001): 30–34.

36. Ibid.

37. Ibid.

38. "Data Privacy Deal," *Journal of Commerce* (March 28, 2000): 4.

39. R. Howells, "Update on Safe Harbor for International Data Transfer," *Direct Marketing* 63, no. 4 (August 2000): 40.

40. Smith, pp. 30–34.

41. Mark Landler and Michael Barbaro, "Wal-Mart Finds That Its Formula Doesn't Fit Every Culture," *New York Times,* August 2, 2006.

42. Geert Hofstede, *Culture's Consequences: International Differences in Work-Related Values* (Beverly Hills, CA: Sage Publications, 1980).

43. George W. England, "Managers and Their Value Systems: A Five-Country Comparative Study," *Columbia Journal of World Business* (Summer 1978): 35–44.

44. Philip R. Harris and Robert T. Moran, *Managing Cultural Differences* (Houston, TX: Gulf Publishing, 2004); Lennie Copeland and Lewis Griggs, *Going International* (New York: Random House, 1985); Boye De Mente, *Japanese Etiquette and Ethics in Business* (Lincolnwood, IL: NTC Business Books, 1989); R. L. Tung, *Business Negotiations with the Japanese* (Lexington, MA: Lexington Books, 1984); W. G. Ouchi and A. M. Jaeger, "Theory Z Organization: Stability in the Midst of Mobility," *Academy of Management Review* 3, no. 2 (1978): 305–314; Fernando Quezada and James E. Boyce, "Latin America," in *Comparative Management*, ed. Raghu Nath (Cambridge, MA: Ballinger Publishing, 1988), pp. 245–270; Simcha Ronen, *Comparative and Multinational Management* (New York: John Wiley and Sons, 1986); and V. Terpstra

and K. David, *The Cultural Environment of International Business*, 3rd ed. (Cincinnati, OH: South-Western, 1991).

45. Akio Kuzuoka, Forty-year Employee at a Japanese Company, quoted in *The Wall Street Journal,* December 29, 2000.

46. R. G. Linowes, "The Japanese Manager's Traumatic Entry in the United States: Understanding the American–Japanese Cultural Divide," *Academy of Management Review* (1993): 21–38.

47. FT Business School, "Go West for a New Mind-Set," *Financial Times,* October 10, 2004.

48. Ibid.

49. Yumiko Ono and William Spindle, "Japan's Long Decline Makes One Thing Rise—Individualism," *The Wall Street Journal*, December 29, 2000, p. 5.

50. E. T. Hall and M. R. Hall, *Understanding Cultural Differences* (Yarmouth, ME: Intercultural Press, 1990), p. 4.

51. P. R. Harris and R. T. Moran, *Managing Cultural Differences*, 4th ed. (Houston, TX: Gulf Publishing Co., 1996).

52. Robert Moore, "Saudi Arabia," Chapter 11, in Harris and Moran.

53. John A. Pearce II and Richard B. Robinson, Jr., "Cultivating *Guanxi* as a Foreign Investor Strategy," *Business Horizons* 43, 1 (January 2000): 31.

54. M. Chen, *Asian Management Systems: Chinese, Japanese and Korean Styles of Business* (New York: Routledge, 1995).

55. Anne Marie Francesco and Barry Allen Gold, *International Organizational Behavior* (Upper Saddle River, NJ: Prentice Hall, 1997).

56. J. Lee, "Culture and Management—A Study of Small Chinese Family Business in Singapore," *Journal of Small Business Management* (July 1996): 17–24.

57. R. Sheng, "Outsiders' Perception of the Chinese," *Columbia Journal of World Business* 14 (2) (Summer 2000): 16–22.

58. Lee, pp. 17–24

59. Ralston et al.

Chapter 4

1. E. T. Hall and M. R. Hall, *Understanding Cultural Differences* (Yarmouth, ME: Intercultural Press, 1990), p. 4.

2. E. Wilmott, "New Media Vision," *New Media Age*, September 9, 1999, p. 8.

3. Hall and Hall; K. Wolfson and W. B. Pearce, "A Crosscultural Comparison of the Implications of Self-discovery on Conversation Logics," *Communication Quarterly* 31 (1983): 249–256.

4. H. Mintzberg, *The Nature of Managerial Work* (New York: Harper and Row, 1973).

5. L. A. Samovar, R. E. Porter, and N. C. Jain, *Understanding Intercultural Communication* (Belmont, CA: Wadsworth Publishing Co., 1981).

6. P. R. Harris and R. T. Moran, *Managing Cultural Differences,* 3rd ed. (Houston, TX: Gulf Publishing, 1991).

7. H. C. Triandis, quoted in *The Blackwell Handbook of Cross-cultural Management,* eds. M. Gannon and K. Newman (Oxford, England: Blackwell Publishers, 2002).

8. Samovar, Porter, and Jain.

9. Hall and Hall, 15.

10. James R. Houghton, Former Chairman of Corning, Inc., quoted in *Organizational Dynamics* 29, no. 4 (Spring 2001).

11. J. Child, "Trust: The Fundamental Bond in Global Collaboration," *Organizaional Dynamics* 29, no. 4 (Spring 2001): 274–288.

12. Ibid.

13. World Values Study Group (1994), *World Values Survey, ICPSR Version* (Ann Arbor, MI: Institute for Social Research); R. Inglehart, M. Basanez, and A. Moreno, *Human Values and Beliefs: A Cross-cultural Sourcebook* (Ann Arbor: University of Michigan Press, 1998).

14. Mansour Javidan and Robert J. House, "Cultural Acumen for the Global Manager," *Organizational Dynamics* 29, no. 4 (Spring 2001), 289–305.

15. Samovar and Porter; Harris and Moran.

16. M. L. Hecht, P. A. Andersen, and S. A. Ribeau, "The Cultural Dimensions of Nonverbal Communication, in *Handbook of International and Intercultural Communication*, ed. M. K. Asante and W. B. Gudykunst (Newbury Park, CA: Sage Publications, 1989), pp. 163–185.

17. H. C. Triandis, *Interpersonal Behavior* (Monterey, CA: Brooks/Cole, 1977).

18. Harris and Moran.

19. Adapted from N. Adler, *International Dimensions of Organizational Behavior,* 2nd ed. (Boston: PWS-Kent, 1991).

20. D. A. Ricks, *Big Business Blunders: Mistakes in Multinational Marketing* (Homewood, IL: Dow Jones–Irwin, 1983).

21. Vern Terpstra and K. David, *The Cultural Environment of International Business*, 3rd ed. (Cincinnati, OH: South-Western, 1991).

22. L. Copeland and L. Griggs, *Going International* (New York: Random House, 1985).

23. J. R. Schermerhorn, "Language Effects in Cross-cultural Management Research: An Empirical Study and a Word of Caution," *National Academy of Management Proceedings* (1987): 103.

24. Jiatao Li, Katherine R. Xin, Anne Tsui, and Donald C. Hambrick, "Building Effective International Joint Venture Leadership Teams in China," *Journal of World Business* 34, no. 1 (1999): 52–68.

25. R. L. Daft, *Organizational Theory and Design*, 3rd ed. (St. Paul, MN: West Publishing, 1989).

26. Li et al., 1999.

27. O. Klineberg, "Emotional Expression in Chinese Literature," *Journal of Abnormal and Social Psychology* 33 (1983): 517–530.

28. P. Ekman and W. V. Friesen, "Constants Across Cultures in the Face and Emotion," *Journal of Personality and Social Psychology* 17 (1971): 124–129.

29. J. Pfeiffer, "How Not to Lose the Trade Wars by Cultural Gaffes," *Smithsonian* 18, no. 10 (January 1988).

30. E. T. Hall, *The Silent Language* (New York: Doubleday, 1959).

31. Hall and Hall.

32. Ibid.

33. N. M. Sussman and H. M. Rosenfeld, "Influence of Culture, Language, and Sex on Conversational Distance," *Journal of Personality and Social Psychology* 42 (1982): 66–74.

34. Copeland and Griggs.

35. Hecht, Andersen, and Ribeau.

36. Li et al., 1999.

37. Pfeiffer.

38. Hall and Hall.

39. Robert Matthews, "Where East Can Never Meet West," *Financial Times,* October 21, 2005.

40. Hall and Hall.

41. Matthews, 2005.

42. Hecht, Andersen, and Ribeau.

43. Hall and Hall.

44. R. Axtell, ed., *Do's and Taboos Around the World*, 2nd ed. (New York: John Wiley and Sons, 1985).

45. Copeland and Griggs.

46. M. K. Nydell, *Understanding Arabs* (Yarmouth, ME: Intercultural Press, 1987).

47. Harris and Moran.

48. E. T. Hall, *The Hidden Dimension* (New York: Doubleday, 1966), p. 15.

49. A. Almaney and A. Alwan, *Communicating with the Arabs* (Prospect Heights, IL: Waveland, 1982).

50. E. T. Hall, "The Silent Language in Overseas Business," *Harvard Business Review* (May–June 1960).

51. Ibid.

52. Based largely on the work of Nydell; and R. T. Moran and P. R. Harris, *Managing Cultural Synergy* (Houston, TX: Gulf Publishing, 1982), pp. 81–82.

53. Ibid.

54. Copeland and Griggs.

55. Hall and Hall.

56. D. C. Barnlund, "Public and Private Self in Communicating with Japan," *Business Horizons* (March–April 1989): 32–40.

57. Hall and Hall.

58. A. Goldman, "The Centrality of 'Ningensei' to Japanese Negotiating and Interpersonal Relationships: Implications for U.S.–Japanese Communication," *International Journal of Intercultural Relations* 18, no. 1 (Winter 1994).

59. Jean-Louis Barsoux and Peter Lawrence, "The Making of a French Manager," *Harvard Business Review* (July–August 1991): 58–67.

60. D. Shand, "All Information Is Local: IT Systems Can Connect Every Corner of the Globe, But IT Managers Are Learning They Have to Pay Attention to Regional Differences," *Computerworld*, April 10, 2000, 88 (1).

61. T. Wilson, "B2B Links, European Style: Integrator Helps Applications Cross Language, Currency and Cultural Barriers," *InternetWeek*, October 9, 2000, p. 27.

62. Shand.

63. Wilmott.

64. *Business Week*, February, 1998, 14–15.

65. Wilson.

66. www.Businessfordiplomaticaction.org, retrieved August 19, 2006.

67. D. Ricks, *Big Business Blunders (Homewood, IL: Dow Jones-Irwin, 1983).*

68. Adler.

69. P. G. W. Keen, "Sorry, Wrong Number," *Business Month* (January 1990): 62–67.

70. R. B. Ruben, "Human Communication and Cross-cultural Effectiveness," in *Intercultural Communication: A Reader*, ed. L. Samovar and R. Porter (Belmont, CA: Wadsworth, 1985), p. 339.

71. D. Ruben and B. D. Ruben, "Cross-cultural Personnel Selection Criteria, Issues and Methods," in *Handbook of*

Intercultural Training, Vol. 1, *Issues in Theory and Design,* ed. D. Landis and R. W. Brislin (New York: Pergamon, 1983), pp. 155–175.

72. Young Yun Kim, *Communication and Cross-cultural Adaptation: An Integrative Theory* (Clevedon, England; Multilingual Matters, 1988).

73. Ibid.

74. R. W. Brislin, *Cross-cultural Encounters: Face-to-Face Interaction* (New York: Pergamon, 1981).

Chapter 5

1. CNN and other newscasts during April, 2001.

2. John Pfeiffer, "How Not to Lose the Trade Wars by Cultural Gaffes," *Smithsonian* 18, no. 10 (January 1988): 145–156.

3. Nancy J. Adler, *International Dimensions of Organizational Behavior,* 4th ed. (Boston: PWS-Kent, 2002), pp. 208–232.

4. Philip R. Harris and Robert T. Moran, *Managing Cultural Differences,* 3rd ed. (Houston, TX: Gulf Publishing, 1991).

5. John L. Graham and Roy A. Herberger, Jr., "Negotiators Abroad—Don't Shoot from the Hip," *Harvard Business Review* (July–August 1983): 160–168; Adler; John L. Graham, "A Hidden Cause of America's Trade Deficit with Japan," *Columbia Journal of World Business* (Fall 1981): 5–15.

6. Phillip D. Grub, "Cultural Keys to Successful Negotiating," in *Global Business Management in the 1990s,* ed. F. Ghader et al. (Washington, DC: Beacham, 1990): 24–32.

7. R. Fisher and W. Ury, *Getting to Yes* (Boston: Houghton Mifflin, 1981).

8. "Soviet Breakup Stymies Foreign Firms," *The Wall Street Journal,* January 23, 1992.

9. S. Weiss, "Negotiating with 'Romans,'" *Sloan Management Review* (Winter 1994): 51–61.

10. John A. Reeder, "When West Meets East: Cultural Aspects of Doing Business in Asia," *Business Horizons* (January–February 1987): 72.

11. Adler, 197.

12. Fisher and Ury.

13. Lennie Copeland and Lewis Griggs, *Going International* (New York: Random House, 1985), p. 85.

14. Adler, 197–198.

15. John L. Graham, "The Influence of Culture on the Process of Business Negotiations in an Exploratory Study," *Journal of International Business Studies* (Spring 1985): 88.

16. Fisher and Ury.

17. R. Tung, "Handshakes Across the Sea," *Organizational Dynamics* (Winter 1991): 30–40.

18. John L. Graham, "The Influence of Culture on Business Negotiations," *Journal of International Business Studies* 16, no. 1 (Spring 1985): 81–96.

19. G. Fisher, *International Negotiation: A Cross-cultural Perspective* (Chicago: Intercultural Press, 1980).

20. Pfeiffer.

21. *The Wall Street Journal,* February 2, 1994.

22. John L. Graham, "Brazilian, Japanese, and American Business Negotiations," *Journal of International Business Studies* (Spring–Summer 1983): 47–61.

23. T. Flannigan, "Successful Negotiating with the Japanese," *Small Business Reports* 15, no. 6 (June 1990): 47–52.

24. Graham, 1983; Boye De Mente, *Japanese Etiquette and Ethics in Business* (Lincolnwood, IL: NTC Business Books, 1989).

25. Robert H. Doktor, "Asian and American CEOs: A Comparative Study," *Organizational Dynamics* (Winter 1990): 49.

26. Harris and Moran, 461.

27. Adler, 181.

28. These profiles are adapted from Pierre Casse, *Managing Intercultural Negotiations: Guidelines for Trainers and Negotiators* (Washington, DC: Society for Intercultural Education, Training and Research, 1985).

29. D. K. Tse, J. Francis, and J. Walls, "Cultural Differences in Conducting Intra- and Inter-Cultural Negotiations: A Sino-Canadian Comparison," *Journal of International Business Studies* (3rd Quarter 1994): 537–555.

30. B. W. Husted, "Bargaining with the Gringos: An Exploratory Study of Negotiations Between Mexican and U.S. Firms," *International Executive* 36, no. 5 (September–October 1994): 625–644.

31. Pierre Casse, *Training for the Cross-cultural Mind,* 2nd ed. (Washington, DC: Society for Intercultural Education, Training, and Research, 1981).

32. Nigel Campbell, John L. Graham, Alain Jolibert, and Hans Meissner, "Marketing Negotiations in France, Germany, the United Kingdom, and the United States," *Journal of Marketing* 52 (April 1988): 49–63.

33. Neil Rackham, "The Behavior of Successful Negotiators" (Reston, VA: Huthwaite Research Group, 1982).

34. J. Teich, H. Wallenius, and J. Wallenius, "World-Wide-Web Technology in Support of Negotiation and Communication," *International Journal of Technology Management* 17, nos. 1/2 (1999): 223–239.

35. Ibid.

36. Ibid.

37. *Newsweek,* May 2001.

38. J. A. Pearce II and R. B. Robinson, Jr., "Cultivating *Guanxi* as a Foreign Investor Strategy," *Business Horizons* 43, no. 1 (January 2000): 31.

39. H. Timmons and D. Greenlees, "The Art of the Deal Meets the China Syndrome," *New York Times,* July 7, 2006, p. C6.

40. Joan H. Coll, "Sino–American Cultural Differences: The Key to Closing a Business Venture with the Chinese," *Mid-Atlantic Journal of Business* 25, no. 2, 3 (December 1988/January 1989): 15–19.

41. M. Loeb, "China: A Time for Caution," *Fortune,* February 20, 1995, pp. 129–130.

42. O. Shenkar and S. Ronen, "The Cultural Context of Negotiations: The Implications of Chinese Interpersonal Norms," *Journal of Applied Behavioral Science* 23, no. 2 (1987): 263–275.

43. Tse et al.

44. J. Brunner, teaching notes, the University of Toledo.

45. Lee, Kam-hon, Yang, Guang, Graham, John L., "Tension and Trust in International Business Negotiations: American Executives Negotiating with Chinese Executives," *Journal of International Business Studies* 37, no. 5 (September 2006) p. 623.

46. Joanna M. Banthin and Leigh Stelzer, "Ethical Dilemmas in Negotiating Across Cultures: Problems in Commercial Negotiations between American Businessmen and the PRC," paper presented at 1st International Conference on East–West Joint Ventures, October 19–20, 1989, State University of New York–Plattsburgh; and J. M. Banthin and L. Stelzer, "'Opening' China: Negotiation Strategies When East Meets West," *The Mid-Atlantic Journal of Business* 25, no. 2, 3 (December 1988/January 1989).

47. Brunner.

48. Pearce and Robinson.

49. Ibid.

50. Ibid.

51. C. Blackman, "An Inside Guide to Negotiating," *China Business Review*, 27, no. 3 (May 2000): 44–45.

52. Brunner.

53. Boye De Mente, *Chinese Etiquette and Ethics in Business* (Lincolnwood, IL: NTC Business Books, 1989), pp. 115–123.

54. S. Stewart and C. F. Keown, "Talking with the Dragon: Negotiating in the People's Republic of China," *Columbia Journal of World Business* 24, no. 3 (Fall 1989): 68–72.

55. Banthin and Stelzer, "'Opening' China."

56. Blackman.

57. Ibid.

58. Lucian Pye, *Chinese Commercial Negotiating Style* (Cambridge, MA: Oelgeschlager, Gunn and Hain, 1982).

59. W. B. Gudykunst and S. Ting Tomey, *Culture and Interpersonal Communication* (Newbury Park, CA: Sage Publications, 1988).

60. L. Copeland and L. Griggs, *Going International* (New York: Random House, 1985), p. 80.

61. M. A. Hitt, B. B. Tyler, and Daewoo Park, "A Cross-cultural Examination of Strategic Decision Models: Comparison of Korean and U.S. Executives," in *Best Papers Proceedings of the 50th Annual Meeting of the Academy of Management* (San Francisco, CA, August 12–15, 1990), pp. 111–115; G. Fisher, *International Negotiation: A Cross-cultural Perspective* (Chicago: Intercultural Press, 1980); G. W. England, "Managers and Their Value Systems: A Five-Country Comparative Study," *Columbia Journal of World Business* 13, no. 2 (Summer 1978); W. Whitely and G. W. England, "Variability in Common Dimensions of Managerial Values Due to Value Orientation and Country Differences," *Personnel Psychology* 33 (1980): 77–89.

62. Hitt, Tyler, and Park, p. 114.

63. B. M. Bass and P. C. Burger, *Assessment of Managers: An International Comparison* (New York: Free Press, 1979), p. 91.

64. D. K. Tse, R. W. Belk, and Nan Zhan, "Learning to Consume: A Longitudinal and Cross-cultural Content Analysis of Print Advertisements from Hong Kong, People's Republic of China and Taiwan," *Journal of Consumer Research* (forthcoming).

65. Copeland and Griggs; M. K. Badawy, "Styles of Mideastern Managers," *California Management Review* 22 (1980): 51–58.

66. N. Namiki and S. P. Sethi, "Japan," in *Comparative Management—A Regional View,* ed. R. Nath (Cambridge, MA: Ballinger Publishing, 1988), pp. 74–76.

67. De Mente, *Japanese Etiquette,* p. 80.

68. S. Naoto, *Management and Industrial Structure in Japan* (New York: Pergamon Press, 1981); Namiki and Sethi.

69. Harris and Moran, 397.

70. S. P. Sethi and N. Namiki, "Japanese-Style Consensus Decision-Making in Matrix Management: Problems and Prospects of Adaptation," in *Matrix Management Systems Handbook*, ed. D. I. Cleland (New York: Van Nostrand, 1984), pp. 431–456.

Chapter 6

1. OECD International Direct Investment Database, www.oecd.org/daf/investment/statistics, August 19, 2006.

2. Pete Engardio, "Emerging Giants," *Business Week,* July 31, 2006, pp.41-49.

3. Ibid.

4. S. Daneshkhu, "U.K. Tops List for Foreign Direct Investment," *Financial Times,* June 29, 2006.

5. D. Kirkpatrick, "A Growing AOL Europe Now Sets Example for U.S.," www.nytimes.com, September 8, 2003.

6. A. MacDonald, A. Lucchetti, and E. Taylor, "Long City-Centric, Financial Exchanges Are Going Global," *Wall Street Journal,* May 27, 2006.

7. M. Maynard, "Foreign Makers, Settled in South, Pace Car Industry," *New York Times, June 22, 2005.*

8. A. E. Serwer, "McDonald's Conquers the World," *Fortune,* October 17, 1994.

9. P. Engardio, "Emerging Giants," *Business Week,* July 31, 2006, pp.41-49.

10. A. K. Gupta and V. Govindarajan, "Managing Global Expansion: A Conceptual Framework," *Business Horizons* (March/April 2000).

11. Dean Foust, "Taking Off Like 'A Rocket Ship'," *Business Week,* April 3, 2006.

12. Ibid.

13. Nanette Byrnes, "Avon: More Than Cosmetic Changes," *Business Week,* March 12, 2007.

14. M. McCarthy, M. Pointer, D. Ricks, and R. Rolfe, "Managers' Views on Potential Investment Opportunities," *Business Horizons* (July–August 1993): 54–58.

15. M. Maynard, "Foreign Makers, Settled in South, Pace Car Industry," New York Times, June 17, 2006.

16. Anant R. Negandhi, *International Management* (Boston: Allyn and Bacon, 1987), 230.

17. Henry Mintzberg, "Strategy Making in Three Modes," *California Management Review* (Winter 1973): 44–53.

18. Arvind V. Phatak, *International Dimensions of Management*, 2nd ed. (Boston: PWS-Kent, 1989).

19. Joseph V. Micallef, "Political Risk Assessment," *Columbia Journal of World Business* 16 (Summer 1981): 47–52; Mark Fitzpatrick, "The Definition and Assessment of Political Risk in International Business: A Review of the Literature," *Academy of Management Review* 8 (1983): 249.

20. M. Porter, *Competitive Strategy* (New York: Free Press, 1980).

21. D. J. Garsombke, "International Competitor Analysis," *Planning Review* 17, no. 3 (May–June 1989): 42–47.

22. A. Swasy, "Procter & Gamble Fixes Aim on Tough Market: The Latin Americans," *Wall Street Journal,* June 15, 1990.

23. W. H. Davidson, "The Role of Global Scanning in Business Planning," *Organizational Dynamics* 19 (Winter 1991).

24. Garsombke.

25. K. R. Andrews, *The Concept of Corporate Strategy* (Homewood, IL: Dow Jones–Irwin, 1979).

26. C. K. Prahalad and Gary Hamel, "The Core Competence of the Corporation," *Harvard Business Review* (May–June 1990): 79–91.

27. Ibid.

28. P. Ghemawat, "Distance Still Matters," *Harvard Business Review,* September 2001: 79 (8): pp.137-147.

29. M. E. Porter, "Changing Patterns of International Competition," in *The Competitive Challenge,* ed. D. J. Teece (Boston: Ballinger, 1987), 29–30.

30. T Chen, "Network Resources for Internationalization," *Journal of Management Studies,* 2003. 40:1107-1130.)

31. Porter, 1987.

32. P. W. Beamish et al., *International Management* (Homewood, IL: Irwin, 1991).

33. A. Palazzo, "B2B Markets—Industry Basics," www.FT.com, January 28, 2001.

34. A. J. Morrison, D. A. Ricks, and K. Roth, "Globalization versus Regionalization: Which Way for the Multinational?" *Organizational Dynamics* 19 (Winter 1991).

35. Ibid.

36. . . . . "Wal-Mart Selling Stores and Leaving South Korea," www.nytimes, March 23, 2006.

37. G. M. Taoka and D. R. Beeman, *International Business* (New York: HarperCollins, 1991).

38. Beamish et al.

39. B. Schlender, "Matsushita Shows How to Go Global," *Fortune,* July 11, 1996.

40. Thomas Friedman, *The World Is Flat,* 2005 (NY: Farrar, Straus and Giroux).

41. Yoram Wind and Susan Douglas, "International Portfolio Analysis and Strategy: The Challenge of the 1980s," *Journal of International Business Studies* (Fall 1991): 69–82.

42. www.ibm.com, April 10, 2001.

43. P. Greenberg, "It's Not a Small eCommerce World, After All," www.ecommercetimes.com, February 23, 2001.

44. Ibid.

45. M. Porter, *The Competitive Advantage of Nations* (New York: Free Press, 1990).

46. S. Butler, "Survivor: B2B Style," www.emarketer.com/analysis/ecommerce, April 13, 2001.

47. "eBusiness Trends," www.idc.com/ebusinesstrends, April 12, 2001.

48. "Fuji–Xerox Teams Up for New E-Marketplace." www.fujixerox.com, April 14, 2001.

49. "Online Auctions Free Procurement Savings," BHP Corporate Services, www.bhp.com, April 20, 2001.

50. "eBay Inc. Outlines Global Business Strategy at 2006 Analyst Conference," *Canada News Wire Group*, May 4, 2006.

51. Ibid.

52. M. Sawhney and S. Mandal, "Go Global," *Business 2.0,* May 2000.

53. Ibid.

54. B. Bright, "E-Commerce: How Do You Say 'Web?' Planning to Take Your Online Business International? Beware: E-Commerce Can Get Lost in Translation," *Wall Street Journal,* May 23, 2005, p.R11.

55. Ibid.

56. Ibid.

57. A. Baxter, "Rewards and Risks of Going Global," *Financial Times,* January 4, 2006.

58. John Garland, Richard N. Farmer, and Marilyn Taylor, *International Dimensions of Business Policy and Strategy,* 2nd ed (Boston:PWS-Kent, 1990), 160.

59. Arvind Phatak, *International Dimensions of Management,* 2nd ed (Boston: PWS-Kent, 1989).

60. R. J. Radway, "International Franchising," in *Global Business Management in the 1990s,* ed. R. at. Moran (Washington, DC: Beacham, 1990), 137.

61. U.S. Department of Commerce, 2005.

62. . . . "Learning to Live with Offshoring," *Business Week,* January 30, 2006, p.122.

63. J. Johnson, "India at Center of Microsoft's World," *Financial Times,* December 8, 2005, p.24

64. William Hoffman, "Trend to IT Outsourcing Slows as Companies Reassess the Benefits," *Shipping Digest, August 28, 2006.*

65. *Hewitt Associates Research Press Release ,*CNBC TV March 5, 2004.

66. S. Hamm, "Big Blue Shift," *Business Week,* June 5, 2006.

67. Manjeet Kripalani,"Call Center? That's So 2004,"*Business Week,* August 7, 2006, p.40-2.

68. Pete Engardio, "The Future of Outsourcing," *Business Week,* January 30, 2006, p. 50.

69. Manjeet Kripalani, "Five Offshore Practices that Pay Off," *Business Week,* January 30, 2006, p.60.

70. S. Zahra and G. Elhagrasey, "Strategic Management of IJVs," *European Management Journal* 12, no. 1 (1994): 83–93.

71. Yigang Pan and Xiaolia Li, "Joint Venture Formation of Very Large Multinational Firms," *Journal of International Business Studies* 31, no. 1 (First Quarter 2000): 179–181.

72. R. Bream and Arkady Ostrovsky, "Merger Leaves Rivals Lagging Behind," *Financial Times,* June 27, 2006, p. 18.

73. Kenichi Ohmae, "The Global Logic of Strategic Alliances," *Harvard Business Review* (March–April 1989): 143–154.

74. Zahra and Elhagrasey.

75. "Lenovo to Lay Off 1,000," www.PCWorld.com, March 16, 2006.

76. P. Meller, "Procter and Gamble Gets European Approval to Buy Gillette," *New York Times,* July 16, 2005.

77. Stefan Wagstyl, "The Next Investment Wave: Companies in East and West Prepare for the Risks and Opportunities of an Enlarged EU," *Financial Times,* April 27, 2004: 13.

78. L. Miller, "Go East, Young Company " www.businessweek.com, October 22, 2003.

79. N. G. Carr, "Managing in the Euro Zone," *Harvard Business Review* (January/February 1999): 47–57.

80. Julia Manea and Robert Pearce, "MNEs' Strategies in Central and Eastern Europe: Key Elements of Subsidiary Behaviour," *Management International Review,* 46, 2, pp. 235-255, 2006.

81. Ibid.

82. N. G. Carr.

83. Ibid.

84. Dana Milbank, "Can Europe Deliver?" *Wall Street Journal,* September 30, 1994: 6.

85. "Creating Global Airlines," www.nytimes.com, October 7, 2003.

86. A. Cowell, "Zeneca Buying Astra as Europe Consolidates," *New York Times,* December 10, 1998.

87. D. Sanger, "Backing Down on Steel Tariffs, U.S. Strengthens Trade Group," www.nytimes.com, December 5, 2003.

88. Daniel Dombey, "Microsoft's Day of Reckoning in Europe," *Financial Times,* March 24, 2004: 3.

89. Syed Anwar, "EU's Competition Policy and the GE-Honeywell Merger Fiasco: Transatlantic Divergence and Consumer and Regulatory Issues," *Thunderbird International Business Review,* Vol. 47, 5, (Sep/Oct 2005): 601–626.

90. Ibid.

91. L. E. Brouthers, S. Werner, and E. Matulich, "The Influence of TRIAD Nations' Environments on Price-quality Product Strategies and MNC Performance," *Journal of International Business Studies* 31, 1 (First quarter, 2000): 39–62.

92. Ibid.

93. Yigang Pan and David K. Tse, "The Hierarchical Model of Market Entry Modes," *Journal of International Business Studies* 31, no. 4 (Fourth Quarter 2000): 535–554.

94. Gupta and Govindarajan.

95. Ibid.

96. A. E. Serwer, "McDonald's Conquers the World," *Fortune,* October 17, 1994.

97. K. R. Harrigan, "Joint Ventures and Global Strategies," *Columbia Journal of World Business* 19, no. 2 (Summer 1984): 7–13.

98. G. Hofstede, *Cultures and Organizations: Software of the Mind* (London: McGraw-Hill, 1991).

99. Pan and Tse.

100. Hofstede.

101. Pan and Tse.

102. Hofstede.

103. Pan and Tse.

Chapter 7

1. B. R. Schlender, "How Toshiba Makes Alliances Work," *Fortune,* October 4, 1993, pp. 116–120.

2. D. Lei and J. W. Slocum, Jr., "Global Strategic Alliances: Payoffs and Pitfalls," *Organizational Dynamics* (Winter 1991).

3. M. A. Hitt, R. D. Ireland, and R. E. Hoskisson, *Strategic Management* (Cincinnati, OH: South-Western, 1999).

4. J. Griffiths, "A Marriage of Two Mindsets," *Financial Times,* March 16, 2005.

5. Ibid.

6. Ibid.

7. J. Tagliabue, "Thomson and TCL to Join TV Units," www.nytimes.com, November 4, 2003.

8. Thomas Friedman, *The World Is Flat* (NY: Farrar, Straus and Giroux, 2005), p. 144.

9. Arvind Parkhe, "Global Business Alliances," *Business Horizons* 43, no. 5 (September 2000): 2.

10. www.covisint.com.

11. "EU Agrees to Rules on Mergers," *Financial Times,* November 28, 2003.

12. Daniel Dombey, "European Takeover Proposals Anger U.S.," *Financial Times,* November 2, 2003, p. 1.

13. "The Return of the Deal," www.businessweek, November 24, 2003.

14. www.e4engineering.com, January 4, 2001.

15. Tim Burt, "Disney's Asian Adventure," *Financial Times,* October 30, 2003, p. 8.

16. Ibid.

17. Ibid.

18. Ibid.

19. Ibid.

20. D. Lei, "Offensive and Defensive Uses of Alliances," in Heidi Vernon-Wortzel and L. H. Wortzel, *Strategic Management in a Global Economy,* 3rd ed. (New York: John Wiley & Sons, 1997).

21. Dave Guilford, "GM's Global Strategy was a Costly Flop; Fiat, Subaru, Isuzu, Suzuki—It Just Didn't Work," *Automotive News,* 80, no. 6201 (May 8, 2006): p. 14.

22. R. N. Osborn and C. C. Baughn, "Forms of Interorganizational Governance for Multinational Alliances," *Academy of Management Journal* 33, no. 3 (1990): 503–519.

23. Lei, 1997.

24. Steve Lohr, "China Poses Trade Worry as It Gains in Technology," www.nytimes.com, January 13, 2004.

25. Lei, 1997.

26. T. L. Wheelen and J. D. Hunger, *Strategic Management and Business Policy,* 6th ed. (Reading, MA: Addison-Wesley, 1998).

27. Lei, 1997.

28. Wheelen and Hunger.

29. N. Buckley, "Rich Rewards for Riding Rollercoaster," Investing in Russia," *Financial Times,* October 11, 2005, Special Report, p. 1.

30. A. Kramer, "Moscow presses BP to Sell a Big Gas Field to Gazprom," The New York Times, June 23, 2007.

31. N. Buckley, "Huge Gains but Also a Lot of Pain," *Financial Times,* October 11, 2005, p. 2.

32. Guy Chazan, "GM Venture in Russia Hits Snag Following Kremlin Involvement," *The Wall Street Journal,* February 18, 2006, p. A7.

33. N. Buckley, "An Unmissable Opportunity," *Financial Times,* April 5, 2005.

34. A. Shama, "After the Meltdown: A Survey of International Firms in Russia," *Business Horizons,* 43, no. 4 (July 2000):73.

35. Ibid.

36. N. Buckley, "Huge Gains but Also a Lot of Pain," *Financial Times,* October 11, 2005, p. 2.

37. M.A. Hitt, D. Ahlstrom, M.T. Dacin, E. Levitas, and L. Svobodina, "The Institutional Effects on Strategic Alliance Partner Selection in Transition Economies: China Versus Russia," *Organization Science* 15, no 2 (March/April 2004): 173–185.

38. A. E. Serwer, "McDonald's Conquers the World," *Fortune,* October 17, 1994.

39. Jack Welch (then CEO of GE) interviewed in *Fortune,* March 8, 1999.

40. P. Engardio, "The Future of Outsourcing," *Business Week,* January 30, 2006, p. 50.

41. Ibid.

42. M. Kripalani, D. Foust, S. Holmes, and P. Enga, "Five Offshore Practices that Pay Off," *Business Week,* January 30, 2006, p. 60.

43. E. Anderson and H. Gatignon, "Modes of Foreign Entry: A Transaction Cost Analysis and Propositions," *Journal of International Business Studies* (Fall 1986): 1–26.

44. J. L. Schaan, "Parent Control and Joint Venture Success: The Case of Mexico," unpublished doctoral dissertation, University of Western Ontario, 1983.

45. J. M. Geringer, "Strategic Determinants of Partner Selection Criteria in International Joint Ventures," *Journal of International Business Studies* (First Quarter 1991): 41–62.

46. J. M. Geringer and L. Hebert, "Control and Performance of International Joint Ventures," *Journal of International Business Studies* 20, no. 2 (Summer 1989).

47. Geringer, 1991.

48. P. Marsh, "Partnerships Feel the Indian Heat," *Financial Times,* June 22, 2006.

49. Ibid.

50. P. W. Beamish et al., *International Management* (Homewood, IL: Irwin, 1991).

51. J. P. Killing, *Strategies for Joint Venture Success* (New York: Praeger, 1983).

52. J. L. Schaan and P. W. Beamish, "Joint Venture General Managers in Less Developed Countries," in *Cooperative Strategies in International Business,* ed. F. Contractor and P. Lorange (Toronto: Lexington Books, 1988), pp. 279–299.

53. Oded Shenkar and Yoram Zeira, "International Joint Ventures: A Tough Test for HR," *Personnel* (January 1990): 26–31.

54. Ibid.

55. Geringer and Hebert, pp. 235–254.

56. M. Geringer, "Criteria for Selecting Partners for Joint Ventures in Industrialized Market Economies," doctoral dissertation, University of Washington, Seattle, 1986; Schaan and Beamish.

57. R. Mead, *International Management* (Cambridge, MA: Blackwell Publishers, 1994).

58. R. Duane Ireland and M. A. Hitt, "Achieving and Maintaining Strategic Competitiveness in the 21st Century: the Role of Strategic Leadership," *The Academy of Management Executive* 19, 4 (2005): 63.

59. R.S. Bhagat, B.L. Kedia, P.D. Harveston, and H.C. Triandis, "Cultural Variations in the Cross-Border Transfer of Organizational Knowledge: An Integrative Framework," *Academy of Management Review* 27, no. 2 (2002): pp. 204–221.

60. Sirmon, D.G., Hitt, M.A., Ireland, R.D., in press. "Managing Firm Resources in Dynamic Environments to Create Value: Looking Inside the Black Box," *Academy of Management Review*, in press, 2006.)

61. M H. Hitt, V. Franklin and Hong Zhu, "Culture, Institutions and International Strategy," *Journal of International Management,* 12, 2, June, 2002, pp. 222–234.

62. I. Berdrow and H. W. Lane, "International Joint Ventures: Creating Value through Successful Knowledge Management," *Journal of World Business,* 38, 1 (February, 2003): 15–30.

63. Ibid.

64. Ibid.

65. "China's New Restrictions on Deals," *Financial Times,* August 10, 2006, p. 2.

66. J. Pura, "Backlash Builds Against Suharto-Lined Firms," *The Wall Street Journal,* May 27, 1998.

67. W. M. Danis, "Differences in Values, Practices, and Systems Among Hungarian Managers and Western Expatriates: An Organizing Framework and Typology," *Journal of World Business* (August 2003): 224–244.

68. R. Schoenberg, "Dealing with a Culture Clash," *Financial Times,* September 23, 2006.

69. Ibid.

70. P. Rosenzweig, "Why Is Managing in the United States so Difficult for European Firms?" *European Management Journal* 12, no. 1 (1994): 31–38.

71. Ibid.

72. "In Alabama, the Soul of a New Mercedes?" *Business Week,* March 31, 1997.

73. Ibid.

74. M. Craze and J. Simmons, "Road from Acrimony to Giant Steel Merger: How Mittal and Arcelor Came to terms," *International Herald Tribune,* July 6, 2006, p. 13.

75. P. Marsh, "Deal Finalised in a Palace, but Sealed in an Airport," *Financial Times,* June 27, 2006.

76. Craze and Simmons, 2006.

77. Ibid.

78. P. Betts, "Steel Deals France a Hard Lesson in Reality," *Financial Times,* June 27, 2006, p.18.

79. H. James, "Europe Rediscovers the Tradition of Family Capitalism," *Financial Times,* July 4, 2006.

80. P. Glader and E. Bellman, "Breaking the Marwari Rules," *The Wall Street Journal,* July 10, 2006.

81. Ibid.

82. Ibid.

83. Ibid.

84. J. A. Pearce II and R. B. Robinson, Jr., "Cultivating *Guanxi* as a Foreign Investor Strategy," *Business Horizons* 43, no 1 (January 2000): 31.

85. Ibid.

86. www.NextLinx.com, September 10, 2001.

87. Ibid.

Chapter 8

1. For additional information on emerging markets and relevant Web sites, see Syed T. Anwar, *Marketing and International Business Links: Emerging Markets,* http://www.wtamu.edu/~sanwar.bus/otherlinks.htm# Emerging_Markets (retrieved on December 5, 2006); Goldman Sachs, *Dreaming with BRICs: The Path to 2050,* (New York: Goldman Sachs, 2003).

2. For more detail, see *The New Global Challengers: How 100 Top Companies from Rapidly Developing Economies Are Changing the World* (Boston, Massachusetts: The Boston Consulting Group, 2006); *Organizing for Global Advantage in China, India, and Other Rapidly Developing Economies* (Boston, Massachusetts: The Boston Consulting Group, 2006); Khanna, Tarun and Krishna Palepu, "Emerging Giants: Building World-Class Companies in Developing Countries," *Harvard Business Review* (October 2006): 60–69.

3. See Syed T. Anwar, "Global Business and Globalization," *Journal of International Management*, 71 (2007): (in press); "Emerging Giants," *Business Week*, July 31, 2006, pp. 40–49.

4. Ibid.

5. Roberto C. Goizueta, (Former) Chairman and CEO, Coca-Cola Company.

6. A. D. Chandler, *Strategy and Structure: Chapters in the History of the American Industrial Enterprise* (Cambridge, MA: MIT Press, 1962); R. E. Miles et al., "Organizational Strategy, Structure, and Process," *Academy of Management Review* 3, no. 3 (July 1978): 546–562; and J. Woodward, *Industrial Organization: Theory and Practice* (Oxford University Press, 1965).

7. C. A. Bartlett and S. Ghoshal, *Managing Across Borders* (Boston: Harvard Business School Press, 1989).

8. J. M. Stopford and L. T. Wells, Jr., *Managing the Multinational Enterprise* (New York: Basic Books, 1972).

9. Alcoa Corporate Information, www.alcoa.com, accessed July 25, 2004.

10. P. Asheghian and B. Ebrahimi, *International Business* (New York: Harper and Row, 1990).

11. Ibid.

12. R. H. Mason and R. S. Spich, *Management: An International Perspective* (Homewood, IL: Irwin, 1987).

13. "Heinz's Johnson to Divest Operations, Scrap Management of Firm by Regions," *The Wall Street Journal*, December 8, 1997, p. B22.

14. www.Nestle.com, December 7, 2000.

15. *Financial Times*, February 22, 2005.

16. Ibid.

17. L. Greenhalgh, "Ford Motor Company's CFO Jac Nasser on Transformational Change, E-Business, and Environmental Responsibility (Interview)," *Academy of Management Executive* 14, no. 13 (August 2001): 46.

18. "Power at Multinationals Shifts to Home Office," *The Wall Street Journal*, September 9, 1994; "Big Blue Wants the World to Know Who's Boss," *Business Week*, September 26, 1994.

19. H. Henzler and W. Rall, "Facing Up to the Globalization Challenge," *McKinsey Quarterly* (Fall 1986): 52–68.

20. T. Levitt, "The Globalization of Markets," *Harvard Business Review* (May–June 1983): 92–102; and S. P. Douglas and Yoram Wind, "The Myth of Globalization," *Columbia Journal of World Business* (Winter 1987): 19–29.

21. Jane Perlez, "Chinese Born Overseas Invest in a Distant Homeland," www.nytimes.com, December 14, 2003.

22. L. Kraar, "The Overseas Chinese," *Fortune*, October 31, 1994.

23. J. Kao, "The Worldwide Web of Chinese Business," *Harvard Business Review* (March–April 1993): 24–35.

24. "Asia's Wealth," *Business Week*, November 29, 1993.

25. Kao.

26. "The New Power in Asia," *Fortune*, October 31, 1994.

27. M. Weidenbaum, "The Rise of Great China: A New Economic Superpower," in *Annual Editions, 1995/96* (Guilford, CT: Dushkin Publishing Group), pp. 180–185.

28. Perlez.

29. Weidenbaum.

30. Kraar.

31. Weidenbaum.

32. Kao.

33. Kraar.

34. P. M. Rosenzweig, "Colgate-Palmolive: Managing International Careers," Harvard Business School Case, 1995.

35. "For Levi's, a Flattering Fit Overseas," *Business Week*, November 5, 1990, pp. 76–77.

36. Ibid.

37. B. R. Schlender, "How Fujitsu Will Tackle the Giants," *Fortune*, July 1, 1991.

38. Oct. 10, 2006.

39. www.pg.com, News releases, November 22, 2006.

40. "Gillette, P&G Team Up for Doubles," *Knight Ridder Tribune Business News*, Washington: January 17, 2006.

41. "P&G Corporate Information: How the Structure Works," www.pg.com, November 22, 2006.

42. Christina Berk, "P&G Is Stronger with Gillette," *Wall Street Journal*, October 11, 2006, p. B5F.

43. "P&G Corporate Information: How the Structure Works," www.pg.com, November 22, 2006.

44. Andy Reinhardt, "Philips: Back on the Beam," www.businessweek.com, May 3, 2004.

45. Press release, www.Philips.com, accessed July 25, 2004.

46. *Financial Times*, February 9, 2005.

47. www.Intel.com, August 18, 2005.

48. S. Ghoshal and C. A. Bartlett, "The Mulinational Corporation as an Interorganizational Network," *Academy of Management Review* 15, no. 4 (1990): 603–625.

49. Mohanbir Sawhney and Sumant Mandal, "Go Global," *Business 2.0* (May 5, 2001): 178–213.

50. J. D. Daniels, L. H. Radebaugh, and D. P. Sullivan, *Globalization and Business* (Upper Saddle River, NJ: Prentice Hall, 2002).

51. "Energizing the Supply Chain," *The Review*, Deloitte & Touche, January 17, 2000, p. 1.

52. C. A. Bartlett and S. Ghoshal, "Organizing for Worldwide Effectiveness: The Transnational Solution," *California Management Review* (Fall 1988): 54–74.

53. R. H. Kilmann, "A Networked Company that Embraces the World," *Information Strategy* 6 (Spring 1990): 23–26.

54. R. B. Reich, "Who Is Them?" *Harvard Business Review* (March–April 1991): 77–88.

55. Ibid.

56. Francesco Caio, CEO, Merloni Elettrodomestici, interview in *Harvard Business Review*, January/February 1999.

57. www.McDonalds.com, February 20, 2001.

58. Andrew Jack, "Russians Wake up to Consumer Capitalism," www.FT.com, January 30, 2001.

59. Ibid.

60. A. V. Phatak, *International Dimensions of Management*, 2nd ed. (Boston: PWS-Kent, 1989).

61. G. Rohrmann, CEO, AEI Corp., press release.

62. Phatak.

63. W. G. Egelhoff, "Patterns of Control in U.S., U.K., and European Multinational Corporations," *Journal of International Business Studies* (Fall 1984): 73–83.

64. Ibid.

65. Ibid.

66. S. Ueno and U. Sekaran, "The Influence of Culture on Budget Control Practices in the U.S.A. and Japan: An Empirical Study," *Journal of International Business Studies* 23 (Winter 1992): 659–674.

67. A. R. Neghandi and M. Welge, *Beyond Theory Z* (Greenwich, CT: J.A.I. Publishers, 1984), p. 18.

68. www.Nestle.com, press release, March 21, 2000.

69. Phatak.

Chapter 9

1. Allan Halcrow, Editor, *Personnel Journal* (February 1996).

2. www.FT.com, March 5, 2001.

3. J. L. Laabs, "HR Pioneers Explore the Road Less Traveled," *Personnel Journal* (February 1996): 70–72, 74, 77–78.

4. Stuart Mathison, Vice President for Strategic Planning, Sprint International.

5. C. A. Bartlett and S. Ghoshal, "Matrix Management: Not a Structure, a Frame of Mind," *Harvard Business Review* (July–August 1990).

6. S. B. Prasad and Y. K. Krishna Shetty, *An Introduction to Multinational Management* (Upper Saddle River, NJ: Prentice Hall, 1979).

7. Rochelle Kopp, "International Human Resource Policies and Practices in Japanese, European, and United States Multinationals," *Human Resource Management* 33, no. 4 (Winter 1994): 581–599.

8. Ibid.

9. Tung, "Selection and Training of Personnel for Overseas Assignments."

10. Dowling and Schuler.

11. S. J. Kobrin, "Expatriate Reduction and Strategic Control in American Multinational Corporations," *Human Resource Management* 27, no. 1 (1988): 63–75.

12. P. J. Dowling, "Hot Issues Overseas," *Personnel Administrator* 34, no. 1 (1989): 66–72.

13. Company information, www.ABB.com, accessed July 26, 2004.

14. Hem C. Jain, "Human Resource Management in Selected Japanese Firms, the Foreign Subsidiaries and Locally Owned Counterparts," *International Labour Review* 129, no. 1 (1990): 73–84; Bartlett and Ghoshal.

15. Mary G. Tye, Peter Y. Chen, "Selection of Expatriates: Decision-making Models used by HR Professionals," *Human Resource Planning*, 28, no. 4 (December 2005): 15.

16. *Personnel Today,* May 23, 2006.

17. M. Mendenhall and G. Oddou, "The Dimensions of Expatriate Acculturation: A Review," *Academy of Management Review* 10, no. 1 (1985): 39–47.

18. Tye and Chen, 2005.

19. ''D. Erbacher, B. D'Netto, and J. Espana, "Expatriate Success in China: Impact of Personal and Situational Factors," *Journal of American Academy of Business* 9, no. 2 (September 2006): 183.

20. www.FT.com, March 5, 2001.

21. Rosalie Tung, "American Expatriates Abroad: From Neophytes to Cosmopolitans," *Journal of World Business,* 33 (1998): 125–144.

22. Business Editors, "International Job Assignment: Boon or Bust for an Employee's Career?" *Business Wire, Inc.*, March 13, 2006.

23. R. D. Hays, "Expatriate Selection: Insuring Success and Avoiding Failure," *Journal of International Business Studies* 5, no. 1 (1974): 25–37; Tung, 1998.

24. His-An Shih, Yun-Hwa Chiang, In-Sook Kim, "Expatriate Performance Management from MNEs of Different National Origins," *International Journal of Manpower,* 26, no. 2 (2005): 161–162.

25. *Business Wire,* 2006.

26. J. S. Black, "Work Role Transitions: A Study of American Expatriate Managers in Japan," *Journal of International Business Studies* 19 (1988): 277–294.

27. *Business Wire,* 2006.

28. Tung, "U.S., European, and Japanese Multinationals."

29. Ibid.

30. B. Wysocki, Jr., "Prior Adjustment: Japanese Executives Going Overseas Take Anti-Shock Courses," *The Wall Street Journal,* December 4, 1987.

31. Mendenhall and Oddou.

32. J. S. Black and M. Mendenhall, "Cross-cultural Training Effectiveness: A Review and a Theoretical Framework for Future Research," *Academy of Management Review* 15, no. 1 (1990): 113–136.

33. K. Oberg, "Culture Shock: Adjustments to New Cultural Environments," *Practical Anthropology* (July–August 1960): 177–182.

34. Ibid.

35. Ibid.

36. P. R. Harris and R. T. Moran, *Managing Cultural Differences,* 4th ed. (Houston, TX: Gulf Publishing, 1996), p. 139.

37. Tung, "Selection and Training of Personnel for Overseas Assignments."

38. Ronen.

39. Ibid.

40. Kealey, 81.

41. R. Peterson, "The Use of Expatriates and Inpatriates in Central and Eastern Europe Since the Wall Came Down," *Journal of World Business,* 38 (2003): 55–69.

42. Christopher Tice, Manager, Global Expatriate Operations, DuPont Inc., quoted in Mark Schoeff, "International Assignments Best Served by Unified Policy," *Workforce Management*, 85, no. 3 (February 13, 2006): 36.

43. Ibid.

44. "Living Expenses," www.economist.com, July 22, 2000; "Runzheimer International Compensation Worksheet," www.runzheimer.com, 2000.

45. *Business Wire,* 2006.

46. B. W. Teague, *Compensating Key Personnel Overseas* (New York: Conference Board, 1992).

47. C. Reynolds, "Compensation of Overseas Personnel," in J. Famularo, *Handbook of Human Resource Administration,* 2ed, 1989, NY: (New York) McGraw-Hill.

48. S. F. Gale, "Taxing Situations for Expatriates," *Workforce,* 82, no. 6 (June 2003): 100.

49. R. B. Peterson, "The Use of Expatriates and Inpatriates in Central and Eastern Europe Since the Wall Came Down," *Journal of World Business* (2003): 55–69.

50. Gina Ruiz, "Kimberly-Clark: Developing Talent in Developing World Markets," *Workforce Management* 85, no. 7 (April 10, 2006): 34.

51. "Seoul Is Supporting a Sizzling Tech Boom," www.businessweek.com, September 25, 2000.

52. P. Damaskopoulos and T. Evgeniou, "Adoption of New Economy Practices by SMEs in Eastern Europe," *European Management Journal,* 21, no. 2, (2003): 133–145.

53. Fay Hansen, "The Great Global Talent Race: One World, One Workforce: Part 1 of 2; Standing out from the crowd to attract and retain the best workers in ever-shifting locales is the global business challenge," 85, no. 7 (April 10, 2006): 1.

54. D. Kiriazov, S. E. Sullivan, and H. S. Tu, "Business Success in Eastern Europe: Understanding and Customizing HRM," *Business Horizons* (January/February 2000): 39–43.

55. Ibid.

56. Y. Ono and W. Spindle, "Japan's Long Decline Makes One Thing Rise: Individualism," *The Wall Street Journal*, January 3, 2001.

57. Ingmar Bjorkman and Yuan Lu, "The Management of Human Resources in Chinese-Western Joint Ventures," *Journal of World Business* 34, no. 3 (Fall 1999): 306.

58. Ibid.

59. "Personnel Demands Attention Overseas," *Mutual Fund Market News*, March 19, 2001, p. 1.

60. Mary Ann Von Glinow, Ellen A. Drost, and Mary B. Teagarden, "Converging on IHRM Best Practices: Lessons Learned from a Globally Distributed Consortium on Theory and Practice," *Human Resource Management*, 41, no. 1 (2002): 133–135.

Chapter 10

1. Alison Maitland, "Top Companies Value Overseas Experience," *Financial Times*, July 3, 2006.

2. Ibid.

3. N. J. Adler, *International Dimensions of Organizational Behavior*, 2nd ed. (Boston: PWS-Kent, 1991); M. Mendenhall, E. Dunbar, and G. Oddou, "Expatriate Selection, Training, and Career-Pathing: A Review and Critique," *Human Resource Management* 26 (1987): 331–345.

4. M. G. Harvey, "Repatriation of Corporate Executives: An Empirical Study," *Journal of International Business Studies* 20 (Spring 1989): 131–144.

5. Rosalie Tung, "Career Issues in International Assignments," *Academy of Management Executive* 2, no. 3 (1988): 241–244.

6. M. Harvey, "Dual-Career Expatriates: Expectations, Adjustments and Satisfaction with International Relocation," *Journal of International Business Studies* 28, no. 3 (1997): 627.

7. Tung.

8. Charlene M. Solomon, "One Assignment, Two Lives," *Personnel Journal* (May 1996): 36–44.

9. Business Editors, "International Job Assignment: Boon or Bust for an Employee's Career?" *Business Wire, Inc.,* (March 13, 2006): 7.

10. Solomon.

11. R. Pascoe, *Surviving Overseas: The Wife's Guide to Successful Living Abroad* (Singapore: Times Publishing, 1992); and R. Pascoe, "Employers Ignore Expatriate Wives at Their Own Peril," *The Wall Street Journal*, March 29, 1992.

12. www.FT.com, March 5, 2001.

13. P. Asheghian and B. Ebrahimi, *International Business* (New York: HarperCollins,1990), 470.

14. Business Editors, "International Job Assignment: Boon or Bust for an Employee's Career?" *Business Wire, Inc.,* (March 13, 2006): 7

15. N. J. Adler, *International Dimensions of Organizational Behavior*, 4th ed (Boston: PWS-Kent, 2002).

16. Excerpted from www.Netscape.com case studies.

17. J. S. Black and H. B. Gregersen, "The Other Half of the Picture: Antecedents of Spouse Cross-cultural Adjustment," *Journal of International Business Studies* (Third Quarter 1992): 461–477.

18. Based on D. C. Feldman, "The Multinational Socialization of Organization Members," *Academy of Management Review* 6, no. 2 (April 1981): 309–318.

19. J. Hamill, "Expatriate Policies in British Multinationals," *Journal of General Management* 14, no. 4 (Summer 1989): 18–33.

20. Based on W. Dyer, *Team Building* (Reading, MA: Addison-Wesley, 1987).

21. T. Gross, E. Turner, and L. Cederholm, "Building Teams for Global Operations," *Management Review* (June 1987): 32–36.

22. www.BritishTelecom.com/cases, February 19, 2001.

23. J. Conger and E. Lawler, "People Skills Still Rule in the Virtual Company," *Financial Times*, August 26, 2005.

24. Based largely on Adler, 2002.

25. T. R. Kayworth and D. E. Leidner, "Leadership Effectiveness in Global Virtual Teams," *Journal of Management Information Systems* 18, no. 3 (Winter 2001–2002): 7–40.

26. C. Solomon, "Building Teams Across Borders," *Global Workforce* (November 1998): 12–17.

27. Ibid.

28. B. Rosen, S. Furst, and R. Blackburn, "Training for Virtual Teams: An Investigation of Current Practices and Future Needs," *Human Resources Management*, 45, no. 2 (Summer 2006): 229–247.

29. T. Brown, "Building a Transnational Team," *Industry Week*, May 16, 1988, p. 13.

30. Ibid.

31. A. Joshi, G. Labianca, P. M. Caligiuri, "Getting Along Long Distance: Understanding Conflict in a Multinational Team Through Network Analysis," *Journal of World Business* 37 (2002): 277–284.

32. I. Ratiu, "International Consulting News," in *Managing Cultural Differences*, 3rd ed., P. R. Harris and R. T. Moran (Houston, TX: Gulf Publishing, 1991).

33. V. Govindarajan and A. K. Gupta, "Bulding an Effective Global Business Team," *MIT Sloan Management Review*, 42, no. 4 (Summer 2001): 63.

34. Ibid.

35. S. Chevrier, "Cross-cultural Management in Multinational Project Groups," *Journal of World Business*, 38, no. 2 (May 2003): 141–149.

36. Ibid.

37. *Business Wire*, 2006.

38. "Global Power 50," *Fortune* (October 16, 2006).

39. R. L. Tung, "Female Expatriates: The Model Global Manager?" *Organizational Dynamics* 33, no. 3 (2004): 243–253.

40. M. Kaminski and J. Paiz, "Japanese Women in Management: Where Are They?" *Human Resource Management* 23, no. 2 (Fall 1984): 277–292.

41. P. Lansing and K. Ready, "Hiring Women Managers in Japan: An Alternative for Foreign Employers," *California Management Review* 26, no. 4 (1988): 112–127.

42. Howard W. French, "Japan's Neglected Resource: Female Workers,"www.nytimes.com, July 24, 2003.

43. G. K. Stahl, E. L. Miller, and R. L. Tung, "Toward the Boundaryless Career: A Closer Look at the Expatriate Career Concept and the Perceived Implications of an International Assignment," *Journal of World Business* 37 (2002): 216–227.

44. Patrick Jenkins and Bettina Wassener, "How Germany Keeps Women off the Board," *Financial Times*, June 15, 2004.

45. Alison Maitland, "The North-South Divide in Europe, Inc.," *Financial Times*, June 14, 2004.

46. Ibid.

47. M. Jelinek N. Adler. "Women: World Class Managers for Global Competition," *Academy of Management Executive* 11, no. 1 (February 1988): 11–19.

48. N. J. Adler and D. N. Izraeli, *Women in Management Worldwide* (Armonk, NY: M. E. Sharpe, 1988), P. 245.

49. Ibid.

50. Jacob Vittorelli, Former Deputy Chairman of Pirelli.

51. P. J. Dowling, R. S. Schuler, and D. E. Welch, *International Dimensions of Human Resource Management,* 2nd ed. (Belmont, CA: Wadsworth, 1994).

52. "A New Deal in Europe?" www.businessweek.com, July 14, 2003.

53. M. R. Czinkota, I. A. Ronkainen, and M. H. Moffett, *International Business,* 3rd ed. (New York: Dryden Press, 1994).

54. Rik Kirkland, "The New Face of Labor," *Fortune* (October 16, 2006).

55. Bureau of Labor Statistics, September 2006.

56. C. K. Prahalad and Y. L. Doz, *The Multinational Mission: Balancing Local Demands and Global Vision* (New York: Free Press, 1987).

57. R. J. Adams, *Industrial Relations Under Liberal Democracy* (University of South Carolina Press, 1995).

58. J. S. Daniels and L. H. Radebaugh, *International Business,* 10th ed. (Reading, MA: Addison-Wesley, 2004).

59. Dowling, Schuler, and Welch.

60. Adams.

61. Ibid.

62. D. Barboza, "China Passed Law to Empower Unions and End Labor Abuse," October 12, 2006.

63. B. Barber, "Workers of the World Are Uniting," *Financial Times,* December 7, 2004.

64. D. Roberts, "Tie-Ups Are a Response to the Challenges of Globalisation," *Financial Times,* July 28, 2005.

65. M. M. Lucio and S. Weston, "New Management Practices in a Multinational Corporation: The Restructuring of Worker Representation and Rights?" *Industrial Relations Journal* 25, no. 2 (2004): 110–121.

66. D. B. Cornfield, "Labor Transnationalism?" *Work and Occupations* 24, no. 3 (August 1997): 278.

67. R. Martin, A. Vidinova, and S. Hill, "Industrial Relations in Transition Economies: Emergent Industrial Relations Institutions in Bulgaria," *British Journal of Industrial Relations* 34, no. 1 (March 1996): 3.

68. "Labour Relations: Themes for the 21st Century," *British Journal of Industrial Relations* 33, no. 4 (December 1995): 515.

69. Daniels and Radebaugh.

70. J. T. Barrett, "Trade Unions in South Africa: Dramatic Change after Apartheid Ends," *Monthly Labor Review*, 199, no. 5 (May 1966): 37.

71. "Culture Clash: South Korea," *The Economist* 342 (7999), January 11, 1997.

72. A. M. Rugman and R. M. Hodgetts, *International Business* (New York: McGraw-Hill, 1995).

73. Daniels and Radebaugh.

74. Richard Milne and H. Williamson, "Selective Bargaining: German Companies Are Driving a Hidden Revolution in Labour Flexibility," *Financial Times*, January 6, 2006.

75. *Financial Times*, January 16, 2004.

76. Milne and Williamson.

77. Gerrit Wiesmann, "Germans Eye U.K. Listings as a Way Out of Worker Law," *Financial Times,* May 24, 2006.

78. Ibid.

79. "A New Deal in Europe?" www.businessweek.com; *BW Online,* July 14, 2003.

80. Milne and Williamson.

81. Ibid.

82. J. Hoerr, "What Should Unions Do?" *Harvard Business Review* (May–June 1991): 30–45.

83. H. C. Katz, "The Decentralization of Collective Bargaining: A Literature Review and Comparative Analysis," *Industrial and Labor Relations Review* 47, no. 1 (October 1993).

84. Williamson, *Financial Times,* July 22, 2004.

85. www.nytimes.com, July 24, 2004.

86. Adams.

87. "The Perils of Cozy Corporatism," *The Economist*, May 21, 1994.

88. Wofgang Streeck, "More Uncertainties: German Unions Facing 1992," *Industrial Relations* (Fall 1991): 30–33.

89. "Germany's Economic Future Is on the Bargaining Table," *Business Week*, March 30, 1992.

Chapter 11

1. S. Michailova, "When Common Sense Becomes Uncommon: Participation and Empowerment in Russian Companies with Western Participation," *Journal of World Business*, 37 (2002): 180–187.

2. F. Rieger and D. Wong-Rieger, "A Configuration Model of National Influence Applied to Southeast Asian Organizations," *Proceedings of the Research Conference on Business in Southeast Asia,* May 12–13, 1990, University of Michigan.

3. R. M. Steers, *Made in Korea: Chung Ju Yung and the Rise of Hyundai* (New York: Routledge, 1999).

4. Meaning of Work International Research Team, *The Meaning of Working: An International Perspective* (New York: Academic Press, 1985).

5. D. Siddiqui and A. Alkhafaji, *The Gulf War: Implications for Global Businesses and Media* (Apollo, PA: Closson Press, 1992): 133–135.

6. Ibid.

7. A. Ali, "The Islamic Work Ethic in Arabia," *Journal of Psychology* 126 (1992): 507–519.

8. Yasamusa Kuroda and Tatsuzo Suzuki, "A Comparative Analysis of the Arab Culture: Arabic, English and Japanese Language and Values," paper presented at the

5th Congress of the International Association of Middle Eastern Studies, Tunis (September 20–24, 1991), quoted in Siddiqui and Alkhafaji.

9. J. R. Hinrichs, "Cross-National Analysis of Work Attitudes," paper presented at the American Psychological Association Meeting, Chicago, 1975.

10. A. Furnham, B. D. Kirkcaldy, and R. Lynn, "National Attitudes to Competitiveness, Money, and Work among Young People: First, Second, and Third World Differences," *Human Relations* 47, no. 1 (1994): 119–132.

11. M. Haire, E. E. Ghiselli, and L. W. Porter, "Cultural Patterns in the Role of the Manager," *Industrial Relations* 12, no. 2 (February 1963): 95–117.

12. S. Ronen, *Comparative and Multinational Management* (New York: John Wiley and Sons, 1986).

13. D. S. Elenkov, "Can American Management Concepts Work in Russia? A Cross-cultural Comparative Study," *California Management Review* 40, no. 4 (Summer 1998): 133–157.

14. E. C. Nevis, "Cultural Assumptions and Productivity: The United States and China," *Sloan Management Review* 24, no. 3 (Spring 1983): 17–29.

15. R. L. Tung, "Patterns of Motivation in Chinese Industrial Enterprises," *Academy of Management Review* 6, no. 3 (1981): 481–489.

16. Swee Hoon Ang, "The Power of Money: A Cross-cultural Analysis of Business-Related Beliefs," *Journal of World Business* 35, no. 1 (Spring 2000): 43.

17. *World Competitiveness Yearbook (1998)* (Lausanne, Switzerland: Institute for Management Development).

18. D. D. White and J. Leon, "The Two-Factor Theory: New Questions, New Answers," *National Academy of Management Proceedings* (1976): 358; D. Macarov, "Work Patterns and Satisfactions in an Israeli Kibbutz: A Test of the Herzberg Hypothesis," *Personnel Psychology* (Autumn 1973): 483–493.

19. P. D. Machungwa and N. Schmitt, "Work Motivation in a Developing Country," *Journal of Applied Psychology* (February 1983): 31–42.

20. G. E. Popp, H. J. Davis, and T. T. Herbert, "An International Study of Intrinsic Motivation Composition," *Management International Review* 26, no. 3 (1986): 28–35.

21. R. N. Kanungo and R. W. Wright, "A Cross-cultural Study of Managerial Job Attitudes," *Journal of International Business Studies* (Fall 1983): 115–129.

22. Ibid., 127–128.

23. J. R. Lincoln, "Employee Work Attitudes and Management Practice in the U.S. and Japan: Evidence from a Large Comparative Survey," *California Management Review* 32, no. 1 (Fall 1989): 89–106.

24. J. R. Lincoln and K. McBride, "Japanese Industrial Organization in Comparative Perspective," *Annual Review of Sociology* 13 (1987): 289–312.

25. Lincoln.

26. "Detroit South," *Business Week,* March 16, 1992.

27. Geert Hofstede, "National Cultures in Four Dimensions," *International Studies of Management and Organization* (Spring–Summer 1983).

28. M. B. Teagarden, M. C. Butler, and M. Von Glinow, "Mexico's Maquiladora Industry: Where Strategic Human Resource Management Makes a Difference," *Organizational Dynamics* (Winter 1992): 34–47.

29. T. T. Herbert, H. Deresky, and G. E. Popp, "On the Potential for Assimilation and Integration of Sub-Culture Members into the U.S. Business System: The Micro-Cultural Effects of the Mexican-American National Origin, Culture, and Personality," *Proceedings of the International Business Association Conference* (London, November 1986).

30. John Condon, *Good Neighbors: Communication with the Mexicans* (Yarmouth, ME: Intercultural Press, 1985).

31. G. K. Stephens and C. R. Greer, "Doing Business in Mexico: Understanding Cultural Differences," *Organizational Dynamics* (Summer 1995): 39–55.

32. Teagarden, Butler, and Von Glinow.

33. Stephens and Greer.

34. Ibid.

35. C. E. Nicholls, H. W. Lane, and M. B. Brechu, "Taking Self-Managed Teams to Mexico," *Academy of Management Executive* 13, 3 (1999): 15–25.

36. Ibid.

37. Ibid.

38. Mariah E. de Forest, "Thinking of a Plant in Mexico?" *Academy of Management Executive* 8, no. 1 (1994): 33–40.

39. Ibid.

40. Ibid.

41. Teagarden, Butler, and Von Glinow.

42. Herbert, Deresky, and Popp; R. S. Bhagat and S. J. McQuaid, "Role of Subjective Culture in Organizations: A Review and Direction for Future Research," *Journal of Applied Psychology Monograph* 67, no. 5 (1982): 669.

43. Malgorzata Tarczynska, "Eastern Europe: How Valid Is Western Reward/Performance Management?" *Benefits and Compensation International* 29, no. 8 (April 2000): 9–16.

44. Snejina Michailova, "When Common Sense Becomes Uncommon: Participation and Empowerment in Russian Companies with Western Participation," *Journal of World Business* 37 (2002), 180–187.

45. M. A. Von Glinow and M. B. Teagarden, "The Transfer of Human Resource Management Technology in Sino–U.S. Cooperative Ventures: Problems and Solutions," *Human Resource Management* 27, no. 2 (1988): 201–229.

46. M. A. Von Glinow and Byung Jae Chung, "Comparative HRM Practices in the U.S., Japan, Korea and the PRC," in *Research in Personnel and HRM—A Research Annual: International HRM*, ed. A. Nedd, G. R. Ferris, and K. M. Rowland (London: JAI Press, 1989).

47. A. Ignatius, "Now if Ms. Wong Insults a Customer, She Gets an Award," *The Wall Street Journal,* January 24, 1989, pp. 1, 15.

48. T. Saywell, "Motive Power: China's State Firms Bank on Incentives to Keep Bosses Operating at Their Peak," *Far Eastern Economic Review* (July 8, 2000): 67–68.

49. Jacques Maisonrouge, IBM World Trade Corporation, 1998.

50. A. Morrison, H. Gregersen, and S. Black, "What Makes Savvy Global Leaders?" *Ivey Business Journal* 64, no. 2 (1999): 44–51; and *Monash Mt. Eliza Business Review* 1, no. 2 (1998).

51. Ibid.

52. Ibid.

53. Morrison et al.; J. W. Gardner, *John W. Gardner on Leadership* (New York: Free Press, 1989); W. Bennis and B. Nanus, *Leaders* (New York: Harper and Row, 1985);

and R. D. Robinson, *Internationalization of Business* (Hinsdale, IL: Drysden Press, 1984), p. 117.

54. R. H. Mason and R. S. Spich, *Management: An International Perspective* (Homewood: IL: Irwin, 1987).

55. Ibid., p. 184.

56. B. M. Bass, *Bass & Stogdill's Handbook of Leadership* (New York: Free Press, 1990).

57. See, for example, M. Mead, *Sex and Temperament in Three Primitive Societies* (New York: Morrow, 1935); M. Mead et al., *Cooperation and Competition among Primitive Peoples* (New York: McGraw-Hill, 1937).

58. L. Copeland and L. Griggs, *Going International* (New York: Random House, 1985), p. 131.

59. D. McGregor, *The Human Side of Enterprise* (New York: McGraw-Hill, 1960). See, for example, R. M. Stogdill, *Manual for the Leader Behavior Description Questionnaire—Form XII* (Columbus: Ohio State University, Bureau of Business Research, 1963); R. R. Blake and J. S. Mouton, *The New Managerial Grid* (Houston, TX: Gulf Publishing, 1978).

60. F. E. Fiedler, "Engineering the Job to Fit the Manager," *Harvard Business Review* 43, no. 5 (1965): 115–122.

61. Den Hartog, N. Deanne, R. J. House, Paul J. Hanges, P. W. Dorfman, S. Antonio Ruiz-Quintanna, et al., "Culture Specific and Cross-culturally Generalizable Implicit Leadership Theories: Are Attributes of Charismatic/Transformational Leadership Universally Endorsed?" *Leadership Quarterly* 10, no. 2 (1999): 219–256.

62. Ibid.

63. R. House et al., "Cultural Influences on Leadership and Organizations: Project GLOBE," *Advances in Global Leadership*, Vol. 1 (JAI Press, 1999).

64. Ibid.

65. Geert Hofstede, "Motivation, Leadership and Organization: Do American Theories Apply Abroad?" *Organizational Dynamics* (Summer 1980): 42–63.

66. Ibid.

67. Geert Hofstede, "Value Systems in Forty Countries," Proceedings of the 4th International Congress of the International Association for Cross-Cultural Psychology (1978).

68. Andre Laurent, "The Cultural Diversity of Western Conceptions of Management," *International Studies of Management and Organization* 13, no. 1–2 (Spring–Summer 1983): 75–96.

69. C. Hampden-Turner and A. Trompenaars, *The Seven Cultures of Capitalism* (New York: Doubleday, 1993).

70. M. Harie, E. E. Ghiselli, and L. W. Porter, *Managerial Thinking: An International Study* (New York: John Wiley and Sons, 1966).

71. S. G. Redding and T. W. Case, "Managerial Beliefs Among Asian Managers," *Proceedings of the Academy of Management* (1975).

72. I. Kenis, "A Cross-cultural Study of Personality and Leadership," *Group and Organization Studies* 2 (1977): 49–60; F. C. Deyo, "The Cultural Patterning of Organizational Development: A Comparative Case Study of Thailand and Chinese Industrial Enterprises," *Human Organization* 37 (1978): 68–72.

73. M. K. Badawy, "Styles of Mid-Eastern Managers," *California Management Review* (Spring 1980): 57; various newscasts, 2001.

74. A. A. Algattan, "Test of the Path-Goal Theory of Leadership in the Multinational Domain," paper presented at the Academy of Management Conference, 1985, San Diego, CA; J. P. Howell and P. W. Dorfman, "A Comparative Study of Leadership and Its Substitutes in a Mixed Cultural Work Setting," unpublished manuscript, 1988.

75. D. H. Welsh, F. Luthans, and S. M. Sommer, "Managing Russian Factory Workers: The Impact of U.S.-Based Behavioral and Participative Techniques," *Academy of Management Journal* 36 (1993): 58–79.

76. A. Maitland, "Le patron, der Chef and the Boss," *Financial Times,* January 9, 2006.

77. Ibid.

78. M. Kets de Vries, K. Korotov, "The Future of an Illusion: In Search of the New European Business Leader," *Organizational Dynamics*, 34, no. 3 (2005): 218–230.

79. Ibid.

80. Maitland.

81. Ibid.

82. R. J. House, *Culture, Leadership and Organizations: The GLOBE Study of 62 Societies* (Thousand Oaks, CA: Sage Publications, 2004).

83. F. C. Brodbeck, M. Frese, and M. Javidan, "Leadership Made in Germany: Low on Compassion, High on Performance," *Academy of Management Executive* 16, no. 1 (2002).

84. Mansour Javidan, Peter W Dorfman, Mary Sully de Luque, Robert J House, "In the Eye of the Beholder: Cross Cultural Lessons in Leadership from Project GLOBE," *The Academy of Management Perspectives* 20, no.1, (2006).

85. R. House and M. Javidan, "Cultural Acumen for the Global Manager: Lessons from Project GLOBE, *Organizational Dynamics* (2001).

86. N. Payton, "Leaderships Skills Hold Britain Back," *The Guardian,* February 22, 2003.

87. Alison Maitland, "An American Leader in Europe," leadership interview with Nancy McKinstry, Wolters Kluwer, *Financial Times*, July 15, 2004, p. 10.

88. Ibid.

89. Ibid.

90. Ibid.

Index